To add a library to a house is to give that house a soul.

                                                                    Cicero

A perfect treat must include a visit to the second hand bookshops.

                                                          Virginia Woolf

The Used Book Lover's Guide to the Pacific Coast States

California, Oregon, Washington, Alaska and Hawaii

By
David S. and Susan Siegel

Book Hunter Press
PO Box 193
Yorktown Heights, NY 10598

The Used Book Lover's Guide To The Pacific Coast States by David S. and Susan Siegel. © Copyright 1996 Book Hunter Press.

All rights reserved. No part of this book may be reproduced or transmitted in any form or by any means, electronic or mechanical, including photocopying, recording, or by an information and retrieval system, without permission in writing from the publisher, except by a reviewer who may quote brief passages in a review to be printed in a magazine or newspaper.

The editors and publisher have made every effort to assure the accuracy of the information contained in this book but assume no legal responsibility for any errors or omissions in this publication, including typographical, clerical or other errors and omissions, and regardless of whether the errors or omissions resulted from negligence, accident or any other cause.

Printed and bound in the United States of America

Library of Congress Catalog Card Number: 95-095014

ISBN 0-9634112-5-X

Acknowledgments

We would like to thank the over 1,350 book dealers listed in this Guide who patiently answered our questionnaire, responded to our phone calls and chatted with us during our visits. Without their cooperation, this book would not have been possible.

We would also like to thank Andrea Drinard, David Brown, Robert Baird, John Perz and Gloria Montlack for their assistance as well as the many other dealers who have compiled regional and local guides for their areas and who have graciously provided us with copies and assisted us in our research efforts.

Also Available From Book Hunter Press

The Used Book Lover's Guide to New England, a guide to over 750 used book dealers in Maine, New Hampshire, Vermont, Massachusetts, Connecticut and Rhode Island.

The Used Book Lover's Guide to the Midwest, a guide to over 1,000 used book dealers in Ohio, Indiana, Illinois, Michigan, Wisconsin, Minnesota, Iowa, Missouri, Kentucky and West Virginia.

The Used Book Lover's Guide to the South Atlantic States, a guide to over 600 used book dealers in Maryland, Washington, DC, Virginia, North Carolina, South Carolina, Georgia and Florida.

The Used Book Lover's Guide to the Mid-Atlantic States, a guide to over 900 used book dealers in New York, New Jersey, Pennsylvania and Delaware.

. . . and available in the near future . . .

The Used Book Lover's Guide to the Central States, a guide to the Rocky Mountain, Prairie, Southwestern and Southcentral States.

If you've found this book useful in your book hunting endeavors and would like information about the other titles in **The Used Book Lover's Guide Series**, contact:

Book Hunter Press
PO Box 193
Yorktown Heights, NY 10598
(914) 245-6608

Table of Contents

List of Maps	2
Introduction	3
How To Get The Most From This Guide	5
Alaska	9
California	15
Hawaii	315
Oregon	319
Washington	376
Specialty Index	449
Keeping Current	474

List of Maps

	Map	Page
Alaska	1	10
California		
State Map	2	38
Berkeley and Oakland	3	52
Central California	4	78
Central Coastal Area	5	235
Los Angeles & Western Area	6	122
Los Angeles Central Area (Orange County and Environs)	7	270
Los Angeles Eastern Area (San Gabriel Valley)	8	168
Los Angeles Northern Area (San Fernando Valley)	9	64
Los Angeles Southern Area	10	253
Northern California	11	289
Riverside and San Bernardino Counties	12	139
Sacramento and Environs	13	189
San Diego	14	203
San Diego Region	15	97
San Francisco	16	212
Downtown	16a	212
Mission & Noe Valley Districts	16b	212
San Francisco Bay Area	17	154
Hawaii	18	315
Oregon		
State Map	19	324
Northwest Oregon/Southwest Washington	20	333
Portland	21	345
Portland Suburbs	22	352
Southwest Oregon	23	366
Washington		
State Map	24	376
Eastern Washington	25	433
Seattle	26	410
Capitol Hill/Eastlake	26a	410
Composite Map	26b	410
Downtown	26c	410
University area	26d	410
Wallingford/Greenwood	26e	410
Tacoma	27	438
Western Washington	28	387

We Keep Going
(Without the benefit of batteries)

Horace Greeley is famous for the advice he gave young men more than a century ago: "Go West."

It took us a while to follow that advice, but after publishing three guides covering the entire Atlantic coast and a fourth to the Midwest, we finally did so ,

Our journey west began in San Diego, California's southern most book city. After visiting the used book shops in that region, we began our trek northward, zigzagging through the entire state of California on our way to Oregon and Washington.

We knew even before we started the research for this guide that the west coast was a treasure trove for the used book lover. What we didn't know, was that there would be so many treasures and that this book would ultimately include over 1,350 dealers.

To those dealers we visited during our travels and who treated us gently, we express our sincerest appreciation for helping to keep our marriage together. Love can go just so far in cementing a relationship. Being no further than 5-10 feet apart from each other 24 hours a day for six solid weeks, driving over 5,800 miles on roads that neither of us had driven before, eating on the run and staying at motels that were conveniently located nearest to the first shop to be visited the following morning, can put a strain on any relationship. Fortunately, ours survived and the guide that resulted from that trip is in now in your hands.

As on our previous trips, during the last weeks of our travels, each of us wondered out loud whether or not another guide would follow: early in the trip, the odds are high, but by the fourth and fifth week, the odds diminish. Fortunately for bookaholics, once the trip is behind us, the odds begin to improve again.

So, if our health and interpersonal relations continue to flourish, and because each of us suffers from "massive compulsion syndrome," we will probably complete our coverage of the "good old USA" with a sixth guide entitled *The Used Book Lover's Guide to the Central States*. While one of us has facetiously subtitled that guide "The rest of the country," the other, more serious member of our team, prefers the subtitle: "The Rocky Mountain, Prairie, Southwest and Southcentral States."

Do you know any good marriage counselors we could meet with prior to undertaking that venture?

David S. and Susan Siegel

How To Get The Most From This Guide

This guide is designed to help you find the books you're looking for, whether you visit used book shops in person or "browse" by mail or phone from the comfort of your home. It's also designed to help you access the collections of the three categories of used book dealers: open shop, by appointment and mail order.

Open shop dealers maintain regular store hours. Their collections can vary in size from less than a 1,000 to more than 100,000 books and can either be a general stock covering most subject categories or a specialized collection limited to one or more specialty areas.

By appointment or chance dealers generally, but not always, have smaller collections, frequently quite specialized. Many of these dealers maintain their collections in their home. By phoning these dealers in advance, avid book hunters can easily combine a trip to open shops and to by appointment dealers in the same region.

Mail order only dealers issue catalogs and/or sell to people on their mailing list or in response to written or phone inquiries.

Antique malls. A growing number of dealers in all three of the above categories also rent space in multi dealer antique malls and some malls have more than one dealer. The size and quality of these collections vary widely from a few hundred fairly common titles to interesting and unusual collections, sometimes as large as what we have seen in individual book shops. While we include antique malls where we knew there were used book dealers, we have not, on a systematic basis, researched most antique malls in the region.

How this book is organized.
Because we believe that the majority of our readers will be people who enjoy taking book hunting trips, we have organized this guide geographically by state, and for open shop and by appointment dealers, within each state by location. Mail order dealers are listed alphabetically at the end of each state chapter.

To help the reader locate specific dealers or locations, at the beginning of each state chapter we have included both an alphabetical listing of all the dealers in that state as well as a geographical listing by location.

Within each listing, we have tried to include the kind of information about book sellers that we have found useful in our own travels.

• A description of the stock: are you likely to find the kind of book you are searching for in this shop? (When collections are a mix of new and used books, and/or hardcover and paperback, we have indicated the estimated percentage of the stock in each category, listing the largest category first.)

• The size of the collection: if the shop has a small collection, should you go out of your way to visit it?

• Detailed travel directions: how can you get to the shop?

• Special services: does the dealer issue a catalog? Accept want lists? Have a search service? Offer other services?

• Payment: will the dealer accept credit cards?

Perhaps the most unique feature of this guide is the *Comments* section that includes our personal observations about the shop. Based on actual visits to the open shops in the region, our comments are designed not to endorse or criticize any of the establishments we visited but rather to place ourselves in the position of our readers and provide useful data or insights.

Also, if you're interested in locating books in very specific categories, you'll want to take a close look at the *Specialty Index* in the back of the book.

Note that the owner's name is included in each listing only when it is different from the name of the business.

Also, in the *Special Services* section, if the dealer issues a catalog, we generally have not listed "mail order" as a separate service.

Maps

The guide includes a series of 34 state, regional and local maps designed to assist readers plan book hunting safaris to open shops and by appointment dealers located near each other.

With a few exceptions, only locations with dealers who have general collections are included on the maps: locations with open shops are shown in bold type while locations that only have by appointment dealers are in italics. Locations of "mostly paperback" shops are not included on the maps. (See "Paperbacks" below.) Also, some locations, "off by themselves" were omitted in order to keep the maps more readable. However, travel directions to these shops are provided.

At the beginning of the California, Oregon and Washington chapters, an outline map of the state indicates how the state was subdivided into regional and local maps while an accompanying page lists the cities that are included on each map. Within each chapter, the map number and page on which the map is located is printed just under the city heading. (Note that because cities are listed alphabetically and not by region, it is not always possible to place regional maps immediately before or after the cities that are included on the map.)

To help first time travelers to some of the major "book" cities in the Pacific Coast states, we have included several city maps which pinpoint more closely the location of open shops with general collections. On these maps, the shops are identified by number and the shop's "map reference" number is shown immediately after the travel directions section.

A few caveats and suggestions before you begin your book hunting safari.

Call ahead. Even when an open shop lists hours and days open, we advise a phone call ahead to be certain that the hours have not changed and that the establishment will indeed be open when you arrive.

Is there a difference between an "antiquarian" and a "used" book store? Yes and no. Many stores we visited call themselves antiquarian but their shelves contain a large stock of books published within the past ten or fifteen years. Likewise, we also found many pre 20th century books in "used" book stores. For that reason, we have used the term "antiquarian" with great caution and only when it was clear to us that the book seller dealt primarily in truly antiquarian books.

Used and Out-of-Print. Some used book purists also make a distinction between "used" books and "out-of-print" books, a distinction which, for the most part, we have avoided. Where appropriate, however, and in order to assist the book hunter, we have tried to indicate the relative vintage of the stock and whether the collection consists of reading copies of popular works or rare and unusual titles.

Paperbacks. The reader should also note that while we do not list shops that are exclusively paperback, we do include "mostly paperback" shops, although these stores are generally not described in great detail. While philosophically we agree with the seasoned book dealer we met in our travels who said, "Books are books and there's a place for people who love to read all kinds of books," because we believe that a majority of our readers are interested in hardcover volumes, we have tried to identify "mostly paperback" shops as a caveat to those who might prefer to shop elsewhere. In those instances where we did visit a "mostly paperback "shop, it was because, based on the initial information we had, we thought the percentage of hardcover volumes was greater than it turned out to be.

Size of the collection. In almost all instances, the information regarding the size of the collection comes directly from the owner. While we did not stop to do an actual count of each collection during our visits, in the few instances where the owner's estimate seemed to be exaggerated, we made note of our observation in the *Comments* section. Readers should note, however, that the number of volumes listed may include books in storage that are not readily accessible.

Readers should also note that with a few exceptions, only dealers who responded to our questionnaire or who we were able to contact by phone are included in the guide. If the dealer did not respond to our multiple inquiries, and if we could not personally verify that the dealer was still in business, the dealer was not listed.

And now to begin your search. Good luck and happy hunting.

Some people will climb to any heights for the right title.

Alaska

Alphabetical Listing By Dealer

Alaska Book Store	14	Gulliver's Books	13
Alaskan Heritage Bookshop	13	Gulliver's Books	12
Alaskan Renaissance Books		Gulliver's Books	12
& Booksearch	11	Gulliver's Books	13
Alaskana Bookshop	11	Lost Horizon Books	14
Bagdad Books & Cafe	13	Martin's Books	13
Bookshop	11	The Observatory	14
C & M Used Books	11	Read Em Again Used Books	12
		Title Wave Used Books	12

Alphabetical Listing By Location

Anchorage
Alaskan Renaissance Books	
& Booksearch	11
Alaskana Bookshop	11
Bookshop	11
C & M Used Books	11
Gulliver's Books	12
Gulliver's Books	12
Read Em Again Used Books	12
Title Wave Used Books	12

Fairbanks
Alaska Book Store	1
Gulliver's Books	13
Gulliver's Books	13
Martin's Books	13

Homer
Bagdad Books & Cafe	13

Juneau
Alaskan Heritage Bookshop	13
The Observatory	14

Seldovia
Lost Horizon Books	14

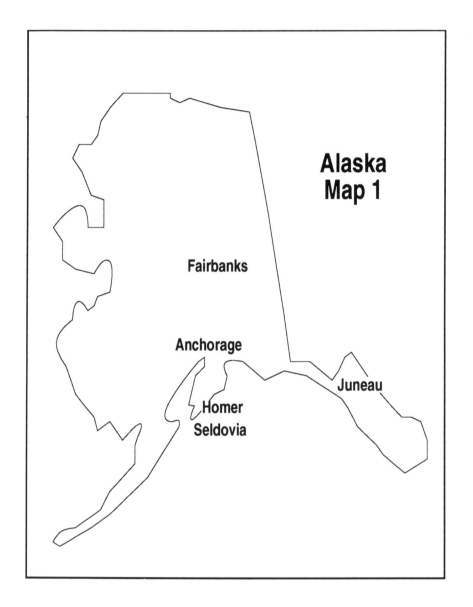

Anchorage

Alaskan Renaissance Books & Booksearch
2837 Wendy's Way 99517

By Appointment
(907) 243-6561

Collection: General stock of hardcover and paperback.
Specialties: Alaska; polar; modern first editions; poetry.
Services: Search service, accepts want lists.
Credit Cards: Yes
Owner: Joe & Mary Buckingham
Year Estab: 1988
Comments: Also displays at an outdoor market in downtown Anchorage every Saturday from May 20th thru first weekend in September, 10-5.30. Market is located at northeast corner of 3rd and E Streets.

Alaskana Bookshop
4617 Arctic Boulevard 99503   Fax: (907) 562-4992

Open Shop
(907) 561-1340

Collection: Specialty
Specialties: Alaska; USGS publications; big game hunting; fishing.
# of Vols: 10,000
Hours: Tue-Sat 1-6 and other times by appointment.
Services: Appraisals, search service, accepts want lists, mail order.
Travel: At corner of 47th Avenue and Arctic Blvd.
Credit Cards: No
Owner: Eugene Short
Year Estab: 1976

Bookshop
750 West Dimond Blvd, #-102-103 99515

Open Shop
(907) 344-1940

Collection: General stock of mostly paperback.
# of Vols: 42,000
Hours: Mon-Fri 10-7. Sat 10-5.

C & M Used Books
217 East Fourth Avenue 99501

Open Shop
(907) 278-9394

Collection: General stock of paperback and hardcover.
# of Vols: 300,000
Hours: Mon-Sat 10-7, except till 6 Wed & Sat.
Services: Mail order.
Travel: Between Barrow and Cordova.
Credit Cards: Yes
Owner: Kathy Cervants & Bob MacArthur
Year Estab: 1974
Comments: Stock is approximately 75% paperback.

Gulliver's Books　　　　　　　　　　　　　　　　　　　　　　　　**Open Shop**
3101 Penland Parkway 99508　　　　　　　　　　　　　　　　　　(907) 278-0084

Collection:　　General stock of paperback and hardcover.
# of Vols:　　 50,000
Hours:　　　　Mon-Fri 10-9. Sat 10-6. Sun 11-6.
Travel:　　　　In Northway Mall at Penland Pky and Airport Heights.
Credit Cards:　Yes
Owner:　　　 Jake Shaw & David Hollingsworth
Comments:　　Stock is approximately 70% paperback.

Gulliver's Books　　　　　　　　　　　　　　　　　　　　　　　　**Open Shop**
701 West 36th Avenue 99503　　　　　　　　　　　　　　　　　　(907) 561-1179

Collection:　　General stock of paperback and hardcover.
# of Vols:　　 60,000
Hours:　　　　Mon-Fri 11-7. Sat 10-6. Sun 12-5.
Travel:　　　　In Olympic Center at 36th Avenue and Arctic.
Credit Cards:　Yes
Owner:　　　 Jake Shaw & David Hollingsworth
Year Estab:　　1980
Comments:　　Stock is approximately 70% paperback.

Read Em Again Used Books　　　　　　　　　　　　　　　　　　**Open Shop**
1427 Muldoon Road 99504　　　　　　　　　　　　　　　　　　　(907) 337-8682

Collection:　　General stock of hardcover and paperback.
# of Vols:　　 25,000+
Hours:　　　　Mon-Fri 11-6:30. Sat 11-6.
Travel:　　　　Muldoon exit off Hwy 1. Proceed south on Muldoon. Shop is between Bebarr and East 20th Avenue.
Credit Cards:　Yes
Year Estab:　　1992
Comments:　　Stock is about evenly divided between hardcover and paperback.

Title Wave Used Books　　　　　　　　　　　　　　　　　　　　**Open Shop**
505 East Northern Lights Blvd. 99503　　　　　　　　　　　　　 (907) 278-9283

Collection:　　General stock of hardcover and paperback.
Specialties:　 Alaska; literature; modern first editions.
# of Vols:　　 100,000
Hours:　　　　Mon-Sat 10:30-6:30. Sun 12-5.
Services:　　 Accepts want lists, mail order.
Travel:　　　　From New Seward Hwy (Gambell St) proceed west on Northern Lights Blvd. Shop is at corner of Eagle St.
Credit Cards:　Yes
Owner:　　　 Steve Lloyd & Julie Drake
Year Estab:　　1991
Comments:　　Stock is evenly divided between hardcover and paperback.

Fairbanks

Gulliver's Books *Open Shop*
1255 Airport Way (907) 456-3657

Collection: General stock used, new and remainders.
Hours: Mon-Fri 10-8. Sat 10-6. Sun 12-6.
Owner: Jake Shaw & David Hollingsworth
Comments: Stock is approximately 75% used, 85% of which is paperback.

Gulliver's Books *Open Shop*
3525 College Road 99709 (907) 474-9574

Collection: General stock used, new and remainders.
Hours: Mon-Fri 10-8. Sat 10-6. Sun 12-6.
Owner: Jake Shaw & David Hollingsworth
Comments: Stock is approximately 75% used, 85% of which is paperback.

Martin's Books *Open Shop*
455 Third Avenue, Ste 115 99701 (907) 456-2240

Collection: Specialty
Specialties: Alaska; Arctic; early sporting in the Arctic.
# of Vols: 2,500
Hours: Apr-Nov only: Mon-Fri 11-5:30.
Services: Search service, accepts want lists, mail order.
Credit Cards: No
Year Estab: 1974

Homer

Bagdad Books & Cafe *Open Shop*
601 East Pioneer, Ste 110 99603 (907) 235-8787

Collection: General stock of mostly paperback.
# of Vols: 15,000-20,000
Hours: Mon-Fri 11-5. Sat 12-4.

Juneau

Alaskan Heritage Bookshop *By Appointment*
PO Box 22165 99802 Fax: (907) 789-8450   (907) 789-8450

Collection: Specialty books and related ephemera.
Specialties: Alaska; Klondike; Robert W. Service.
# of Vols: 8,000
Services: Appraisals, accepts want lists, mail order.
Credit Cards: No
Owner: Richard A. Wood
Year Estab: 1982

The Observatory   **Open Shop**
235 2nd Street 99801   Fax: (907) 586-9676 (907) 586-9676

Collection: General stock.
Specialties: Polar; Alaska; maps.
# of Vols: 7,000
Hours: Winter: Mon-Sat 12-5:30. Summer: Mon-Sat- 10-5:30.
Services: Appraisals, search service, accepts want lists, mail order.
Travel: In downtown, at corner of Franklin and 2nd St.
Credit Cards: Yes
Owner: Dee Longenbaugh
Year Estab: 1977

Seldovia

Lost Horizon Books   **Open Shop**
235 Main Street   (907) 234-7839
Mailing Address: PO Box 42 Seldovia 99663

Collection: General stock of hardcover and paperback.
Specialties: Alaska
# of Vols: 10,000
Hours: Mon-Sat 10-5. Sun 12-5. (Mid May-mid Sept.)
Services: Accepts want lists.
Travel: Located on tip of the Kenai Peninsula, across Kachemak Bay from Homer. Tour boats make daily trips from Homer Spit.
Credit Cards: Yes
Owner: Dan & Eva Wilson
Year Estab: 1990
Comments: Stock is approximately 75% hardcover.

Mail Order Dealers

Alaska Book Store   (907) 455-6539
PO Box 71651 Fairbanks 99707   Fax: (907) 457- 3615
    E-mail: howardgh@aol.com

Collection: Specialty books and ephemera.
Specialties: Alaska; Arctic.
Services: Appraisals, search service, accepts want lists, mail order.
Owner: Howard G. Henry, Jr.
Year Estab: 1971

California

Alphabetical Listing By Dealer

A

Dealer	Page
A Clean Well-Lighted Place For Books	77
A Time For Books	198
A to Z Books	101
A Wrinkle In Time	78
Aaben Books	211
Aardvark Books	199
Aardvark Books	211
Abandoned Planet Bookstore	213
Abbey Bookshop	290
Noreen Abbot Books	290
Acorn Books	213
Acquitania Gallery	213
Acres of Books	116
Adams Angling and Hunting Books	50
Adams Avenue Bookstore	199
Adobe Bookshop	213
Affordable Books & Collectibles	136
Aftermore Books	117
Afterwords	238
Again Books	242
Aladdin Books	94
Albatross Book Co.	214
Aldine Books	120
Alibi Mystery	258
Robert Allen/Books	168
Alouette Antiques	200
Allred Books	278
Almost Perfect Bookstore	187
Almost Perfect Used Books	89
Almost Perfect Used Books	83
Alpine Bookstore	266
Alta's	290
Altair-4 (Knights Cross Books)	159
Am Here Books	174
Amadeus Books	110
American Bookstore	92
American-European Books	120
Ames Bookstore	101
An Oasis Bookstore	200
Anacapa Books	51
Anacapa House	242
Ananda Bookbuyers	145
Anchor Book Shop	91
Ander's Attic	185
Anderson Valley Books	58
Anderson's Bookshop	284
Andersonville Books	186
Andy's Books	290
Anmar's Children's Series Books	184
Another World Comics & Books	120
The Antiquarian Archive	119
Antique Arcade	183
Antique Marketplace	173
The Antique Trove	187
Antique Trove	198
Antiques West Mall & Gallery	201
Apex Books	290
Apollo Book Shop	74
The Aquatic Book Shop	291
Aracia Avenue Books	260
Arcana: Books on the Arts	249
Arcata Books	45
Archaeologia	155
The Archives Bookshop	169
Argonaut Book Shop	214
Argus Books & Graphics	188
Arkadyan Books & Prints	215
The Armchair Adventurer Bookstore	43
Armchair Bookshop	162
Armchair Sailor Bookstore	256
Armenian Coins & Books	174
Around The World	215
Arrow Books	99
Art Books Only	243
Arundel Books	120
Athena's Book Shop	132
Atlantis Book Shop	59
Attic City Book Shop	117
Austen Books	215

Auto-Bound Inc.	41	Bibliomania	155
Automotive Book Stop	60	Barbara Bilson-Books	250
Automotive Information	291	Black Ace Books	121
Stephen Avedikian Fine &		Black Moon Books	202
Rare Books	216	Black Oak Books	51
Aviation Bookmobile/H Miller Books	152	Black Swan	155
Avon Book Shop	60	Blake's Books	133
Avons Research Publications	291	Bleak House Books	267
AG Access	79	Roy Bleiweiss-Fine Books	
B		and Autographs	292
B & L Rootenberg Rare Books	259	Blenheim Books	257
Bad Moon Books	291	Carl Blomgren-Fine Books	239
Balbontin Books	172	Bloody Dagger Books	202
Ronald J. Ballou, Bookman	187	Blue Sky Books	216
Alan S. Bamberger Books	216	Bluff Park Rare Books	117
Barber Books	89	Bob E's Books	104
Bargain Books	277	Bodhi Tree Bookstore	123
Bargain Books	273	Bogbean Books & Music	179
Bargain Bookshop	117	Bogey's Books	79
Bargain Bookstore	201	Bolerium Books	216
Bargain Lovers Used Books	188	Bonanza St. Books	280
Barnaby Rudge Bookseller	111	Bonanza Used Books	286
Barnstormer Books	87	Bonnie's Bookworm	48
Bart's Books	158	Book Again	268
Basement Books	291	Book Alert	292
Basset Books	114	Book Alley of Old Pasadena	169
Bay Books	241	Book Attic	69
Bay Books	71	Book Barrel	77
Bayside Books	249	Book Barn	249
Bearded Giraffe	256	Book Barn	66
Bearly Used Books	281	Book Baron	43
Beaver Books	292	Book Bay	217
Stan Beecher	292	Book Box	189
Beers Book Center	188	The Book Broker	202
Beever's Antiques, Used		Book Carnival	159
Furniture & Books	175	Book Cellar	179
Being Books Inc.	151	The Book Center	152
Don Belew Antiques	169	Book City Of Burbank	60
Bell Rose Used Book Store	49	Book City Of Hollywood	105
Bell's Book Store	165	The Book Collector	190
Bell, Book & Candle	143	Book Corner	287
Benedikt & Salmon	201	Book Corral	137
Stuart Bennett Rare Books	135	Book Country	180
Berkelouw Books	121	The Book Den	243
Charles Lewis Best	201	Book Depot	51
Best Books	113	The Book Drop	266
Best Friends Books	232	The Book End	140
Bethel Antiquarian Books	292	The Book Exchange	132
Betty's Bargain Books	107	Book Exchange	104
Betty's Bookstore	202	Book Exchange	44
Bev's Bookworm & Coffee House	101	Book Exchange	203

State Listings

Book Exchange	73	Book World	260
Book Exchange	144	The Bookworm	161
Book Exchange	277	Book Worm	195
Book Exchange	49	Book'Em	52
Book Exchange	164	Book-Go-Round	256
The Book Faire	175	Bookaneer	268
The Book Gallery	196	Bookends	255
Book Garden	272	Bookery	176
Book Gems	293	The Bookie Joint	184
Book Harbor	95	Bookland	133
The Book Hotel & Cafe	92	Booklegger	86
Book Jam	170	Booklovers Exchange	279
The Book Juggler	285	Booklover's Haven	273
Book King	74	Bookman Basement	160
The Book Ladies of Feather River	287	Bookman	160
Book Lady	115	The Bookmark	156
Book Loft	246	Bookmine	190
Book Lovers	47	Bookmonger	217
Book Mall of Ventura	274	Books	136
Book Mark	49	Books	95
Book Market	234	Books & Company	217
The Book Merchant	146	Books & Things	140
The Book Nest	119	Books & Treasures	176
Book Nook	93	Books Bohemian	123
Book Nook	70	Books By Mail	204
The Book Nook	84	Books, Etc.	111
The Book Nook	158	Books Fantastique	284
Book Nook	82	Books For Less	249
Book Oasis	114	Books For Libraries	246
Book Passage Used & Rare Books	73	Books From Bree	149
The Bookplace by C & H	83	Books In Transit	269
The Book Rack	90	Books of Paradise	168
Book Re-View	112	Books On The Boulevard	259
The Book Review	190	Books on Sports	123
The Book Seller	263	Books Past & Present	83
The Book Shelf	293	Books Plus	160
The Book Shop	280	Books Redux	287
The Book Shop	103	Books Revisited	239
The Book Shop	76	Books Then & Now	195
The Book Stall	93	Books Unlimited	237
The Book Store	75	Books, Etc.	218
Book Stop	112	The Booksmith	101
Book Stop	110	The Bookstall	218
The Book House	287	Booksville	143
The Book Store	177	Booktrader	191
The Book Symposium	293	Bookworm	286
Book Time	159	Bookworm	71
Book Treasury	118	Bookworm	88
The Book Tree	72	Bookworm	179
Book Village	139	Bookworm	88
Book Works	80	Bookworm	69

Boomerang Books	70	Charmed Circle Books	191
Boulder Creek Book Co.	59	Chelsea Books	220
Boulevard Books	293	Chimaera Books & Music	166
Bound For Pleasure Book	191	Chimney Sweep Books	246
Bountiful Books	204	Christian Discount Book Center	284
Brand Bookshop	98	Christian Discount Book Center	77
Brannan Books	96	Christian Discount Book Center	283
The Brick Row Book Shop	219	Churchilliana Co.	192
Brigadoon Books	147	Claremont Books & Prints	71
Brindles Bookstore	271	Cliff's Books/Records/Comics	170
Broad Street Books	147	Coalesce... A Bookstore & More	144
Broadway Booksellers	204	Coarsegold Book Peddler	71
Brooks Books	72	Cobblestone Books	192
The Brown Study Bookshop	178	Coffee & Classics	79
Wm Burgett Booksellers	205	John Cole's Book Shop	107
Virginia Burgman Rare Books	293	Collected Thoughts Bookshop	53
Burlingame Book Browse	62	Collectors' Library	148
John R. Butterworth	294	Collectors Book Store	105
Buy The Book	294	Collectors Ink	70
By The Book	103	Columbus Books	220
By The Way Books	172	Don Conner Fine Books	192
Byron's Magic Books	234	Controversial Bookstore	205
		Barbara Cook Modern 1st Editions	295
C		The Cook Book Lady	295
Dirk Cable, Bookseller	170	Dorothy G. Cook-Rare Children's	
Caernarvon Press	294	Books & Ephemera	247
Cahill's Book Store	91	Grayson D. Cook, Bookseller	124
John Caius-Books	219	Cook Books - By Janet Jarvits,	
Cal's Books	180	Bookseller	61
Calico Cat Bookshop	275	Copper Dragon Books	265
Califia Books	219	Copperfield's Annex	258
California Collectible Books	133	Copperfield's Annex	254
Richard Callaway, Rare Books		Copperfield's Books	173
and Autographs	294	Copperfield's Books	146
Camelot Books	97	Cornerstone Books	242
Camelot Books	279	Cosmopolitan Book Shop	124
Donald W. Cannon Bookseller	96	Counterpoint Records & Books	105
Cape Cod Clutter	205	Crabtree's Collection	89
Caravan Book Store	123	Craig Books	295
Carroll's Books	220	Craig & Craig Booksellers	165
Cartesian Bookstore	53	J. Crawford's Books	192
Casey's Books	136	Crawford-Peters Aeronautica	295
Cassidy's Bargain Bookshelf	237	Crystal Cave	161
Barry Cassidy Rare Books	191	Curious Bookshop	131
Castle Books	269	Curran & Hermes Books	295
Cecchettini's Books & Things	81	Curt's Books	104
Celebrity Bookstore	164	**D**	
Chamasha Books	294	Robert Dagg Rare Books	296
Channel Island Books	294	W & V Dailey	124
Channel Isles Books	177	Danville Books	78
Chanticleer Books	261	Ursula C. Davidson Books	239
Chapters	84		

Name	Page
L. Clarice Davis	296
Tom Davis Books	44
Dawson's Book Shop	125
Day's Past	179
Gene de Chene, Bookseller	282
Derail Books	254
Desert Used Books	80
Harold B. Diamond, Bookseller	61
Diesel, A Bookstore	155
Dieterly Books	296
Discount Textbooks	221
Discoveries Music & Books	173
Carol Docheff-Bookseller	110
Dog Eared Books	221
Steven G. Doi-Books	296
The Dollar Book Store	63
James M. Dourgarian, Bookman	280
Drama Books	221
Drew's Books	243
Dutton's Brentwood Books	282
Dutton's Books/Arco Plaza	125
Dutton's Books/Burbank	61
Dutton's Books/North Hollywood	149
D & J Book Barn	48

E

Name	Page
East Bay Book Co.	234
East West Bookshop	134
The Eclectic Collector	104
F. Wayne Edmunds - Bookseller	47
871 Fine Arts Gallery and Bookstore	222
El Dorado Books	125
Elaine's Books	187
Eldorado Books	296
Elsewhere Books	222
Encore Books	182
Encore! Books	81
Encyclopedias Bought & Sold	242
Essence Gallery	297
Estates Gallery	90
Ethnographic Arts Publications	136
Eureka Books	86
Exotica Fine Books	297
Exploded Views Books	150
Eye of the Cat	118

F

Name	Page
Family Book Center	93
Fantasy Etc.	222
Far Mountain Books	197
Fat City Books	264
Peter R. Feltus	53
Ferndale Books	88
Fields Book Store	223
Fifth Avenue Books	205
57th Street Antique Mall	193
Fifty Thousand Books	82
First Street Books & Antiques	297
Flashback Books	297
Flights of Fantasy Books	250
Flip Side	266
Florey's Book Co.	163
J. Joseph Flynn Rare Books	297
Folk Motif	298
The Fool's Progress	298
FootNote Books	206
Forest Books	223
Forever After Books	223
Foster Book Form	72
Frenchman's Den Bookshelf	105
Friends of the Library Bookstore	263
Friends of the San Diego Public Library	206
Theodore Front Musical Literature	274
Fuhrman & Fuhrman	298

G

Name	Page
Galactic Archives	43
Gallery Bookshop	134
Garcia-Garst, Booksellers	271
V.L.T. Gardner	244
Gaslamp Books, Prints & Antiques	206
Gateways Book & Gift	247
Geiger's Books	298
The Gemmary Inc.	182
Geoscience Books & Prints	298
Lois Gereghty Books, Et Al	149
Michael Gibbs, Books	298
Richard Gilbo-Bookseller	69
Ginkgo Leaf	286
Edwin V. Glaser Rare Books	256
Peter Glaser Bookseller	257
Richard Glassman Books	73
Globus Slavic Bookstore	223
Phillip Gold-221 Books	299
Golden Bough Bookstore	144
Golden Legend	126
Goodwin Goldfaden	259
Thomas A. Goldwasser Rare Books	224
Goldwasser & Wilkinson Books	224
Michael Good, Fine/Rare Books	195
The Good Book Company	299
Good Books Limited	67
Grand Slam Sports Books	299
Grapevine Books	237

CALIFORNIA

Gray Whale Book Store	258
Great Overland Book Co.	257
Green Apple Books	224
Green Ginger Bookshop	66
Greyhavens Books	183
Sol J. Grossman, Bookseller	275
Grounds for Murder Mystery Book Store	207

H

Half Price Books	53
Half Price Books	54
John T. Hamilton III	108
Hammons Archives	193
Jim Hansen Books	67
The Happy Booker	197
Emmett Harrington Rare Books	299
Harvard Used Book Store	264
David Hecht Antiquarian Books	225
Heldfond Book Gallery	196
Hennessey & Ingalls	250
Dave Henson-Books	299
Heritage Book Shop	126
Heritage Books	85
Herland Book-Cafe	247
Heron House	300
Heros & Legends	41
Willis E. Herr, Bookseller	300
Arnold Herr	126
Hessel and Taylor Books	180
Richard Hilkert, Bookseller	225
E. Louis Hinrichs	116
Historicana	63
History Focused	300
Michael S. Hollander Rare Books	240
Hollywood Movie Posters	106
Hooked On Books	281
Julia Houdek Books & Search Service	80
Houle Rare Books & Autographs	126
House Of Books	275
House of Fiction	171
Household Words	300
Hyacinths for the Soul	67
Hein & Co.	177

I

I Love A Mystery	300
I Love Books-Bookstore	279
Iliad Bookshop	150
Inkworks Rare & Collectible Books	300
Inn Of The Beginning	76
Insomnia Books	284
The Invisible Bookman	301
Isla Vista Bookstore	100
It Is Written Bookstore	113

J

Jack London Bookstore	98
Jack's Music & Books	153
Jan's Book Nook	81
Jan's Paperbacks	48
Jan's Paperbacks	187
Java Point	102
Pauline Jenkins Rare Books	163
Johnson Books & Collectibles	244
Johnson's Antiques & Books	80
Josef's Books	185
Joseph the Provider/Books	244
Joyful Word Discount	85
Julie's Books	137
Just Books And...	301

K

Kaiser Bill's Military Emporium	178
George Robert Kane, Fine Books	247
Kenneth Karmiole, Bookseller	250
Howard Karno Books	273
Elliot Katt, Bookseller	127
Samuel W. Katz	127
Kenrich Co.	267
Key Bookshop	156
Keynote Used Books and Records	263
Gerry Kleier	301
Susan J. Klein, Bookseller	232
Eric Chaim Kline Bookseller	251
Knight's Books	255
Know Knew Books	166
George Frederick Kolbe	77
Kongo Square Gallery & Gift Shop	128
Valerie Kraft, Fine Books	164
Krieger's Antiques	128
Krown & Spellman, Booksellers	58
Gen Krueger Books	301
Hans Kuperus-Periodicals	163
J.B. Kennedy, Bookseller	182

L

L & L Book Store	82
La Mesa Used Books	109
Larkfield Book Company	255
Larry Edmunds Cinema & Theatre Book Shop	106
Larry's Books & Autographs	301
Last Grenadier	61
The Last Post Military Antiques	173

Last Seen Reading	302	Megabooks	167
Latin Blood Books	302	Paul Melzer, Rare Books &	
Lawrence's Books	302	Autographs	181
Lee-Gannon Booksellers	142	Memorabilia of San Jose	233
Lemon Grove Bookstore	114	Merlin's Bookshop	116
Leon's Bookstore	236	Meyer Boswell Books	227
Barry R. Levin Science Fiction		Mike's Memories	303
& Fantasy Literature	251	Frank Mikesh	281
Levin & Company, Community		Minerva Books	167
Booksellers	104	Mission Valley Books	92
Libros Latinos	181	Mitchell Books	171
Lighthouse Books	141	Mockingbird Books	44
Lilly Books	138	Mockingbird Books	303
Limelight Bookstore	225	Moe's Books	54
Lincoln Avenue Books	232	Monkey House Books	176
Linda's Used Books	278	Monroe Books	93
The Literary Guillotine	248	Monroe Stahr Books	259
Little Old Bookshop	285	Moondance Bookshop	252
Live Oak Booksellers	99	Mountain Light Books	153
Lodestar Books	225	Mountain House Books	147
Logos Books	248	Movie World	62
Lorson's Books & Prints	96	Mr. Good Books	111
Los Osos Book Exchange	131	Mr. Nichols	254
Lost Horizon Bookstore	244	P.F. Mullins Books	108
E. Lubbe Books	302	J. B. Muns Fine Arts Books	54
Lynn's of Alameda	41	Murphy's Books	145
Jim Lyons Historical Newspapers	302	Murphy's Stage Stop	145

M

		My Book Heaven	41
The Magazine	225	Mysterious Bookshop West	281
Magazine Baron	43	Mystery & Imagination Bookshop	99

N

Magnolia Park Book Shop	62		
Main Street Books	194	Nan's Pre-Owned Books	43
Malibu Books & Co.	132	Natural History Books	150
Malter Galleries	84	Netkin Fine Arts	303
Mandrake Bookshop	240	Maurice F. Neville Rare Books	245
Margaret Mannatt Fine Books	207	New Age World Services & Books	107
Manning's Books	163	New Albion Bookshop	88
Manzanita Books & Records	226	New and Not So New Book Shop	148
Marlow's Bookshop	251	New Harmony Book Cafe	148
Dennis B. Marquand	128	M.C. Newburn Books	42
Mary Mason Bookseller	303	Nick Adams & Co Rare Books	187
Susan Mast Enterprises	303	9th Avenue Books	227
Carl Mautz, Vintage Photographs	147	Nix Books	161
Maxwell's Bookmark	265	Jeremy Norman & Co.	227
McDonald's Bookshop	118	Northwest Books	156
McDonald's Bookshop	226	Nothing's New	198
Laurence McGilvery	108	Now & Then	184
McWilliams & Chee Old &		Kai Nygaard, Bookseller	303

O

Rare Books	141		
The Media Shack	65	Ocean Beach Books	207

Ocean Books	102	Phantom Bookshop	276
The Odyssey Bookshop	240	The Phoenix Bookstore	252
Old California Store	276	Phoenix Books and Music	227
Old Capitol Books	142	Phoenix Books/Mind & Body	130
Old Master Gallery	113	Phoenix Bookstore	236
Old Monterey Book Co.	142	Pictus Orbis Collectors Books	267
Old Town Books	115	Plaza Books	262
Old Town News & Used Books	103	Pleiadian Dreams	45
Oliver's Books	196	Ken Prag Paper Americana	63
On The Cover	132	Wallace D. Pratt, Bookseller	305
Once Read Books	112	Richard L. Press, Fine and	
One Way Book Shop	87	Scholarly Books on the Arts	193
Open Secret Bookstore	241	The Prince and the Pauper	
Opera Shop of Los Angeles	128	Collectible Children's Books	208
Jim Orbaugh, Bookseller	304	Printed Matter	116
Oriental Book Store	172	The Printers' Shop	306
Otento Books	207	Prufrock Books and Etc.	172
The Other Change of Hobbit	55	Diane Pyke-Books	306
Other Times Books	282	R. Franklin Pyke, Bookseller	48
"Our Shop"	85	Pyramid Books	134

Q

Out-Of-State Book Service	304		
Outlet Books	55	Quest Rare Books	263
Outpost Coffeehouse & Bookshop	265		

R

		R.G.I. Book Co.	137

P

Pa-Has-Ka Books	304	Randall House	245
Pacific Rim Galleries	68	Rare Oriental Book Co.	45
Pacific Shore Maps	208	Ravens Bookshop	272
Pages of Time	137	Ravenscar Books	306
Pandora's Books	185	Read It Again Sam	283
Papa's Used Books	165	Reade Moore Books	173
Paper Collectibles	304	The Reader's Edge Bookshop	143
Paperback Alley	245	Recyclepedia Bookstore	252
Paperback Bookstore	178	Recycle Bookstore	233
Paperback Emporium	67	Recycled Romances & Other	
The Paperback Exchange	70	Used Books	75
Paperback Trading Co.	112	Red House Books	227
Papyrus Books	304	Red Star Military Museum & Sales	77
David Park Books	305	Regent Press	157
Parmer Books	208	Renaissance Bookshop	186
Past Times Bookshop	65	Renaissance Bookstore	167
Kevin Patrick Books	42	Kenneth W. Rendell Gallery	58
Peabody's Books	49	River City Books	193
Pegasus Books & CDs	55	Robinson Book Store	75
Pegasus Books	281	J. Arthur Robinson, Bookseller	287
Pendragon Books	156	John Roby	306
Pepper & Stern Rare Books	305	Rock of Ages	306
Robert Perata	305	Rocky's Antiques, Books &	
Peri Lithon Books	305	Collectibles	208
Joan Perkal-Books	305	Rodden's Used Bookshop	119
Diane Peterson - Booklady	134	Romance World	82
Pettler & Lieberman Booksellers	128	Roseboro House	68

Bernard M. Rosenthal	55
Roskie & Wallace Bookstore	234
Robert Ross & Co.	63
Ross Valley Book Co.	56
Barry Lawrence Ruderman Old Historic Maps & Prints	108
Russian Hill Bookstore	228
Rykken And Scull	102

S

S & J Books	307
D.A. Sachs - Books	157
Sacramento Surplus Book Room	194
Safari Out of Print Bookstore & Search Service	209
Safari Press	307
Sagebrush Press Bookstore	288
Saint Adrian Company	228
St. Francis Book Store	198
Saint Vincent De Paul Society Store	258
Sally's Attic (Salvation Army)	209
Salty's Record Attic	138
Sam and Gene Jones-Books	199
Sam's Book City	151
Sam's Book Company	286
Sam's Books & Gifts	49
Sam: Johnson's Bookshop	129
San Diego Model Railroad Museum	307
San Fernando Book Co.	211
San Francisco Mystery Bookstore	228
Sandcastle Books	106
Sandpiper Books	268
Myrna Sapunar Books	307
Scattergood Research	307
Schoyer's Books	307
John Scopazzi Gallery	229
Seabreeze Limited	209
Sebastopol Mall Books	258
Secondhand Prose	46
Second Edition Books	268
2nd Edition Books	69
Second Harvest Books	308
Second Time Around	135
The Second Time Around Bookshop	276
Second Time 'Round Quality Used Books	308
Secret Staircase Bookshop	183
Select Press	74
Selected Favorites	46
Serendipity Books	56
Seven Authors Bookshop	78
Shakespeare & Co.	56

Shambhala Booksellers	57
Martin A. Silver, Musical Literature	100
Skyline Books	89
Sleepy Hollow Books	308
Small Planet Books	87
Ed Smith Books	152
Smith & Co. Booksellers	266
Solvang Book Company	260
Southwest Instrument Co.	238
The Spectator Bookstore	42
The Spectator Bookstore	157
Marvin Stanley, Bookseller	153
Kenneth Starosciak	229
Starworld	106
Christophe Stickel Autographs	308
Jack L. Stone, Bookseller	262
Ivan Stormgart-Books	309
William Stout, Books	229
Sullivan Goss Books & Prints	245
Sun Dance Books	309
Sun Moon Bear Rare Books	309
Sundance Books	66
Sunrise Bookshop	57
Sunset Bookstore	229
Super Collector	91
Sylvester & Orphanos Booksellers	309
Szwede Slavic Books	167

T

Joseph Tabler Books	210
Tall Stories	230
Tanner Candles & Antiques	50
Taugher Books	50
Tavistock Books	309
D.W. Taylor Books	310
Ted's Used Books & Collectibles	246
Ten O'CLock Books	310
That Book Place	261
The Bookstore	90
Theater Book Shop	310
Thelema Publications	310
Thinker Used Books	75
Third World Ethnic Books	129
This Old House Bookshop	140
Jeffrey Thomas, Fine & Rare Books	230
William Thomas	310
Michael R. Thompson, Bookseller	129
Rik Thompson Books	311
Thompson's Book Shop	277
Thorn Books	143
Tiger Lilly Books	96
Time Tested Books	194

Name	Page
Tin Can Mailman	46
To & Again Books	311
Toad Hall	311
Top of the Heap	248
Torrance Book Buddy	269
Town Center Book Gallery	136
Toyon Books	104
Treehorn Books	255
Trophy Room Books	41
Truckee Books	269
Turn Table Books	81
Turtle Island Booksellers	57
Tustin Used Books	271
Twelfth Street Booksellers	132
Twice Sold Tales	174
Twice Told Tales	151

U

Name	Page
Uncle David's Family Fun Store	158
Len Unger-Rare Books	130
Universal Books	186
University Press Books	58
Uptown Books	262

V

Name	Page
Vacaville Book Co.	272
Vagabond Books	59
Valdez Books & Bindery	285
Valley Book Center	94
Van Norman-Booksellers	311
Graeme Vanderstoel	312
B. Vasin Bookseller	312
Vicarious Experience Books	76
Vigne Co.	68
Village Book Cafe	257
Village Book Exchange	272
Village Book Shop	100
Village Books	94
Vinegar Hill Books	238
Virtual Book Shop	312
Visions & Dreams	75
Volkoff & von Hohenlohe	312
Volume One Used Books	146
Paul von Ahnen Books	312

W

Name	Page
Wahrenbrock's Book House	210
Walden Pond Books	157
Wall Street Books	313
The Warehouse Book Store	162
Warm Springs Book Co.	92
Waverley Books	252
We Buy Estates Store	181
Jeff Weber Rare Books	99
Donald J. Weinstock Books	313
Weinstein & Ruhl Fine Books	65
Wessex Books & Records	134
West L.A. Book Center	283
West Portal Books	230
West Wind Books	241
Western Sport Shop	241
Westside Books	130
Whaling Research	313
The White Rose Bookstore	102
Whyte's Booksmith	196
William Byrd Aviation Books	115
D.G. Wills Books	109
Wilshire Books	253
John Windle Antiquarian Bookseller	231
Windmill Books	65
Windsong Used Books	90
Wings Bookstore	145
Witch's Brew	100
Alan Wofsy Fine Arts	231
Wonderland Books	83
Woodie's Collectibles	313
Woodruff & Thrush Twice Read Books	233
Word Has It	175
Wordsworth Used Books	273
World Wide Hunting Books	313
Worn Bookworm	314
Writer's Bookstore	231

Y

Name	Page
Donald Yates	314
Ye Bookstore	278
Ye Olde Book Shoppe	47
Yesterdays Used Books & Coffee House	183
Yesterday's Books	144
Yesterday's Books	138
Yesterdaze Bookshop	50

Z

Name	Page
Zeitlin Periodicals Co.	130
Zeno's	232

Alphabetical Listing By Location

Agoura Hills
Heros & Legends 41
Trophy Room Books 41
Alameda
Auto-Bound Inc. 41
Lynn's of Alameda 41
My Book Heaven 41
Kevin Patrick Books 42
The Spectator Bookstore 42
Tavistock Books 309
Albany
M.C. Newburn Books 42
Alpine
The Armchair Adventurer Bookstore 43
Anaheim
Bad Moon Books 291
Book Baron 43
Galactic Archives 43
Magazine Baron 43
Apple Valley
Book Exchange 44
Aptos
Tom Davis Books 44
Mockingbird Books 44
Rare Oriental Book Co. 45
Arcata
Arcata Books 45
Pleiadian Dreams 45
Secondhand Prose 46
Tin Can Mailman 46
Arroyo Grande
Nan's Pre-Owned Books 43
William Thomas 310
Atascadero
Selected Favorites 46
Ye Olde Book Shoppe 47
Atwater
F. Wayne Edmunds - Bookseller 47
Auburn
Book Lovers 47
D & J Book Barn 48
Jan's Paperbacks 48
Avalon
R. Franklin Pyke, Bookseller 48
Bakersfield
Bonnie's Bookworm 48
Book Exchange 49

Book Mark 49
Peabody's Books 49
Sam's Books & Gifts 49
Bellflower
Bell Rose Used Book Store 49
Belmont
Book Alert 292
Taugher Books 50
Benicia
Tanner Candles & Antiques 50
Yesterdaze Bookshop 50
Berkeley
Adams Angling and Hunting Books 50
Anacapa Books 51
Black Oak Books 51
Roy Bleiweiss-Fine Books and Autographs 292
Book Depot 51
Book'Em 52
Cartesian Bookstore 53
Collected Thoughts Bookshop 53
Peter R. Feltus 53
Half Price Books 53, 54
Household Words 300
The Invisible Bookman 301
Moe's Books 54
J. B. Muns Fine Arts Books 54
The Other Change of Hobbit 55
Outlet Books 55
Pegasus Books & CDs 55
Bernard M. Rosenthal 55
Ross Valley Book Co. 56
Schoyer's Books 307
Serendipity Books 56
Shakespeare & Co. 56
Shambhala Booksellers 57
Sunrise Bookshop 57
Toad Hall 311
Turtle Island Booksellers 57
University Press Books 58
Whaling Research 313
Beverly Hills
Krown & Spellman, Booksellers 58
Kenneth W. Rendell Gallery 58
Big Pine
Worn Bookworm 314
Boonville
Anderson Valley Books 58

Boulder Creek
Boulder Creek Book Co.   59
Brentwood
Vagabond Books   59
Burbank
Atlantis Book Shop   59
Automotive Book Stop   60
Avon Book Shop   60
Book City Of Burbank   60
Cook Books - By Janet Jarvits, Bookseller   61
Harold B. Diamond, Bookseller   61
Dutton's Books/Burbank   61
Last Grenadier   61
Magnolia Park Book Shop   62
Movie World   62
Burlingame
Burlingame Book Browse   62
Historicana   63
Ken Prag Paper Americana   63
Calabasas
Robert Ross & Co.   63
Camarillo
The Dollar Book Store   63
Past Times Bookshop   65
Cambria
The Media Shack   65
Weinstein & Ruhl Fine Books   65
Windmill Books   65
Cameron Park
Sundance Books   66
Camino
Book Barn   66
Canoga Park
Green Ginger Bookshop   66
Canyon Country
Paperback Emporium   67
Carlsbad
Good Books Limited   67
Jim Hansen Books   67
Hyacinths for the Soul   67
Roseboro House   68
Vigne Co.   68
Carmel
Pacific Rim Galleries   68
Carmichael
Book Attic   69
Bookworm   69
Carpinteria
Richard Gilbo-Bookseller   69

Ceres
2nd Edition Books   69
Chico
Collectors Ink   70
The Paperback Exchange   70
Chino
Book Nook   70
Citrus Heights
Boomerang Books   70
Claremont
John R. Butterworth   294
Claremont Books & Prints   71
Clovis
Bookworm   71
Coarsegold
Coarsegold Book Peddler   71
Cobb Mountain
Second Harvest Books   308
Concord
Bay Books   71
The Book Tree   72
Brooks Books   72
Corning
Foster Book Form   72
Corona
Book Exchange   73
Corte Madera
Book Passage Used & Rare Books   73
Curran & Hermes Books   295
Richard Glassman Books   73
Select Press   74
Costa Mesa
Apollo Book Shop   74
Book King   74
The Book Store   75
Recycled Romances & Other Used Books   75
Robinson Book Store   75
Thinker Used Books   75
Visions & Dreams   75
Cotati
Inn Of The Beginning   76
Vicarious Experience Books   76
Covina
The Book Shop   76
Christian Discount Book Center   77
Crestline
George Frederick Kolbe   77

Culver City
Book Barrel 77
Grand Slam Sports Books 299
Red Star Military Museum & Sales 77
Cupertino
A Clean Well-Lighted Place For Books 77
A Wrinkle In Time 78
Seven Authors Bookshop 78
Cypress
Andy's Books 290
Daly City
Beaver Books 292
Danville
Bethel Antiquarian Books 292
Danville Books 78
Davis
AG Access 79
Bogey's Books 79
Coffee & Classics 79
Del Mar
Book Works 80
Denair
Johnson's Antiques & Books 80
Desert Hot Springs
Desert Used Books 80
Julia Houdek Books & Search Service 80
Diamond Bar
Encore! Books 81
Downieville
Jan's Book Nook 81
Dunsmuir
Cecchettini's Books & Things 81
Turn Table Books 81
El Cajon
Fifty Thousand Books 82
L & L Book Store 82
Romance World 82
El Centro
Book Nook 82
El Cerrito
Graeme Vanderstoel 312
Wonderland Books 83
Elk Grove
Almost Perfect Used Books 83
The Bookplace by C & H 83
Ten O'CLock Books 310
Encinitas
Books Past & Present 83

Encino
Malter Galleries 84
Escondido
The Book Nook 84
Chapters 84
Heritage Books 85
Joyful Word Discount 85
Kai Nygaard, Bookseller 303
"Our Shop" 85
Eureka
Booklegger 86
Eureka Books 86
One Way Book Shop 87
Small Planet Books 87
Fair Oaks
Barnstormer Books 87
Bookworm 88
Bookworm 88
Fairfax
New Albion Bookshop 88
Fallbrook
S & J Books 307
Ferndale
Ferndale Books 88
Folsom
Almost Perfect Used Books 89
Barber Books 89
Crabtree's Collection 89
Forest Knolls
Skyline Books 89
Fort Bragg
Estates Gallery 90
The Bookstore 90
Windsong Used Books 90
Fortuna
The Book Rack 90
Fountain Valley
Anchor Book Shop 91
Cahill's Book Store 91
Super Collector 91
Fremont
Mission Valley Books 92
Papyrus Books 304
Warm Springs Book Co. 92
Fresno
American Bookstore 92
The Book Hotel & Cafe 92
Book Nook 93
The Book Stall 93

Family Book Center	93	**Hanford**	
Monroe Books	93	Old Town News & Used Books	103
Valley Book Center	94	**Hawaiian Gardens**	
Village Books	94	To & Again Books	311
Fullerton		**Hayward**	
Aladdin Books	94	The Book Shop	103
Book Harbor	95	By The Book	103
Books	95	**Healdsburg**	
Donald W. Cannon Bookseller	96	Levin & Company	104
Lorson's Books & Prints	96	Toyon Books	104
Garberville		**Hemet**	
Brannan Books	96	Bob E's Books	104
Tiger Lilly Books	96	Book Exchange	104
Garden Grove		Curt's Books	104
Camelot Books	97	**Hermosa Beach**	
Geyserville		The Eclectic Collector	104
Sun Moon Bear Rare Books	309	**Hesperia**	
Glen Ellen		Frenchman's Den Bookshelf	105
Jack London Bookstore	98	**Hollywood**	
Glendale		Book City Of Hollywood	105
The Book Symposium	293	Collectors Book Store	105
Brand Bookshop	98	Counterpoint Records & Books	105
Exotica Fine Books	297	Hollywood Movie Posters	106
Mystery & Imagination Bookshop	99	Larry Edmunds Cinema/Theatre Books	106
Jeff Weber Rare Books	99	Starworld	106
Glendora		Sun Dance Books	309
Arrow Books	99	Sylvester & Orphanos Booksellers	309
Live Oak Booksellers	99	**Huntington Beach**	
Village Book Shop	100	Safari Press	307
Goleta		Sandcastle Books	106
Isla Vista Bookstore	100	Donald J. Weinstock Books	313
Martin A. Silver, Musical Literature	100	**Indio**	
Graeagle		Betty's Bargain Books	107
Witch's Brew	100	**Joshua Tree**	
Granite Bay		New Age World Services & Books	107
Bev's Bookworm & Coffee House	101	**Kensington**	
Grass Valley		Scattergood Research	307
Ames Bookstore	101	**Kings Beach**	
The Booksmith	101	Thelema Publications	310
Grover Beach		**La Canada**	
A to Z Books	101	Avons Research Publications	291
Gualala		**La Jolla**	
Java Point	102	John Cole's Book Shop	107
Guerneville		John T. Hamilton III	108
Rykken And Scull	102	Laurence McGilvery	108
Gustine		P.F. Mullins Books	108
The White Rose Bookstore	102	Barry L. Ruderman Maps & Prints	108
Half Moon Bay		D.G. Wills Books	109
Ocean Books	102		

La Mesa	
Automotive Information	291
La Mesa Used Books	109
La Selva Beach	
Myrna Sapunar Books	307
La Verne	
Book Stop	110
Lafayette	
Amadeus Books	110
Chamasha Books	294
Carol Docheff-Bookseller	110
Larry's Books & Autographs	301
Laguna Beach	
Barnaby Rudge Bookseller	111
Laguna Hills	
Books, Etc.	111
Mr. Good Books	111
Laguna Niguel	
Paperback Trading Co.	112
Lakeport	
Book Stop	112
Lakewood	
Book Re-View	112
Once Read Books	112
Lancaster	
Best Books	113
Lawndale	
Old Master Gallery	113
Lemon Grove	
It Is Written Bookstore	113
Lemon Grove Bookstore	114
Lewiston	
D.W. Taylor Books	310
Livermore	
Basset Books	114
Book Oasis	114
Lodi	
Book Lady	115
Old Town Books	115
Lomita	
William Byrd Aviation Books	115
Lompoc	
E. Louis Hinrichs	116
Merlin's Bookshop	116
Printed Matter	116
Long Beach	
Acres of Books	116
Aftermore Books	117
Attic City Book Shop	117
Bargain Bookshop	117
Bluff Park Rare Books	117
Book Treasury	118
Eye of the Cat	118
Folk Motif	298
McDonald's Bookshop	118
Rodden's Used Bookshop	119
World Wide Hunting Books	313
Los Altos	
The Antiquarian Archive	119
The Book Nest	119
First Street Books & Antiques	297
The Printers' Shop	306
Los Angeles	
Abbey Bookshop	290
Aldine Books	120
American-European Books	120
Another World Comics & Books	120
Arundel Books	120
Berkelouw Books	121
Black Ace Books	121
Bodhi Tree Bookstore	123
Books Bohemian	123
Books on Sports	123
Caravan Book Store	123
Grayson D. Cook, Bookseller	124
Cosmopolitan Book Shop	124
W & V Dailey	124
Dawson's Book Shop	125
Dutton's Books/Arco Plaza	125
El Dorado Books	125
J. Joseph Flynn Rare Books	297
Golden Legend	126
Heritage Book Shop	126
Arnold Herr	126
Houle Rare Books & Autographs	126
Inkworks Rare & Collectible Books	300
Elliot Katt, Bookseller	127
Samuel W. Katz	127
Kongo Square Gallery & Gift Shop	128
Krieger's Antiques	128
Dennis B. Marquand	128
Opera Shop of Los Angeles	128
Pettler & Lieberman Booksellers	128
Sam: Johnson's Bookshop	129
Third World Ethnic Books	129
Michael R. Thompson, Bookseller	129
Len Unger-Rare Books	130
Wall Street Books	313
Westside Books	130
Zeitlin Periodicals Co.	130

Los Banos
Phoenix Books/Mind & Body	130

Los Gatos
Curious Bookshop	131
Michael Gibbs, Books	298
Paul von Ahnen Books	312

Los Osos
Los Osos Book Exchange	131

Malibu
Malibu Books & Co.	132

Manteca
The Book Exchange	132
On The Cover	132

Marina
Athena's Book Shop	132

Marina Del Rey
Twelfth Street Booksellers	132

Martinez
Basement Books	291
California Collectible Books	133
The Cook Book Lady	295

Marysville
Bookland	133

McKinleyville
Blake's Books	133

Mendocino
Gallery Bookshop	134

Menlo Park
East West Bookshop	134
Diane Peterson - Booklady	134
Pyramid Books	134
Wessex Books & Records	134

Merced
Second Time Around	135

Mill Valley
Stuart Bennett Rare Books	135
Books	136
Ethnographic Arts Publications	136

Millbrae
Casey's Books	136

Milpitas
Rik Thompson Books	311
Town Center Book Gallery	136

Mission Hills
Affordable Books & Collectibles	136
R.G.I. Book Co.	137

Mission Viejo
Book Corral	137

Modesto
Julie's Books	137
Pages of Time	137
Salty's Record Attic	138
Yesterday's Books	138

Mokelumne Hill
Lilly Books	138

Monrovia
Book Village	139

Montclair
Mockingbird Books	303
This Old House Bookshop	140

Monterey
The Book End	140
Books & Things	140
Lighthouse Books	141
McWilliams & Chee Old & Rare Books	141
Old Capitol Books	142
Old Monterey Book Co.	142

Monterey Park
Lee-Gannon Booksellers	142

Montrose
Booksville	143
The Reader's Edge Bookshop	143

Moorpark
Bell, Book & Candle	143
Thorn Books	143

Moraga
Sleepy Hollow Books	308
Woodie's Collectibles	313

Moreno Valley
Book Exchange	144
Dieterly Books	296

Morro Bay
Coalesce... A Bookstore & More	144

Moss Landing
Yesterday's Books	144

Mount Shasta
Golden Bough Bookstore	144
Wings Bookstore	145

Mountain View
Ananda Bookbuyers	145
Jim Lyons Historical Newspapers	302
Netkin Fine Arts	303

Murphys
Murphy's Books	145
Murphy's Stage Stop	145

Napa
The Book Merchant	146

State Listings

Copperfield's Books	146
Volume One Used Books	146
Nevada City	
Brigadoon Books	147
Broad Street Books	147
Carl Mautz, Vintage Photographs	147
Mountain House Books	147
New Harmony Book Cafe	148
Newcastle	
New and Not So New Book Shop	148
Newport Beach	
The Book Shelf	293
Collectors' Library	148
North Hills	
Lois Gereghty Books, Et Al	149
North Hollywood	
Books From Bree	149
Dutton's Books/North Hollywood	149
Exploded Views Books	150
Iliad Bookshop	150
Natural History Books	150
Sam's Book City	151
Twice Told Tales	151
Northridge	
Being Books Inc.	151
Norwalk	
Aviation Bookmobile/H Miller Books	152
Oak View	
Ed Smith Books	152
Oakdale	
The Book Center	152
Jack's Music & Books	153
Marvin Stanley, Bookseller	153
Oakhurst	
Mountain Light Books	153
Oakland	
Archaeologia	155
Bibliomania	155
Black Swan	155
The Bookmark	156
Diesel, A Bookstore	155
Key Bookshop	156
Northwest Books	156
Pendragon Books	156
Regent Press	157
D.A. Sachs - Books	157
The Spectator Bookstore	157
Walden Pond Books	157
Occidental	
Uncle David's Family Fun Store	158

Oildale	
The Book Nook	158
Ojai	
Bart's Books	158
The Good Book Company	299
Orange	
Altair-4 (Knights Cross Books)	159
Book Carnival	159
Book Time	159
Bookman Basement	160
Bookman	160
Books Plus	160
Crystal Cave	161
Nix Books	161
Oroville	
The Bookworm	161
Oxnard	
The Warehouse Book Store	162
Pacific Grove	
Armchair Bookshop	162
Christophe Stickel Autographs	308
Pacifica	
Florey's Book Co.	163
Manning's Books	163
Diane Pyke-Books	306
Pacoima	
Pauline Jenkins Rare Books	163
Hans Kuperus-Periodicals	163
Palm Desert	
Valerie Kraft, Fine Books	164
Palm Springs	
Book Exchange	164
Celebrity Bookstore	164
Craig & Craig Booksellers	165
Palmdale	
Papa's Used Books	165
Palo Alto	
Bell's Book Store	165
Chimaera Books & Music	166
Know Knew Books	166
Last Seen Reading	302
Megabooks	167
Minerva Books	167
Renaissance Bookstore	167
Szwede Slavic Books	167
Paradise	
Books of Paradise	168
Pasadena	
Robert Allen/Books	168

The Archives Bookshop	169
Don Belew Antiques	169
Book Alley of Old Pasadena	169
Book Jam	170
Dirk Cable, Bookseller	170
Cliff's Books/Records/Comics	170
House of Fiction	171
Mitchell Books	171
Oriental Book Store	172
Prufrock Books and Etc.	172
Paso Robles	
Balbontin Books	172
Penn Valley	
By The Way Books	172
Petaluma	
Antique Marketplace	173
Copperfield's Books	173
Discoveries Music & Books	173
Flashback Books	297
The Last Post Military Antiques	173
Reade Moore Books	173
Philo	
Am Here Books	174
Pico Rivera	
Armenian Coins & Books	174
Pine Grove	
Twice Sold Tales	174
Pismo Beach	
Word Has It	175
Placentia	
The Book Faire	175
Placerville	
The Aquatic Book Shop	291
Beever's Antiques & Books	175
Bookery	176
Pleasant Hill	
Monkey House Books	176
Pleasant Valley	
Books & Treasures	176
Pleasanton	
The Book Store	177
Plymouth	
Hein & Co.	177
Point Hueneme	
Channel Isles Books	177
Point Reyes Station	
The Brown Study Bookshop	178
Pomona	
Kaiser Bill's Military Emporium	178
Poway	
Paperback Bookstore	178
Quincy	
Day's Past	179
Rancho Cordova	
Bookworm	179
Rancho Santa Fe	
Book Cellar	179
Redding	
Bogbean Books & Music	179
Book Country	180
Cal's Books	180
Redlands	
Hessel and Taylor Books	180
Libros Latinos	181
Paul Melzer, Rare Books & Autographs	181
We Buy Estates Store	181
Redondo Beach	
Encore Books	182
The Gemmary Inc.	182
J.B. Kennedy, Bookseller	182
Yesterdays Used Books & Coffee House	183
Redwood City	
Antique Arcade	183
Buy The Book	294
Greyhavens Books	183
Secret Staircase Bookshop	183
Reseda	
The Bookie Joint	184
Rheem Valley	
Anmar's Children's Series Books	184
Rio Linda	
Now & Then	184
Riverside	
Ander's Attic	185
Stan Beecher	292
Josef's Books	185
Pandora's Books	185
Renaissance Bookshop	186
Universal Books	186
Rocklin	
Andersonville Books	186
Elaine's Books	187
Jan's Paperbacks	187
Nick Adams & Co Rare Books	187
Virtual Book Shop	312
Roseville	
Almost Perfect Bookstore	187
The Antique Trove	187

Ronald J. Ballou, Bookman	187	**San Diego**	
Sacramento		Aardvark Books	199
Argus Books & Graphics	188	Adams Avenue Bookstore	199
Bargain Lovers Used Books	188	Alouette Antiques	200
Beers Book Center	188	An Oasis Bookstore	200
Book Box	189	Antiques West Mall & Gallery	201
The Book Collector	190	Bargain Bookstore	201
The Book Review	190	Benedikt & Salmon	201
Bookmine	190	Charles Lewis Best	201
Booktrader	191	Betty's Bookstore	202
Bound For Pleasure Book	191	Black Moon Books	202
Barry Cassidy Rare Books	191	Bloody Dagger Books	202
Charmed Circle Books	191	The Book Broker	202
Churchilliana Co.	192	Book Exchange	203
Cobblestone Books	192	Books By Mail	204
Don Conner Fine Books	192	Bountiful Books	204
Barbara Cook Modern 1st Editions	295	Broadway Booksellers	204
J. Crawford's Books	192	Wm Burgett Booksellers	205
57th Street Antique Mall	193	Caernarvon Press	294
Hammons Archives	193	Cape Cod Clutter	205
Just Books And...	301	Controversial Bookstore	205
Richard L. Press, Fine and		Crawford-Peters Aeronautica	295
Scholarly Books on the Arts	193	Fifth Avenue Books	205
River City Books	193	FootNote Books	206
Sacramento Surplus Book Room	194	Friends of the San Diego	
Time Tested Books	194	Public Library	206
Saint Helena		Gaslamp Books, Prints & Antiques	206
Main Street Books	194	Grounds for Murder Mystery	
Donald Yates	314	Book Store	207
Salinas		Willis E. Herr, Bookseller	300
Book Worm	195	History Focused	300
Books Then & Now	195	Margaret Mannatt Fine Books	207
San Anselmo		Mary Mason Bookseller	303
Michael Good, Fine/Rare Books	195	Ocean Beach Books	207
Heldfond Book Gallery	196	Otento Books	207
Oliver's Books	196	Pacific Shore Maps	208
Whyte's Booksmith	196	Parmer Books	208
San Bernardino		Peri Lithon Books	305
The Book Gallery	196	The Prince and the Pauper Books	208
Far Mountain Books	197	John Roby	306
The Happy Booker	197	Rocky's Antiques & Books	208
St. Francis Book Store	198	Safari Out of Print Bookstore	209
San Bruno		Sally's Attic (Salvation Army)	209
Nothing's New	198	San Diego Model Railroad Museum	307
San Carlos		Seabreeze Limited	209
A Time For Books	198	Second Time 'Round Qlty Used Books	308
Antique Trove	198	Joseph Tabler Books	210
San Clemente		Van Norman-Booksellers	311
Sam and Gene Jones-Books	199	Wahrenbrock's Book House	210
Out-Of-State Book Service	304	**San Fernando**	
		San Fernando Book Co.	211

San Francisco

Aaben Books	211
Aardvark Books	211
Abandoned Planet Bookstore	213
Noreen Abbot Books	290
Acorn Books	213
Acquitania Gallery	213
Adobe Bookshop	213
Albatross Book Co.	214
Argonaut Book Shop	214
Arkadyan Books & Prints	215
Around The World	215
Austen Books	215
Stephen Avedikian Fine & Rare Books	216
Alan S. Bamberger Books	216
Blue Sky Books	216
Bolerium Books	216
Book Bay	217
Bookmonger	217
Books & Company	217
Books, Etc.	218
The Bookstall	218
The Brick Row Book Shop	219
John Caius-Books	219
Califia Books	219
Carroll's Books	220
Chelsea Books	220
Columbus Books	220
Craig Books	295
Discount Textbooks	221
Dog Eared Books	221
Drama Books	221
871 Fine Arts Gallery and Bookstore	222
Eldorado Books	296
Elsewhere Books	222
Fantasy Etc.	222
Fields Book Store	223
The Fool's Progress	298
Forest Books	223
Forever After Books	223
Globus Slavic Bookstore	223
Thomas A. Goldwasser Rare Books	224
Goldwasser & Wilkinson Books	224
Green Apple Books	224
Emmett Harrington Rare Books	299
David Hecht Antiquarian Books	225
Heron House	300
Richard Hilkert, Bookseller	225
Limelight Bookstore	225
Lodestar Books	225
E. Lubbe Books	302
The Magazine	225
Manzanita Books & Records	226
McDonald's Bookshop	226
Meyer Boswell Books	227
9th Avenue Books	227
Jeremy Norman & Co.	227
David Park Books	305
Phoenix Books and Music	227
Wallace D. Pratt, Bookseller	305
Red House Books	227
Russian Hill Bookstore	228
Saint Adrian Company	228
San Francisco Mystery Bookstore	228
John Scopazzi Gallery	229
Kenneth Starosciak	229
Ivan Stormgart-Books	309
William Stout, Books	229
Sunset Bookstore	229
Tall Stories	230
Jeffrey Thomas, Fine & Rare Books	230
West Portal Books	230
John Windle Antiquarian Bookseller	231
Alan Wofsy Fine Arts	231
Writer's Bookstore	231
Zeno's	232

San Jose

Best Friends Books	232
Steven G. Doi-Books	296
Susan J. Klein, Bookseller	232
Lincoln Avenue Books	232
Memorabilia of San Jose	233
Recycle Bookstore	233
Woodruff & Thrush Twice Read Books	233

San Leandro

Book Market	234
Byron's Magic Books	234
East Bay Book Co.	234
Roskie & Wallace Bookstore	234

San Luis Obispo

Leon's Bookstore	236
Phoenix Bookstore	236

San Marcos

Cassidy's Bargain Bookshelf	237

San Mateo

Books Unlimited	237
Grapevine Books	237

San Pedro

Richard Callaway, Rare Books	294
Southwest Instrument Co.	238
Vinegar Hill Books	238

San Rafael
Afterwords	238
Carl Blomgren-Fine Books	239
Books Revisited	239
Ursula C. Davidson Books	239
Michael S. Hollander Rare Books	240
Mandrake Bookshop	240
The Odyssey Bookshop	240
Open Secret Bookstore	241
West Wind Books	241
Western Sport Shop	241

San Ramon
Bay Books	241

Santa Ana
Cornerstone Books	242
Encyclopedias Bought & Sold	242
Dave Henson-Books	299

Santa Barbara
Again Books	242
Anacapa House	242
Art Books Only	243
The Book Den	243
Book Gems	293
Channel Island Books	294
Robert Dagg Rare Books	296
Drew's Books	243
V.L.T. Gardner	244
Johnson Books & Collectibles	244
Joseph the Provider/Books	244
Lost Horizon Bookstore	244
Maurice F. Neville Rare Books	245
Paperback Alley	245
Pepper & Stern Rare Books	305
Randall House	245
Sullivan Goss Books & Prints	245
Ted's Used Books & Collectibles	246

Santa Clarita
Books For Libraries	246

Santa Cruz
Book Loft	246
Chimney Sweep Books	246
Dorothy G. Cook-Rare Children's Books & Ephemera	247
Gateways Book & Gift	247
Herland Book-Cafe	247
George Robert Kane, Fine Books	247
The Literary Guillotine	248
Logos Books	248
Susan Mast Enterprises	303
Theater Book Shop	310
Top of the Heap	248

Santa Maria
Book Barn	249
Books For Less	249

Santa Monica
Arcana: Books on the Arts	249
Bayside Books	249
Barbara Bilson-Books	250
Flights of Fantasy Books	250
Hennessey & Ingalls	250
Kenneth Karmiole, Bookseller	250
Eric Chaim Kline Bookseller	251
Barry R. Levin Science Fiction & Fantasy Literature	251
Marlow's Bookshop	251
Moondance Bookshop	252
The Phoenix Bookstore	252
Recyclepedia Bookstore	252
Waverley Books	252
Wilshire Books	253

Santa Paula
Mr. Nichols	254

Santa Rosa
Virginia Burgman Rare Books	293
Copperfield's Annex	254
Derail Books	254
Fuhrman & Fuhrman	298
Knight's Books	255
Larkfield Book Company	255
Robert Perata	305
Treehorn Books	255

Santa Ynez
Bookends	255

Saratoga
Book-Go-Round	256

Sausalito
Armchair Sailor Bookstore	256
Bearded Giraffe	256
Edwin V. Glaser Rare Books	256
Peter Glaser Bookseller	257
Great Overland Book Co.	257

Scotts Valley
Geiger's Books	298
Village Book Cafe	257

Seaside
Blenheim Books	257
Paper Collectibles	304
Saint Vincent De Paul Society Store	258

Sebastopol
Alibi Mystery	258
Copperfield's Annex	258
Sebastopol Mall Books	258

Shell Beach
Gray Whale Book Store 258
Sherman Oaks
B & L Rootenberg Rare Books 259
Books On The Boulevard 259
L. Clarice Davis 296
Goodwin Goldfaden 259
Monroe Stahr Books 259
Ravenscar Books 306
Simi Valley
Book World 260
Solana Beach
Aracia Avenue Books 260
Solvang
Solvang Book Company 260
That Book Place 261
Volkoff & von Hohenlohe 312
Sonoma
Apex Books 290
Chanticleer Books 261
Plaza Books 262
Sonora
Alta's 290
Jack L. Stone, Bookseller 262
Uptown Books 262
South Lake Tahoe
Keynote Used Books and Records 263
South Pasadena
Friends of the Library Bookstore 263
Stanford
Quest Rare Books 263
Stockton
The Book Seller 263
Fat City Books 264
Harvard Used Book Store 264
Maxwell's Bookmark 265
Outpost Coffeehouse & Bookshop 265
Studio City
I Love A Mystery 300
Sunland
Gen Krueger Books 301
Sunnyvale
Copper Dragon Books 265
Smith & Co. Booksellers 266
Tahoe City
Alpine Bookstore 266
Tarzana
Flip Side 266

Temecula
The Book Drop 266
Pictus Orbis Collectors Books 267
Temple City
Kenrich Co. 267
Thousand Oaks
Bleak House Books 267
Bookaneer 268
Second Edition Books 268
Topanga
Boulevard Books 293
Torrance
Book Again 268
Lawrence's Books 302
Sandpiper Books 268
Torrance Book Buddy 269
Truckee
Truckee Books 269
Turlock
Books In Transit 269
Castle Books 269
Garcia-Garst, Booksellers 271
Tustin
Brindles Bookstore 271
Rock of Ages 306
Tustin Used Books 271
Twentynine Palms
Ravens Bookshop 272
Ukiah
Village Book Exchange 272
Upland
Book Garden 272
Vacaville
Vacaville Book Co. 272
Wordsworth Used Books 273
Vallejo
Booklover's Haven 273
Gerry Kleier 301
Valley Center
Essence Gallery 297
Howard Karno Books 273
Van Nuys
Bargain Books 273
Theodore Front Musical Literature 274
Latin Blood Books 302
B. Vasin Bookseller 312
Ventura
Book Mall of Ventura 274
Calico Cat Bookshop 275

Sol J. Grossman, Bookseller	275	**Westchester**	
House Of Books	275	Read It Again Sam	283
Old California Store	276	**Westlake Village**	
Joan Perkal-Books	305	Phillip Gold-221 Books	299
Phantom Bookshop	276	**Westminster**	
The Second Time Around Bookshop	276	Christian Discount Book Center	283
Victorville		**Whittier**	
Book Exchange	277	Anderson's Bookshop/Books Fantastique	284
Thompson's Book Shop	277	Christian Discount Book Center	284
Visalia		Insomnia Books	284
Bargain Books	277	Little Old Bookshop	285
Linda's Used Books	278	Valdez Books & Bindery	285
Ye Bookstore	278	**Willits**	
Vista		The Book Juggler	285
Allred Books	278	**Wofford Heights**	
Booklovers Exchange	279	Bookworm	286
Camelot Books	279	**Woodland**	
I Love Books-Bookstore	279	Bonanza Used Books	286
Jim Orbaugh, Bookseller	304	**Woodland Hills**	
Walnut Creek		Ginkgo Leaf	286
Bonanza St. Books	280	Sam's Book Company	286
The Book Shop	280	**Yorba Linda**	
James M. Dourgarian, Bookman	280	Book Corner	287
Hooked On Books	281	Books Redux	287
Frank Mikesh	281	**Yuba City**	
Pegasus Books	281	The Book Ladies of Feather River	287
West Covina		The Book House	287
Bearly Used Books	281	**Yucaipa**	
West Hills		Geoscience Books & Prints	298
Pa-Has-Ka Books	304	**Yucca Valley**	
West Hollywood		J. Arthur Robinson, Bookseller	287
Mike's Memories	303	Sagebrush Press Bookstore	288
Mysterious Bookshop West	281		
West Los Angeles			
Gene de Chene, Bookseller	282		
Dutton's Brentwood Books	282		
Other Times Books	282		
West L.A. Book Center	283		

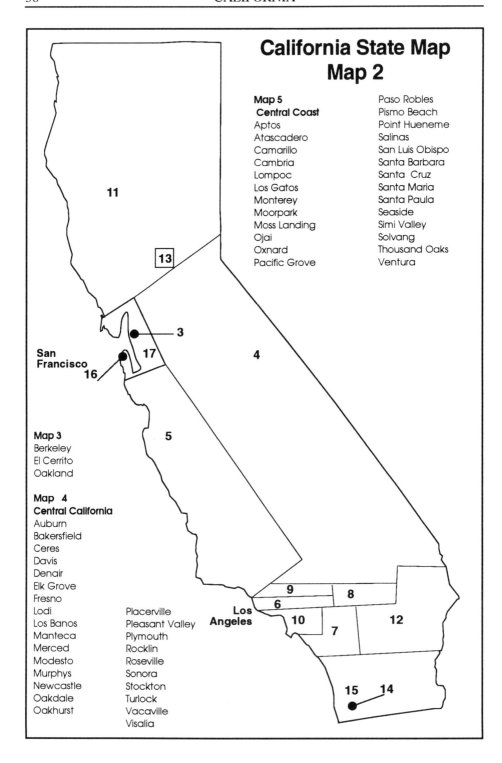

State Listings

Map 6: LA & Western Area
Beverly Hills
Brentwood
Culver City
Hollywood
Los Angeles
Santa Monica
West Los Angeles

Map 7: LA Central Area
Anaheim
Costa Mesa
Fountain Valley
Fullerton
Garden Grove
Huntington Beach
Laguna Hills
Newport Beach
Norwalk
Orange
Placentia
Tustin
Whittier
Yorba Linda

Map 8: LA Eastern Area
Covina
Glendora
La Verne
Monrovia
Monterey Park
Pasadena
Temple City

Map 9: LA Northern Area
Burbank
Canoga Park
Glendale
Mission Hills
Montrose
North Hills
North Hollywood
Pacoima
Reseda
Sherman Oaks
Van Nuys
Woodland Hills

Map 10: LA Southern Area
Bellflower
Hermosa Beach
Lakewood
Lawndale
Long Beach
Redondo Beach
San Pedro
Torrance
Westchester

Map 11: Northern California
Arcata
Boonville
Cotati
Chico
Corning
Downieville
Dunsmuir
Eureka
Ferndale
Fort Bragg
Fortuna
Garberville
Glen Ellen
Grass Valley
Gualala
Healdsburg
Lakeport
Marysville
Mendocino
Napa
Nevada City
Oroville
Paradise
Petaluma
Quincy
Redding
Santa Rosa
Sebastopol
Sonoma
Ukiah
Willits

Map 12: Riverside/San Bernardino Areas
Apple Valley
Chino
Claremont
Desert Hot Springs
Diamond Bar
Hesperia
Indio
Joshua Tree
Lancaster
Montclair
Moreno Valley
Palm Springs
Palmdale
Redlands
Riverside
San Bernardino
Temecula
Twentynine Palms
Upland
Victorville
Yucca Valley

Map 13: Sacramento Area
Carmichael
Fair Oaks
Folsom
Sacramento

Map 14: San Diego

Map 15: San Diego Area
Carlsbad
Del Mar
El Cajon
Encinitas
Escondido
La Jolla
La Mesa
Lemon Grove
San Clemente
Solana Beach
Vista

Map 16: San Francisco

Map 17: Bay Area
Alameda
Benicia
Berkeley
Burlingame
Concord
Corte Madera
Danville
El Cerrito
Fairfax
Fremont
Half Moon Bay
Hayward
Lafayette
Livermore
Los Altos
Martinez
Menlo Park
Mill Valley
Millbrae
Mountain View
Oakland
Pacifica
Palo Alto
Pleasant Hill
Pleasanton
Point Reyes Station
Redwood City
San Anselmo
San Carlos
San Jose
San Leandro
San Mateo
San Rafael
San Ramon
Sausalito
Vallejo
Walnut Creek

A bi-level shop with class

Agoura Hills

Heros & Legends — **Open Shop**
28884 Roadside Drive (818) 991-5979
Mailing Address: PO Box 1038 Agoura Hills 91301 Fax: (818) 780-8477

Collection: Specialty hardcover and paperback.
Specialties: Science fiction; fantasy; occult; autographs (Hollywood).
# of Vols: 50,000
Hours: Daily 11-7.
Services: Appraisals, search service, catalog, accepts want lists.
Credit Cards: Yes
Owner: Myron Ross
Year Estab: 1963
Comments: Stock is approximately 80% hardcover.

Trophy Room Books — **By Appointment**
PO Box 3041 91301 Fax: (818) 889-4849 (818) 889-2469

Collection: Specialty. Mostly used and ephemera.
Specialties: Big game hunting; travel and exploration in Africa, Arabia and Central Asia; Sir Richard Burton (first editions).
Services: Appraisals, accepts want lists.
Credit Cards: Yes
Owner: E. Herring
Year Estab: 1971

Alameda
(Map 17, page 154)

Auto-Bound Inc. — **Open Shop**
2313 Santa Clara Avenue 94501 Fax: (510) 521-8755 (510) 521-8630

Collection: Specialty. Mostly new and some used.
Specialties: Automotive
Hours: Mon-Fri 9-5:30. Sat 10-4.
Year Estab: 1978

Lynn's of Alameda — **Open Shop**
2807 Encinal 94501 (510) 523-2383

Collection: See Comments.
Hours: Mon-Sat 11-5. Sun 10-2.
Comments: A consignment shop that does estate liquidations. Best to call ahead to determine if there are likely to be books available at the time of your planned visit.

My Book Heaven — **Open Shop**
2406 Lincoln Avenue 94501 (510) 521-0373

Collection: General stock of hardcover and paperback.

Specialties:	Fiction; children's illustrated; vintage paperbacks.
# of Vols:	7,500
Hours:	Mon-Sat 10-6.
Services:	Catalog, accepts want lists.
Travel:	23rd St exit off I-80. West on Park to end into South Shore shopping mall.
Credit Cards:	Yes
Year Estab:	1989

Kevin Patrick Books **Open Shop**
2170 Encinal 94501 (510) 865-3880

Collection:	General stock of paperback and hardcover.
# of Vols:	75,000
Hours:	Mon-Sat 11-6. Sun 12-4.
Travel:	I-880 northbound: High St exit. West on High, left on Encinal. I-880 southbound: 23rd exit. Follow traffic to Park. Right on Park, right on Encinal.
Credit Cards:	No
Year Estab:	1989
Comments:	Stock is approximately 75% paperback.

The Spectator Bookstore **Open Shop**
1358 Park Street 94505 (510) 522-4018

Collection:	General stock of used, new and remainders.
Hours:	Mon-Sat 10-9. Sun 10-6.
Services:	Search service.
Travel:	23rd Ave exit off I-980 south. Cross Park St bridge into Alameda.
Credit Cards:	Yes
Owner:	Fred & Yvette Schmalz-Riedt
Year Estab:	1993
Comments:	The stock is approximately 80% hardcover. The owners operate a second shop with a similar stock in Oakland.

Albany

M.C. Newburn Books **Open Shop**
950 San Pablo 94706 (510) 524-1370

Collection:	Specialty new and used paperback and hardcover.
Specialties:	Mystery
# of Vols:	8,000 (used)
Hours:	Mon-Sat 10:30-6. Sun 12-4.
Travel:	Buchannan exit off I-80. East on Buchannan then left on San Pablo.
Credit Cards:	Yes
Year Estab:	1989
Comments:	Used stock is approximately 40% hardcover.

Alpine

The Armchair Adventurer Bookstore **Open Shop**
2357 Alpine Boulevard (619) 445-6146
Mailing Address: 11870 Rocoso Road Lakeside 92040

Collection: General stock of paperback and hardcover.
Hours: Tue-Sat 10-5.

Anaheim
(Map 7, page 270)

Book Baron **Open Shop**
1236 South Magnolia Avenue 92804 (714) 527-7022

Collection: General stock of hardcover and paperback.
Specialties: Modern first editions; magazines.
# of Vols: 400,000
Hours: Mon-Sat 9:30-6, except Fri till 7. Sun 11:30-5.
Services: Appraisals, search service, occasional catalog.
Travel: Magnolia exit off 91 Fwy. Proceed south on Magnolia to Ball Rd. Shop is located on the left, in a shopping center just south of Ball.
Credit Cards: Yes
Owner: Bob & Lois Weinstein
Year Estab: 1975
Comments: One doesn't usually find a store of this vast size in a shopping center. (The shop might almost be described as a mini supermarket for used and some new books.) There is something here for almost everyone's taste, particularly if you're into popular culture. In addition to the specialties listed above, the shop is strong in entertainment, mystery, science fiction and has a good selection of signed books and collectibles under glass. Definitely worth a visit unless your interests are highly specialized or in the realm of the scholarly.

Galactic Archives **Open Shop**
5219 East Orangethorpe 92807 Fax: (714) 693-9459 (714) 693-0673

Collection: General stock of paperback and hardcover.
Specialties: Science fiction; fantasy.
# of Vols: 3,000
Hours: Mon-Sat 11-7, except Fri till 8. Sun 11-5.
Travel: Near Lakeview exit off 91 Fwy.
Credit Cards: Yes
Owner: Mac McMahon
Year Estab: 1989

Magazine Baron **Open Shop**
1236 South Magnolia Avenue 92804 (714) 527-0358

Collection: Specialty

Specialties:	Magazines
Hours:	Mon-Sat 9:30-6, except Fri till 7. Sun 11:30-5.
Services:	Appraisals, search service, accepts want lists.
Travel:	See Book Baron above.
Credit Cards:	Yes
Owner:	Jim Kremer
Year Estab:	1993

Apple Valley
(Map 12, page 139)

Book Exchange — **Open Shop**
20162-J Highway 18 92307 — (619) 242-4077

Collection:	General stock of paperback and hardcover.
Hours:	Mon-Sat 10-6. Sun 11-3.
Travel:	Off I-15, in Hughes Shopping Center.
Comments:	Stock is approximately 70% paperback.

Aptos
(Map 5, page 235)

Tom Davis Books — **By Appointment**
PO Box 1107 95001 — (408) 475-8341

Collection:	Specialty new and used hardcover and paperback.
Specialties:	Kennedy assassination; intelligence community; mind control; UFOs; ruling class.
# of Vols:	2,000
Hours:	Mon-Fri 10-6.
Services:	Search service, catalog, accepts want lists.
Credit Cards:	Yes
Owner:	Tom Davis & Tom Davis, Jr.
Year Estab:	1974
Comments:	Stock is approximately 25% used and total stock is evenly divided between paperback and hardcover.

Mockingbird Books — **Open Shop**
8045 Soquel Drive 95003 — (408) 689-9113

Collection:	General stock of hardcover and paperback.
# of Vols:	10,000
Hours:	Tue-Sat 10-6. Sun 11-5.
Travel:	Sea Cliff Beach/Aptos exit off Hwy 1. Proceed east on State Park Dr to Soquel. Right on Soquel. Shop is on corner of Soquel and Trout Gulch Rd.
Credit Cards:	No
Owner:	Mark Bradlyn & Claire Sherard
Year Estab:	1995
Comments:	Stock is approximately 75% hardcover.

Rare Oriental Book Co.   **By Appointment**
PO Box 1599 95001   Fax: (408) 761-1350   (408) 724-4911

Collection:	Specialty books and ephemera.
Specialties:	Asia; Far East; Southeast Asia.
# of Vols:	20,000
Hours:	Mon-Fri 9-7.
Services:	Appraisals, search service, catalog, accepts want lists.
Credit Cards:	Yes
Owner:	J.G. Stanoff
Year Estab:	1967

Arcata
(Map 11, page 289)

Arcata Books   **Open Shop**
959 H Street 95536   Fax: (707) 786-9155   (707) 822-1024

Collection:	General stock of hardcover and paperback.
# of Vols:	30,000
Hours:	Mon-Sat 9:30-9. Sun 10-6.
Travel:	Northbound of Hwy 101: Samoa exit. Right on G St, left on 10th, left on H. Southbound: Arcata/Humboldt State exit. Proceed straight to H St.
Credit Cards:	No
Owner:	Carlos E. & Marilyn F. Benemann
Year Estab:	1991
Comments:	One large room with much the same appearance as the owners' Ferndale shop and an equally large second room that was not completely stocked at the time of our visit. Of the owners' three locations (Ferndale, Eureka and Arcata), our impression was that their better books were located in Eureka and Ferndale. Which does not, by any means, mean that you would be disappointed if you visited here. Again, like the other two shops, the bookcases are filled from floor to ceiling and labeled in a manner that makes browsing quite easy.

Pleiadian Dreams   **Open Shop**
1360 G Street 95521   (707) 822-0422

Collection:	Specialty used and new, hardcover and paperback and ephemera.
Specialties:	Metaphysics; occult; gemology.
# of Vols:	900
Hours:	Mon-Sat 12-6.
Services:	Search service, catalog.
Travel:	Northbound on Hwy 101: 14th St/Humboldt State exit. Left on 14th St, left on H St, left on 13th St, right on G St.
Credit Cards:	No
Owner:	Liane Turchyn
Year Estab:	1991

Secondhand Prose **Open Shop**
600 F Street 95521 Fax: (707) 826-7873 (707) 822-3471

Collection:	General stock of hardcover and paperback.
Specialties:	Western Americana; nature; mystery.
# of Vols:	20,000
Hours:	Mon-Sat 10-6. Sun 11-5.
Services:	Accepts want lists.
Travel:	Samoa Blvd exit off Hwy 101. Right on F St. Shop is in a shopping center.
Credit Cards:	Yes
Owner:	Gloria Gordon
Year Estab:	1979
Comments:	A small shop that makes maximum use of its space by creating upwards of 13 little alcoves, each with its own specialty. Paperbacks and hardcovers are shelved together. With some exceptions, most of the books we saw appeared to be reading copies of primarily newer vintage titles.

Tin Can Mailman **Open Shop**
1000 H Street 95521 (707) 822-1307

Collection:	General stock of hardcover and paperback.
Specialties:	California
# of Vols:	130,000
Hours:	Mon-Sat 10:30-9. Sun 12-6.
Services:	Appraisals
Travel:	See Arcata Books above. Shop is at 10th & H St.
Credit Cards:	Yes
Owner:	Richard Sanborn
Year Estab:	1972
Comments:	A bi-level shop with a good selection of books in most categories. The emphasis is on fairly recent titles but there are enough older items to make your visit worthwhile. Well labeled shelves and a helpful staff. Better books are located in a separate back room.

Arroyo Grande

Nan's Pre-Owned Books **Open Shop**
1405 Grand Avenue 93420 (805) 489-8223

Collection:	General stock of primarily paperback.
Hours:	Mon-Sat 10-5. Sun 1-5.

Atascadero
(Map 5, page 235)

Selected Favorites **By Appointment**
5825 Ridgeway Court (805) 466-0707
Mailing Address: PO Box 155 Atascadero 93423

Collection:	General stock of hardcover and paperback.

# of Vols:	20,000
Credit Cards:	No
Owner:	Russell C. Goodrich
Comments:	Books are also on display at Rick Butler's Office Machines, 5914 Entrada, Atascadero. Stock is approximately 75% hardcover.

Ye Olde Book Shoppe   **Open Shop**
4303 El Camino Real 93422   (805) 466-3000

Collection:	General stock of hardcover and paperback.
# of Vols:	20,000
Hours:	Tue-Sat 9-5. Other times by appointment.
Services:	Search service, accepts want lists.
Travel:	San Anselmo exit off Hwy 101. Proceed east for one block to El Camino Real, then north one block.
Credit Cards:	No
Owner:	Sally J. McFarlane
Year Estab:	1991
Comments:	Stock is evenly divided between hardcover and paperback.

Atwater

F. Wayne Edmunds - Bookseller   **Antique Mall**
At Castle Antique Mall, 1300 Broadway   (209) 358-6271
Mailing Address: PO Box 397 Livingston 95334

Collection:	Specialty books and ephemera.
Specialties:	Western Americana; native Americans.
# of Vols:	2,000
Hours:	Mon-Sat 10-5. Sun 11-2.
Services:	Accepts want lists.
Travel:	Briggsmore/Winton Way exit off Hwy 99. Proceed east to Broadway. Right on Broadway. Shop is one block ahead.
Credit Cards:	Yes
Year Estab:	1983

Auburn
(Map 4, page 78)

Book Lovers   **Open Shop**
878 High Street 95603   (916) 885-7393

Collection:	General stock of hardcover and paperback.
# of Vols:	22,000
Hours:	Mon-Sat 9:30-6. Sun 11-4.
Services:	Accepts want lists, mail order.
Travel:	Elm St exit off I-80. Proceed south on Elm then right on High.
Credit Cards:	Yes

Owner: Dave Miskel & Linda Huggins
Year Estab: 1990
Comments: An attractive shop with a modest collection of mostly recent hardcover books that were in good condition and a smaller section at the rear of the shop for paperbacks. The shop is easy to browse and the shelves are well labeled. The store also sells some remainders.

D & J Book Barn   **Open Shop**
2535 Bell Road 95603   (916) 887-0901

Collection: General stock of mostly used paperback.
Hours: Mon-Fri 10-6. Sat 12-5. Sun 12-4.

Jan's Paperbacks   **Open Shop**
1209 Grass Valley Highway 95603   (916) 885-3170

Collection: General stock of mostly paperback.
Hours: Mon-Fri 10-6. Sat 10-5.

Avalon

R. Franklin Pyke, Bookseller   **Open Shop**
228 Metropole   * (310) 510-2588
Mailing Address: PO Box 514 Avalon 90704

Collection: General stock of hardcover and paperback.
Specialties: Santa Catalina Island; southern California history and native Americans; 1920's art pottery; maps.
Hours: Tue-Sun 10-5.
Services: Appraisals, search service, accepts want lists.
Travel: One hour boat ride from Long Beach, San Pedro or Newport Beach.
Credit Cards: Yes
Owner: Ron Pyke
Year Estab: 1983
Comments: Stock is approximately 70% hardcover.

Bakersfield
(Map 4, page 78)

Bonnie's Bookworm   **Open Shop**
2800 Chester Avenue 93301   (805) 323-6980

Collection: General stock of paperback and hardcover.
# of Vols: 25,000
Hours: Mon-Fri 10-5:30. Sat 10-5.
Travel: Rosedale Hwy exit off Hwy 99. East on Rosedale than left on Chester.
Credit Cards: Yes
Owner: Bonnie Dowda
Year Estab: 1980
Comments: Stock is approximately 70% paperback.

* In 1996, some 310 codes change to 562

Book Exchange   **Open Shop**
2007 H Street 93301   (805) 327-1041

Collection:	General of paperback and hardcover.
# of Vols:	90,000
Hours:	Tue-Sat 10-5.
Travel:	Rosedale/24th St/downtown exit off Hwy 99. East on 24th, south on H St.
Year Estab:	1975
Comments:	Stock is approximately 70% paperback.

Book Mark   **Open Shop**
6300 White Lane, Ste. C 93309   (805) 835-8483

Collection:	General stock of mostly paperback.
Hours:	Mon-Fri 10-8. Sat 10-6. Sun 11-5.

Peabody's Books   **Open Shop**
2315 Edison Highway 93307   (805) 322-8382

Collection:	General stock of paperback, hardcover, comics, magazines and records.
# of Vols:	60,000
Hours:	Mon-Sat 10-5. Sun 1-5.
Travel:	Mt. Vernon exit off Hwy 58. North on Mt. Vernon, east on California and north on Exchange. Shop is on corner of Exchange and Edison Hwy.
Owner:	Mrs. Willie Peabody
Year Estab:	1989
Comments:	Stock is approximately 60% paperback.

Sam's Books & Gifts   **Open Shop**
2491 Edison Highway 93307   (805) 323-3798

Collection:	General stock of paperback and hardcover.
# of Vols:	30,000+
Hours:	Tue-Sun 9-5.
Travel:	See Peadoby's Books above. Right on Edison.
Year Estab:	1964
Comments:	Stock is approximately 75% paperback.

Bellflower
(Map 10, page 253)

Bell Rose Used Book Store   **Open Shop**
10108 East Rosecrans Avenue 90706   * (310) 925-8634

Collection:	General stock of hardcover and paperback.
Hours:	Mon-Fri 10-7. Sat 10-6.
Travel:	Rosecrans exit off 605 Fwy. West on Rosecrans. Shop is on left in a small strip mall.
Credit Cards:	Yes
Year Estab:	1985
Comments:	Stock is divided equally between hardcover and paperback.

Belmont

Taugher Books   **By Appointment**
2550 Somerset Drive 94002   (415) 591-8366
E-mail: taugher@batnet.com

Collection: Specialty. Mostly used and some ephemera.
Specialties: Modern first editions; detective; mystery; black literature; book collecting; price guides.
# of Vols: 2,000
Services: Catalog
Credit Cards: Yes
Owner: Dennis Taugher
Year Estab: 1991

Benicia
(Map 17, page 154)

Tanner Candles & Antiques   **Open Shop**
615 First Street 94510   (707) 745-2396

Collection: General stock of paperback and hardcover.
# of Vols: 9,000
Hours: Sat & Sun 11-6. Other times by appointment.
Travel: East Second St exit off I-780. Shop is 1/2 block from old state capitol.
Credit Cards: No
Owner: Ruth B. Tanner
Year Estab: 1970
Comments: Stock is approximately 60% paperback.

Yesterdaze Bookshop   **Open Shop**
374 First Street 94510   (707) 745-2309

Collection: General stock of mostly paperback.
Hours: Mon-Thu 10:30-5:30. Fri & Sat 10:30-5. Sun 12-4.

Berkeley
(Map 3, page 52 & Map 17, page 154)

Adams Angling and Hunting Books   **By Appointment**
1170 Keeler Avenue 94708   Fax: (510) 548-0313   (510) 849-1324

Collection: Specialty
Specialties: Fishing; hunting and related natural history.
# of Vols: 7,000
Services: Appraisals, search service, catalog, accepts want lists.
Credit Cards: Yes
Owner: Jim R. Adams
Year Estab: 1977

Anacapa Books
3090 Claremont Avenue 94705

Open Shop

(510) 601-7739 (510) 654-3517

Collection:	Specialty
Specialties:	20th century fiction; poetry; first editions.
# of Vols:	25,000
Hours:	Mon-Fri 10-5.
Services:	Catalog, accepts want lists.
Travel:	Between College and Ashby.
Credit Cards:	No
Owner:	David S. Wirshup
Year Estab:	1980
Comments:	A modest sized shop with a focused collection in the specialties listed above. The above notwithstanding, when we visited the shop, we clearly saw titles of a more general nature as well as other specialty areas, e.g., a collection dealing with Freudian psychology. If you're visiting Berkeley bookstores and the specialties are of interest to you, we advise a stop.

Black Oak Books
1491 Shattuck Avenue 94709

Open Shop

(510) 486-0698

Collection:	General stock of used and new. Mostly hardcover.
Specialties:	Greek and Latin; medieval history; science; math; modern first editions.
# of Vols:	60,000+ (used)
Hours:	Daily 10-10.
Services:	Appraisals, search service, accepts want lists, mail order.
Travel:	Between Vine & Rose.
Map Ref:	Map 3, page 52, #1.
Credit Cards:	Yes
Owner:	Bob Brown, Don Pretari & Herb Bivins
Year Estab:	1983
Comments:	One of Berkeley's three or four better general open used book shops. Most of the used books (some paperback but mostly hardcover) were in a large separate room to the rear of the shop while rare books (and in this case we mean rare) were behind glass in several different sections.

Book Depot
1805 Second Street 94710

Open Shop

(510) 843-2951

Collection:	General stock of mostly hardcover.
Specialties:	Military; World War I & II; Civil War; Western Americana; San Francisco; California; Americana; Europe; Asia.
# of Vols:	40,000
Hours:	Tue-Sat 1:30-5:30.
Travel:	Between Hearst & Virginia.
Map Ref:	Map 3, page 52, #2.
Credit Cards:	No
Owner:	Frank Murdoch
Year Estab:	1979
Comments:	Unfortunately, this shop is closed Mondays, the day we visited Berkeley.

52   CALIFORNIA

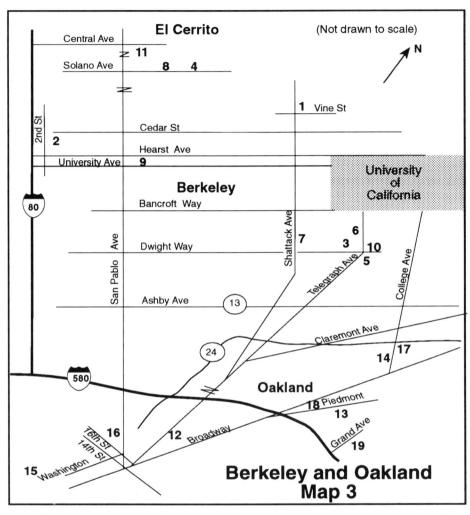

Book'Em   **Open Shop**
At Strawberry Creek Design Center, 1250 Addison Street, #103
Mailing Address: PO Box 92 Belmont 94002-0092

Collection: Specialty hardcover and paperback.
Specialties: Vintage paperbacks; modern first editions; signed; limited editions; mystery.
# of Vols: 3,000
Hours: Thu 12-8. Sat 12-6. Other times by appointment.
Services: Search service, accepts want lists, mail order.
Travel: University Ave exit off I-80. Proceed east on University. Right on Bonar. Left on Addison.
Owner: Lori Ubell
Year Estab: 1993

Cartesian Bookstore
2445 Dwight Way 94704

Open Shop
(510) 549-3973

Collection:	General stock.
Specialties:	Emphasis on scholarly subjects.
# of Vols:	5,000
Hours:	Mon-Sat 11-7:30. Sun 12-5.
Travel:	Between Telegraph and Dana.
Map Ref:	Map 3, page 52, #3.
Credit Cards:	Yes
Owner:	Wayne Brown
Year Estab:	1978
Comments:	A rather small shop with a limited number of books, almost exclusively of a scholarly nature, e.g., language, history, philosophy, etc. If this is your cup of tea, drink from it.

Collected Thoughts Bookshop
1816 Euclid Avenue 94709

Open Shop
(510) 843-1816

Collection:	Specialty new and used paperback and hardcover and some ephemera.
Specialties:	Literature; poetry; politics; travel; performing arts; history; theology.
# of Vols:	10,000
Hours:	Daily 9-9.
Services:	Search service, accepts wants lists, mail order.
Travel:	University exit off I-80. Right on University. Left on Oxford, Right on Hearst. Left on Euclid.
Credit Cards:	Yes
Owner:	Lorraine Zimmerman
Year Estab:	1995
Comments:	We visited this shop shortly after it had opened and found a nice supply of paperbacks with titles in good taste, a rather small number of hardcover books (probably less then 200 at the time of our visit) and newspapers.

Peter R. Feltus
PO Box 5339 94705

By Appointment
(510) 658-9627

Collection:	Specialty used and some new.
Specialties:	Egyptian and Sudanese history and philately; Baedecker, Cook and Murray travel guides..
# of Vols:	500
Services:	Appraisals, search service, lists, accepts want lists, mail order.
Credit Cards:	No
Year Estab:	1970

Half Price Books
1849 Solano 94707

Open Shop
(510) 526-6080

Collection:	General stock of new, used and remainders.
Hours:	Daily 10-10.
Travel:	In north Berkeley. See Pegasus Books below.
Map Ref:	Map 3, page 52, #4.

(Berkeley)

Comments: This store is quite similar to the other Half Price Book shops we've visited in other regions in that in addition to new books sold at discount prices and remainders, there's also a reasonable selection of mixed vintage used hardcover books in mixed condition. As with our experience elsewhere, one never knows what books may be offered to the local shop and therefore what books you'll see when you visit. Since another used book dealer is just steps away from this site, a visit here will put you in touch with two used book collections for the price of one.

Half Price Books   Open Shop
2525 Telegraph Avenue 94704   (510) 843-6412

Collection: General stock of new, used and remainders.
Hours: Daily 10-10.
Travel: Between Parker and Dwight Way.
Map Ref: Map 3, page 52, #5

Moe's Books   Open Shop
2476 Telegraph Avenue 94704   Fax: (510) 849-9938   (510) 849-2087
Rare book room: (510) 849-2133
E-mail: moe@moesbooks.com

Collection: General stock of mostly used hardcover and paperback and remainders.
Specialties: Photography; art; architecture.
# of Vols: 500,000+
Hours: Daily 10am-11pm, except till midnight on Fri & Sat. (See Comments)
Services: Appraisals, search service, catalog (electronic only), accepts want lists.
Travel: Ashby exit (Hwy 13) off I-80. Proceed east on Ashby, then left on Telegraph. Shop is between Dwight Way and Haste.
Map Ref: Map 3, page 52, #6.
Credit Cards: Yes
Owner: Morris Moskowitz
Year Estab: 1964
Comments: An interesting mix of new books and remainders (mostly on the first and second floors) and used volumes (mostly on the 3rd and 4th floors.) The size of the collection makes a visit to this store worth the time invested. We saw lots of interesting titles, most of a more recent nature and almost all in very good condition. The shop's more valuable and rare books are located in a separate room on the 4th floor which is open daily between 12-6.

J. B. Muns Fine Arts Books   By Appointment
1162 Shattuck Avenue 94707   Fax: (510) 525-1126   (510) 525-2420

Collection: Specialty
Specialties: Art; architecture; photography; music; dance; musical autographs.
# of Vols: 2,500
Services: Catalog, search service, accepts want lists.
Year Estab: 1964

The Other Change of Hobbit
2020 Shattuck Avenue 94704

Open Shop
(510) 848-0413

Collection:	Specialty new and used, hardcover and paperback.
Specialties:	Science fiction; fantasy and related subjects.
Hours:	Mon-Sat 11-7. Sun 1-6.
Services:	Appraisals, search service, catalog, accepts want lists.
Travel:	University Ave exit off I-80. East on University. Right on Shattuck.
Owner:	David Nee, Debbie Notkin & Thomas Whitmore
Year Estab:	1975
Comments:	Used stock (about 30% of total stock) is about evenly divided between hardcover and paperback.

Outlet Books
2349 Shattuck Avenue 94704

Open Shop
(510) 649-1230

Collection:	General stock of mostly "hurt books," remainders and some used.
# of Vols:	75,000
Hours:	Daily 9-9.
Travel:	At Durant.
Map Ref:	Map 3, page 52, #7.
Credit Cards:	Yes
Owner:	Matt Wyse, president. Amy Thomas, president.

Pegasus Books & CDs
1855 Solano Avenue 94707

Open Shop
(510) 525-6888

Collection:	General stock of used paperback and hardcover, new books and remainders.
# of Vols:	50,000-70,000
Hours:	Mon-Thu 8am-10pm. Fri & Sat 8-10:45pm. Sun 10-10.
Travel:	Albany exit off I-80. Proceed east to San Pablo, left on San Pablo and right on Solano. Shop is between Colusa and Alameda in north Berkeley.
Map Ref:	Map 3, page 52, #8.
Credit Cards:	Yes
Owner:	Matt Wyse, owner. Amy Thomas, presdient.
Comments:	Entering this shop one gets the impression that it sells primarily new books. A walk around, however, reveals several bookcases that do indeed carry used volumes, the majority of which consist of reading copies of fairly recent fiction and non fiction titles. We suppose it is possible that if you visit the shop "on your lucky day" you may find just the volume you've been looking for. However, if that volume is truly scarce, we wouldn't give odds on it

Bernard M. Rosenthal
PO Box 5279 94705

By Appointment
(510) 549-2532

Collection:	Specialty
Specialties:	Continental books before 1600.
Services:	Appraisals in specialty field only.
Year Estab:	1953

56   CALIFORNIA

(Berkeley)

Ross Valley Book Co.   **Open Shop**
3360 Adeline Street 94703   (510) 547-3680

Collection: Specialty used and new hardcover and paperback.
Specialties: Western Americana.
# of Vols: 4,000 (used)
Hours: Tue-Sat 10-6.
Services: Appraisals, accepts want lists, mail order.
Travel: Ashby Ave exit off I-80. Proceed east on Ashby then right on Martin Luther King. Shop is at corner of Martin Luther King and Adeline.
Credit Cards: No
Owner: Robert Hawley
Year Estab: 1978
Comments: Used stock is approximately 60% hardcover.

Serendipity Books   **Open Shop**
1201 University Avenue 94702   (510) 841-7455

Collection: General stock.
Specialties: First editions; modern American fiction and poetry; bibliography; books on books; Western Americana; detective; science fiction; literature; medieval studies; literature in translation.
# of Vols: 400,000
Hours: Mon-Sat 9-5.
Services: Appraisals, occasional catalog, mail order, accepts want lists.
Travel: University Ave exit off I-80. Shop is between Curtis and Chestnut.
Map Ref: Map 3, page 52, #9.
Credit Cards: Yes
Owner: Peter B. Howard
Year Estab: 1963
Comments: Regardless of your taste in books, if you don't visit here, you'll be missing out on an experience of a lifetime. Your first impression as you enter this establishment is that the authors of this book must be crazy as you'll see books piled in no discernible order, shelves that are not obviously labeled and a general sense of disarray. Before you jump to conclusions, though, walk around the front of the shop and eyeball the titles on some of the shelves. When you do, you'll see far more unusual and hard-to-find titles than common ones. You'll also spot truly antiquarian volumes. And, if the owner is on the premises and you ask him to either show you books in your special areas of interest, you'll soon realize, as we did, that the shop does indeed hold in excess of 400,000 volumes (many stored in moveable library-like storage shelves). In other words, there is far more than meets the eye in this storehouse of books and what exists is worth seeing.

Shakespeare & Co.   **Open Shop**
2499 Telegraph Avenue 94704   (510) 841-8916

Collection: General stock of hardcover and paperback.

# of Vols:	100,000+
Hours:	Daily 10-10.
Services:	Appraisals, search service.
Travel:	See Moe's above. Shop is at Dwight Way.
Map Ref:	Map 3, page 52, #10.
Credit Cards:	Yes
Owner:	Harvey Segal & Jackie Miskel
Year Estab:	1965
Comments:	An interesting selection of mixed vintage books in mixed condition with an emphasis on the scholarly although popular culture is represented. The shop was somewhat crowded and while the shelves were well labeled, in some cases, the books were so tightly shelved it was difficult to slide one out to look at.

Shambhala Booksellers   Open Shop
2482 Telegraph Avenue 94704   (510) 848-8443

Collection:	Specialty. Mostly new paperback and hardcover.
Specialties:	Eastern religions; metaphysics; religion; psychology; health.
# of Vols:	15,000+
Hours:	Daily 10-7.
Services:	Mail order.
Travel:	See Moe's above.
Credit Cards:	Yes
Owner:	Samuel Bercholz & Philip Barry
Year Estab:	1968

Sunrise Bookshop   Open Shop
3054 Telegraph Avenue 94705   (510) 841-6372

Collection:	Specialty new and used.
Specialties:	Philosophy; religion.
# of Vols:	3,0000 (used)
Hours:	Mon & Tue 10-6. Wed-Fri 10-7. Sat 10-6. Sun 12-5.
Travel:	Between Ashby and Prince.

Turtle Island Booksellers   Open Shop
2067 Center Street 94704   Fax: (510) 540-5461   (510) 540-5422

Collection:	Specialty
Specialties:	Art; architecture; photography; modern first editions; literature; mediaeval studies; classical studies; linguistics; scholarly books in all fields.
# of Vols:	25,00
Hours:	Tue-Sat 10-6.
Services:	Appraisals, catalog.
Travel:	University Ave exit off I-80. Proceed east on University, right on Shattuck, then right on Center.
Credit Cards:	Yes
Owner:	Roger Wicker & Michael Hackenberg
Year Estab:	1990

University Press Books　　　　　　　　　　　　　　　　　　　　　　　　**Open Shop**
2430 Bancroft Way 94704　　　　　　　　　　　　　　(800) 676-8722 (510) 548-0585
　　　　　　　　　　　　　　　　　　　　　　　　　　　　　　　　　Fax: (510) 849-9214

Collection: 　　Specialty new and used, paperback and hardcover.
Specialties:　　University press books.
# of Vols:　　　30,000
Hours:　　　　Mon-Fri 10-8. Sat 10-6. Sun 12-5.
Services:　　　Accepts want lists, mail order.
Travel:　　　　University Ave exit off I-80. Proceed east on University to end. Right on Oxford, left on Durant, left on Telegraph, left on Bancroft.
Credit Cards:　Yes
Owner:　　　　Bill & Karen McClung
Year Estab:　　1974
Comments:　　Stock is approximately 20% used.

Beverly Hills
(Map 6, page 122)

Krown & Spellman, Booksellers　　　　　　　　　　　　　　　　　**Open Shop**
323 South Robertson Boulevard 90211　　　　　　　　　　　　　* (310) 659-4306

Collection:　　Specialty
Specialties:　　Rare; scholarly; manuscript leaves; early printed books.
Hours:　　　　Mon-Sat 10-5.
Services:　　　Appraisals, catalog.
Travel:　　　　One half block north of Olympic.
Map Ref:　　　Map 6, page 122, #27.
Credit Cards:　Yes
Owner:　　　　Franklin V. Spellman
Year Estab:　　1978
Comments:　　Unfortunately, we attempted to visit this dealer at his former location in Santa Monica only to learn that the shop had moved to the above address.

Kenneth W. Rendell Gallery　　　　　　　　　　　　　　　　　　　**Open Shop**
309 North Beverly Drive 90210　　　　　　　　　　　　　　　　* (310) 550-1812

Collection:　　Specialty
Specialties:　　Signed books; autographs.
Hours:　　　　Tue-Sat 10-6.
Travel:　　　　Between Dayton Way and Brighton.

Boonville
(Map 11, page 289)

Anderson Valley Books　　　　　　　　　　　　　　　　　　　　　　**Open Shop**
14125 Highway 128　　　　　　　　　　　　　　　　　　　　　　　(707) 895-2415
Mailing Address: PO Box 889 Boonville 95415　　　　　　　　Fax: (707) 895-2545

Collection:　　General stock of hardcover and paperback and ephemera.
Specialties:　　California; Western Americana; natural history; radical and labor history.

* In 1996, some 310 codes change to 562

# of Vols:	12,000
Hours:	Wed-Mon 11-7. (Often open Tue in summer.)
Services:	Search service, catalog, accepts want lists.
Travel:	Southbound on Hwy 101: Hwy 253 exit from Ukiah. Northbound on Hwy 101: Hwy 128 exit west from Cloverdale. Shop is in downtown.
Credit Cards:	Yes
Owner:	Carl Hammarskjold
Year Estab:	1992
Comments:	The stock is about evenly divided between hardcover and paperback.

Boulder Creek

Boulder Creek Book Co.   **Open Shop**
13155 Central Avenue 95006   (408) 338-9155

Collection:	General stock of new and mostly paperback used.
Hours:	Daily 10-6, except closed Wed.

Brentwood
(Map 6, page 122)

Vagabond Books   **Open Shop**
11706 San Vicente Boulevard 90049   * (310) 442--2665   (310) 475-2700
           Fax: (310) 475-2856

Collection:	General stock of mostly hardcover.
Specialties:	Modern first editions; art; mystery; science fiction; signed.
# of Vols:	75,000
Hours:	Mon-Sat 11-7. Sun 12-5.
Services:	Appraisals, search service, catalog, accepts want lists.
Travel:	Wilshire west exit off 405 Fwy. Proceed west on Wilshire to San Vicente, then continue on San Vicente to Barrington.
Map Ref:	Map 6, page 122, #14.
Credit Cards:	Yes
Owner:	Pat & Craig Graham
Year Estab:	1978
Comments:	When we attempted to visit this shop at its old location on Westwood Boulevard in Los Angeles, we discovered a sign on the door informing would be customers that the shop had relocated to the above address.

Burbank
(Map 9, page 64)

Atlantis Book Shop   **Open Shop**
144 South San Fernando Boulevard 91502   Fax: (818) 845-0460   (818) 845-6467

Collection:	General stock.
Specialties:	Politics; history; true crime; UFOs; military; secret societies; Central Intelligence Agency; conspiracy; assassination.

(Burbank)

# of Vols:	30,000
Hours:	Mon-Sat 10-6, except Sat till 8. Sun 12-5.
Services:	Search service, accepts want lists, mail order.
Travel:	Near intersection of 5 Fwy and 1st St, about five blocks from Media Center shopping mall.
Credit Cards:	Yes
Owner:	Paul Hunt
Year Estab:	1978

Automotive Book Stop **Open Shop**
1508A West Magnolia Boulevard 91505 (818) 845-1202

Collection:	Specialty
Specialties:	Automobiles; aviation.
# of Vols:	2,000-3,000
Hours:	Tue-Fri 12-6. Sat 10-5.
Credit Cards:	No
Owner:	Fred Chaparro
Year Estab:	1985

Avon Book Shop **Open Shop**
3604 West Magnolia Boulevard 91505 (818) 842-6816

Collection:	General stock.
Specialties:	History
# of Vols:	25,000
Hours:	Mon-Sat 10-6, except Fri till 8.
Services:	Search service.
Travel:	Near intersection of Magnolia and Hollywood Way.
Credit Cards:	Yes
Owner:	Paul Hunt
Year Estab:	1995
Comments:	An interesting shop with books representing most subject areas. The majority of books we saw were in good condition with some titles certainly fitting the category of "the unusual" and a majority of the books likely to be of interest to specialists. Since there are two other shops within a three block radius, it certainly makes sense to visit all of them. Your luck is bound to reward you in one or more of these visits.

Book City Of Burbank **Open Shop**
308 North San Fernando Boulevard 91502 Fax: (818) 848-5615 (818) 848-4417

Collection:	General stock of mostly hardcover.
Specialties:	Performing arts; fine art; photography; graphics; illustrated.
# of Vols:	150,000
Hours:	Mon-Sat 10-9. Sun 11-9.
Services:	Appraisals, search service, catalog for screen plays; accepts want lists, mail order.

Travel: Olive exit off I-5 northbound. East on Olive then north on San Fernando.
Credit Cards: Yes
Owner: Mitch Siegel
Year Estab: 1981
Comments: The same layout and organizational pattern as the shop's sister store in Hollywood (see Hollywood listings), the only difference being that this collection is a bit smaller.

Cook Books - By Janet Jarvits, Bookseller
321 North San Fernando Boulevard
Mailing Address: PO Box 11327 Burbank 91510

Open Shop
(818) 848-4630
Fax: (818) 845-0460

Collection: Specialty
Specialties: Cookbooks; wine.
# of Vols: 10,000
Hours: Mon-Sat 11-7. Sun 12-7.
Services: Appraisals, search service, catalog, accepts want lists.
Travel: From I-5 north: Olive exit. Continue along frontage road. Right on Orange Grove, left on San Fernando Blvd. From I-5 south: Verdugo Rd exit.
Credit Cards: Yes
Year Estab: 1989

Harold B. Diamond, Bookseller
PO Box 1193 91507

By Appointment
(818) 846-0342

Collection: General stock.
Specialties: English and American literature; foreign language literature; history; signed; presentation copies; law; art; Judaica; natural history; medicine; Western Americana; economics; social science; political science; science fiction; fantasy; books about books; World War I; Darwin; erotica.
Services: Occasional catalog, accepts want lists.
Year Estab: 1964

Dutton's Books/Burbank
3806 West Magnolia Boulevard 91505

Open Shop
(818) 840-8003

Collection: General stock of new and used, paperback and hardcover.
# of Vols: 30,000 (used)
Hours: Mon-Sat 9:30-6.
Services: Accepts want lists, mail order.
Travel: Hollywood Way exit off Ventura Fwy. Proceed north on Hollywood Way. Left on West Magnolia Blvd.
Credit Cards: Yes
Owner: Davis & Judy Dutton
Year Estab: 1984
Comments: The stock is approximately 40% used, 60% of which is hardcover.

Last Grenadier
335 North San Fernando Boulevard 91502

Open Shop
(818) 848-9144

Collection: Specialty. Mostly used and some new.

Specialties:	Military.
Hours:	Mon-Fri 11:30-7, except Fri till 9. Sat 11-7. Sun 11-6.
Services:	Accepts want lists, mail order.
Travel:	See Book City of Burbank above.
Credit Cards:	Yes
Owner:	Christopher Johnston
Year Estab:	1976

Magnolia Park Book Shop   **Open Shop**
3508 West Magnolia Boulevard 91505   Fax: (818) 556-3449   (818) 556-3441

Collection:	General stock of mostly hardcover.
Specialties:	Military; children's; reference.
# of Vols:	50,000
Hours:	Mon-Sat 11-7, except Fri till 9. Sun 12-5.
Services:	Accepts want lists, mail order.
Travel:	Near Hollywood Way and 134 Fwy.
Credit Cards:	Yes
Owner:	Paul Hunt
Year Estab:	1945
Comments:	Sometimes you can learn about a store you visit by watching its customers. When we visited this shop, we couldn't help but note a young man moving from aisle to aisle with a rather large pile of books in his arms. When the books were brought to the front counter they were far from light reading. Based on our own stroll through the several aisles of this spacious shop, we believe it fair to say that there is something available for almost every taste in this shop and that although we did not spot (perhaps due to our own ineptitude) many antiquarian or truly rare titles, we did find a large selection of good reading copies at reasonable prices.

Movie World   **Open Shop**
212 North San Fernando Boulevard 91502   (818) 846-0459

Collection:	Specialty books (mostly used), magazines and ephemera.
Specialties:	Film; theater; dance; biography.
Hours:	Mon-Sat 10-8. Sun 10-6.
Services:	Accepts want lists.
Travel:	See Book City of Burbank above.
Credit Cards:	Yes
Owner:	Steve Edrington
Year Estab:	1984

Burlingame
(Map 17, page 154)

Burlingame Book Browse   **Open Shop**
1101 Juanita Avenue 94010   (415) 579-2665

Collection:	General stock of hardcover and paperback.
# of Vols:	40,000

Hours:	Tue-Fri 12-5. Sat 11-6. Sun 12-5.
Travel:	Broadway exit off Hwy 101. Proceed west on Broadway, then right on California and left on Juanita.
Credit Cards:	Yes
Owner:	Steve Feldman
Year Estab:	1989
Comments:	Visiting this shop gives one the feeling of being in a really classic "old time book shop" in that one can wander from room to room (we counted at least six of them) and from corridor to corridor (we lost track of how many after awhile) to find books, books and more books in almost every subject imaginable. The majority of the books were in good condition, with some older items on hand including books that could certainly be classified as antiquarian and/or collectible. The variety and depth in most subjects should make your visit to this shop truly a worthwhile experience. We wish we could have stayed longer.

Historicana By Appointment
1200 Edgehill Drive 94044 Fax: (415) 579-6014 (415) 343-9578

Collection:	Specialty
Specialties:	Americana; literature; Judaica.
Services:	Catalog
Owner:	Irvin Unger

Ken Prag Paper Americana By Appointment
PO Box 531 94011 (415) 566-6400

Collection:	Ephemera
Services:	Appraisals, catalog, accepts want lists.
Credit Cards:	No
Year Estab:	1972

Calabasas

Robert Ross & Co. By Appointment
PO Box 8362 91372 Fax: (818) 348-7867 (818) 348-7867

Collection:	Specialty
Specialties:	Maps; atlases; geographies (new and old); cartographic references.
Services:	Appraisals, search service, catalog.
Credit Cards:	No
Year Estab:	1980

Camarillo
(Map 5, page 235)

The Dollar Book Store Open Shop
330 North Lantana 93010 (805) 484-8085

Collection:	General stock of mostly paperback.
Hours:	Mon-Sat 10-6. Sun 11-3.

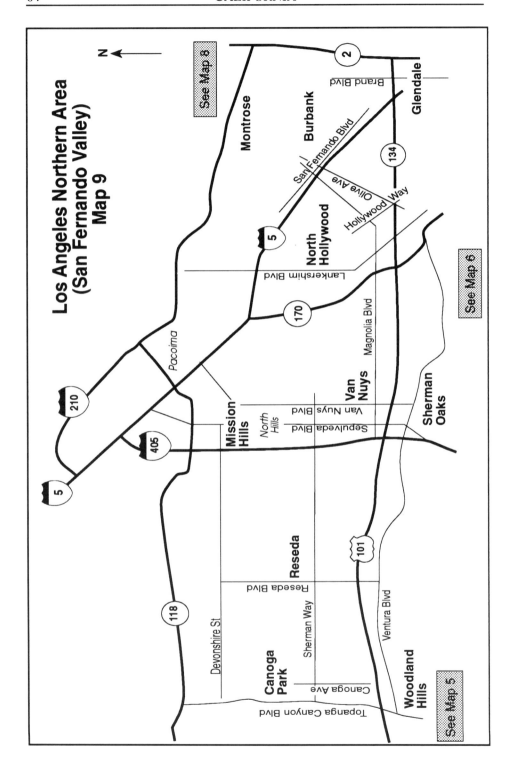

Past Times Bookshop **Open Shop**
2312 Ventura Boulevard 93010 (805 388-9970

Collection: General stock.
Specialties: Modern first editions; Americana; California.
# of Vols: 10,000
Hours: Tue-Fri 11-6. Sat 10-5.
Services: Appraisals, accepts want lists, mail order.
Travel: Northbound on 101 Fwy: Lewis Rd exit. Immediate left on Daily Dr, then left at first light on Arniell Rd. Shop is at intersection of Arniell and Ventura Blvd. Southbound on 101 Fwy: Carmen Dr exit. Proceed straight on Ventura Blvd to Arniell. Shop is on the right.
Credit Cards: No
Owner: Roger Jaep
Year Estab: 1992
Comments: For a small community book store we were pleasantly surprised at the variety and quality of the titles available here for perusal. Clearly, the size of the shop precluded depth in any area, but if you're on the road and nearby, a brief stop here could prove satisfying to your book buying tastes.

Cambria
(Map 5, page 235)

The Media Shack **Open Shop**
852 Main 93428 (805) 927-0134

Collection: General stock of hardcover and paperback.
# of Vols: 25,000+
Hours: Daily 10-6.
Travel: Main St exit off Hwy 1.
Credit Cards: No
Owner: John Wilson
Year Estab: 1995
Comments: A new owner (with new books and even new bookcases) on the site of a shop that went out of business after suffering severe flood damage. Most of the books we saw, a mix of hardcover reading copies and paperbacks, were of mixed vintage and in mixed condition. We saw little we could say really stood out in the way of being out of the ordinary.

Weinstein & Ruhl Fine Books **By Appointment**
601 Canterbury Lane 93428 (805) 927-0209

Collection: Specialty
Specialties: Literature (pre 20th cent.); fine and applied art; African American literature.
# of Vols: 40,000
Services: Catalog, appraisals, accepts want lists.
Credit Cards: No
Owner: Jerry Weinstein & Sidney Ruhl
Year Estab: 1993

Windmill Books	**Open Shop**
821 Cornwall Street 93428	Fax: (805) 927-3969 (805) 927-3900

Collection: General stock of mostly hardcover.
# of Vols: 3,000
Hours: Tue-Sun 11-5.
Travel: Main St exit off Hwy 1. Shop is just off Main St.
Credit Cards: No
Owner: Susan Hoffman
Year Estab: 1993
Comments: A rather small shop located in the heart of a tourist town. What you see is what there is and it shouldn't take you more than a few minutes to view what is there. Although the stock is limited, we were able to leave with at least one item in our area of interest in quite good condition and at a most reasonable price.

Cameron Park

Sundance Books	**Open Shop**
3450 Palmer Drive, Ste 9 95682	(916) 677-4217

Collection: General stock of new and mostly paperback used.
Hours: Mon-Thu & Sat 10-7. Fri 10-9. Sun 12-5.

Camino

Book Barn	**Open Shop**
4123 Carson Road	(916) 644-3499

Mailing Address: PO Box 163123 Sacramento 95816

Collection: General stock of mostly paperback.
Hours: Mon-Sat 10-4.

Canoga Park
(Map 9, page 64)

Green Ginger Bookshop	**Open Shop**
21710 Sherman Way 91303	(818) 713-1601

Collection: General stock of hardcover and paperback and records.
Specialties: Americana; Western Americana; art; nautical; automobile repair; technical; cookbooks.
# of Vols: 60,000+
Hours: Mon-Sat 11-7.
Travel: Topanga Canyon Blvd exit off 101 Fwy. Proceed north on Topanga Canyon Blvd for about three miles, then right on Sherman Way.
Credit Cards: Yes
Owner: Eve Klein
Year Estab: 1994

Comments: If you're looking for a specific title and know the author, that may not be enough to find the book here. While the shelves are labeled, the books are not all shelved in alphabetical order. Thus, one has to scan an entire section to see if the desired author is one hand. If you like volume, you should be pleased with a visit here as the store is certainly strong in this feature - to the point where many shelves are double stacked, a factor that adds to the time required to search for the titles you may be seeking. Despite the aforementioned caveats, we made three purchases here and paid very little. The books were in mixed vintage and of mixed condition.

Canyon Country

Paperback Emporium *Open Shop*
18970 Soledad Canyon Road 91350 (805) 251-4508

Collection: General stock of mostly paperback.
Hours: Tue-Fri 10-5:30. Sat 10-5.

Carlsbad
(Map 15, page 97)

Good Books Limited *Open Shop*
3095-A State Street 92008 (619) 729-8384

Collection: General stock of new and used hardcover and paperback.
# of Vols: 8,000-10,000
Hours: Wed-Sun 11-5.
Travel: Carlsbad Village Dr exit off I-5. West on Carlsbad. Left on State.
Credit Cards: No
Owner: Jodi Pendry Good
Year Estab: 1994
Comments: A relatively new shop at the time of our visit offering fairly common titles in popular fiction and non fiction.

Jim Hansen Books *By Appointment*
3514 Highland Drive 92008 Fax: (619) 729-8797 (619) 729-3383

Collection: General stock of mostly used.
Specialties: Scholarly and academic; California; Southwest Americana; Baja California.
# of Vols: 10,000
Services: Catalog
Credit Cards: No
Year Estab: 1975

Hyacinths for the Soul *Open Shop*
2984 State Street 92008 (619) 729-9040

Collection: General stock.
# of Vols: 8,000
Hours: Tue-Sun 11-5.
Services: Appraisals, accepts want lists, mail order.

68   CALIFORNIA

Travel: Carlsbad Village Dr exit off I-5. West on Carlsbad, then right on State.
Credit Cards: Yes
Owner: Judy & Dean Heyenga
Year Estab: 1993
Comments: A relatively small, easy to browse shop with books in rather good condition. If a book you're looking for is here, it shouldn't take you long to locate it.

Roseboro House   **Open Shop**
2971 State Street   (619) 729-3667
Mailing Address: PO Box 1863 Carlsbad 92008

Collection: General stock and ephemera.
# of Vols: 17,000
Hours: Mon-Fri 10-3. Sat 10-4.
Services: Search service, accepts want lists, mail order.
Travel: See Hyacinths for the Soul above.
Credit Cards: Yes
Owner: Joseph & Barbara Hurwitz
Year Estab: 1978
Comments: This combination used book/antique shop has a nice selection of books, although there were fewer volumes on hand to browse than the number indicated above. The titles we saw were mixed in terms of vintage, condition and value. Since the owners have computerized their stock, if you're looking for a specific title, you might save some time by calling ahead.

Vigne Co.   **Open Shop**
505 Oak Avenue 92008   (619) 729-7081

Collection: General stock.
Specialties: Art; Western Americana; literature; Franklin Mint editions.
# of Vols: 10,000
Hours: Daily 12-5 but best to call ahead.
Services: Appraisals, accepts want lists.
Travel: See Good Books Limited above. Proceed to end of State St.
Credit Cards: No
Owner: Tom Vigne
Year Estab: 1960
Comments: A combination book/collectibles shop with the books very much like those seen in multi dealer antique malls. There were plenty of titles. There was even a semblance of organization. But, the books were difficult to view as there were so many other "collectibles" in the way. We saw little that would whet the taste of an avid book person.

Carmel

Pacific Rim Galleries   **By Appointment**
3548 Greenfield Place 93923   (408) 625-2669

Collection: Specialty

Specialties:	Ansel Adams; Mary Austin; Robinson Jeffers; Henry Miller; John Steinbeck; Edward Weston.
Services:	Mail order.
Credit Cards:	No
Owner:	James H. Johnson
Year Estab:	1981

Carmichael
(Map 13, page 189)

Book Attic   **By Appointment**
PO Box 1094 95608   (916) 944-1635

Collection:	General stock.
# of Vols:	500
Services:	Search service, mail order.
Owner:	Carolyn Garrison
Year Estab:	1977

Bookworm   **Open Shop**
4132 Manzanita 95608   (916) 485-1284

Collection:	General stock of mostly paperback.
Hours:	Mon-Sat 10-5:30. Sun 1-5.

Carpinteria

Richard Gilbo-Bookseller   **By Appointment**
PO Box 12 93014   (805) 684-2892

Collection:	Specialty
Specialties:	Modern first editions; black studies; mountaineering; travel; hunting; fishing; cookbooks.
# of Vols:	3,500
Services:	Catalog, accepts want lists.
Credit Cards:	No
Owner:	Richard & Patricia Gilbo
Year Estab:	1985

Ceres
(Map 4, page 78)

2nd Edition Books   **Open Shop**
2517-E Mitchell Road 95307   (209) 538-4870

Collection:	General stock of paperback and hardcover.
Specialties:	Civil War; Western Americana; mystery; science fiction.
# of Vols:	50,000
Hours:	Mon-Sat 9-6, except Thu till 8.
Travel:	Mitchell Rd exit off Hwy 99. Proceed north on Mitchell for about 3/4 mile. Shop is located in Whitmore Plaza shopping center.

Credit Cards: No
Owner: Martin & Georgia Johnson
Year Estab: 1992
Comments: This shop carries more paperbacks than hardcover books with the hardcover titles representing a mix of both vintage and condition. The shelves are clearly labeled and the size of the shop makes browsing an activity that can be completed in a reasonably short period. Our impression was that a majority of the books were reading copies and that this is an establishment that provides good reading support for the community it serves.

Chico
(Map 11, page 289)

Collectors Ink — **Open Shop**
932 West 8th Avenue, Ste A 95926   (916) 345-0958

Collection: General stock of new and some used paperback and hardcover.
# of Vols: 200+ (used)
Hours: Tue-Sat 10-5:30.

The Paperback Exchange — **Open Shop**
951 Nord Avenue, Ste. 1 95926   (916) 343-6106

Collection: General stock of paperback and hardcover.
Hours: Mon-Sat 10-5. Sun 12-5.
Comments: Stock is approximately 60% paperback.

Chino
(Map 12, page 139)

Book Nook — **Open Shop**
12085 Central Avenue 91710   (909) 590-2110

Collection: General stock of hardcover and paperback.
# of Vols: 40,000+
Hours: Mon-Thu 10-7. Fri & Sat 10-9. Sun 12-6.
Travel: Central Ave exit off 60 Fwy. North on Central to Philadelphia.
Credit Cards: Yes
Owner: Marilyn Waters
Year Estab: 1993
Comments: Stock is approximately 50% paperback.

Citrus Heights

Boomerang Books — **Open Shop**
6632 Greenback Lane 95621   (916) 722-6133

Collection: General stock of mostly paperback.
Hours: Mon-Fri 1-6. Sat 10-5.

Claremont
(Map 12, page 139)

Claremont Books & Prints — **Open Shop**
128 Yale Avenue (upstairs) 91711   (909) 624-0757

Collection:	General stock of hardcover and some paperback.
Specialties:	Scholarly books; Western Americana; press books; social sciences; literature.
# of Vols:	10,000
Hours:	Tue-Sat 10:30-5:30.
Services:	Appraisals, lists, accepts wants lists, mail order.
Travel:	Indian Hill exit off 10 Fwy. North on Indian Hill, right on 2nd St, right on Yale.
Credit Cards:	Yes
Owner:	Charles A. Goldsmid
Year Estab:	1983
Comments:	Stock is approximately 70% hardcover.

Clovis

Bookworm — **Open Shop**
516 Fifth Street 93612   (209) 298-7650

Collection:	General stock of mostly paperback.
Hours:	Mon-Sat 10-5, except Fri till 6:30 (May-Sept).

Coarsegold

Coarsegold Book Peddler — **Open Shop**
35430 Highway 41   (209) 683-8024
Mailing Address: PO Box 1062 Coarsegold 93614

Collection:	General stock of mostly paperback.
Hours:	Mon 12-3. Tue-Fri 10-5. Sat 10-4.

Concord
(Map 17, page 154)

Bay Books — **Open Shop**
1669 Willow Pass Road 94520   (510) 671-2245

Collection:	General stock of mostly used hardcover and paperback.
# of Vols:	75,000+
Hours:	Mon-Fri 10-8. Sat 10-7. Sun 11-5.
Services:	Search service.
Travel:	Willow Pass Rd exit off I-680. Proceed east on Willow Pass. Shop is in shopping center between Market and Concord.
Credit Cards:	Yes
Owner:	Donna Davidson

Year Estab: 1990
Comments: A large shop (both wide and deep) with mostly new books displayed up front and used books (more hardcover than paperback) taking up the remainder of the shop. Many first editions, some leather bindings, a few sets and even an old encyclopedia and reference volumes. Some vintage items as well as collectibles under glass. Well organized and attractively displayed. The owner has a second similar, although smaller, shop in San Ramon.

The Book Tree **Open Shop**
1828 Salvio Street 94518 (510) 687-7343

Collection: General stock of paperback and hardcover.
Specialties: Children's.
Hours: Mon-Fri 10-7. Sat 10-6. Sun 11-5.
Services: Accepts want lists.
Travel: See Bay Books above. Shop is at end of the shopping center in rear.
Credit Cards: Yes
Owner: Virginia Larson & Sandra Longworth
Year Estab: 1975
Comments: The majority of the books were paperback with a limited selection of hardcover books, most of which were of quite recent vintage. Some Franklin Mint/Easton leather bindings.

Brooks Books **By Appointment**
1343 New Hampshire Drive (510) 672-4566
Mailing Address: PO Box 21473 Concord 94521 Fax: (510) 672-3338

Collection: Specialty
Specialties: Botany; horticulture; landscape architecture; gardening; cacti and succulents; plant hunting; forestry; orchids; roses; fruit; floras; herbs.
# of Vols: 5,000
Services: Search service, catalog, accepts want lists.
Credit Cards: Yes
Owner: Philip & Martha Nesty
Year Estab: 1986

Corning
(Map 11, page 289)

Foster Book Form **By Appointment**
25079 Ohio Avenue 96021 Fax: (916) 824-2614 (916) 824-2614

Collection: General stock.
Specialties: Pre-1900 books.
# of Vols: "Small"
Services: Accepts want lists, mail order.
Credit Cards: No
Owner: Dorth Foster
Year Estab: 1970

Corona

Book Exchange   **Open Shop**
1390 West 6th Street, #108 91720   (909) 736-6603

Collection: General stock of mostly paperback.
Hours: Mon-Sat 10-6. Sun 11-3.

Corte Madera
(Map 17, page 154)

Book Passage Used & Rare Books   **Open Shop**
51 Tamal Vista Boulevard 94925   (800) 999-7909 (415) 927-0960
Fax: (415) 924-3838

Collection: General stock of primarily new and some used paperback and hardcover.
Specialties: Mystery.
# of Vols: 10,000+
Hours: Daily 9am-10pm, except Fri & Sat till 11pm.
Services: Search service, mail order.
Travel: Northbound on Hwy 101: Paradise Dr exit. Left and crossover freeway. Right at third light. Continue to Market Place Shopping Center. Southbound on Hwy 101: Madera Blvd exit. Turn right at stop sign.
Credit Cards: Yes
Owner: Elaine & Bill Petrocelli
Year Estab: 1976
Comments: Far from a typical used book shop. How could it be since the majority of the books offered for sale are new? Despite that caveat, if you're a mystery aficionado, you should find this a delightful place to visit as its out-of-print selections (mostly more recent issues) represent a respectable offering. And, if you play your cards right and can time your visit appropriately (call ahead for dates), you might even arrive during the shop's annual mystery writer's conference and have an opportunity to meet and/or have a book autographed by an eminent writer. The shop is large, has an adjacent annex that sells coffee plus magazines and newspapers and has an upbeat style. Who knows? Pardon us for suggesting it, but you may even purchase a new book here.

Richard Glassman Books   **Open Shop**
15 First Street 94925   (415) 924-0410

Collection: General stock.
Specialties: Literary biography; poetry; gardening; birding; nature; fine printing; history; travel; children's; cooking; needlework; fiction; Modern Library.
# of Vols: 8,000
Hours: Saturday afternoons and other times by appointment.
Travel: Corte Madera exit off Hwy 101. West on Tamalpais Dr, left on Corte Madera and left on First.
Credit Cards: No
Year Estab: 1978

Select Press **By Appointment**
PO Box 37 94976 (415) 433-3325

Collection: Specialty
Specialties: Children's series.
# of Vols: 2,000
Services: Accepts want lists.
Credit Cards: Yes
Owner: R. Crandall
Year Estab: 1977

Costa Mesa
(Map 7, page 270)

Apollo Book Shop **Open Shop**
1670 Westminster Avenue 92627 (714) 646-7045

Collection: General stock of hardcover and paperback.
Specialties: Maritime; Hawaii; South Seas; Alaska; California.
# of Vols: 15,000+
Hours: Mon-Fri 10-7. Sat 10-6.
Services: Appraisals, occasional catalog, search service, accepts want lists, mail order.
Travel: Newport Blvd exit off 55 Fwy. Proceed south (toward ocean). Left on 17th St, then right on Westminster (a small street just after Orange that appears to cut through the shopping center). Shop is in rear of shopping center.
Credit Cards: No
Owner: James L. Currie
Year Estab: 1961
Comments: Once you locate this shop (hidden behind a shopping center) you'll find a collection of older books in a difficult-to-browse set up. Either the shop needs to be at least twice its current size in order to accommodate the number of books we saw piled in the aisles or at least one half the books should be stored elsewhere in order for the browser to be able to comfortably view the titles. This is a frustrating situation because there could be some real winners here. But unless you have the patience of a Job, you're not likely to find them. (We didn't see any labels on the shelves.)

Book King **Open Shop**
103 East 17th Street 92627 (714) 631-3838

Collection: General stock of mostly hardcover.
Specialties: Modern first editions; mystery; science fiction.
# of Vols: 20,000
Hours: Mon-Thu 10-6. Fri 10-7. Sat 10-6. Sun 11-5.
Services: Search service, catalog, accepts want lists.
Travel: Hwy 55 south to Newport Blvd, then Newport Blvd to 17th St. Right on 17th and an immediate left into shopping center.
Credit Cards: Yes
Owner: Barry Pines & Roy Robbins
Year Estab: 1994

Comments: Two signs in the front window read: "Romances 50¢" and "Come In And See Our $1 Specials." Despite the message conveyed by these two signs and one's initial impression upon entering the shop, the owner does maintain a separate room in the back of the shop marked "Rare Books" in which, in addition to copies of some current new books, there are also some first editions of older titles. In conclusion, one might observe that while the general stock is limited, if you're interested in one of the specialties listed above, you could find an item here worth adding to your collection.

The Book Store
130 East 17th Street, Ste. L 92627

Open Shop
(714) 645-5496

Collection:	General stock.
Specialties:	First editions.
# of Vols:	7,500
Hours:	Tue-Fri 10-7. Sat 10-6. Sun: Call.
Travel:	55 Fwy to end which becomes Newport Blvd. Left on 17th St and make first possible U turn. Shop is in a strip shopping center.
Credit Cards:	No
Owner:	Brad & Nancy Wilson
Year Estab:	1992
Comments:	Unfortunately, our schedule brought us to Costa Mesa on a Monday when this shop is normally closed.

Recycled Romances & Other Used Books
145/147 Broadway 92627

Open Shop
(714) 645-0529

Collection:	General stock of primarily used paperback.
Hours:	Tue-Sat 10-5:30.

Robinson Book Store
1125 Victoria, Unit P 92627

Open Shop
(714) 631-6113

Collection:	General stock of mostly hardcover.
# of Vols:	10,000
Hours:	Tue-Sun 11-7.
Services:	Appraisals, search service, mail order, accepts want lists.
Travel:	Victoria exit off 55 Fwy. Proceed west on Victoria.
Credit Cards:	No
Owner:	Mark Robinson
Year Estab:	1994
Comments:	Unfortunately, another shop that was closed on Monday.

Thinker Used Books
1525 Mesa Verde Drive East 92626

Open Shop
(714) 540-7771

Collection:	General stock of mostly paperback.
Hours:	Mon-Sat 10-5:30.

Visions & Dreams
1804 Newport Boulevard 92627

Open Shop
(714) 650-0730

Collection:	Specialty. Primarily new with some used.

Specialties:	Metaphysics.
Hours:	Mon-Sat 10-9. Sun 10-7.
Travel:	55 Fwy to end in Newport Beach. Continue on Newport Blvd.

Cotati
(Map 11, page 289)

Inn Of The Beginning   **Open Shop**
8201 Old Redwood Highway 94931   (707) 794-9453

Collection:	General stock of mostly paperback.
Hours:	Daily 9am-midnight.

Vicarious Experience Books   **Open Shop**
60 West Sierra Avenue 94931   (707) 795-6457

Collection:	General stock of hardcover and paperback.
Specialties:	Metaphysics.
# of Vols:	6,000+
Hours:	Mon, Thu, Sat 12-5. Other times by appointment.
Services:	Accepts want lists.
Travel:	West Sierra exit off Hwy 101. Proceed east on West Sierra.
Credit Cards:	No
Owner:	Jon Wobber
Year Estab:	1979
Comments:	Stock is approximately 50% paperback.

Covina
(Map 8, page 168)

The Book Shop   **Open Shop**
134 North Citrus 91723   (818) 967-1888   (800) 507-7323

Collection:	General stock of hardcover and paperback.
Specialties:	California; Western Americana; literary first editions; science fiction first editions; jazz and jazz musicians.
# of Vols:	30,000
Hours:	Mon-Thu 10-9. Fri & Sat 10-10. Sun 12-6.
Services:	Appraisals, search service, catalog, accepts want lists (from collectors only).
Travel:	Citrus exit off 10 Fwy. Proceed north on Citrus.
Credit Cards:	Yes
Owner:	Roger Gozdecki
Year Estab:	1981
Comments:	The shop has a nice selection of books, most of which are in good condition and ran the gamut from mostly recent editions to some vintage items. At least half of the stock on display is paperback. Notwithstanding that observation, the hardcover titles we saw and the appearance of the shop suggest that unless your needs are highly esoteric and/or scholarly to the nth degree, a visit here should be worth the time invested.

Open Shops and By Appointment Dealers 77

Christian Discount Book Center   **Open Shop**
1010 East Arrow Highway 91724   (818) 967-2893

Collection: Specialty new and used.
Specialties: Religion
Hours: Mon-Sat 9-9.

Crestline

George Frederick Kolbe   **By Appointment**
PO Drawer 3100 92325   Fax: (909) 338-6980   (909) 338-6527

Collection: Specialty books and periodicals.
Specialties: Numismatics (all languages and periods).
# of Vols: 10,000+
Services: Appraisals, catalog, accepts want lists.
Credit Cards: Yes
Year Estab: 1967

Culver City
(Map 6, page 122)

Book Barrel   **Open Shop**
6273 Bristol Parkway 90230   * (310) 641-6889

Collection: General stock of paperback and hardcover.
# of Vols: 70,000
Hours: Mon-Sat. Call for hours.
Travel: At Sepulveda and Green Valley Circle.
Map Ref   Map 6, page 122, #15.
Year Estab: 1985
Comments: Stock is approximately 65% paperback.

Red Star Military Museum & Sales   **Open Shop**
11018 Washington Boulevard 90232   Fax: (310) 559-5530   * (310) 559-7730

Collection: Specialty used and new books and related items.
Specialties: Military.
# of Vols: 10,000+
Hours: Mon-Sat 11-5.
Services: Accepts want lists, mail order.
Travel: Four blocks east of 405 Fwy.
Credit Cards: Yes
Owner: Loren Relin
Year Estab: 1975
Comments: Stock is approximately 60% used.

Cupertino

A Clean Well-Lighted Place For Books   **Open Shop**
21269 Stevens Creek Boulevard 95014   (408) 255-7600

Collection: General stock of mostly paperback new and used.

* Some 310 area codes change to 562 in 1996

Hours: Sun-Thu 10am-11pm. Fri & Sat 10am-midnight.

A Wrinkle In Time   **Open Shop**
19970 Homestead Road 95014   (408) 255-9406

Collection: Specialty used and new. Mostly paperback.
Specialties: Science fiction; horror; fantasy.
Hours: Daily 11-10, except Fri & Sat till midnight.

Seven Authors Bookshop   **Open Shop**
10961 North Wolfe Road 95014   (408) 252-5662

Collection: Specialty. Primarily new.
Specialties: American authors: the land and people; children's.

Danville
(Map 17, page 154)

Danville Books   **By Appointment**
404 Hartz Avenue 94526   (510) 837-4200

Collection: General stock.

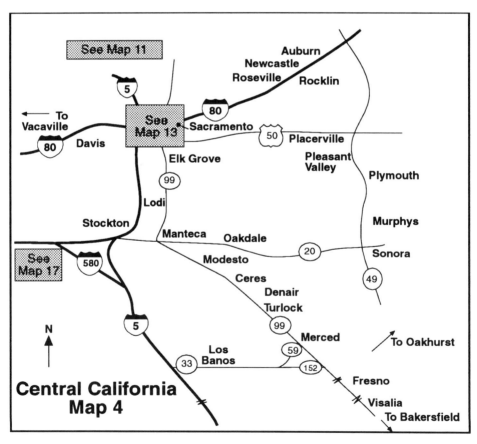

Davis
(Map 4, page 78)

AG Access   **Open Shop**
603 4th Street 95616   Fax: (916) 756-7188   (916) 756-7177

Collection:	Specialty. Mostly new.
Specialties:	Agriculture; horticulture; forestry; water issues; land use.
Hours:	Mon-Fri 9-5:30. Sat 10-4.
Services:	Mail order.
Travel:	See Bogey's Books below. Shop is at corner of 4th & E Streets.
Owner:	Karen Van Epen
Year Estab:	1984

Bogey's Books   **Open Shop**
223 E. Street 95828   Fax: (916)757-6127   (916) 757-6127

Collection:	General stock of mostly used hardcover and paperback.
# of Vols:	20,000
Hours:	Sun-Thu 10-10. Fri & Sat 10-11.
Travel:	Richards Blvd exit off I-80. Proceed on Richards under bridge. Right on E.
Credit Cards:	Yes
Owner:	Mark Nemmers
Year Estab:	1990
Comments:	A generously proportioned shop that intershelves its collection of paperbacks and hardcover volumes. We saw a few older items, some nice classics and many of the titles one would expect in a college town. Most of the items were of fairly recent vintage and none, at least that we could spot, would fit into the rare and/or collectible category. Basically, a nice bookshop that serves the needs of its community.

Coffee & Classics   **Open Shop**
132 E Street, #1B 95616   (916) 758-7358

Collection:	General stock of hardcover and paperback.
Specialties:	Science; literature; scholarly; university press; history.
# of Vols:	20,000
Hours:	Mon-Fri 7:30am-10pm. Sat 8am-10pm. Sun 9am-6pm.
Travel:	See Bogey's above. Shop is one block ahead in Mansion Square Complex.
Credit Cards:	No
Owner:	Cathy & Dale Richardson
Year Estab:	1992
Comments:	Like so many other combination book/coffee shops, you're more likely to get a good cup of espresso and pastry here than a rare book. We saw paperbacks and hardcover volumes intershelved and at the time of our visit would doubt that there were half the number of volumes suggested above on display. One sign cautioning buyers to beware that dictionaries for sale had pages missing (hence, the lower price) caught our eye and perhaps said something about the shop itself.

Del Mar
(Map 15, page 97)

Book Works   **Open Shop**
2670 Via de la Valle 92014   (619) 755-3735

Collection: General stock of mostly new books.
# of Vols: 600+ (used)
Hours: Mon-Thu 10-10. Fri & Sat 10-11. Sun 10-8.
Comments: Used stock is approximately 60% paperback.

Denair
(Map 4, page 78)

Johnson's Antiques & Books   **Open Shop**
5401 Hickman Road 95316   (209) 632-1774

Collection: General stock.
# of Vols: 3,000
Hours: Mon-Sat 10-5.
Travel: Keys Rd exit off Hwy 99. Southeast on Keys Rd. Right on Hickman.

Desert Hot Springs
(Map 12, page 139)

Desert Used Books   **Open Shop**
11625F Palm Drive   (619) 329-4499
Mailing Address: 11761 Mesquite Ave. Desert Hot Springs 92240-3729

Collection: General stock of mostly paperback.
# of Vols: 7,000+
Hours: Mon-Sat 9-5.
Travel: Palm Dr off 10 Fwy. Proceed north to 3rd St. Shop is on left.
Credit Cards: No
Owner: Louise E. Hammari
Year Estab: 1994
Comments: We regret to say that the extra miles required to get to Desert Hot Springs is not, in our humble view, worth the drive time. The shop is crowded with approximately 95% paperback titles and the few hardcover books on display are not distinguishable in any manner.

Julia Houdek Books & Search Service   **By Appointment**
68250 Club Circle Drive 92240   (619) 329-4706

Collection: General stock.
Specialties: Literature; history.
# of Vols: 10,000
Services: Search service, accepts want lists, mail order.
Credit Cards: No
Year Estab: 1980

Diamond Bar
(Map 12, page 139)

Encore! Books　　　　　　　　　　　　　　　　　　**Open Shop**
1135 South Grand Avenue 91765　　　　　　　　　　　(909) 860-7448

Collection:　General stock of hardcover and paperback.
# of Vols:　35,000
Hours:　Mon-Sat 10-7. Sun 10-5.
Travel:　Grand Ave exit off 57 Fwy. East on Grand.
Comments:　Stock is approximately 60% paperback.

Downieville
(Map 11, page 289)

Jan's Book Nook　　　　　　　　　　　　　　　　　**Open Shop**
201 Main Street 95936　　　　　　　　　　　　　　　(916) 289-3347

Collection:　General stock of hardcover and some paperback.
Specialties:　Western Americana.
# of Vols:　2,000
Hours:　Mon-Sun 9:30-5:30.
Travel:　On Hwy 49.
Owner:　Jan Powell
Year Estab:　1993

Dunsmuir
(Map 11, page 289)

Cecchettini's Books & Things　　　　　　　　　　　**Open Shop**
5835 Dunsmuir Avenue 96025　　　　　　　　　　　　(916) 235-4047

Collection:　General stock of paperback and hardcover.
# of Vols:　15,000
Hours:　Mon & Tue 10-6. Thu-Sat 9-8. Sun 11-5.
Travel:　Central Dunsmuir exit off I-5. Follow signs for business district.
Owner:　Ron & Judi Cecchettini
Year Estab:　1994
Comments:　A rather small display of hardcover books and paperbacks, mostly reading copies, a shelf of first editions and in general very few books in the categories identified by the shelf labels. Most of the items appeared to be of recent vintage. The owner indicates that he has additional "rare" books which he will show to visitors upon request.

Turn Table Books　　　　　　　　　　　　　　　　**Open Shop**
4118 Pine Street 96025　　　　　　　　　　　　　　　(916) 235-2665

Collection:　General stock of new and used hardcover and paperback.
Specialties:　Railroads
# of Vols:　5,000
Hours:　Wed-Thu 11-4. Fri & Sat 11-7:30. Sun 11-4.
Travel:　See Cecchettini's Books & Things above. Left on Pine.

Credit Cards: Yes
Owner: Laurence Cook
Year Estab: 1994
Comments: If you like the wonders of nature and want to visit Mt. Shasta sometime during your trip, you might want to take a few minutes off and stop at this bookshop which is rather close by. The hardcover volumes were of mixed vintage with the owner trying to build a specialty in railroads. The stock, at least when we visited, was not large enough to offer much variety, but we did see some quality items.

El Cajon
(Map 15, page 97)

Fifty Thousand Books Open Shop
116 East Main Street 92020 (619) 444-6191

Collection: General stock of used and new paperback and hardcover.
Specialties: Science fiction; metaphysics; military; children's.
# of Vols: 90,000 (used)
Hours: Mon-Fri 10-7. Sat 10-6. Sun 11-5.
Travel: Magnolia exit off 8 Fwy. Right on Magnolia. Left on East Main.
Credit Cards: Yes
Owner: Tom Chambers
Year Estab: 1987
Comments: Stock is approximately 70% paperback.

L & L Book Store Open Shop
2990 Jamacha Road, #-152 92019 (619) 660-8646

Collection: General stock of paperback and hardcover.
# of Vols: 20,000
Hours: Mon-Fri 10-7. Sat 10-6.
Travel: 94 Fwy to Jamacha. Shop is in Plaza Rancho San Diego shopping center.
Credit Cards: Yes
Year Estab: 1992
Comments: Stock is approximately 75% paperback.

Romance World Open Shop
929 East Main Street 92021 (619) 588-5494

Collection: General stock of mostly paperback.
Hours: Mon-Fri 10-6. Sat 10-5. Sun 10-4.

El Centro

Book Nook Open Shop
617 Main Street 92243 (619) 352-3955

Collection: General stock of mostly new and some used paperbacks.
Hours: Mon-Fri 7:30am-7pm. Sat 8-5.

El Cerrito
(Map 3, page 52 & Map 17, page 154)

Wonderland Books   **Open Shop**
7511 Fairmount Avenue 94530   (510) 528-8475
E-mail: alland@dnai.com

Collection: General stock of mostly hardcover and ephemera.
Specialties: Children's; Western Americana; illustrated; first editions.
# of Vols: 10,000
Hours: Tue-Sun 12-5. Other times by appointment.
Services: Search service, mail order.
Travel: Central Ave exit off I-80. Proceed east on Central to end. Right on Ashbury. Left at first light on Fairmount. Shop is about two blocks ahead.
Map Ref: Map 3, page 52, #11.
Credit Cards: Yes
Owner: Allan Friedman
Year Estab: 1993
Comments: A small shop with a mix of hardcover collectibles, vintage paperbacks and ephemera. If you have a sharp eye, you stand a reasonable chance of finding a treasure here. The shop is just a few minutes north of Berkeley and if you can spare the extra time, we think it's worth it.

Elk Grove
(Map 4, page 78)

Almost Perfect Used Books   **Open Shop**
8459 Elk Grove Boulevard 95758   (916) 684-7272

Collection: General stock of mostly used paperback.
Hours: Mon-Sat 10-9. Sun 10-6.

The Bookplace by C & H   **Open Shop**
9673 Elk Grove-Florin Road 95624   (916) 985-6256

Collection: General stock of paperback and hardcover.
# of Vols: 21,000+
Hours: Mon-Fri 10:30-6:30. Sat 10:30-5:30.
Travel: Elk Grove Blvd exit off Hwy 99. Proceed east on Elk Grove for four lights. Right on Elk Grove-Florin Rd. Left at next light into shopping center.
Owner: Jodi Wyner-Holmes & Laurie Chaidez
Year Estab: 1993
Comments: Stock is approximately 70% paperback.

Encinitas
(Map 15, page 97)

Books Past & Present   **Open Shop**
292 North El Camino Real 92024   (619) 942-4265

Collection: General stock of hardcover and paperback.

Specialties: Art; metaphysics.
# of Vols: 60,000
Hours: Mon-Sat 10-9. Sun 10-5.
Services: Appraisals, search service, accepts want lists.
Travel: Encinitas Blvd exit off I-5. Proceed east on Encinitas, left on El Camino Real, then left on Via Montoro into shopping center.
Credit Cards: Yes
Comments: Because of a mix up in communications, we didn't get a chance to visit this shop which we're told carries a more collectible quality stock than the owner's other location in Vista. (See I Love Books-Bookstore.)

Encino

Malter Galleries   **Open Shop**
17005 Ventura Boulevard 91316   (818) 784-7772

Collection: Specialty new and used.
Specialties: Numismatics; archeology.
# of Vols: 3,000
Hours: Mon-Fri 10-5. Sat by appointment.
Services: Appraisals, catalog.
Travel: Off Ventura Fwy at Balboa.
Owner: Joel Malter
Year Estab: 1961

Escondido
(Map 15, page 97)

The Book Nook   **Open Shop**
415 West Grand Avenue 92025   Fax: (619) 741-1007   (619) 746-9797

Collection: General stock of hardcover and paperback.
Specialties: Cookbooks; metaphysics; classics.
# of Vols: 60,000
Hours: Tue-Thu 9-3. Fri 12-6. Sat 9-3.
Services: Accepts want lists, mail order.
Travel: Valley Pky exit off I-15. Proceed east on Valley Pky, then north on Centre City and east on Grand. Shop is one block ahead.
Credit Cards: No
Owner: Judith Nowicki
Year Estab: 1968
Comments: Every shop owner is entitled to change hours. When we visited, the hours listed above were posted on the door. However, the hours provided to us earlier were different. Had we followed our own advice, we would have called ahead and avoided finding the shop closed during our visit to Escondido.

Chapters   **Open Shop**
142 South Juniper Street 92025   (619) 480-9453

Collection: General stock of hardcover and paperback.

# of Vols:	20,000
Hours:	Mon-Sat 11-5.
Services:	Appraisals, accepts want lists, mail order.
Travel:	Valley Pky exit off I-15. Proceed east on Valley Pky which becomes 2nd St. Left on Juniper.
Credit Cards:	Yes
Owner:	Tom & Bonnie Shine
Year Estab:	1988
Comments:	Considering the limited space available in this neighborhood shop, the number of volumes on display was impressive. Except for a good number of Franklin Mints and a selection of limited edition reprints, most of the stock consisted of a mix of paperbacks, trade paperbacks and hardcover books in various stages of condition. Some of the hardcover titles looked quite intriguing while others were of a more ordinary variety. Finding the books of your choice is always a gamble. However, we would hesitate to name the odds should you decide to visit here.

Heritage Books   **Open Shop**
1785 South Escondido Boulevard, #E 92025   (619) 746-6601

Collection:	General stock.
Specialties:	Children's illustrated; early literature; history; art; first editions.
# of Vols:	30,000+
Hours:	Mon-Sat 11:30-6:30.
Travel:	Center City Pky exit off I-15. Proceed north on Center City, right on Felicita and right on Escondido.
Credit Cards:	Yes
Owner:	Lydia Nikuls
Year Estab:	1966
Comments:	A rather crowded shop not at all easy to work your way around (even if you are slimmer than the authors). The books we saw were mostly in very good to fine condition with as many unusual titles as common ones. It is clear that the books in this shop have been well taken care of and their prices reflect this factor.

Joyful Word Discount   **Open Shop**
754 South Escondido 92025   (619) 743-2836

Collection:	General stock of primarily new and some used paperback and hardcover.
# of Vols:	2,000-3,000 (used)
Hours:	Mon-Fri 10-6. Sat 10-5:30.
Travel:	9th Ave exit off I-15. Proceed east on 9th, then left on Escondido.
Owner:	Donna Bennett
Comments:	Used stock is approximately 75% paperback.

"Our Shop"   **Open Shop**
239 South Kalmia Street 92025   (619) 741-4832

Collection:	General stock of hardcover and paperback.
Hours:	Mon-Sat 10-4.

Travel:	East Valley Pky off I-15. Proceed east on 2nd St, then right on Kalmia.
Comments:	Shop is operated by the Friends of the Escondido Public Library.

Eureka
(Map 11, page 289)

Booklegger   **Open Shop**
402 Second Street 95501   (707) 445-1344

Collection:	General stock of used and some new, paperback and hardcover, and some ephemera.
Specialties:	Children's; modern first editions; women's studies; art; popular fiction.
# of Vols:	37,500
Hours:	Mon-Sat 10-5:30. Sun 12-5.
Services:	Appraisals, search service.
Travel:	Located at corner of Second and E Streets in "Old Town" Eureka.
Credit Cards:	No
Owner:	Nancy Short & Jennifer McFadden
Year Estab:	1981
Comments:	A corner shop less than a half block away from a first class book dealer (see below). The stock here falls mostly into the "reading copy" category although there were some items that might be at home on the shelves of a more "collectible" quality dealer. Paperbacks and hardcover volumes were intershelved with the latter being a mix of older and newer items with an emphasis on the newer. The tightly packed nature of the shop, while providing customers an opportunity to view more titles, unfortunately, detracts from the shop's ambience.

Eureka Books   **Open Shop**
426 Second Street 95501   (707) 444-9593

Collection:	General stock.
Specialties:	Music; California; Western Americana.
# of Vols:	50,000
Hours:	Mon-Sat 10-6. Sun 12-5.
Travel:	Located in "Old Town" Eureka.
Services:	Appraisals, search service.
Credit Cards:	No
Owner:	Marilyn F. & Carlos E. Benemann
Year Estab:	1987
Comments:	When one enters this bi-level shop, one gets the impression of being in a large Victorian library: there is a sense of neatness, order and elegance about the shop. The shelves are well labeled and the books we saw were in generally good condition. The stock covered a wide range of areas making for a most pleasant visit, particularly if you enjoy browsing outside of what may be your own special interests. We did sense (based on an examination of several titles and comparing them with similar volumes in similar condition seen elsewhere) that prices here were slightly higher. Perhaps this is a reflection on the care taken to select the books or on the upkeep necessary

to keep the shop looking so good? We had the same observation about the owners' other shops in Arcata and Ferndale.

One Way Book Shop **Open Shop**
1707 E Street 95501 (707) 442-4004

Collection: Specialty new and used.
Specialties: Religion (Christian).
# of Vols: 2,000 (used)
Hours: Mon-Sat 9:30-5:30.

Small Planet Books **Open Shop**
236 G Street 95501 (707) 443-9463

Collection: General stock of used and new hardcover and paperback.
# of Vols: 5,000-10,000 (used)
Hours: Mon-Sat 10-7.
Services: Search service, accepts want lists.
Travel: Hwy 101 becomes Broadway and then 5th or 4th street in town. From 5th St, turn left on G St. From 4th St, turn right on G.
Owner: Steve Shirley & Kay Moroski
Year Estab: 1994
Comments: A block or two away from most of the other visitor oriented shops in "Old Town," this rather small shop carries a mix of attractive hardcover volumes (several dealing with art), some more common used hardcover items, paperbacks and some new books. When we visited, the shop had only been in operation for eight months, many shelves had an empty look and we would estimate that the stock on hand was less than the number cited above.

Fair Oaks
(Map 13, page 189)

Barnstormer Books **Open Shop**
10239 Fair Oaks Boulevard 95628   Fax: (916) 961-2615   (916) 961-3703

Collection: General stock of hardcover and paperback and ephemera.
Specialties: Aviation; children's.
# of Vols: 10,000
Hours: Mon-Sat 10-5. Sun 11-4.
Services: Appraisals, search service, catalog, accepts want lists.
Travel: Sunrise Blvd exit off Hwy 50. Proceed north on Sunrise. Right on Winding Way. Shop is located at intersection of Winding Way and Fair Oaks Blvd.
Map Ref: Map 13, page 189, #9.
Credit Cards: Yes
Owner: Sheri Plummer-Raphael
Year Estab: 1984
Comments: A really nice shop with much more depth to it than is initially apparent. The books we saw were well cared for, the shelves were well labeled, the books reasonably priced and the shop both easy and pleasant to browse. Well worth going out of your way for.

Bookworm
8050 Madison 95628

Open Shop
(916) 961-0542

Collection: General stock of mostly paperback.
Hours: Mon-Sat 10-5:30. Sun 1-5.

Bookworm
8121 Madison 95628

Open Shop
(916) 967-1247

Collection: General stock of mostly paperback.
Hours: Mon-Sat 10-5:30. Sun 1-5.

Fairfax
(Map 17, page 154)

New Albion Bookshop
1820 Sir Francis Drake Boulevard 94930

Open Shop
(415) 456-1464

Collection: General stock of paperback, hardcover and comics.
Specialties: Science fiction; mystery.
# of Vols: 10,000-12,000
Hours: Tue-Sat 12-6.
Travel: Five miles west of San Rafael. In center of town, across from theater.
Credit Cards: No
Owner: Hal Bertram
Year Estab: 1966

Ferndale
(Map 11, page 289)

Ferndale Books
405 Main Street
Mailing Address: PO Box 1034 Ferndale 95536

Open Shop
(707) 786-9135
Fax: (707) 786-9155

Collection: General stock.
Specialties: Latin America; California; Western Americana.
# of Vols: 20,000
Hours: Daily 10-6.
Services: Appraisals, search service.
Travel: Five miles off Hwy 101.
Credit Cards: No
Owner: Carlos E. & Marilyn F. Benemann
Year Estab: 1982
Comments: A nice looking shop with a good selection of books in most areas, although few areas were represented in any great depth. The books reached up to the shop's 20 foot+ ceiling but there were plenty of ladders on hand to assist the hearty browser. The books represented a mix of recent and older volumes, all of which appeared to be in good condition.

Folsom
(Map 13, page 189)

Almost Perfect Used Books   **Open Shop**
711-15 East Bidwell Street 95630   (916) 983-3636

Collection: General stock of mostly used paperback.
Hours: Mon-Sat 10-9. Sun 10-6.

Barber Books   **Open Shop**
6610 Folsom-Auburn Road, #10 95630   Fax: (916) 987-6225   (916) 987-2818

Collection: General stock of hardcover and paperback.
# of Vols: 15,000
Hours: Mon-Thu 10-6. Sat 10-6. Sun 12-5. Longer hours in summer.
Services: Appraisals, search service, accepts want lists.
Travel: Douglas Blvd exit off I-80. East on Douglas, right (south) on Folsom-Auburn to Greenback Lane. Shop is in shopping center.
Map Ref: Map 13, page 189, #10.
Credit Cards: Yes
Owner: Harry Barber
Year Estab: 1995
Comments: We found this shop to be "above average" in its offerings, both hardcover (mostly more recent titles) and paperbacks. The number of volumes was modest but their condition was above average. Easy to browse and pleasant to visit.

Crabtree's Collection   **Antique Mall**
At Sheepish Grin Antiques Market, 625 Sutter St.   Mall: (916) 985-0257
Mailing Address: 1850 Dormity Road Rescue 95672   Home: (916) 676-8453

Collection: General stock.
Specialties: Nature
# of Vols: 4,000
Hours: Daily 10:30-5.
Services: Appraisals, search service, accepts want lists.
Travel: Hwy 50 east from Sacramento. Folsom Blvd exit north to Sutter St.
Owner: Allen & Penny Crabtree
Year Estab: 1983

Forest Knolls

Skyline Books   **By Appointment**
PO Box T 94933   (415) 488-9491

Collection: Specialty books and ephemera.
Specialties: Beat generation; counter culture; modern literature.
# of Vols: 2,500
Services: Catalog, accepts want lists.
Owner: James Musser

Fort Bragg
(Map 11, page 289)

Estates Gallery
335 North Franklin 95437

Open Shop
(707) 964-7634

Collection:	General stock of paperback and hardcover.
Specialties:	Military; metaphysics; first editions.
# of Vols:	55,000
Hours:	Mon-Sat 10-5. Sun 11-whenever.
Services:	Appraisals, search service, accepts want lists.
Travel:	From Hwy 1 in Fort Bragg, turn east on Laurel than right on North Franklin.
Credit Cards:	Yes
Owner:	Diana & Richard Lina
Year Estab:	1982
Comments:	Stock is approximately 65% paperback.

The Bookstore
223 East Redwood Avenue 95437

Open Shop
(707) 964-6559

Collection:	General stock of paperback and hardcover.
# of Vols:	6,500
Hours:	Mon-Fri 10-6. Sat 10-4.
Travel:	1½ blocks east of Hwy 1 which is Main St in Fort Bragg.
Credit Cards:	No
Owner:	Jennifer Wolfman
Year Estab:	1980
Comments:	The stock is approximately 60% paperback.

Windsong Used Books
324 North Main Street 95437

Open Shop
(707) 964-2050

Collection:	General stock of mostly used paperback.
Hours:	Mon-Sat 10-5:30. Sun 10-4.

Fortuna
(Map 11, page 289)

The Book Rack
1711 Main Street 95540

Open Shop
(707) 725-5892

Collection:	General stock of paperback and hardcover.
# of Vols:	15,000
Hours:	Mon-Fri 10-5:30. Sat 11-4:30.
Services:	Accepts want lists.
Travel:	Main St exit off Hwy 101. Proceed east on Main for two miles.
Credit Cards:	Yes
Owner:	Keith Plant
Year Estab:	1988
Comments:	Stock is approximately 75% paperback.

Fountain Valley
(Map 7, page 270)

Anchor Book Shop — **Open Shop**
18440 Brookhurst Street 92708 (714) 963-3882

Collection:	General stock of hardcover and paperback.
Specialties:	Art
# of Vols:	25,000
Hours:	Mon-Sat 10-6. Sun 12-5.
Travel:	Brookhurst exit off 405 Fwy. Proceed south on Brookhurst for about 1/2 mile. Left into Valley Garden Shopping Center.
Credit Cards:	Yes
Owner:	Don Mitchell
Year Estab:	1979
Comments:	A well organized and attractive shop with most of the hardcover books in quite good condition with shiny dust jackets pleading to be purchased. The hardcover items are of mostly recent vintage with few older items and few items that could truly be classified as rare. About 20% of the stock consisted of paperbacks.

Cahill's Book Store — **Open Shop**
18838 Brookhurst Street 92708 (714) 963-3122

Collection:	General stock of hardcover and paperback and ephemera.
Specialties:	Modern first editions; California; Western Americana.
# of Vols:	150,000
Hours:	Mon-Sat 10-6. Sun 11-4.
Services:	Appraisals, search service, catalog, accepts want lists.
Travel:	Brookhurst exit off 405 Fwy. Proceed south on Brookhurst for one mile. Shop is on left, south of Ellis, in Fountain Plaza shopping center.
Credit Cards:	Yes
Owner:	Michael & Ida Cahill
Year Estab:	1986
Comments:	A Class A shop that should not be missed. The quality and selection of hardcover books, particularly in the non fiction sections, is quite high. When we visited, there were several volumes of presidential papers for three recent inhabitants of the White House. It was clear to us from the condition of the books that they were selected with great care and we would be greatly surprised if any readers did not share our own enthusiasm for this shop. The collection is meticulously organized and the shelves clearly labeled by category and subcategory.

Super Collector — **Open Shop**
16547 Brookhurst Street 92708 (714) -83-9-3693

Collection:	Specialty paperbacks and collectibles. Mostly new.
Specialties:	Science fiction; film.
Hours:	Mon 12-8. Tue-Sat 11-8. Sun 11-6.

Fremont
(Map 17, page 154)

Mission Valley Books — Open Shop
40061 Mission Boulevard 94539 — (510) 770-0388

Collection:	General stock of paperback and hardcover.
# of Vols:	30,000
Hours:	Mon-Sat 11-7. Sun 12-5.
Travel:	Mission Blvd exit off I-680. Proceed north on Mission for about one mile to Mission Valley Shopping Center.
Credit Cards:	Yes
Owner:	Pat Cushing
Year Estab:	1993
Comments:	Stock is approximately 70% paperback.

Warm Springs Book Co. — Open Shop
46695 Mission Boulevard 94539 — (510) 683-9038

Collection:	General stock of mostly used paperback.
Hours:	Mon-Sat 11-8. Sun 11:30-6.

Fresno
(Map 4, page 78)

American Bookstore — Open Shop
608 East Olive 93728 — (209) 264-2648

Collection:	General stock of hardcover and paperback.
Specialties:	Western Americana; military (American wars); history; religion; science; children's; literature; poetry; arts and crafts; do-it-yourself.
# of Vols:	40,000
Hours:	Mon-Sat 10:30-5.
Services:	Search service, accepts want lists, mail order.
Travel:	Olive exit off Hwy 99. Proceed east for two miles.
Credit Cards:	No
Owner:	Marilyn Affeldt
Year Estab:	1976
Comments:	In our judgment, a shop worth a visit. Although the collection on hand is modest in size (while we didn't count the books on display, we'd be surprised if the number on hand reached the owner's estimate) the shop does have a number of older items which we think are worth examining. The condition of the books ranged from quite good to books that were worn and could have used more care. Prices were reasonable. Many subjects were covered. Your visit here should not take too long.

The Book Hotel & Cafe — Open Shop
2767 West Shaw, #126 93711 — (209) 229-6601

Collection:	General stock of paperback and hardcover.

# of Vols:	100,000
Hours:	Mon-Sat 8am-9pm. Sun 8am-5pm.
Services:	Search service.
Travel:	Shaw Ave exit off Hwy 99. Proceed east for two miles. Shop is in Pepper Tree Plaza.
Credit Cards:	Yes
Owner:	Nancy P. Caldwell
Year Estab:	1993

Book Nook   **Open Shop**
6735 North First, #109 93710   Fax: (209) 438-1239 (209) 438-6502

Collection:	General stock of mostly paperback.
Hours:	Mon-Fri 10-6. Sat 10-5.

The Book Stall   **Open Shop**
931 North Blackstone 93701   (209) 266-1344

Collection:	General stock of hardcover and paperback.
Hours:	Mon-Sat 10-5:30.
Travel:	Blackstone exit off Hwy 41. Proceed one block to Abby. Left on Abby. Left on Lewis and left on Blackstone. Shop is on right.
Credit Cards:	Yes
Owner:	Marilyn Ward
Year Estab:	1975
Comments:	The shop was closed on the holiday weekend we visited Fresno. According to the owner, the collection is spread out over a 13 room house.

Family Book Center   **Open Shop**
4159 East Ashlan 93726   (209) 227-2339

Collection:	General stock of paperback and hardcover.
Hours:	Mon-Sat 10-6.
Travel:	Ashlan exit off Hwy 41. Proceed east on Ashlan.
Credit Cards:	No
Comments:	Stock is approximately 65% paperback.

Monroe Books   **Open Shop**
359 East Shaw Ave, Ste 102 93710   (209) 224-7000

Collection:	General stock.
Specialties:	California (Fresno and San Joaquim Valley); Western Americana, with emphasis on outlaws and lawmen; William Saroyan; children's; Civil War.
# of Vols:	20,000
Hours:	Mon 12-5. Tue-Sat 10:30-5.
Services:	Appraisals, search service, catalog, accepts want lists.
Travel:	Shaw exit off Hwy 41. Right on Shaw and immediate right into Mission Village shopping center.
Credit Cards:	Yes
Owner:	John Perz
Year Estab:	1972

94　　　　　　　　　　　　　　　CALIFORNIA

Comments:　　If you're schedule is tight and you can make only one stop in Fresno, this is the place you should visit. The shop's stock is not enormous but there are quality books here in most subject areas. The store is well organized and pleasant to visit and if you've ever read a Saroyan story or seen one of his plays, you'll be impressed by the strong Saroyan collection offered here. Reasonably priced.

Valley Book Center　　　　　　　　　　　　　　　　　　　　　　**Open Shop**
838 East Olive 93728　　　　　　　　　　　　　　　　　　　　(209) 237-5050

Collection:　　General stock of mostly paperback.
Hours:　　Mon-Fri 10-5:30. Sat 10-5.

Village Books　　　　　　　　　　　　　　　　　　　　　　　　**Open Shop**
1474 North Van Ness 93728　　　　　　　　　　　　　　　　　(209) 442-0244

Collection:　　General stock.
Specialties:　　*National Geographics.*
# of Vols:　　20,000
Hours:　　Mon-Sat 10-3.
Services:　　Search service.
Travel:　　McKinley exit off Hwy 41. Proceed west on McKinley.
Credit Cards:　　No
Owner:　　Norm Wolf
Year Estab:　　1987
Comments:　　A good sized collection with shelves labeled and at least three sections marked off for books dealing with religion. Some leather bindings. Most of the stock was of mixed vintage and in mixed condition and contained little that stood out as being rare. If you're in Fresno making the rounds and you know specifically what you're looking for, it should not take long to find out whether that elusive item you're searching for is here.

Fullerton
(Map 7, page 270)

Aladdin Books　　　　　　　　　　　　　　　　　　　　　　　**Open Shop**
122 West Commonwealth Avenue　　　　　　　　　　　　　(714) 738-6115
Mailing Address: PO Box 152 Fullerton 92632　　　　　Fax: (714) 738-6288

Collection:　　General stock of used and new, hardcover and paperback.
Specialties:　　Film; magic; performing arts; art; photography; literature; science fiction; fantasy; mystery; pop culture; circus.
# of Vols:　　20,000
Hours:　　Wed-Fri 11-6. Sat 10-5. Sun 12-4. (Sunday hours may vary.)
Services:　　Mail order.
Travel:　　Harbor Blvd exit off 91 Fwy. Proceed north on Harbor for about one mile. Left on Commonwealth (first light after railroad underpass).
Credit Cards:　　Yes
Owner:　　John T. Cannon
Year Estab:　　1982

Comments: Confession time. This is one of those shops that Susan had to drag me out of kicking and screaming because I wanted to stay longer and buy more books. True, the shop does have a specialty flair and it carries some new titles as well as used books (and I bought several of each). I guess, if you're smitten with the germ it doesn't matter; you see titles you want to own and even though you're 3,000 miles from home and know you'll have to ship the books, you pile them up, pay for them and keep thinking about the day you'll get home and will be able to savor the books you've just purchased. Note: the circus collection can be viewed on a by appointment basis.

Book Harbor **Open Shop**
116½ West Wilshire 92632 (714) 738-1941

Collection: General stock of used and new hardcover and paperback.
Specialties: Fiction; literature.
# of Vols: 125,000 (used)
Hours: Daily. Call for hours. (See Comments)
Services: Catalog, appraisals, search service.
Travel: Harbor Rd exit off Hwy 91. North on Harbor. The shop is in the rear.
Credit Cards: Yes
Owner: Al Ralston
Year Estab: 1976
Comments: At the time of our visit, the owner was very busy shelving books at this new location and questions regarding store hours were answered by the comment that the shop would be open seven days a week and that if one had further questions, a phone call might provide additional information. If you fail to get a clarification on hours when you do call (all we got was a message giving us the shop's new location), you may take the chance (as we did) that someone will be there when you visit. Based on our brief stay, and with the recognition that the shop had newly opened, we would recommend a stop on the premise that book people don't mind being ignored by a busy owner as long as they can browse the shelves in the hope of finding some long list treasure.

Books **Open Shop**
1051 South Lemon Street, #D 92632 (714) 879-9420

Collection: General stock of paperback and hardcover.
# of Vols: 40,000
Hours: Jul 1-Labor Day: Mon-Thu 11:30-9:30. Fri & Sat 11-11. Sun 11-8. Labor Day-June 30: Mon-Thu 11:30-9. Fri & Sat 11-11. Sun 11-7:30.
Travel: Harbor exit off 91 Fwy. Proceed north on Harbor then right on Southgate into shopping center.
Credit Cards: No
Owner: Paris Domenici, II
Year Estab: 1993
Comments: Stock is approximately 75% paperback.

Donald W. Cannon, Bookseller   **By Appointment**
PO Box 152 92632   (714) 449-1739

Collection: Specialty
Specialties: Film; television; science fiction; horror; fantasy; mystery.
# of Vols: 5,000
Services: Catalog in planning stage, accepts want lists, mail order.
Year Estab: 1985

Lorson's Books & Prints   **Open Shop**
116 West Wilshire Avenue 92632   Fax: (714) 526-8127   (714) 526-2523

Collection: General stock, ephemera and some new children's books.
Specialties: California; Western Americana; miniature books; private press.
# of Vols: 5,000
Hours: Mon-Fri 10-5:30. Sat 10-5.
Services: Catalog
Travel: Harbor Blvd exit off 91 Fwy. Proceed north on Harbor. Left on Wilshire.
Credit Cards: Yes
Year Estab: 1977
Comments: Unfortunately, our itinerary took us to Fullerton on a Sunday when this shop is closed.

Garberville
(Map 11, page 289)

Brannan Books   **By Appointment**
PO Box 475 95542   Fax: (707) 923-2560   (707) 923-3552

Collection: Specialty
Specialties: Art (European, American, Oriental).
# of Vols: 9,000
Services: Search service, catalog, accepts want lists.
Credit Cards: No
Owner: Paul Brannan
Year Estab: 1979

Tiger Lilly Books   **Open Shop**
355 Sprowel Creek Road 95542   (707) 923-4488

Collection: General stock of new and used hardcover and paperback.
# of Vols: 10,000 (used)
Hours: Mon-Fri 11:30-8. Sat 12:30-7.
Travel: Garberville exit off Hwy 101. First left after the exit.
Credit Cards: No
Owner: Paul Encmier
Year Estab: 1985
Comments: Stock is approximately 65% hardcover.

Open Shops and By Appointment Dealers 97

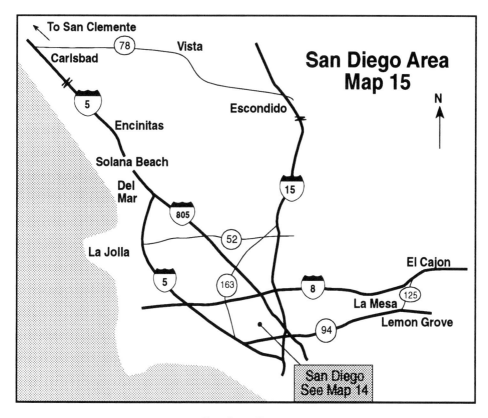

Garden Grove
(Map 7, page 270)

Camelot Books **Open Shop**
12873 Harbor Boulevard 92640 (714) 539-7550

Collection: General stock of mostly used hardcover and paperback.
# of Vols: 75,000 (used)
Hours: Mon-Sat 10-7. Sun 11-5.
Services: Search service, accepts want lists, mail order.
Travel: Harbor Blvd exit off 22 Fwy. Proceed north on Harbor for about 6/10 of a mile. The shop is along Harbor Blvd in the front of the Town and Country Shopping Center.
Credit Cards: Yes
Owner: Sherry Wendell & Bill Phillips
Year Estab: 1994
Comments: The owner was doing a bit of refurbishing when we arrived on the scene but put down his tools and took the time to show us around and discuss the book trade and his expansion plans. The stock, during our visit, consisted of a mix of paperbacks and hardcover titles with enough hardcover volumes in different categories and in mixed condition to make a visit here worth a stop.

Glen Ellen
(Map 11, page 289)

Jack London Bookstore   **Open Shop**
14300 Arnold Avenue   (707) 996-2888
Mailing Address: PO Box 337 Glen Ellen 95442   Fax: (707) 996-4107

Collection: General stock.
Specialties: Jack London (new and used); California; Hawaii; Klondike.
# of Vols: 20,000
Hours: Wed-Mon 10:30-5.
Services: Mail order.
Travel: Hwy 101 to Hwy 37 then north on Hwy 121 through Sonoma. Follow signs for Jack London State Park. The shop is 1/2 mile from center of Glen Ellen.
Credit Cards: Yes
Owner: Winifred Kingman
Year Estab: 1972
Comments: Clearly if you happen to be a Jack London fan this is the shop for you. There is little written by or about London that you could not find here. Beyond this author, the shop does maintain a fair sized general stock, including two sections of fiction, one for fiction published prior to 1950 and a second for works published after 1950. Both are extensive and contained books in generally mixed condition with the majority of them being in good condition. The shop is the headquarters for the Jack London Foundation.

Glendale
(Map 9, page 64)

Brand Bookshop   **Open Shop**
231 North Brand Boulevard 91203   (818) 507-5943

Collection: General stock of mostly hardcover.
# of Vols: 100,000
Hours: Sun-Thu 10-9. Fri & Sat 10am-11pm.
Services: Catalog, accepts want lists.
Travel: Westbound on 134 Fwy: Brand/Central exit. Left on Brand. Eastbound on 134 Fwy: Brand/Central exit. Right on Brand.
Credit Cards: Yes
Owner: Jerome Joseph
Year Estab: 1985
Comments: The shop carries a large collection of hardcover books in addition to some paperbacks and records. The store has both depth and width and it would be a mistake for any serious book person not to check all the aisles before leaving as there are lots of good titles throughout the shop. A good portion of the books are newer items and these are in generally good condition. We found the prices to be most reasonable.

Mystery & Imagination Bookshop
515½ East Broadway 91205

Open Shop
(818) 545-0206

Collection: Specialty books and ephemera.
Specialties: Modern first editions; literature; science fiction; mystery; children's; illustrated; fiction; poetry; literary biography; horror.
# of Vols: 20,000
Hours: Mon-Sat 12-6.
Services: Search service, catalog, accepts want lists.
Travel: Glendale Ave exit off 134 Fwy. Turn right and proceed south for six lights. Right (west) on East Broadway. Shop is 1½ blocks ahead.
Credit Cards: Yes
Owner: Christine & Malcolm Bell
Year Estab: 1977
Comments: As the name of this establishment suggests, most of its books fall into the mystery, science fiction and fantasy categories. With limited exceptions, the selection is broad with a mix of newer and vintage titles, however newer titles are in the majority. Most of the books we saw were in quite good condition. If this field is one that you're a devotee of, you'll certainly enjoy visiting. If you don't see what you're looking for, ask as only a portion of the dealer's collection is on display at the shop. If you can't stop by, the telephone is a marvelous invention.

Jeff Weber Rare Books
1923 Foothill Drive 91201

By Appointment
(818) 848-9704

Collection: General stock.
Specialties: Science; medicine; fore-edge paintings; bibliography.
# of Vols: 6,000
Services: Appraisals, catalog.
Credit Cards: Yes
Year Estab: 1988

Glendora
(Map 8, page 168)

Arrow Books
529 East Arrow Highway 91740

Open Shop
(818) 963-6983

Collection: General stock of mostly paperback.
Hours: Mon-Fri 10-7. Sat & Sun 12-6.

Live Oak Booksellers
110 West Foothill Boulevard 91741

Open Shop
(818) 914-6494

Collection: General stock and ephemera.
Specialties: California, Western Americana; technical; older fiction.
# of Vols: 20,000
Hours: Tue-Sat 10-6.
Services: Mail order.

Travel:	Grand Ave exit off 210 Fwy. Proceed north on Grand then east on Foothill for five blocks to Glendora Ave. Shop is in shopping center.
Credit Cards:	Yes
Owner:	G. Franklin Shirbroun
Year Estab:	1993
Comments:	We can certify that the sign in the front window of this establishment advertising that the store sells used out-of-print and rare books is absolutely accurate. While the collection could hardly be classified as huge, the titles on hand in every subject exhibited are for the most part books that are in good condition, unusual and would make a fine addition to the library of most serious collectors. And to top all that, they're affordably priced.

Village Book Shop   **Open Shop**
125 North Glendora Avenue 91741   (818) 335-5720

Collection:	General stock of mostly new and some used paperback and hardcover.
# of Vols:	20,000
Hours:	Mon-Sat 9-6.
Travel:	North of corner of Foothill Blvd and Glendora Ave.
Credit Cards:	Yes
Owner:	Wanda Lea Bradley
Year Estab:	1970
Comments:	Stock is approximately 20% used, 75% of which is paperback.

Goleta

Isla Vista Bookstore   **Open Shop**
6553 Pardall Road 93117   (805) 968-3600

Collection:	General stock of primarily used textbooks.
# of Vols:	70,000
Hours:	Regular hours: Mon-Thu 8-6:30. Fri 8-5:30. Sat 9-5:30. Hours when school is not in session: Mon-Fri 10-5:30. Sat 10-5.

Martin A. Silver, Musical Literature   **By Appointment**
7221 Del Norte Drive 93117   Fax: (805) 961-8290   (805) 961-8190

Collection:	Specialty
Specialties:	Dance; musical literature; music.
# of Vols:	4,000
Services:	Appraisals, search service, catalog, accepts want lists.
Year Estab:	1969

Graeagle

Witch's Brew   **Open Shop**
109 Highway 89   (916) 836-0554
Mailing Address: PO Box 20773 Graeagle 96103

Collection:	General stock of mostly used paperback.
Hours:	Jan-mid May: Thu-Sun 11-4. Mid May-Dec: Daily 10-5.

Granite Bay

Bev's Bookworm & Coffee House　　　　　　　　　　**Open Shop**
7097 Douglas Boulevard 95746　　　　　　　　　　　　(916) 791-5115

Collection:　　General stock of mostly used paperback.
Hours:　　　　Mon-Fri 7-7. Sat 8-7. Sun 9-6. (Later hours in summer)

Grass Valley
(Map 11, page 289)

Ames Bookstore　　　　　　　　　　　　　　　　　　**Open Shop**
309 Neal Street 95945　　　　　　　　　　　　　　　　(916) 273-9261

Collection:　　　General stock of hardcover and paperback.
Specialties:　　Children's; Western Americana.
# of Vols:　　　300,000
Hours:　　　　　Mon-Sat 10-6. Sun 12-5.
Services:　　　 Appraisals, accepts want lists.
Travel:　　　　 Grass Valley exit off Hwy 49. Follow signs to downtown.
Credit Cards:　 Yes
Owner:　　　　 Richard & Delores Slavin
Year Estab:　　1968
Comments:　　Almost universally, the owners of other book stores in this region spoke highly of this shop. When we finally visited, we understood why. The store actually consists of three separate shops, all on the same site. The main shop stocks a mix of hardcover volumes in mixed condition and paperbacks shelved together. The shelves were well labeled and most sections had good depth of coverage. Some items were priced quite reasonably and a few (in our humble opinion) were priced a bit higher than we have seen elsewhere. If you're looking for a broad selection, you'll find it here. A second "shop" contains collectible and rare books and a third stocks mostly technical titles.

The Booksmith　　　　　　　　　　　　　　　　　　　**Open Shop**
10021-C Wolf Road 95949　　　　Fax: (916) 268-1794 (916) 268-1793

Collection:　　General stock of new and mostly paperback used.
Hours:　　　　Mon-Sat 10-6.

Grover Beach

A to Z Books　　　　　　　　　　　　　　　　　　　　**Open Shop**
1526 Grand Avenue 93433　　　　　　　　　　　　　　(805) 489-8653

Collection:　　General stock of new and mostly used paperback.
Hours:　　　　Mon-Fri 10-6. Sat 10-5. Sun 1-5.

Gualala
(Map 11, page 289)

Java Point   **Open Shop**
Seaclift Center on Highway 1   (707) 884-9020
Mailing Address: PO Box 1512 Gualala 95445

Collection: General stock of hardcover and paperback.
# of Vols: 3,000
Hours: Daily 8-5.
Travel: On Hwy 1.
Comments: Stock is about evenly divided between hardcover and paperback.

Guerneville

Rykken And Scull   **By Appointment**
PO Box 1979 95446   Fax: (707) 869-9173 (707) 869-2030

Collection: Specialty books and some ephemera.
Specialties: Illustrated; children's; black studies; Edward S. Curtis photogravures; signed.
# of Vols: 2,200
Services: Catalog, accepts want lists.
Credit Cards: No
Owner: Dick Rykken & Wolf Scull
Year Estab: 1974

Gustine

The White Rose Bookstore   **Open Shop**
417 Fifth Street 95322   (209) 854-6104

Collection: General stock of mostly used paperback.
Hours: Tue-Fri 10:30-4:30. Sat 11-2.

Half Moon Bay
(Map 17, page 154)

Ocean Books   **Open Shop**
500C Purissima 94019   (415) 726-2665

Collection: General stock of mostly used hardcover and paperback.
# of Vols: 80,000
Hours: Mon-Fri 10-7. Sat & Sun 10-6.
Services: Search service, accepts want lists.
Travel: Kelly exit off Hwy 1. East on Kelly, then right on Purissima.
Credit Cards: Yes
Owner: David Fenstemaker & Jellina Teo
Year Estab: 1992

Comments: Aesthetically, this was one of the more attractive shops we have visited. In terms of its collection, we saw many many subjects covered but very few in great depth. (Unless the shop has additional books in storage, we would guess that the number of volumes was half the number estimated above.) The vast majority of the books were of recent vintage and in very good condition. Prices were moderate. Indeed other book dealers have been known to make purchases here only to sell the same volumes at substantial mark-ups. While you may not find a rare book here, it is clear that the shop serves the reading needs of its community quite well. A second floor mezzanine is devoted exclusively to paperbacks.

Hanford

Old Town News & Used Books   **Open Shop**
308 North Irwin Street 93230   (209) 582-6552

Collection: General stock of primarily paperback.
Hours: Mon-Fri 9:30-5:30. Sat 9:30-4. Sun 9:30-1:30.

Hayward
(Map 17, page 154)

The Book Shop   **Open Shop**
1007 B Street 94541   (510) 538-3943

Collection: General stock of used and new paperback and hardcover.
# of Vols: 25,000 (used)
Hours: Mon-Fri 10-6. Sat 9-5. Sun 12-4.
Travel: A St exit off I-880. East on A St, right on Foothill and right on B St.
Credit Cards: Yes
Owner: Hank Maschal
Year Estab: 1961
Comments: Stock is approximately 75% used, 75% of which is paperback.

By The Book   **Open Shop**
25825 Mission Boulevard 94544   (510) 537-7200

Collection: General stock of paperback and hardcover.
# of Vols: 18,000
Hours: Thu-Mon 10-6, except till 9 most Mon & Fri. (Call after 6pm to check on late closing.)
Travel: Jackson Ave exit off I-880. Proceed east on Jackson to Mission Blvd. Right on Mission and proceed for about 1¼ mile.
Credit Cards: No
Owner: Eric & Denise Campbell
Year Estab: 1990
Comments: The stock is approximately 70% paperback. The owner also operates a doll shop on the premises.

Healdsburg
(Map 11, page 289)

Levin & Company, Community Booksellers   **Open Shop**
306 Center Street 95448   (707) 433-1118

Collection: General stock of new and mostly used paperback.
Hours: Mon-Wed 9-9. Thu-Sat 9am-10pm. Sun 9-6.

Toyon Books   **Open Shop**
104 Matheson Street 95448   (707) 433-9270

Collection: General stock of primarily new books and mostly used paperback.
Hours: Mon-Sat 9am-10pm. Sat 10-6.

Hemet

Bob E's Books   **Open Shop**
263 East Stetson Avenue 92543   (909) 652-9021

Collection: General stock of mostly paperback.
Hours: Mon. Tue, Thu 9:30-5:30. Wed & Fri 9:30-7. Sat 9:30-5.

Book Exchange   **Open Shop**
2063 East Florida Avenue 92344   (909) 652-8824

Collection: General stock of mostly paperback.
Hours: Mon-Sat 9-5.

Curt's Books   **Open Shop**
219 East Stetson Avenue 92543   (909) 652-7509

Collection: General stock of mostly paperback.
Hours: Mon-Fri 9-5. Sat 9-2.

Hermosa Beach
(Map 10, page 253)

The Eclectic Collector   **Open Shop**
1116 Hermosa Avenue 90254   * (310) 374-4240

Collection: General stock of hardcover and paperback.
Specialties: Art; World War II, Civil War; biography.
# of Vols: 16,000
Hours: Mon-Sat 11-6:30. Sun 12-6.
Services: Search service, appraisals, mail order, accepts want lists.
Travel: Rosecrans exit off 5 Fwy. West on Rosecrans, south on Sepulveda Blvd, west on Pier Ave then south on Hermosa.
Credit Cards: Yes
Owner: Randolph M. Moss
Year Estab: 1983
Comments: Stock is approximately 70% hardcover.

* Some 310 codes change to 562 in 1996

Hesperia
(Map 12, page 139)

Frenchman's Den Bookshelf — **Open Shop**
16689 Yucca Street 92345 — (619) 244-3323

Collection: General stock.
# of Vols: 3,000
Hours: Mon-Sat 10-5.
Services: Appraisals, accepts want lists, mail order.
Travel: Main St exit off 15 Fwy. East on Main, left on C Ave then left on Yucca.
Credit Cards: No
Owner: George Bulat
Year Estab: 1977

Hollywood
(Map 6, page 122)

Book City Of Hollywood — **Open Shop**
6627 Hollywood Boulevard 90028 — (213) 466-2525

Collection: General stock of hardcover and paperback.
Specialties: Performing arts.
# of Vols: 150,000+
Hours: Mon-Thu 10-10. Fri & Sat 9-9. Sun 10-8.
Travel: Between Cherokee and Whitley.
Map Ref: Map 6, page 122, #16.
Credit Cards: Yes
Comments: When we initially entered this shop, we anticipated seeing books devoted mostly to show business. Indeed, the shop does have an excellent selection in this field. To our pleasant surprise, however, this rather large collection also includes a very fine general stock as well, with books in good condition covering almost every subject. There was even a rare book room with first editions, fine bindings, etc.

Collectors Book Store — **Open Shop**
1708 North Vine Street 90028 — (213) 467-3296

Collection: Specialty
Specialties: Film; television; entertainment.
# of Vols: 2,000-3,000
Hours: Tue-Fri 10-5. Sat 10-5:30.
Services: Mail order.
Travel: At intersection of Hollywood and Vine.
Credit Cards: Yes
Year Estab: 1968

Counterpoint Records & Books — **Open Shop**
5911 Franklin Avenue 90028 — (213) 957-7965

Collection: General stock of hardcover and paperback and records.

Specialties:	Literature; the arts; poetry.
# of Vols:	5,000-8,000
Hours:	Mon-Sat 1pm-11pm. Sun 1pm-8pm.
Travel:	Hollywood exit off 101 Fwy. Proceed west one block to Bronson, then north for two blocks to Franklin. Left on Franklin.
Map Ref:	Map 6, page 122, #17.
Credit Cards:	Yes
Owner:	John & Susan Polifronio
Year Estab:	1979
Comments:	Far more in the way of records and CDs than books-but-the book collection is respectable with most of the volumes of fairly recent vintage and in mixed condition. We noted an emphasis on entertainment, but other subjects are clearly represented.

Hollywood Movie Posters Open Shop
6727 5/8 Hollywood Boulevard 90028 (213) 463-1792

Collection:	General stock of mostly paperback.
Hours:	Mon-Sat 11-5.

Larry Edmunds Cinema & Theatre Book Shop Open Shop
6644 Hollywood Boulevard 90028 (213) 463-3273

Collection:	Specialty new and used, hardcover and paperback.
Specialties:	Film; theater.
Hours:	Mon-Sat 10-6.
Services:	Mail order, accepts want lists.
Travel:	Three blocks east of Highland at Cherokee.
Credit Cards:	Yes
Owner:	Din & Phil Luboviski & Git Polin
Year Estab:	1941
Comments:	Stock is approximately 30% used, 75% of which is hardcover.

Starworld Open Shop
6665 Hollywood Boulevard 90028 Fax: (213) 469-9007 (213) 469-0757

Collection:	Specialty paperbacks and collectibles.
Specialties:	Film
Hours:	Daily 11-8.
Credit Cards:	Yes
Owner:	David Elkouby
Year Estab:	1983

Huntington Beach
(Map 7, page 270)

Sandcastle Books Open Shop
16582 Gothard Street, #E 92647 (714) -84-7-9944

Collection:	General stock of hardcover and paperback.
# of Vols:	25,000
Hours:	Mon-Fri 10-7. Sat 10-5.

Services: Search service, accepts want lists, mail order.
Travel: From 405 Fwy southbound: Beach Blvd/Huntington Beach exit. Proceed south on Beach Blvd, right on Heil and left on Gothard. From 405 Fwy northbound: Huntington Beach/Westminster exit. From off ramp, take Huntington Beach exit which leads to Beach Blvd southbound. Follow directions above.
Credit Cards: No
Year Estab: 1979
Comments: Based on the stock we saw during our visit, we have no doubt that this shop serves the community quite well. Some of the used books were in such good condition it was hard to tell them from new books. The shop offers a little bit of almost every subject with few subjects covered in depth.

Indio
(Map 12, page 139)

Betty's Bargain Books   **Open Shop**
45130 Oasis Street 92201   (619) 347-4225

Collection: General stock of paperback and hardcover.
# of Vols: 82,000
Hours: Mon-Fri 9:30-4:30. Sat 9-12.
Travel: Oasis St exit off Hwy 111. Proceed north on Oasis.
Owner: Betty Jacobsen
Year Estab: 1981
Comments: Stock is approximately 70% paperback.

Joshua Tree
(Map 12, page 139)

New Age World Services & Books   **Open Shop**
62091 Valley View Circle 92252   Fax: (619) 365-9067 (619) 366-2833

Collection: General stock of used and new hardcover and paperback.
Specialties: Occult; metaphysics; UFOs; new age; lost continents; yoga; astrology.
Hours: Mon-Fri 10-5. Sat 10-4. Other times by appointment.
Services: Search service, catalog, accepts want lists.
Travel: Off Hwy 62.
Credit Cards: No
Owner: Victoria E. Vandertuin
Comments: Stock is approximately 75% used.

La Jolla
(Map 15, page 97)

John Cole's Book Shop   **Open Shop**
780 Prospect Street 92037   Fax: (619) 454-8377 (619) 454-4766

Collection: General stock of mostly new.
Specialties: Baja California.

# of Vols:	Limited used selection.
Hours:	Mon-Sat 9:30-5:30.
Services:	Search service, accepts want lists, mail order.
Credit Cards:	Yes
Owner:	Barbara T. Cole
Year Estab:	1946

John T. Hamilton III   **By Appointment**
PO Box 2191 92038   (619) 454-4546

Collection:	Specialty
Specialties:	Business directories; commercial credit rating books (pre-1930); numismatics.
Year Estab:	1978

Laurence McGilvery   **By Appointment**
PO Box 852 92038   (619) 454-4443

Collection:	Specialty
Specialties:	Art: reference, exhibition catalogues; art periodicals.
# of Vols:	100,000
Services:	Occasional catalog, accepts want lists, mail order.
Credit Cards:	Yes
Owner:	Laurence & Geraldine McGilvery
Year Estab:	1960

P.F. Mullins Books   **Open Shop**
7426 Girard 92037   (619) 456-1645

Collection:	General stock of hardcover and paperback.
Specialties:	Literature; first editions; California; military; black studies; John Steinbeck; James Baldwin.
# of Vols:	25,000
Hours:	Mon-Thu 10-9. Fri 10-6. Sat 6pm-10pm. Sun 12-9.
Services:	Accepts want lists, mail order.
Travel:	From I-5 southbound: Ardath Rd exit. Proceed to Torrey Pines Rd. South on Torrey Pines. Left on Girard. From I-5 northbound: La Jolla Village Dr exit. Proceed west to Torrey Pines Rd. Left on Girard.
Credit Cards:	Yes
Owner:	Paul F. Mullins
Year Estab:	1979
Comments:	A nice selection of used hardcover volumes, mostly in good condition and reasonably priced along with both vintage paperbacks and paperback titles of a more common variety. First editions, signed copies and fine bindings are displayed behind glass. In addition to the specialties listed above, we noted a strong selection of books dealing with art, architecture and design.

Barry Lawrence Ruderman Old Historic Maps & Prints   **By Appointment**
6141 Soledad Mountain Road 92037   Fax: (619) 456-4095 (619) 456-7667

Collection:	Specialty

Specialties: Antiquarian maps; prints, atlases, cartographic references; limited Western Americana with maps.
Services: Appraisals, catalog, accepts want lists.
Credit Cards: Yes
Owner: Barry & Denise Ruderman
Year Estab: 1991

D.G. Wills Books   **Open Shop**
7461 Girard Avenue 92037   (619) 456-1800

Collection: General stock of new and used hardcover and paperback.
Specialties: Philosophy; history of science; literature; poetry.
# of Vols: 50,000
Hours: Sun-Thu 10-9. Fri & Sat 10-10.
Travel: See P.F. Mullins Books above.
Credit Cards: Yes
Year Estab: 1979
Comments: If you don't mind searching for used titles intermixed with new books on the same shelves, and, if you're fascinated by objects that some might define as "clutter" and others as "charm," this bookstore may be right for you. At any event, don't arrive too early as the store may not always open at the 10am opening time listed above. (At least it didn't on the day we visited.) Based on the photographs and announcements on display, the shop is apparently a mecca for local readings and signings. With another high quality used bookstore almost directly across the street, it would be foolish for you not to stop here and perhaps find an item of interest.

La Mesa
(Map 15, page 97)

La Mesa Used Books   **Open Shop**
8274 La Mesa Boulevard 91941   (619) 465-8733

Collection: General stock of hardcover and paperback and records.
Specialties: Metaphysics; religion; psychology; Alcohol Anonymous; magazines.
# of Vols: 70,000
Hours: Mon-Fri 11-6, except Fri till 9. Sat & Sun 1-5.
Services: Accepts want lists.
Travel: Eastbound on I-8. Spring St exit. Proceed south on Spring, then left on La Mesa Blvd. Westbound on I-8. La Mesa Blvd exit. Left at bottom of ramp and proceed west on La Mesa.
Credit Cards: No
Owner: Lee Ashmore
Year Estab: 1991
Comments: A neighborhood shop with a plus. Translation: a shop with a better than average sized collection considering its neighborhood location. Lots of paperbacks, but a good number of hardcover volumes as well, with most areas represented and reasonably priced.

La Verne
(Map 8, page 168)

Book Stop **Open Shop**
2316 D Street 91750 Fax: (909) 593-3638 (909) 593-3638

Collection: General stock of mostly paperback.
# of Vols: 65,000+
Hours: Mon-Fri 10-8. Sat 10-5. Sun 12-5.
Services: Search service, accepts want lists.
Travel: East of the 210/57 Fwy. Proceed east on Arrow Hwy, then left on D St.
Credit Cards: Yes
Owner: Jim Kilgore
Year Estab: 1985
Comments: At least 90-95% of the stock is paperback with the remaining hardcover items made up either of very recent best sellers in the romance or mystery genre and about 1,000 or so older items that represented fairly common titles.

Lafayette
(Map 17, page 154)

Amadeus Books **Open Shop**
3369 Mount Diablo Boulevard 94549 Fax: (510) 284-4625 (510) 284-2665

Collection: General stock of mostly hardcover.
Specialties: Military; Western Americana.
# of Vols: 20,000
Hours: Mon-Sat 12-5:30.
Services: Search service, accepts want lists.
Travel: Westbound on Hwy 24: Central Lafayette exit. Left on Mt. Diablo. Shop is about 1/2 mile ahead on right. Eastbound on Hwy 24: Mt. Diablo exit.
Credit Cards: Yes
Owner: Victor Prada
Year Estab: 1990
Comments: A modest collection of mixed vintage titles, most in good condition, with several collectibles. If you look sharply, while the number of volumes is not overwhelming, the quality in terms of titles makes this shop one that could turn out to be a worthwhile stop for you.

Carol Docheff-Bookseller **By Appointment**
1390 Reliez Valley Road 94549 (510) 935-9595

Collection: Specialty
Specialties: Children's, including first editions and original art.
# of Vols: 10,000
Services: Search service, catalog, accepts want lists.
Credit Cards: Yes
Year Estab: 1978

Laguna Beach

Barnaby Rudge Bookseller **Open Shop**
1479 Glenneyre Street 92651 (714) 497-4079

Collection:	Specialty
Specialties:	Children's illustrated; Civil War; fine bindings; early printed books; maps; prints.
# of Vols:	2,500
Hours:	Tue-Sat 11-5:30. Mon & Sun by appointment.
Services:	Appraisals, mail auction catalog, search service, accepts want lists.
Travel:	From Pacific Coast Hwy, turn south on Hwy 133 and proceed for about one mile. Left on Calliope. Shop is at corner of Calliope and Glenneyre.
Credit Cards:	Yes
Owner:	Bonnie MacMillan
Year Estab:	1992

Laguna Hills
(Map 7, page 270)

Books Etc. **Open Shop**
23016 Lake Forest Drive, Ste G 92653 (714) 855-8242

Collection:	General stock of used paperback and hardcover and some new.
# of Vols:	15,000 (used)
Hours:	Mon-Fri 10-7. Sat 10-6:30. Sun 11-5:30.
Services:	Accepts want lists, mail order.
Travel:	Located in a shopping center on ocean side of 405/5 Fwy.
Credit Cards:	Yes
Owner:	Christy Compton
Year Estab:	1994
Comments:	"New & Used Books Bought & Sold" is the sign on the front windows of this attractive neighborhood shop that carries a healthy collection of recent best sellers with the majority of the hardcover volumes selling for between $1-$6. We saw considerably fewer than the 15,000 used volumes indicated above by the owner.

Mr. Good Books **Open Shop**
24881 Alicia Parkway, #C 92652 (714) 951-3966

Collection:	General stock of hardcover and paperback.
# of Vols:	20,000
Hours:	Mon-Fri 10-6. Sat 10-5. Sun 12-5.
Services:	Search service, accepts want lists.
Travel:	Alicia exit off 5 Fwy. Turn toward the ocean and proceed one block. Shop is in Laguna Hills Plaza.
Credit Cards:	Yes
Owner:	Barbara A. Otaki
Year Estab:	1983

112 CALIFORNIA

Comments: Another neighborhood shop with a larger collection of hardcover books than paperbacks. The books were in good condition with the owner emphasizing non fiction over fiction and offering first edition fiction whenever possible.

Laguna Niguel

Paperback Trading Co. **Open Shop**
27601 Forbes Road 92677 (714) 582-1320

Collection: General stock of mostly paperback.
Hours: Mon-Fri 10-6. Sat 10-4.

Lakeport
(Map 11, page 289)

Book Stop **Open Shop**
305 North Main 95453 (707) 263-5787

Collection: General stock of used and new, paperback and hardcover.
Specialties: Military; biography.
# of Vols: 23,000 (used)
Hours: Mon-Sat 10-5:30. Sun 11-4.
Travel: Lakeport exit off Hwy 29. Follow signs to museum. Shop is next to museum.
Credit Cards: Yes
Owner: Anita Sombs
Year Estab: 1988
Comments: Stock is approximately 70% used, 70% of which is paperback.

Lakewood
(Map 10, page 253)

Book Re-View **Open Shop**
5609 South Street 90713 * (310) 920-2708

Collection: General stock of mostly used hardcover.
Specialties: Literature; non fiction.
# of Vols: 7,000 (hardcover)
Hours: Mon-Sat 10-5:30.
Travel: Bellflower exit off 405 Fwy. North on Bellflower, right on South.
Credit Cards: Yes
Owner: Marilyn Abbate
Year Estab: 1987
Comments: A small shop with some nice books, both in terms of quality and condition, where it's possible to find a title "worth having" as the stock does not appear to have been picked over.

Once Read Books **Open Shop**
4174 Woodruff Boulevard 90713 * (310) 420-1034

Collection: General stock of hardcover and paperback.
Specialties: Military; Western Americana; nature.

* *Some 310 codes change to 562 in 1996*

# of Vols:	25,000
Hours:	Mon-Sat 10-7. Sun 12-5.
Travel:	Carson exit off 605 Fwy southbound. Right on Carson, right on Woodruff and immediate right into shopping center. Shop is in the back of the center.
Credit Cards:	Yes
Owner:	Roger Grunke
Year Estab:	1987
Comments:	The hardcover volumes were mostly reading copies, although there were a few rare items behind glass. While the books were organized by subject, there was not much depth. The shop also sells magazines and comics.

Lancaster
(Map 12, page 139)

Best Books — **Open Shop**
2054 West Avenue K 93536 (805) 723-5335

Collection:	General stock of hardcover and paperback.
Specialties:	Religion; cookbooks.
# of Vols:	50,000
Hours:	Daily 10-8.
Services:	Search service, accepts want lists, mail order.
Travel:	Ave K exit off 14 Fwy. Proceed west on K for about 1/2 mile through signal at 20th St west. Make next left into shopping center.
Owner:	Mary & Peter Price
Year Estab:	1992
Comments:	Stock is approximately 65% paperback.

Lawndale
(Map 10, page 253)

Old Master Gallery — **Open Shop**
15438 South Hawthorne Boulevard 90260 * (310) 679-2525

Collection:	General stock of new and used hardcover.
Specialties:	Art
# of Vols:	3,000 (used)
Hours:	Mon-Wed and Fri & Sat 10-6.
Services:	Appraisals, accepts want lists.
Travel:	Hawthorne Blvd exit off 405 Fwy.
Credit Cards:	Yes
Owner:	Norman Davies
Year Estab:	1975

Lemon Grove
(Map 15, page 97)

It Is Written Bookstore — **Open Shop**
6934 Federal Boulevard 91945 (619) 697-4173

Collection:	Specialty. Mostly new and some used hardcover and paperback.

Specialties: Black studies.
Hours: Mon-Sat 10-7.
Travel: College exit off I-94. West on Federal. Shop is in a small shopping center.
Credit Cards: Yes
Owner: Martha Roberts
Year Estab: 1993
Comments: Stock is approximately 25% used, 60% of which is hardcover.

Lemon Grove Bookstore **Open Shop**
7904 Broadway 91945 (619) 463-2503

Collection: General stock of hardcover and paperback.
Specialties: Literature; history; art; scholarly.
# of Vols: 100,000
Hours: Mon-Fri 11-6. Sat 10-5.
Travel: Hwy 94 exit off I-5. Proceed east on 94 to Lemon Grove. South (right) on Lemon Grove, then left on Broadway. Shop is just ahead on left.
Credit Cards: Yes
Owner: William Burgett
Year Estab: 1980
Comments: Not as large or as well stocked as the owner's downtown San Diego shop but the books here certainly provide a good selection of well cared for volumes in most categories. And, as in similar circumstances where one person owns more than one shop, it is not unusual to find titles in the smaller establishment that were not seen in the larger one.

Livermore
(Map 17, page 154)

Basset Books **Open Shop**
212 South L Street 94550 (510) 371-6280

Collection: General stock of hardcover and paperback.
# of Vols: 10,000
Hours: Sun-Thu 10-6. Fri & Sat 10-midnight.
Travel: North Livermore exit off I-580. Proceed south on North Livermore to 1st St, right on 1st St, left on L St.
Credit Cards: No
Owner: Jack Liske
Year Estab: 1994
Comments: Stock is approximately 60% hardcover.

Book Oasis **Open Shop**
160 South K Street 94550 (510) 606-7876
E-mail: bigbird@netcom.com

Collection: General stock of paperback and hardcover.
Specialties: Science fiction; fantasy.
# of Vols: 45,000
Hours: Tue-Fri 10-6. Sat 10-5.

Services: Appraisals, search service, accepts want lists.
Travel: North Livermore Ave exit off I-580 north. Continue on North Livermore. Right on Second St, then right on K St.
Credit Cards: Yes
Owner: Larry Burdick
Year Estab: 1990
Comments: Stock is approximately 70% paperback.

Lodi
(Map 4, page 78)

Book Lady   Open Shop
440 East Kettleman Lane 95240   (209) 368-8018

Collection: General stock of paperback and hardcover.
# of Vols: 20,000
Hours: Mon-Sat 10-5:30.
Travel: Kettleman exit off Hwy 99. West on Kettleman (Hwy 12) for one mile.
Credit Cards: No
Owner: Clara Heller
Year Estab: 1976
Comments: A small, crowded shop filled to capacity with paperbacks and a limited number of hardcover titles, some old and interesting, most recent and common. The shop also sells records, cards, souvenirs, etc.

Old Town Books   Open Shop
121 South School Street 95240   (209) 339-8454

Collection: General stock of new and used paperback and hardcover.
# of Vols: 8,000+ (used)
Hours: Tue-Fri 10-5:30. Sat 10-4.
Services: Accepts want lists.
Travel: Hwy 12 exit off Hwy 99. West on Hwy 12, then north on School.
Credit Cards: Yes
Owner: Tim Vallem
Year Estab: 1987
Comments: The used stock is approximately 75% paperback.

Lomita

William Byrd Aviation Books   Open Shop
1945 Pacific Coast Highway 90717   * (310) 326-3341

Collection: Specialty new and used.
Specialties: Aviation
Hours: Mon-Sat 10-6, except Thu till 7. Sun 11-5.
Services: Search service, mail order, accepts want lists.
Credit Cards: Yes
Owner: Rene Grebe & Andres Rodriguez
Year Estab: 1992

* Some 310 codes change to 562 in 1996

Lompoc
(Map 5, page 235)

E. Louis Hinrichs   **By Appointment**
PO Box 1090 93438   (805) 735-4761

Collection:	General stock.
Specialties:	Astronomy; physics; math; engineering; computers; health; conspiracy; Hungarian books.
# of Vols:	20,000
Services:	Catalog, accepts want lists.
Credit Cards:	No
Year Estab:	1987

Merlin's Bookshop   **By Appointment**
1236 Orchid Street   (805) 736-2234
Mailing Address: PO Box 1747 Lompoc 93438

Collection:	Specialty
Specialties:	First editions; science fiction; fantasy; horror; mathematics; physics; history of physical sciences.
# of Vols:	5,000
Services:	Search service, catalog, signature service for science fiction and fantasy books
Credit Cards:	No
Owner:	Merlin D. & Flora Schwegman
Year Estab:	1975

Printed Matter   **Open Shop**
107 South H Street 93436   (805) 736-0797

Collection:	General stock of mostly used hardcover and paperback.
# of Vols:	40,000
Hours:	Sun & Mon 10-6. Tue-Sat 10-8.
Travel:	Lompoc exit off Hwy 101. West on Hwy 101 which becomes Ocean. Left on H St.
Credit Cards:	Yes
Year Estab:	1992
Comments:	Stock is evenly divided between hardcover and paperback.

Long Beach
(Map 10, page 253)

Acres of Books   **Open Shop**
240 Long Beach Boulevard 90802   * (310) 437-6980

Collection:	General stock of hardcover and some paperback.
# of Vols:	750,000+
Hours:	Tue-Sat 9:15-5.
Travel:	Broadway east exit off 710 Fwy. East on Broadway. Left on Long Beach Blvd. Shop is just ahead on right. Parking is available in rear.

* *Some 310 codes change to 562 in 1996*

Credit Cards: No
Owner: Philip & Jacqueline Smith
Year Estab: 1934
Comments: Come early and plan to stay late as this store is aptly named. Once you've identified your areas of interest and are pointed in the right direction you can spend quite a bit of time browsing and discovering titles you never knew existed. The books are priced most reasonably. Condition of the books varies greatly. Many older titles.

Aftermore Books
155 Nieto Avenue 90803

By Appointment
* (310) 439-1937

Collection: General stock of mostly hardcover.
Specialties: Conspiracy; Hollywood; art; royalty; history; religion.
# of Vols: 40,000
Services: Catalog, accepts want lists.
Credit Cards: No
Owner: David Pearce
Year Estab: 1990

Attic City Book Shop
4226 Atlantic 90805

Open Shop

Collection: ??
Comments: We are assured by dealers in the area that this shop does exist although the owner may not keep regular hours. As the shop does not have a phone, we're afraid you're on your own here. If you're the adventurous type, let us know what you find.

Bargain Bookshop
3325 South Street 90805

Open Shop
* (310) 531-6909

Collection: General stock of hardcover and paperback.
# of Vols: 50,000
Hours: Tue-Sat 12 noon-6.
Travel: Downey Ave exit off 91 Fwy. South on Downey, then right on South.
Credit Cards: No
Year Estab: 1965
Comments: The stock is approximately 65% hardcover.

Bluff Park Rare Books
2535 East Broadway 90803

Open Shop
* (310) 438-9830

Collection: Specialty books, ephemera and Hollywood collectibles.
Specialties: Hollywood; children's; mystery; literature; archaeology; poetry.
# of Vols: 20,000
Hours: Mon-Sat 11-6.
Services: Search service, accepts want lists, mail order.
Travel: 405 Fwy to 710 Fwy south. Broadway exit. Proceed one mile. Shop is between Cherry and Temple.
Credit Cards: No

Owner: Joe Hix
Year Estab: 1986

Book Treasury
246 Long Beach Boulevard
Mailing Address: PO Box 20033 Long Beach 90801

Open Shop
* (310) 435-7383
Fax: (310) 435-6513

Collection:	General stock of hardcover and paperback.
Specialties:	Modern first editions; Oz; children's illustrated.
# of Vols:	15,000 (hardcover)
Hours:	Mon-Sat 10-6. Sun 12-5.
Services:	Catalog.
Travel:	See Acres of Books above. At corner of 3rd. Parking is available in rear.
Credit Cards:	Yes
Owner:	Jon Gentilman
Year Estab:	1975
Comments:	Substantially smaller than its immediate neighbor (see Acres of Books above) which means you can be in and out of here in far less time. The hardcover books, however, are of a far different quality: they are, for the most part, almost entirely in good to fine condition and priced accordingly. Most subjects are represented, though not in great depth. When we visited, the owner was in the process of laying carpet and shelving books in an adjoining space. Based on our observations, this should be a most attractive shop to visit and combining a visit here with the one next door will provide the book person with an expanded opportunity.

Eye of the Cat
3314 East Broadway 90803

Open Shop
* (310) 438-3569

Collection:	Specialty. Primarily new books and related items.
Specialties:	Occult
Hours:	Mon-Fri 9-7. Sat & Sun 11-7.

McDonald's Bookshop
129 West 5th Street 90802

Open Shop
* (310) 435-5438

Collection:	General stock of paperback and hardcover, magazines and comics.
# of Vols:	500,000
Hours:	Mon-Sat 9-5.
Services:	Accepts want lists, mail order.
Travel:	6th St exit off 710 Fwy. Proceed on 6th for about three lights. Right on Pacific, then left on Fifth.
Credit Cards:	No
Owner:	Jeri McDonald
Year Estab:	1975
Comments:	Like its sister store (see Rodden's Used Bookshop below) owned by the same person, this shop is predominately paperback with a few thousand hardcover books located in the same general areas (albeit usually on the upper shelves) as the paperbacks. Lots of volume if you're a paperback junkie but sadly not a lot of quality if you're looking for hard-to-find hardcover books.

* *Some 310 codes change to 562 in 1996*

Rodden's Used Bookshop **Open Shop**
500 East Broadway 90802 * (310) 432-5896

Collection:	General stock of paperback and hardcover.
# of Vols:	300,000
Hours:	Mon-Sat 9-5.
Services:	Accepts want lists, mail order.
Travel:	Broadway exit off 710 Fwy. Proceed on Broadway for about eight blocks. Shop is at corner of Linden and Broadway.
Credit Cards:	No
Owner:	Jeri McDonald
Year Estab:	1950's
Comments:	After visiting the shop, we have no doubt that the estimate of 300,000 items is accurate. The problem is that about 280,000 of the items are in the form of paperbacks and magazines and the hardcover items (at least the ones we viewed) looked very ordinary to us. Most of the hardcover volumes were in mixed condition.

Los Altos
(Map 17, page 154)

The Antiquarian Archive **Open Shop**
379 State Street 94022 (415) 949-1593

Collection:	General stock of mostly hardcover.
Specialties:	Military; Western Americana; transportation; Roycroft Press.
# of Vols:	15,000-20,000.
Hours:	Tue-Sat 9-5:30. Sun and Mon by appointment or chance.
Services:	Appraisals, search service, accepts want lists.
Credit Cards:	Yes
Owner:	David B. Ogle
Year Estab:	1983
Comments:	An interesting shop with a nice selection of books, in good condition and reasonably priced. The owner uses his limited space in a very efficient manner. A fun shop to browse.

The Book Nest **Open Shop**
366 Second Street 94022 (415) 948-4724

Collection:	General stock of mostly hardcover.
Specialties:	John Steinbeck.
# of Vols:	10,000
Hours:	Tue-Sat 10-5:30.
Services:	Search service, accepts want lists.
Travel:	El Monte east exit off Hwy 280. Proceed to Foothill Blvd. Left on Foothill, right on Main St, right on Second St.
Credit Cards:	Yes
Owner:	Edwin Schmitz
Year Estab:	1978

Comments: Located in what was once a small private house, the hardcover books we saw were in good condition and represented mixed periods. One bookcase adjacent to the front counter contained first editions. Since the collection is modest in size and the books are shelved in a manner that makes browsing quite simple, you won't need to spend a great deal of time visiting here.

Los Angeles
(Map 6, page 122)

Aldine Books
4663 Hollywood Boulevard 90027

Open Shop
(213) 666-2690

Collection:	General stock.
Specialties:	Art; natural history.
# of Vols:	20,000+
Hours:	Daily 11-8.
Services:	Appraisals, search service, accepts want lists, mail order.
Travel:	Corner of Hollywood and Vermont.
Map Ref:	Map 6, page 122, #1.
Credit Cards:	Yes
Owner:	Darrel Thede
Year Estab:	1975

American-European Books
1816 North Mariposa Avenue, #2 90027

By Appointment
(213) 666-9866

Collection:	Specialty hardcover and paperback.
Specialties:	Europe (all subjects); military; Civil War; Southern Americana; American history and politics; Judaica.
# of Vols:	30,000
Services:	Appraisals, search service, catalog, accepts want lists.
Credit Cards:	No
Owner:	Paul Dawson
Year Estab:	1989

Another World Comics & Books
1615 Colorado Boulevard 90041

Open Shop
(213) 257-7757

Collection:	Specialty paperbacks.
Specialties:	Science Fiction.
Hours:	Tue-Thu 12-7. Fri 10-7. Sat 10-6. Sun 1-5.
Comments:	Primarily a comics store with a few hundred used paperbacks.

Arundel Books
8380 Beverly Boulevard 90048

Open Shop
Fax: (213) 852-9853 (213) 852-9852

Collection:	General stock of hardcover and paperback.
Specialties:	Art; architecture; literature; private press.
# of Vols:	10,000-15,000
Hours:	Mon-Sat 9-6.

Services: Appraisals, accepts want lists, occasional catalog, mail order.
Travel: Three blocks east of La Cienega, between Orlando and Kind Rd.
Map Ref: Map 6, page 122, #2.
Credit Cards: Yes
Owner: Phillip Bevis
Year Estab: 1985
Comments: It's always embarrassing to salivate in public. However, we must admit that we came very close to it when visiting this shop. Its size was modest; its stock was not. While one entire wall was filled with beautiful volumes dealing with art, much of the remaining stock contained a selection of literature which we can only describe as exceptional. First editions abound and books that are truly classic in their field are seen here almost commonly in their first printing. If you love literature and fine books, you'll certainly enjoy your visit here. If you happen to suffer from vertigo, one of the store's employees will be more than willing to climb the ladders to search the higher shelves for titles that may hold your interest.

Berkelouw Books **Open Shop**
830 North Highland Avenue 90038 Fax: (213) 460-2922 (213) 466-3321

Collection: General stock.
Specialties: Southseas; Pacific; exploration.
# of Vols: 100,000+
Hours: Mon-Sat 10-5.
Travel: Between Melrose and Santa Monica Blvd.
Map Ref: Map 6, page 122, #3.
Credit Cards: Yes
Owner: Henry Berkelouw
Year Estab: 1985
Comments: Another nice "traditional" used book shop with five generations of book people responsible for the current collection which is large, varied, well organized and worth visiting. The books, which are mixed both in vintage and condition, are moderately priced.

Black Ace Books **Open Shop**
1658 Griffith Park Boulevard 90026 (213) 661-5052

Collection: Specialty. Mostly paperback.
Specialties: Vintage paperbacks; beat generation; counter culture.
# of Vols: 20,000
Hours: Mon-Fri 10-6. Occasional Saturdays.
Services: Catalog, accepts want lists, co-sponsors annual paperback collectibles show, vintage paperback auctions.
Travel: In Silverlake area. Call for directions.
Credit Cards: No
Owner: Rose Idlet & Tony Scibella
Year Estab: 1990

122 CALIFORNIA

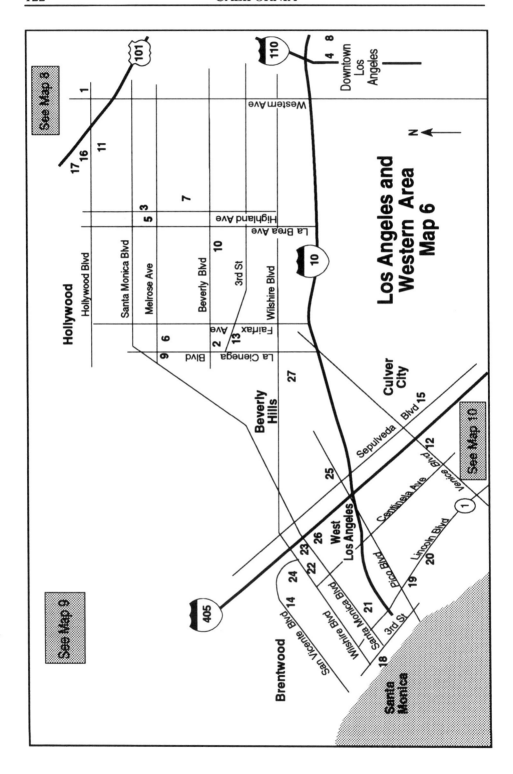

Bodhi Tree Bookstore **Open Shop**
8585 Melrose Avenue 90069 (800) 825-9798 * (310) 659-3227
Fax: (310) 659-0178

Collection:	Specialty new and used.
Specialties:	Metaphysics; occult; religion.
# of Vols:	15,000
Hours:	Daily 11-7 (Used books only).
Services:	Catalog, accepts want lists.
Travel:	La Cienega exit off 10 Fwy. North La Cienega, west on Melrose.
Credit Cards:	Yes
Owner:	Phil Thompson & Stan Madson
Year Estab:	1970
Comments:	Used books are located in a separate building behind the "new" bookshop.

Books Bohemian **By Appointment**
PO Box 17218 90017 (213) 385-6761

Collection:	Specialty
Specialties:	Homosexuality
Hours:	Daily, 12-8.
Services:	Search service, catalog.
Credit Cards:	Yes
Owner:	Robert J. Manners
Year Estab:	1977

Books on Sports **Open Shop**
8302 Melrose Avenue 90069 (213) 651-2334

Collection:	Specialty new and used books and ephemera.
Specialties:	Sports
# of Vols:	50,000
Hours:	Mon-Sat 10-6. Sun 12-4.
Services:	Appraisals, search service, accepts want lists, specific catalogs.
Credit Cards:	Yes
Owner:	Neil Victor
Year Estab:	1991

Caravan Book Store **Open Shop**
550 South Grand Avenue 90071 (213) 626-9944

Collection:	General stock and ephemera.
Specialties:	Western Americana; California; railroads; ships and sea; cookbooks; wine; fine bindings; limited editions; broadsides.
Hours:	Mon-Fri 11-6. Sat 11-6. Other times by appointment.
Services:	Search service, accepts want lists, mail order.
Travel:	Downtown, a few blocks from 6th St exit off Harbor Fwy.
Map Ref:	Map 6, page 122, #4.
Credit Cards:	No
Owner:	L. Bernstein
Year Estab:	1954

* Some 310 codes change to 562 in 1996

(Los Angeles)

Grayson D. Cook, Bookseller
367 W. Avenue 42 90065

By Appointment
(213) 227-8899

Collection:	General stock.
Specialties:	Film; American and English first editions; illustrated; mystery.
# of Vols:	10,000
Hours:	Evenings and weekends.
Services:	Mail order.
Credit Cards:	No
Year Estab:	1972

Cosmopolitan Book Shop
7017 Melrose Avenue 90038

Open Shop
(213) 938-7119

Collection:	General stock of mostly hardcover and records.
# of Vols:	500,000
Hours:	Daily 11:30-6.
Services:	Accepts want lists.
Travel:	La Brea Ave north exit off I-10. North on La Brea. Right on Melrose.
Map Ref:	Map 6, page 122, #5.
Credit Cards:	No
Owner:	Eli Goodman
Year Estab:	1958
Comments:	If you like the atmosphere of older, more traditional crowded book shops with large selections where you can find both familiar titles as well as titles you've never seen before but might like to own, we suggest a stop here. At the time of our visit, the owner was planning to expand the shop to an adjoining storefront.

W & V Dailey
8216 Melrose Avenue 90046

Open Shop
(213) 658-8515

Collection:	Specialty
Specialties:	First editions; rare and early printed books; art; illustrated.
# of Vols:	8,000
Hours:	Tue-Sat 10:30-5:30.
Services:	Appraisals, catalog, accepts want lists.
Travel:	Between Crescent and La Brea.
Map Ref:	Map 6, page 122, #6.
Credit Cards:	Yes
Owner:	William & Victoria Dailey
Year Estab:	1974
Comments:	One of the pleasures of visiting the West Los Angeles area is covering more quality book dealers concentrated in a region than we have seen in most of our travels to other major cities. This shop fits this description. Many of the books on display are rare, desirable and presented in an attractive fashion (bindings and decorative slip cases). This is not a typical "walk-in" shop. If your pocket book matches your tastes, you should enjoy

Open Shops and By Appointment Dealers

visiting here. If you can't visit, contact the owners and request one of their several attractive catalogs.

Dawson's Book Shop   **Open Shop**
535 North Larchmont Boulevard 90004   Fax: (213) 469-9553   (213) 469-2186

Collection: Specialty
Specialties: Western Americana; history of photography; fine printing; miniature books.
# of Vols: 25,000
Hours: Tue-Sat 9-5.
Services: Catalog, accepts want lists.
Travel: Between Beverly and Melrose.
Map Ref: Map 6, page 122, #7.
Credit Cards: Yes
Owner: Muir Dawson
Year Estab: 1905
Comments: If you happen to be driving down Larchmont Boulevard, don't be surprised if you pass right by this shop without realizing you have done so. The shop (set back from the street) offers convenient parking for its customers right at its front door but does not (at least when we visited) have any sign indicating that a used book business is located at the site. Perhaps it's because the shop's specialties (see above) are so well represented in both volume and character that possibly most of the shop's business is done via mail order? This is definitely not a place for the casual browser. On the other hand, if the subjects are of interest to you, a visit would be far more instructive (and enjoyable) than simply looking through a catalog.

Dutton's Books/Arco Plaza   **Open Shop**
515 South Flower Street 90017   (213) 683-1199

Collection: General stock of mostly new and some used hardcover and paperback.
# of Vols: 5,000 (used)
Hours: Mon-Fri 9:30-5.
Services: Accepts want lists, mail order.
Travel: Downtown at 5th.
Map Ref: Map 6, page 122, #8.
Credit Cards: Yes
Owner: Davis & Judy Dutton
Year Estab: 1987

El Dorado Books (Bill McClatchey)   **By Appointment**
2237 North Berendo Street 90027   (213) 662-l045

Collection: Specialty
Specialties: Hunting; fishing; military; arms and armor; Western Americana; cowboys; native Americana; sports; California; children's; illustrated; travel; exploration; pirates; photography; occult; nautical.
# of Vols: 6,000+
Services: Appraisals, search service, catalog, accepts want lists.
Year Estab: 1971

(Los Angeles)

Golden Legend **Open Shop**
7615 Sunset Boulevard 90046 (213) 850-5520

Collection: Specialty
Specialties: Theater; dance; costume.
# of Vols: 5,000
Hours: Tue-Sat 10-5:30. Other times by appointment.
Services: Appraisals, catalog, accepts want lists.
Travel: Between Fairfax and La Brea.
Credit Cards: Yes
Owner: Gordon Hollis
Year Estab: 1980

Heritage Book Shop **Open Shop**
8540 Melrose Avenue 90069 * (310) 659-3674

Collection: Specialty
Specialties: 19th century literature; fine and rare books.
# of Vols: 10,000
Hours: Mon by appointment. Tue-Fri 9:30-5:30. Sat 10-4:30.
Services: Appraisals, catalog, accepts want lists, book binding
Travel: La Cienega exit off 10 Fwy. North on La Cienega, then west on Melrose.
Map Ref: Map 6, page 122, #9.
Credit Cards: Yes
Owner: Louis & Ben Weinstein
Year Estab: 1964
Comments: You don't have to be extremely wealthy to purchase a book here but it would surely help. If you love good books, regardless of the subject area, and if you have an affinity for fine bindings, first editions (including those of Bronte, Dickens and other literary greats), you'll find a visit to this establishment almost like a visit to paradise. If you can't stop, you may want to get on the shop's mailing list and receive one of its attractive catalogs or subjects lists in your area of interest. We have visited a number of very fine book dealers, many of them with high quality stock, but few in our judgement can compare with what you'll see here.

Arnold Herr **By Appointment**
1026½ North Western Avenue 90029 (213) 469-6817

Collection: General stock mostly hardcover.
# of Vols: 30,000
Services: Appraisals, accepts want lists, mail order.
Credit Cards: No
Year Estab: 1990

Houle Rare Books & Autographs **Open Shop**
7260 Beverly Boulevard 90036 Fax: (213) 937-0091 (213) 937-5858

Collection: Specialty

Specialties:	19th and 20th century literature; sets; fine bindings; Americana; Zane Grey; autographs and signed photographs; performing arts; autographs.
# of Vols:	10,000-15,000
Hours:	Tue-Fri 10-6. Sat 10-3.
Services:	Appraisals, catalog, accepts want lists.
Travel:	La Brea exit off 10 Fwy. Proceed on north on La Brea, then left on Beverly.
Map Ref:	Map 6, page 122, #10.
Credit Cards:	Yes
Owner:	G.J. Houle
Year Estab:	1976
Comments:	In appearance, this shop is delightful to visit. The books are for the most part quality items, well maintained and very nicely displayed. You'll find everything here that might ordinarily be found in a general book shop, from entertainment, literature and history to cookbooks and mysteries. The difference is that almost all of the books in this shop are cataloged and priced with a history to justify the books' cost. We're not experts in every field but we do believe that many of the items we examined could probably be purchased elsewhere at a slightly lower cost. Notwithstanding the above observation, if you have a taste for good books and want to see a substantial selection, we would definitely recommend a visit.

Elliot Katt, Bookseller   Open Shop
8568 Melrose Avenue 90069   Fax: (310) 652-2778 * (310) 652-5178

Collection:	Specialty
Specialties:	Film; music; dance; theatre; costumes; circus; vaudeville and burlesque.
# of Vols:	10,000
Hours:	Mon-Fri 11-6. Sat 11-5.
Services:	Search service, catalog, accepts want lists.
Travel:	See Heritage Books above.
Year Estab:	1980
Comments:	If you're into the world of film or theater, there's an excellent chance you'll be able to locate a book by, and or about your favorite actor, director or subject at this location. The shop's titles are on computer, so if you can't travel, call ahead and you may still be able to acquire the book via Uncle Sam's post office.

Samuel W. Katz   By Appointment
PO Box 241487 90024   * (310) 208-7934

Collection:	General stock.
Specialties:	Early Italian printing; early illustrated; Mexican art.
# of Vols:	3,000-4,00
Services:	Appraisals, mail order, accepts want lists.
Credit Cards:	No
Year Estab:	1970's

* Some 310 codes change to 562 in 1996

(Los Angeles)

Kongo Square Gallery & Gift Shop
4334 Degnan Boulevard

Open Shop
(213) 291-6878

Collection:	Specialty hardcover and paperback and ephemera.
Specialties:	Black studies; Caribbean; Third World.
# of Vols:	1,000+
Hours:	Tue-Sun 11-7.

Krieger's Antiques
1606 Gower 90028

Open Shop
(213) 461-9463

Collection:	General stock.
# of Vols:	4,000
Hours:	Wed-Sat 12-6.
Travel:	Three blocks east of Hollywood and Vine.
Map Ref:	Map 6, page 122, #11.
Credit Cards:	No
Owner:	Nancy Krieger
Comments:	Majority of books are pre-1930.

Dennis B. Marquand
3536 Centinela
Mailing Address: PO Box 1187 Culver City 90232

By Appointment
* (310) 313-0177
Fax: (310) 915-9922

Collection:	Specialty. Mostly used.
Specialties:	Oriental rugs and textiles; pre-Columbian-Navajo textiles; historical textiles.
# of Vols:	1,000
Hours:	Mon-Sat 9-8. Sun 2-5.
Services:	Appraisals, search service, catalog, accepts want lists.
Credit Cards:	No
Year Estab:	1980

Opera Shop of Los Angeles
8384 Beverly Boulevard 90048

Open Shop
(213) 658-5811

Collection:	Specialty new and used hardcover and paperback.
Specialties:	Opera; music; dance.
# of Vols:	1,000
Hours:	Mon-Sat 10-6.
Services:	Accepts want lists, mail order.
Credit Cards:	Yes
Owner:	Larry Rappaport
Year Estab:	1987

Pettler & Lieberman Booksellers
2345 Westwood Boulevard, #3 90064
Mailing address: 8033 Sunset Boulevard, #977, Los Angeles 90046

Open Shop
* (310) 474-2479

Collection:	Specialty

* *Some 310 codes change to 562 in 1996*

Specialties: Modern first editions.
# of Vols: 8,000
Hours: Wed-Sat 12-6.
Services: Appraisals, search service, catalog, accepts want lists.
Travel: Pico Blvd exit off 405 Fwy. East on Pico, then north on Westward.
Credit Cards: Yes
Owner: Robert Pettler
Year Estab: 1978

Sam: Johnson's Bookshop
12310 Venice Boulevard 90066

Open Shop
* (310) 391-5047

Collection: General stock.
Specialties: Literature; scholarly; ghost stories; fantasy; mystery; music.
# of Vols: 10,000
Hours: Mon-Sat 11-6. Sun 12-5.
Services: Appraisals, accepts want lists.
Travel: Venice exit off 405 Fwy. Shop is between Centinela and Grandview.
Map Ref: Map 6, page 122, #12.
Credit Cards: Yes
Owner: Robert E. Klein & Lawrence D. Myers
Year Estab: 1977
Comments: While this shop does offer a general selection of hardcover titles, it is particularly strong in the specialties listed above and, for a change, the titles available in these areas are far from ordinary. The books we saw were in good to excellent condition and most reasonably priced. If these are areas that are of interest to you, we strongly urge a visit.

Third World Ethnic Books
3617 Montclair Street 90018

Open Shop
(213) 737-3292

Collection: Specialty. Mostly used hardcover.
Specialties: Black studies.
# of Vols: 15,000
Hours: Mon-Sat 10-6.
Services: Appraisals, search service, mail order, accepts want lists.
Travel: Arlington exit off 10 Fwy. South on Arlington. Right on Montclair.
Credit Cards: No
Owner: L. Clayton
Year Estab: 1972

Michael R. Thompson, Bookseller
8312 West 3rd Street 90048

Open Shop
Fax: (213) 658-5380   (213) 658-1901

Collection: General stock.
Specialties: Western philosophy; foreign literature in translation; history; art; music; "think books."
# of Vols: 20,000
Hours: Mon-Sat 10-6. Sun 12-5.
Services: Appraisals, catalog, accepts want lists.

Travel: Between La Cienega and Fairfax.
Map Ref: Map 6, page 122, #13.
Credit Cards: Yes
Owner: Michael R. and Kathleen Thompson & Carol Sanberg
Year Estab: 1972
Comments: The sign on the front window of this establishment reads: "Good Used, Scholarly, Antiquarian, Fine, Rare Books." After visiting the shop we would agree that all the aforementioned descriptors accurately apply to the collection. We would add a single world of our own: "Affordable."

Len Unger-Rare Books **By Appointment**
631 North Wilcox Avenue, #3B (213) 962-7929
Mailing Address: PO Box 5858 Sherman Oaks 91413 Fax: (213) 962-7929

Collection: Specialty
Specialties: First editions of literature; mystery; western literature; signed.
Services: Catalog
Credit Cards: Yes
Year Estab: 1981

Westside Books **By Appointment**
1615 Wellesley Avenue 90025 * (310) 479-8434

Collection: Specialty
Specialties: Signed books: by presidents and people in the miliary, sport and movies.
# of Vols: 1,000
Services: Occasional catalog.
Credit Cards: No
Owner: Nathaniel Connor
Year Estab: 1989

Zeitlin Periodicals Co. **By Appointment**
817 South La Brea Avenue 90230 (213) 933-7175

Collection: Specialty
Specialties: Magazines
# of Vols: 2 million
Hours: Mon-Fri 7-4.
Owner: Stanley Zeitlin
Year Estab: 1925

Los Banos
(Map 4, page 78)

Phoenix Books/Mind & Body **Open Shop**
936 6th 93635 Fax: (209) 826-1514 (209) 826-3797

Collection: General stock of new and mostly paperback used.
Specialties: Horses
# of Vols: 20,000+
Hours: Mon-Fri 8:30-5, except Fri till 6. Sat 9-4.
Services: Search service, catalog, accepts want lists.

* Some 310 codes change to 562 in 1996

Travel: Hwy 152 exit off I-5. In Los Banos, turn north on 6th St.
Credit Cards: Yes
Owner: Joanne Hoefer
Year Estab: 1977
Comments: A small community shop with at least 90% of the stock consisting of paperbacks. Most of the hardcover books we saw were new and fairly common. This is not the spot where one is likely to find rare books, unless your interests happens to turn to the equestrian field, the owner's specialty.

Los Gatos
(Map 5, page 235)

Curious Bookshop   **Open Shop**
23 East Main Street 95032   (408) 354-5560

Collection: General stock.
# of Vols: 20,000
Hours: Mon-Sat 9:30-6. Sun 12-5.
Services: Appraisals, accepts want lists, mail order.
Travel: Southbound on Hwy 17 (from San Jose): East Los Gatos exit. Right on Main. Northbound on Hwy 17: Los Gatos exit. Proceed north on Santa Cruz Ave to Main. Right on Main.
Credit Cards: Yes
Owner: Richard P. Balch
Year Estab: 1974
Comments: On several occasions, we have visited shops in the process of "getting set up" and had to make allowances for things if everything wasn't exactly as one might expect. In this instance, we visited a shop that was fully operational but would be moving to a new location. (The new address is listed above.) At it's "old" location, the shop had a strong stock in most areas, the books were in generally good to better condition and the collection was well organized and easy to browse. We assume, based on a conversation with the owner, that his new location will easily accommodate the stock we saw plus allow for growth. If his prediction turns out to be correct, you should enjoy visiting the new site.

Los Osos

Los Osos Book Exchange   **Open Shop**
2149 10th Street 93402   (805) 528-1614

Collection: General stock of mostly paperback.
Specialties: Military technical manuals, with emphasis from 1930-1960 (See Comments below.)
Hours: Mon-Fri 11-6. Sat 11-5. Sun 12-4.
Owner: George Kastner
Comments: The collection on display at the shop is approximately 90% paperback. If you're interested in viewing the military collection, call ahead as this collection is not located in the shop.

Malibu

Malibu Books & Co.   **Open Shop**
23410 Civic Center Way 90265   * (310) 456-1375

Collection: General stock of primarily new and some used hardcover.
Hours: Mon-Sat 10-6. Sun 11-5.

Manteca
(Map 4, page 78)

The Book Exchange   **Open Shop**
347 North Main Street 95336   (209) 823-2938

Collection: General stock of mostly paperback.
Hours: Mon-Sat 10-6, except till 8 on Thu. Sun 12-4:30.

On The Cover   **Open Shop**
311 West Yosemite Boulevard 95336   Fax: (209) 825-1569   (209) 825-1565

Collection: General stock, ephemera and magazines.
Specialties: Sports
# of Vols: 3,00-5,000
Hours: Mon, Wed, Thu, Sun 10-6. Fri & Sat 10-9.
Travel: Hwy 120 into center of town.
Credit Cards: Yes
Owner: Rod Oldfield
Year Estab: 1995
Comments: This shop had only recently opened when we visited. The collection was limited with some collectibles and an emphasis on sports and nostalgia.

Marina

Athena's Book Shop   **Open Shop**
265 Reservation Road 93933   (408) 883-9323

Collection: General stock of mostly paperback.
Hours: Mon-Sat 10-8. Sun 11-6.

Marina Del Rey

Twelfth Street Booksellers   **By Appointment**
14021 Marquesas Way, #308C   * (310) 822-1505
Mailing Address: PO Box 3103 Santa Monica 90408

Collection: Specialty books and ephemera.
Specialties: Jewelry; gemology; gem hunting adventures.
# of Vols: 600
Services: Appraisals, search service, catalog, accepts want lists.
Credit Cards: No
Owner: Lillian Cole
Year Estab: 1985

* Some 310 codes change to 562 in 1996

Martinez
(Map 17, page 154)

California Collectible Books   **Open Shop**
3503 Alhambra Avenue 94553   Fax: (510) 229-3005 (510) 229-4878

Collection:	Specialty (with limited general stock).
Specialties:	First editions; California; California authors.
# of Vols:	10,000
Hours:	Tue-Sat 10-6.
Services:	Search service, catalog, accepts want lists.
Travel:	From I-680, west on Hwy 4 to Alhambra exit. Right on Alhambra.
Credit Cards:	Yes
Owner:	Lloyd Mason
Year Estab:	1993
Comments:	Every book buyer dreams of finding a shop that appears not to have been picked over by scouts and other buyers before their own arrival. We hope that aforementioned statement doesn't result in "spoiling" this shop for you as we found the shop to be a veritable treasure chest for the specialty areas identified above as well as several other general areas. This is a real antiquarian used book shop that certainly can take its place among other dealers in rare and collectible items.

Marysville
(Map 11, page 289)

Bookland   **Open Shop**
501 D Street 95901   (916) 743-2642

Collection:	General stock of new and used paperback and hardcover.
# of Vols:	10,000 (used)
Hours:	Mon-Thu 9-6. Fri 9-8. Sat 10-6. Sun 11-4.
Travel:	Hwy 5 north to Hwy 99/70, then Hwy 70 to Marysville. Right on 5th.
Credit Cards:	Yes
Owner:	Stephen & Jayne White
Year Estab:	1970
Comments:	A step up from most similar shops in that the used hardcover books here, while smaller in number (perhaps 2,000-3,000) then the number given to us by the owner, contain a nice mix of vintage items in addition to more recent volumes. There were even some sets and a bookcase filled with leather bound books.

McKinleyville

Blake's Books   **Open Shop**
Central Avenue at Gwin   (707) 839-8800
Mailing Address: PO Box 2083 McKinleyville 95521   Fax: (707) 839-8892

Collection:	General stock of mostly used paperback.
Hours:	Mon-Sat 10-7. Sun 12-5.

Mendocino
(Map 11, page 289)

Gallery Bookshop — Open Shop
Main & Kaston Streets (707) 937-2665
Mailing Address: PO Box 270 Mendocino 95460

Collection: General stock of mostly new and some used paperback and hardcover.
Hours: Daily 10-6, except Fri & Sat till 9.
Services: Mail order.
Travel: From Hwy 101 at Cloverdale, take Hwy 128 to coast.
Credit Cards: Yes
Owner: Anthony Miksak
Year Estab: 1980
Comments: Stock is approximately 20% used and 60% paperback.

Menlo Park
(Map 17, page 154)

East West Bookshop — Open Shop
1170 El Camino Real 94025 (415) 325-5709

Collection: Specialty. Mostly new and some used.
Specialties: New age; metaphysics..
Hours: Mon-Sat 10-9. Sun 1-5:30.

Diane Peterson - Booklady — By Appointment
PO Box 2544 94026 (415) 324-1201

Collection: General stock.
Specialties: John Steinbeck; Wallace Stegner; John Muir; modern literary first editions; Western Americana; miniature books; science fiction; fantasy.
Hours: Available Sept-May only.
Services: Collection development for Steinbeck, Stegner and Muir.
Credit Cards: Yes
Year Estab: 1976

Pyramid Books — Open Shop
1047 El Camino Real 94025 (415) 326-1888

Collection: General stock mostly used paperback.
Hours: Sun-Tue 11-7. Wed-Sat 10-10.

Wessex Books & Records — Open Shop
558 Santa Cruz Avenue 94025   Fax: (415) 856-1984   (415) 321-1333

Collection: General stock of hardcover and some paperback and records.
Specialties: Literature; modern fiction; literary criticism; history; scholarly; university press.
# of Vols: 75,000
Hours: Mon-Thu 11-6. Fri & Sat 11-9. Sun 12-5.

Travel:	Southbound on Hwy 101: Marsh Rd exit. West on Marsh, left on Middlefield, right on Oak Grove, left on Merrill (immediately after railroad tracks). Proceed one block to stop sign. Wessex is to the right around the corner. Northbound on Hwy 101: Willow Rd exit. West on Willow, right on Middlefield, left on Ravenswood then right on Merrill. Proceed one block to Santa Cruz. Wessex is ahead on left
Credit Cards:	Yes
Owner:	Tom Haydon
Year Estab:	1975
Comments:	Quite a respectable collection. In addition to the specialties listed above, all of which were quite well represented, the rest of the collection was also quite nice. We did not see a single book that was not in good to better condition and since condition is a major factor in both book buying and collecting, we don't think you can go wrong visiting this shop.

Merced
(Map 4, page 78)

Second Time Around
515 West Main Street 95340

Open Shop
(209) 723-0925

Collection:	General stock of hardcover and paperback.
# of Vols:	50,000
Hours:	Mon-Sat 10-5:30, except Thu till 9 in summer.
Services:	Search service, accepts want lists, mail order.
Travel:	Martin Luther King Jr Way exit off Hwy 99. Proceed east on Martin Luther King Jr, then left on Main.
Credit Cards:	No
Owner:	Mary Casados
Year Estab:	1984
Comments:	The hardcover books fall into two categories: older titles (many of which have seen better days, but many of which also may well be considered collectible or worthwhile titles) and newer volumes in better condition. The shelves are not always clearly labeled, except perhaps for some of the paperbacks which make up at least half of the stock. We felt that several of the books we examined were slightly overpriced.

Mill Valley
(Map 17, page 154)

Stuart Bennett Rare Books
PO Box 878 94942

By Appointment
Fax: (415) 380-8945 (415) 380-8945

Collection:	Specialty books and ephemera.
Specialties:	English books printed before 1850, mostly literary, with emphasis on philosophy, fiction, poetry, satire and social history.
# of Vols:	1,500
Services:	Appraisals, catalog, accepts want lists.
Year Estab:	1980

Books **Open Shop**
10 Locust Avenue 94941 (415) 389-6612

Collection: General stock of paperback and hardcover.
Hours: Mon-Sat 11-6. Sun 12-4.
Travel: Near intersection of Miller and Locust.
Comments: Stock is about evenly divided between paperback and hardcover.

Ethnographic Arts Publications **By Appointment**
1040 Erica Road 94941 (415) 332-1646 (415) 383-2998
Fax: (415) 388-8708

Collection: Specialty used and some new, hardcover and paperback.
Specialties: Tribal and primitive art; cultural anthropology; art of Africa, the Pacific, Southeast Asia, Arctic regions, North and South America and art and archaeology of North American Indians, pre-Columbian and Latin American peoples.
# of Vols: 12,000
Services: Appraisals, catalog, accepts want lists.
Credit Cards: Yes
Owner: Arnold Rogoff
Year Estab: 1978

Millbrae
(Map 17, page 154)

Casey's Books **Open Shop**
373 El Camino Real 94030 (415) 697-5659

Collection: General stock of paperback and hardcover and comics
# of Vols: 5,000
Hours: Mon-Sat 11-7. Sun 11-6.
Travel: Millbrae Ave exit off Hwy 101. West on Millbrae, north on El Camino.
Year Estab: 1990
Comments: Stock is approximately 65% paperback.

Milpitas

Town Center Book Gallery **Open Shop**
597 East Calaveras Boulevard 95035 (408) 262-0249

Collection: General stock of new and mostly paperback used.
Hours: Mon-Thu 11-9. Fri 10-10. Sun 12-7.

Mission Hills
(Map 9, page 64)

Affordable Books & Collectibles **Open Shop**
10324-B Sepulveda Boulevard 91345 (818) 365-1190

Collection: General stock of hardcover and paperback.

Specialties: Children's; illustrated; literature.
# of Vols: 20,000
Hours: Mon-Fri 11-7. Sat 10-6.
Services: Appraisals, search service, accepts want lists, mail order.
Travel: From 405 Fwy: Devonshire St exit. Proceed east for 1/4 mile. Shop is located in Mission Hill Plaza shopping center.
Credit Cards: No
Owner: Mary Watanabe
Year Estab: 1989
Comments: An owner who apparently takes her 11 o'clock posted opening with a grain of salt, at least on the day we tried to visit and the shop was still not open when we left at 11:15.

R.G.I. Book Co.   **By Appointment**
PO Box 950553 91395   (818) 361-8889

Collection: Specialty. Mostly new and some used.
Specialties: Horses; pets; agribusiness; gardening; western art and Americana; farm animals and management.
Services: Search service, accepts want lists.
Credit Cards: No
Owner: Robert P. Griset
Year Estab: 1975
Comments: Stock is approximately 90% new. Horse titles make up about 80% of the dealer's business.

Mission Viejo

Book Corral   **Open Shop**
25571 Jeronimo Road, #9 92691   (714) 855-8054

Collection: General stock of mostly paperback.
Hours: Tue-Fri 10-7. Sat 10-6.

Modesto
(Map 4, page 78)

Julie's Books   **Open Shop**
2900 Standiford   (209) 571-1410
Mailing Address: 901 Carpenter, #32 Modesto 95351

Collection: General stock of mostly paperback.
Hours: Mon-Sat 10-6. Sun 12-5.

Pages of Time   **By Appointment**
321 Camellia Way 95354   (209) 529-4667

Collection: Specialty
Specialties: Theology; fiction; children's; cookbooks; hymn books; poetry.
# of Vols: 700
Services: Subject lists, mail order, accepts want lists.
Credit Cards: No

Owner: Richard & Dorothea Duroy
Year Estab: 1993

Salty's Record Attic **Open Shop**
1326 9th Street 95354 (209) 527-4010

Collection:	Specialty. Mostly used hardcover and paperback.
Specialties:	Entertainment; music; children's.
# of Vols:	10,000-15,000 (Used. See Comments)
Hours:	Tue-Sat 10-5.
Services:	Appraisals, search service, accepts want lists, mail order.
Travel:	Kansas exit off Hwy 99. Proceed east on Kansas, then south on 9th.
Credit Cards:	Yes
Owner:	Ramona Saben
Year Estab:	1976
Comments:	If you're looking for used LPs or cassettes, we suspect you might be able to find what you're looking for here. On the other hand, if you're interested in either hardcover or paperback books dealing with the above specialties, the selection (at least on display) is very limited. You could save a lot of time by calling ahead to see if the owner has what you're looking for.

Yesterday's Books **Open Shop**
3457 McHenry Avenue 95350 (209) 521-9623

Collection:	General stock of paperback and hardcover.
Specialties:	Biblical studies; automotive; music; literature; science fiction.
# of Vols:	110,000
Hours:	Mon-Sat 9-6, except Thu till 8.
Services:	Search service, mail order.
Travel:	Standiford Ave exit off Fwy 99. Proceed east for about four miles to McHenry, then right on McHenry. Shop is second building on right.
Credit Cards:	Yes
Owner:	Larry & Kathleen Dorman
Year Estab:	1980
Comments:	If you're traveling in central California, we believe you'll find a visit to this shop one of the highlights of your book hunting experience. This is a Class A shop. The shop is large, the shelves meticulously organized and labeled, the books in very good condition and the shop spacious enough for you to browse comfortably and leisurely. We were most impressed and would be surprised if our readers did not come to a similar conclusion.

Mokelumne Hill

Lilly Books **Open Shop**
8085 Highway 26 & 49 (209) 286-1324
Mailing Address: PO Box 70 Mokelumne Hill 95245 Fax: (209) 667-8876

Collection:	General stock of new and mostly paperback used.
Hours:	Mon-Sat 10-7. Sun 1-7.

Monrovia
(Map 8, page 168)

Book Village **Open Shop**
103 West Foothill Boulevard 91016 (818) 359-7811

Collection: General stock of mostly paperback and comics.
# of Vols: 10,000+
Hours: Mon-Sat 10-5. Sun 11-2.
Travel: Myrtle exit off 210 Fwy. North on Myrtle. Left on Foothill.
Credit Cards: No
Owner: Gloria Adachi Knight
Year Estab: 1980
Comments: Upon entering the shop it was difficult to determine if the owner dealt exclusively in comics and magazines. We did see some hardcover books in mixed condition in various categories but unfortunately little that grabbed our attention nor do we believe the attention of most non comic or popular culture collectors.

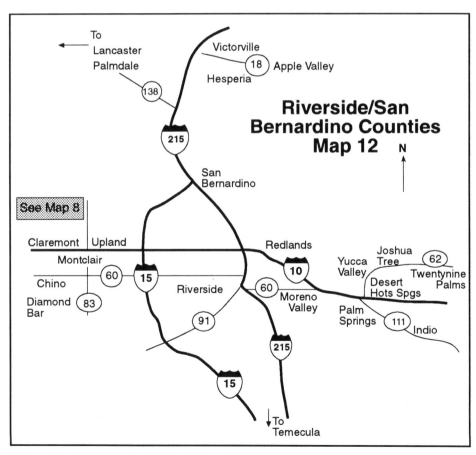

Montclair
(Map 12, page 139)

This Old House Bookshop **Open Shop**
5399 West Holt Boulevard 91763 (909) 624-5144

Collection: General stock of hardcover and paperback.
# of Vols: 40,000
Hours: Daily 9-5 but best to call ahead.
Services: Search service, accepts want lists.
Travel: Central exit off 10 Fwy. South on Central and east on Holt.
Owner: Thomas Harold Guthormsen
Year Estab: 1956
Comments: The good news is that the shop is located immediately behind the owner's home and even if it isn't open when you approach, a honk of the horn will bring the owner around and he'll be happy to show you his stock. The bad news is that the vast majority of the hardcover books we saw were weather beaten and worn and clearly not well cared for. If you have any idea of the titles you're looking for, with a little help from the owner who correctly maintains that the shelves are organized (although not labeled) you might be lucky. Unless you have a lot of time and are willing to overlook condition and the thousands of paperbacks that clutter the aisles, you'll probably do better hunting elsewhere.

Monterey
(Map 5, page 235)

The Book End **Open Shop**
245 Pearl Street 93940 (408) 375-6214

Collection: General stock of hardcover and paperback.
Specialties: Classics; children's; foreign language; art; California.
# of Vols: 14,000
Hours: Mon-Sat 10:30-5:30. Sun 12:30-4:30.
Travel: Fremont exit off Hwy 1. Proceed west on Freemont, north on Munras and right on Pearl.
Credit Cards: No
Owner: Sylvia Anderson
Year Estab: 1976
Comments: The books were of mixed vintage and in mixed condition with the majority of them in slightly better condition. None of the specialties listed above, at least in our judgment, were represented by a very large selection of titles. For the most part, the books could be classified as reading copies.

Books & Things **Open Shop**
224 Lighthouse Avenue 93940 (408) 655-8784

Collection: General stock of hardcover and paperback.
# of Vols: 70,000

Hours: Mon-Sat 11-6. Sun 12-6.
Travel: Monterey exit off Hwy 1. Follow signs to Cannery Row, staying on Lighthouse Ave after tunnel. Shop is between Dickman and Reeside.
Credit Cards: No
Year Estab: 1990
Comments: When we arrived at this shop at 11 o'clock, we found a note on the door indicating that because of a doctor's appointment the shop would open at 11:30. We immediately viewed the owner as a kindly, considerate person for at least letting prospective customers know that he/she is not habitually late in opening. A cursory glance through the front window revealed that while the shop offers a good supply of paperbacks, the shop also has an ample supply of hardcover books. We regret that our tight schedule prevented us from waiting an additional half hour for the shop to open.

Lighthouse Books

801 Lighthouse Avenue 93921

Open Shop
(408) 372-0653

Collection: General stock of hardcover and paperback.
Specialties: John Steinbeck; Henry Miller; photography.
# of Vols: 3,000-4,000
Hours: Daily 11-6:30, except Tue 12-4.
Services: Accepts want lists, mail order.
Travel: See Books & Things above. Shop is between Prescott and David.
Credit Cards: No
Owner: Ron Marek
Year Estab: 1993
Comments: While the size of the collection is small, a good many of the books could be classified as "collectible." The shop is easy to browse as many of the books are displayed face up on tables in the center of the store.

McWilliams & Chee Old & Rare Books

In Canery Row Antique Mall, 471 Wave Street 93940

Antique Mall
(408) 656-9264

Collection: General stock.
# of Vols: 2,000+
Hours: Mon-Fri 10:30-5:30. Sat 10-6. Sun 11-6.
Services: Search service, accepts want lists, catalog.
Travel: One block from Canery Row.
Owner: "Mac" McWilliams
Year Estab: 1995
Comments: Alas, when we were in Monterey the only address we had for this shop (from the phone book) was "Canery Row" and we were unable to find the shop in the famous street's labyrinth of boutiques and gift shops, many of which are located in multi dealer malls in old factory buildings and warehouses. We were equally unsuccessful in locating a public phone that was a) in working order or, b) not busy so that we could call the owner and ask for directions. Pressed for time, we reluctantly gave up our search.

Old Capitol Books
639-A Lighthouse Avenue 93940

Open Shop
(408) 375-2665

Collection:	General stock.
# of Vols:	50,000
Hours:	Mon-Sat 10:30-6.
Services:	Mail order.
Travel:	See Books & Things above. Shop is between Hoffman and Prescott.
Credit Cards:	No
Owner:	C.J. Sundt
Year Estab:	1983
Comments:	A good sized selection with most of the books showing that they have been cared for (even the older volumes). The shop offers a wide selection in the areas of fiction and a more than reasonable representation in other categories. The shelves are easy to browse, clean and neat and the shop is a pleasure to visit.

Old Monterey Book Co.
136 Bonifacio Place 93940

Open Shop
(408) 372-3111

Collection:	General stock.
# of Vols:	10,000
Hours:	Tue-Sat 10-5.
Services:	Appraisals, search service, accepts want lists, mail order, book binding.
Travel:	Freemont exit off Hwy 1. Proceed west on Freemont, north on Munras which leads into Alvarado and right on Bonifacio.
Credit Cards:	Yes
Owner:	Jean O'Brien
Year Estab:	1955
Comments:	We're always delighted to find a shop that opens on schedule and so we were most pleased to see the owner of this 400 square foot bi-level shop put her key in the door a couple of minutes before opening time. During our brief chat, the owner stressed the fact that hers was a "general shop" with no specialities and after browsing the collection we certainly agree. The shelves are crammed with volumes (both fiction and non fiction) that are in generally good condition, nicely organized and reasonably priced. Whether or not you find a book that meets your taste, a visit here should prove most enjoyable.

Monterey Park
(Map 8, page 168)

Lee-Gannon Booksellers
450 East Potrero Grande Drive 91755

By Appointment
Fax: (213) 725-7730   (213) 725-7730

Collection:	General stock.
Specialties:	Literary first editions; black studies; natural history.
# of Vols:	10,000-20,000
Services:	Appraisals, catalog, search service, accepts want lists.
Owner:	Yoonjeong Lee & James Gannon
Year Estab:	1994

Montrose
(Map 9, page 64)

Booksville   **Open Shop**
2626 Honolulu Avenue 91020   (818) 248-9149

Collection:	General stock of paperback and hardcover.
# of Vols:	15,000
Hours:	Wed-Mon 9:30-7.
Travel:	Pennsylvania exit off 210 Fwy. Proceed south on Pennsylvania which becomes Honolulu Ave. (Do not make right on Honolulu.)
Credit Cards:	No
Owner:	Shirley McCormick
Year Estab:	1983
Comments:	Lots and lots of paperbacks of all description and far less in the way of hardcover items. When we find titles like *Head Hunters of the Solomon Islands* and Peter Freuchen's *Book of the Seas* shelved with novels, we know we're in a neighborhood book store.

The Reader's Edge Bookshop   **Open Shop**
2329 Honolulu Avenue 91020   (818) 249-5546

Collection:	General stock of new and used hardcover and paperback.
# of Vols:	35,000
Hours:	Mon-Sat 10-7. Sun 12-5.
Travel:	Ocean View exit off 210 Fwy. South on Ocean View. West on Honolulu.
Credit Cards:	Yes
Owner:	Diane & Ed Tellefsen
Year Estab:	1988
Comments:	Stock is approximately 40% used, 70% of which is hardcover.

Moorpark
(Map 5, page 235)

Bell, Book & Candle   **Open Shop**
17 East High Street 93021   (805) 532-1104

Collection:	General stock.
# of Vols:	2,000
Hours:	Wed-Sat 11-5.
Travel:	New Los Angeles Ave exit off 23 Fwy. Proceed west on New Los Angeles, then right on Moorpark. After crossing High St, park in first lot.
Credit Cards:	No
Owner:	Crystal Koofman
Year Estab:	1993

Thorn Books   **By Appointment**
624 Moorpark Avenue   (805) 529-7610
Mailing Address: PO Box 1244 Moorpark 93020

Collection:	General stock.

Specialties: California; Western Americana; King Arthur; early Roman Britain.
# of Vols: 10,000
Services: Appraisals, catalog, accepts want lists, book repair.
Credit Cards: Yes
Owner: Lynne Owens
Year Estab: 1988

Moreno Valley
(Map 12, page 139)

Book Exchange   Open Shop
11875 Pigeon Pass Road 92587   (909) 247-5453

Collection: General stock of paperback and hardcover.
Hours: Mon-Sat 10-6. Sun 11-3.
Travel: Pigeon Pass exit off 60 Fwy. North on Pigeon Pass. In Lucky Center.
Comments: Stock is approximately 70% paperback.

Morro Bay

Coalesce...A Bookstore & More   Open Shop
845 Main Street 93442   (805) 772-2880

Collection: General stock of new and used, mostly paperback.
Hours: Mon-Sat 10-5:30. Sun 11-4. Open occasional evenings and by appointment.

Moss Landing
(Map 5, page 235)

Yesterday's Books   Open Shop
7902 East Sandholdt Road   (408) 633-8033
Mailing Address: PO Box 322 Moss Landing 95039

Collection: General stock of all hardcover.
# of Vols: 10,000
Hours: Mon-Fri 11-4. Sat & Sun 10-5.
Travel: Moss Landing Rd off Hwy 1.
Credit Cards: No
Owner: Guy Rodiguez
Year Estab: 1973

Mount Shasta

Golden Bough Bookstore   Open Shop
219 North Mt. Shasta Boulevard 96067   (916) 926-3228

Collection: Specialty. Mostly new with some used.
Specialties: Metaphysics
Hours: Mon-Sat 10-5. Sun 11-3.

Wings Bookstore **Open Shop**
226 North Mt. Shasta Boulevard 96067 (916) 926-3041

Collection: General stock of new and mostly paperback used.
Hours: Mon-Sat 10-5:30. Sun by chance.

Mountain View
(Map 17, page 154)

Ananda Bookbuyers **Open Shop**
317 Castro Street 94041 (415) 968-7323

Collection: General stock mostly used hardcover and paperback and records.
# of Vols: 250,000
Hours: Mon-Thu 11-11. Fri & Sat 10-midnight. Sun 10-10.
Travel: Moffet Blvd exit off Hwy 101. West on Moffet which becomes Castro.
Credit Cards: Yes
Year Estab: 1990
Comments: Stock is approximately 80% hardcover.

Murphys
(Map 4, page 78)

Murphy's Books **Open Shop**
Sierra Hills Shopping Center, Highway 4 (209) 728-9207
Mailing Address: PO Box 303 Murphys 95247 Fax: (209) 728-8479

Collection: General stock of mostly used hardcover and paperback.
Specialties: California; Western Americana; hunting; fishing; art; architecture; first editions.
# of Vols: 20,000
Hours: Daily 11-6.
Services: Appraisals, search service, accepts want lists, mail order.
Travel: On Hwy 4.
Credit Cards: Yes
Owner: Paul Groh
Year Estab: 1992
Comments: The stock is approximately 65% hardcover.

Murphy's Stage Stop **Open Shop**
416 Main Street (209) 728-2200
Mailing Address: PO Box 867 Murphys 95247

Collection: General stock of new and used hardcover and paperback.
Specialties: California, especially Indians, flora and fauna, gold rush and early exploration.
# of Vols: 11,000
Hours: Daily 10:30-5.
Services: Search service, accepts want lists.
Travel: From Hwy 49, proceed north or south to Angles Camp, then east on Hwy 4 to Murphy's historic Main St.

Credit Cards: Yes
Owner: Lawrence Pugno
Year Estab: 1977
Comments: The stock is 40% used and about evenly divided between hardcover and paperback.

Napa
(Map 11, page 289)

The Book Merchant
At Soscol Antiques, 1551 Soscol Avenue
Mailing Address: 2295 Kathleen Drive Napa 94558

Open Shop
Shop: (707) 254-9897
Home: (707) 259-1326

Collection: General stock.
Specialties: Modern first editions; Western Americana.
Hours: Mon-Sat 10-5.
Services: Appraisals, search service, catalog, accepts want lists.
Travel: Hwy 121 exit off I-80. Proceed north on Hwy 121 to Napa Lake Berryessa turnoff. Continue toward Napa where road becomes Soscol.
Credit Cards: No
Owner: R.D. Mulins
Year Estab: 1994

Copperfield's Books
1303 Randolf Street 94559

Open Shop
(707) 252-8002

Collection: General stock of used and remainders and some new.
# of Vols: 21,000
Hours: Mon-Wed 9:30-8. Thu-Sat 9:30-9. Sun 12-6.
Services: Appraisals, search service, catalog, accepts want lists.
Travel: First St/downtown exit off Hwy 29. Left on Second St and proceed to Randolf. Left on Randolf. Shop is at corner of 1st and Randolf.

Volume One Used Books
1405 Second Street 94559

Open Shop
(707) 252-1466

Collection: General stock of paperback and hardcover.
Specialties: Cookbooks; children's.
# of Vols: 25,000
Hours: Tue-Sat 10-5:30.
Travel: First St exit off Hwy 29 north. Proceed east, following signs for downtown.
Credit Cards: No
Owner: Judith Hart Wolcott
Year Estab: 1975
Comments: Mea culpa. We misread our own notes and arrived in Napa on a Monday when the shop is normally closed. A cursory view through the front window made it clear that in addition to paperbacks and hardcovers (there appeared to be somewhat more of the former than the latter), the shop also sold used jigsaw puzzles. The hardcover volumes appeared to be of fairly recent vintage. We also spotted two cats patrolling the empty shop.

Nevada City
(Map 11, page 289)

Brigadoon Books   **Open Shop**
421 Broad Street 95959   (916) 265-3450

Collection:	General stock of hardcover and paperback.
Specialties:	British, Irish and Scottish literature.
# of Vols:	40,000
Hours:	Mon-Sat 10-5. Sun 12-5.
Travel:	Broad St exit off Hwy 20/49.
Credit Cards:	Yes
Owner:	Gary & Clarinda Stollery
Year Estab:	1989
Comments:	Set back a few feet from the main street, this shop has an excellent selection of hardcover volumes in most areas with quite interesting titles and several volumes that would certainly fit the antiquarian and/or rare category. A nice shop with a most helpful owner.

Broad Street Books   **Open Shop**
426 Broad Street 95959   (916) 265-4204

Collection:	General stock of hardcover and paperback.
# of Vols:	30,000
Hours:	Daily 7-7.
Travel:	See Brigadoon Books above.
Credit Cards:	No
Owner:	Bob & Konnie Warburton
Year Estab:	1993
Comments:	A combination espresso bar/book shop with a mix (about 50/50) of paperbacks and hardcover reading copies in mixed condition. The pastries looked scrumptious.

Carl Mautz, Vintage Photographs   **By Appointment**
228 Commercial Street, #522 95959   Fax: (916) 478-0466   (916) 478-1610

Collection:	Specialty
Specialties:	Photography
Services:	Appraisals, search service, accepts want lists, mail order.
Credit Cards:	Yes
Year Estab:	1973

Mountain House Books   **Open Shop**
418 Broad Street 95959   Fax: (916) 265-5836   (916) 265-0241

Collection:	General stock.
Specialties:	California; Western Americana; gold rush.
# of Vols:	10,000
Hours:	Mon & Wed-Sat 12-5.
Services:	Appraisals, search service, catalog, accepts want lists, collection development.

Travel:	See Brigadoon Books above.
Credit Cards:	Yes
Owner:	Leonard Berardi & Phyllis Butz
Year Estab:	1983
Comments:	A small shop with quality books in the areas identified above as specialties, along with first editions and some older volumes. Even if your visit is short, if you appreciate fine books, you won't regret having stopped here.

New Harmony Book Cafe   **Open Shop**
727 Zion Street 95959   (916) 265-3002

Collection:	General stock of paperback and hardcover.
# of Vols:	10,000
Hours:	Mon-Sat 10-6. Sun 12-6.
Services:	Search service, accepts want lists.
Travel:	Gold Flat exit off Hwy 49 north. Turn left across the highway and right at second stop sign on Zion St. Shop is 1½ blocks ahead on right.
Credit Cards:	Yes
Owner:	Eric Tomb
Year Estab:	1994
Comments:	If ever the word eclectic fit a description of a smaller bookshop, it fits here. In addition to a 23 volume set of the works of John Burroughs available for $100, we saw other sets of important writers as well as an assortment of more common material, both older and newer, plus paperbacks, LPs, cassettes, CDs and a light menu if you're hungry. What more can one ask for?

Newcastle
(Map 4, page 78)

New and Not So New Book Shop   **Open Shop**
455 Main Street   (916) 663-3633
Mailing Address: PO Box 958 Newcastle 95658

Collection:	General stock of mostly used paperback and hardcover.
Hours:	Tue-Sat 9:30-5.
Travel:	Newcastle exit off I-80. Shop is two blocks from Hwy.
Credit Cards:	No
Owner:	Cecelia A. Brodt
Year Estab:	1980
Comments:	The stock is approximately 75% used, 75% of which is paperback.

Newport Beach
(Map 7, page 270)

Collectors' Library   **Open Shop**
3405 Via Oporto, Lido Village 92663   (714) 675-0686

Collection:	General stock.
Specialties:	First editions; signed.

# of Vols:	6,000
Hours:	Tue-Sun 10-5:30.
Services:	Search service.
Travel:	55 Fwy to end. Continue on Newport Blvd. Left on Via Lido (first left after crossing Hwy 1), then left on Via Oporto.
Credit Cards:	Yes
Owner:	Jan Wilhelm
Year Estab:	1995
Comments:	Unfortunately our travels brought us to Newport Beach on a Monday when this shop is normally closed

North Hills
(Map 9, page 64)

Lois Gereghty Books, Et Al **By Appointment**
9521 Orion Avenue 91343 Fax: (818) 892-1073 (818) 892-1053

Collection:	General stock.
# of Vols:	10,000
Services:	Search service, accepts want lists.
Credit Cards:	No
Year Estab:	1972

North Hollywood
(Map 9, page 64)

Books From Bree **By Appointment**
6716 Clyburn Avenue, #153 91606 (818) 766-5156
E-mail: shoshana@auldbooks.com

Collection:	Specialty
Specialties:	Life and physical sciences; technical.
# of Vols:	5,000
Services:	Catalog, appraisals, search service, accepts want lists.
Credit Cards:	No
Owner:	Shoshana Edwards
Year Estab:	1988

Dutton's Books/North Hollywood **Open Shop**
5146 Laurel Canyon Boulevard 91607 (213) 877-9222

Collection:	General stock of used and new hardcover and paperback.
Specialties:	Modern first editions.
# of Vols:	90,000 (used)
Hours:	Mon-Fri 9:30-9. Sat 9:30-6. Sun 10-6.
Services:	Appraisals, accepts want lists, mail order.
Travel:	Laurel Canyon/Studio City exit off 101 Fwy. North on Laurel Canyon.
Credit Cards:	Yes
Owner:	David & Judy Dutton

Year Estab:	1961
Comments:	If you live in the area and like books you might find this a "neat" shop to visit as the number of books to browse is large and, at least during our visit, new books were being sold at 20% off the cover price. We must admit that we found the shop a bit cramped in terms of the space between bookcases and also because in some sections it was difficult to view specific titles. Sometimes it was difficult to distinguish the new from the old. We saw a number of Franklin Mint/Easton volumes and were advised by the owner that upon request his selection of rare (16th-19th century editions) could be viewed.

Exploded Views Books   By Appointment
5708 Cahuenga Boulevard 91601   Fax: (818) 769-9958   (818) 760-6463

Collection:	Specialty
Specialties:	Modern literature; counter culture; beat generation; erotica; magazines; William S. Burroughs.
# of Vols:	5,000
Services:	Search service, catalog, accepts want lists.
Credit Cards:	No
Owner:	Joe & Lucy Zinnato
Year Estab:	1987

Iliad Bookshop   Open Shop
4820 Vineland Avenue 91601   (818) 509-2665
                                                          E-mail: ac506@lafn.org

Collection:	General stock of hardcover and paperback and some new books.
Specialties:	Literature; art; photography; film; music; counter culture.
# of Vols:	100,000
Hours:	Mon-Sat 10-10. Sun 12-6.
Services:	Search service, accepts want lists.
Travel:	From 101 Fwy north: Lankershim exit. North on Lankershim for two miles. Veer right on Vineland. From 134 Fwy westbound: Lankershim exit. Right on Lankershim. Proceed for 1/2 mile, then veer right on Vineland.
Credit Cards:	Yes
Owner:	Dan Weinstein
Year Estab:	1987
Comments:	For some people books run in their blood. This has to be the case with the owner of this shop whose father, uncle and cousin are also used book dealers in California. The shop here is roomy, the books are nicely displayed and are in generally good condition. Most subjects are covered. Prices are reasonable and the shop can be a fun browse.

Natural History Books   By Appointment
6821 Babcock Avenue 91605   Fax: (818) 982-1619   (818) 982-4911

Collection:	Specialty. Mostly used.
Specialties:	Natural history, including mammals, birds, reptiles, fish, insects, arachnids, zoology, naturalist's biographies and naturalist's travels and voyages.
# of Vols:	4,500-5,000

Hours: By chance, daily 10-10 and by appointment.
Services: Appraisals, search service, catalog, accepts want lists.
Credit Cards: Yes
Owner: Rudolph Wm. Sabbot
Year Estab: 1965

Sam's Book City **Open Shop**
5249 Lankershim Boulevard 91601 (818) 985-6911

Collection: General stock of hardcover and paperback.
Specialties: Film; performing arts; children's; literature; modern first editions; art; sports, with an emphasis on baseball.
# of Vols: 75,000
Hours: Mon-Fri 10-7. Sat 10-6. Sun 11-5.
Services: Accepts want lists.
Travel: Northbound on 101 Fwy to Hwy 170. Magnolia exit off Hwy 170. Right on Magnolia, then left on Lankershim. Southbound on 101 Fwy: Tujunga exit. Right on Tujunga, right on Magnolia and left on Lankershim.
Credit Cards: Yes
Owner: Craig Klapman
Year Estab: 1973
Comments: A spacious shop with a 30% paperback/70% hardcover mix. Most of the hardcovers were of recent vintage and in generally good condition. Reasonable prices. If your interests are in the fields listed above as specialties you should find a visit here worthwhile.

Twice Told Tales **Open Shop**
11223½ Magnolia Blvd 91601 (818) 980-7506

Collection: General stock.
# of Vols: 10,000
Hours: Call for hours
Travel: See Sam's Book City above. Shop is on corner of Magnolia and Lankershim.
Owner: Ty Stanley
Year Estab: 1995

Northridge

Being Books Inc. **By Appointment**
19834 Gresham Street 91324 (818) 341-0283

Collection: Specialty, Mostly used hardcover.
Specialties: Psychology; psychiatry; psychotherapy; marital and family therapy; philosophy; religion; metaphysics.
# of Vols: 50,000
Hours: By chance daily before 3pm and by appointment.
Services: Appraisals, search service, catalog, accepts want lists.
Credit Cards: No
Owner: Clinton Ellis Weyand, PhD.
Year Estab: 1975

Norwalk
(Map 7, page 270)

Aviation Bookmobile/H.N. Miller Books   **Open Shop**
12142 East Front   * (310) 864-4116
Mailing Address: PO Box U Norwalk 90651-5023   (800) 865-4116

Collection: General stock of used and new hardcover and paperback.
Specialties: Aviation; military; space; transportation.
# of Vols: 80,000
Hours: Sun & Mon 2-5. Tue-Sat 11-5. Mornings by appointment.
Services: Appraisals, mail order, search service, catalog in planning stage.
Travel: Southbound on 5 Fwy: Pioneer Blvd exit. South on Pioneer, east on Firestone, right on Clarkdale. Store is at dead end. Northbound on 5 Fwy: Imperial exit. East on Imperial, right on Firestone, right on Clarkdale.
Owner: Harold Norman Miller
Year Estab: 1960

Oak View

Ed Smith Books   **By Appointment**
PO Box 66 93022   Fax: (805) 649-2863   (805) 649-2844

Collection: Specialty
Specialties: 20th century literature; photography; signed; literary biographies; proofs.
Services: Appraisals, catalog.
Credit Cards: Yes
Owner: Ed Smith & Ellen Boughn
Year Estab: 1990

Oakdale
(Map 4, page 78)

The Book Center   **Open Shop**
1275 East F Street, Ste. 2 95358   (209) 847-8286

Collection: General stock of paperback and hardcover.
# of Vols: 50,000
Hours: Mon-Sat 10-7. Sun 10-5.
Services: Search service, accepts want lists.
Travel: Located in a shopping center on Hwy 108/120 just east of downtown.
Credit Cards: No
Owner: Wayne P. Burton
Year Estab: 1991
Comments: A respectable, well organized community bookshop with about 50%-75% of its stock consisting of paperback mysteries, romance, etc. and the balance reading copies of hardcover books. Some nice volumes. Some ordinary volumes.

* Some 310 codes change to 562 in 1996

Jack's Music & Books **Open Shop**
326 East F Street 95361 (209) 847-1858
Collection: General stock of mostly paperback.
Hours: Daily 11-7.

Marvin Stanley, Bookseller **Open Shop**
7450 River Road, #6 95361 (209) 847-8706
Collection: General stock, ephemera and records.
Specialties: Black studies; religion; history; cookbooks; vintage paperbacks; magazines.
# of Vols: 30,000
Hours: Tue-Sat 12-5.
Services: Appraisals, accepts want lists.
Travel: Located at intersection of Hwy 120 and River Rd. Proceeding east on Hwy 120, shop is just before Oakdale.
Credit Cards: No
Year Estab: 1975
Comments: If neatness is your thing, this shop may not be for you. When the very kind owner opened his shop a bit early to accommodate our schedule, we were greeted by piles and piles of books, some in the aisles and some in boxes and walking around the aisles was a real challenge. A majority of the books were older volumes in mixed condition. Despite the difficulties encountered in navigating the shop, we were still able to find two books worth purchasing. If you enjoy a challenge, you might want to stop here. Note: The phone number listed above is the owner's home number; there is no phone in the shop.

Oakhurst
(Map 4, page 78)

Mountain Light Books **Open Shop**
40177 Highway 41 (209) 683-2665
Mailing Address: PO Box 1229 North Fork 93643
Collection: General stock of used and new.
Specialties: Local history, art; performing arts; literature; history.
# of Vols: 10,000 (used)
Hours: Memorial Day-Labor Day: Tue Sat 11-5. Sun 11-3. Remainder of year: Tue-Sat only 11-5.
Services: Mail order, search service, accepts want lists.
Travel: Approximately 40 miles north of Fresno, near south gate to Yosemite National Park.
Credit Cards: Yes
Owner: Emily Susann
Year Estab: 1987
Comments: The stock is approximately 80% hardcover.

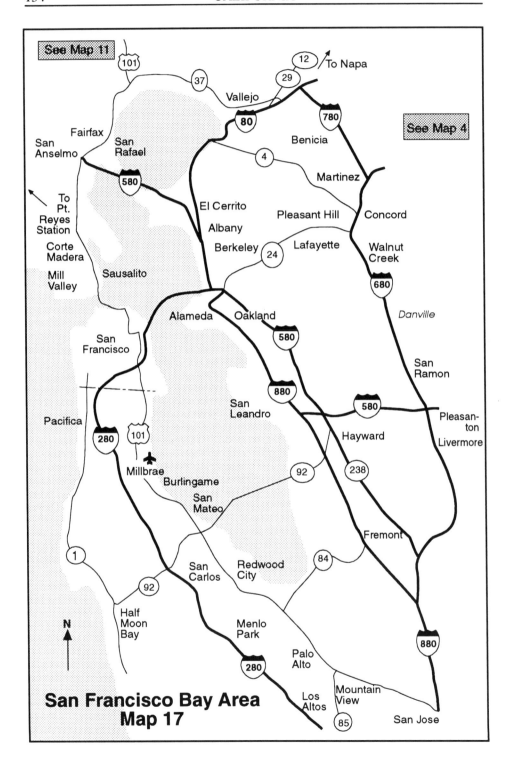

Oakland
(Map 3, page 52 and Map 17, page 154)

Archaeologia **By Appointment**
707 Carlston Avenue 94610 Fax: (510) 832-1410 (510) 832-1405

Collection: Specialty
Specialties: Archeology; ancient history; ancient art; ancient religion; ancient medicine; ancient languages.
# of Vols: 8,000-10,000
Services: Catalog, search service, accepts want lists.
Credit Cards: Yes
Owner: Andrew Gordon & Arthur Richter
Year Estab: 1983

Bibliomania **Open Shop**
1816 Telegraph Avenue 94612 (510) 835-5733

Collection: General stock and ephemera.
Specialties: Social movements; black studies; military history with emphasis on Spanish Civil War and Vietnam War; modern literature; children's; sports, with an emphasis on baseball and golf; cats.
# of Vols: 40,000+
Hours: Mon-Sat 11-5. Sun by chance or appointment.
Services: Appraisals, search service, catalog, accepts want lists.
Travel: SE corner of Telegraph at 19th, one block from Broadway.
Map Ref: Map 3, page 52, #12.
Credit Cards: Yes
Owner: Daryl & Jean Van Fleet
Year Estab: 1974

Black Swan **Open Shop**
4236 Piedmont Avenue 94611 (510) 428-2881

Collection: General stock of mostly hardcover.
Specialties: Children's; modern first editions; military; photography.
# of Vols: 65,000
Hours: Tue-Sat 11-6. Sun 12-6.
Services: Appraisals, search service.
Travel: MacArthur Blvd exit off I-580. East on MacArthur for three miles. Left on Piedmont Ave. Shop is about seven blocks ahead in a private house.
Map Ref: Map 3, page 52, #13.
Credit Cards: No
Owner: Martin Neil
Year Estab: 1986

Diesel, A Bookstore **Open Shop**
5433 College Avenue 94618 (510) 653-9965

Collection: General stock of new and used.
Specialties: Contemporary fiction; poetry; children's.

(Oakland)

Hours:	Mon-Sat 9am-10pm. Sun 10-6.
Travel:	Claremont exit off Hwy 24 eastbound. Proceed straight across Claremont on Clifton to dead end at College. Left on College. Westbound on Hwy 24: College Ave exit. Proceed to College Ave. Left on College.
Map Ref:	Map 3, page 52, #14.
Credit Cards:	Yes
Owner:	John Evans & Alison Reid
Year Estab:	1989
Comments:	Approximately 30% of the stock is used.

The Bookmark
721 Washington Street 94607

Open Shop
(510) 444-0473

Collection:	General stock.
Hours:	Tue-Sat 10:30-5.
Travel:	Between 7th & 8th St.
Map Ref:	Map 3, page 52, #15
Comments:	Operated by Friends of the Public Library.

Key Bookshop
531 16th Street 94612

Open Shop
(510) 444-2915

Collection:	General stock of mostly used hardcover and paperback.
Specialties:	Black studies.
# of Vols:	20,000 (used)
Hours:	Mon-Sat 11-5. Sun 12-3.
Travel:	Two blocks from 14th & Broadway.
Map Ref:	Map 3, page 52, #16.
Credit Cards:	No
Owner:	Kokavulu Lumukanda
Year Estab:	1990
Comments:	Used stock is approximately 70% hardcover.

Northwest Books
3814 Lyon Avenue 94601

By Appointment
(510) 532-5227

Collection:	Specialty
Specialties:	Western Americana; lithographs.
# of Vols:	3,000
Services:	Appraisals, accepts want lists, mail order.
Credit Cards:	No
Owner:	Don McKinney
Year Estab:	1956

Pendragon Books
5560 College Avenue 94618

Open Shop
(510) 652-6259

Collection:	General stock of used paperback and hardcover, new and remainders.

# of Vols: 30,000
Hours: Mon-Sat 9am-10:45pm. Sun 10-10.
Travel: Claremont exit off Hwy 24. North on Claremont, south on College.
Map Ref: Map 3, page 52, #17.
Credit Cards: Yes
Owner: Matt Wyse, owner. Amy Thomas, presdient.
Year Estab: 1975
Comments: Stock is approximately 70% paperback.

Regent Press
6020-A Adeline 94608

By Appointment
Fax: (510) 547-6357   (510) 547-7602

Collection: General stock.
Specialties: Dreams
# of Vols: 1,000
Services: Mail order.
Credit Cards: Yes
Owner: Mark Weiman
Year Estab: 1978

D.A. Sachs - Books
PO Box 10267 94610

By Appointment
(510) 832-3115

Collection: General stock.
Specialties: Area studies; foreign language books; pamphlets; social movements; unusual materials in many fields.
# of Vols: "Large"
Credit Cards: No
Year Estab: 1970

The Spectator Bookstore
4163 Piedmont Avenue 94611

Open Shop
(510) 653-7300

Collection: General stock of used, new and remainders.
Hours: Mon-Thu 10-9. Fri & Sat 10am-11pm. Sun 10-8.
Services: Search service.
Travel: Broadway exit off Hwy 24 south. Follow Broadway to MacArthur. Left on MacArthur, then left on Piedmont.
Map Ref: Map 3, page 52, #18.
Credit Cards: Yes
Owner: Fred & Yvette Schmalz-Riedt
Year Estab: 1993
Comments: The used stock is approximately 70% hardcover. The owners have a second shop with a similar stock in Alameda.

Walden Pond Books
3316 Grand Avenue 94610

Open Shop
Fax: (510) 832-4010   (510) 832-4438

Collection: General stock of new and used, hardcover and paperback.
Specialties: Fiction; radical literature; art; photography; railroads.
# of Vols: 150,000

Hours:	Daily 10-10.
Travel:	Grand Ave exit off I-580. Left on Grand.
Map Ref:	Map 3, page 52, #19.
Credit Cards:	Yes
Owner:	M. Curatolo
Year Estab:	1975
Comments:	The stock is approximately 50% used and 50% hardcover.

Occidental

Uncle David's Family Fun Store   **Open Shop**
123 Main Street   (707) 874-3449
Mailing Address: PO Box 272 Occidental 95465

Collection:	General stock of mostly paperback.
Hours:	Mon-Fri 11-6. Sat 10-6. Sun 12-6.

Oildale

The Book Nook   **Open Shop**
911 North Chester 93308   (805) 393-4911

Collection:	General stock of new and used paperback and hardcover.
Specialties:	Americana; political; non fiction.
# of Vols:	30,000+
Hours:	Tue-Sat 10-5.
Services:	Accepts want lists.
Travel:	Olive Dr exit off Fwy 99. East on Olive. Right on Roberts. Left on North Chester. Shop is about seven blocks ahead on left.
Credit Cards:	No
Owner:	Claire Smeed
Year Estab:	1990
Comments:	Stock is about 75% paperback and is evenly divided between new and used.

Ojai
(Map 5, page 235)

Bart's Books   **Open Shop**
302 West Matilija Street 93023   (805) 646-3755

Collection:	General stock of hardcover and paperback.
Specialties:	Occult; history; religion; literature.
# of Vols:	125,000+
Hours:	Tue-Sun 10-5:30.
Services:	Search service.
Travel:	Hwy 33 to Ojai. When Hwy 33 forks, bear right following signs to downtown. Left on Canada. Shop is one block ahead.

Credit Cards: Yes
Owner: Gary Schlichter
Year Estab: 1964
Comments: We strongly urge a visit here and suggest that you not reach any conclusions about the quality of the stock based purely on your initial observations. One's first reaction is that one is visiting a flea market because so many of the books displayed outside show signs of wear (even though they are sheltered by plastic overhangs.) Overall, the number of books is large, the shelves are labeled, paperbacks are separated from hardcover volumes and there are lots of inexpensively priced hardcover books. Most of the books are older, and, as previously indicated, do show their age. However, don't leave without visiting the two completely enclosed buildings, one appropriately called the "gallery" as it houses a selection of hardcover books (in quite good condition) dealing with art and art related topics. Both buildings offer some real treats: behind glass, we saw some absolutely wonderful and truly rare first editions (Truman Capote, Virginia Woolf, etc.) in very good condition, some 17th and 18th century volumes, an entire section of other first editions (some signed) and even a clean rest room for the weary traveler.

Orange
(Map 7, page 270)

Altair-4 (Knights Cross Books) **Open Shop**
870 Tustin Avenue 92667 (714) 639-5736

Collection: Specialty. Mostly used.
Specialties: Fantasy; science fiction; pulps; military.
# of Vols: 12,000
Hours: Mon-Fri 11-7. Sat 11-6. Sun by appointment.
Travel: Katella exit off 55 Fwy. West on Katella, left on Tustin.

Book Carnival **Open Shop**
348 South Tustin Street 92666 Fax: (714) 538-3210 (714) 538-3210

Collection: Specialty used and new, hardcover and paperback.
Specialties: Mystery; detective; science fiction; fantasy; dark suspense.
# of Vols: 15,000
Hours: Mon-Fri 11-6, except Fri till 7. Sat 10-5.
Services: Appraisals, mail order.
Travel: Near intersection of 55 and 22 Fwys.
Credit Cards: Yes
Owner: Ed & Pat Thomas
Year Estab: 1981
Comments: Stock is approximately 70% used and 60% hardcover.

Book Time **Open Shop**
456 South Main Street 92668 Fax: (714) 978-9143 (714) 978-2708

Collection: General stock of hardcover and paperback.

(Orange)

Specialties:	Modern first editions; signed; Western Americana; art; literature; mystery.
# of Vols:	100,000
Hours:	Mon-Fri 10-7. Sat 10-6.
Services:	Search service, catalog, accepts want lists.
Travel:	Main St exit off 5 Fwy. Proceed south on Main.
Credit Cards:	Yes
Owner:	Jerry & Lloyd Griffin
Year Estab:	1993
Comments:	This shop is set up like two separate stores with one room devoted primarily to paperbacks and a second almost exclusively to hardcover books, a majority of which were of recent vintage but with a fair representation of older volumes. More expensive and/or unusual items are kept under glass. The variety of the stock was sufficient for us to suggest that a visit here is in order.

Bookman   **Open Shop**
840 North Tustin Avenue 92667   (714) 538-0166

Collection:	General stock of mostly used hardcover and paperback.
# of Vols:	250,000
Hours:	Mon-Fri 10-8. Sat 10-6. Sun 12-5.
Services:	Search service, accepts want lists.
Travel:	Chapman/Orange exit off 55 Fwy. Proceed west on Chapman, then north on Tustin. The shop is located in a strip shopping center.
Credit Cards:	Yes
Owner:	Donald Hess & Paul Bonaventure
Year Estab:	1990
Comments:	About three quarters of this large shop is devoted to used hardcover items in almost every conceivable area ranging from reading copies to fine editions to more difficult-to-locate items. We found some winners here and don't believe we overpaid for them. A smaller bargain annex is located just a few doors down from the main shop.

Bookman Basement   **Open Shop**
806 North Tustin Avenue 92667   (714) 744-2665

Collection:	General stock of hardcover and paperback.
Hours:	Mon-Fri 10-6, except Fri till 8. Sat 10-6. Sun 12-5.
Comments:	See Bookman above. The books here are generally priced at $5 or less.

Books Plus   **Open Shop**
725 North Tustin Avenue 92667   (714) 633-3928

Collection:	General stock of hardcover and paperback.
# of Vols:	5,000
Hours:	Mon-Sat 10-6.
Travel:	At corner of Tustin and Mayfair.
Credit Cards:	Yes
Owner:	Monica Ray

Year Estab:	1995
Comments:	A neighborhood book store with a neighborhood flavor and a mix of hardcover and paperbacks. The vast majority of the hardcover books were recent best sellers. Nothing out of the ordinary.

Crystal Cave   **Open Shop**
777 South Main Street, #2   92668   (714) 543-0551

Collection:	Specialty. Mostly new. Mostly paperback.
Specialties:	Metaphysics, new age; alternative healing; eastern philosophy.
Hours:	Mon-Sat 10-6, except Fri till 7. Sun 12-5.

Nix Books   **Open Shop**
2820 East Chapman Avenue   92669   (714) 997-5242

Collection:	General stock of mostly hardcover.
Specialties:	Modern first editions; history; literature.
# of Vols:	100,000
Hours:	Mon-Sat 10-6.
Services:	Appraisals, catalog, search service, accepts want lists.
Travel:	East Chapman exit off 55 Fwy. Proceed east on East Chapman, right on Malena and right into parking lot. Shop is in the rear of the shopping center and is not visible from Chapman.
Credit Cards:	Yes
Owner:	Dennis Nix
Year Estab:	1991
Comments:	As you immediately enter this shop you'll find two rooms that have books displayed in a manner that makes browsing quite easy. The rest of the shop is crowded to the point where it is possible to overlook a title that you may have wished to purchase had you seen it. During our visit, some of the fiction was being discounted at 50% and there were paperbacks being sold for as little as 25¢ each. We found a title we had been looking for for quite some time and wish you equal luck although we recognize, as in Las Vegas, that the odds may be against you. If you're interested in truly rare items, or very scholarly titles, this is probably not your cup of tea. We estimate there were fewer books on display than the number indicated above.

Oroville
(Map 11, page 289)

The Bookworm   **Open Shop**
2310 Montgomery Street   95965   (916) 534-1974

Collection:	General stock of paperback and hardcover.
# of Vols:	50,000+
Hours:	Daily 9-6.
Travel:	Montgomery St exit off Hwy 70.
Credit Cards:	No
Owner:	Ron Hearn
Comments:	Approximately 80-85% of the stock consists of paperbacks and the hardcover items we saw were of little distinction.

Oxnard
(Map 5, page 235)

The Warehouse Book Store — **Open Shop**
1830 Lockwood Street, #106 93030 (805) 983-2143

Collection: General stock of paperback and hardcover and magazines.
# of Vols: 125,000+
Hours: Daily 10-6.
Travel: Rose Ave exit off Hwy 101. Proceed south on Rose to first light, then left on Lockwood. Shop is in a renovated warehouse.
Credit Cards: Yes
Year Estab: 1993
Comments: While the owner maintains that half his stock is hardcover (and we can hardly lay claim to having done an accurate count that would have challenged that assertion) one's immediate impression is that the paperback selection, which is enormous, far outweighs the hardcover books. The vast majority of the hardcover volumes we did see were older volumes in rather mixed condition, not organized by subject and priced very inexpensively. Other bookcases contained *Readers Digest* condensations and some labeled shelves of technical manuals and some non fiction categories. If you want to buy a lot of books inexpensively this is a place to shop. If you're a serious book person looking for a special title or titles in your field, you may not feel comfortable here. On the other hand, there are legends told about book scouts picking up valuable editions at thrift shops and flea markets, etc. So, "you never know."

Pacific Grove
(Map 5, page 235)

Armchair Bookshop — **Open Shop**
170 Grand Avenue 93950 (408) 644-9318

Collection: General stock of hardcover and paperback.
# of Vols: 5,000
Hours: Tue-Sat 10:30-5.
Travel: Lighthouse Ave in Monterey becomes Central Ave in Pacific Grove. Continue on Central, then left on Grand.
Credit Cards: No
Owner: Annabelle Ruedemann
Year Estab: 1993
Comments: A rather small shop, not much larger than a good sized living room. Most of the books we saw were rather ordinary and quite a number of them were in less than satisfactory condition. If you have time after visiting the other book stores in the region and want to stop by, it's always conceivable that you might find a book (particularly if you're looking for an older volume) of interest. If you're on a tight schedule, we believe time spent here might be better invested elsewhere.

Pacificia
(Map 17, page 154))

Florey's Book Co.   **By Appointment**
2316 Palmetto 94044   (415) 355-8811

Collection:	General stock of used and new.
# of Vols:	5,000-10,000
Hours:	Mon-Sat 10-6.
Travel:	Northbound on Hwy 1: Clarendon exit. Left under freeway and proceed to dead end. Right on Palmetto. Southbound on Hwy 1: Franciscan Blvd exit. Right at stop sign and proceed one block, then left on Palmetto.
Credit Cards:	Yes
Owner:	Mary Palmetto
Year Estab:	1975
Comments:	Once you've walked through one or two rooms displaying new books (hardcover and paperback), gift items and charming little souvenirs, you'll eventually come to two more rooms that do indeed carry used hardcover books. Most of these books are in mixed condition and of mixed vintage. While we were unable to find any truly rare items and would guess that the store basically provides reading copies for the community, one never knows what books may be on the shelves at the time of your visit.

Manning's Books   **Open Shop**
580-M Crespi 94044   Fax: (415) 355-1851   (415) 355-6325

Collection:	Specialty
Specialties:	Antique maps and prints.
Hours:	Tue-Fri 8-6. Other times by appointment in San Francisco.
Services:	Catalog, accepts want lists.
Travel:	Crespi Dr exit off Hwy 1. East on Crespi, then right into Crespi Center.
Credit Cards:	No
Owner:	Kathleen Manning
Year Estab:	1972

Pacoima
(Map 9, page 64)

Pauline Jenkins Rare Books   **By Appointment**
13301 Van Nuys Blvd, #2 91331   (818) 899-2153

Collection:	General stock.
# of Vols:	200,000

Hans Kuperus-Periodicals   **By Appointment**
11254 Bradley Avenue 91331   (818) 890-1503

Collection:	Specialty
Specialties:	Magazines
Credit Cards:	No
Year Estab:	1983

Palm Desert

Valerie Kraft, Fine Books   **By Appointment**
41-617 Armanac Court   (619) 340-4674
Mailing Address: PO Box 12932 Palm Desert 92255

Collection: Specialty
Specialties: Children's; illustrated; sports; cookbooks; art; art reference.
# of Vols: 7,000
Services: Mail order.
Year Estab: 1971

Palm Springs
(Map 12, page 139)

Book Exchange   **Open Shop**
611 South Palm Canyon Drive, #19   92264   (619) 325-6200

Collection: General stock of paperback and hardcover.
# of Vols: 15,000
Hours: Mon-Sat 9-5.
Travel: Hwy 111 exit off 10 Fwy. Stay on Hwy 111 which becomes Palm Canyon Dr (first north then south). Shop is in Sun Center shopping plaza just after crossing Ramon Rd.
Owner: Christine M. Lowe
Comments: One of a chain of eight shops all with the same name. At the time of our visit, this shop provided a pleasant surprise as the hardcover volumes we are used to seeing in "mostly paperback" shops in shopping centers consist primarily of book club editions, modern best sellers, remainders, etc. Indeed, the vast majority of the books in this shop are paperbacks, but the 2,000-3,000 hardcovers on display did represent a balance not ordinarily seen in shops of this type and some might well tempt the traveling buyer.

Celebrity Bookstore   **Open Shop**
170 East Tahquitz Canyon   92262   (800) 320-6575   (619) 320-6575
Fax: (619) 320-6575

Collection: General stock of hardcover and paperback.
Specialties: Books by and about celebrities.
# of Vols: 15,000
Hours: Mon-Thu 10-7. Fri & Sat 10-9. Sun 10-4. Summer hours: Call ahead or by appointment.
Travel: Left turn off North Palm Canyon Dr.
Credit Cards: Yes
Owner: Darrell & Shirley Meeks
Year Estab: 1980
Comments: Although the owner of this establishment tries to stock books reflecting the careers of well known personalities (biographies and autobiographies), the shop's general stock is nothing to sneeze at. The books seemed well cared for and were displayed in an attractive fashion.

Craig & Craig Booksellers
333 North Palm Canyon Drive 92262

Open Shop
(619) 323-7379

Collection: General stock of hardcover and paperback.
Specialties: Modern first editions; non fiction.
# of Vols: 30,000
Hours: Mon-Thu 10-6. Fri & Sat 10-10. Sun 11-5. Call for summer hours.
Services: Appraisals, search service, accepts want lists, mail order.
Travel: See Book Exchange above.
Credit Cards: Yes
Owner: Gary & Donna Craig
Year Estab: 1987
Comments: A neat, attractively laid out book shop with nice titles, even in our own areas of interest (which are not always readily on view). Moderately priced. A pleasure to browse.

Palmdale
(Map 12, page 139)

Papa's Used Books
1645 Palmdale Boulevard, Ste. L 93550

Open Shop
(805) 274-1420

Collection: General stock of paperback and hardcover.
# of Vols: 45,000-50,000
Hours: Mon-Sat 9-6. Sun 10-4.
Services: Accepts want lists, mail order.
Travel: Palmdale Blvd exit off Hwy 14. Proceed east on Palmdale to 17th St.
Credit Cards: Yes
Owner: Warren Powers
Year Estab: 1993
Comments: Stock is approximately 75% paperback.

Palo Alto
(Map 17, page 154)

Bell's Book Store
536 Emerson Street 94301

Open Shop
(415) 323-7822

Collection: General stock.
Specialties: Gardening; roses; children's; music; scholarly.
# of Vols: 100,000
Hours: Mon-Thu 9:30-5:30. Fri 9:30-9. Sat 9:30-5.
Services: Search service, mail order.
Travel: University Ave exit off Hwy 82 (El Camino Real) or Hwy 101. West on University. Left on Emerson.
Credit Cards: Yes
Owner: Valeria Bell
Year Estab: 1934

(Palo Alto)

Comments: A delightful bi-level shop and one that certainly should not be missed. The collection is substantial, although clearly much stronger in the specialties identified above. One problem for the browser who likes to eyeball as many titles as possible is that the height of some of the shelves on the first floor makes one's willingness to climb a ladder the key to one's browsing success.

Chimaera Books & Music **Open Shop**
165 University Avenue 94301 (415) 327-1122

Collection: General stock of hardcover and paperback and records.
Specialties: Scholarly; classics; arts; history; humanities.
# of Vols: 50,000
Hours: Daily 10am-midnight.
Services: Appraisals
Travel: See Bell's Book Store above.
Credit Cards: Yes
Owner: Walter Martin
Year Estab: 1970
Comments: The emphasis here is on the scholarly, even in the literature section. Most of the books we saw were in very good condition with about 20% of the stock consisting of new books, some of which may have been priced at a discount. While it may not be appropriate to generalize, we noticed both a Book of the Month Club item and a library discard at prices that we thought a bit steep. We suspect that a good portion of the shop's stock is probably in storage as considerably fewer than the 50,000 volumes noted above were available for browsing at the time of our visit.

Know Knew Books **Open Shop**
415 California 94306 (415) 326-9355

Collection: General stock of paperback and hardcover.
Specialties: Science fiction; horror.
# of Vols: 100,000+
Hours: Mon-Sat 10-10. Sun 12-8.
Services: Accepts want lists, mail order.
Travel: Oregon Expy exit off Hwy 101. Proceed on Oregon to El Camino. Right on El Camino then right on California.
Credit Cards: Yes
Owner: Bill Burruss & Paul Willis
Year Estab: 1989
Comments: The estimate of the number of volumes listed above is probably close to target, with the majority of the stock being paperback. Most subjects were covered with paperbacks and hardcovers (with some exceptions) generally shelved together. Most of the hardcover volumes we saw were reading copies, and again, with exceptions, seemed to be reasonably priced. As always, it's helpful for the buyer to have some sense of what a particular book might be worth.

Megabooks
444 University Avenue 94301

Open Shop
(415) 326-4730

Collection:	General stock of paperback and hardcover.
# of Vols:	25,000
Hours:	Mon-Sat 10-6. Longer evening hours on Fri & Sat in summer.
Travel:	See Bell's Book Store above. Shop is on left between Cowper & Waverly.
Credit Cards:	Yes
Owner:	G. Marsullo
Year Estab:	1968
Comments:	The emphasis here was clearly on popular paperbacks (mystery, science fiction, etc.) while many of the hardcover sections contained more academically oriented subjects. Perhaps this shop meets local needs; we wouldn't recommend traveling far out of one's way for a visit.

Minerva Books
1027 Alma 94301

Open Shop
(415) 326-2006

Collection:	Specialty. Primarily new and some used.
Specialties:	Metaphysics
# of Vols:	2,000 (used)
Hours:	Mon-Sat 11-6, except Thu till 8. Sun 1-5.
Travel:	Embarcadero exit off Hwy 101. Proceed west on Embarcadero. At underpass, proceed on frontage road, then right on Alma.
Comments:	Used stock is approximately 70% paperback.

Renaissance Bookstore
230 Hamilton Avenue 94301

Open Shop
(415) 321-2846

Collection:	General stock of mostly used paperback and hardcover.
# of Vols:	50,000
Hours:	Mon-Sat 10-9. Sun 12-6.
Travel:	See Bell's Book Store above. Left on Ramona and right on Hamilton.
Credit Cards:	Yes
Owner:	John Hally
Year Estab:	1991
Comments:	More of a "peoples" store, in that its stock, while a mix of paperback and hardcover (intershelved) has older volumes and a higher ratio of paperbacks to hardcover. While many subjects were covered, popular culture gets a break here. Reasonably priced.

Szwede Slavic Books
2233 El Camino Real
Mailing Address: PO Box 1214 Palo Alto 94302

Open Shop
(415) 851-0748   (415) 327-5590
Fax: (415) 327-8957

Collection:	Specialty new and used.
Specialties:	Books in slavic languages; books in English about slavic countries, including literature; literary criticism; history; heraldry; dictionaries.
# of Vols:	100,000+
Hours:	Tue-Sat 10-5.
Services:	Limited search service, catalog, accepts want lists.

Travel:	One block south of Stanford University.
Credit Cards:	No
Owner:	Dr. Irena Szwede
Year Estab:	1959
Comments:	Stock is approximately 75% new.

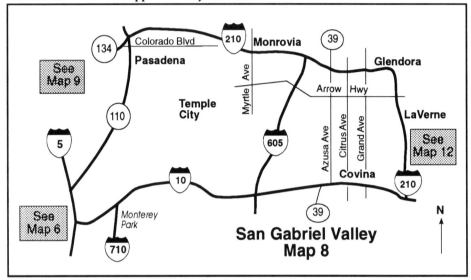

Paradise
(Map 11, page 189)

Books of Paradise — Open Shop
6141 Skyway 95969 — (916) 877-8741

Collection:	General stock of paperback and hardcover.
# of Vols:	50,00
Hours:	Mon-Fri 9:30-5:30. Sat 10-4.
Travel:	Skyway exit off Hwy 99. Follow signs to Paradise.
Credit Cards:	No
Owner:	Paul Shelley
Year Estab:	1988
Comments:	Stock is approximately 60% paperback.

Pasadena
(Map 8, page 168)

Robert Allen/Books — Open Shop
1393 East Washington Boulevard — (818) 794-4210
Mailing Address: PO Box 582 Altadena 91001

Collection:	General stock and ephemera.
Specialties:	Literature before 1915; children's; California.

# of Vols: 5,000
Hours: Tue-Sat 10:30-5:30.
Services: Appraisals, catalog, accepts want lists.
Travel: Hill St exit off 210 Fwy. Proceed north on Hill St for one mile. Shop is at northwest corner of Hill and Washington.
Credit Cards: Yes
Year Estab: 1977
Comments: A small shop with a small collection located on the same premises as Mitchell Books. (see below). Lots of interesting ephemera but not enough volumes in any one subject area to make a description of the shop's collection viable. If you're interested in any of the specialties listed above, a phone call would be a far more economical way of determining if the shop is for you - unless you're in the neighborhood and would simply like to drop in.

The Archives Bookshop **Open Shop**
1387 East Washington Boulevard 91104   Fax: (818) 797-5237   (818) 797-4756

Collection: Specialty. Mostly used and some new, hardcover and paperback.
Specialties: Bible; religion; philosophy; church history.
# of Vols: 40,000
Hours: Mon-Sat 10-6.
Services: Appraisals, catalog, accepts want lists.
Travel: See Robert Allen Books above.
Credit Cards: Yes
Owner: John Wipf
Year Estab: 1980

Don Belew Antiques **Antique Mall**
At Pasadena Antique Center   (818) 449-7706
480 South Fair Oaks Avenue   91105

Collection: General stock.
Hours: Daily 10-6.

Book Alley of Old Pasadena **Open Shop**
36 West Colorado boulevard 91105   (818) 683-8083

Collection: General stock of mostly hardcover.
Specialties: Western Americana; California; film; theater; art; photography.
# of Vols: 25,000
Hours: Daily noon-10pm.
Services: Appraisals, search service, accepts want lists.
Travel: Fair Oak Ave exit off 134 Fwy. Proceed south on Fair Oak for about three blocks. Shop is located in Mills Place Alley.
Credit Cards: Yes
Owner: Peter Hay & Dorthea Atwater
Year Estab: 1992
Comments: As its name suggests, this shop is located in an alley between the number 30

(Pasadena)

and 40 on West Colorado. Once we made this elementary discovery (after two unsuccessful trips around the block in search of number 36), we found a shop displaying a good sized collection of more recent publications, most in good condition. The store is both easy and pleasant to browse.

Book Jam   **Open Shop**
659 East Colorado Boulevard 91101   (818) 585-8308

Collection: General stock of hardcover and paperback.
# of Vols: 15,000
Hours: Mon-Sat 10-9. Sun 10-5.
Services: Search service, accepts want lists, mail order.
Travel: See Cliff's Books below.
Credit Cards: Yes
Owner: Angel Arellano, Jr.
Year Estab: 1991
Comments: A corner shop with mostly relatively recent titles in mixed condition. While winners can be found in any shop and in any environment, we saw few if any that could be characterized as such here. Moderately priced.

Dirk Cable, Bookseller   **Open Shop**
350 South Lake Avenue, #113 91101   (818) 449-7001

Collection: General stock and ephemera.
Specialties: Western Americana; California; history; travel; books about books; Americana; English and American literature.
# of Vols: 5,00-7,000
Hours: Mon-Sat 10-6.
Services: Appraisals, mail order.
Travel: 110 Fwy north to end at Arroyo Pky. Continue north to California Blvd, then right on California and right on Lake. Shop is between Del Mar and San Pasqual in Colonade Mall.
Credit Cards: Yes
Year Estab: 1980
Comments: This is a shop that one can admire even without entering as there are four large windows that allow the passing viewer to appreciate the ambience of the establishment. Once entering the shop, one's initial impressions are reinforced as each bookcase contains carefully selected titles both in the shop's speciality areas and in other areas that reveal the owner's good taste. Despite the modest size of the collections, the shop provides the serious buyer with lots of interesting choices. Don't look for paperbacks here.

Cliff's Books/Records/Comics   **Open Shop**
628-632 East Colorado Boulevard 91101   (818) 449-9541

Collection: General stock of mostly used hardcover and paperback and ephemera.
Specialties: Science; technology; metaphysics; occult; children's; literature; cookbooks; vintage paperbacks.

# of Vols: 250,000
Hours: Mon-Sat 10-midnight. Sun 11-midnight.
Services: Appraisals, search service, accepts want lists, mail order.
Travel: Lake Ave exit off 210 Fwy. South on Lake. Right on Colorado.
Credit Cards: Yes
Owner: Cliff Gildart
Year Estab: 1959
Comments: The hardcover volumes are of relatively recent vintage with few that we would judge as being rare or difficult to find.

House of Fiction
663 East Colorado Boulevard 91101

Open Shop
(818) 499-9861

Collection: General stock of hardcover and paperback.
Specialties: Literature; history; baseball.
# of Vols: 10,000
Hours: Mon-Thu 10-9. Fri & Sat 10-10. Sun 12-5.
Services: Appraisals
Travel: See Cliff's Books below. Shop is between Lake and El Molino.
Credit Cards: No
Owner: Bill Tunilla
Year Estab: 1979
Comments: Perhaps it was our imagination, but we sensed a strange aroma upon entering this shop. Most of the books we saw were older volumes, not all in the best condition. It is possible that had the shop been a bit cleaner, one might have had a better impression of the books while browsing. This does not mean that you might not find a winner here. What it does mean is that browsing may be more of a chore.

Mitchell Books
1395 East Washington Boulevard 91104

Open Shop
(818) 798-4438

Collection: Specialty hardcover and paperback.
Specialties: Mystery; detective; spy; crime fiction.
# of Vols: 40,000
Hours: Tue-Sat 10:30-5:30.
Services: Search service, accepts want lists, mail order.
Travel: See Robert Allen Books above.
Credit Cards: Yes
Owner: John Mitchell
Year Estab: 1981
Comments: If you're a mystery buff (and one of us readily confesses to that addiction), and particularly if you're interested in older, out-of-print titles, you're sure to find a visit to this shop a delight. Its expansive shelves, meticulously alphabetized, offer thousands of titles (both recent and vintage) that should keep you happy for decades. Prices vary (as one might expect) depending upon the condition and rarity of the volumes. Even if you can't make a personal visit, if this is your field, a phone call or letter to the owner inquiring about a particular title could produce pure gold.

Oriental Book Store **Open Shop**
1713 East Colorado Boulevard 91106 (818) 577-2413

Collection: Specialty new and used, hardcover and paperback.
Specialties: Middle East; Asia; Pacific and Asian Americans.
# of Vols: 60,000
Hours: Mon-Sat 11-5:30.
Travel: Between Hill and Allen, 1/2 block east of Pasadena City College.
Credit Cards: No
Owner: Frank Mosher
Year Estab: 1936
Comments: Stock is evenly divided between new and used, hardcover and paperback.

Prufrock Books and Etc. **By Appointment**
531 South Marengo Avenue 91101 (818) 795-3558

Collection: Specialty
Specialties: Art; architecture; literature; black literature; cookbooks; illustrated.
Services: Accepts want lists.
Credit Cards: No
Owner: Robert L. Wilkerson
Year Estab: 1979

Paso Robles
(Map 5, page 235)

Balbontin Books **Antique Mall**
At Great American Antiques, 1305 Spring Street 93446 Mall: (805) 239-1203
  Home: (805) 466-6319

Collection: General stock.
Specialties: Children's
# of Vols: 2,000
Hours: Daily 10-5.
Credit Cards: Yes
Owner: Rosann Balbontin
Year Estab: 1990
Comments: Collection can also be viewed by appointment.

Penn Valley

By The Way Books **By Appointment**
PO Box 1759 95946 Fax: (916) 432-4949   (916) 432-4442

Collection: Specialty used and new, hardcover and paperback.
Specialties: Mysticism; philosophy; religion; psychology; spirituality; literature; poetry; Gurddjieff/Ouspensky and The Fourth Way; Thomas Merton; Walt Whitman; eastern thought.
# of Vols: 5,000
Services: Search service, catalog, accepts want lists.
Credit Cards: Yes

Owner: James & Elizabeth Evans
Year Estab: 1988

Petaluma
(Map 11, page 289)

Antique Marketplace
304 Petaluma Boulevard North 94952

Open Shop
(707) 765-1155

Collection:	General stock.
# of Vols:	30,000
Hours:	Daily 10-5.
Travel:	Located on the lower level of an antique mall.
Comments:	The lower level, referred to as "The Library" is devoted to the collection of a single dealer with an "all hardcover" collection.

Copperfield's Books
140 Kentucky Street 94952

Open Shop
(707) 762-0563

Collection:	General stock of new, remainders and used.
# of Vols:	25,000+ (used)
Hours:	Mon-Sat 9-9. Sun 10-6.
Travel:	Washington St exit off Hwy 101. West on Washington for about two miles. Left on Petaluma Blvd, right on Western and right on Kentucky.
Comments:	The used books are located on the lower level.

Discoveries Music & Books
627 East Washington 94952

Open Shop
(707) 778-3898

Collection:	General stock of hardcover and paperback.
Specialties:	Children's
# of Vols:	5,000
Hours:	Tue-Sat 10-7. Sun 11-7.
Travel:	East Washington exit off Hwy 101. Proceed west on East Washington.
Year Estab:	1995
Comments:	Stock is approximately 55% hardcover.

The Last Post Military Antiques
At Petaluma Collective
260 Petaluma Boulevard North 94952

Antique Mall
(707) 763-2220

Collection:	Specialty new and used.
Specialties:	Military.
Hours:	Mon-Sat 10-5:30. Sun 11-5:30.
Travel:	Washington exit off Hwy 101. West on Washington, then right on Petaluma.

Reade Moore Books
1 Fourth Street 94952

Open Shop
(707) 762-2215

Collection:	General stock of hardcover and paperback and ephemera.
Specialties:	Pre-1910 technology.
# of Vols:	60,000

Hours:	Mon-Sat 10-7. Sun 12-5.
Services:	Appraisals, search service, catalog, accepts want lists, book restoration.
Travel:	Washington St exit off Hwy 101. West on Washington, left on Petaluma Blvd, right on B St and right again on 4th St.
Credit Cards:	No
Owner:	Ruth Walker
Year Estab:	1987
Comments:	A bi-level shop that appears to have a much stronger selection of non fiction than fiction, with an emphasis on books dealing with various sections of the United States and the world, science and technology and relatively smaller selections in the areas of fiction and popular culture. Some older items that could be considered collectibles. The books were well organized and the shelves well labeled. Most of the books appeared to be in relatively good condition. Neither a shop to go out of the way for nor to avoid.

Philo

Am Here Books Open Shop
7501 Highway 128 (707) 895-2369
Mailing Address: PO Box 574 Philo 65466

Collection:	Specialty
Specialties:	First edition poetry.
# of Vols:	100,000
Hours:	Mon-Fri 10-4. Weekends by appointment.
Services:	Catalog, appraisals, search service, accepts want lists.
Travel:	Hwy 128 exit off Hwy 101. West on Hwy 128. Shop is in a metal building.
Credit Cards:	Yes
Owner:	Richard Aaron
Year Estab:	1971
Comments:	Stock is approximately 80% hardcover.

Pico Rivera

Armenian Coins & Books By Appointment
8511 Beverly Park Pace 90660 * (310) 695-0380

Collection:	Specialty. Primarily new and some used.
Specialties:	Armenia (all subjects).
Services:	Catalog

Pine Grove

Twice Sold Tales Open Shop
19698-C Highway 88 95265 (209) 296-4453

Collection:	General stock of mostly paperback.
Hours:	Mon-Fri 9-5. Sat 9:30-3.

* Some 310 codes change to 562 in 1996

Pismo Beach
(Map 5, page 235)

Word Has It   **Open Shop**
519 Five Cities Drive 93449   (805) 773-3312

Collection: General stock of paperback and hardcover.
# of Vols: 40,000
Hours: Mon-Fri 11-8. Sat 10-6. Sun 12-5.
Travel: Hwy 101 northbound: 4th St exit. Proceed on 4th St, cross freeway, turn right on Five Cities Dr, then left into shopping center. Southbound: Cross Five Cities Dr and the shopping center is straight ahead.
Year Estab: 1995
Comments: Stock is approximately 65% paperback.

Placentia
(Map 7, page 270)

The Book Faire   **Open Shop**
1848 North Placentia Avenue 92670   (714) 996-6725

Collection: General stock of mostly used hardcover and paperback.
# of Vols: 30,000
Hours: Mon-Fri 10:30-8. Sat 10-6. Sun 11-5.
Travel: Yorba Linda exit off Hwy 57. East on Yorba Linda then north on Placentia. Shop is two blocks ahead, on right, in shopping center.
Credit Cards: Yes
Owner: Sam & Penny Weinstein
Year Estab: 1989
Comments: Although the shop carries a goodly number of paperbacks, hardcovers did dominate. The latter volumes varied from more recent titles to vintage items. Most subjects were represented. The collection was well organized and the shelves well labeled for easy browsing.

Placerville
(Map 4, page 78)

Beever's Antiques, Used Furniture & Books   **Open Shop**
462 Main Street 95667   (916) 626-3314

Collection: General stock and ephemera.
# of Vols: 4,000
Hours: Daily 10-6.
Services: Accepts want lists, mail order.
Travel: See Bookery below.
Credit Cards: Yes
Owner: Jerry & Lucille Beever
Year Estab: 1981
Comments: A small shop that sells collectibles, some older hardcover books, sheet music and comics. You might, as we did, find some older items of interest.

Bookery	**Open Shop**
326 Main Street 95667	(916) 626-6454

Collection:	General stock of paperback and hardcover.
# of Vols:	15,000
Hours:	Mon-Fri 10-5:30. Sat 10-4:30. Sun 12-4.
Services:	Search service, mail order.
Travel:	Hwy 49 exit off Hwy 50. South on Hwy 49 for about 1/2 block then east on Main.
Credit Cards:	No
Owner:	Celia Starkey & Nancy Heidt
Year Estab:	1983
Comments:	A shop that carries a mix of paperbacks and mostly reading copy hardcover volumes. If there were collectibles or rare books here, we failed to spot them.

Pleasant Hill
(Map 17, page 154))

Monkey House Books	**Open Shop**
236 Golf Club Road 94523	(510) 602-0679

Collection:	General stock of mostly used hardcover.
# of Vols:	20,000 (used)
Hours:	Mon-Fri 10-8. Sat 11-6. Sun 12-5.
Travel:	Willow Pass exit off I-680. East on Willow Pass, north on Contra Costa Blvd and left on Golf Club Rd.
Credit Cards:	No
Owner:	John McDermott
Year Estab:	1994

Pleasant Valley
(Map 4, page 78)

Books & Treasures	**Open Shop**
4570 Pleasant Valley Road	(916) 644-5427
Mailing Address: 4570 Pleasant Valley Road Placerville 95667	

Collection:	General stock of mostly paperback.
# of Vols:	40,000
Hours:	Tue-Thu 11-6. Fri & Sat 11-6:30.
Travel:	Missouri Flat Rd exit off Hwy 50. South on Missouri Flat Rd, then left on Pleasant Valley Rd. Shop is about eight miles ahead in shopping center.
Credit Cards:	No
Owner:	Sam Ross
Year Estab:	1989
Comments:	We frequently argue about the wisdom of driving to "out of the way" places when there are so many shops to see and our travel time is limited. The directions to this store are from Placerville, a lovely tourist town with plenty of interesting attractions. If you decide to drive the additional 12

miles (24 round trip) to visit this store, we suspect you'll regret it unless, that is, you're attracted to shops where the stock is 80% paperback and 20% fairly common hardcover titles.

Pleasanton
(Map 17, page 154))

The Book Store **Open Shop**
2911 Hopyard Road 94566 (510) 426-8255

Collection:	General stock of mostly paperback.
# of Vols:	20,000
Hours:	Mon-Sat 11-6.
Travel:	Hopyard exit off I-580. Proceed south on Hopyard. Shop is in a stand alone building in the front of the shopping center.
Credit Cards:	No
Owner:	Dorothy Mackey
Year Estab:	1988
Comments:	As we approached this shop, we were greeted by a sign indicating that the owner sold "Used & Rare" books. Once inside, we saw lots of used paperbacks (upwards to 80% of the stock) and a mix of used hardcover items, mostly with rather common titles. If there were rare books on hand, we probably missed them. This is a shop that meets the reading needs of its immediate community.

Plymouth
(Map 4, page 78)

Hein & Co. **Open Shop**
9369 Main Street 95669 (209) 245-5028

Collection:	General stock.
Specialties:	Emphasis on non fiction; California; gold rush.
# of Vols:	40,000-50,000
Hours:	Daily, except closed Tue, 10-6.
Travel:	Off Hwy 49.
Credit Cards:	No
Owner:	Wolfgang & Rolf Hein
Year Estab:	1991

Point Hueneme
(Map 5, page 235)

Channel Isles Books **By Appointment**
274 East Fiesta Green 93041 Fax: (805) 985-1921 (805) 985-1921

Collection:	General stock.
Specialties:	First editions; military; maritime; Irish; history.
# of Vols:	9,000

Services: Appraisals, accepts want lists, mail order.
Credit Cards: No
Year Estab: 1986

Point Reyes Station
(Map 17, page 154))

The Brown Study Bookshop   **Open Shop**
11315 State Route 1 94956   (415) 663-1633
Mailing Address: PO Box 313 Point Reyes Station

Collection: General stock of new and used, hardcover and paperback.
# of Vols: 15,000-20,000
Hours: Daily 10-5.
Services: Accepts want lists, mail order.
Travel: In the center of town, 35 miles north of San Francisco.
Credit Cards: No
Owner: Jill Westley
Year Estab: 1984
Comments: At the time of our visit, there seemed to be a greater number of used volumes on hand although the owner indicated that she tries to keep a roughly equal balance between new and used books. Every subject was covered although with the exception of a section dealing with natural history and related topics, not in any great depth. The books we saw were in generally good condition and were of mixed vintage.

Pomona

Kaiser Bill's Military Emporium   **Open Shop**
224 East Second Street   (909) 622-5046
Mailing Address: PO Box 741 San Dimas 91773

Collection: Specialty
Specialties: Military
# of Vols: 400-500
Hours: Mon & Wed 9:30-3. Thu-Sun 9:30-4:30.
Services: Accepts want lists, mail order.
Travel: Garvey exit off I-10. Proceed south for about 2½ miles. Left on Second St.
Credit Cards: Yes
Owner: David George
Year Estab: 1980

Poway

Paperback Bookstore   **Open Shop**
12845 Poway Road 92064   (619) 486-1440

Collection: General stock of mostly paperback.
Hours: Mon-Sat 10-6. Sun 12-5:30.

Quincy
(Map 11, page 289)

Day's Past — **Open Shop**
2163 East Main — (916) 283-3291
Mailing Address: PO Box 1846 Quincy 95971

Collection:	General stock of hardcover and paperback.
Specialties:	Western Americana; mining; hunting; fishing; firearms; automotive.
# of Vols:	10,000
Hours:	Mon-Sat 10:30-5:30. Closed Jan & Feb.
Services:	Search service, accepts want lists.
Travel:	Located on Hwy 70.
Credit Cards:	Yes
Owner:	Pat Day
Year Estab:	1979
Comments:	Stock is about evenly divided between hardcover and paperback.

Rancho Cordova

Bookworm — **Open Shop**
11050 Coloma Road 95670 — (916) 852-8525

Collection:	General stock of mostly paperback.
Hours:	Mon-Sat 10-5:30. Sun 1-5.

Rancho Sante Fe

Book Cellar — **Open Shop**
17040 Avenida de Acacias 92067 — (619) 756-4780

Collection:	General stock of hardcover and paperback.
Hours:	Mon-Sat 10-4.
Comments:	Operated by the Friends of the Public Library.

Redding
(Map 11, page 289)

Bogbean Books & Music — **Open Shop**
1740 California Street 96001 — (916) 246-8657

Collection:	General stock of paperback and hardcover and CDs.
# of Vols:	5,000+
Hours:	Mon-Thu 10-8. Fri & Sat 10-9. Sun 10-6.
Travel:	Hwy 299 exit off I-5. West on Hwy 299 to Redding. Left on California.
Credit Cards:	Yes
Owner:	Benjamin Bambauer
Year Estab:	1991
Comments:	When we arrived at this shop at 10:45 on a Sunday morning we found the shop closed despite the sign posted on the front door confirming that the

shop's Sunday hours were 10-5. Evidently, the person responsible for opening the shop that Sunday was not overly concerned about meeting his or her responsibilities. Through the window we saw a mix of paperbacks, hardcover titles, books on tapes and lots of cassettes. Who knows? Perhaps, had the shop been open, we might have located the find of the century.

Book Country *Open Shop*
96 Hartnell Avenue 96002 (916) 224-0854

Collection: General stock of hardcover and paperback.
# of Vols: 10,000
Hours: Mon-Fri 9-5:30. Sat 10-5.
Travel: Cypress exit off I-5. West on Cypress, then south on Hartnell. Shop is in Cobblestone Shopping Center.
Comments: Stock is approximately 50% paperback.

Cal's Books *Open Shop*
5242 Westside Road 96001 (916) 243-5499

Collection: General stock of paperback, hardcover, comics and ephemera.
Specialties: Metaphysics
# of Vols: 250,000
Hours: Daily 10-5.
Services: Search service, accepts want lists.
Travel: South Bonnyview exit off I-5. West on Bonnyview to Hwy 273 (S. Market St). Right on Hwy 273. Left on Branstetter and immediate right on Westside.
Credit Cards: No
Owner: Cal Kearn
Year Estab: 1969
Comments: An interesting shop that probably does have over 250,000 items. While the majority of the stock was clearly paperback, there was a reasonable collection of hardcover volumes, both vintage (in mixed condition) and more recent items (in much better condition). Although ladders were available in one portion of the store, browsers would have to use their ingenuity to reach the higher shelves elsewhere in the shop. If you don't mind a laid-back, unadorned, underlit warehouse-like atmosphere in book stores, you could well find a treasure in what might be viewed as an overlooked mine.

Redlands
(Map 12, page 139)

Hessel and Taylor Books *Open Shop*
423 East State Street 92373 Shop: (909) 793-8263
 Home: (909) 335-5766

Collection: General stock.
Specialties: Religion
# of Vols: 10,000-15,000
Hours: Mon-Fri 10-5:30, except Thu till 8. Sat 10-2:30.

Services: Appraisals, accepts want lists, search service, mail order.
Travel: 10 Fwy eastbound: Orange exit. South on Orange, left on State. Westbound: 6th St exit. South on 6th, left on State.
Credit Cards: No
Owner: William & Esther Hessel
Year Estab: 1990
Comments: Most of the books (almost all hardcover) appeared to be either recent titles or older books that were in good condition. Many subjects were represented but few, except for the specialty listed above, were in great depth.

Libros Latinos **By Appointment**
301 9th Street, Ste B (909) 793-8423
Mailing Address: PO Box 1103 Redlands 92373 Fax: (909) 335-9945

Collection: General stock of new and used.
Specialties: Latin America; Mexico; Spanish art; archaeology.
# of Vols: 40,000
Services: Appraisals, search service, catalog, accepts want lists.
Credit Cards: Yes
Owner: Alfonso J. Vijil
Year Estab: 1973
Comments: Stock is approximately 50% used.

Paul Melzer, Rare Books & Autographs **Open Shop**
12 East Vine Street 92373 Fax: (909) 792-7299 (909) 792-7299

Collection: General stock.
# of Vols: 10,000
Hours: Thu-Sat 12-6. Other times by chance or appointment.
Services: Appraisals, search service, catalog, accepts want lists.
Travel: Eastbound on 10 Fwy: Orange exit. Turn right and proceed 1/2 mile to Vine. Left on Vine. Westbound on 10 Fwy: 6th St exit. Turn left and proceed 1/2 mile to Vine. Right on Vine.
Credit Cards: Yes
Year Estab: 1985
Comments: A small shop with high quality books. If you're simply walking past shelves scanning titles, it will not take you long to visit this shop. On the other hand, if you're attracted by unusual titles in very good condition, your visit should last a bit longer.

We Buy Estates Store **Open Shop**
204 East State Street 92373 (909) 792-6732

Collection: General stock of new and used paperback and hardcover.
# of Vols: 1,000 (used hardcover)
Hours: Mon-Sat 10-6.
Travel: Westbound on I-10: 6th St exit. Proceed south on 6th, then left on State. Eastbound on I-10: Orange St exit. Continue on frontage road to 6th, then south on 6th and left on State.

Redondo Beach
(Map 10, page 253)

Encore Books **Open Shop**
1704 South Pacific Coast Highway 90277 (800) 340-1106 * (310) 540-1106

Collection: General stock of mostly hardcover.
Specialties: Art; first editions; literature; cookbooks; children's; technical; Civil War; World War II; Americana.
# of Vols: 17,500
Hours: Tue-Sat 10:30-6:30. Sun 12-4.
Services: Search service, accepts want lists, mail order.
Travel: Hawthorne Blvd exit off I-405. Proceed south to Pacific Coast Hwy. Right on highway and proceed for two miles.
Credit Cards: Yes
Owner: Joe Moeller
Year Estab: 1993
Comments: A roomy, airy atmosphere with a good selection, particularly in fiction. Some firsts. Most of the books were in quite good condition. A step up from the traditional neighborhood selection.

The Gemmary Inc. **By Appointment**
PO Box 816 90277 Fax: (310) 372-5969 * (310) 372-6149

Collection: Specialty
Specialties: Mining; mineralogy; gemology; jewelry; history of science; physical sciences; antique scientific instruments; microscopy.
# of Vols: 2,500
Services: Search service, catalog, accepts want lists.
Credit Cards: Yes
Owner: R.C. Blankenhorn
Year Estab: 1979

J.B. Kennedy, Bookseller **Open Shop**
614 Torrance Boulevard 90277 * (310) 316-1168

Collection: General stock.
# of Vols: 5,000
Hours: Sun & Mon 1-7. Tue-Sat 12-9.
Services: Appraisals, accepts want lists.
Travel: Pacific Coast Hwy to Torrance Blvd, then east on Torrance. Shop is on right, a few blocks ahead in a small cluster of stores.
Credit Cards: No
Year Estab: 1945
Comments: A rather small selection of books in a rather small store. The books on display (all hardcover) were in generally good condition and ran the gamut from mystery to a dozen or so books on history (including an incomplete set of Durant's). Generally speaking, you're not likely to find a book that has been eluding you for years in this shop. (Famous last words.)

* Some 310 codes change to 562 in 1996

Yesterdays Used Books & Coffee House　　　　　　　　　　　**Open Shop**
126 North Catalina Avenue 90277　　　　　　　　　　　　　　* (310) 318-2499

Collection:	General stock of paperback and hardcover.
Specialties:	Science fiction; mystery.
# of Vols:	20,000
Hours:	Daily 6am-11pm.
Travel:	Crenshaw exit off 405 Fwy. Proceed south on Crenshaw, west on 190th, south on Pacific Coast Hwy, west on Torrance Blvd and north on Catalina.
Credit Cards:	No
Year Estab:	1993
Comments:	The stock is approximately 75% paperback.

Redwood City
(Map 17, page 154)

Antique Arcade　　　　　　　　　　　　　　　　　　　　**Antique Mall**
1823 El Camino Real 94063　　　　　　　　　　　　　　　　(415) 368-8267

Collection:	General stock of hardcover and paperback.
Hours:	Mon-Sat 10-6. Sun 11-5.

Greyhavens Books　　　　　　　　　　　　　　　　　　　**Antique Mall**
At Antique Arcade, 1823 El Camino Real　　　　　　　　　　(415) 368-8267
Mailing Address: PO Box 22513 Carmel 93922

Collection:	General stock.
Specialties:	Travel; history; illustrated; antiques; art reference; military; naval.
# of Vols:	1,000
Hours:	Mon-Sat 10-5. Sun 12-5.
Travel:	Woodside/Hwy 84 exit off Hwy 101. Proceed west to El Camino Real.
Credit Cards:	Yes
Owner:	Richard Smith
Year Estab:	1988

Secret Staircase Bookshop　　　　　　　　　　　　　　　**Open Shop**
2223 Broadway 94062　　　　　　　　　　　　　　　　　　(415) 366-1222

Collection:	General stock of mostly new and some used paperback and hardcover.
# of Vols:	12,000
Hours:	Mon-Sat 9:30-5:30.
Travel:	Rte 101 southbound to Whipple. Keep straight for about six blocks. Right on Middlefield, right on Broadway. Rte 101 northbound to Woodside Rd. Proceed west for two blocks then right on Broadway.
Credit Cards:	Yes
Year Estab:	1992
Comments:	A small shop that sells more new books than used and seems to concentrate on mysteries and children's books. Most of the used hardcover books were located on the shop's second floor. As the owner was reorganizing the used book section during the time of our visit, we were unable to view the titles

and consequently are unable to make any judgments as to the wisdom of visiting here. Be advised, however, that the number of used hardcover volumes on hand was not great.

Reseda
(Map 9, page 64)

The Bookie Joint — **Open Shop**
7246 Reseda Boulevard (818) 343-1055
Mailing Address: 19138 Topham St Tarzana 91356   E-mail: ffdog@earthlink.new

Collection:	General stock of hardcover and paperback
Specialties:	Popular culture; scholarly; magazines.
# of Vols:	80,000
Hours:	Mon-Fri 10:30-6. Sat 10:30-5:30.
Services:	Search service, catalog, accepts want lists.
Travel:	Reseda exit off 101 Fwy. Proceed north on Reseda for about two miles.
Credit Cards:	Yes
Owner:	Jerry & Rose Blaz
Year Estab:	1975
Comments:	A fun shop to visit with an owner who knows her stock and respects the book trade. Plan to spend a reasonable amount of time here for in addition to a large number of paperback items, the shop carries a substantial number of hardcover volumes in all areas but with particular strength in mystery and science fiction. Ephemera is another strong area, and if you're looking for pulp magazines and/or long runs of some of the more popular magazines (many beginning with Volume 1, Number 1) you just might find that elusive item at this location.

Rheem Valley

Anmar's Children's Series Books — **By Appointment**
PO Box 6422 94570   Fax: (510) 376-1573   (510) 376-1573

Collection:	Specialty
Specialties:	Children's series.
# of Vols:	3,000
Services:	Search service, accepts want lists.
Credit Cards:	No
Owner:	Anthony & Mary Carpentieri
Year Estab:	1993

Rio Linda

Now & Then — **Open Shop**
6808 Front Street 95673   (916) 992-1615

Collection:	General stock of mostly used paperback.
Hours:	Tue-Fri 11-6. Sat 11-5.

Open Shops and By Appointment Dealers 185

Riverside
(Map 12, page 139)

Ander's Attic
9980 Indiana Avenue, Ste #4
Mailing Address: PO Box 4281 Riverside 92514

Open Shop
(909) 785-4331

Collection:	General stock and ephemera.
Specialties:	Military; children's; magazines.
# of Vols:	50,000
Hours:	Mon-Fri 11-4. Sat 12- 4. Other times by appointment.
Services:	Limited search service, accepts want lists.
Travel:	Van Buren exit off 91 Fwy. Turn south on Van Buren, then first right on Indiana Ave. After Harrison, turn left into business complex.
Credit Cards:	No
Owner:	Joseph & Lorraine Anders
Year Estab:	1963
Comments:	A large collection of older books in mixed condition. Once you pass through the small vestibule type entrance and finish chatting with the owner, you'll enter a room that has long narrow aisles filled with books from floor to ceiling. Although the sections are adequately labeled, if you're looking for a particular subject, you're better off inquiring as to the location before you begin your browsing.

Josef's Books
3769 Mission Inn Avenue 92506

Open Shop
(909) 788-3063

Collection:	General stock.
Specialties:	Religion; children's; Western Americana.
# of Vols:	45,000
Hours:	Mon-Sat 10-6. Sun 12-4.
Services:	Appraisals, search service, accepts want lists.
Travel:	Mission Inn Ave exit off 91 Fwy. West on Mission Inn to corner of Market.
Credit Cards:	Yes
Owner:	Josef Purkart
Year Estab:	1984
Comments:	Don't let the specialties of this shop mislead you. In addition to a very strong selection of books dealing with religion, we found the rest of the shop overflowing with good books in every subject and in fine condition. Most reasonably priced. The shop is easy to browse and the owner is friendly.

Pandora's Books
5225 Canyon Crest Drive 92507

Open Shop
(909) 686-3312

Collection:	General stock of new, mostly hardcover used and ephemera.
Specialties:	Emphasis is on non fiction.
# of Vols:	15,000 (used)
Hours:	Tue-Fri 11-9. Sat-Mon 11-6.
Travel:	Between 60 and 215 Fwys in Canyon Crest Towne Centre. From 215 Fwy: Central exit. From 60 Fwy: Pennsylvania exit.

Credit Cards: Yes
Owner: Frank & Esther Krance
Year Estab: 1990

Renaissance Bookshop   **Open Shop**
6639 Magnolia Avenue   (909) 369-8843
Mailing Address: PO Box 2451 Riverside 92516-2451

Collection:	Specialty. Mostly used paperback and hardcover.
Specialties:	Libertarian; free market economics; science fiction; philosophy; European literature and history; Asian literature and history; books in German, French and Spanish.
# of Vols:	15,000
Hours:	Mon-Sat 11-7.
Services:	Catalog, accepts want lists.
Travel:	Central Ave exit off I-91. West on Central. South on Magnolia.
Credit Cards:	No
Owner:	Gene Berkman & Janet Henson
Year Estab:	1983

Universal Books   **Open Shop**
3582 Main Street 92501   (909) 682-1082

Collection:	General stock of hardcover and paperback.
# of Vols:	50,000
Hours:	Mon-Sat 10-6. Sun 10-4.
Travel:	91 Fwy to Riverside. West on 7th St, right on Market, right on 6th, left on Main. The entrance is on the side of the building.
Credit Cards:	No
Owner:	Paula Peters & Diane Ferree
Year Estab:	1978
Comments:	An interesting but hardly unusual collection. Most of the hardcover books are on the first floor with the basement devoted almost exclusively to paperbacks. The books are in mixed condition with few that could really be classified as "cared for." In a collection like this, there's always the possibility of a hidden gem. Since most subjects are covered and the shop is not far from another quality shop (see Josef's Books above) we think it worth a visit.

Rocklin
(Map 4, page 78)

Andersonville Books   **Open Shop**
5035 Pacific Street 95677   (916) 632-9186

Collection:	General stock of new and used hardcover.
# of Vols:	5,000 (used)
Hours:	Daily 9:30-6:30.
Travel:	Rocklin Rd exit off I-80. Proceed east on Rocklin, then right on Pacific.

Credit Cards: Yes
Year Estab: 1994

Elaine's Books — **By Appointment**
3933 Rawhide Road 95747 — (916) 632-2624

Collection: General stock.
Specialties: Children's; cookbooks; Western Americana.
# of Vols: 4,000-5,000
Services: Subject lists, mail order, accepts want lists.
Credit Cards: No
Owner: Elaine Madsen
Year Estab: 1992
Comments: Also displays in Antique Troves in Roseville and The Book Collector in Sacramento.

Jan's Paperbacks — **Open Shop**
4877 Granite Drive 95677 — (916) 624-4363

Collection: General stock of mostly paperback.
Hours: Mon-Sat 10-6. Sun 12-4.

Nick Adams & Co Rare Books — **By Appointment**
PO Box 54 95677 — (916) 632-2068

Collection: Specialty
Specialties: Literary first editions; Hemingway; Steinbeck; mystery; detective; literary manuscripts.
# of Vols: 10,000
Services: Appraisals, catalog, accepts want lists.
Credit Cards: No
Owner: David Meeker
Year Estab: 1986

Roseville
(Map 4, page 78)

Almost Perfect Bookstore — **Open Shop**
1911 Douglas Boulevard, Ste 82 95661 — (916) 781-7935

Collection: General stock of mostly paperback.
Hours: Mon-Sat 10-7. Sun 10-5.

The Antique Trove — **Antique Mall**
238 Vernon Street 95678 — (916) 786-2777

Collection: General stock of hardcover and paperback.
Hours: Daily 10-6.

Ronald J. Ballou, Bookman — **Open Shop**
124 Riverside Avenue 95678 — (916) 786-8219

Collection: General stock.

Specialties: California; Western Americana; native Americans; fine bindings; modern first editions; literary biography; art; military; railroads; children's; illustrated; Civil War; music.
# of Vols: 7,500
Hours: Mon-Fri 10-6.
Services: Appraisals, search service, accepts want lists, book repair.
Travel: Riverside Ave exit off I-80. North on Riverside for about one mile.
Credit Cards: Yes
Year Estab: 1990
Comments: A rather small shop with exclusively hardcover volumes in very good to excellent condition. The books ranged from fine bindings to small press, limited editions, first editions (some signed), etc. If you like good books and you're not interested in the "warehouse" approach, a visit here should leave you feeling satisfied.

Sacramento
(Map 13, page 189)

Argus Books & Graphics
1311 21st Street 95814

Open Shop
(916) 443-2223

Collection: Specialty books and ephemera.
Specialties: California; Western Americana; mining; Yosemite; archaic skills; trade catalogs.
# of Vols: 10,000
Hours: Mon-Sat 10-6, except Tue till 9.
Services: Catalog, accepts want lists.
Travel: 15th St exit off Bus I-80 eastbound. Left on 16th St. Right on N. Left on 21st.
Credit Cards: Yes
Owner: William Ewald
Year Estab: 1971

Bargain Lovers Used Books
5413 Palm Avenue 95841

Open Shop
(916) 334-1192

Collection: General stock of mostly paperback.
Hours: Mon-Fri 10-6. Sat 10-3.

Beers Book Center
1431 L. Street 95814

Open Shop
(916) 443-9148

Collection: General stock of new and used, paperback and hardcover.
# of Vols: 30,000-40,000
Hours: Mon-Wed 10-6. Thu-Sat 10-9. Sun 11-5.
Services: Search service, accepts want lists.
Travel: At corner of 15th.
Map Ref: Map 13, page 189, #1.
Credit Cards: Yes

Owner: Jim Naify
Year Estab: 1936
Comments: A spacious shop with a well organized collection of books in mixed condition and of mostly recent vintage. We don't believe this is a shop that offers much in the way of collectibles or rare items, but we could have missed some gems.

Book Box **Open Shop**
5619 H Street 95819 Fax:(916) 737-1251 (916) 737-1919

Collection: General stock of mostly paperback.
Specialties: Cookbooks
# of Vols: 80,000
Hours: Tue-Fri 10:30-6. Sat 11-5.
Travel: Located in East Sacramento, at corner of 56th St & H St.
Map Ref: Map 13, page 189, #11.
Credit Cards: Yes
Owner: Phyllis Foster
Year Estab: 1988
Comments: Paperbacks account for about 80% of this shop's stock. We would classify the hardcover volumes we saw as reading copies of mixed vintage (although most of them were fairly recent) in mixed condition. We noted the word "Collectible" on one shelf of cookbooks; we wouldn't quarrel with the sign.

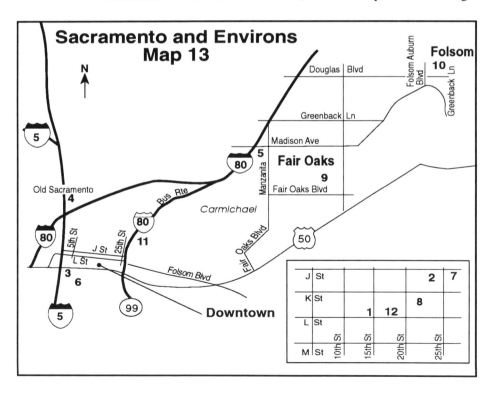

(Sacramento)

The Book Collector
1008 24th Street 95816

Open Shop
(916) 442-9295

Collection:	General stock.
Specialties:	Modern first editions; Western Americana; art; native Americans; children's.
# of Vols:	10,000
Hours:	May-Sep: Mon-Fri 11-7. Sat 11-8. Sun 11-5. Oct-Apr: Mon-Fri 10-6. Sat 10-7. Sun 11-5.
Services:	Search service, accepts want lists, mail order.
Travel:	Between J & K Streets.
Map Ref:	Map 13, page 189, #2.
Credit Cards:	Yes
Owner:	Rachel R. Justman
Year Estab:	1994
Comments:	As with other group shops, the dealers here try to put their best foot forward by displaying their better books. We saw some interesting vintage titles as well as newer volumes and truly collectible items. Depending on your own special interests, you may well find some delights here.

The Book Review
3233 Riverside Boulevard 95818

Open Shop
(916) 443-7984

Collection:	General stock of paperback and hardcover.
Specialties:	Children's; foreign languages; religion.
# of Vols:	15,000
Hours:	Mon-Sat 12-7. Sun 12-5.
Services:	Modified search service, accepts want lists.
Travel:	Southbound on I-5: Sutterville Rd exit. Right on Riverside. Northbound on I-5: 12th Ave exit.
Map Ref:	Map 13, page 189, #3.
Credit Cards:	No
Owner:	Genevieve Flett
Year Estab:	1979
Comments:	A typical neighborhood bookstore with a larger proportion of paperbacks than hardcover volumes. The books were in fair condition. We noted lots of self help items.

Bookmine
1015 Second Street 95814

Open Shop
(916) 441-4609
E-mail: books4u@aol.com

Collection:	General stock.
Specialties:	Western Americana; railroads.
# of Vols:	6,000
Hours:	Daily 10-5, except Thu-Sat till 9.
Services:	Appraisals, catalog, search service, accepts want lists.
Travel:	J St exit off I-5. Follow signs to Old Sacramento.
Map Ref:	Map 13, page 189, #4.

Credit Cards:	Yes
Owner:	Steve Mauer
Year Estab:	1984
Comments:	Quite strong in the specialty areas designated above, plus a more modest general stock. Certainly many of the items we saw fit into the rare and collectible category. If you happen to be visiting Old Sacramento and you're a real book person, you should enjoy a stop here.

Booktrader

9219 Folsom Boulevard 95826

Open Shop
(916) 363-9996

Collection:	General stock of mostly paperback.
Hours:	Mon 10-7. Tue-Sat 10-5.

Bound For Pleasure Book

At Antique Tresores
1510 16th Street

Antique Mall
Mall: (916) 446-6960
Home: (916) 454-1693

Collection:	General stock.
Hours:	Daily 10-6.
Owner:	Dion Kissinger
Comments:	Also displays at The Book Collector. (See above)

Barry Cassidy Rare Books

2005 T Street 95814

Open Shop
(916) 456-6307

Collection:	Specialty books and ephemera.
Specialties:	Western Americana; literature; books about books; Civil War; voyages; travel.
# of Vols:	4,000
Hours:	Mon-Sat 9:30-4.
Travel:	From I-5: Q St exit. Proceed east on Q St, then south on 20th St. From Bus 80: 16th St exit. North on 16th St, then east on T.
Credit Cards:	Yes
Year Estab:	1975

Charmed Circle Books

1729½ L Street, 2nd Fl. 95814

Open Shop
(916) 444-1468

Collection:	General stock.
Specialties:	Modern first editions; signed; American expatriates living in Paris from 1900-1930's (Stein, Joyce, etc.).
# of Vols:	3,000-4,000
Hours:	Fri & Sat 11-6. Other times by appointment.
Services:	Search service, catalog, accepts want lists.
Travel:	15th St exit off I-80 eastbound. Proceed to 21st St. Left on 21st St, then left on L St. Shop is near corner of 18th & L on second floor.
Map Ref:	Map 13, page 189, #12.
Credit Cards:	No
Owner:	Dorothy Rangel & Teresa Hansen
Year Estab:	1993

(Sacramento)

Churchilliana Co.
4629 Sunset Drive 95822

By Appointment
(916) 448-7053

Collection:	Specialty new and used.
Specialties:	Winston Churchill.
Services:	Accepts want lists, mail order.
Credit Cards:	No
Owner:	Mrs. E. Dalton-Newfield
Year Estab:	1976

Cobblestone Books
5111 College Oak Drive 95841

Open Shop
(916) 332-3347

Collection:	General stock of hardcover and paperback.
Specialties:	Science fiction; mystery; fantasy; horror.
# of Vols:	20,000
Hours:	Mon-Sat 10-6. Sun 11-4.
Services:	Appraisals, catalog, search service, accepts want lists.
Travel:	Proceeding east on I-80: Madison exit. Proceed right on Madison then right on College Oak Dr.
Map Ref:	Map 13, page 189, #5.
Credit Cards:	Yes
Owner:	Steve Adamovich
Year Estab:	1989
Comments:	All too often our experience when visiting a shop that lists the specialties cited above is disappointing as we have found such places to be overwhelmingly paperback. We are therefore delighted to report that this shop was a most pleasant exception to that experience. In addition to the obligatory paper stock, the shop's shelves were filled with hardcover volumes of mixed vintage that were quite representative of the specialties. We also saw some rare and collectibles items under glass, a large number of uncorrected proofs, a healthy supply of collectible pulps and a respectable general stock.

Don Conner Fine Books
1311 21st Street 95814

Open Shop
(916) 443-2223

Collection:	Specialty
Specialties:	Natural history; fishing; hunting; Darwiniana; Teddy Roosevelt.
Hours:	Mon-Sat 10-6. Tue till 9.
Travel:	See Argus Books above.
Services:	Catalog, appraisals, search service, accepts want lists.
Credit Cards:	Yes

J. Crawford's Books
5011 Freeport Boulevard 95822

Open Shop
(916) 731-8001

Collection:	General stock of hardcover and paperback.
# of Vols:	50,000

Hours:	Mon-Sat 10-6. Sun 12-5.
Travel:	Fruitridge Rd exit off I-5. Proceed east on Fruitridge and left on Freeport.
Map Ref:	Map 13, page 189, #6.
Credit Cards:	Yes
Owner:	Jim & George Crawford
Year Estab:	1983
Comments:	Stock is approximately 50% paperback.

57th Street Antique Mall
875 57th Street 95819

Antique Mall
(916) 451-3110

Collection:	General stock of hardcover and paperback.
Hours:	Daily 10-5.

Hammons Archives
1115 Front Street 95814

Open Shop
(916) 446-1782

Collection:	Specialty new and used and ephemera.
Specialties:	Western Americana; railroads, mining; geology; Japan.
# of Vols:	2,000+
Hours:	Tue-Sun 12-6.
Services:	Appraisals, catalog, accepts want lists.
Travel:	Located in Old Sacramento. See Bookmine above.
Credit Cards:	Yes
Owner:	Wendell P. Hammon
Year Estab:	1975
Comments:	If you happen to be a railroad buff, you might find this place of interest. Or, if you just like old books and curios, it's conceivable that you might find something that strikes your fancy here. During our short visit, we saw little that struck ours.

Richard L. Press, Fine and Scholarly Books on the Arts
1727½ I Street 95814

Open Shop
(916) 447-3413

Collection:	Specialty
Specialties:	Art; architecture; photography; decorative arts; book arts; Islamic art; Judaica.
# of Vols:	3,50
Hours:	Mon-Sat 10:30-6. Other times by appointment.
Services:	Appraisals, search service, catalog, accepts want lists.
Travel:	Eastbound on Bus I-80: 15th St/downtown exit. Turn left and proceed one block to 16th St. Right at J St, left at 18th St. Shop is between 17th & 18th.
Credit Cards:	No
Year Estab:	1979

River City Books
2527 J Street 95816

Open Shop
(916) 446-9055

Collection:	General stock of hardcover and paperback.
# of Vols:	40,000
Hours:	Mon-Sat 11-6. Sun 11-5.

Travel:	Between 25th & 26th Streets.
Map Ref:	Map 13, page 189, #7.
Credit Cards:	Yes
Owner:	Fran Levin
Year Estab:	1989
Comments:	A better than average shop with better than average stock. The books, most of which appeared to be of relatively recent vintage, were well organized and in excellent condition. There were several collectibles under glass, some leather bindings (Franklin Mints) and a modest number of paperbacks. While few categories were covered in depth, the titles on hand seemed to be quality items.

Sacramento Surplus Book Room   **Open Shop**
4121 Power Inn Road   (916) 454-3459
Mailing Address: PO Box 192002 Sacramento 95819

Collection:	General stock of mostly used hardcover.
Specialties:	School texts; encyclopedias; braille and other large print books; atlases.
Hours:	Wed 1-5. Thu 5-8. Sat 10-2. Closed Dec & Jan.
Travel:	Power Inn Rd exit off Hwy 50. Proceed 1/2 mile.
Credit Cards:	No
Owner:	Matine Snelling, Director
Year Estab:	1991
Comments:	A non profit business "designed to save school books and library books from destruction. Seventy percent of the books are free to the public."

Time Tested Books   **Open Shop**
1114 21st Street 95814   (916) 447-5696

Collection:	General stock of mostly used hardcover and paperback.
Specialties:	History; politics; California; Western Americana.
# of Vols:	25,000+
Hours:	Mon, Tue, Fri 11-5:30. Wed & Thu 11-7:30. Sat 10-4.
Services:	Search service, accepts want lists, mail order.
Travel:	Between L & K Streets.
Map Ref:	Map 13, page 189, #8.
Credit Cards:	Yes
Owner:	Peter Keat
Year Estab:	1981
Comments:	A most respectable collection of predominately hardcover items in generally good condition with a majority of the titles of post 1970 vintage. A few older items and some sets. Reasonably priced.

Saint Helena

Main Street Books   **Open Shop**
1371 Main Street 94574   (707) 963-1338

Collection:	General stock of mostly new books and primarily used paperback.
Hours:	Mon-Sat 10-5:30. Sun 12-4.

Salinas
(Map 5, page 235)

Book Worm **Open Shop**
342 Main Street 93901 (408) 753-2099

Collection:	General stock of hardcover and paperback.
Specialties:	Poetry; philosophy; eastern religions; literature.
# of Vols:	28,000
Hours:	Mon-Sat 11-6. Sun 11-4.
Services:	Limited search service, accepts want lists.
Travel:	John St exit off Hwy 101. Proceed on John St towards downtown. At end of John, right on Main. Shop is three blocks ahead.
Credit Cards:	No
Owner:	C.J. Benejam
Year Estab:	1991
Comments:	It may take a minute or two but eventually the browser will get used to seeing paperbacks and hardcover titles (about evenly mixed) shelved together by subject. The condition of most of the hardcover books was good. Whether you'll find the long lost item you've been seeking in this shop is speculative, but the shop is interesting enough to make a visit here worth your while unless it requires a really long or out of the way drive.

Books Then & Now **Open Shop**
956 Park Row 93901 (408) 753-0658

Collection:	General stock of paperback and hardcover.
# of Vols:	7,000
Hours:	Mon-Sat 10:30-5:30.
Travel:	Between Romie Lane and Acacia, parallel to South Main.
Credit Cards:	No
Owner:	Fred Marcal
Year Estab:	1995
Comments:	Stock is approximately 70% paperback.

San Anselmo
(Map 17, page 154)

Michael Good, Fine/Rare Books **Open Shop**
35 San Anselmo Avenue 94960 (415) 459-6092

Collection:	General stock.
# of Vols:	10,000
Hours:	Mon-Sat 10-5.
Services:	Appraisals, occasional catalog, accepts want lists, mail order.
Travel:	See Whyte's Booksmith above. From Sir Francis Drake Blvd, left on Bolanis and right on San Anselmo.
Credit Cards:	Yes
Year Estab:	1981

Heldfond Book Gallery   **Open Shop**
310 San Anselmo Avenue 94960   Fax: (415) 383-3310 (415) 456-8194

Collection: Specialty
Specialties: Illustrated.
# of Vols: 6,000-7,000
Hours: Mon-Sat 10-6. Sun 12-5.
Services: Appraisals; catalog, book repair and rebinding.
Travel: See Whyte's Booksmith below. Shop is at corner of Ross and San Anselmo.
Credit Cards: Yes
Owner: Erik & Lane Heldfond
Year Estab: 1991

Oliver's Books   **Open Shop**
645 San Anselmo Avenue 94960   (415) 454-4421

Collection: General stock of used and new hardcover and paperback.
Specialties: Literature
# of Vols: 15,000
Hours: Mon 10-6. Tue & Wed 10-9. Thu-Sat 10-10. Sun 12-5.
Services: Search service, accepts want lists.
Travel: See Whyte's Booksmith below.
Credit Cards: Yes
Owner: Kathleen Lanphier
Year Estab: 1990
Comments: We don't usually see 20th century first editions (although not necessarily in the best condition), illustrated collectibles, literary sets and other signs of a fine used book collection on the premises of a shop that sells as many new books as this one does. The winners are those book people who live nearby and who can therefore take advantage of both the many good new and used volumes this shop has to offer.

Whyte's Booksmith   **Open Shop**
615 San Anselmo Avenue 94960   (415) 459-7323

Collection: General stock of new and used hardcover and paperback.
# of Vols: 5,000-10,000 (used)
Hours: Daily 10-10.
Travel: Sir Francis Drake Blvd exit off Hwy 101. Proceed west on Sir Francis Drake, left on Tunstead, then first right on San Anselmo.
Credit Cards: Yes
Owner: Michael Whyte
Year Estab: 1980
Comments: Used stock is about evenly divided between hardcover and paperback.

San Bernardino
(Map 12, page 139)

The Book Gallery   **Open Shop**
1179 E Street North 92410   (909) 885-6182

Collection: General stock of hardcover and paperback, ephemera and magazines.

Specialties:	History; the sciences; religion, fiction, art.
# of Vols:	50,000
Hours:	Mon-Sat 11:30-5:30. Other times by appointment.
Services:	Search service, accepts want lists, mail order.
Travel:	Baseline exit off 15 Fwy. East on 13th, left on Baseline and right on E.
Credit Cards:	No
Owner:	John & Patricia Price
Year Estab:	1974
Comments:	Almost two different stores on the same premises. A large room to the left as one enters the shop is almost exclusively paperback with just 1,000 or so hardcover books (newer titles, mysteries, best sellers, etc.) A second room resembles more of a traditional used book shop with a mix of newer and vintage hardcover items covering most subject areas and enough interesting titles to make a visit worthwhile.

Far Mountain Books
Open Shop
416 West Highland Avenue 92405
(909) 886-9621

Collection:	General stock of mostly paperback.
Specialties:	Science fiction; fantasy.
# of Vols:	20,000
Hours:	Mon-Sat 11-6.
Travel:	Between D and E Streets, five blocks east of 215 Fwy.
Credit Cards:	No
Owner:	D. Vance Lizza
Year Estab:	1990
Comments:	A mostly paperback shop with a few hardcover volumes on hand. If you're interested in an out-of-print science fiction or fantasy title that once appeared in paperback, there's a better than even chance you may find it here. On the other hand, if you're looking for truly esoteric titles in hardcover editions, even in the shop's specialties, call ahead and save yourself a trip.

The Happy Booker
Open Shop
4096 North Sierra Way Avenue 92407
(909) 883-6110

Collection:	General stock of hardcover and paperback.
# of Vols:	10,000
Hours:	Mon-Fri 9:30-5. Sat 10-5.
Travel:	Waterman exit off I-30. North on Waterman to 40th St, then west (left) on 40th and right on Sierra Way.
Credit Cards:	No
Owner:	Ruth E. Petersen
Year Estab:	1973
Comments:	A shop with mostly reading copies on hand and many hardcover volumes that were rescued from public libraries. Occasionally our eye caught a section that collectors might well be attracted to, i.e., several volumes in the American Rivers Series.

St. Francis Book Store　　　　　　　　　　　　　　　　　　　　　　　**Open Shop**
462 West Highland Avenue 92405　　　　　　　　　　　　　　　　　(909) 886-8371

Collection:　　Specialty. Mostly new and some used.
Specialties:　Religion
Hours:　　　　Mon-Fri 10-5. Sat 10-4.

San Bruno

Nothing's New　　　　　　　　　　　　　　　　　　　　　　　　　　**Open Shop**
851 Cherry Avenue, #23 94066　　　　　　　　Fax: (415) 871-6062 (415) 871-6063

Collection:　　Specialty
Specialties:　Film; nostalgia.
# of Vols:　　 300-500
Hours:　　　　Mon-Sat 9-9.
Travel:　　　　From I-280: northbound, San Bruno Ave exit. Southbound, Sneath Lane/San Bruno Ave. From either direction, turn into Bayhill Shopping Center.
Owner:　　　　Roger & Louredes Hill
Year Estab:　 1995

San Carlos
(Map 17, page 154)

A Time For Books　　　　　　　　　　　　　　　　　　　　　　　　**Open Shop**
733 Laurel Street 94070　　　　　　　　　　　Fax: (415) 592-2664 (415) 592-2665

Collection:　　General stock of new and used hardcover and paperback.
Specialties:　Antiques; autographs (signed photos).
# of Vols:　　 35,000
Hours:　　　　Mon-Sat 10:30-5:30.
Services:　　 Appraisals, search service, accepts want lists.
Travel:　　　　Holly St/San Carlos exit off Hwy 101. Proceed west for about 1/2 mile. Left on Laurel. Shop is 2½ blocks ahead.
Credit Cards: Yes
Owner:　　　　T.E. Christensen
Year Estab:　 1988
Comments:　　Interesting contrasts. As one enters the shop and looks immediately behind the owner's counter, one can see older, antiquarian, rare and collectible items in various categories. The main part of the shop is devoted to new books, paperbacks and hardcover reading copies that are, for the most part, in good condition and of fairly recent vintage. This is a shop were one can spend $1, or, if it hasn't been sold by the time you arrive, $10,000 for a rare volume on torture.

Antique Trove　　　　　　　　　　　　　　　　　　　　　　　　　　**Antique Mall**
1119 Industrial Way 94070　　　　　　　　　　　　　　　　　　　　(415) 593-1300

Collection:　　General stock of hardcover and paperback.
Hours:　　　　Daily 11-6.

San Clemente
(Map 15, page 97)

Sam and Gene Jones-Books   **Open Shop**
200 South Ola Vista 92672   (714) 492-0210

Collection:	General stock of hardcover and paperback.
# of Vols:	25,000
Hours:	Daily 11-7.
Services:	Search service, accepts want lists.
Travel:	Southbound of 5 Fwy: Palizada exit. Right on Palizada, left on El Camino, then right on Granada. Shop is on corner of Ola Vista and Granada.
Credit Cards:	No
Owner:	W. Gene Jones
Year Estab:	1977
Comments:	The vast majority of the books here were hardcover and consisted of a mix of new and vintage volumes in varied condition. The shelves were labeled for easy browsing and while there were no areas of great depth, several section did have some interesting titles. One room was devoted to children's books. The owner, a most accommodating transplanted southerner, is carrying on her late husband's business.

San Diego
(Map 14 page 203)

Aardvark Books   **Open Shop**
3342 Adams Avenue 92116   (619) 284-7715

Collection:	General stock of hardcover and paperback.
Specialties:	Mystery; science fiction.
# of Vols:	15,000
Hours:	Mon-Sat 11-7. Sun 12-6.
Travel:	See Book Broker below.
Map Ref:	Map 14, page 203, #1.
Credit Cards:	No
Owner:	Anne & Forrest Curo
Year Estab:	1985
Comments:	The hardcover books we saw were in mixed condition, strong in travel, with a reasonable selection in most other areas. The shelves were well labeled and the shop is an easy place to browse.

Adams Avenue Bookstore   **Open Shop**
3502 Adams Avenue 92116   (619) 281-3330

Collection:	General stock of hardcover and paperback.
Specialties:	Theology; philosophy; western Americana; literature.
# of Vols:	120,000
Hours:	Mon-Sat 10-6. Sun 12-5.
Travel:	See Book Broker below.

(San Diego)

Map Ref: Map 14, page 203, #2.
Services: Appraisals, search service, accepts want lists, mail order.
Credit Cards: Yes
Owner: Brian Lucas
Year Estab: 1960's
Comments: A real neat store with an owner who cares enough about his customers to provide them with an excellent map to help navigate through the shop's two floors. The books were attractively displayed and were, for the most part, in good condition and moderately priced. We noted a nice display of antiquarian volumes behind glass immediately behind the front counter.

Alouette Antiques
2936 Adams Avenue 92116

Open Shop
(619) 284-9408

Collection: General stock and ephemera (medicine).
Specialties: Children's; biography; medicine.
# of Vols: 3,000
Hours: Fri & Sat 12:30-4:30.
Travel: See Book Broker below, except left turn on Adams.
Map Ref: Map 14, page 203, #3.
Credit Cards: No
Owner: Yvette Ancell & Charles Molnar, Jr.
Year Estab: 1978

An Oasis Bookstore
3911 3rd Avenue 92103

Open Shop
(619) 299-8941
E-mail: jamesd@cg57.esnet.com

Collection: General stock of hardcover and paperback.
Specialties: Science fiction; mystery; metaphysics; children's.
# of Vols: 45,000
Hours: Daily 11-7.
Services: Search service, accepts want lists, catalog (E-mail only)
Travel: Northbound on Hwy 163: Washington St exit. Proceed on Washington and make first possible U turn. Continue west on Washington, then left on 3rd. Shop is one block ahead. Southbound on Hwy 163: University Ave exit. Right at light, then proceed west on University. Parking available in rear.
Map Ref: Map 14, page 203, #4.
Credit Cards: No
Owner: Cheryl Davis
Year Estab: 1992
Comments: An almost even mix of hardcover and paperbacks with the quality of the hardcover volumes well worth including the shop on your list of stops, particularly since there are so many other used book dealers in the immediate vicinity. The books were reasonably priced.

Antiques West Mall & Gallery
4905 Newport Avenue 92107

Open Shop
(619) 222-7500

Collection:	General stock of primarily used.
# of Vols:	3,000
Hours:	Daily 10-5:30.
Services:	Search service, accepts want lists, mail order.
Travel:	I-8 exit off I-5 northbound, then Sunset Cliff Blvd exit off I-8. Left on Sunset Cliff. Right on Newport.
Map Ref:	Map 14, page 203, #5.
Credit Cards:	Yes
Owner:	Ann-Marie & Brian Boyce
Year Estab:	1990

Bargain Bookstore
1053 Eighth Avenue 92101

Open Shop
(619) 234-5380

Collection:	General stock of hardcover and paperback and some ephemera.
# of Vols:	100,000
Hours:	Mon-Sat 10:30-4. Sunday by appointment.
Travel:	See Broadway Booksellers below. Left on Eighth Ave.
Map Ref:	Map 14, page 203, #6.
Credit Cards:	No
Owner:	Jim & Nancy Lindstrom
Year Estab:	1926
Comments:	A stop here should be worth the bending and occasional ladder climbing. The books ranged in condition from dusty to fine editions and were reasonably priced.

Benedikt & Salmon
3020 Meade Avenue 92116

Open Shop
Fax: (619) 281-3345 (619) 281-3345

Collection:	Specialty new and used.
Specialties:	Music; performing arts; autographs; magazines; scores; librettos.
Hours:	Mon-Sat 12-6.
Services:	Catalog, appraisals, search service, accepts want lists.
Credit Cards:	Yes
Owner:	Gerri Benedikt & Bob Salmon
Year Estab:	1981

Charles Lewis Best
854 Rosecrans 92106

By Appointment
Fax: (619) 224-0785 (619) 223-3418

Collection:	Specialty
Specialties:	California; maritime; history of the Pacific.
# of Vols:	2,000
Services:	Appraisals, catalog, search service, accepts want lists.
Credit Cards:	No
Year Estab:	1988

Betty's Bookstore
3533 Adams Avenue 92116

Open Shop
(619) 283-6222

Collection:	General stock of paperback and hardcover.
Specialties:	Mystery; science fiction; women's studies.
Hours:	Mon & Tue 12-8. Wed-Sat 10-8. Sun 11-6.
Travel:	See Book Broker below.
Map Ref:	Map 14, page 203, #7.
Services:	Search service, accepts want lists.
Credit Cards:	No
Year Estab:	1990
Comments:	A neighborhood used book shop with a goodly amount of paperbacks, book club editions and popular literature. There's little chance of finding a rare item here, but, as the shop is located directly across the street from a "don't miss" shop (see Adams Avenue Bookstore above), it's worth a brief stop.

Black Moon Books
PO Box 159-001-192 92175

By Appointment
(619) 466-6010

Collection:	Specialty used and new hardcover and paperback.
Specialties:	Vampire literature; horror.
# of Vols:	2,000
Services:	Appraisals, search service, catalog, accepts want lists.
Credit Cards:	No
Owner:	Blaza
Year Estab:	1970
Comments:	Also displays at Fifth Avenue Books in San Diego.

Bloody Dagger Books
3817 Shasta Street, #D 92109

Open Shop
(619) 581-9134

Collection:	Specialty. Mostly hardcover.
Specialties:	Mystery; crime; detective.
# of Vols:	8,000
Hours:	Mon-Sat 9-6.
Services:	Search service, accepts want lists, mail order. Publishes *Bloody Dagger Reference-A Price Guide to Mystery-Crime Detective Fiction.*
Credit Cards:	No
Owner:	Nick Pappas
Year Estab:	1992

The Book Broker
3341 Adams Avenue 92116

Open Shop
(619) 280-2665

Collection:	General stock of hardcover and some paperback.
Specialties:	Modern fiction; literature; art; architecture; Americana; military.
# of Vols:	25,000
Hours:	Mon-Sat 10-6. Sun 11-5.
Services:	Search service, mail order.

Travel: From 805 Fwy southbound: Adams Ave exit. Proceed east on Adams for eight blocks. From 805 Fwy northbound: El Cajon Blvd exit. Proceed east on El Cajon for one block, then left on 33rd St, right on Adams.
Map Ref: Map 14, page 203, #8.
Credit Cards: Yes
Owner: Robin Weber & Wendy Schink
Year Estab: 1992
Comments: What this shop lacks in size it more than makes up for in the quality of its collection. The majority of the books, regardless of their vintage, were in fine condition, most having dust jackets and most well cared for. A good supply of firsts on hand, along with a most pleasant ambience.

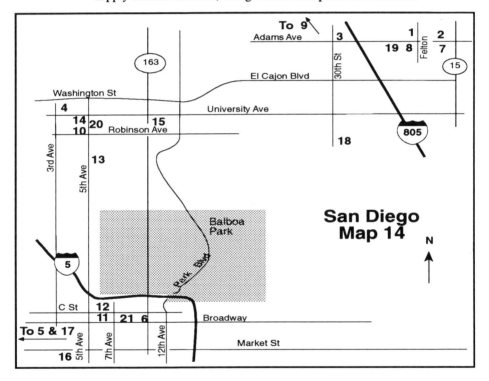

Book Exchange   **Open Shop**
11295 Camino Ruiz 92126   (619) 695-0447

Collection: General stock of paperback and hardcover.
# of Vols: 45,000
Hours: Mon-Fri 2-6:30. Sat 10-5.
Travel: Mira Mesa Blvd exit off 15 Fwy. West on Mira Mesa, north on Camino Ruiz. Shop is on right, in Camino Village shopping center.
Map Ref: Map 14, page 203, #9.
Year Estab: 1991
Comments: Stock is about evenly divided between paperback and hardcover.

(San Diego)

Books By Mail **By Appointment**
6315 Connie Drive 92115 (619) 582-0894

Collection:	Specialty
Specialties:	California; Baja California; Southwest Americana; ornithology; gardening.
Services:	Accepts want lists, mail order.
Credit Cards:	No
Owner:	Rosalie C. Davidson
Year Estab:	1978
Comments:	Also displays at Newport Antique Center in Ocean Beach.

Bountiful Books **Open Shop**
3834 5th Avenue 92103 (619) 491-0664

Collection:	General stock of hardcover and paperback.
# of Vols:	20,000
Hours:	Daily 11-9:30.
Services:	Appraisals, search service, accepts want lists, mail order.
Travel:	Hwy 163 to University exit. Shop is two blocks from exit, between Robinson and University.
Map Ref:	Map 14, page 203, #10.
Credit Cards:	Yes
Owner:	Rhea Kuhlman
Year Estab:	1992
Comments:	A nice selection of books covering most subject areas. During our visit, we noticed several vintage Oz titles as well as other rare children's items. The books were generally well cared for and the shop, while not overly large, has enough interest to keep the browser attentive.

Broadway Booksellers **Open Shop**
632 Broadway 92101 (619) 232-8331

Collection:	General stock of hardcover and paperback.
Specialties:	Military; beat literature; art; religion.
# of Vols:	10,000
Hours:	Mon-Sat 10-6. Sun 12-5.
Services:	Appraisals, search service, accepts want lists, mail order.
Travel:	I-5 southbound.: 10th St exit. Proceed south on 10th to Broadway. Right on Broadway. I-5 Northbound: 6th Ave exit. Proceed south on 6th then left on Broadway.
Map Ref:	Map 14, page 203, #11.
Credit Cards:	Yes
Owner:	Garrick Ryan, Manager
Year Estab:	1994
Comments:	Considering the fact that we were able to visit four other used book dealers within two-three blocks of this shop, all of whom were open at their posted hour, you may not miss much if you share the experience we did of finding the shop still closed twenty minutes after its posted opening time. The front

windows displayed popular recent titles but beyond that, we are unable to speculate as to what you may find inside.

Wm Burgett Booksellers   Open Shop
640 C Street 92101   (619) 238-7323

Collection:	General stock or hardcover and paperback.
# of Vols:	100,000
Hours:	Mon-Sat 10-6. Sun 12-5.
Services:	Appraisals, search service, accepts want lists, mail order.
Travel:	See Broadway Booksellers above. Shop is between 6th and 7th Avenues.
Map Ref:	Map 14, page 203, #12.
Credit Cards:	Yes
Owner:	William Burgett
Year Estab:	1980
Comments:	At the time of our visit the owner was settling into a new, more expansive shop, just a few blocks away from his old location. Most of the books we saw were in good to excellent condition with a few in lesser health. Almost every subject was represented. Some of the books were priced at levels that suggested, at least to us, that the owner was optimistic regarding their value. The selection was such that we would definitely recommend a visit.

Cape Cod Clutter   Open Shop
3523 Fifth Avenue 92103   (619) 291-8088

Collection:	General stock.
Specialties:	New England, maritime; travel history; literature.
# of Vols:	10,000
Hours:	Mon-Sat 12:30-7.
Services:	Appraisals, accepts want lists.
Travel:	Downtown exit off I-8, then University exit. Right at fifth light on Fifth.
Map Ref:	Map 14, page 203, #13.
Credit Cards:	No
Owner:	Sandee Gillis
Year Estab:	1974
Comments:	A relatively small shop with quality titles, most of which were quite reasonably priced. Lots of subjects covered with books representing various eras and more than a few collectibles for those with a quick eye.

Controversial Bookstore   Open Shop
3021 University Avenue 92104   (619) 296-1560

Collection:	Specialty. Primarily new with some used.
Specialties:	Metaphysics
Hours:	Mon-Sat 9:30-6. Sun 11-4.

Fifth Avenue Books   Open Shop
3840 Fifth Avenue 92103   (619) 291-4660
E-mail: rms@cts.com

Collection:	General stock of hardcover and paperback.

(San Diego)

# of Vols:	20,000
Hours:	Mon-Sat 11-9:30. Sun 11-6.
Travel:	From downtown, take Fifth Ave 2½ miles north.
Map Ref:	Map 14, page 203, #14.
Credit Cards:	Yes
Comments:	A mix of hardcover and paperback, most in generally good condition. We noted strong sections in fiction, mystery and horror but few titles not seen elsewhere. There are enough books here, and enough variety, to keep you looking.

FootNote Books
1627 University Avenue 92103

Open Shop
(619) 294-8455

Collection:	General stock of paperback and hardcover and records.
Specialties:	Books about comics; science fiction (hardcover); fantasy (hardcover).
# of Vols:	15,000
Hours:	Mon-Sat 10:30-8. Sun 11-5:30.
Travel:	University exit off Hwy 163 south. East on University. Shop is at 16th Ave.
Map Ref:	Map 14, page 203, #15.
Credit Cards:	Yes
Owner:	Troy Beaver
Year Estab:	1987

Friends of the San Diego Public Library
4193 Park Boulevard 92103

Open Shop
(619) 542-1724

Collection:	General stock of hardcover and paperback.
Hours:	Tue & Thu 9-1.
Travel:	At corner of Howard and Park, on the lower level of the University Heights branch library.
Comments:	This location is the headquarters for 39 individual "Friends" groups located at branch libraries.

Gaslamp Books, Prints & Antiques
413 Market Street 92101

Open Shop
(619) 237-1492

Collection:	General stock and memorabilia.
Specialties:	Military; Southwest Americana.
# of Vols:	5,000
Hours:	Sun-Thu 12-7. Fri & Sat 12-9.
Services:	Appraisals, accepts want lists, mail order.
Travel:	Front St exit off I-5 southbound. Proceed on Front to Market. Left on Market.
Map Ref:	Map 14, page 203, #16.
Credit Cards:	Yes
Owner:	Ken & Jennifer Cilch
Year Estab:	1992
Comments:	A small shop with lots of interesting San Diego, gambling and west coast

memorabilia. Whether or not you buy a book here, you should still find the shop of interest because of its focus on nostalgia.

Grounds for Murder Mystery Book Store
3858 Fifth Avenue 92103

Open Shop
(619) 299-9500

Collection: Specialty new and used.
Specialties: Mystery
# of Vols: 30,000 (used)
Hours: Tue-Sun 11-6.
Services: Occasional catalog, appraisals, accepts want lists.
Travel: Between University and Robinson. (Enter from courtyard on Fifth Ave.)
Credit Cards: Yes
Owner: Phyllis Brown
Year Estab: 1980

Margaret Mannatt Fine Books
PO Box 16243 92176

By Appointment
Fax: (619) 283-2127 (619) 283-3062

Collection: General stock and ephemera.
Specialties: Illustrated; children's; modern first editions; Egypt; theatrical design, especially costume.
# of Vols: 5,000
Services: Appraisals, search service, catalog, accepts want lists, bookbinding and repair.
Credit Cards: No
Year Estab: 1981

Ocean Beach Books
1917 Cable Street 92107

Open Shop
(619) 222-7923

Collection: General stock of paperback and hardcover.
Specialties: Literature.
# of Vols: 10,000
Hours: Tue-Sun 10-5:30.
Travel: Northbound on 8 Fwy: Sunset Cliffs exit. South on Sunset Cliffs, right on Newport and right on Cable. Southbound: Sea World Dr exit. Proceed straight on Sea World Dr which becomes Sunset Cliffs. Follow as above
Map Ref: Map 14, page 203, #17.
Credit Cards: Yes
Owner: Keith Finley
Year Estab: 1985
Comments: Stock is about evenly divided between hardcover and paperback.

Otento Books
4756 Terrace Drive 92116

By Appointment
(619) 281-8962

Collection: General stock.
Specialties: Cookbooks; children's; art; picture books.
# of Vols: 8,000
Services: Search service, catalog, accepts want lists.

(San Diego)

Credit Cards: Yes
Owner: Barbara Gelink
Year Estab: 1963
Comments: Also displays at four antique malls on Newport Avenue in Ocean Beach.

Pacific Shore Maps **By Appointment**
5664 Menorca Drive 92124 Fax: (619) 571-2031 (619) 571-2031

Collection: Specialty
Specialties: Maps and sea charts from 17th century to post World War II. Special focus on maps of Pacific Rim countries.
Services: Appraisals, accepts want lists, mail order.
Credit Cards: No
Owner: Capt. Richard Cloward
Year Estab: 1991

Parmer Books **By Appointment**
7644 Forrestal Road 92120 Fax: (619) 287-6135 (619) 287-0693
E-mail: parmerbook@aol.com

Collection: Specialty
Specialties: Arctic; Antarctic; Alaska; voyages; South Pacific; Americana.
# of Vols: 5,000
Hours: Mon-Sat 9-5.
Services: Search service, catalog, accepts want lists.
Credit Cards: Yes
Owner: Jean Marie & Jerome F. Parmer
Year Estab: 1983

The Prince and the Pauper Collectible Children's Books **Open Shop**
3201 Adams Avenue 92116 Fax: (619) 283-4666 (619) 283-4380
E-mail: keeline@cerf.net

Collection: Specialty. Primarily used hardcover.
Specialties: Children's; children's series; Oz; Little Golden Books.
# of Vols: 50,000+
Hours: Mon-Sat 10-7.
Services: Appraisals, search service, occasional catalog, accepts want lists, mail order.
Travel: See Book Broker above. Shop is at corner of 32nd St and Adams.
Credit Cards: Yes
Owner: Jack Hastings, owner. James D. Keeline, manager
Year Estab: 1988

Rocky's Antiques, Books & Collectibles **Open Shop**
2367 30th Street 92104 (619) 280-3806

Collection: General stock of mostly hardcover.
Specialties: Gardening; cookbooks; children's.
# of Vols: 10,000

Hours: Tue-Sun 10-6.
Services: Appraisals, search service, mail order, accepts want lists.
Travel: 30th St exit off Hwy 94. Proceed north on 30th.
Map Ref: Map 14, page 203, #18.
Credit Cards: No
Owner: Rocky Best
Year Estab: 1985
Comments: Despite its out-of-the way location (i.e., not near the city's other book dealers), we stopped by here and were not surprised to find almost as many non book collectibles as books. The books we did see, mostly older volumes, seemed fairly ordinary to our eye, although we recognize that in the world of book hunting, gems can turn up in the most unlikely places.

Safari Out of Print Bookstore & Search Service **Open Shop**
3311 Adams Avenue 92116   Fax: (619) 584-4399   (619) 584-4381

Collection: General stock of mostly hardcover.
Specialties: Alcoholics Anonymous; books on books.
# of Vols: 200,000
Hours: Daily 10-7.
Services: Search service, accepts want lists.
Travel: See Book Broker above.
Map Ref: Map 14, page 203, #19.
Credit Cards: Yes
Owner: Jeff Bohannon & Charles Morris
Year Estab: 1988
Comments: A shop with a large collection of used books which would be a pleasure to visit even if it were the only shop in town. Visitors to this shop have the additional bonus of finding two other shops less than a block away, with two more shops just another two to three blocks beyond that. The books are reasonably priced, if not all in pristine condition. This is a shop with lots of stock, lots of variety and certainly lots of interesting titles.

Sally's Attic (Salvation Army) **Open Shop**
901 Twelfth Avenue 92101   (619) 696-1560

Collection: General stock of hardcover and paperback.
Hours: Mon-Sat 9-6.

Seabreeze Limited **Open Shop**
1254 Scott Street 92106   (619) 223-8989

Collection: Specialty. New and used books and related items.
Specialties: Nautical
# of Vols: 2,000 (used)
Hours: Mon- Sat 9-5:30.
Services: Mail order.
Travel: Rosecrans exit off I-5. Proceed south on Rosecrans to Harbor Dr. Left on Harbor, then right on Scott.

Credit Cards: Yes
Owner: John & Suzanne Pew
Year Estab: 1984

Joseph Tabler Books
3817 Fifth Avenue 92103

Open Shop
(619) 296-1424

Collection:	General stock of hardcover and paperback.
Specialties:	Surfing; architecture; history.
# of Vols:	25,000
Hours:	Daily 11-9:30.
Services:	Mail order, accepts want lists.
Travel:	University Ave exit off Hwy 163. Proceed south on University to 4th, left on 4th, left on Robinson and left on 5th.
Map Ref:	Map 14, page 203, #20.
Credit Cards:	Yes
Owner:	Joseph Tabler
Year Estab:	1955
Comments:	The largest of three shops, all within 50 yards of one another. While the shop had lots of volume, a good deal of it was devoted to paperbacks, with the hardcover books representing items of mixed vintage and in mixed condition. Standing alone, this shop is typical of many older establishments. Considering the ambience of the neighborhood, it could probably benefit from a face-lift.

Wahrenbrock's Book House
726 Broadway 92101

Open Shop
(800) 315-8643   (619) 232-0132
Fax: (619) 232-3808

Collection:	General stock.
Specialties:	Literature; voyages; travel; first editions; western Americana; California; Mexico.
# of Vols:	250,000
Hours:	Mon-Fri 9:30-5:30. Sat 9-5. Rare Book Room: Mon & Sat 10-4 and by appointment.
Services:	Appraisals, catalog, accepts want lists.
Travel:	See Broadway Booksellers above.
Map Ref:	Map 14, page 203, #21.
Credit Cards:	Yes
Owner:	C.A. Valverde
Year Estab:	1935
Comments:	This is a must visit for anyone traveling to San Diego. Three floors of books, meticulously organized and most reasonably priced greet both the casual and intense browser. If you don't leave having made at least one modest purchase we would be surprised. The quality of the books range from frequently seen titles to truly antiquarian items with many an unusual title in between.

San Fernando

San Fernando Book Co.
PO Box 447 91342

Antique Mall
(818) 362-2173

Collection:	General stock of new and some used.
Specialties:	Antiques and collectibles reference and price guides.
# of Vols:	2,500
Owner:	Emil N. Eusanio
Year Estab:	1972
Comments:	Books are sold at eight antique malls. For names and locations call the owner at the number listed above.

San Francisco
(Map 16, page 212)

Aaben Books
1546 California 94109

Open Shop
(415) 563-3525

Collection:	General stock of hardcover and paperback.
# of Vols:	20,000
Hours:	Mon-Sat 10-10, except Sat till midnight . Sun 10-10.
Travel:	In Polk Street district between Polk & Larkin.
Map Ref:	Map 16a, page 212, #1.
Credit Cards:	Yes
Owner:	James Noonan
Year Estab:	1993
Comments:	A good sized shop with a friendly feline owning owner. A mix of hardcover and paperback with some vintage paperbacks and hardcover books representing several eras. A nice collection but one that requires a little time to check out because the books are so compactly shelved. (At the time of our visit, the owner was planning an expansion to a second room in the rear of the shop.)

Aardvark Books
227 Church Street 94114

Open Shop
(415) 552-6733

Collection:	General stock of mostly used, paperback and hardcover.
# of Vols:	70,000
Hours:	Mon-Sat 10:30-10:30. Sun 9:30-9.
Travel:	Between Market & 15th.
Map Ref:	Map 16b, page 212, #2.
Credit Cards:	Yes
Year Estab:	1978
Comments:	A majority of the books appeared to be in good condition and of fairly recent vintage. The shop had lots of browsers on hand when we visited. The shelves were well organized and the titles seemed interesting, with some collectible and rare books.

212 CALIFORNIA

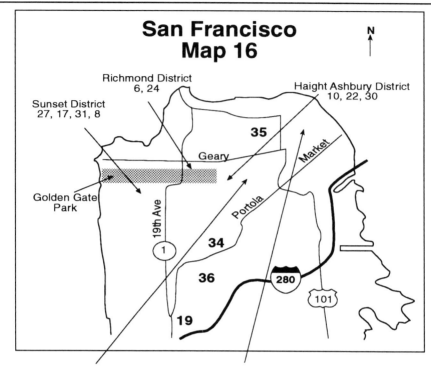
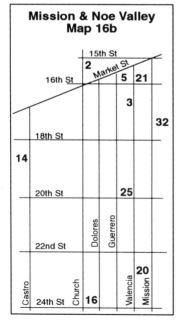
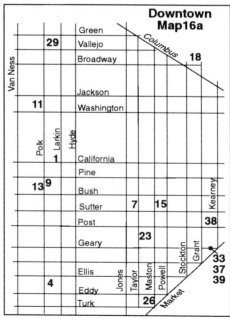

Abandoned Planet Bookstore
518 Valencia Street 94110

Open Shop
(415) 861-4695

Collection:	General stock of paperback and hardcover.
Specialties:	Literature; the arts.
# of Vols:	10,000-15,000
Hours:	Daily 12-11pm.
Travel:	In Mission district between 16th & 17th Streets.
Map Ref:	Map 16b, page 212, #3.
Credit Cards:	Yes
Owner:	Scott Harrison
Year Estab:	1993
Comments:	The stock is approximately 70% paperback.

Acorn Books
740 Polk Street 94109

Open Shop
(415) 563-1736
E-mail: acornbks@netcom.com

Collection:	General stock of hardcover and paperback.
Specialties:	Western Americana; modern first editions; art; railroads; military.
# of Vols:	100,000+
Hours:	Mon-Sat 10:30-8. Sun 12-7.
Services:	Internet search service, catalog, accepts want lists.
Travel:	Near Civic Center, between Eddy and Ellis.
Map Ref:	Map 16a, page 212, #4.
Credit Cards:	Yes
Owner:	Joel McKee Chapman
Year Estab:	1980
Comments:	Our kind of shop: large, with a very nice mix of books, mostly hardcover but with a healthy supply of paperbacks. The books we saw were in generally good condition and represented both vintage and more recent titles. The shop is easy to browse (lots of ladders and stools). Getting lost here would not be a tragedy.

Acquitania Gallery
158 Carl Street 94117

By Appointment
Fax: (415) 664-2707 (415) 664-2707

Collection:	Specialty
Specialties:	Maps (16th-18th century); prints; art; travel; children's illustrated; San Francisco.
# of Vols:	1,000
Services:	Catalog, accepts want lists.
Credit Cards:	Yes
Owner:	Diane D. Vasica
Year Estab:	1984

Adobe Bookshop
3166 16th Street 94103

Open Shop
(415) 864-3936

Collection:	General stock of hardcover and paperback.

(San Francisco)

Specialties:	Art; philosophy; scholarly.
# of Vols:	20,000
Hours:	Daily 12-10.
Services:	Appraisals, accepts want lists.
Travel:	In Mission district, between Valencia and Guerrero.
Map Ref:	Map 16b, page 212, #5.
Credit Cards:	Yes
Owner:	Andrew McKinley
Year Estab:	1989
Comments:	A roomy shop with as many paperback titles as hardcover volumes and several stuffed chairs in sight inviting customers to sit and read. Many of the books seemed "arty" and/or new age-like which, based on our assessment of the neighborhood, would mean that the shop fits right in.

Albatross Book Co.   **Open Shop**
143 Clement 94118   (415) 752-8611

Collection:	General stock.
Specialties:	Wine; cookbooks; Western Americana.
# of Vols:	10,000
Hours:	Sun-Thu 11-8. Fri & Sat 11-10.
Services:	Appraisals, accepts want lists, mail order.
Travel:	In Richmond district, between 2nd & 3rd Avenues.
Map Ref:	Map 16, page 212, #6.
Credit Cards:	Yes
Owner:	Rick Wilkinson
Year Estab:	1965
Comments:	A collection of interesting titles (mostly hardcover) and collectibles. Most of the items we saw were in good condition. A shop that definitely holds enough interest to make us feel it is worth a visit.

Argonaut Book Shop   **Open Shop**
786 Sutter Street 94109   (415) 474-9067

Collection:	General stock and ephemera.
Specialties:	California; Western Americana.
# of Vols:	10,000
Hours:	Mon-Fri 9-5. Sat 10-4.
Services:	Appraisals, catalog, accepts want lists.
Travel:	Between Jones & Taylor.
Map Ref:	Map 16a, page 212, #7.
Credit Cards:	Yes
Owner:	Robert D. Haines, Jr.
Year Estab:	1941
Comments:	A small shop that offers quality titles, particularly in its specialty areas, and more than its share of rare and antiquarian items. We were impressed by the condition of the books.

Arkadyan Books & Prints

938 Irving Street 94122

Open Shop

(415) 664-6212

Collection: General stock.
Specialties: Children's; illustrated; fine bindings; 19th century maps and prints.
# of Vols: 2,000
Hours: Mon-Sat 12-6.
Travel: In Sunset district, between 10th & 11th.
Map Ref: Map 16, page 212, #8.
Credit Cards: Yes
Owner: Gerald Webb
Year Estab: 1974
Comments: This shop was closed when we visited San Francisco. Visitors should note that the entrance to the front door is up one flight and we suspect that the actual shop may be up an additional flight.

Around The World

1346 Polk Street 94109

Open Shop

(415) 474-5568

Collection: General stock of mostly used hardcover and paperback.
# of Vols: 25,000
Hours: Daily 12-8.
Travel: At Pine St, one block from California cable car.
Map Ref: Map 16a, page 212, #9.
Credit Cards: Yes
Owner: Lloyd Mooney
Year Estab: 1985
Comments: A shop that looks almost "lived in" with books on the shelves that might have come from a library of the one of the neighborhood's residents. The books were in mixed condition (many without dust jackets) and while many subjects were represented, few were represented in depth. Paperbacks and records were available on the second floor and some of the shelves on the first floor were hard to get to.

Austen Books

1687 Haight Street 94117

Open Shop

(415) 552-4122

Collection: General stock of hardcover and paperback.
# of Vols: 10,000-15,000.
Hours: Tue-Sat 11-6. Sun & Mon 12-6.
Travel: In Haight Ashbury district, at Cole.
Map Ref: Map 16, page 212, #10.
Credit Cards: Yes
Owner: Brian Beard
Comments: A modest sized shop with a good collection of hardcover volumes, paperbacks and trade paperbacks, mostly of newer vintage. Lots of materials that fit the flavor of what one would normally associate with the Haight district.

(San Francisco)

Stephen Avedikian Fine & Rare Books
815 York Street 94110

By Appointment
Fax: (415) 642-0780   (415) 642-0780

Collection:	Specialty
Specialties:	Fine and rare book in all fields.
# of Vols:	5,000
Services:	Appraisals, occasional catalog, accepts want lists, mail order.
Credit Cards:	Yes
Year Estab:	1988

Alan S. Bamberger Books
2510 Bush Street 94115

By Appointment
Fax: (415) 9223-580   (415) 931-7875

Collection:	Specialty books and ephemera.
Specialties:	Art; architecture; photography; design; decoration; antiques.
# of Vols:	5,000
Services:	Appraisals, search service, accepts want lists, mail order.
Credit Cards:	No
Year Estab:	1978

Blue Sky Books
1819 Polk Street 94109

Open Shop
(415) 441-4519

Collection:	General stock of hardcover and paperback.
Specialties:	Mystery.
# of Vols:	20,000
Hours:	Mon-Sat 11-6. Sun 12-6.
Services:	Catalog, accepts want lists.
Travel:	Between Jackson and Washington.
Map Ref:	Map 16a, page 212, #11.
Credit Cards:	Yes
Owner:	William J. Mooney
Year Estab:	1981
Comments:	The shop shares space with a used record shop. The casual visitor will see a relatively general collection of paperbacks and hardcover volumes to the rear of the records while the real book person, once identifying himself as a true aficionado, may be fortunate enough to visit the locked back room where a more extensive collection of both recent and vintage hardcover mysteries can be found. The back room also has vintage paperbacks and other rare items of a more general nature. If mystery is your cup of tea, you'll enjoy the flavor of your visit here.

Bolerium Books
2141 Mission Street, Ste 300 94110

Open Shop
Fax: (415) 255-6499   (415) 863-6353
E-mail: bolerium@connex.com   8003266353

Collection:	Specialty books and ephemera.
Specialties:	American labor and radical history; black studies; homosexuality; Spanish Civil War; federal writer's project; chess; Troyskyism; anarchism; Americana; books about books.

# of Vols:	20,000+
Hours:	Mon-Sat 12-6.
Services:	Appraisals, catalog, accepts want lists.
Travel:	In Mission district, between 17th & 18th Streets. Ring buzzer for entry into building.
Credit Cards:	Yes
Owner:	John Durham & Mike Pincus
Year Estab:	1981
Comments:	Confession time. As on one or two other occasions when visiting certain neighborhoods in urban centers, one of us becomes somewhat nervous about the surroundings. During our visit to this neighborhood, that member preferred to keep an eye on our car (and enjoy the safety of its four locked doors) while the more courageous distaff member of the team was admitted to the locked building by ringing an outside buzzer (not the usual means of entry into a book shop) and visited this specialty dealer as well as the group shop next door (See Tall Stories below). While Susan kindly attributes to David the "books sense" portion of our team, she has visited enough shops herself to have been most impressed with the quality of the titles she observed at this shop and has no reservations about recommending the shop to anyone seeking books dealing with the shop's specialties. For book hunters who can't make it to San Francisco, or who are too "suburbanized" to want to venture here, the owner is more than willing to send a catalog.

Book Bay   Open Shop
Building C, Fort Mason in Golden Gate National Recreation Area   (415) 771-1076

Collection:	General stock of hardcover and paperback.
Hours:	Wed-Sun 11-5, except Thu till 8.
Comments:	Operated by the Friends of the San Francisco Public Library.

Bookmonger   Open Shop
2411 Clement 94121   (415) 387-2332

Collection:	General stock of mostly paperback.
Hours:	Mon-Fri 1-9. Sat & Sun 11-9.

Books & Company   Open Shop
1323 Polk Street 94109   (415) 441-2929

Collection:	General stock of new and used hardcover and paperback.
Specialties:	Art; cookbooks; homosexuality.
# of Vols:	15,000-20,000
Hours:	Mon-Sat 11-4.
Travel:	Between Bush and Pine Streets.
Map Ref:	Map 16a, page 212, #13.
Credit Cards:	No
Owner:	G. Bennett
Year Estab:	1935

(San Francisco)

Comments: Sometimes it was difficult to tell the difference between the shop's new and used books as the latter were in such good condition and most of the titles seemed to be quite recent. In making inquiries, the owner advised us that he intershelved his new and used books, but that his new books were offered at 40% off their listed price. If you're looking for interesting titles in art, photography or general fiction and the titles you're seeking are relatively recent, the chances of acquiring a copy here are fairly good.

Books, Etc. **Open Shop**
538 Castro Street 94114 Fax: (415) 387-7162 (415) 621-8631

Collection: General stock of hardcover and paperback.
Specialties: Homosexuality; Modern Library; first editions; Anne Rice.
# of Vols: 30,000
Hours: Daily 11am-10pm, except Fri & Sat till midnight.
Services: Catalog
Travel: In Mission district, between 18th & 19th Streets.
Map Ref: Map 16b, page 212, #14.
Credit Cards: Yes
Owner: H. Toledano
Year Estab: 1985
Comments: Quite a healthy mix of first editions, leather bindings and literary sets together with lots of paperback titles and hardcover fiction and non fiction. Most of the books were in good condition. A nice shop to visit and one where, if you're of a mind to do so, you can easily make a purchase or two. Note: many of the first editions in the owner's stock are housed elsewhere and are available through catalog or mail order sales.

The Bookstall **Open Shop**
570 Sutter Street 94102 Fax: (415) 362-1503 (415) 362-6353

Collection: General stock.
Specialties: Children's; illustrated; history of science; medicine; California; literature; exploration.
# of Vols: 10,000
Hours: Mon-Sat 11-6.
Services: Appraisals, catalog, accepts want lists.
Travel: One half block from Union Square between Powell and Mason.
Map Ref: Map 16a, page 212, #15.
Credit Cards: Yes
Owner: Henry & Louise Moises
Year Estab: 1975
Comments: When we visited San Francisco in early July and arrived at this shop, we found a sign in the window indicating that the shop was closed for vacation for a two week period. We believe that everyone is entitled to a vacation (even book people who use their vacation time to visit other bookstores

only to find them closed). Clearly, the owners had a good reason for not leaving someone in charge of their shop while they were gone. A very superficial examination of the shop's stock from the front and side windows revealed hardcover titles that fell into the "collectible" category, lots of vintage material and many items that we would have loved to have examined more closely. If you're planning a trip to San Francisco, we recommend this shop - but definitely urge you to call ahead to make sure someone will be on hand when you arrive.

The Brick Row Book Shop **Open Shop**
49 Geary Street, #235 94108 Fax: (415) 398-0435 (415) 398-0414

Collection: Specialty
Specialties: Rare and antiquarian books in all fields, especially 18th and 19th century English and American literature; modern first editions; bibliography.
# of Vols: 8,000+
Hours: Mon-Fri 9:30-5:30. Sat 10:30-4. Other times by appointment.
Services: Appraisals, catalog, accepts want lists.
Travel: Between Grant and Kearney.
Map Ref: Map 16a, page 212, #39.
Credit Cards: Yes
Owner: John Crichton
Year Estab: 1915
Comments: Located on the second floor of an office building, this "ain't" your typical used book shop. While it is certainly possible to find a few less expensive items here, even some titles seen elsewhere, most of the books we saw were in the upscale, collectible category with more than a few fine bindings, sets, rare titles, first editions, etc. If you're a serious collector and want to view quality titles, a visit here would certainly be in order.

John Caius-Books **By Appointment**
PO Box 640309 94164 Fax: (415) 776-6669 (415) 775-5646

Collection: Specialty books and ephemera.
Specialties: Early and rare books dealing with medicine; science; occult; "modern" bibliographies and reference works in specialty areas.
# of Vols: 3,000
Services: Catalog
Year Estab: 1983

Califia Books **Open Shop**
20 Hawthorne Street 94105 (415) 284-0314

Collection: Specialty
Specialties: Fine press; artist books.
Hours: Tue, Fri, Sat 12-5. Other times by appointment.
Services: Appraisals, catalog.
Travel: South of Market, between Hoard and Folsom.
Credit Cards: Yes

(San Francisco)

Owner: Edwina Leggett
Year Estab: 1984

Carroll's Books
1193 Church 94114

Open Shop
(415) 647-3020

Collection:	General stock of hardcover and paperback.
Specialties:	Ireland
# of Vols:	30,000
Hours:	Mon-Thu 10-9. Fri-Sun 10-10.
Travel:	In Noe Valley district at corner of 24th St and Church.
Map Ref:	Map 16b, page 212, #16.
Credit Cards:	Yes
Owner:	Jim Carroll
Year Estab:	1990
Comments:	You can usually tell if a shop is popular in its neighborhood when you find several people comfortably browsing its shelves. This is such a shop. The shop offers hardcover volumes (and some paperbacks) of every description and in almost every subject category. The shelves are well labeled and the books (primarily reading copies) are nicely displayed.

Chelsea Books
637 Irving Street 94122

Open Shop
(415) 566-0507

Collection:	General stock of mostly hardcover.
Specialties:	Art; literature.
# of Vols:	5,000
Hours:	Daily 10-10.
Travel:	In Inner Sunset district, between 7th & 8th Ave.
Map Ref:	Map 16, page 212, #17.
Credit Cards:	Yes
Owner:	Bryan Bilby
Year Estab:	1995
Comments:	At the time of our visit the shop had only been open for about three months which perhaps explains the fact that several of the shelves were void of books. The books that were on hand were mostly recent titles in reasonably good condition. Unfortunately, we were not able to spot any titles that we viewed as worth hunting for a parking space to view.

Columbus Books
540 Broadway 94133

Open Shop
(415) 986-3872

Collection:	General stock of hardcover and paperback.
Specialties:	Literature; foreign language.
# of Vols:	50,000+
Hours:	Mon-Thu 10:30am-11pm. Fri & Sat 10am-midnight. Sun 11am-10pm.
Travel:	In North Beach district between Grant and Kearney.
Map Ref:	Map 16a, page 212, #18.

Credit Cards: Yes
Owner: Gary Palister
Year Estab: 1987
Comments: A well organized collection with many scholarly titles as well as a balanced general stock. The store is large and easy to browse. Foreign language, science and technical subjects are located on a second level. If you're lucky enough to find a place to park (or use public transportation) include this shop on your San Francisco itinerary.

Discount Textbooks   Open Shop
3950 19th Avenue 94132   (415) 585-2665

Collection: General stock of paperback and hardcover.
# of Vols: 50,000 (used, non textbooks)
Hours: Mon-Thu & Sat 10-7. Fri & Sun 10-5.
Travel: Near San Francisco State.
Map Ref: Map 16, page 212, #19.

Dog Eared Books   Open Shop
1173 Valencia 94110   (415) 282-1901

Collection: General stock of mostly used hardcover and paperback.
# of Vols: 10,000-15,000
Hours: Mon-Sat 10-9. Sun 11-6.
Travel: At 23rd, in Mission district.
Map Ref: Map 16b, page 212, #20.
Credit Cards: Yes
Owner: Kate Rosenberger
Year Estab: 1993
Comments: The name of the shop doesn't quite do the books justice as the books are a bit better than "dog eared." Indeed, some of the items are almost in near to new condition. There are at least an equal number of books devoted to scholarly subjects as to fiction and popular culture although most of the titles are of fairly recent vintage. We saw little that could be classified as rare or collectible.

Drama Books   Open Shop
134 9th Street 94103   Fax: (415) 255-0605 (415) 255-0604

Collection: Specialty used and new (mostly hardcover) and ephemera.
Specialties: Film; theater; dance; musical comedy; writing; design; costume design; plays; acting criticism; biography.
Hours: Mon-Sat 10-5. (See Comments)
Services: Accepts want lists, mail order.
Travel: Civic Center exit off Hwy 101 or I-80.
Credit Cards: Yes
Owner: Andrew DeShore
Year Estab: 1975
Comments: Stock is approximately 55% used. Ephemera can be viewed by appointment.

(San Francisco)

871 Fine Arts Gallery and Bookstore
49 Geary Street, Ste. 513 94108

Open Shop
(415) 543-5812 (415) 543-5155
Fax: (415) 398-9388

Collection:	Specialty used and new.
Specialties:	Art; photography; exhibition catalogs; artist's books.
# of Vols:	8,000
Hours:	Tue-Sat 10:30-5:30.
Services:	Appraisals, lists; search service, accepts want lists, mail order.
Travel:	Between Grant and Kearney.
Credit Cards:	Yes
Owner:	Adrienne Fish
Year Estab:	1986
Comments:	Stock is approximately 75% used.

Elsewhere Books
260 Judah Street 94122

Open Shop
(415) 661-2535

Collection:	Specialty hardcover and paperback.
Specialties:	Mystery; science fiction; horror; fantasy.
# of Vols:	20,000
Hours:	Wed, Fri, Sat 10:30-6. Thu 12-7. Sun 12-5.
Services:	Subject catalogs, accepts want lists, appraisals.
Travel:	In Inner Sunset neighborhood, at corner of Judah and 8th Ave.
Credit Cards:	No
Owner:	Amy Beasom
Year Estab:	1978
Comments:	If, like ourselves, you're addicted to older mysteries and/or fantasy, you should either visit this shop if you're in San Francisco or write to the owner and request a catalog. Unlike so many other shops that specialize in these fields, this establishment really concentrates on vintage material and the selection on hand when we visited was truly mouth watering — but again, only if your tastes are for vintage materials and not the latest whodunit. The shop is strong in hardcover volumes, paperbacks and pulps.

Fantasy Etc.
808 Larkin Street 94109

Open Shop
(415) 441-7617

Collection:	Specialty. Mostly new and some used.
Specialties:	Science fiction; fantasy; horror; mystery; detective; adventure.
Hours:	Mon-Sat 12-7. Sun 12-6.
Services:	Accepts want lists, mail order.
Travel:	Near the Civic Center District.
Owner:	Charlie Cockey
Year Estab:	1976

Fields Book Store
1419 Polk Street 94109

Open Shop
(415) 673-2027

Collection: Specialty. Primarily new and some used.
Specialties: Metaphysics; occult; eastern philosophy.
Hours: Tue-Sat 11-6.

Forest Books
3080 16th Street 94103

Open Shop
(415) 863-2755

Collection: General stock of hardcover and paperback.
Specialties: Eastern art, religion, culture.
# of Vols: 20,000
Hours: Daily 11-9.
Services: Appraisals, catalog, accepts want lists.
Travel: In Mission district at Valencia.
Map Ref: Map 16b, page 212, #21.
Credit Cards: Yes
Owner: Gregory A. Wood
Year Estab: 1989
Comments: A roomy shop with mostly newer titles. The shelves were well organized, the shop easy to browse and the owner reader friendly. If you're looking for rare or esoteric books, this may not be the place to find them.

Forever After Books
1475 Haight Street 94117

Open Shop
(415) 431-8299

Collection: General stock of hardcover and paperback.
# of Vols: 30,000+
Hours: Mon-Sat 10:30-9:30. Sun 11-9:30. Hours are approximate.
Travel: In Haight Ashbury district between Ashbury and Masonic.
Map Ref: Map 16, page 212, #22.
Credit Cards: Yes
Year Estab: 1985
Comments: We saw more interesting titles here than elsewhere on the same street and had we not been limited by a tight schedule we could have spent a bit more time browsing here. The number of volumes was substantial and the shelves so crammed full that in some cases books were placed in front of books. If you're not intimidated by the Haight Ashbury flavor, you could enjoy a visit here.

Globus Slavic Bookstore
332 Balboa 94118

Open Shop
(415) 668-4723

Collection: Specialty new and used.
Specialties: Russian language books; Slavic language books in English translation.
Hours: Tue-Sat 12-5. Other times by appointment.
Services: Catalog
Travel: In Richmond district between 4th & 5th Avenues.
Comments: Stock is approximately 40% used.

(San Francisco)

Thomas A. Goldwasser Rare Books
126 Post Street, Ste 407 94108

Open Shop
(415) 981-4100

Collection:	Specialty
Specialties:	English, American and continental literature; first editions; illustrated; fine bindings.
# of Vols:	6,000
Hours:	Mon-Fri 10-5:30. Sat 11-4.
Services:	Appraisals, catalog.
Travel:	Between Grant and Kearney.
Map Ref:	Map 16a, page 212, #38.
Credit Cards:	Yes
Year Estab:	1990
Comments:	Located on the 4th floor of an office building, this establishment offers a modest sized collection of volumes in the rare and/or collectible category (both fiction and non fiction). If you're interested in a particular title and/or author, our advice is to phone ahead to determine if the item is in stock as browsing here may not be the best way of spending your valuable book hunting time.

Goldwasser & Wilkinson Books
486 Geary Street 94102

Open Shop
(415) 292-4698

Collection:	General stock.
Specialties:	First editions; art; fine press; California; the West; travel; wine and food; photography.
# of Vols:	3,000-5,000
Hours:	Mon-Thu 10-6. Fri 10-7. Sat & Sun 10-6.
Travel:	Between Taylor and Mason.
Map Ref:	Map 16a, page 212, #23.
Credit Cards:	Yes
Owner:	Thomas A. Goldwasser & Rick Wilkinson
Comments:	A relatively small shop with an interesting mix of books that ran the gamut from rare quality items in a number of areas to limited editions to more frequently viewed titles. This is a shop where you can spend as much or as little as your wallet can afford and still leave with an item worth having.

Green Apple Books
506 Clement 94118

Open Shop
(415) 387-2272

Collection:	General stock of used and new hardcover and paperback.
# of Vols:	150,000+ (used)
Hours:	Sun-Thu 9:30am-11pm. Fri & Sat 9:30am-midnight.
Services:	Mail order.
Travel:	In Richmond district between 6th & 7th Avenues.
Map Ref:	Map 16, page 212, #24.
Credit Cards:	Yes
Owner:	Richard Savoy

Year Estab: 1967
Comments: A large bi-level shop, plus mezzanine. While most of the books appeared to be of recent vintage, the selection was large enough and varied enough to make the shop worth a visit for all but the most sober antiquarian. We would include this shop on our list of "places to see while in San Francisco."

David Hecht Antiquarian Books
115 Gates Street 94110

By Appointment
(415) 826-4274

Collection: General stock.
Specialties: Early printed books; Americana; voyages; travel; pamphlets and manuscripts.
Services: Accepts want lists, mail order, subject lists.
Credit Cards: No
Year Estab: 1982

Richard Hilkert, Bookseller
333 Hayes Street 94102

Open Shop
Fax: (415) 863-7780 (415) 863-3339

Collection: Specialty. Primarily new and some used and ephemera.
Specialties: Interior design; architecture.
# of Vols: 8,000-10,000
Hours: Mon-Fri 9-5. Sat 11-5. Occasional Sun. Evenings by appointment.
Services: Occasional catalog, informal search service, accepts want lists, mail order.
Travel: In Civic Center area, between Franklin and Gough.
Credit Cards: Yes
Year Estab: 1981

Limelight Bookstore
1803 Market Street 94103

Open Shop
(415) 864-2265

Collection: Specialty. Mostly new and ephemera.
Specialties: Film; theater; television.
# of Vols: 20,000
Hours: Mon-Sat 10-6. Sun 12-5.
Services: Search service, accepts want lists, mail order.
Credit Cards: Yes
Owner: Roy A. Johnson
Year Estab: 197

Lodestar Books
313 Noe 94114

Open Shop
(415) 864-3746

Collection: Specialty. Mostly new.
Specialties: Metaphysics
Hours: Daily 12-10, except Fri & Sat till midnight.

The Magazine
920 Larkin Street 94109

Open Shop
(415) 441-7737

Collection: Specialty
Specialties: Magazines (1900 to present).

(San Francisco)

Hours:	Mon-Sat 12-7.
Services:	Accepts want lists, mail order.
Travel:	In downtown, approximately six blocks west of Union Square.
Credit Cards:	Yes
Owner:	Trent Dunphy
Year Estab:	1973

Manzanita Books & Records **Open Shop**
3686 20th Street 94110 (415) 648-0957

Collection:	General stock of hardcover and paperback.
# of Vols:	10,000
Hours:	Daily 12-9.
Travel:	In Mission district between Valencia and Guerrero.
Map Ref:	Map 16b, page 212, #25.
Credit Cards:	No
Owner:	Wayne Holder
Year Estab:	1988
Comments:	A small shop with the owner taking advantage of almost every square inch of space (a large mirror behind the cashier gives one the impression of an even roomier shop). The books had clearly been selected with care and the shelves were well organized. We spotted some very interesting titles and had we been able to find a parking spot nearby we would have stayed longer.

McDonald's Bookshop **Open Shop**
48 Turk Street 94102 (415) 673-2235

Collection:	General stock of hardcover and paperback and magazines.
Specialties:	Magazines.
# of Vols:	1 million+
Hours:	Mon, Tue, Thu 10-6. Wed, Fri, Sat 10:30-6:45.
Travel:	One half block off Market between Mason & Taylor.
Map Ref:	Map 16a, page 212, #26.
Year Estab:	1926
Comments:	After viewing the owner's sidewalk sign: "A Dirty, Poorly Lit Place For Books" (which we later learned was inspired by the contrasting name of a "new" bookshop) and noting an adult movie house several feet away from the shop (as well as the general ambience of the neighborhood), we must confess that our stop here consisted of parking in front of the shop and viewing lots and lots of paperbacks through the open front door. If any of our readers exercise greater courage or curiosity by visiting, we sincerely hope they will write to us and provide us with a more accurate description of what this shop has to offer so that we can add the information in a future Supplement.

Meyer Boswell Books

2141 Mission Street, 3rd Fl. 94110

Open Shop

Fax: (415) 255-6499   (415) 255-6400

Collection:	Specialty
Specialties:	Law and legal history.
# of Vols:	6,000
Hours:	Mon-Fri 9-5.
Services:	Catalog
Travel:	In Mission district between 17th & 18th Streets. Ring bell for admittance.
Credit Cards:	Yes
Owner:	Jordan D. Luttrell
Year Estab:	1976

9th Avenue Books

1348 9th Avenue 94122

Open Shop

(415) 665-2938

Collection:	General stock of used and new hardcover and paperback.
# of Vols:	15,000+ (used)
Hours:	Sun-Thu 10-9. Fri & Sat 10-10.
Travel:	In Inner Sunset district, between Irving & Judah.
Map Ref:	Map 16, page 212, #27.
Credit Cards:	Yes
Owner:	Richard Savoy
Year Estab:	1986
Comments:	A large shop with lots if display space. We assume the shop is popular in the community as it was crowded when we visited. Most of the books we saw were of relatively recent vintage but the selection was large enough for a serious collector (unless you're interests are of a more narrow scholarly nature) to find browsing worth the stop.

Jeremy Norman & Co.

720 Market Street, 3rd Fl. 94102

Open Shop

(415) 781-6402

Collection:	Specialty
Specialties:	Medicine; science; natural history; technology.
# of Vols:	10,000
Hours:	Mon-Fri 9:30-5:30.
Services:	Appraisals, catalog, accepts want lists.
Travel:	Between 3rd & 4th Streets.
Credit Cards:	Yes
Year Estab:	1970

Phoenix Books and Music

3850 24th Street 94114

Open Shop

(415) 821-3477

Collection:	General stock of new and primarily paperback used.
Hours:	Daily 10-10

Red House Books

PO Box 460267 94146

By Appointment

(415) 282-8933

Collection:	Specialty

(San Francisco)

Specialties:	Beat generation; 1960's; modern literature.
# of Vols:	5,000-10,000
Services:	Appraisals, catalog, search service, accepts want lists.
Credit Cards:	No
Owner:	Andrew Stafford
Year Estab:	1985

Russian Hill Bookstore
2234 Polk Street 94109

Open Shop
(415) 929-0997

Collection:	General stock of mostly used hardcover and paperback.
Specialties:	Art; history.
# of Vols:	30,000
Hours:	Daily 10-10.
Services:	Accepts want lists, mail order.
Travel:	Two blocks north of Broadway tunnel and one block east of Van Ness Ave, between Vallejo and Green.
Map Ref:	Map 16a, page 212, #29.
Credit Cards:	Yes
Owner:	Richard & Carol Martucci
Year Estab:	1993
Comments:	A much easier shop to browse than the owner's other location (see Sunset Bookstore below), perhaps because of the way the books are shelved or perhaps because there are fewer space restrictions. The books on hand were similar to the other location: we noted some Franklin Mints and Easton leather bindings, some older titles and a large assortment of "neat" books in many subject areas.

Saint Adrian Company
1334 Haight Street 94117

Open Shop
(415) 255-1490

Collection:	General stock of paperback and hardcover.
Specialties:	Counter culture; beat generation; poetry; magazines (1950's-1960's).
Hours:	Mon-Sat 11-7. Sun 12-about 6.
Services:	Accepts want lists, mail order.
Travel:	Located in Haight Ashbury district, between Masonic and Central.
Map Ref:	Map 16, page 212, #30.
Year Estab:	1988
Comments:	Stock is approximately 70% paperback.

San Francisco Mystery Bookstore
746 Diamond 94114

Open Shop
(415) 282-7444

Collection:	Specialty new and used paperback and hardcover.
Specialties:	Mystery
# of Vols:	10,000
Hours:	Wed-Sun 11:30-5:30.

Services:	Appraisals, catalog, search service, accepts want lists.
Travel:	In Noe Valley district at corner of 24th Street.
Credit Cards:	Yes
Owner:	Bruce Taylor
Year Estab:	1977
Comments:	Stock is approximately 50% used, 25% of which is hardcover.

John Scopazzi Gallery   **Open Shop**
130 Maiden Lane 94108   (415) 362-5708

Collection:	Specialty
Specialties:	Literature; fine printing; illustrated; antique maps and prints.
Hours:	Mon-Fri 10-5. Sat 10-4.
Travel:	Between Stockton and Grant. Shop is located on mezzanine. For elevator, use entrance at 233 Post St.
Credit Cards:	Yes
Owner:	Jill Scopazzi
Year Estab:	1955

Kenneth Starosciak   **By Appointment**
117 Wilmot Mews 94115   (415) 346-0650

Collection:	Specialty
Specialties:	Architecture; American art; modern European art; decorative arts; textiles.
Services:	Appraisals, search service, catalog, accepts want lists.
Credit Cards:	No
Year Estab:	1972

William Stout, Books   **Open Shop**
804 Montgomery 94133   (415) 391-6757

Collection:	Specialty new and out-of-print.
Specialties:	Architecture; design; landscape architecture.
Hours:	Mon-Sat 10-5:30.
Services:	Catalog, appraisals.
Travel:	At Jackson.
Credit Cards:	Yes
Year Estab:	1975

Sunset Bookstore   **Open Shop**
2161 Irving Street 94122   (415) 664-3644

Collection:	General stock of hardcover and paperback and sheet music.
Specialties:	Art
# of Vols:	50,000
Hours:	Daily 9-9.
Travel:	In Sunset district, between 22nd & 23rd Ave.
Map Ref:	Map 16, page 212, #31.
Credit Cards:	Yes
Owner:	Richard & Carol Martucci
Year Estab:	1974

(San Francisco)

Comments: A tightly packed shop with narrow aisles, high shelves and interesting titles. We noted several shelves of books dealing with crafts, e.g., knitting, sewing, crocheting. The owners have a second shop with a similar stock. (See Russian Hill Bookstore above).

Tall Stories **Open Shop**
2141 Mission, #301 94110 (415) 255-1915

Collection: General stock.
Specialties: Modern first editions; science fiction; mystery; military; aviation; theater; illustrated; children's.
# of Vols: 30,000
Hours: Mon-Sat 11-6.
Travel: In Mission district between 17th & 18th St. Ring the buzzer for entry into the lobby.
Services: Catalog
Map Ref: Map 16b, page 212, #32.
Credit Cards: Yes
Owner: Donna Rankin
Year Estab: 1991
Comments: See Comments under Bolerium Books above. It's unfortunate that a group shop of this caliber could not be located on another street in the Mission District where more book buyers would feel more comfortable. Susan was impressed with this shop: the collection was interesting, the shop easy to browse (with comfortable chairs) and the owner most gracious. Unless you suffer from the "suburban syndrome," this is a shop you'll want to visit.

Jeffrey Thomas, Fine & Rare Books **Open Shop**
49 Geary, #230 94108 Fax: (415) 956-2738 (415) 956-3272

Collection: General stock.
Specialties: Americana; first editions; illustrated; travel; fine press.
# of Vols: 10,000
Hours: Mon-Fri 9-5.
Services: Appraisals, occasional catalog, accepts want lists, mail order.
Travel: Between Grant and Kearney.
Map Ref: Map 16a, page 212, #33.
Credit Cards: Yes
Year Estab: 1981

West Portal Books **Open Shop**
111 West Portal Avenue 94127 (415) 731-5291

Collection: General stock of hardcover and paperback.
Specialties: True crime; biography; modern first editions; illustrated; art; comics (1960's and earlier); *Mad Magazine* collectibles; San Francisco.
# of Vols: 30,000
Hours: Mon-Sat 10-7. Sun 12-6.

Services:	Accepts want lists, mail order.
Travel:	From Hwy 1 (19th Ave): Turn east on Sloat Blvd, then left at West Portal Ave. From downtown: Continue west on Market St (which becomes Portola Dr) to 14th Ave. Right on 14th to West Portal.
Map Ref:	Map 16, page 212, #34.
Credit Cards:	Yes
Owner:	Jeffrey & Diane Goodman
Year Estab:	1992
Comments:	A bi-level shop with books of mixed condition and vintage. Lots of subjects covered but not many in depth. Notwithstanding the above, we saw several unusual titles that could be considered collectibles. Worth a visit.

John Windle Antiquarian Bookseller
Open Shop
49 Geary Street, Ste. 233 94108   Fax: (415) 986-5827   (415) 986-5826

Collection:	Specialty
Specialties:	Antiquarian (15th-19th centuries); fine printing; illustrated.
Hours:	Mon-Fri 10-5:30. Sat 10-4.
Services:	Catalog, appraisals, accepts want lists.
Map Ref:	Map 16a, page 212, #37.
Credit Cards:	No
Year Estab:	1975
Comments:	This is a shop for the serious collector with a healthy pocketbook; not the casual browser. You would probably get a far more accurate sense of the type of books sold here by requesting a copy of the dealer's catalog.

Alan Wofsy Fine Arts
Open Shop
1109 Geary Boulevard 94109   (415) 292-6500

Collection:	Specialty used and some new.
Specialties:	Art; architecture; prints.
# of Vols:	5,000
Hours:	Mon-Fri 10-5.
Services:	Catalog, appraisals.
Travel:	Between Franklin and Van Ness.
Credit Cards:	Yes
Year Estab:	1969

Writer's Bookstore
Open Shop
2848 Webster 94123   (415) 921-2620

Collection:	General stock of new and used hardcover and paperback.
Hours:	Daily 11-6.
Travel:	Between Green and Union in Marina/Pacific Hts district.
Map Ref:	Map 16, page 212, #35.
Credit Cards:	Yes
Owner:	John Capman
Year Estab:	1969
Comments:	The stock is evenly divided between new and used, hardcover and paperback.

Zeno's
1935 Ocean Avenue 94127

Open Shop
(415) 585-5309

Collection: General stock of hardcover and paperback.
Specialties: World literature.
# of Vols: 50,000
Hours: Tue-Fri 12-6. Sat 10-6. Sun 12-5.
Services: Catalog, accepts want lists.
Travel: In Ingleside neighborhood between City College and San Francisco State, or between Keystone and Fairfield Way.
Map Ref: Map 16, page 212, #36.
Credit Cards: No
Owner: Robert Rosenberg
Year Estab: 1992

San Jose
(Map 17, page 154)

Best Friends Books
180 West San Carlos 95113

Open Shop
(408) 275-1515

Collection:
Hours: Tue & Wed 1-8. Thu & Fri 1-4:30. Sat 10-4:30.
Travel: Bird exit off I-280. North on Bird, right on San Carlos to public library.
Comments: Operated by Friends of the Library.

Susan J. Klein, Bookseller
4431 Calle De Farrar 95118

By Appointment
Fax: (408) 265-1528 (408) 978-5497

Collection: Specialty
Specialties: 20th century literature in first editions.
# of Vols: 3,000
Services: Appraisals, catalog, accepts want lists.
Credit Cards: Yes
Owner: Susan J. Klein & William F. Ahearn
Year Estab: 1992

Lincoln Avenue Books
2194 Lincoln Avenue 95125

Open Shop
(408) 448-0373

Collection: General stock of hardcover and paperback and ephemera.
Specialties: History of costumes; textiles; local history; children's.
# of Vols: 25,000
Hours: Tue-Sat 11-6.
Services: Appraisals, accepts want lists, mail order.
Travel: Hwy 87 south exit off I-280. Proceed on Hwy 87 to Curtner. Right on Curtner then right on Lincoln.
Year Estab: 1977
Comments: A neat shop that has as many paperbacks (or perhaps a bit more) as hardcover volumes, with the latter books for the most part being in good

condition and displaying interesting titles. The shelves are easy to browse and we were able to find several items (in different categories) of sufficient interest to cause us to part with some dollars. We wish our readers the same good fortune.

Memorabilia of San Jose   Open Shop
250 West St. John Street 95110   Fax: (408) 292-0417 (408) 298-5711

Collection: Specialty books and ephemera.
Specialties: San Jose; Western Americana.
# of Vols: 600
Hours: Mon-Fri 9-4. Sat and evenings by appointment.
Services: Appraisals, catalog, accepts want lists.
Travel: In downtown, just off Hwy 87.
Credit Cards: No
Owner: Leonard McKay
Year Estab: 1986
Comments: Research facilities are available in the owner's private library.

Recycle Bookstore   Open Shop
138 East Santa Clara Street 95113   (408) 286-6279

Collection: General stock of mostly paperback.
Hours: Mon 10-6. Tue-Thu 10-9. Fri & Sat 10-7. Sun 12-6.

Woodruff & Thrush Twice Read Books   Open Shop
81 East San Fernando 95113   (408) 294-3768

Collection: General stock of hardcover, paperbacks and magazines.
# of Vols: 1,000,000+
Hours: Mon-Fri 11:30-5:30. Sat 11:30-4:30.
Travel: Virginia St exit off I-280 southbound. Follow signs for Hwy 82. Proceed three blocks. Right on 3rd St. Left on San Fernando.
Credit Cards: Yes
Year Estab: 1928
Comments: I was looking forward to visiting this shop. What book person wouldn't want to browse through a shop that claimed to have a million or so volumes? When I arrived at 5:05 (while the other member of our team scouted out a parking spot) and saw a sign confirming that the shop was open till 5:30, I was relieved that I would still have time to see what the shop held in store for the typical bookaholic. Upon entering, the owner asked me if I had any questions. After introducing myself and indicating why I wanted to "look around," the owner's response was that he was getting ready to close, had just "neatened up" and could not allow anyone into the shop. When I indicated that I would do my best to be brief and unobtrusive and that the visit was designed to provide our readers with some insight as to what to expect should they decide to visit here, the owner expressed his impatience, again saying he was closing and didn't care what we told our readers. Following this experience, we can only say that if you desire to visit this shop, we hope you have a more pleasant experience than we did.

San Leandro
(Map 17, page 154)

Book Market **Open Shop**
1786 East 14th Street 94577 (510) 357-8915

Collection: General stock of paperback and hardcover.
# of Vols: 35,000
Hours: Mon-Fri 10-6. Sat 10-5.
Travel: Davis St exit off I-880. Proceed east on Davis then right on East 14th St.
Credit Cards: No
Owner: Will & Agnes Jacobs
Year Estab: 1992
Comments: A neighborhood shop with hardcover volumes of mostly recent vintage and in generally good condition. Few items that we would view as truly rare or collectible.

Byron's Magic Books **By Appointment**
PO Box 3186 94578 (510) 276-1854

Collection: Specialty. Mostly used and some new.
Specialties: Magic; ventriloquism; juggling; automata; gambling.
Services: Appraisals, catalog, accepts want lists.
Credit Cards: No
Owner: Byron Walker
Year Estab: 1975

East Bay Book Co. **Open Shop**
1555 Washington 94577 Fax: (510) 357-1337 (510) 483-3990

Collection: General stock of new and used paperback and hardcover.
# of Vols: 75,000 (used)
Hours: Mon-Fri 9-8. Sat 10-5. Sun 11-5.
Services: Mail order, search service, accepts want lists.
Travel: Marina exit off I-880. Proceed east on Marina to end. Left on Washington.
Credit Cards: Yes
Owner: Barbara Keenan
Year Estab: 1984
Comments: Used stock is about evenly divided between hardcover and paperback.

Roskie & Wallace Bookstore **Open Shop**
14595 East 14th Street 94578 (510) 483-4163

Collection: General stock of primarily used paperback and hardcover.
# of Vols: 500,000+
Hours: Tue-Sat 10-6.
Travel: 150th Ave exit off I-580. Proceed south on 150th then right on East 14th.
Credit Cards: Yes
Owner: George von Glahn
Year Estab: 1930's

Open Shops and By Appointment Dealers

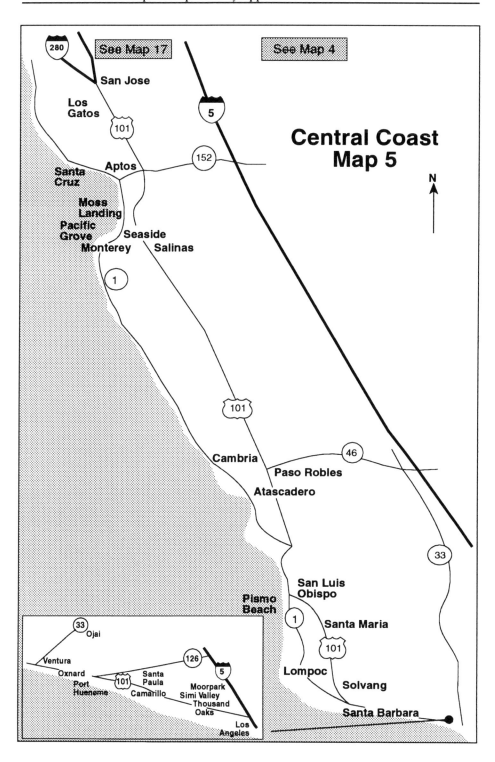

Central Coast Map 5

Comments: You have to see it to believe it: as we approached the entrance of this multi room warehouse-like building, we saw several United States Postal Service sorting bins each filled with books being offered at bargain prices and several customers bending over the bins in search of some treasure. Once you begin your tour of this huge establishment, don't expect to find books in pristine condition. What you'll see, if you're willing to walk from room to room, will be books and titles that are available, albeit in lesser quantity (and probably at higher prices), at other book dealers. In summary, what is available here is volume. But, if you're patient and careful in the selections you make, you may be able to find some quality items at reasonable prices.

San Luis Obispo
(Map 5, page 235)

Leon's Bookstore **Open Shop**
659 Higuera Street 93401 (805) 543-5039

Collection:	General stock of hardcover and paperback.
# of Vols:	150,000
Hours:	Mon-Sat 9:30-9. Sun 10-5.
Services:	Search service, accepts want lists.
Travel:	Marsh St exit off Hwy 101. North on Marsh, left on Broad. Left on Higuera.
Credit Cards:	Yes
Owner:	Rick & Cathy Wiegers
Year Estab:	1969
Comments:	A most pleasant surprise. This establishment is in reality two shops separated from one another but immediately adjacent to each other. While the shop on the right is primarily paperback with some hardcover items and a concentration on popular fiction, the shop on the left could hold rich treasures for patient browsers. The books here are well organized and include a healthy mix between vintage and newer titles. The majority of the books are in good condition and the prices are quite reasonable. This is a deep shop with enough long aisles and high shelves (ladders and stools provided) to make your search a real pleasure.

Phoenix Bookstore **Open Shop**
990 Monterey Street 93401 Fax: (805) 543-7432 (805) 543-5171

Collection:	General stock of mostly used hardcover and paperback.
Specialties:	Political science; architecture; photography; homosexuality; art; literature; history; science.
# of Vols:	25,000
Hours:	Sun-Wed 10-9. Thu-Sat 10-10.
Services:	Appraisals
Travel:	From Hwy 101 north: Osos St exit, then right on Monterey St. From Hwy 101 south: Santa Rosa St exit, then left on Santa Rosa and right on Monterey.
Credit Cards:	Yes
Owner:	Bruce Miller
Year Estab:	1981

Comments: A bi-level shop with a good sized collection in the areas listed above as specialties. Some of the selections we saw on the literature shelves were items not ordinarily found in larger stores. But even if you're a general book person whose interests may go beyond those specialties you should still find a visit to this stop enjoyable. With another fine book store in town, we think you can't go wrong by visiting both.

San Marcos

Cassidy's Bargain Bookshelf   **Open Shop**
339 Rancho Santa Fe 92069   (619) 471-9111

Collection: General stock of mostly paperback.
Hours: Mon-Sat 9:30-5:30.

San Mateo
(Map 17, page 154)

Books Unlimited   **Open Shop**
22 East 25th Avenue 94403   (415) 574-5377

Collection: General stock of mostly used paperback and hardcover.
# of Vols: 75,000
Hours: Tue-Sat 10-5.
Travel: South El Camino Real exit off Hwy 92. Proceed south on El Camino Real then east on 25th Ave. Parking available in rear.
Credit Cards: Yes
Owner: Hollie Ransdell
Year Estab: 1983
Comments: On the day of our visit, the shop had apparently acquired several thousand new volumes (mostly paperback) which the owner had not yet had an opportunity to sort and shelve. This created some traffic problems in the aisles that were already rather narrow. Clearly, the owner is trying to display as many books as possible in a shop that has limited space. Hence, the appropriateness of the recycled traffic sign: "One Lane-No Passing." While the vast majority of the books on view were paperback, the shop does carry hardcover volumes in most subjects, if not in great depth. We also spotted some older volumes which would certainly fit the category of rare and/or collectible, although the number of such items was limited. Our sense is that most the shop's regular customers are interested in reading copies of popular fiction but that the shop does make an effort to accommodate the more serious reader.

Grapevine Books   **By Appointment**
PO Box 1134 94403   (415) 341-7009

Collection: General stock.
Specialties: Children's; Americana; cookbooks; fiction.
# of Vols: 6,000
Hours: (Please phone between 9-5, Mon-Fri.)

Services: Search service, accepts want lists, mail order.
Credit Cards: No
Owner: Sharalyn Spiteri
Year Estab: 1972

San Pedro
(Map 10, page 253)

Southwest Instrument Co.   **Open Shop**
235 West 7th Street 90731   * (310) 519-7800

Collection: Specialty new and used.
Specialties: Nautical
Hours: Mon-Fri 9-5. Sat 9-12.
Services: Appraisals, mail order.
Travel: South on 110 Fwy to end. Continue south on Gaffey to 7th St. Left on 7th.
Credit Cards: Yes
Owner: Norbert Cupp & Steven Moisen
Year Estab: 1926
Comments: Stock is approximately 30% used.

Vinegar Hill Books   **Open Shop**
381 West 6th Street 90731   Fax: (310) 548-0332 * (310) 548-0332

Collection: General stock of hardcover and paperback.
# of Vols: 20,000
Hours: Mon-Sat 10-6. Sun by appointment.
Services: Search service, accepts want lists, mail order, book binding and repair.
Travel: From Hwy 110 southbound: Harbor Blvd exit. Bear right on exit ramp. Right on Harbor and proceed to 6th St. Right on 6th.
Credit Cards: Yes
Owner: Andrea Kowalski
Year Estab: 1993
Comments: A neat little shop that's easy to browse. Small in size but not necessarily in quality. Far more hardcovers than paperbacks. Reasonably priced.

San Rafael
(Map 17, page 154)

Afterwords   **Open Shop**
1321 4th Street 94901   (415) 453-1888

Collection: General stock.
Specialties: Art
# of Vols: 10,000-12,000
Hours: Tue, Wed, Sat 9-6. Thu & Fri 9-9. Sun 12-5.
Services: Search service, accepts want lists.
Travel: See Books Revisited below. Shop is between C & D.
Credit Cards: Yes
Owner: Kathleen May
Year Estab: 1995

* *Some 310 codes change to 562 in 1996*

Comments:	We were most fortunate to find the owner in (and preparing coffee) a half hour before the normal Sunday opening time. A visit to this shop was an upbeat experience and we think the shop would meet any experts' judgment of a truly quality book store. Though the size of its collection was modest, we failed to notice a single volume that was not in prime condition. In addition to seeing plenty of hardcover dust jacketed recent volumes, glass cases held a number of older, rare and collectible items. One exceptionally bound large volume particularly caught our eye as did several other "non run of the mill" leather bindings. If you're in San Rafael, stop by, have a cup of coffee and enjoy the great books.

Carl Blomgren-Fine Books   **By Appointment**
PO Box 3597 94912   Fax: (415) 453-1085 (415) 456-1471

Collection:	General stock, posters and prints.
Specialties:	Art; architecture; photography.
Services:	Accepts want lists, mail order.

Books Revisited   **Open Shop**
1122 Fourth Street 94901   Fax: (415) 459-7634 (415) 459-5788

Collection:	General stock of mostly used paperback and hardcover.
Specialties:	Signed first editions; proofs; signed.
# of Vols:	200,000
Hours:	Mon-Thu 7am-10pm. Fri-Sun 7am-midnight.
Services:	Search service, accepts want lists, catalog.
Travel:	Central Rafael exit off Hwy 101. West on Fourth. Shop is between A & B.
Credit Cards:	Yes
Owner:	Byron J. Spooner, President
Year Estab:	1982
Comments:	The good news is that this bi-level combination book store/coffee house actually has a substantial collection of both hardcover and paperback books (with an emphasis on paperback) although not quite as many as the number suggested above. (As there is plenty of room for expansion, there could be that many books on display when you visit.) In looking at the titles more closely, we noted what we believe to be a tendency to price items slightly higher than we have seen elsewhere. Perhaps this is a reflection of the upscale nature of the community and the tourist trade it serves? While the books were in both mixed condition and of mixed vintage, the majority of them were a bit more recent. The shop hosts live music on the weekends as well as readings and other literary events.

Ursula C. Davidson Books   **By Appointment**
134 Linden Lane 94901   Fax: (415) 454-1087 (415) 454-3939

Collection:	Specialty
Specialties:	19th & 20th century children's; illustrated.
Services:	Appraisals, search service, catalog, accepts want lists.
Credit Cards:	Yes
Year Estab:	1982

(San Rafael)

Comments:	Also displays at A Clean Well Lighted Place For Books, 2417 Larkspur Landing in Larkspur (415-461-0171). Hours: Daily 10am-11pm, except till midnight on weekends.

Michael S. Hollander Rare Books   **By Appointment**
PO Box 2729 94912   (415) 459-4224

Collection:	General stock.
Specialties:	Travel; Asia; fine press; art.
# of Vols:	2,000
Services:	Appraisals, catalog, accepts want lists.
Credit Cards:	No
Year Estab:	1971

Mandrake Bookshop   **Open Shop**
910 Lincoln 94901   (415) 453-3484

Collection:	General stock of mostly hardcover.
# of Vols:	80,000
Hours:	Mon 10-6. Tue-Sat 10-9. Sun 11-5.
Travel:	See Books Revisited above. Right on Lincoln.
Owner:	Harold Bertram
Year Estab:	1960's
Comments:	Off the main street that houses most of this town's other used book shops but well worth going the few blocks out of your way for. While this shop has its share of special leather bindings, we liked it particularly because it has an extensive collection of vintage items as well as newer fiction and non fiction. Scholarly books are also on hand as are books in the areas of popular culture. If you're an old style book person, plan to spend a bit more time here as the shelves are worthy of the browsing time you'll require. You'll also find several bargains.

The Odyssey Bookshop   **Open Shop**
1109 Fourth Street 94901   (415) 453-8701

Collection:	General stock of hardcover and paperback.
Specialties:	Literature; performing arts; art; travel; history; natural history; philosophy.
# of Vols:	35,000
Hours:	Mon-Sat 10-6. Sun 11-4.
Services:	Appraisals, catalog, accepts want lists.
Travel:	See Books Revisited above. Shop is between A and B Streets.
Credit Cards:	Yes
Owner:	Peter McMillan
Year Estab:	1991
Comments:	This shop had recently doubled in size at the time of our visit and the owner has clearly used his additional space wisely with one small room devoted to paperbacks and the entire balance of the shop (two good sized rooms and a connecting corridor) devoted to a well balanced selection of hardcover

volumes in almost every category. This is one of San Rafael's better book shops and one that you should not miss, even if your time in this community is limited.

Open Secret Bookstore   **Open Shop**
923 C Street 94901   Fax: (415) 457-4193 (415) 457-4191

Collection: Specialty. Mostly new. Mostly paperback.
Specialties: Spirituality; humanities; metaphysics.
Hours: Mon-Sat 10-9. Sun 12-5.
Year Estab: 1981
Comments: The owners maintain a resource library with rare and out of print titles.

West Wind Books   **Open Shop**
1006 Tamalpais Avenue 94901   (415) 456-6322

Collection: General stock of hardcover and paperback.
# of Vols: 17,500
Hours: Mon-Sat 11-6.
Travel: See Books Revisited above. Right on Tamalpais (before railroad tracks).
Credit Cards: No
Owner: Barbara A. Lee
Year Estab: 1986
Comments: Unfortunately, this shop is not open on Sundays, the day our itinerary brought us to San Rafael.

Western Sport Shop   **Open Shop**
902 Third Street 94901   Fax: (415) 456-2577 (415) 456-5454

Collection: Specialty used and new.
Specialties: Hunting; fishing; guns; nature; cookbooks (game).
Hours: Mon-Wed 9-6. Thu 9-8. Fri & Sat 6am-6pm. Sun 10-4.
Services: Appraisals, search service, accepts want lists, mail order.
Travel: See Books Revisited above. Turn west on Third St.
Credit Cards: Yes
Owner: James Edgar
Year Estab: 1947

San Ramon
(Map 17, page 154)

Bay Books   **Open Shop**
2415 San Ramon Boulevard 94583   (510) 855-1524

Collection: General stock of mostly used hardcover and paperback.
# of Vols: 50,000
Hours: Mon-Fri 10-8. Sat 10-7. Sun 11-5.
Services: Search service.
Travel: Crow Canyon exit off I-680. West on Crow Canyon. Left on San Ramon.
Credit Cards: Yes

Owner: Donna Davidson
Comments: Similar to the owner's other shop, Bay Books, in Concord. See above.

Santa Ana

Cornerstone Books By Appointment
PO Box 28224 92799 (714) 668-1718

Collection:	Specialty
Specialties:	Theology; biblical studies.
# of Vols:	15,000
Services:	Catalog, search service, accepts want lists.
Credit Cards:	No
Owner:	Phil Jackson
Year Estab:	1989

Encyclopedias Bought & Sold By Appointment
14071 Windsor Place 92705 Fax: (714) 731-5223 (714) 838-3643

Collection:	Specialty
Specialties:	Encyclopedias; classical literature.
Services:	Accepts want lists, mail order.
Credit Cards:	Yes
Owner:	Kathleen Italiane
Year Estab:	1965

Santa Barbara
(Map 5, page 235)

Again Books Open Shop
16A Helena Avenue 93101 (805) 966-9312

Collection:	General stock of hardcover and paperback.
Specialties:	Military; religion (Christian faith); children's; Santa Barbara.
# of Vols:	25,000
Hours:	Mon-Sat 1:30-9. Sun 4-9.
Travel:	Garden St exit off Hwy 101. Proceed south on Garden to beach. Right on Cabrillo Blvd, then right on Helena. Shop is about 1/2 block ahead.
Credit Cards:	No
Owner:	John M. Sloan
Year Estab:	1978
Comments:	A small, crowded shop. With the exception of the specialties listed above, the other books on display were quite limited in terms of depth. As the shop is located about 1/2 block from the beach, one might easily find some beach reading here. Most of the books were saw were older volumes.

Anacapa House By Appointment
1727 Anacapa Street 93101 (805) 682-6948

Collection:	Specialty
Specialties:	Modern first editions; women's literature.

# of Vols: 2,000
Services: Search Service, catalog, accepts want lists.
Credit Cards: No
Owner: Catherine Manset
Year Estab: 1992

Art Books Only   Open Shop
715 State Street   (805) 962-5893
Mailing Address: PO Box 30564 Santa Barbara 93130   Fax: (805) 966-0563

Collection: Specialty
Specialties: Fine art; artist monographs, decorative art; applied arts.
# of Vols: 10,000
Hours: Tue-Sun. Afternoons only.
Services: Catalog, accepts want lists.
Travel: Garden St exit off Hwy 101. Left on Ortega St. Continue to State.
Credit Cards: Yes
Owner: Jeffrey Akard
Year Estab: 1980

The Book Den   Open Shop
11 East Anapamu Street   (805) 962-3321
Mailing Address: PO Box 733 Santa Barbara 93102   Fax: (805) 965-2844
                                                                E-mail: ekelley@rain.org

Collection: General stock of hardcover and paperback.
Specialties: California; Santa Barbara; architecture, especially California, Spain and Mexico.
# of Vols: 40,000
Hours: Mon-Sat 10-9. Sun 12-5.
Services: Appraisals, search service, mail order, accepts want lists.
Travel: Garden St exit off Hwy 101. Proceed on Garden away from ocean. Left on Anapamu St. Shop is 2½ blocks ahead.
Credit Cards: Yes
Owner: Eric E. Kelley
Year Estab: 1902
Comments: A large, spacious and easy to browse shop that sells newspapers, popular magazines and some new books but which also carries a sizeable selection of used items. The books are, for the most part, in good condition and reasonably priced. There's a healthy balance between fiction and nonfiction, with a wide selection of reading copies in almost every subject area.

Drew's Books   By Appointment
PO Box 163 93101   (805) 682-3610

Collection: General stock.
# of Vols: 40,000
Owner: Warren & Mary Ann Drew

(Santa Barbara)

V.L.T. Gardner
625 East Victoria Street 93101

By Appointment
(805) 966-0246

Collection:	Specialty
Specialties:	Gardening; horticulture.
Owner:	Virginia Gardner

Johnson Books & Collectibles
At Hightower Galleries, 528 Brinkerhoff Avenue
Mailing Address: 14 McKevett Heights Santa Paula 93060

Antique Mall
Mall: (805) 965-5687
Home: (805) 525-8955

Collection:	General stock and specialty.
Specialties:	Technical (See Comments)
Hours:	Daily 10-5.
Travel:	Bath or Castillo exit off Hwy 101. North to Halley, then east to Brinkerhoff.
Owner:	Delton & Margaret Johnson
Year Estab:	1984
Comments:	Also displays at Country Antique Fair Mall in Saugus. Technical books are sold at the Radio Swapmeet held on the last Saturday of each month from 7am-11am at Aviation and Marine Blvd in Manhattan Beach.

Joseph the Provider/Books
10 West Micheltorena Street 93101

Open Shop
(805) 962-6862

Collection:	Specialty
Specialties:	Modern literary first editions.
# of Vols:	5,000
Hours:	Mon-Fri 10-5. Sat by appointment.
Services:	Appraisals, accepts want lists, catalog.
Travel:	Garden St exit off Hwy 101.
Credit Cards:	Yes
Owner:	Ralph Sipper & Lee Campbell
Year Estab:	1970

Lost Horizon Bookstore
703 Anacapa Street 93101

Open Shop
(805) 962-4606

Collection:	General stock.
Specialties:	Decorative arts; art; architecture; western Americana; California.
# of Vols:	9,000
Hours:	Mon-Sat 10-6. Sun 11-5.
Services:	Appraisals, search service, catalog, accepts want lists.
Travel:	Carrillo St exit off Hwy 101. Proceed toward downtown. Right on Anacapa.
Credit Cards:	Yes
Owner:	Jerry Jacobs & Angela Perko
Year Estab:	1983
Comments:	An attractive, easy to browse shop with quality items. The books are in quite good condition and the specialties listed above are well represented.

Maurice F. Neville Rare Books
PO Box 50509 93150

By Appointment
(805) 969-1563

Collection: Specialty
Specialties: Modern first editions; mystery and detective; bull fighting.
# of Vols: 8,000
Services: Accepts want lists, mail order.
Credit Cards: Yes
Year Estab: 1977

Paperback Alley
5840 Hollister Avenue 93117

Open Shop
(805) 967-1051

Collection: General stock of mostly paperback.
Hours: Mon-Sat 10:30-5. Sun 12-4.

Randall House
835 Laguna Street 93101

Open Shop
Fax: (805) 963-1650 (805) 963-1909

Collection: Specialty books, paintings and prints.
Specialties: Fine and rare books in all fields; autographs; original illustrations; paintings and prints of a literary or historical nature..
# of Vols: 5,000
Hours: Mon-Fri 9:30-5. Sat 10-2.
Services: Appraisals, catalog, accepts want lists.
Travel: Laguna/Garden St exit off Hwy 101. Turn away from ocean and proceed six blocks. Shop is at corner of Canon Perdido and Laguna. Parking is available up the driveway.
Credit Cards: Yes
Owner: Ronald R. Randall
Year Estab: 1975
Comments: We do not advise readers who are interested in more mundane subjects to attempt a visit to this shop which is located within a national historic landmark (an adobe house built in 1825) and which is adjacent to the owner's private residence. The collection consists of scholarly, truly rare and antiquarian items. If you have the means and are in the process of building a collection in almost any field, we believe that this dealer should be able to assist you in making your dream come true.

Sullivan Goss Books & Prints
7 East Anapamu Street 93101

Open Shop
Fax: (805) 730-1462 (805) 730-1460

Collection: Specialty. New and used books and original prints.
Specialties: Art; California; Western Americana; art of the print.
Hours: Mon-Sat 10-9. Sun 11-6.
Services: Search service, catalog, accepts want lists.
Travel: Shop is across from the Santa Barbara Art Museum.
Credit Cards: Yes
Owner: Patricia Sullivan Goss & Frank Goss
Year Estab: 1983
Comments: The shop also features a gallery and sculpture garden.

Ted's Used Books & Collectibles **Open Shop**
2008 De La Vina Street 93105 (805) 682-6733

Collection: ??
Comments: Another dealer we were unable to reach but who, we were advised by area dealers, is open for business, although with irregular hours.

Santa Clarita

Books For Libraries **By Appointment**
28064 Avenue Stanford, Unit L 91355 (805) 294-9704

Collection: General stock.
Specialties: See Comments.
Owner: James F. Stitzinger
Comments: Sells only large quantities of used books to academic institutions. Note: minimum order is for 5,000 books. Order can be for a specific subject category or a range of subjects.

Santa Cruz
(Map 5, page 235)

Book Loft **Open Shop**
1207 Soquel Avenue 95062 (408) 429-1812

Collection: General stock.
# of Vols: 15,000
Hours: Tue-Sat 10-10. Sun 12-6. Mon 10-6.
Services: Search service, accepts want lists.
Travel: Morressey Ave exit off Hwy 1. From Morressey, turn right on Water, then left on Seabright and right on Soquel. Parking is available in the first lot on Soquel although the shop is 1/2 block away.
Credit Cards: Yes
Owner: Jeff Rickard
Year Estab: 1983
Comments: A bi-level shop that carries a mix of hardcover volumes and paperbacks and some offbeat (but quite interesting) greeting cards. While the number of volumes is limited and at least one half of the stock is paperback, there are enough hardcover titles of interest to keep the browser busy for a short visit. Prices are most reasonable.

Chimney Sweep Books **Open Shop**
419 Cedar Street 95060 (408) 458-1044
E-mail: chimney@cruzio.com

Collection: General stock.
Specialties: Women's studies; gardening; religion.
# of Vols: 50,000
Hours: Wed-Sat 12-5 but best to call ahead.
Services: Appraisals, search service, catalog, accepts want lists.

Travel: See Literary Guillotine below. Located at corner of Cedar and Elm Streets.
Credit Cards: Yes
Owner: Lillian S. Kaiser
Year Estab: 1975
Comments: Most of the stock consists of serious titles in several categories of non fiction. However, there are also at least two bookcases devoted to fiction and one each devoted to cooking and theater (subjects some intellects might view as less than serious). Depending on the nature of your interests, you may or may not find this shop challenging your book buying habits. Certainly if you're a reader of scholarly titles, you'll not want to miss this shop.

Dorothy G. Cook-Rare Children's Books & Ephemera   By Appointment
80 Hollins Drive 95060   (408) 426-1119

Collection: Specialty books and ephemera.
Specialties: 19th century children's; Kate Greenaway, P. Cox; costume and fashion (books and magazines); toys.
# of Vols: 2,000
Services: Lists, mail order.
Credit Cards: No
Year Estab: 1962

Gateways Book & Gift   Open Shop
1018 Pacific 95060   (408) 429-9600

Collection: Specialty new and used paperback and hardcover.
Specialties: Metaphysics
# of Vols: 3,500 (used)
Hours: Sun-Thu 10-8. Fri & Sat 10-10.
Comments: Used stock is approximately 75% paperback.

Herland Book-Cafe   Open Shop
902 Center Street 95060   (408) 429-6636

Collection: Specialty. Mostly paperback.
Specialties: Books by women.
Hours: Book shop hours. Summer: Mon-Thu 10-6. Fri-Sun 10-8. Winter: 6pm closing time. Cafe is open earlier and stays open later.

George Robert Kane, Fine Books   By Appointment
252 Third Avenue 95062   (408) 426-4133

Collection: Specialty books and some ephemera.
Specialties: Private press, illustrated; children's early printed books; pochoir illustrated; printing; typography; fore-edge paintings; California.
# of Vols: 9,000
Services: Appraisals, accepts want lists, mail order.
Credit Cards: Yes
Year Estab: 1978

(Santa Cruz)

The Literary Guillotine
204 Locust Street 95060

Open Shop
(408) 457-1195

Collection:	Specialty hardcover and paperback.
Specialties:	Literary criticism; philosophy; general academic.
# of Vols:	18,000
Hours:	Mon-Sat 10-6.
Services:	Appraisals, search service, catalog, accepts want lists.
Travel:	From intersection of Hwy 1 & Hwy 17, take Ocean St west to Water St. Right on Water. Left on Cedar. Right on Locust.
Credit Cards:	Yes
Owner:	David S. Watson
Year Estab:	1990
Comments:	This shop is a god-send for the local serious book person who is also somewhat of a scholar. Most of the fiction fits into the category of "quality literature" or "the classics." The rest of the shop's titles are divided between scholarly volumes on history, language, criticism, social issues, etc. and a number of mostly trade paperback new titles published by various university presses.

Logos Books
1117 Pacific Avenue 95060

Open Shop
Fax: (408) 427-5107   (408) 427-5100

Collection:	General stock of mostly used paperback and hardcover, records, CDs and cassettes.
# of Vols:	100,000+
Hours:	Daily 10-10.
Travel:	See Literary Guillotine above. Continue on Cedar to parking lot at Cathcart St. Store can be entered from parking lot.
Credit Cards:	Yes
Owner:	John Livingston
Year Estab:	1969
Comments:	The largest used book dealer in town and indeed for several towns nearby. Most of the books available on the first floor (an elevator is available) are new, with some used titles intershelved. The lower level is devoted almost entirely to used hardcover volumes and paperbacks with close to a 60/40 mix respectively. Most of hardcover titles are newer but the selection is large enough and enough topics are covered to give the patient browser an opportunity to find books he or she might never know existed.

Top of the Heap
2228 Soquel Avenue 95062

Open Shop
(408) 475-6364

Collection:	General stock of paperback and hardcover.
# of Vols:	20,000
Hours:	Mon-Sat 10-5. Sun 11-4.
Travel:	Soquel Ave exit off Hwy 1. Proceed north on Soquel.
Credit Cards:	No

Owner:	Melissa Gregg
Year Estab:	1991
Comments:	Stock is approximately 70% paperback.

Santa Maria
(Map 5, page 235)

Book Barn   **Open Shop**
220 West Main Street 93454   (805) 922-7477

Collection:	General stock of paperback and hardcover.
# of Vols:	100,000
Hours:	Mon-Sat 10-5.
Travel:	Main St exit off Hwy 101. Proceed west on Main.
Credit Cards:	No
Owner:	Jo Ann Woods
Year Estab:	1980
Comments:	Stock is approximately 65% paperback.

Books For Less   **Open Shop**
1157 East Clark Avenue, Ste. J 93455   (805) 934-1388

Collection:	General stock of used and new paperback and hardcover.
# of Vols:	34,00 (used)
Hours:	Mon-Sat 9:30-6.
Travel:	Clark Ave exit off 101 Fwy. Proceed west on Clark for about one mile.
Credit Cards:	No
Year Estab:	1989
Comments:	Used stock is approximately 60% paperback.

Santa Monica
(Map 6, page 122)

Arcana: Books on the Arts   **Open Shop**
1229 3rd Street Promenade 90401   Fax: (310) 458-9014 * (310) 458-1499

Collection:	Specialty used and new.
Specialties:	Late 19th-20th century art; architecture; photography; design.
# of Vols:	9,000 (used)
Hours:	Mon-Sat 10-6. Sun 12-6.
Services:	Search service, accepts want lists, mail order.
Travel:	4th St exit off 10 Fwy westbound. North on 4th St. Left on 3rd St.
Credit Cards:	Yes
Owner:	Lee C. Kaplan
Year Estab:	1984

Bayside Books   **Open Shop**
1234 3rd Street 90401   (310) 394-8311

Collection:	General stock of used and some new hardcover and paperback.
# of Vols:	5,000

* *Some 310 codes change to 562 in 1996*

(Santa Monica)

Hours:	Tue-Sun 12-6.
Travel:	See Arcana above.
Map Ref:	Map 6, page 122, #18.
Credit Cards:	No
Owner:	Hal Kemp
Year Estab:	1987
Comments:	A neat little shop that is overflowing with books in every category but which is particularly strong in biography and entertainment. We didn't see any rare books here but did see books in generally good condition, and, if you enjoy "people watching," you can also treat yourself to some refreshments at one of the many outdoor cafes along the promenade.

Barbara Bilson-Books

2619 Pearl Street 90405

By Appointment
* (310) 450-4744

Collection:	General stock.
Specialties:	Women writers; African American writers; mystery; books made into film.
# of Vols:	3,000
Services:	Occasional catalog, search service, accepts want lists, mail order.
Year Estab:	1984

Flights of Fantasy Books

523 Santa Monica Boulevard 90401

Open Shop
* (310) 917-9112

Collection:	Specialty new and used hardcover and paperback.
Specialties:	Science fiction; fantasy; horror.
# of Vols:	10,000 (used)
Hours:	Mon-Sat 11-8. Sun 12-6.
Travel:	Between 5th & 6th.
Credit Cards:	Yes
Year Estab:	1993

Hennessey & Ingalls

1254 3rd Street Promenade 90401

Open Shop
* (310) 458-9074

Collection:	Specialty. Mostly new.
Specialties:	Art; architecture.
Hours:	Daily 10-6.
Services:	Mail order, accepts want lists.
Credit Cards:	Yes
Owner:	Mark Hennessey
Year Estab:	1962

Kenneth Karmiole, Bookseller

509 Wilshire Boulevard
Mailing Address: PO Box 464 Santa Monica 90406

By Appointment
* (310) 451-4342
Fax: (310) 458-5930

Collection:	Specialty
Specialties:	Antiquarian; early printed books; art; architecture; travel; fine printing.

# of Vols:	3,000
Hours:	Usually, Tue-Sat 10-5.
Services:	Appraisals, catalog.
Credit Cards:	Yes
Year Estab:	1977
Comments:	While we don't always have the time in our travels to visit small specialty shops, we thought it would be nice to stop at this location, especially as it was located close to our other stops in Santa Monica. At 3pm on a Tuesday, despite the hours listed above that were sent to us by the owner, the shop was closed and a drawn iron gate (and no sign or message on the front door) greeted us. If you're planning a visit here, we strongly urge you to call head.
	Perhaps as a result of the experience we had when we tried to visit this establishment (see above), the owner, in a subsequent phone conversation, decided to change his listing from "open shop" to "by appointment" so as not to disappoint traveling book people.

Eric Chaim Kline Bookseller   By Appointment
PO Box 829   90406   Fax: (310) 395-8825   *   (310) 395-4747

Collection:	General stock.
Specialties:	Judaica; archeology; ancient Near East; German language books; architecture; photography; decorative arts; art; illustrated; children's.
# of Vols:	30,000
Services:	Appraisals, catalog, search service in specialty areas, accepts want lists.
Credit Cards:	Yes
Year Estab:	1985

Barry R. Levin Science Fiction & Fantasy Literature   Open Shop
720 Santa Monica Boulevard   90401   *   (310) 458-6111

Collection:	Specialty (used hardcover)
Specialties:	Science fiction; fantasy; horror. (First and rare editions, manuscripts and original art.)
Hours:	Mon-Thu 10-6. Sun 12-5. (Closed Fri & Sat).
Services:	Catalog, accepts want lists, newsletter.
Travel:	Lincoln Blvd exit off 10 Fwy. Right on Lincoln. Left on Santa Monica.
Year Estab:	1973

Marlow's Bookshop   Open Shop
2314 Lincoln Boulevard   90405   *   (310) 392-9161

Collection:	General stock of new and used hardcover and paperback.
# of Vols:	50,000
Hours:	Mon-Fri 10-8. Sat 10-6. Sun 1-6.
Services:	Appraisals, accepts want lists, mail order.
Travel:	Lincoln Blvd exit off 10 Fwy. South on Lincoln. Shop is between Pico and Ocean.
Map Ref:	Map 6, page 122, #19.
Credit Cards:	Yes

* Some 310 codes change to 562 in 1996

(Santa Monica)

Owner:	Harvey Hodge
Year Estab:	1969
Comments:	Stock is approximately one third used, two thirds of which is hardcover.

Moondance Bookshop   **Open Shop**
1512 16th Street 90404   * (310) 394-3440

Collection:	General stock of mostly hardcover.
Specialties:	Modern first editions; black studies; signed.
# of Vols:	15,000
Hours:	Mon, Tue, Thu-Sat 12-6.
Services:	Accepts want lists, mail order.
Travel:	Lincoln exit off 10 Fwy, North on Lincoln, right on Broadway, right on 16th.
Map Ref:	Map 6, page 122, #21.
Credit Cards:	No
Owner:	C. Edward Moondance
Year Estab:	1987

The Phoenix Bookstore   **Open Shop**
1514 Fifth Street 90401   * (310) 395-9516

Collection:	Specialty. Mostly new.
Specialties:	Metaphysics; occult; philosophy; psychology.
Hours:	Mon-Sat 10-9. Sun 11-7.

Recyclepedia Bookstore   **Open Shop**
3006 Lincoln Boulevard   * (310) 392-6917

Collection:	General stock of mostly used hardcover and paperback.
Specialties:	Vintage paperbacks.
Hours:	Mon-Fri 12-7. Sat & Sun 12-5.
Travel:	See Marlow's Bookshop above. Shop is between Ocean and Rose.
Map Ref:	Map 6, page 122, #20.
Credit Cards:	No
Year Estab:	1994
Comments:	Stock is approximately 75% hardcover.

Waverley Books   **By Appointment**
948 9th Street 90403   * (310) 393-4593

Collection:	Specialty
Specialties:	Modern first editions; mystery; detective; fantasy; baseball novels; black literature; westerns; native American literature; Latin American and Chicano literature; Vietnam fiction; Hollywood and show business.
# of Vols:	15,000
Services:	Appraisals, catalog, accepts want lists.
Credit Cards:	Yes
Owner:	Dan Adams
Year Estab:	1981

* Some 310 codes change to 562 in 1996

Wilshire Books   **Open Shop**
3018 Wilshire Boulevard 90403   * (310) 828-3115

Collection: General stock.
# of Vols: 30,000
Hours: Mon-Sat 12-7. Sun 12-5.
Travel: Wilshire exit off 10 Fwy. West on Wilshire. Shop is between 26th & Centinela.
Map Ref: Map 6, page 122, #22.
Credit Cards: Yes
Year Estab: 1968
Comments: The owner uses almost every square inch of space in this relatively small shop for display which means that in order to browse all the shelves one has to squeeze in and out of narrow aisles. The plus is an abundance of books, most of which were in good condition. The minus is that one has to wait one's turn to view a section of books when another browser gets there before you (which can be frustrating when the browser does not move on.) You have to be willing and patient if you hope to find what you're looking for here. The books may be present but it is hardly the most comfortable shop we have visited.

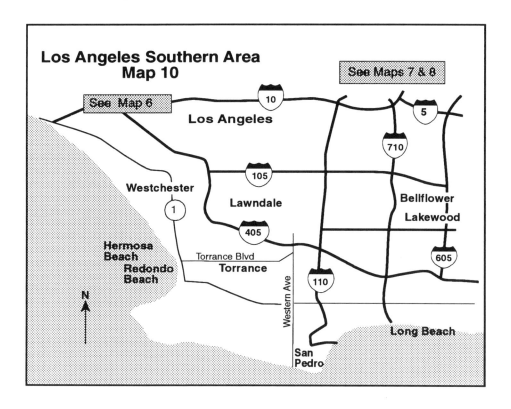

Santa Paula
(Map 5, page 235)

Mr. Nichols   **Open Shop**
901 East Main Street 93060   Fax: (805) 933-2548   (805) 525-7804

Collection: General stock of mostly used hardcover and paperback and ephemera.
Specialties: Citrus labels; photography.
# of Vols: 10,000
Hours: Mon-Sat 10-5.
Travel: 10th St exit off hwy 126. North on 10th, then west on Main.
Credit Cards: Yes
Owner: John Nichols
Year Estab: 1984
Comments: Stock is approximately 75% hardcover.

Santa Rosa
(Map 11, page 289)

Copperfield's Annex   **Open Shop**
650 Fourth Street 95404   (707) 545-5326

Collection: General stock of used and remainders and some new.
Specialties: Western Americana; first editions.
# of Vols: 85,000
Hours: Mon-Sat 9-9. Sun 10-6.
Services: Appraisals, search service, mail order.
Travel: Downtown Santa Rosa exit off Hwy 101. East on 3rd St, then north on D.
Credit Cards: Yes
Year Estab: 1985
Comments: Almost directly across the street form another fine shop, we sensed that a majority of the titles in this attractive shop were remainders, although the new and used books are intershelved. If you have particular interests and don't see the item/s you're looking for, either on the large main level or on the mezzanine, you might ask for permission to view the books in the shop's rare book room where some more expensive items, collectibles, firsts and unusual titles are offered. When we visited, we saw a set of Luther Burbank volumes that horticultural specialists would be pleased to have.

Derail Books   **By Appointment**
448 Denton Way   (707) -57-3-0751
Mailing Address: PO Box 15026 Santa Rosa 95402

Collection: Specialty
Specialties: Railroads; some California and Western Americana.
# of Vols: 2,000-3,000
Hours: Mon-Fri 10-5.
Services: Appraisals, search service, catalog, accepts want lists.
Credit Cards: No

Owner: David L. Dorranc
Year Estab: 1992

Knight's Books   **Antique Mall**
At Whistle Stop Antiques, 130 4th Street 95403   Mall: (707) 542-9474
Business: (707) 526-5611

Collection: General stock and magazines.
# of Vols: 8,000
Hours: Tue-Fri 2-5. Sat & Sun 12-4:30.
Credit Cards: Yes
Owner: Lanny Davidson
Year Estab: 1978

Larkfield Book Company   **Open Shop**
420 Larkfield Center 95403   (707) 542-2665

Collection: General stock of paperback and hardcover.
Hours: Mon-Fri 10-6. Sat 10-5. (Hours may be longer)
Travel: River Rd exit off Hwy 101. East on River Rd. Left on Old Redwood Hwy.
Credit Cards: Yes
Year Estab: 1994
Comments: Stock is approximately 70% paperback.

Treehorn Books   **Open Shop**
625 Fourth Street 95404   (707) 525-1782

Collection: General stock of mostly used hardcover and paperback, plus some ephemera and new books.
Specialties: Jack London; wine; cookbooks; Western Americana; socialist movements.
# of Vols: 75,000
Hours: Mon-Sat 10-9:30. Sun 12-6.
Services: Appraisals, search service, mail order.
Travel: See Copperfield's above.
Credit Cards: Yes
Owner: Keith Hotaling & Michael Stephens
Year Estab: 1979
Comments: We envy the people of Santa Rosa for having two quality used book dealers almost directly across the street from each other. While this shop carries some new books (discounted), it also has quite a respectable selection of used items, most in good condition and quite reasonably priced. The shop is easy to browse and the staff most helpful. One can spend a good deal of time looking at shelf after shelf of titles and truly appreciate the selections.

Santa Ynez

Bookends   **By Appointment**
3450 Baseline   (805) 686-9778
Mailing Address: PO Box 445 Los Olivos 93441   Fax: (805) 688-0307

Collection: Specialty books and related art.

Specialties:	Horses; cowboys; westerns; sighthound dogs.
# of Vols:	600-800
Services:	Search service, catalog, accepts want lists.
Credit Cards:	Yes
Owner:	Linda L. Paich
Year Estab:	1974
Comments:	Formerly Pony Tracks Gallery.

Saratoga

Book-Go-Round *Open Shop*
14410 Oak Street 95070 (408) 867-5552
E-mail: BookGoRndaol.com

Collection:	General stock of hardcover and paperback.
# of Vols:	10,000
Hours:	Wed-Sat 10-4. Sun 1-4.
Services:	Fall and Spring auction catalog of rare and collectible books.
Travel:	Saratoga Ave exit off Hwy 85. South on Saratoga to downtown. Left on Saratoga/Los Gatos Rd. Right on Oak.
Comments:	Shop is operated by the Friends of the Saratoga Library.

Sausalito
(Map 17, page 154)

Armchair Sailor Bookstore *Open Shop*
42 Caledonia Street 94965 Fax: (415) 332-7608 (415) 332-7505

Collection:	Specialty. Mostly new.
Specialties:	Nautical
# of Vols:	3,000
Hours:	Mon-Sat 9-6. Sun 12-5.
Services:	Mail order.
Travel:	Off Hwy 101.
Credit Cards:	Yes
Owner:	David Kennedy
Year Estab:	1985

Bearded Giraffe *Open Shop*
1115 Bridgeway 94965 (415) 332-4503

Collection:	Specialty. Mostly new paperbacks.
Specialties:	Metaphysics
Hours:	Thu-Mon 11-7.

Edwin V. Glaser Rare Books *By Appointment*
PO Box 1765 94966 Fax: (415) 332-5024 (415) 332-1194

Collection:	Specialty
Specialties:	Medicine; science.
# of Vols:	5,000

Services: Appraisals, catalog.
Credit Cards: Yes
Year Estab: 1964

Peter Glaser Bookseller   **By Appointment**
PO Box 404 94966   (415) 331-9064

Collection:	Specialty
Specialties:	History of medicine and science; food and drink.
# of Vols:	1,000
Services:	Appraisals, catalog, accepts want lists.
Credit Cards:	No
Year Estab:	1995

Great Overland Book Co.   **Open Shop**
215 Caledonia 94965   (415) 332-1532

Collection:	General stock of paperback and hardcover.
Specialties:	Modern first editions; native Americans; California.
# of Vols:	7,000
Hours:	Daily 11-7.
Travel:	Sausalito exit off Hwy 101. Proceed on Bridgeway toward town. Turn west on Turney, then right on Caledonia.
Owner:	Eric Flaherty & Beau Solsoeil
Year Estab:	1995
Comments:	Stock is approximately 60% paperback.

Scotts Valley

Village Book Cafe   **Open Shop**
245-J Mt. Hermon Road 95066   (408) 438-2442

Collection:	General stock of new and primarily paperback used.
Hours:	Mon-Wed 8-8. Thu & Fri 8-9. Sat 9-9. Sun 10-6.

Seaside
(Map 5, page 235)

Blenheim Books   **By Appointment**
1119 Malta Court   (408) 899-1992
Mailing Address: PO Box 164 Seaside 93955   Fax: (408) 394-8652

Collection:	Specialty
Specialties:	Winston Churchill; military.
# of Vols:	3,000
Services:	Appraisals (Churchill only), catalog, search service, accepts want lists.
Credit Cards:	Yes
Owner:	Marvin S. Nicely
Year Estab:	1985

258   CALIFORNIA

Saint Vincent De Paul Society Store   **Open Shop**
1269 Fremont Boulevard 93955   (408) 899-2211

Collection: General stock of hardcover and paperback.
Hours: Mon-Sat 10-5.
Travel: Del Rey exit off Hwy 1. East on Canyon Del Rey, then south on Fremont.
Comments: All books are donated.

Sebastopol
(Map 11, page 289)

Alibi Mystery   **Open Shop**
7824 Covert Lane 95436   (707) 829-0819

Collection: Specialty. All used, paperback and hardcover.
Specialties: Mystery
# of Vols: 7,500
Hours: Mon-Sat 9:30-5. Sun 11:30-4:30.
Travel: Located on Hwy 116 in Fiesta Shopping Center.
Credit Cards: No
Owner: M. Graham
Year Estab: 1981

Copperfield's Annex   **Open Shop**
146 North Main Street 95472   Fax: (707) 823-3271 (707) 829-0429

Collection: General stock of used and remainders.
# of Vols: 16,000
Hours: Mon-Sat 9-9. Sun 10-6.
Services: Appraisals, search service, accepts want lists, mail order.
Travel: Hwy 116 exit off Hwy 101. Proceed west on Hwy 116 to Sebastopol.
Credit Cards: Yes
Year Estab: 1992

Sebastopol Mall Books   **Antique Mall**
755 Petaluma 95472   (707) 824-9604

Collection: General stock of hardcover and paperback.
Hours: Daily 10-6.

Shell Beach

Gray Whale Book Store   **Open Shop**
1327 Shell Beach Road 93449   (805) 773-5357

Collection: General stock of new and mostly paperback used.
Hours: Mon-Sat 8-5. Sun 10-5.

Sherman Oaks
(Map 9, page 64)

B & L Rootenberg Rare Books
15422 Sutton Street
Mailing Address: PO Box 5049 Sherman Oaks 91403

By Appointment
(818) 788-7765
Fax: (818) 788-8839
E mail: blroot@pacificnet.net

Collection:	Specialty
Specialties:	History of science; medicine; technology; natural history; manuscripts. (Books and manuscripts range from 15th-20th century.)
# of Vols:	1,200
Services:	Appraisals, catalog.
Credit Cards:	Yes
Owner:	Barbara Rootenberg
Year Estab:	1968

Books On The Boulevard
13357 Ventura Boulevard 91423

Open Shop
(818) 905-0988

Collection:	General stock of mostly hardcover.
Specialties:	Performing arts; film; literature; art.
# of Vols:	18,000
Hours:	Mon-Sat 11-7. Sun 11-5.
Travel:	Woodman exit off 101 Fwy. South on Woodman, then left on Ventura. Shop is between Ventura Canyon and Fulton.
Credit Cards:	Yes
Owner:	Keith Perez & Lisa Kingsley
Year Estab:	1995
Comments:	A second shop owned by the proprietor of Sam's Book Company in Woodland Hills. While we didn't have a chance to visit this recently opened shop, we were told by the owner that the collection was similar to his other location.

Goodwin Goldfaden
4463 Calhoun Avenue
Mailing Address: PO Box 48677 Los Angeles 90048

By Appointment
(818) 986-4914

Collection:	Specialty books, magazines and programs.
Specialties:	Sports (1860 to date).
# of Vols:	50,000
Services:	Search service, mail order.
Year Estab:	1947

Monroe Stahr Books
4420 Ventura Canyon # 2 91423

By Appointment
Fax: (818) 995-0866   (818) 784-0870

Collection:	Specialty
Specialties:	Modern first editions; detective; the Hollywood novel; surfing; uncorrected proofs and advance reading copies.

# of Vols:	4,000
Services:	Catalog, accepts want lists.
Credit Cards:	No
Owner:	Tom Rusch
Year Estab:	1982

Simi Valley
(Map 5, page 235)

Book World   **Open Shop**
2311 Tapo Street, #E 93063   (805) 526-0129

Collection:	General stock of paperback and hardcover.
# of Vols:	50,000
Hours:	Mon-Thu 9-7. Fri 9-8. Sat 9-6. Sun 10-5.
Travel:	Stern exit off 118 Fwy. Proceed on Stern, then left on Cochran and left on Tapo. Shop is in shopping center on right.
Credit Cards:	Yes
Year Estab:	1985
Comments:	Stock is approximately 65% paperback.

Solana Beach
(Map 15, page 97)

Aracia Avenue Books   **Open Shop**
132 North Acacia Avenue 92075   (619) 481-6455

Collection:	General stock of hardcover and paperback.
Specialties:	Modern first editions; biography.
# of Vols:	30,000
Hours:	Mon-Sat 10:30-5:30.
Services:	Appraisals, search service, accepts want lists, mail order.
Travel:	Lomas Sante Fe exit off I-5. West on Lomas Sante Fe. Turn right on Acacia which is first street west of Hwy 101. Shop is 1/2 block ahead on right.
Credit Cards:	Yes
Owner:	Myrna Roberts
Year Estab:	1990
Comments:	The hardcover books (about half the stock) we saw in this shop were almost exclusively newer titles, most with dust jackets and often best sellers, popular titles and reprints in leather bindings. If you're looking for a current title or classic you stand a good chance of finding it here. If you're looking for technical items or unusual or rare titles, we don't think the odds are good that it will be located at this site.

Solvang
(Map 5, page 235)

Solvang Book Company   **Open Shop**
1680 Mission Drive 93463   (805) 688-6010

Collection:	General stock.

Specialties: Children's; Western Americana; Scandinavia.
# of Vols: 10,000
Hours: Daily 9-6.
Services: Appraisals, search service.
Travel: Hwy 246 off Hwy 101. Hwy 246 becomes Mission St in downtown.
Credit Cards: Yes
Owner: Gary Mullins
Year Estab: 1970
Comments: Planning a vacation? Want to visit a semi authentic Danish village along California's south central coast? Combine your visit to Solvang with a stop on the second floor of this otherwise new book shop. The collection is small but very nice and reasonably priced. The shop's second floor is also the home of the Hans Christian Anderson Museum which displays original manuscripts, first editions, research materials and other literature related to the famous writer.

That Book Place   **Open Shop**
636 Alamo Pintado Road 93463   (805) 686-8561

Collection: General stock of paperback and hardcover.
# of Vols: 25,000
Hours: Tue, Wed, Fri 11-5:30. Sat 10:30-5. Some Sun hours in summer.
Services: Search service, accepts want lists, mail order.
Travel: Alamo Pintado exit off Hwy 246. Proceed north on Alamo Pintado.
Credit Cards: No
Owner: Patricia Greschner-Nedry
Year Estab: 1991
Comments: Stock is approximately 75% paperback.

Sonoma
(Map 11, page 289)

Chanticleer Books   **Open Shop**
552 Broadway Street 95476   Fax: (707) 996-2376   (707) 996-5364

Collection: General stock.
Specialties: Art; literature; cookbooks; history; first editions.
# of Vols: 5,000-10,000
Hours: Mon-Sat 10-6. Sun 11-5.
Services: Appraisals, search service, accepts want lists, mail order.
Travel: On Hwy 12 (Broadway), one half block off Sonoma Plaza.
Credit Cards: Yes
Owner: Stephen Blackmer
Year Estab: 1994
Comments: A neat and easy to browse shop with books ranging from Franklin Mint bindings to older collectibles, some first editions and everything in between. Most of the books we saw were well cared for. What the shop lacks in depth it makes up for in character.

Plaza Books
40 West Spain Street 95476

Open Shop
(707) 996-8474

Collection: General stock.
Specialties: Western Americana; Jack London; wine.
# of Vols: 12,500
Hours: Daily 11-6.
Services: Appraisals, catalog.
Travel: Hwy 37 off Hwy 101. Proceed east on Hwy 37, north on Hwy 121. Shop is in the center of town on the plaza.
Credit Cards: Yes
Owner: Boris Bruton
Year Estab: 1988
Comments: A good selection of unusual titles in almost every field. Hardly "run of the mill" selections. The books were well cared for and there were lots of nooks and crannies where you could continue to browse just about when you thought you had exhausted all the space you thought was in the shop. Whether or not you find a book you're looking for, you should be fascinated by the items you do see.

Sonora
(Map 4, page 78)

Jack L. Stone, Bookseller
20913 Phoenix Lake Road 95370

By Appointment
(209) 536-1166

Collection: Specialty
Specialties: California; Western Americana.
# of Vols: 2,800+
Hours: Daily 8-5.
Services: Appraisals, catalog, accepts want lists.
Credit Cards: No
Year Estab: 1981

Uptown Books
68 North Washington Street 95370

Open Shop
(209) 533-0713

Collection: General stock of new and some used (mostly hardcover).
Specialties: Regional history; self help; reference; camping and hiking guides; gold mining.
Hours: Mon-Fri 9:30-5. Sat 10-4. Sun by chance.
Services: Appraisals, search service.
Travel: In downtown Sonora, on Hwy 49, one block south of historic red church.
Credit Cards: Yes
Owner: Joseph E. Ross
Year Estab: 1979
Comments: The stock is 30% used.

South Lake Tahoe

Keynote Used Books and Records   **Open Shop**
2719 Highway 50   (800) 416-6967
Mailing Address: PO Box 16696 South Lake Tahoe 96151

Collection: General stock of hardcover and paperback.
# of Vols: 7,000
Hours: Mon-Sat 11-5.
Credit Cards: Yes
Owner: Ray Hadley
Year Estab: 1986
Comments: The stock is about evenly divided between hardcover and paperback.

South Pasadena

Friends of the Library Bookstore   **Open Shop**
1100 Oxley Street 91030   (818) 441-5294

Collection: General stock of hardcover and paperback.
Hours: Mon-Wed 11-5. Thu & Fri 10-5. Sat 10-4:30. Sun 1-4.
Travel: Fair Oaks exit off Pasadena Fwy. Proceed south on Fair Oaks to Oxley, then right on Oxley. Shop is in library building.

Stanford

Quest Rare Books   **By Appointment**
774 Santa Ynez 94305   (415) 324-3119

Collection: Specialty
Specialties: Gardening; landscaping and related subjects.
# of Vols: 1,500
Services: Appraisals, search service, catalog.
Credit Cards: No
Owner: Gretl Meier
Year Estab: 1985

Stockton
(Map 4, page 78)

The Book Seller   **Open Shop**
1551 North Broadway Avenue 95205   (209) 466-0445

Collection: General stock of hardcover and paperback.
# of Vols: 100,000
Hours: Mon-Sat 11-5. Sometimes earlier. Most times later.
Services: Book repair, restoration and rebinding.
Travel: Fremont or Waterloo exits off Hwy 99. Proceed west to Broadway (the first street west of Hwy 99).

(Stockton)

Credit Cards: No
Owner: Paul Gauthier
Year Estab: 1963
Comments: We followed the directions to the above address and discovered that the street was in an industrial area with warehouses lining the road. Unfortunately, once we found the warehouse containing this shop, the gate surrounding the building was locked and all we could see was a sign on the building that read: "Bookbinding, Maps, Magazines." We strongly urge you to call ahead to avoid the same experience we had. And, if you do get to see the books, please let us know what we missed.

Fat City Books **Open Shop**
535 West Harding Way 95204 (209) 465-8335

Collection: General stock of hardcover and paperback.
Specialties: Bull fighting; wine.
# of Vols: 12,000
Hours: Mon-Sat 11-6. Other times by appointment.
Services: Appraisals, search service, accepts want lists, mail order.
Travel: Pershing exit off I-5 northbound. North on Pershing. Right on Harding.
Credit Cards: Yes
Owner: Kelly Rego
Year Estab: 1992
Comments: An interesting assortment of mostly recent hardcover titles with about half of the stock consisting of paperbacks. The shop is clean, neat and easy to browse. A few collectibles. Little out of the ordinary.

Harvard Used Book Store **Open Shop**
336 East Market 95202 (209) 464-4866

Collection: General stock of hardcover and paperback.
Specialties: Nautical
# of Vols: 1 million+
Hours: Mon-Fri 9:30-5. Sat 10-4.
Services: Appraisals, accepts want lists.
Travel: Downtown exit off I-5. Proceed north on Eldorado then east on Market.
Credit Cards: No
Owner: Richard Young
Year Estab: 1990
Comments: If you're looking for volume, you'll certainly find it here. We walked through the shop and found room after room after room of hardcover books, paperbacks and magazines. Most of what we saw were fairly ordinary and in rather mixed condition. The entire second floor was devoted to paperbacks which the owner classified as of collectible quality. We saw little that we would consider truly rare. However, with the number of books on hand, and the number of subjects covered, it's always possible that a collector will find "just what he's looking for" here. We didn't.

Maxwell's Bookmark
Open Shop
2103 Pacific Avenue 95204 Fax: (209) 466-0262 (209) 466-0194

Collection:	General stock of used and new hardcover.
Specialties:	California; Western Americana; golf.
# of Vols:	10,000+
Hours:	Mon-Sat 9:30-6, except Thu till 9.
Services:	Appraisals, search service, catalog, accepts want lists.
Travel:	Pershing exit off I-5 north. Proceed north on Pershing, right on Harding, left on Pacific to Dorris. Shop is located on northwest corner.
Credit Cards:	Yes
Owner:	William & Wendi Maxwell
Year Estab:	1939
Comments:	Quite a nice, easy to browse shop with the majority of the books in very good to excellent condition. The books on display show good taste on the part of the owners and thus enhance the choices available to the serious book buyer. In addition to the general stock, we noted several attractive literary sets.

Outpost Coffeehouse & Bookshop
Open Shop
535 West Harding Way 95204 (209) 466-3857

Collection:	General stock of hardcover and paperback.
# of Vols:	8,000-10,000
Hours:	Daily 10-midnight.
Travel:	See Fat City Books above.
Credit Cards:	No
Owner:	Stanley Fagundes
Year Estab:	1994
Comments:	Like many coffee houses that also sell books, we would guess that patrons stop here primarily for refreshments, and if their reading habits are not overly specialized, they might find an item that satisfies their taste. The books we saw were in fair to good condition with little that one could classify as worthy of a special trip, unless, that is, you happen to be visiting Fat City, the used book shop next door.

Sunnyvale

Copper Dragon Books
By Appointment
1706 Wright Avenue 94087 Fax: (408) 733-5435 (408) 733-1984

Collection:	Specialty
Specialties:	Horror; science fiction; fantasy. (Primarily first editions, signed and limited editions.)
# of Vols:	3,000
Services:	Occasional catalog, appraisals, search service, accepts want lists.
Credit Cards:	Yes
Owner:	Mark Anderson
Year Estab:	1986

Smith & Co. Booksellers 1706 Wright Avenue 94087

By Appointment Fax: (408) 733-5435 (408) 733-5435

Collection: Specialty
Specialties: Children's; pop ups; fairy tales; vampires; Sherlock Holmes; serial killers.
# of Vols: 10,000
Services: Search service, accepts want lists, mail order.
Credit Cards: Yes
Owner: Kim Smith
Year Estab: 1989

Tahoe City

Alpine Bookstore 600 North Lake Boulevard 96145

Open Shop (916) 581-4136

Collection: General stock of used and new hardcover and paperback.
# of Vols: 15,000
Hours: Daily 10-6.
Travel: Hwy 89 exit off I-80. Proceed south on Hwy 89 than north on Hwy 28 which becomes North Lake Blvd in Tahoe City.
Credit Cards: Yes
Year Estab: 1988
Comments: The stock is approximately 60% used, 60% of which is hardcover.

Tarzana

Flip Side 18551 Ventura Boulevard 91356

Open Shop (818) 758-9103

Collection: Specialty books (mostly paperback) and comics.
Specialties: Science fiction; fantasy.
# of Vols: Limited
Hours: Mon-Thu 11-7. Fri & Sat 11-9. Sun 12-6.

Temecula
(Map 12, page 139)

The Book Drop 27457 Jefferson Avenue 92590

Open Shop (909) 676-9616

Collection: General stock of mostly used paperback and hardcover.
# of Vols: 50,000 (used)
Hours: Mon-Fri 10-5:30. Sat 10-5.
Travel: Winchester exit off 15 Fwy. West on Winchester and left on Jefferson.
Credit Cards: Yes
Owner: Annette Smith
Year Estab: 1988
Comments: Stock is approximately 65% paperback.

Pictus Orbis Collectors Books   **Open Shop**
42031 Main Street 92590   Fax: (909) 699-4969 (909) 695-3139

Collection:	Specialty
Specialties:	Children's; illustrated; toys; fine art.
# of Vols:	20,000
Hours:	Wed-Sun 11-5.
Services:	Appraisals, search service, accepts want lists.
Travel:	Rancho California exit off I-15. Proceed west on Rancho California then left on Front and right on Main. The shop is located upstairs.
Credit Cards:	No
Owner:	Phyllis Barton
Year Estab:	1991
Comments:	Whether you're buying for a special child you know or for the child in you, we believe you'll be thoroughly enchanted as you enter this delightful shop. The children's books range from old classics to pop ups to Dr. Seuss and everything in between. Don't look for inexpensive items here. The owner takes great pride in the quality of her stock and refuses to carry less than first class material.

Temple City
(Map 8, page 168)

Kenrich Co.   **Open Shop**
9418 Las Tunas 91780   (818) 286-3888

Collection:	Primarily ephemera and limited general stock of books.
Hours:	Tue-Sat 10-6.
Travel:	210 Fwy to Rosemead exit. South on Rosemead, then left on Las Tunas.
Credit Cards:	Yes
Owner:	William Colby
Year Estab:	1962

Thousand Oaks
(Map 5, page 235)

Bleak House Books   **By Appointment**
PO Box 1465 91358   (805) 373-9332

Collection:	General stock.
Specialties:	Literature; Mark Twain; poetry.
# of Vols:	8,000
Services:	Catalog, accepts want lists.
Credit Cards:	No
Owner:	Marion Wood
Year Estab:	1994

Bookaneer   **Open Shop**
3186 Thousand Oaks Boulevard 91362   (805) 379-9667

Collection: General stock of mostly paperback.
Hours: Tue-Sat 11-6.

Second Edition Books   **Open Shop**
368 Thousand Oaks Boulevard 91360   Fax: (805) 498-2018   (805) 497-9727

Collection: General stock of mostly paperback.
# of Vols: 20,000
Hours: Mon-Fri 10-5:30. Sat 10-4.
Services: Search service, accepts want lists.
Travel: Moorpark exit off 101 Fwy. North on Moorpark. Right on Thousand Oaks Blvd. Shop is in Vogue Plaza.
Credit Cards: Yes
Owner: Patricia A. Swindle
Year Estab: 1980
Comments: Paperbacks predominate in this neighborhood store in a neighborhood shopping center. The row and a half of hardcover books were undistinguished in terms of collectibility or desirability. Need we say more.

Torrance
(Map 10, page 253)

Book Again   **Open Shop**
5039 Torrance Boulevard 90503   * (310) 542-1156

Collection: General stock of paperback and hardcover.
# of Vols: 10,000+
Hours: Tue-Sat 11-6. Sun 12-5.
Travel: Between Anza and Palos Verdes Blvd.
Credit Cards: Yes
Year Estab: 1985

Sandpiper Books   **Open Shop**
4665 Torrance Boulevard 90503   * (310) 371-2002

Collection: General stock of hardcover and paperback.
# of Vols: 10,000
Hours: Mon-Sat 10-7.
Travel: Located in shopping center at corner of Anza Ave and Torrance Blvd.
Credit Cards: Yes
Owner: Christine Anderson
Year Estab: 1991
Comments: A pleasant shop with a warm and inviting ambience. Most of the books we saw were in good to very good condition. While many subjects were covered, none were represented in depth. A majority of the books were of recent vintage. There were some shelves marked "old books" and some additional items that would fit the antiquarian label.

* Some 310 codes change to 562 in 1996

Torrance Book Buddy
1328 Sartori Avenue 90501

Open Shop
* (310) 328-1134

Collection:	General stock of hardcover and paperback.
Specialties:	History; art; film; fantasy.
# of Vols:	30,000
Hours:	Mon-Sat 10-4, plus Fri from 6pm to . . . Other evenings by chance or appointment.
Travel:	Western Ave exit off I-405. Proceed south on Western Ave for one mile to Torrance Blvd. From I-110: proceed west on Torrance Blvd for one mile past Western Ave. Proceed under railroad bridge to railroad station. Turn left at first light on Cabrillo Ave, then right on Sartori.
Credit Cards:	No
Owner:	W.F. Wilson
Year Estab:	1960
Comments:	Quite a nice shop with a modest but "worth browsing" collection. Most subjects covered. Books are reasonably priced. Definitely worth a visit.

Truckee

Truckee Books
10009 West River Street 96161

Open Shop
(916) 582-8302

Collection:	General stock of new and mostly paperback used.
Hours:	Daily 9:30-6.

Turlock
(Map 4, page 78)

Books In Transit
2830 Case Way 95382

By Appointment
(209) 632-6984

Collection:	Specialty
Specialties:	Arts and crafts.
Services:	Catalog, accepts want lists.
Credit Cards:	No
Owner:	Mary T. Peterson
Year Estab:	1975

Castle Books
334 North Center 95380

Open Shop
(209) 667-7795

Collection:	General stock of paperback and hardcover.
# of Vols:	50,000
Hours:	Mon-Sat 10-6.
Travel:	Falkerth exit off Hwy 99. Proceed east on Falkerth, right on Golden State Blvd, left on North Center. Shop is in North Center Plaza.
Credit Cards:	Yes
Year Estab:	1991
Comments:	Stock is about evenly divided between paperback and hardcover.

CALIFORNIA

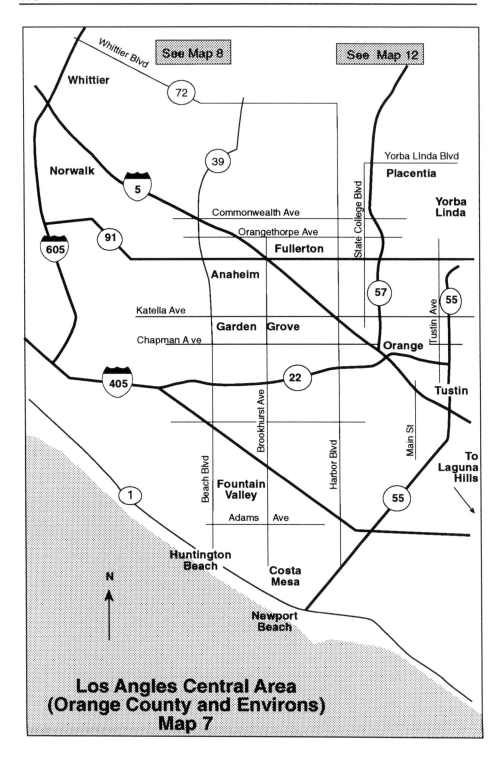

Garcia-Garst, Booksellers   **Open Shop**
2857 Geer Road, Suite C 95382   Fax: (209) 632-0805   (209) 632-5054

Collection: General stock.
Specialties: Children's; children's series; illustrated; Western Americana; California.
# of Vols: 20,000
Hours: Mon-Sat 11-5 but a call ahead is recommended.
Services: Appraisals, search service, catalog, accepts want lists.
Travel: Monte Vista exit off Hwy 99. Proceed east on Monte Vista, then right on Geer. Proceed one block, then right on Regis St and left into College Park Business Center. Follow driveway as it curves back to Geer.
Credit Cards: Yes
Owner: Kenneth & Beverly Garst
Year Estab: 1978
Comments: The shop is modest in size but not in quality. The specialties identified above are clearly not exaggerated and the number of children's books on hand would delight most collectors in this area. Condition ranged from fair to excellent and everywhere in between. The rest of the collection provides a fair, if limited, representation in more general areas. If the shop's specialties are your thing, a visit would certainly be appropriate.

Tustin
(Map 7, page 270)

Brindles Bookstore   **Open Shop**
13721 Newport Avenue 92680   Fax: (714) 258-7116,   (714) 731-5773

Collection: General stock of mostly used hardcover and paperback.
# of Vols: 100,000
Hours: Daily 9-9.
Travel: Southbound on 5 Fwy: Newport exit. Left on Newport. Northbound on 5 Fwy: Redhill exit. Right on Redhill, left on El Camino and right on Newport. Shop is in Tustin Plaza.
Credit Cards: Yes
Owner: Julie Allen
Year Estab: 1994
Comments: Large in size and attractive and easy to browse with well labeled shelves. Most of the used books were items that had been published in the past 10-20 years. A very small number of vintage volumes which, depending on your taste, can be either a blessing or a curse. Reasonably priced.

Tustin Used Books   **Open Shop**
215 West 1st St, #102 92680   (714) 731-6103

Collection: General stock of mostly paperback.
Hours: Tue-Sat 10-5:30.

Twentynine Palms
(Map 12, page 139)

Ravens Bookshop — Open Shop
69225 29 Palms Highway 92277 — (619) 362-4900

Collection:	General stock of hardcover and paperback.
Specialties:	Science fiction; mystery; metaphysics; deserts.
# of Vols:	20,000
Hours:	Mon, Tue, Thu, Fri 11-5:30. Sat 11-5. Sun 12-5.
Travel:	On Hwy 62, between Lear Ave and Indian Cove Rd.
Credit Cards:	No
Owner:	Cliff Ingram
Year Estab:	1990

Ukiah
(Map 11, page 289)

Village Book Exchange — Open Shop
344 North State Street 95482 — (707) 468-5355

Collection:	General stock of paperback and hardcover.
# of Vols:	60,000
Hours:	Mon-Fri 20-5:30. Sat 10-4.
Comments:	Stock is about 70% paperback.

Upland
(Map 12, page 139)

Book Garden — Open Shop
1651 West Foothill Boulevard, Ste. J 91786 — (909) 982-0292

Collection:	General stock of hardcover and paperback.
# of Vols:	20,000
Hours:	Mon-Sat 10-7:30.
Travel:	Central Ave exit off 10 Fwy. North on Central. Right on Foothill.
Credit Cards:	No
Owner:	Jeff Blum
Year Estab:	1995
Comments:	Stock is about evenly divided between hardcover and paperback.

Vacaville
(Map 4, page 78)

Vacaville Book Co. — Open Shop
1315 Main 95688 — (707) 449-0550

Collection:	General stock of new and used paperback and hardcover.
# of Vols:	1,000 (used)
Hours:	Mon-Thu 10-8. Fri & Sat 8-10.
Comments:	Used stock is 75% paperback.

Wordsworth Used Books **Open Shop**
1015 Alamo Drive 95687 (707) 452-9022

Collection: General stock of mostly paperback.
Hours: Wed-Sat 10-6. Sun 12-4.

Vallejo
(Map 17, page 154)

Booklover's Haven **Open Shop**
1614 Sonoma Boulevard 94590 (707) 557-4190

Collection: General stock of hardcover and paperback.
# of Vols: 30,000
Hours: Mon-Fri 7:30am-6pm. Sat 8am-10pm.
Travel: Sonoma Blvd exit off I-80. Proceed on Sonoma (Hwy 29) toward old downtown.
Credit Cards: No
Owner: Greg & Veronica Morris
Year Estab: 1991
Comments: At the time of our visit, the owner was in the process of remodeling the shop which was located adjacent to a coffee shop. Most of the books we saw were reading copies and the shop only had room to display a portion of the volumes noted above. In some sections, paperbacks and hardcover volumes were shelved together. We also saw some old encyclopedias and other outdated reference materials. We were not able to identify what we would call any really exciting titles here but, because of the nature of the shop and community, we certainly feel that a knowledgeable book person could, if he visits the shop at the right time, find an underpriced item of value.

Valley Center

Howard Karno Books **By Appointment**
PO Box 2100 92082 Fax: (619) 749-4390 (619) 749-2304

Collection: Specialty used and new.
Specialties: Latin America, especially the arts, archaeology, history, reference and anthropology.
# of Vols: 12,000-15,000
Services: Appraisals, search service, catalog, accepts want lists.
Credit Cards: Yes
Year Estab: 1973

Van Nuys
(Map 9, page 64)

Bargain Books **Open Shop**
14426 Friar Street 91401 (818) 782-2782

Collection: General stock of used and new, hardcover and paperback.

Specialties:	Art; technical; children's; cookbooks; aviation.
# of Vols:	150,000+
Hours:	Tue-Fri 10-6. Sat 10-5.
Travel:	Near 405 Fwy. One half block east of Van Nuys Blvd and one block south of Victory.
Credit Cards:	Yes
Owner:	Bill Wirt & Diane Sharrar
Year Estab:	1958
Comments:	A long narrow shop with two aisles of books from floor to ceiling and shelves that are very well marked by category and subcategory. The majority of the books we saw were more recent but the shop does have older items. The owner maintains a separate storeroom where books are even more meticulously shelved and from which prospective buyers (with some assistance) may be able to locate additional titles not readily found in the main part of the shop. The good thing about browsing here is that once you've identified the subject you're seeking, it should be relatively easy to determine whether you're going to make a purchase. The negative is that with so many books in a fairly limited space, if you're doing general browsing, depending on the number of other visitors in the stop, you may not be able to view all the shelves in a comfortable manner.

Theodore Front Musical Literature   Open Shop
16122 Cohasset Street 91406   (818) 994-1902

Collection:	Specialty new and used.
Specialties:	Music; sheet music.
Hours:	Mon-Fri 9-5. Sat 12-5.
Services:	Appraisals, search service, catalog, accepts want lists.
Travel:	Sherman Way/Reseda exit off 405 Fwy. Proceed west on Sherman Way, right on Woodley and left on Cohasset.
Credit Cards:	Yes
Year Estab:	1961
Comments:	Stock is approximately 30% used.

Ventura
(Map 5, page 235)

Book Mall of Ventura   Open Shop
424 East Main Street 93001   Fax: (805) 643-4854   (805) 641-2665

Collection:	General stock.
Specialties:	Western Americana; signed; modern first editions; cookbooks; art.
# of Vols:	10,000
Hours:	Mon-Fri 10-5. Sat 10-6. Sun 11-5.
Services:	Appraisals, search service, catalog, accepts want lists.
Travel:	See Calico Cat Bookshop below. Left on Main.
Credit Cards:	Yes
Owner:	Diane L. Neveu

Year Estab: 1990
Comments: Lots of interesting items on view in this group shop, from hardcover volumes of mixed vintage and in mixed condition to ephemera, vintage paperbacks, etc. The store is fun to browse, and, if you like the sound of mother nature's natural singers, you'll enjoy the chirping of the owner's pet birds.

Calico Cat Bookshop
495 East Main Street 93001

Open Shop
(805) 643-7849

Collection: General stock of mostly hardcover.
Specialties: California; history; cookbooks; classics; mysticism; maps.
# of Vols: 25,000
Hours: Mon-Sat 10-6. Sun 12-4. Other times by appointment.
Services: Appraisals, search service, occasional catalog, accepts want lists.
Travel: Northbound on Hwy 101: California St exit. Right on California. Proceed to Main St. Southbound on Hwy 101: Main St exit. Proceed south on Main to California. Shop is on corner of California and Main.
Credit Cards: Yes
Owner: Peter Margenat
Year Estab: 1976
Comments: An attractive store to shop, whether you're a tourist or a serious book person. The books are in generally good condition. As noted in the specialties listed above, the shop's emphasis is on non fiction. We also saw a fair number of sets and fine leather bindings, e.g., Franklin Mints and Eastons.

Sol J. Grossman, Bookseller
171 South California Street 93001

By Appointment
Fax: (805) 643-2030   (805) 648-3276

Collection: Specialty
Specialties: Small western presses; Leo Politi; children's illustrated; children's signed; Limited Editions Club; Alcoholics Anonymous.
# of Vols: 2,000
Hours: Usually Mon-Fri 9:30-3:30.
Services: Appraisals
Credit Cards: No
Year Estab: 1992

House Of Books
9184 Neath Street
Mailing Address: PO Box 3083 Ventura 93006

By Appointment
(805) 647-3344

Collection: General stock of hardcover and paperback.
Specialties: Mystery; modern first editions.
# of Vols: 11,000
Services: Accepts want lists, mail order.
Credit Cards: No
Owner: David N. & Lynda M. Gallup
Year Estab: 1991

(Ventura)

Old California Store
1528 East Thompson Boulevard 93001

Open Shop
(805) 643-4217

Collection:	Specialty
Specialties:	California, with emphasis on art, history, architecture, ranching, cowboys; Baja California.
# of Vols:	500
Hours:	Fri-Sun 11-5. Other times by appointment.
Travel:	Seaward exit off Hwy 101. North on Seaward, then left on Thompson.
Credit Cards:	No
Owner:	Don Shorts
Year Estab:	1980

Phantom Bookshop
451 East Main Street 93001

Open Shop
Fax: (805) 641-1246 (805) 641-3844
E-mail: phantom@fishnet.net

Collection:	General stock of mostly hardcover.
Specialties:	Jack London; Frank Baum; Wizard of Oz; H. Rider Haggard; children's; E. Stanley Gardner.
# of Vols:	10,000
Hours:	Daily 11-5.
Travel:	See Calico Cat Bookshop above. Left on Main.
Credit Cards:	Yes
Owner:	John Anthony Miller
Year Estab:	1992
Comments:	The owner makes the most of this deep but narrow shop with both hardcover and paperback books abounding on every wall. In addition to the specialties listed above, the shop appears to have a strong collection of fantasy items. We saw many interesting titles and noted what we conclude was a mixed priced structure with some items priced quite reasonably and others slightly higher than we have seen elsewhere. If you know your subject and recognize that condition as well as rarity is the key to price structure, you could come away from this shop with several items that may have heretofore alluded you.

The Second Time Around Bookshop
391 East Main Street 93001

Open Shop
(805) 643-3154

Collection:	General stock of hardcover and paperback.
Specialties:	UFOs; magazines; metaphysics; new age.
# of Vols:	35,000
Hours:	Daily 10-5.
Services:	Appraisals, search service, accepts want lists.
Travel:	See Calico Cat Bookshop above. Left on Main.
Credit Cards:	Yes
Owner:	James Staley, Manager
Year Estab:	1971

Comments: This shop stocks a selection of hardcover items, paperbacks, comic books, magazines and records. In examining some of the volumes marked "first editions," we noticed several titles (without dust jackets) that had seen far better days and that were priced substantially higher than the same volumes we have seen elsewhere. We were hard pressed to find, on any of the shelves, items of substantial interest (at least to us). However, considering the fact that there are at least three other used book dealers along the same street, why not visit and judge for yourself.

Victorville
(Map 12, page 139)

Book Exchange — Open Shop
15024 Bear Valley Road 92392 — (619) 241-0465

Collection: General stock of paperback and hardcover.
Hours: Mon-Sat 10-6.
Travel: Bear Valley Rd exit off 15 Fwy. East on Bear Valley.
Comments: Stock is approximately 70% paperback.

Thompson's Book Shop — Open Shop
15581 Seventh Street 92392 — (619) 241-1544

Collection: General stock of hardcover and paperback.
# of Vols: 10,000
Hours: Wed-Sat 11-4. Other times by appointment.
Travel: D St exit off I-15. Turn east and proceed to 7th St.
Credit Cards: No
Owner: Richard & Kathy Thompson
Year Estab: 1990
Comments: Stock is about evenly divided between hardcover and paperback.

Visalia
(Map 4, page 78)

Bargain Books — Open Shop
4129 West Mineral King Highway 93277 — (209) 635-4657

Collection: General stock of paperback and hardcover.
Specialties: Modern first editions; children's.
# of Vols: 15,000-20,000
Hours: Mon-Fri 10-6. Sat 10-5. Sun 10:30-4:30.
Services: Accepts want lists.
Travel: Hwy 198 exit off Hwy 99. East on Hwy 198 (Mineral King Highway) for about four miles. Right on Chinowth, then immediate right into shopping center.
Credit Cards: Yes
Owner: Harold, Sheila & Jon Butterworth
Year Estab: 1993

Comments: The stock is primarily paperback with a modest collection of hardcover books, including a good number of classics, Franklin Mint and Easton leather bindings. Many of the hardcover titles are located on the higher shelves above paperbacks of the same subject. Several of the items we saw were very reasonably priced.

Linda's Used Books **Open Shop**
1107 East Houston Avenue 93292 (209) 734-1043

Collection: General stock of mostly paperback.
Hours: Tue-Sat 10-5.

Ye Bookstore **Open Shop**
104 South Church Street 93291 (209) 732-3229

Collection: General stock.
Specialties: Primarily non fiction and literature.
# of Vols: 25,000
Hours: Mon-Sat 9:30-5:30.
Services: Appraisals
Travel: Downtown exit off Hwy 198. Follow signs for downtown. Left on Main, then right on Church.
Credit Cards: No
Owner: J.P. Beavers
Year Estab: 1975
Comments: Perhaps the owner of this shop believes that his customers should share is sense of humor. When we arrived at this shop at its posted 9:30 opening (having taken our own advice and called ahead the day before to determine if the shop would be open the following day) we found the shop closed (despite the "Open" sign on the door) and a tongue in cheek message about hours posted on the window. When one travels a distance to be at a shop at the published opening time and the shop is not open at that time, or 15 minutes later, one's sense of humor is blunted.

Vista
(Map 15, page 97)

Allred Books **Open Shop**
209 East Broadway 92084 (619) 726-8914

Collection: General stock of hardcover and paperback.
Specialties: History; native Americans; literature; science; art; poetry; mystery.
# of Vols: 35,000
Hours: Mon-Sat 10-5.
Services: Accepts want lists, minor book repairs.
Travel: Escondido exit off 78 Fwy. Proceed north on Escondido, left on Eucalyptus, right on Citrus and left on East Broadway. Shop is 1½ blocks ahead.
Credit Cards: Yes
Owner: Janet Allred

Year Estab: 1993
Comments: At the time of our visit, the shop could best be described as a "work in progress" and the owner was expanding, modernizing and reorganizing her shop. Most of the hardcover titles we saw (about half the stock) were newer and few could be classified as rare or antiquarian. We noted several items that were underpriced suggesting to us that for the person who knows his books, items of interest found here could turn out to be good buys.

Booklovers Exchange   Open Shop
1611-D South Melrose Drive 92083   (619) 727-5040

Collection: General stock of paperback and hardcover.
# of Vols: 35,000
Hours: Tue-Sun 10-8.
Travel: Two miles south of Fwy 78 in shopping center.
Credit Cards: Yes
Owner: Russell C. Lawrence
Year Estab: 1994
Comments: Stock is approximately 70% paperback.

Camelot Books   Open Shop
1011 South Santa Fe, Ste. H   (619) 940-9472
Mailing Address: PO Box 2883 Vista 92085

Collection: General stock of mostly hardcover.
Specialties: Arthurian legend; mystery and suspense (from 1960).
# of Vols: 30,000
Hours: Mon-Sat 10-6.
Services: Appraisals, search service and lists (Arthurian only), mail order.
Travel: Escondido Ave exit off 78 Fwy. North on Escondido. Right on South Santa Fe. Shop is 1½ blocks ahead in Santa Fe Square shopping center.
Credit Cards: No
Owner: Charles Wyatt
Year Estab: 1975
Comments: One wonders if the owner of this shop refuses books offered to him. We saw books in every condition from modern editions to older items. On the plus side, you can get books inexpensively here. On the minus side, the books you acquire will not necessarily be fine copies. Of course, there are exceptions to the above.

I Love Books-Bookstore   Open Shop
707 East Vista Way 92084   (619) 945-7718

Collection: General stock of hardcover and paperback.
# of Vols: 80,000
Hours: Mon-Sun 10-6.
Services: Appraisals, search service, accepts want lists.
Travel: Escondido Ave exit off 78 Fwy. Proceed west on Escondido, then right on Vista Way. Shop is just ahead on right in a small shopping center.
Credit Cards: Yes

Year Estab: 1985
Comments: The hardcover books were of mixed vintage and mixed condition. While we were not able to spot titles here that might be considered truly rare, we were advised that the owner's second location in Encinitas (see Books Past & Present above) does carry more items that would fall into the rare and collectible category.

Walnut Creek
(Map 17, page 154)

Bonanza St. Books   Open Shop
1605 Bonanza Street 94596   Fax: (510) 932-2459   (510) 932-2466

Collection: General stock of used, new and remainders.
Specialties: California
# of Vols: 100,000+
Hours: Sun-Thu 9am-9:30pm. Fri & Sat 9am-11pm.
Services: Search service.
Travel: Northbound on I-680: Walnut Creek exit. Proceed on Mt. Diablo Blvd, then left on Bonanza St. Southbound on I-680: Walnut Creek exit. Proceed south on Main, then right on Bonanza.
Credit Cards: Yes
Owner: Jackie Miskel
Year Estab: 1987
Comments: Three shops in one: a coffee shop, a shop that sells new books, remainders, magazines and cards and a shop that carries used books. The used books, at least during our visit, represented about half the total number of books on hand and ran the gamut from some collectible items behind glass to leather bindings to a general assortment of hardcover reading copies, the majority of which were of a more recent vintage, and paperbacks.

The Book Shop   By Appointment
2687 Cherry Lane 94596   (510) 937-5040

Collection: General stock.
Specialties: D.H. Lawrence; literary biography.
Services: Appraisals, search service, catalog, accepts want lists.
Credit Cards: No
Owner: Larry Kimmich
Year Estab: 1987

James M. Dourgarian, Bookman   By Appointment
1595-A Third Avenue 94596   (510) 935-5033

Collection: Specialty and ephemera related to authors carried.
Specialties: Primarily fiction first editions from 1900: John Steinbeck; Jack London; Wallace Stegner; Richard Brautigan; armed services editions.
# of Vols: 5,000
Hours: Daily 9:30-4.
Services: Appraisals, search service, catalog, accepts want lists.

Credit Cards: No
Year Estab: 1980

Hooked On Books   **Open Shop**
1854 Tice Valley Boulevard 94595   (510) 933-1025

Collection: General stock of mostly paperback.
Hours: Mon-Fri 9:30-5:30. Sat 9-5. Sun 11-5.

Frank Mikesh   **By Appointment**
1356 Walden Road 94596   (510) 934-9243

Collection: Specialty
Specialties: Natural history; hunting; fishing; sports; wildlife art.
# of Vols: 13,000+ (9,000 in natural history)
Services: Search service, catalog, accepts want lists.
Credit Cards: No
Year Estab: 1973

Pegasus Books   **Open Shop**
1333 North Main 94596   (510) 934-4449

Collection: General stock of used hardcover and paperback, new and remainders.
# of Vols: 50,000+
Hours: Daily 10-10.
Travel: Walnut Creek exit off Hwy 24. East on Mt. Diablo Blvd then left on Main.
Credit Cards: Yes
Owner: Matt Wyse, owner. Amy Thomas, president.
Comments: Similar to Pegasus Books in Berkeley with a slightly smaller stock.

West Covina

Bearly Used Books   **Open Shop**
1013 South Glendora Avenue 91790   (818) 338-1939

Collection: General stock of mostly paperback.
Hours: Mon, Tue, Thu 11-6. Wed & Fri 11-8. Sat 10-6. Sun 12-5.

West Hollywood

Mysterious Bookshop West   **Open Shop**
8763 Beverly Boulevard 90048   Fax: (310) 659-2962 * (310) 659-2959

Collection: Specialty used and new.
Specialties: Mystery
# of Vols: 10,000+ (used)
Hours: Mon-Sat 10-6. Sun 12-5.
Services: Catalog, search service, accepts want lists, appraisals.
Travel: Robertson exit off 10 Fwy. North on Robertson, then right on Beverly.
Credit Cards: Yes
Owner: Sheldon McArthur

* Some 310 codes change to 562 in 1996

Year Estab: 1989
Comments: Used stock is primarily of collectible quality.

West Los Angeles
(Map 6, page 122)

Gene de Chene, Bookseller
11556 Santa Monica Boulevard 90025

Open Shop
* (310) 477-8734

Collection: General stock of hardcover and paperback.
Specialties: Literature; women's studies.
# of Vols: 20,000
Hours: Mon-Sat 10:30-7:30.
Travel: Santa Monica Blvd exit off 405 Fwy. Proceed west on Santa Monica Blvd. Shop is between Colby and Federal.
Map Ref: Map 6, page 122, #23.
Credit Cards: Yes
Year Estab: 1968
Comments: A more traditional used book dealer with about a 50/50 mix of hardcover and paperback. The books were of mixed vintage and in mixed condition. Reasonably priced. The selection is limited but as with many shops of this nature, sometimes one can locate an attractive rose among the thorns.

Dutton's Brentwood Books
11975 San Vicente Boulevard 90049

Open Shop
* (310) 476-6263

Collection: General stock of new and used, hardcover and paperback.
# of Vols: 15,000 (used)
Hours: Mon-Fri 9-9. Sat 9-6. Sun 11-5.
Travel: Wilshire exit off 405 Fwy. West on Wilshire. Right on San Vicente.
Map Ref: Map 6, page 122, #24.
Credit Cards: Yes
Owner: Doug Dutton
Year Estab: 1985

Other Times Books
10617 West Pico Boulevard 90064

Open Shop
(213) 475-2547

Collection: General stock of mostly hardcover.
Specialties: Literature; pop culture; film.
# of Vols: 10,000
Hours: Tue-Sat 12-6.
Services: Accepts want lists, mail order.
Travel: Olympic/Pico exit off 405 Fwy. Proceed east on Pico. Shop is between Westwood and Century City.
Map Ref: Map 6, page 122, #25.
Credit Cards: No
Owner: Andrew Dowdy
Year Estab: 1975

* Some 310 codes change to 562 in 1996

Comments: A relatively small shop emphasizing books dealing with show business (film, theater, dance, etc.) and a limited number of books that might be classified as general, e.g., literature, history, etc. A nice selection, particularly if the specialty is one of interest to you.

West L.A. Book Center   **Open Shop**
1650 South Sawtelle Boulevard 90025   * (310) 473-4442

Collection:	General stock of hardcover and paperback.
Specialties:	Art; literature.
# of Vols:	22,000
Hours:	Mon-Fri 12-7. Sat 12-6. Sun 1-5.
Travel:	One half block south of Santa Monica Blvd and one block west of I-405.
Map Ref:	Map 6, page 122, #26.
Credit Cards:	No
Owner:	K.M. Hyre
Year Estab:	1959
Comments:	At first glance, this shop gives the casual visitor the impression of being an ordinary book shop with about one third of the stock consisting of paperbacks. The hardcover items we saw were of mixed vintage and condition and reasonably priced. Some interesting titles are available for the browser willing to take the time needed to scrutinize the stock. If you're lucky, the owner may invite you into his "inner sanctum" where a collection of fine bindings, first editions and other worthwhile items can be viewed.

Westchester
(Map 10, page 253)

Read It Again Sam   **Open Shop**
6227 West 87th Street 90045   * (310) 641-2665

Collection:	General stock of paperback and hardcover.
# of Vols:	17,000
Hours:	Summer: Mon- 12-4. Tue, Thu Fri 10-6. Wed 8:30-6. Sat 10-5. Winter: Mon 12-5. Tue, Thu, Fri, Sat 10-5. Wed 8:30-5.
Travel:	La Tijera exit off 405 Fwy. West on La Tijera for 2 miles. Right on Truxton, left on 87th.
Comments:	Stock is approximately 65% paperback.

Westminster

Christian Discount Book Center   **Open Shop**
16595 Magnolia Street 92683   (714) 847-0396

Collection:	Specialty new and used.
Specialties:	Religion
Hours:	Mon-Sat 9-9.

Whittier
(Map 7, page 270)

Anderson's Bookshop/Books Fantastique   **Open Shop**
7043 Greenleaf Avenue   * (310) 693-4408
Mailing Address: Books Fantastique, PO Box 510 Whittier 90608

Collection:	General stock of used and new hardcover and paperback.
Specialties:	Stephen King; Clive Barker; science fiction; fantasy; horror; mystery; Western Americana.
# of Vols:	250,000
Hours:	Mon-Sat 11-7. Other times by appointment.
Services:	Search service for science fiction, horror and fantasy only, occasional catalog.
Travel:	Whittier Blvd east exit off 605 Fwy. East on Whittier. Left on Greenleaf.
Credit Cards:	No
Owner:	Dorothea Anderson & Michael Autrey
Year Estab:	1975
Comments:	Some shops are fun to visit regardless of their physical appearance. This is one such establishment. Books abound on shelf after shelf and in aisle after aisle in most categories that one would normally expect to find in a shop of this size. We saw a mix of older and newer titles (some unusual, some common) with a majority of the volumes in good to better condition. The ownership of the store and its stock is shared by two experienced book people, one of whom (Michael Autrey) is a leading Stephen King/Clive Barker authority. By and large, a visit to this shop should prove to be an enjoyable experience and you should leave with an acquisition or two.

Christian Discount Book Center   **Open Shop**
8401 S. Pioneer Boulevard 90606   * (310) 692-1296

Collection:	Specialty new and used.
Specialties:	Religion
Hours:	Mon-Sat 9-9.

Insomnia Books   **Open Shop**
13013 Philadelphia 90601   (310) 698-9595

Collection:	General stock of used and new paperback and hardcover.
# of Vols:	8,000-10,000
Hours:	Mon-Thu 11-9. Fri & Sat 11-10. Sun 11-6.
Services:	Search service, accepts want lists, mail order.
Travel:	From Greenleaf, left on Philadelphia. Shop is just ahead on left.
Credit Cards:	Yes
Owner:	Rocco Ingala, Jr.
Year Estab:	1993
Comments:	A small general shop with particular strength in the literature of the beat generation as exemplified by the generation's writers, musicians and artists. The shop also functions as an art gallery, making for an interesting visit while in town.

* Some 310 codes change to 562 in 1996

Little Old Bookshop **Open Shop**
6546 Greenleaf Avenue 90601 * (310) 698-1934

Collection:	General stock of hardcover and paperback.
# of Vols:	100,000
Hours:	Daily 10-10.
Services:	Appraisals, accepts want lists, mail order.
Travel:	Beverly exit off 605 Fwy. Proceed east on Beverly then right on Greenleaf.
Credit Cards:	No
Owner:	Charles Jimenez
Year Estab:	1976
Comments:	One should never be discouraged when an employee tells you that the shop has no books in the category you're looking for. That was our experience when we visited this shop - despite the fact that five minutes later, and with little trouble, we spotted at least half a dozen books in the category we had initially inquired about. Indeed, one of the titles was on our want list. Conclusion: this is a shop that does have worthwhile titles, but unless the owner is on hand, you may have to do your own search, which afterall, is half the fun.

Valdez Books & Bindery **Open Shop**
6747A South Greenleaf Avenue 90601 * (310) 693-6684

Collection:	General stock.
Specialties:	Western Americana; 19th century English literature; biography; Charles Dickens; books on books; Latin literature.
# of Vols:	40,000
Hours:	Mon-Thu 12-9. Fri & Sat 12-10.
Services:	Appraisals, accepts want lists, book binding and restoration.
Travel:	See Anderson's Bookshop above.
Credit Cards:	Yes
Owner:	Dr. R.F. Valdez
Year Estab:	1981
Comments:	In addition to the shop's several specialties, this establishment also has several hundred old *Life* magazines and a mixed selection of fiction and non fiction hardcover titles worth browsing. With at least three other book shops in town, you can't go wrong stopping at each of them.

Willits
(Map 11, page 289)

The Book Juggler **Open Shop**
182 South Main Street 95490 (707) 459-4075

Collection:	General stock of paperback and hardcover and records.
# of Vols:	60,000
Hours:	Mon-Sat 10-5:30. Sun 12-5.
Travel:	On Hwy 101 in downtown.
Credit Cards:	Yes

Owner: Steve & Susan Grimes
Year Estab: 1984
Comments: A shop that is much deeper than is initially apparent. While at least half of the entry area is taken up with comic related material, the other half is devoted to a mix of paperback and hardcover fiction shelved together. A back room is devoted to hardcover non fiction and magazines. Most of the items were reading copies.

Wofford Heights

Bookworm   **Open Shop**
6925 Wofford Boulevard 93285   (619) 376-2199

Collection: General stock of mostly paperback.
Hours: Tue-Sat 10-4.

Woodland

Bonanza Used Books   **Open Shop**
417 First Street 95695   (916) 661-0636

Collection: General stock of mostly paperback.
Hours: Mon-Sat 10-5.

Woodland Hills
(Map 9, page 64)

Ginkgo Leaf   **Open Shop**
21109 Costanso Street 91364   (818) 716-6332

Collection: Specialty. Primarily new and some used.
Specialties: Self help; ecology; psychology.

Sam's Book Company   **Open Shop**
21016 Ventura Boulevard 91364   Fax: (818) 781-1244   (818) 999-6962

Collection: General stock.
Specialties: Modern first editions; art; literature; philosophy; psychology; poetry; history; mystery; science fiction.
# of Vols: 20,000
Hours: Mon-Sat 11-7. Sun 11-5.
Services: Search service, accepts want lists, mail order.
Travel: Desoto exit off 101 Fwy north. Proceed south to Ventura Blvd. Right on Ventura. Shop is 1½ blocks ahead. Parking available in rear.
Credit Cards: Yes
Owner: Keith Perez
Year Estab: 1985
Comments: Fastidious is the way we would describe both the books on the shelves and the manner in which they are organized. We may be mistaken, but we don't think we saw a single volume *sans* dust jacket. While this shop was

not particularly large in terms of volume or square footage, the books on hand reflect quality. The owner has a second shop in Sherman Oaks. (See Books On The Boulevard above.)

Yorba Linda
(Map 7, page 270)

Book Corner   **Open Shop**
18181 Imperial Highway 92686   (714) 693-5044

Collection: General stock of hardcover and paperback.
Hours: Mon 10-7:30. Tue, Thu, Fri, Sat 10-4. Wed 1-4.
Travel: Imperial Hwy exit off 91 Fwy. North on Imperial. Shop is in public library.
Comments: Operated by Friends of the Yorba Linda Public Library.

Books Redux   **Open Shop**
21520-F Yorba Linda Boulevard 92687   (714) 970-2957

Collection: General stock of mostly used hardcover and paperback.
# of Vols: 30,000
Hours: Mon-Fri 10-6:30. Sat 11-6. Sun 11-4.
Travel: Yorba Linda Blvd exit off 91 Fwy. North on Yorba Linda Rd. Shop is at intersection of Yorba Linda and New River Rd in shopping center.
Credit Cards: Yes
Owner: Marian Hawley & Fred Cannizzaro
Year Estab: 1993
Comments: The shop uses its limited space quite economically. The used stock is about evenly divided between hardcover and paperback. In addition to the standard Stephen King titles, there was a respectable number of older, and in several cases, more unusual hardcover titles.

Yuba City

The Book Ladies of Feather River   **Open Shop**
431 Center Street 95991   (916) 673-3323

Collection: General stock of mostly paperback.
Hours: Winter: Mon-Fri 10-4:30. Sat 10-2. Summer: Mon-Fri 10-4:30. Sat 8-2.

The Book House   **Open Shop**
211 Percy 95991   (916) 674-7680

Collection: General stock of mostly paperback.
Hours: Mon-Fri 10-6. Sat 10-4.

Yucca Valley
(Map 12, page 139)

J. Arthur Robinson, Bookseller   **Open Shop**
57492 Twentynine Palms Highway 92284   Fax: (619) 365-1851   (619) 365-1861

Collection: General stock of new and used, hardcover and paperback.

Specialties: Deserts
# of Vols: 15,000
Hours: Mon-Fri 9-5:30. Sat 10-5. (Closed Dec 25-Jan 1).
Services: Search service, accepts want lists, mail order.
Travel: Located at corner of Airway and Hwy 62 (Twentynine Palms Hwy).
Credit Cards: Yes
Owner: Connie L. & J. Arthur Robinson
Year Estab: 1979
Comments: A combination new/used shop at a ratio of about 50% each. Except for the shop's specialty, most of the books we saw were of a fairly common variety.

Sagebrush Press Bookstore **Open Shop**
55198 Twentynine Palms Highway (619) 365-5671
Mailing Address: PO Box 87 Morongo Valley 92256

Collection: General stock of hardcover and paperback.
Specialties: Western Americana; deserts.
# of Vols: 20,000
Hours: Wed-Sat 12-6. Other times by appointment. Summer hours may vary so best to call ahead.
Services: Catalog, accepts want lists.
Travel: On Hwy 62, at west end of Yucca Valley.
Credit Cards: No
Owner: Dan & Janet Cronkhite
Year Estab: 1991
Comments: There's actually more to this shop than one might suppose considering the modest exterior. In addition to the shop's specialties, there's a nice variety of books in most other subject areas with several titles not seen elsewhere If you're in the mood for a desert drive, a stop here should prove refreshing.

Open Shops and By Appointment Dealers

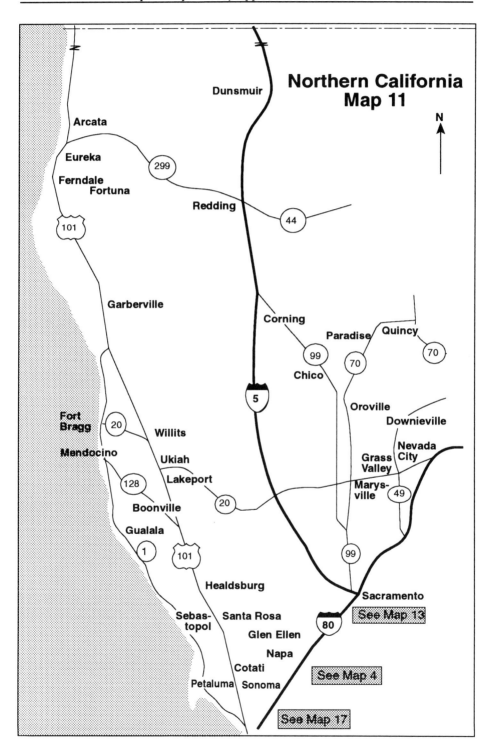

Abbey Bookshop
* (310) 470-2296

PO Box 64384 Los Angeles 90064

Collection:	General stock.
Specialties:	Primarily non fiction.
# of Vols:	30,000
Services:	Appraisals, search service, catalog, accepts want lists.
Credit Cards:	No
Owner:	Gideon Berman
Year Estab:	1948

Noreen Abbot Books
(415) 664-9464

2666-44th Avenue San Francisco 94116

Collection:	Specialty
Specialties:	Children's; illustrated.
# of Vols:	2,000
Services:	Search service, catalog, accepts want lists.
Credit Cards:	No
Year Estab:	1987

Alta's
(209) 532-6151

20418 Green Acres Road Sonora 95370

Collection:	General stock of mostly hardcover.
Specialties:	Children's; railroads.
# of Vols:	10,000
Services:	Search service, catalog, accepts want lists.
Credit Cards:	No
Owner:	Alta Matthews
Year Estab:	1985

Andy's Books
(714) 527-6935
Fax: (714) 527-4263

PO Box 2686 Cypress 90630

Collection:	Specialty new and used hardcover.
Specialties:	Mystery; horror (signed first editions); modern first editions.
# of Vols:	2,500
Services:	Search service, catalog, accepts want lists.
Credit Cards:	Yes
Owner:	Andy & Janis Langwiser
Year Estab:	1991

Apex Books
(707) 996-7205   (707) 996-4769
Fax: (707) 996-7205

PO Box 1576 Sonoma 95476

Collection:	Specialty hardcover and paperback and ephemera.
Specialties:	Science fiction; fantasy; horror; modern first editions; mystery; westerns; children's; UFOs; metaphysics; Hollywood; vintage paperbacks.
# of Vols:	15,000
Services:	Catalog, accepts want lists.
Owner:	Dennis L. White
Year Estab:	1987

* Some 310 codes change to 562 in 1996

The Aquatic Book Shop
3050 Countryside Drive Placerville 95667

(916) 622-7547
Fax: (916) 622-7157

Collection: Specialty. Mostly new and some used books and related items.
Specialties: Aquarium and fish related.
# of Vols: 10,000
Services: Search service, catalog, accepts want lists.
Credit Cards: Yes
Owner: Jim Forshey
Year Estab: 1988

Automotive Information
PO Box 1746 La Mesa 91944

(619) 447-7200
Fax: (619) 447-8080

Collection: Specialty
Specialties: Automobiles
# of Vols: 800,000+
Credit Cards: Yes
Year Estab: 1978
Comments: Stock is totally computerized. All inquiries must have a self addressed stamped envelope.

Avons Research Publications
PO Box 40 La Canada 91011

(818) 790-5370

Collection: Specialty
Specialties: Avon hobby collecting; depression glass.
Services: Catalog
Credit Cards: No
Owner: Dorothy Rudolph
Year Estab: 1968

Bad Moon Books
724 South Falcon Street Anaheim 92804

(714) 533-1828

Collection: Specialty hardcover.
Specialties: Horror; science fiction; mystery; modern first editions.
Services: Catalog, accepts want lists.
Credit Cards: Yes
Owner: Roy K. Robbins
Year Estab: 1990

Basement Books
75 Millthwait Drive Martinez 94553

(510) 228-3666

Collection: Specialty
Specialties: Science fiction, fantasy; horror.
Services: Catalog
Owner: Donna Rankin
Comments: Also displays at Tall Stories in San Francisco.

Beaver Books
PO Box 974 Daly City 94017

Collection:	Specialty
Specialties:	Fur trade and related exploration.
# of Vols:	2,500
Services:	Search service, catalog, accepts want lists.
Credit Cards:	No
Owner:	E.L. Weber
Year Estab:	1972

Stan Beecher (909) 687-0982
9433 Bruce Avenue Riverside 92503

Collection:	Specialty
Specialties:	Mystery; science fiction; modern first editions; autographs; Disneyania.
# of Vols:	5,000
Services:	Accepts want lists.
Credit Cards:	No
Year Estab:	1994

Bethel Antiquarian Books Fax: (510) 945-020
PO Box 2071 Danville 9452

Collection:	Specialty books and ephemera.
Specialties:	Watchtower publications; Jehovah's Witnesses.
# of Vols:	5,000
Services:	Catalog, accepts want lists.
Credit Cards:	No
Owner:	Kamil Marcinka
Year Estab:	1988

Roy Bleiweiss-Fine Books and Autographs (510) 548-1624
92 Northgate Avenue Berkeley 94708

Collection:	Specialty
Specialties:	Fine printing; private press; Americana; art; architecture; first editions; smoking and anti-tobacco; autographs; manuscripts.
# of Vols:	3,500
Services:	Appraisals, catalog, accepts want lists.
Year Estab:	1974

Book Alert (415) 391-3114
1081 Alameda de las Pulgas Belmont 94002

Collection:	General stock.
# of Vols:	900
Services:	Search service, accepts want lists.
Credit Cards:	No
Owner:	Marion Hill
Year Estab:	1990

Book Gems
(805) 967-4238
PO Box 60532 Santa Barbara 93160

Collection: General stock.
# of Vols: 5,000
Services: Appraisals, search service, accepts want lists.
Credit Cards: No
Owner: Joanne Wightman
Year Estab: 1993

The Book Shelf
(714) 642-5619
1308 Sussex Lane Newport Beach 92660
Fax: (714) 642-5619

Collection: Specialty
Specialties: Modern first editions specializing in literature, women writers, African American literature and mystery; signed.
Services: Catalog
Credit Cards: Yes
Owner: Steve & Judi Johnson
Year Estab: 1988

The Book Symposium
(818) 242-4818
1745 Kenneth Road Glendale 91201

Collection: Specialty hardcover and paperback and some ephemera.
Specialties: Science fiction; fantasy; H.P. Lovecraft; Clark Aston Smith; Robert E. Howard; Ras Press; Arkham House.
# of Vols: 3,000
Services: Appraisals, catalog, accepts want lists.
Credit Cards: Yes
Owner: Terence A. McVicker
Year Estab: 1976

Boulevard Books
* (310) 455-1036
PO Box 89 Topanga 90290

Collection: Specialty
Specialties: Mystery; plays.
# of Vols: 25,000
Services: Catalog, accepts want lists.
Credit Cards: No
Owner: Clifford McCarty
Year Estab: 1958

Virginia Burgman Rare Books
(707) 526-2482
3198 Hidden Valley Drive Santa Rosa 95404

Collection: Specialty
Specialties: Children's (early); signed first editions; Americana; magazines.
Services: Search service, catalog, accepts want lists (preferably in large print).
Credit Cards: No
Year Estab: 1958

* *Some 310 codes change to 562 in 1996*

John R. Butterworth (909) 626-0763
742 West 11th Street Claremont 91711

Collection:	Specialty
Specialties:	Modern first editions.
# of Vols:	10,000
Services:	Occasional catalog.
Year Estab:	1975

Buy The Book (415) 366-6001
40 Woodhue Court Redwood City 94062

Collection:	General stock.
Specialties:	Modern first editions.
# of Vols:	2,500
Owner:	Wendy & Dave Redfern
Year Estab:	1994

Caernarvon Press (619) 299-1341
4665 Mississippi Street, #1 San Diego 92116

Collection:	General stock.
Specialties:	Emphasis on fiction; science fiction; mystery.
# of Vols:	4,000
Services:	Occasional catalog, search service, accepts want lists.
Credit Cards:	No
Owner:	Terry Hertzler
Year Estab:	1985

Richard Callaway, Rare Books and Autographs * (310) 831-5542
PO Box 590 San Pedro 90733 Fax: (310) 831-5350

Collection:	Specialty
Specialties:	Primarily 19th century: first editions; fine bindings; illustrated; autographs.
# of Vols:	15,000
Services:	Accepts want lists.
Credit Cards:	No
Year Estab:	1980

Chamasha Books (510) 283-0201
PO Box 1836 Lafayette 94549

Collection:	Specialty
Specialties:	Maritime, including hard hat diving; ocean salvage; work boats; steam navigation.
# of Vols:	5,000
Services:	Catalog, accepts want lists.
Credit Cards:	No
Owner:	Charles W. Shambaugh
Year Estab:	1986

Channel Island Books (805) 569-1200
PO Box 3325 Santa Barbara 93130

Collection:	Specialty

* *Some 310 codes change to 562 in 1996*

Specialties:	Modern first editions; signed; literary autographs.	
# of Vols:	3,000	
Services:	Appraisals, catalog, search service, accepts want lists.	
Credit Cards:	No	
Owner:	Gary Staneff	
Year Estab:	1993	

Barbara Cook Modern 1st Editions (916) 454-4850
2939 25th Street Sacramento 95818

Collection:	Specialty
Specialties:	Modern first editions; dance.
# of Vols:	5,000
Services:	Accepts want lists.
Credit Cards:	Yes
Year Estab:	1989
Comments:	Also displays at The Book Collector in Sacramento.

The Cook Book Lady (510) 687-1029
253 Magda Way Martinez 94553

Collection:	Specialty
Specialties:	Cookbooks
# of Vols:	1,700
Services:	Catalog, search service, accepts want lists.
Credit Cards:	No
Owner:	Lori Huges
Year Estab:	1989

Craig Books (415) 661-3064
103 Mendosa Avenue San Francisco 94116

Collection:	Specialty
Specialties:	Cooking
Credit Cards:	No
Owner:	Elaine Craig
Year Estab:	1992

Crawford-Peters Aeronautica (619) 287-3933
PO Box 152528 San Diego 92195

Collection:	Specialty
Specialties:	Aviation; space.
# of Vols:	11,000
Services:	Catalog, search service, accepts want lists.
Credit Cards:	No
Owner:	James P. Peters & Mike Crawford
Year Estab:	1985

Curran & Hermes Books (415) 927-3036
PO Box 278 Corte Madera 94976

Collection:	General stock.
Specialties:	Natural history (mainly birds); cookbooks; wine.

# of Vols:	6,000
Services:	Search service, accepts want lists.
Credit Cards:	No
Owner:	Ann Kidd
Year Estab:	1990

Robert Dagg Rare Books (805) 966-4318
PO Box 4758 Santa Barbara 93140 Fax: (805) 966-5046

Collection:	Specialty
Specialties:	Modern first editions; signed and inscribed.
# of Vols:	1,000
Services:	Catalog, accepts want lists.
Credit Cards:	Yes
Year Estab:	1989
Comments:	Collection may also be viewed by appointment.

L. Clarice Davis (818) 787-1322
PO Box 56054 Sherman Oaks 91413 Fax: (818) 780-3281

Collection:	Specialty
Specialties:	Fine and applied arts; art history; decorative arts; photography; architecture; exhibition catalogs.
# of Vols:	10,000
Services:	Appraisals, catalog.
Credit Cards:	No
Year Estab:	1972
Comments:	Collection may also be viewed by appointment.

Dieterly Books (909) 924-1678
PO Box 8334 Moreno Valley 92552

Collection:	General stock.
# of Vols:	10,000
Services:	Appraisals, search service.
Credit Cards:	No
Owner:	Duncan Dieterly
Year Estab:	1992

Steven G. Doi-Books (408) 265-8351
PO Box 7845 San Jose 95150

Collection:	Specialty
Specialties:	Asians in America; Asian immigration; refugees; Chinatowns; Japanese American internment during WW II.
# of Vols:	2,000
Services:	Search service, catalog, accepts want lists.
Credit Cards:	No
Year Estab:	1981

Eldorado Books (415) 552-8122
PO Box 14036 San Francisco 94114

Collection:	General stock.

# of Vols:	2,000-3,000
Services:	Appraisals, accepts want lists.
Credit Cards:	No
Owner:	Irving Eidenberg
Year Estab:	1954

Essence Gallery (619) 749-9352
PO Box 1800 Valley Center 92082   Fax: (619) 749-9352

Collection:	Specialty
Specialties:	Art, specializing in equine, western, southwestern, California impressionism, 19th -20th century.
Services:	Search service, accepts want lists.
Credit Cards:	No
Owner:	M.H. Parkinson
Year Estab:	1990

Exotica Fine Books (818) 507-5142
329 North Brank Boulevard Glendale 91203

Collection:	Specialty
Specialties:	True crime; occult; radical studies.
# of Vols:	7,000
Services:	Catalog, accepts want lists.
Credit Cards:	Yes
Owner:	Jerome Joseph
Year Estab:	1994

First Street Books & Antiques (415) 948-8903
14510 Manuella Road Los Altos 94022

Collection:	Specialty
Specialties:	Modern first editions; children's; illustrated; Wallace Stegner.
# of Vols:	2,500
Owner:	Sylvia Asendorf
Year Estab:	1981

Flashback Books (707) 762-4714
40 Fourth Street, Ste. 260 Petaluma 94952

Collection:	Specialty
Specialties:	60's counter culture; drug literature.
# of Vols:	3,000
Services:	Catalog, accepts want lists.
Credit Cards:	No
Owner:	Michael Horowitz
Year Estab:	1988

J. Joseph Flynn Rare Books * (310) 440-3979
2220 Mandeville Canyon Road Los Angeles 90049   Fax: (310) 440-3979

Collection:	Specialty
Specialties:	George MacDonald; C.S. Lewis; Charles Williams; J.R.R. Tolkien.
Services:	Search service, catalog, accepts want lists.

* Some 310 codes change to 562 in 1996

Folk Motif
* (310) 439-7380
PO Box 14755 Long Beach 90803

Collection: Specialty. Mostly new and some used.
Specialties: Folk arts and traditions.
Services: Catalog

The Fool's Progress
(415) 752-3490
PO Box 591596 San Francisco 94159

Collection: General stock.
Specialties: Modern fiction; beat generation; counter culture; erotica.
# of Vols: 5,000
Services: Catalog, search service, accepts want lists.
Credit Cards: No
Owner: Rocky Heck
Year Estab: 1995
Comments: Also displays at Tall Stories in San Francisco.

Fuhrman & Fuhrman
(707) 541-0399
106 Pierce Street Santa Rosa 95404

Collection: Specialty
Specialties: Modern first editions, with emphasis on mystery.
# of Vols: 2,000
Services: Appraisals, accepts want lists.
Credit Cards: Yes
Owner: Harry & Mary Fuhrman
Year Estab: 1992

Geiger's Books
(408) 335-5870
PO Box 66223 Scotts Valley 95067
E-mail: geigers@cruzio.com

Collection: Specialty
Specialties: Western Americana; California; modern first editions; mystery.
Services: Search service, accepts want lists.
Credit Cards: No
Owner: Gary Decker

Geoscience Books & Prints
(909) 797-1650
13057 California Street Yucaipa 92399

Collection: Specialty books and ephemera.
Specialties: Mining; mineralogy; gemology.
# of Vols: "Moderate"
Services: Accepts want lists.
Credit Cards: No
Year Estab: 1980

Michael Gibbs, Books
(800) 475-0869   (408) 395-1937
PO Box 33271 Los Gatos 95031
Fax: (408) 395-1937

Collection: Specialty
Specialties: Western Americana.

* *Some 310 codes change to 562 in 1996*

# of Vols: 10,000
Services: Catalog, appraisals, search service.
Credit Cards: No
Year Estab: 1978

Phillip Gold-221 Books (818) 889-2640
760 Carlisle Canyon Road Westlake Village 91361   Fax: (818) 889-2640

Collection: General stock.
Specialties: Sherlock Holmes; Arthur Conan Doyle; H. Rider Haggard; H.G. Wells; science fiction; mystery; literature.
# of Vols: 5,000
Credit Cards: No
Year Estab: 1991

The Good Book Company (805) 646-7106
136 South Arnaz Ojai 93023

Collection: General stock.
Services: Catalog in planning stage, search service, accepts want lists.
Credit Cards: Yes
Owner: Victor & Virginia Garner
Year Estab: 1992

Grand Slam Sports Books * (310) 822-5789
PO Box 4369 Culver City 90230   Home: (310) 277-5972

Collection: Specialty books, magazines and ephemera.
Specialties: Sports
# of Vols: 10,000
Services: Occasional catalog, appraisals, search service, accepts want lists.
Credit Cards: Yes
Owner: Arthur S. Keith
Year Estab: 1970
Comments: Collection can be viewed by appointment.

Emmett Harrington Rare Books (415) 587-4604
PO Box 27326 San Francisco 94127

Collection: Specialty
Specialties: Americana, especially Western Americana and California.
Services: Catalog, accepts want lists.
Credit Cards: Yes
Year Estab: 1989

Dave Henson-Books (714) 542-8839
PO Box 11402 Santa Ana 92711

Collection: Specialty
Specialties: California; Western Americana.
Credit Cards: No
Year Estab: 1959

Heron House (415) 564-5241
2101 15th Avenue San Francisco 94116

Collection:	Specialty books and ephemera.
Specialties:	Books about books; fine printing.
# of Vols:	2,000
Services:	Accepts want lists.
Credit Cards:	No
Owner:	Earl Emelson
Year Estab:	1986

Willis E. Herr, Bookseller (619) 268-3550
7004 Camino Pacheco San Diego 92111

Collection:	General stock of new and used.
Specialties:	Mystery; fiction.
Services:	Catalog, accepts want lists.
Credit Cards:	No
Year Estab:	1992

History Focused (619) 672-2593
PO Box 720101 San Diego 92172

Collection:	Specialty
Specialties:	Civil War (books and photographic).
# of Vols:	100
Services:	Search service, accepts want lists.
Credit Cards:	No
Owner:	David J. Tooley
Year Estab:	1990

Household Words (510) 524-8859
PO Box 7231 Berkeley 94707

Collection:	Specialty hardcover and paperback.
Specialties:	Cookbooks; wine.
Services:	Appraisals, search service, catalog, accepts want lists.
Credit Cards:	No
Owner:	Kay Caughren
Year Estab:	1976

I Love A Mystery (818) 508-6979
4312 Babcock Avenue, #5 Studio City 91604
Fax: (818) 508-5336

Collection:	Specialty. Mostly hardcover.
Specialties:	Mystery and detective fiction and non fiction.
Services:	Catalog, accepts want lists.
Credit Cards:	No
Owner:	Sally Powers
Year Estab:	1992

Inkworks Rare & Collectible Books
3700 Eagle Rock Boulevard Los Angeles 90065

Collection:	Specialty

Specialties: Science fiction; horror; fantasy. All first, limited or sighed editions.
# of Vols: 500
Services: Catalog, appraisals, accepts want lists.
Credit Cards: Yes
Owner: John Dorman
Year Estab: 1990

The Invisible Bookman (510) 524-7823
97 Franciscan Way Berkeley 94707

Collection: Specialty books and ephemera.
Specialties: Poetry; first books of authors; black literature; modern first editions (with emphasis on poetry, fiction and drama); literary criticism.
# of Vols: 2,000
Services: Appraisals, search service, accepts want lists.
Credit Cards: No
Owner: Allan Covici
Year Estab: 1963

Just Books And... (916) 482-7493
3630 La Habra Way Sacramento 95864

Collection: General stock.
# of Vols: 4,000
Services: Search service, accepts want lists.
Credit Cards: No
Owner: Frank Just
Year Estab: 1977

Gerry Kleier (707) 554-6123
322 Manhattan Drive Vallejo 94591

Collection: General stock.
Specialties: Modern first editions; mystery; science fiction.
# of Vols: 5,000
Services: Catalog
Credit Cards: No
Year Estab: 1989

Gen Krueger Books (818) 353-0525
7840 McGroarty Street Sunland 91040

Collection: General stock.
Specialties: Children's
# of Vols: 15,000
Services: Occasional catalog, search service, accepts want lists.
Credit Cards: No
Year Estab: 1982

Larry's Books & Autographs (510) 935-4131
PO Box 1018 Lafayette 94549 Fax: (510) 935-0407

Collection: Specialty
Specialties: Modern first editions; poetry; autographs of jazz and big band personalities.

# of Vols: 500-1,000
Services: Catalog, accepts want lists.
Owner: Larry Rafferty

Last Seen Reading (415) 321-3348
PO Box 1423 Palo Alto 94302

Collection: Specialty
Specialties: Mystery; children's.
Services: Catalog, accepts want lists.
Credit Cards: No
Owner: Bonnie & David Pollard

Latin Blood Books (818) 344-1613
PO Box 7733 Van Nuys 91409

Collection: Specialty
Specialties: Mystery; crime; Latin American literature; modern fiction. Approximately 95% of stock is signed or inscribed..
# of Vols: 2,000
Services: Search service, catalog, accepts want lists.
Credit Cards: No
Owner: Dale Carter
Year Estab: 1986

Lawrence's Books * (310) 316-8134
22433 Redbeam Avenue Torrance 90505

Collection: General stock of hardcover and paperback.
Specialties: Literary first editions; technical; military.
# of Vols: 17,000
Services: Accepts want lists.
Credit Cards: No
Owner: Larry Schmidt
Year Estab: 1995

E. Lubbe Books (415) -46-7-0811
PO Box 347294 San Francisco 94134

Collection: General stock.
Specialties: Western Americana; California; military.
# of Vols: 15,000
Services: Accepts want lists.
Credit Cards: No
Owner: Ernest Lubbe
Year Estab: 1971

Jim Lyons Historical Newspapers (415) 969-6612
970 Terra Bella, Ste 3 Mountain View 94043

Collection: Specialty
Specialties: Newspapers, predominately United States from colonial times.
Services: Catalog
Credit Cards: No

* *Some 310 codes change to 562 in 1996*

Year Estab: 1972
Comments: Collection can be viewed by appointment.

Mary Mason Bookseller (619) 287-2299
PO Box 15804 San Diego 92175

Collection: Specialty. Mostly used hardcover.
Specialties: Mystery; signed; cookbooks.
# of Vols: 10,000
Services: Search service, catalog, accepts want lists.
Credit Cards: No
Year Estab: 1991

Susan Mast Enterprises (408) 423-9786
849 Almar Avenue, #C-270 Santa Cruz 95060

Collection: Specialty
Specialties: Hawaii

Mike's Memories * (310) 659-4955
939 Palm Avenue, #201 West Hollywood 90069 Fax: (310) 659-4955

Collection: General stock and ephemera.
Specialties: Charles Burowksi; beat generation; modern literature.
Services: Search service, catalog, accepts want lists.
Credit Cards: No
Owner: Michael Artura
Year Estab: 1987

Mockingbird Books (909) 621-5758
5426 Denver Street Montclair 91763

Collection: General stock.
# of Vols: 10,000
Services: Subject lists, search service, accepts want lists.
Credit Cards: No
Owner: Mike Friedman
Year Estab: 1990

Netkin Fine Arts (415) 962-0720
1375 Montecito Avenue, #32 Mountain View 94043

Collection: Specialty
Specialties: Art; photography; dance; Japanese and Chinese art and culture.
Services: Catalog, accepts want lists.
Comments: Collection may also be viewed by appointment.

Kai Nygaard, Bookseller (619) 746-9039
19421 Eighth Place Escondido 92029

Collection: Specialty hardcover and paperback.
Specialties: Science fiction; fantasy; horror. (First Editions).
# of Vols: 7,000+
Services: Catalog, accepts want lists.

Credit Cards: No
Year Estab: 1985

Jim Orbaugh, Bookseller (619) 598-2734
1500 Shadowridge Drive, #125 Vista 92083

Collection: Specialty paperback and hardcover books and related magazines.
Specialties: Horror; small press; signed; limited editions.
# of Vols: 4,000-5,000
Services: Search service, catalog, accepts want lists.
Credit Cards: No
Year Estab: 1986
Comments: Stock is primarily used with some new United Kingdom titles.

Out-Of-State Book Service (714) 492-2976
PO Box 3253-B San Clemente 92674

Collection: General stock.
# of Vols: 3,000
Services: Search service, accepts want lists.
Credit Cards: No
Owner: A. Spigler
Year Estab: 1958

Pa-Has-Ka Books (818) 348-9795
8436 Samra Drive West Hills 91304

Collection: Specialty
Specialties: Western Americana.
# of Vols: 1,500
Services: Catalog, search service, accepts want lists.
Credit Cards: No
Owner: Art & Chris Sowin
Year Estab: 1985

Paper Collectibles (408) 646-5204
PO Box 1159 Seaside 93955

Collection: Ephemera
Specialties: 19th century engravings - all subjects.
Services: Search service, accepts want lists, mail order.
Credit Cards: No
Owner: John Barbier
Year Estab: 1986

Papyrus Books (510) 790-1342
34372 Dunhill Drive Fremont 94555

Collection: Specialty
Specialties: Ancient art, archaeology; numismatics.
# of Vols: 2,000
Services: Catalog, search service, accepts want lists.
Owner: Nancy Katsouras
Year Estab: 1992

David Park Books (415) 621-6654
3456 17th Street San Francisco 94110

Collection:	Specialty
Specialties:	Conspiracy; CIA; John F. Kennedy.
# of Vols:	3,000
Services:	Catalog
Year Estab:	1989

Pepper & Stern Rare Books (805) 963-1025
1980 Cliff Drive, Ste. 224 Santa Barbara 93109

Collection:	Specialty
Specialties:	American and English first editions (mostly 20th century, some 19th century); mystery; detective; Sherlock Holmes; autographed and signed copies; film.
Services:	Catalog
Credit Cards:	Yes
Owner:	James Pepper

Robert Perata (707) 575-3731
2204 Sartori Drive Santa Rosa 95405

Collection:	Specialty books and ephemera.
Specialties:	Western Americana; books on books; press books.
# of Vols:	1,500-2,000
Services:	Catalog, appraisals, accepts want lists.
Credit Cards:	No
Year Estab:	1969

Peri Lithon Books (619) 488-6904
PO Box 9996 San Diego 92169

Collection:	Specialty hardcover and paperback and ephemera.
Specialties:	Geosciences; geology; paleontology; mining; mineralogy; gemology; jewelry; microscopes.
# of Vols:	9,000
Services:	Catalog, accepts want lists, mail order.
Owner:	John & Marjorie Sinkankas
Year Estab:	1971

Joan Perkal-Books (805) 653-6868
193 Aliso Street Ventura 93001 Fax: (805) 653-6879

Collection:	Specialty
Specialties:	Children's; illustrated.
# of Vols:	5,000
Services:	Search service, accepts want lists.
Comments:	Also displays at The Book Mall in Ventura and Magnolia Park Books in Burbank.

Wallace D. Pratt, Bookseller (415) 673-0178
1801 Gough Street, #304 San Francisco 94109

Collection:	Specialty

Specialties: Civil War; Indian Wars; military.
# of Vols: 4,000
Services: Catalog, accepts want lists.
Credit Cards: No
Year Estab: 1987

The Printers' Shop
4546 El Camino Real, B10, Ste 207 Los Altos 94022

(415) 941-0433
Fax: (415) 941-0596

Collection: Specialty
Specialties: Book arts; printing; bookbinding; papermaking; typography; fine printing; miniature books.
# of Vols: 1,500
Services: Catalog, accepts want lists.
Credit Cards: Yes
Owner: Frederica Postman
Year Estab: 1974

Diane Pyke-Books
1107 Glacier Avenue Pacifica 94044

(415) 355-7611

Collection: General stock.
Specialties: French books.
Services: Search service, accepts want lists.
Credit Cards: No
Year Estab: 1988

Ravenscar Books
14431 Ventura Boulevard, Ste. 210 Sherman Oaks 91423

(818) 786-1040
Fax: (818) 786-5363

Collection: General stock.
Specialties: Mystery; fiction.
Services: Catalog, accepts want lists.
Credit Cards: No
Owner: David & Kathleen Scherman
Year Estab: 1992

John Roby
3703 Nassau Drive San Diego 92115

(619) 583-4264
Fax: (619) 286-2425

Collection: Specialty
Specialties: Aviation (technical and non technical).
Services: Search service, catalog, accepts want lists.
Credit Cards: No
Year Estab: 1960

Rock of Ages
PO Box 3503 Tustin 92681

(714) 730-8948
Fax: (714) 730-1644

Collection: Specialty. Mostly used and some new.
Specialties: Mining (history and technology); mineralogy; geology (no fuels); gemology; jewelry; metallurgy; crystallography; meteoritics; USGS publications.
# of Vols: 2,000
Services: Catalog, accepts want lists, mail order.

Credit Cards: Yes
Owner: John & Linda Stimson
Year Estab: 1987

S & J Books (619) 728-9668
PO Box 464 Fallbrook 92088

Collection: General stock.
# of Vols: 5,000
Credit Cards: No
Owner: Stephen Spears
Year Estab: 1977

Safari Press (714) 894-9080
15621 Chemical Lane, #B Huntington Beach 92649 Fax: (714) 894-4949

Collection: Specialty
Specialties: Big game hunting.
# of Vols: 1,500
Services: Appraisals, search service, catalog, accepts want lists.
Credit Cards: Yes
Owner: Ludo J. Wurfbain
Year Estab: 1984

San Diego Model Railroad Museum (619) 696-0199
1649 El Prado San Diego 92101

Collection: Specialty magazines.
Specialties: Railroads
Comments: The museum is open Tue-Sun 11-4. The gift shop sells new books as well as old magazines.

Myrna Sapunar Books (408) 688-7389
34 Mar Monte Avenue La Selva Beach 95076

Collection: General stock.
# of Vols: 2,000

Scattergood Research (510) 525-5454
77 Stratford Road Kensington 94707 E-mail: mayi@netcom.com

Collection: Specialty
Specialties: Russia and Soviet Union, including history, literature and art; Middle East; propaganda; Spanish Civil War.
# of Vols: 3,000
Services: Accepts want lists.
Credit Cards: No
Owner: Irwin Mayers
Year Estab: 1985

Schoyer's Books 1 (800) 356-2199
Berkeley (See Comments) Fax: 1 (800) 439-2199
E-mail: dsbooks@eworld.com

Collection: Specialty

Specialties:	California; Western Americana; Federal Writers Project; travel; Balkan; Middle East; Asia; Africa; women's studies; Americana.
# of Vols:	5,00-7,000
Services:	Catalog, collection development.
Owner:	Donnis deCamp & Marc Selvaggio
Year Estab:	1952
Comments:	The owners will be relocating to Berkeley in early 1996 from Pittsburgh, PA. Prior to their move, they can be reached at the above '800' numbers or by E-mail.

Second Harvest Books (800) 928-5206
PO Box 1388 Cobb Mountain 95426 Fax:(800) 928-5206

Collection:	General stock.
Specialties:	Wine
# of Vols:	2,000
Services:	Search service, catalog, accepts want lists.
Credit Cards:	No
Owner:	Warren R. Johnson
Year Estab:	1992

Second Time 'Round Quality Used Books (619) 273-9571
PO Box 9658 San Diego 92169

Collection:	General stock of hardcover and paperback and ephemera.
Specialties:	Mystery; cookbooks; science fiction.
Services:	Accepts want lists.
Credit Cards:	No
Owner:	M.E. & M.L. Shelley & R.N. Anderson
Year Estab:	1980

Sleepy Hollow Books (510) 376-9235
1455 Camino Peral Moraga 94556

Collection:	General stock.
Specialties:	19th & 20th century fiction; Western Americana; mystery; private press; science fiction; children's; California; books about books; Sherlock Holmes.
# of Vols:	10,000
Services:	Appraisals, search service, catalog, accepts want lists.
Credit Cards:	No
Owner:	Richard G. Allen
Year Estab:	1980

Christophe Stickel Autographs (408) 656-0111
167-B Central Avenue Pacific Grove 93950

Collection:	Specialty
Specialties:	Autographs; signed books.
Services:	Catalog
Credit Cards:	Yes
Year Estab:	1980

Ivan Stormgart-Books (415) 931-6746
PO Box 470883 San Francisco 94147

Collection:	Specialty. Mostly used hardcover.
Specialties:	Sexology; erotica.
# of Vols:	10,000
Services:	Appraisals; search service, catalog, accepts want lists.
Credit Cards:	No
Year Estab:	1979

Sun Dance Books (213) 654-2383
1520 North Crescent Heights Hollywood 90046

Collection:	Specialty
Specialties:	Southwestern Americana; Mexico; Latin America; Chicano studies; Asian America; natives Americans of southwest.
# of Vols:	2,500
Services:	Appraisals
Credit Cards:	No
Owner:	A. Adrian
Year Estab:	1972

Sun Moon Bear Rare Books (707) 433-2625
17807 Lytton Station Road Geyserville 95441

Collection:	Specialty books and ephemera.
Specialties:	Poetry (20th century American and British); modern fiction; hyper modern first editions; bilingual literature; beat generation; San Francisco; private press.
# of Vols:	5,000
Services:	Search service, catalog, accepts want lists, collection development
Credit Cards:	No
Owner:	Lee Perron
Year Estab:	1981

Sylvester & Orphanos Booksellers (213) 461-1194
PO Box 2567 Hollywood 90078-2567

Collection:	General stock of mostly first editions.
Specialties:	Modern literary first editions; black studies. Also publishes literary limited signed editions.
# of Vols:	40,000
Services:	Appraisals, catalog, search service, accepts want lists.
Credit Cards:	No
Owner:	Ralph Sylvester & Stathis Orphanos
Year Estab:	1970's

Tavistock Books (510) 814-0480
PO Box 5096 Alameda 94501 Fax: (510) 814-0480

Collection:	General stock and ephemera.
Specialties:	Focus on 19th century books, especially Charles Dickens; also Vietnam first editions.

# of Vols:	2,000
Services:	Appraisals, search service, catalog, accepts want lists.
Credit Cards:	Yes
Owner:	Vic Zoschak, Jr.
Year Estab:	1989
Comments:	Collection may also be viewed by appointment.

D.W. Taylor Books (916) 778-3178
PO Box 127 Lewiston 96052

Collection:	General stock.
# of Vols:	500+
Services:	Search service, accepts want lists, mail order.
Credit Cards:	No
Owner:	Diana Taylor
Year Estab:	1992
Comments:	Collection may also be viewed by appointment.

Ten O'CLock Books (916) 685-8219
8839 Kelsey Drive Elk Grove 95624

Collection:	Specialty
Specialties:	Out-of-print books in Spanish and in English translation in humanities and literature.
Services:	Catalog
Credit Cards:	No
Owner:	J.A. Grenzeback
Year Estab:	1973

Theater Book Shop (408) 429-6874
PO Box 1182 Santa Cruz 95061

Collection:	Specialty used and some new.
Specialties:	Theater, including biographies and autobiographies of theater personalities.
Services:	Appraisals, occasional catalog, mail order.
Credit Cards:	No
Owner:	Lisa Pollock
Year Estab:	1975

Thelema Publications
PO Box 1393 Kings Beach 96143

Collection:	Specialty
Specialties:	Occult; Aleister Crowley; thelema.
Services:	Search service, accepts want lists.
Credit Cards:	No
Owner:	H. Parsons Smith
Year Estab:	1970

William Thomas (805) 489-8386
259 Oakwood Court Arroyo Grande 93420

Collection:	Specialty

Specialties: Historical facsimiles in all subject fields.
# of Vols: 3,000
Services: Appraisals, catalog, accepts want lists.
Credit Cards: No
Year Estab: 1980
Comments: Collection can also be viewed by appointment.

Rik Thompson Books (408) 262-4673
PO Box 361420 Milpitas 95035

Collection: Specialty
Specialties: Science fiction; mystery. Primarily first editions and signed editions.
# of Vols: 20,000
Services: Occasional catalog, accepts want lists.
Credit Cards: No
Year Estab: 1972
Comments: Also displays at Tall Stories in San Francisco.

To & Again Books * (310) 809-1373
PO Box 1821 Hawaiian Gardens 90716

Collection: Specialty
Specialties: Children's
# of Vols: 4,000
Services: Appraisals, catalog, search service, accepts want lists.
Credit Cards: No
Owner: Cliff Erickson
Year Estab: 1981

Toad Hall (510) 540-0172
PO Box 902 Berkeley 94701

Collection: General stock.
Specialties: Garden history and design; mountaineering; children's; fine bindings; literature.
# of Vols: 1,000
Services: Search service, catalog, accepts want lists.
Credit Cards: No
Owner: J.A. Baker
Year Estab: 1976

Van Norman-Booksellers (619) 296-6451
4047 Bay View Court San Diego 92103

Collection: Specialty
Specialties: Western Americana; architecture; photography; dance; natural history; children's illustrated; art; nautical; mountaineering; books on books; biography.
# of Vols: 20,000
Services: Catalog, accepts want lists.
Credit Cards: No
Owner: Allen Van Norman
Year Estab: 1980

* *Some 310 codes change to 562 in 1996*

Graeme Vanderstoel (510) 527-2882
PO Box 599 El Cerrito 94530

Collection:	Specialty
Specialties:	Asia; Asian art; performing arts of Asia.
# of Vols:	3,000
Services:	Appraisals; search service, catalog, accepts want lists.
Credit Cards:	No
Year Estab:	1962

B. Vasin Bookseller (818) 780-4060
7007 DeCelis Place Van Nuys 91406

Collection:	Specialty
Specialties:	Costume design; vintage clothing; textiles and allied interests.
# of Vols:	4,000-5,000
Services:	Subject lists.
Credit Cards:	No
Year Estab:	1965

Virtual Book Shop (916) 632-9770
2351 Sunset Blvd, Ste 170-307 Rocklin 95765

Collection:	General stock.
# of Vols:	50,000
Owner:	Steve Armstrong
Comments:	A first for Book Hunter Press. A mail order dealer that is exclusively on line, i.e., you can only order via the Internet. In addition to his own stock, the dealer provides Internet access to other dealers in the United States and overseas. The stock ranges from 13th century illuminated manuscripts to more recent horror fiction.

Volkoff & von Hohenlohe (805) 686-1567
1696 Nordentoft Way Solvang 93463 Fax: (805) 686-1882

Collection:	Specialty
Specialties:	Central European political science from 1450-1950; Slavica; humanism and reformation; women's studies; history of science; Napoleon (including documents); Judaica (cultural and historical up to 1933).
Services:	Subject lists
Credit Cards:	No
Owner:	Ivan Volkoff & Adelheid A. von Hohenlohe
Year Estab:	1953
Comments:	Specializes in large subject collections to institutions.

Paul von Ahnen Books (408) 353-1939
22220 Old Santa Cruz Highway Los Gatos 95030

Collection:	General stock.
Specialties:	California; Western Americana; native Americans; literature; literary criticism.
# of Vols:	8,000
Services:	Catalog, accepts want lists.

Credit Cards: No
Year Estab: 1983

Wall Street Books * (310) 476-6732
PO Box 24 A 06 Los Angeles 90024

Collection: Specialty books and related memorabilia.
Specialties: Stock market, futures market; financiers; Wall Street history.
# of Vols: 5,000+
Services: Search service, appraisals, catalog, accepts want lists.
Credit Cards: No
Owner: R.G. Klein
Year Estab: 1983

Donald J. Weinstock Books (714) 848-1128
PO Box 2051 Huntington Beach 92647

Collection: General stock.
Specialties: Literature; social and behavioral sciences; history; religion; philosophy; theater; film; music; mystery; science fiction.
# of Vols: 30,000+
Services: Occasional catalog, accepts want lists.
Credit Cards: No
Year Estab: 1971

Whaling Research
PO Box 5034 Berkeley 94705

Collection: Specialty books and ephemera.
Specialties: Whaling; sea and ships.
# of Vols: 3,000-5,000
Services: Search service, occasional catalog, accepts want lists.
Credit Cards: Yes
Owner: E.M. McDermott
Year Estab: 1963

Woodie's Collectibles (510) 631-6632
PO Box 102 Moraga 94556

Collection: Specialty
Specialties: Children's, with emphasis on Disney, Oz and comic characters.
# of Vols: 700-1,000
Services: Lists, accepts want lists.
Credit Cards: No
Owner: Gary Wood
Year Estab: 1980

World Wide Hunting Books (714) 894-9080
PO Box 3095 Long Beach 90803   Fax: (714) 894-4949

Collection: Specialty
Specialties: Hunting; big game hunting; firearms.
# of Vols: 2,000
Services: Catalog, accepts want lists, appraisals.

* *Some 310 codes change to 562 in 1996*

Credit Cards: Yes
Owner: Ludo Wurfbain
Year Estab: 1985

Worn Bookworm (619) 938-2894
PO Box 45 Big Pine 93513 Fax: (619) 938-2894

Collection: General stock.
# of Vols: 20,000
Services: Search service, accepts want lists.
Credit Cards: Yes
Owner: Jean Holt
Year Estab: 1982

Donald Yates (707) 963-0201
555 Canon Park Drive Saint Helena 94574

Collection: Specialty
Specialties: Mystery; detective magazines; fiction.
# of Vols: 300
Services: Accepts want lists.
Credit Cards: Yes
Year Estab: 1990

Not all literary finds are confined to stuffy environments.

Hawaii

Alphabetical Listing By Dealer

Basically Books/Book Finders of Hawaii	316
Island Books	317
Jelly's	316
Jelly's	316
Kauai Fine Arts	317
Maui Friends of the Library Used Bookstore	318
Paperbacks Plus	318
Rainbow Books and Records	316
Tusitala Bookshop	316

Alphabetical Listing By Location

Aiea
Jelly's 316
Rainbow Books and Records 316

Hilo
Basically Books/Book Finders of Hawaii 316

Honolulu
Jelly's 316

Kailua
Tusitala Bookshop 316

Kauai
Kauai Fine Arts 317

Kealakekua
Island Books 317

Wailluku
Maui Friends of the Library Used Bookstore 318
Paperbacks Plus 318

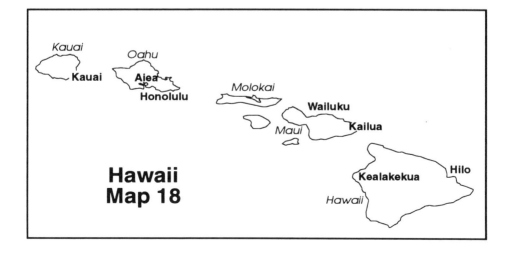

Hawaii Map 18

Aiea
(Oahu Island)

Jelly's — Open Shop
98-199 Kamehameha Highway 96701 — (808) 486-5600

Collection: General stock of paperback and hardcover.
Hours: Mon-Thu 10am-11pm. Fri & Sat 10am-midnight. Sun 10-10.
Travel: In Pearl Kai shopping center.
Comments: Stock is approximately 75% paperback.

Rainbow Books and Records — Open Shop
99-080 Kauhale Street, # C7 96701 — (808) 487-8867

Collection: General stock of mostly paperback.
Hours: Daily 10-8.

Hilo
(Hawaii Island)

Basically Books/Book Finders of Hawaii — Open Shop
46 Waianuenue Avenue 96720 — Fax: (808) 935-1553 (808) 961-0144

Collection: Specialty. Mostly new and some used books.
Specialties: Hawaii; travel; maps.
Hours: Mon-Fri 9-5. Sat 10-4.
Services: Search service, mail order.
Travel: From Hwy 19, turn into downtown Hilo and proceed up Waianuenue Ave.
Credit Cards: Yes
Owner: David & Christine Reed
Year Estab: 1970

Honolulu
(Oahu Island)

Jelly's — Open Shop
2919 Kapiolani Boulevard 96826 — (808) 735-7676

Collection: General stock of mostly paperback.
Hours: Mon-Sat 10-10. Sun 10-7.
Travel: In Market City Shopping Center off Kapiolani Blvd and King St.

Kailua
(Maui Island)

Tusitala Bookshop — Open Shop
116 Hekili Street 96734 — (808) 262-6343

Collection: General stock of hardcover and paperback and ephemera.
Specialties: Hawaii; South Pacific islands; military; Asian art and history.

# of Vols: 22,000
Hours: Mon-Sat 10-5:30. Sun 10-4.
Services: Accepts want lists.
Travel: From Hwy 61, turn right at Hamakua Dr, then next left on Hekili St. Shop is on left.
Credit Cards: Yes
Owner: B. Lee Reeve & Nancy M. Abe
Year Estab: 1976
Comments: Approximately 75% of the stock is used.

Kauai
(Kauai Island)

Kauai Fine Arts **Open Shop**
3848 Hanapepe Road (808) 332-8508
Mailing Address: PO Box 1079 Lawai 96765 Fax: (808) 332-9808

Collection: Specialty books, maps and prints.
Specialties: Travel; maps and prints; Americana; West Indies; Pacific.
# of Vols: Small
Hours: Mon-Fri 10-6. Other times by appointment.
Services: Catalog
Credit Cards: Yes
Owner: Paul & Mona Nicholas
Year Estab: 1977
Comments: A second gallery is located in Old Koloa Town in Koloa, Kaui

Kealakekua
(Hawaii Island)

Island Books **Open Shop**
79-7360 Mamalahoa Highway (808) 322-2006
Mailing Address: PO Box 645 Kealakekua 96750 Fax: (808) 322-2006

Collection: General stock of paperback and hardcover.
Specialties: Hawaii
# of Vols: 4,000
Hours: Mon-Sat 10-6.
Services: Search service.
Travel: Ten miles south of Kailua-Kona on Hwy 11 in Kainaliu.
Credit Cards: Yes
Owner: Jonathan & Jev Thomson
Year Estab: 1994

Wailuku
(Maui Island)

Maui Friends of the Library Used Bookstore **Open Shop**
PO Box 1017 96793 (808) 871-6563

Collection: General stock of hardcover and paperback.
# of Vols: 50,000+
Hours: Mon-Sat 8-4.
Travel: Call for directions.

Paperbacks Plus **Open Shop**
1977 Main Street 96793 (808) 242-7135

Collection: General stock new and used hardcover and paperback.
Hours: Mon-Fri 8:30-5:30. Sat 9-5.
Travel: On main street of island.

What would Poe have to say about this literary feline?

OREGON

Alphabetical Listing By Dealer

...and Books, too!	371	The Book Habit	367
Gerry Aboud-Back Issue Magazines	370	The Book Man	328
a.k.a. Used Books & Records	332	The Book Station	334
Albany Book Company	325	Books 'N Bears	337
An-Tiki Books and Collectables	372	Books Welred	367
Antiques & Artifacts	373	Books/Art	351
Antiques, Etc.	369	Booksmart	342
Leila White	325	Booktique	343
Armchair Family Bookstore	350	Brady Books	343
Joe Armstrong	373	Buck's Book Barn	369
Artifacts	340	Buck's Book Store	334
Ashland Books & Music	326	Budget Books	367
Ashurst Books	342	Cal's Books and Wares	351
The Author's Bookstore	350	Cameron's Books	353
Author's Ink	350	Canyonville Books & Videos	330
Authors Of The West	333	Cellar of Books	374
Autumn Leaves Bookstore	350	Channel Book Shop	332
Avocet Used Books	331	Chapter II Bookstore	337
Backroom Bookstore	327	Christian Discount Books	341
Backstage Books	373	Coffee House Books	339
Bargain Barn Books	371	Collectors Antique Marketplace	353
Carol Barnett, Books	373	Columbia Books	374
Bartlett Street Book Store	346	Daniel Conner	335
Basin Book Trader	343	Corls Books	374
The Bay Window	337	Country Store	338
Beehive Books and Arts	349	Barbara Cutts-UK/USA Bookdealer	353
Betty's Books	328	Dave's Book Barn	331
Beth L. Bibby-Books	373	Dee's Books & More	353
Black Sun Books	334	Richard Dix, Illustrated Books	329
Blue Dragon Bookshop	326	Dog Eared Editions	346
Blue Goose Books	326	Edna's Book Exchange	326
Blumenkron & Ramirez Books	351	Eldora's Books	374
The Book Bin	367	Excalibur Books & Comics	354
The Book Bin	331	Fritzler's Books	354
The Book Bin	325	Future Dreams/Burnside	354
Book City Paradise	351	Future Dreams/Gateway	354
The Book Fair	334	Charles Garvin, Books	354

Robert Gavora, Bookseller	355	Panurge Emporium Books	360
Godfather's Books & Espresso Bar	328	The Paper Moon Bookstore	360
Golden Gull Bookstore	338	Marc Paulsen Bookseller	375
Great Outdoors Book Exchange	374	Per USED Books	349
The Great Northwest Bookstore	355	Periodicals Paradise	360
Lawrence Hamman Fine Books	375	Pilgrim Discount Book & Bible Supply	360
Hanson's Books	355	Philip J. Pirages Rare Books	344
Hawthorne Boulevard Books	356	Pirate Cove	348
Hey Joe Used Books & Records	356	R. Plapinger Baseball Books	327
Holland's Books	356	Powell's Books	329
Hungry Head Books	335	Powell's Books for Cooks	361
In Between Times	349	Powell's City of Books	361
Interzone Comics	339	Powell's on Hawthorne	362
Irvington Booknook	357	Powell's Technical Books	362
J. Michaels Books	335	Powell's Travel Store	362
Jacksonville Books	341	Larry W. Price Books	375
Jane's Books	329	Truman Price	375
Jewell Collector Reference Books	367	Rainy Day Books	372
Jim's Trading Post	338	Readers Guide to Recycled Literature	368
JP Books	357	Reedsport Books & Tapes	365
Jupiter Rare & Used Books	330	Robert's Book Shop	344
K & D Main Street Books	340	Rogue Books	327
Wayne Kee Books	365	Sandy's Corner Book Nook	372
Raymond Kimeldorf	357	Dale C. Schmidt-Books	369
Klindts, Booksellers	371	Second Chance Books	346
L & M Treasures	344	Second Story Booksellers	363
La Pine Book Exchange Plus	343	Second Time Around Books	370
Lang Syne Books	339	Charles Seluzicki Fine and Rare Books	363
Lonesome Water Books	370	Shakespeare & Co - A Bookstore	327
Longfellow's Books	357	Smith Family Bookstore	336
Magic Door Books	368	Smith Family Bookstore II	336
Main Street Books	375	Stayton Books	371
Main Street Books	370	Nancy Stewart-Books	329
Michael's Book Shop	368	Bill Swing Rare & Fine Books	363
Mike's Books & Espresso	347	The Three Gables Antiques	342
David Morrison Books	358	Title Wave Bookstore	363
Murder By The Book	358	Turner House Antiques	342
Murder By The Book	358	U Shop	370
Mystery Treasure House	347	Village Books	346
Nautical Wheelers Books & Gifts	372	Waking Dream Books	364
Newport Book Center	348	Webfoot Bookman	364
Nineteenth Century Prints	359	Western Book Company	338
Nye Book House	348	Joy A. Wheeler-Books	333
Old Friends Library	359	While Away Books	365
Old Oregon Book Store	359	Windows Booksellers	336
The Old Trunk	340	Wrigley-Cross Books	364
The Open Book	330	Yellow Pages Used Books	338
Oregon Tertitorial Books	371	Yesterday's Books	348
T.W. Palmer Books	335		

Alphabetical Listing By Location

Albany
Albany Book Company 325
The Book Bin 325
Applegate
Leila White 325
Ashland
Ashland Books & Music 326
Blue Dragon Bookshop 326
Blue Goose Books 326
Edna's Book Exchange 326
R. Plapinger Baseball Books 327
Rogue Books 327
Shakespeare & Co - A Bookstore 327
Astoria
Backroom Bookstore 327
Godfather's Books & Espresso Bar 328
Baker City
Betty's Books 328
The Book Man 328
Bandon
Jane's Books 329
Beaverton
Richard Dix, Illustrated Books 329
Lawrence Hamman Fine Books 375
Powell's Books 329
Nancy Stewart-Books 329
Bend
The Open Book 330
Cannon Beach
Jupiter Rare & Used Books 330
Canyonville
Canyonville Books & Videos 330
Dave's Book Barn 331
Corvallis
Avocet Used Books 331
The Book Bin 331
Corls Books 374
Cottage Grove
a.k.a. Used Books & Records 332
Depoe Bay
Channel Book Shop 332
Dundee
Authors Of The West 333
Elgin
Joy A. Wheeler-Books 333

Eugene
Joe Armstrong 373
Backstage Books 373
Black Sun Books 334
The Book Fair 334
The Book Station 334
Buck's Book Store 334
Cellar of Books 374
Daniel Conner 335
Hungry Head Books 335
J. Michaels Books 335
T.W. Palmer Books 335
Smith Family Bookstore 336
Smith Family Bookstore II 336
Windows Booksellers 336
Florence
The Bay Window 337
Books 'N Bears 337
Forest Grove
Chapter II Bookstore 337
Garibaldi
Country Store 338
Gaston
Western Book Company 338
Gold Hill
Beth L. Bibby-Books 373
Grand Ronde
Jim's Trading Post 338
Grants Pass
Golden Gull Bookstore 338
Yellow Pages Used Books 338
Gresham
Coffee House Books 339
Interzone Comics 339
Lang Syne Books 339
Hillsboro
K & D Main Street Books 340
Hood River
Artifacts 340
The Old Trunk 340
Jacksonville
Christian Discount Books 341
Jacksonville Books 341
The Three Gables Antiques 342
Turner House Antiques 342

OREGON

Keizer
Booksmart — 342
Klamath Falls
Ashurst Books — 342
Basin Book Trader — 343
La Pine
La Pine Book Exchange Plus — 343
Lake Oswego
Booktique — 343
Columbia Books — 374
Great Outdoors Book Exchange — 374
Lincoln City
Brady Books — 343
L & M Treasures — 344
Robert's Book Shop — 344
McMinnville
Philip J. Pirages Rare Books — 344
Medford
Bartlett Street Book Store — 346
Village Books — 346
Monmouth
Dog Eared Editions — 346
Truman Price — 375
Second Chance Books — 346
Myrtle Creek
Mike's Books & Espresso — 347
Nehalem
Mystery Treasure House — 347
Newberg
Eldora's Books — 374
Newport
Newport Book Center — 348
North Bend
Nye Book House — 348
Pirate Cove — 348
Yesterday's Books — 348
Noti
Antiques & Artifacts — 373
Ontario
Per USED Books — 349
Philomath
Beehive Books and Arts — 349
In Between Times — 349
Portland
Armchair Family Bookstore — 350
The Author's Bookstore — 350
Author's Ink — 350
Autumn Leaves Bookstore — 350
Carol Barnett, Books — 373
Blumenkron & Ramirez Books — 351
Book City Paradise — 351
Books/Art — 351
Cal's Books and Wares — 351
Cameron's Books — 353
Collectors Antique Marketplace — 353
Barbara Cutts-UK/USA Bookdealer — 353
Dee's Books & More — 353
Excalibur Books & Comics — 354
Fritzler's Books — 354
Future Dreams/Burnside — 354
Future Dreams/Gateway — 354
Charles Garvin, Books — 354
Robert Gavora, Bookseller — 355
The Great Northwest Bookstore — 355
Hanson's Books — 355
Hawthorne Boulevard Books — 356
Hey Joe Used Books & Records — 356
Holland's Books — 356
Irvington Booknook — 357
JP Books — 357
Raymond Kimeldorf — 357
Longfellow's Books — 357
David Morrison Books — 358
Murder By The Book — 358
Murder By The Book — 358
Nineteenth Century Prints — 359
Old Friends Library — 359
Old Oregon Book Store — 359
Panurge Emporium Books — 360
The Paper Moon Bookstore — 360
Marc Paulsen Bookseller — 375
Periodicals Paradise — 360
Pilgrim Discount Book & Bible Supply — 360
Powell's Books for Cooks — 361
Powell's City of Books — 361
Powell's on Hawthorne — 362
Powell's Technical Books — 362
Powell's Travel Store — 362
Larry W. Price Books — 375
Second Story Booksellers — 363
Charles Seluzicki Fine and Rare Books — 363
Bill Swing Rare & Fine Books — 363
Title Wave Bookstore — 363
Waking Dream Books — 364
Webfoot Bookman — 364
Wrigley-Cross Books — 364
Prineville
Wayne Kee Books — 365

Reedsport
Reedsport Books & Tapes 365
Roseburg
While Away Books 365
Salem
The Book Bin 367
The Book Habit 367
Books Welred 367
Budget Books 367
Jewell Collector Reference Books 367
Magic Door Books 368
Michael's Book Shop 368
Readers Guide to Recycled Literature 368
Dale C. Schmidt-Books 369
Seal Rock
Antiques, Etc. 369
Seaside
Buck's Book Barn 369
U Shop 370
Sheridan
Main Street Books 370
Sherwood
Second Time Around Books 370

Sisters
Lonesome Water Books 370
Stayton
Gerry Aboud-Back Issue Magazines 370
Oregon Tertitorial Books 371
Stayton Books 371
The Dalles
Bargain Barn Books 371
Klindts, Booksellers 371
Tigard
...and Books, too! 371
Tillamook
An-Tiki Books and Collectables 372
Rainy Day Books 372
Toledo
Main Street Books 375
Waldport
Nautical Wheelers Books & Gifts 372
Winston
Sandy's Corner Book Nook 372

Oregon
Map 19

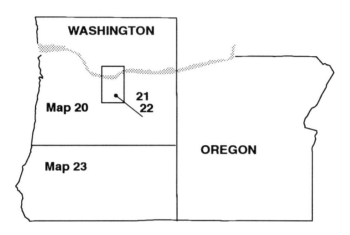

Map 20
**Northwest Oregon &
Southwest Washington**
Albany
Astoria
Bend
Cannon Beach
Corvallis
Depoe Bay
Forest Grove
Grand Ronde
Hood River
Lincoln City
Newport
Philomath
Salem
Seal Rock
Seaside
Sisters
The Dalles
Tillamook
Waldport

Long Beach, WA
Vancouver, WA
Woodland, WA

Map 21
Portland

Map 22
Portland suburbs
Beaverton
Gresham
Hillsboro
Lake Oswego
Portland

Vancouver, WA

Map 23
Southwest Oregon
Applegate
Ashland
Bandon
Canyonville
Cottage Grove
Eugene
Florence
Grants Pass
Jacksonville
Klamath Falls
Medford
Myrtle Creek
North Bend
Roseburg

Albany
(Map 20, page 345)

Albany Book Company — **Open Shop**
1425 Pacific Boulevard, SE 97321 — (541) 926-2612

Collection: General stock of paperback and hardcover, magazines and ephemera.
Specialties: Military; World War II; Oregon; Americana.
# of Vols: 50,000
Hours: Mon-Sat 9:30-6, except Fri till 8.
Services: Appraisals, search service, accepts want lists.
Travel: From I-5 southbound: first Albany exit. Off ramp becomes Pacific Blvd. Northbound: first Albany exit. Proceed on Santiam, then left on Pacific.
Credit Cards: Yes
Owner: Carl Chrisco
Year Estab: 1992
Comments: While paperbacks certainly dominate this shop (there was even a small room devoted entirely to romance paperbacks), the number of hardcover books, and the subjects represented in both older and newer volumes, makes this shop worth a brief stop, particularly if there are some vintage titles on your want list. Prices were most reasonable.

The Book Bin — **Open Shop**
415 West 1st Street 97321 — (541) 926-6869

Collection: General stock of hardcover and paperback.
# of Vols: 100,000
Hours: Mon-Sat 9:30-6. Sun 12-6.
Travel: Hwy 20 exit off I-5. Proceed to Main St. North on Main, left on 1st St.
Credit Cards: Yes
Owner: Robert Baird
Year Estab: 1971
Comments: While the number of paperbacks in this shop is a bit larger than in the Corvallis store (see below), the hardcover books were of a similar condition and type: most were in relatively good condition and of recent vintage with an alcove housing "older" volumes. The number of books (both hardcover and certainly paperback) and the varied selection provides lots of opportunity for both the local resident and out of town visitor to find something here of interest, if not a very rare item.

Applegate
(Map 23, page 333)

Leila White — **By Appointment**
PO Box 3260 97530 — (541) 846-6609

Collection: General stock.
# of Vols: 2,500
Services: Book binding and restoration.
Year Estab: 1983

Ashland
(Map 23, page 333)

Ashland Books & Music　　　　　　　　　　　　　　　　　　　　　　　**Open Shop**
247 East Main Street 97520　　　　　　　　　　　　　　　　　　　　　(541) 482-2759

Collection:	General stock of hardcover and paperback.
# of Vols:	15,000
Hours:	Mon-Sat 10-6. Sun 10-5.
Services:	Appraisals, search service, accepts want lists.
Travel:	Valley View Rd off I-5. Proceed west on Valley View, then left on North Main which becomes East Main. Shop is between 1st & 2nd Sts.
Credit Cards:	Yes
Owner:	Stanley B. & Jean Jones
Year Estab:	1993
Comments:	A well organized, well labeled shop with mostly newer books.

Blue Dragon Bookshop　　　　　　　　　　　　　　　　　　　　　　　　**Open Shop**
297 East Main Street　　　　　　　　　　　　　　　　　　　　　　　　　(541) 482-2142
Mailing Address: PO Box 216 Ashland 97520

Collection:	General stock of mostly hardcover.
Specialties:	Metaphysics; polar; mountaineering; Shakespeare.
# of Vols:	40,000
Hours:	Jun-Oct: Daily 10:30-5. Nov-May: Mon-Sat 10:30-5. Sun 12-5.
Services:	Appraisals, catalog, search service, accepts want lists.
Travel:	See Ashland Books & Music above.
Credit Cards:	Yes
Owner:	Bob Peterson
Year Estab:	1981
Comments:	A very nice shop with a good selection of books in almost every category, including many titles not seen elsewhere in our travels. The books were in very good condition and most reasonably priced. Worth a visit.

Blue Goose Books　　　　　　　　　　　　　　　　　　　　　　　　**By Appointment**
489 Allison Street 97520　　　　　　　　　　　　　　　　　　　　　　(541) 488-2300

Collection:	Specialty
Specialties:	Modern first editions; children's illustrated.
Services:	Catalog, accepts want lists.
Credit Cards:	No
Owner:	Elizabeth L. Jones
Year Estab:	1971

Edna's Book Exchange　　　　　　　　　　　　　　　　　　　　　　　　**Open Shop**
89 Oak Street 97520　　　　　　　　　　　　　　　　　　　　　　　　　(541) 482-1675

Collection:	General stock of mostly paperback.
Hours:	Summer: Daily: 10-5:30. Winter: Tue-Sat 10-5.

R. Plapinger Baseball Books
PO Box 1062 97520

By Appointment
(541) 488-1220

Collection: Specialty books and ephemera.
Specialties: Primarily baseball (fiction and non fiction) and a small selection of other sports.
# of Vols: 4,000+
Services: Appraisals, search service, catalog (separate catalogs for baseball fiction and non fiction), accepts want lists.
Credit Cards: No
Year Estab: 1986

Rogue Books
107 East Main 97520

Open Shop
(541) 482-0272

Collection: General stock of mostly used hardcover and paperback.
# of Vols: 5,000-10,000
Hours: Summer: Mon-Sat 10-5. Sun 11-5. Remainder of year: Tue-Sat 10-5.
Travel: See Ashland Books & Music above.
Credit Cards: Yes
Owner: Sharon Davenport
Year Estab: 1990
Comments: Down a flight of stairs, this shop offers a rather modest stock with little if any depth in any of the subject areas represented on the shelves. Prices were quite reasonable.

Shakespeare & Co - A Bookstore
154 East Main Street 97520

Open Shop
(541) 488-1474

Collection: General stock.
Specialties: Shakespeare; theater; James Joyce.
# of Vols: 25,000
Hours: Tue-Sat 10:30-5:30.
Services: Accepts want lists, mail order.
Travel: See Ashland Books & Music above.
Credit Cards: Yes
Owner: Les Jensen
Year Estab: 1990
Comments: Unfortunately, our schedule brought us to Ashland on a Sunday when this shop is normally closed.

Astoria
(Map 20, page 345)

Backroom Bookstore
At Phog Bounder's Antique Mall, 1052 Commercial 97103

Open Shop
(503) 325-9722

Collection: General stock.
# of Vols: 25,000
Hours: Mon-Sat 10-5:30. Sun 12-5.

Travel: Hwy 101 to center of town.
Credit Cards: No
Owner: Mary Lewis
Year Estab: 1990
Comments: As the name implies, this shop is located in the back room of an antique mall. But don't be misled into equating the shop with a "booth" at a multi dealer antique mall. It's not. In square footage and number of volumes on hand, it's large enough to be a store by itself. The collection (all hardcover) consisted of mostly older books in mixed condition. Pricing was also mixed: some items were on target while others were priced slightly higher than we have seen elsewhere.

Godfather's Books & Espresso Bar **Open Shop**
1108 Commercial Street 97103 (503) 325-8143

Collection: General stock of new and used, paperback and hardcover.
Specialties: Literature; regional; art; sports.
# of Vols: 5,000-10,000
Hours: Mon-Sat 9-5:30. Sun 11-4.
Services: Appraisals, search service, accepts want lists, mail order.
Travel: See Backroom Bookstore above. Shop is at corner of 11th St.
Credit Cards: Yes
Owner: Charlie Holboke
Year Estab: 1993
Comments: An attractive, if somewhat limited, combination new/used shop with little that we have not seen in greater numbers in either all new or all used book stores. New and used books are intershelved, with the majority of the books being new.

Baker City

Betty's Books **Open Shop**
1813 Main Street 97814 (541) 523-7551

Collection: General stock of mostly new and some used hardcover.
Hours: Mon-Sat 8:30-5:30.

The Book Man **Open Shop**
2376 Broadway 97814

Collection: General stock of hardcover and paperback.
# of Vols: 17,000
Hours: Mon-Fri 10:30-5.
Services: Accepts want lists, mail order.
Credit Cards: No
Owner: Mark Alderson
Year Estab: 1991
Comments: Stock is evenly divided between hardcover and paperback.

Bandon
(Map 23, page 333)

Jane's Books   **Open Shop**
122 2nd Street 97411

Collection: General stock.
Specialties: Cookbooks.
# of Vols: 3,000
Hours: Daily 10-5:30. (See Comments)
Comments: This owner did not return our Information Sheet and does not have a telephone. However, as other dealers in the area confirmed that the shop is in business, we are including the shop in this guide and listing the shop's last published hours. Good luck.

Beaverton
(Map 22, page 366)

Richard Dix, Illustrated Books   **By Appointment**
13660 SW Brightwood 97005   (503) 646-1780

Collection: Specialty
Specialties: Illustrated; children's; fantasy; art.
# of Vols: 2,500
Services: Search service, accepts want lists, mail order.
Credit Cards: No
Year Estab: 1985

Powell's Books   **Open Shop**
8775 SW Cascade Avenue 97008   (503) 643-3131

Collection: General stock of new, used and remainders.
# of Vols: 100,000+ (used)
Hours: Mon-Sat 9-9. Sun 10-6.
Travel: Northbound on Hwy 217: Sholls Ferry Rd. Left at signal then right on Cascade. Southbound: Progress exit. At light, cross Hall Blvd onto Cascade.
Credit Cards: Yes
Comments: See Portland listings for the main Powell's store.

Nancy Stewart-Books   **By Appointment**
1188 NW Weybridge Way 97006   (503) 645-9779

Collection: General stock.
Specialties: Children's (turn of the century); illustrated; modern first editions; Americana.
# of Vols: 5,000
Services: Catalog
Credit Cards: No
Year Estab: 1985

Bend
(Map 20, page 345)

The Open Book — **Open Shop**
155 NE Greenwood Avenue 97701 (541) 388-3249

Collection: General stock of paperback and hardcover.
# of Vols: 37,000
Hours: Mon-Sat 10:30-5:30.
Travel: From Hwy 97, turn west on Greenwood.
Credit Cards: Yes
Year Estab: 1985
Comments: Stock is approximately 65% paperback.

Cannon Beach
(Map 20, page 345)

Jupiter Rare & Used Books — **Open Shop**
244 North Spruce (503) 436-2915
Mailing Address: PO Box 1222 Cannon Beach 97110

Collection: General stock of hardcover and paperback.
# of Vols: 15,000
Hours: Daily "around" 10 to "about" 5.
Travel: Heading south on Hwy 101, take first Cannon Beach exit.
Credit Cards: No
Owner: Billy L. Hults
Year Estab: 1990
Comments: The owner informed us that his hours are "from about 10 to about 5." Having previously driven long distances only to find shops closed, we decided to take our own advice, especially since it was already 4:15 and it would take us at least 45 minutes to reach the shop. After four unsuccessful attempts to phone the shop (the line was busy each time we called) we decided to head off in a different direction and visit two other shops that were open till 6. We hope that any of our readers who do visit this shop will share their impressions with us.

Canyonville
(Map 23, page 333)

Canyonville Books & Videos — **Open Shop**
430 South Main Avenue 97417 (541) 839-6110

Collection: Specialty new and used.
Specialties: Genealogy; religion; Oregon and Applegate trails.
# of Vols: 2,000 (used)
Hours: Sun-Fri 10-5.
Year Estab: 1994

Dave's Book Barn **Open Shop**
211 Leland (541) 839-4878
Mailing Address: PO Box 219 Canyonville 97417

Collection:	General stock of hardcover and paperback and records.
# of Vols:	100,000
Hours:	Daily 11-5. Best to call ahead.
Travel:	Exit 98 off I-5. If northbound, proceed under freeway, turn right on frontage road, left at stop sign and right on Leland. If southbound, turn right at stop sign at end of exit ramp then right at Leland.
Credit Cards:	No
Owner:	Dave & Zee Roberts
Year Estab:	1986
Comments:	The closest thing we have seen on the Pacific Coast to a New England style book barn. A large collection with a ratio of what we would guess to be 40% hardcover and 60% paperback. Whether or not you find the book/s you're looking for, if you like to browse used book shops, we think you should enjoy a visit here. Most of what we saw were reading copies in mixed condition but there could be some gems hidden on the well labeled shelves.

Corvallis
(Map 20, page 345)

Avocet Used Books **Open Shop**
614 SW 3rd Street 97333 (541) 753-4119

Collection:	General stock of hardcover and paperback.
Specialties:	First editions; Americana; literature; cookbooks; science; technology; natural history; children's; art.
# of Vols:	40,000
Hours:	Mon-Sat 9:30-7.
Services:	Search service, accepts want lists.
Travel:	Corvallis exit (Hwy 34) off I-5. As you approach Corvallis, when Hwy 34 turns left, continue straight on Harrison to 4th St. Left on 4th, left on Jackson and left on 3rd.
Credit Cards:	No
Owner:	Howard & Saundra Mills
Year Estab:	1979
Comments:	A tightly packed shop with hardcover volumes (about two thirds of the stock) of mixed vintage and in generally good condition. If you like the challenge of browsing in tight quarters, you should enjoy a visit here.

The Book Bin **Open Shop**
228 SW 3rd Street 97333 Fax: (541) 752-0045 (541) 752-0040

Collection:	General stock of hardcover and paperback.
Specialties:	Pacific Islands; Hawaii.
# of Vols:	100,000
Hours:	Mon-Fri 9:30-8. Sat 9:30-6. Sun 12-6.

Services:	Appraisals, search service.
Travel:	See Avocet Used Books above. Left on 4th St. Shop is between Madison and Jefferson Sts.
Credit Cards:	Yes
Owner:	Robert Baird
Year Estab:	1981
Comments:	An interesting collection of both vintage and more recent items in a spacious and attractive shop that is well organized for easy browsing. If your interests are in the shop's specialties, you may be lucky enough to be allowed to visit the shop's second level where these books are shelved. Note: The owner operates a second Book Bin in Corvallis that sells college texts.

Cottage Grove
(Map 23, page 333)

a.k.a. Used Books & Records   **Open Shop**
726 East Main Street 97424   (541) 942-7423

Collection:	General stock of paperback, hardcover and comics.
Hours:	Mon-Fri 10:30-6. Sat 10-6.
Services:	Main Cottage Grove exit off I-5. Right off exit. Right on Main.
Credit Cards:	Yes
Owner:	Mary Landers & Marti Grissom
Year Estab:	1988
Comments:	Stock is approximately 60% paperback.

Depoe Bay
(Map 20, page 345)

Channel Book Shop   **Open Shop**
246 Ellingson   (541) 765-2352
Mailing Address: PO Box 376 Depoe Bay 97341

Collection:	General stock of hardcover and paperback.
Specialties:	Native Americans; metaphysics.
# of Vols:	100,000
Hours:	Daily 9-5.
Services:	Accepts want lists, mail order.
Travel:	Corner of Hwy 101 and Ellingson.
Credit Cards:	Yes
Owner:	Nola Stanek
Year Estab:	1955
Comments:	A real sleeper and definitely worth visiting. One of the nicer used book shops along the coast in terms of number of volumes, selection and price and with an emphasis on vintage items. We saw many volumes here that were priced substantially higher elsewhere. You may have to spend a bit more time rummaging round the shelves to find what you're looking for, and some of the aisles are narrow, but that simply provides more space for the large number of books you'll be able to select here.

Dundee

Authors Of The West **By Appointment**
191 Dogwood Drive 97115 (503) 538-8132

Collection: Specialty
Specialties: Western American literature; Oregon/California Trail in fact and fiction; C.S. Lewis and the Inklings; British and American first editions.
# of Vols: 4,000
Services: Appraisals, search service, catalog, accepts want lists.
Credit Cards: No
Owner: Lee & Grayce Nash
Year Estab: 1973

Elgin

Joy A. Wheeler-Books **By Appointment**
69612 Wheeler Lane 97827 (541) 437-8641

Collection: General stock and some ephemera.
Specialties: Oregon; children's; cookbooks.
# of Vols: 2,000
Services: Search service, catalog, accepts want lists.
Credit Cards: No
Year Estab: 1980

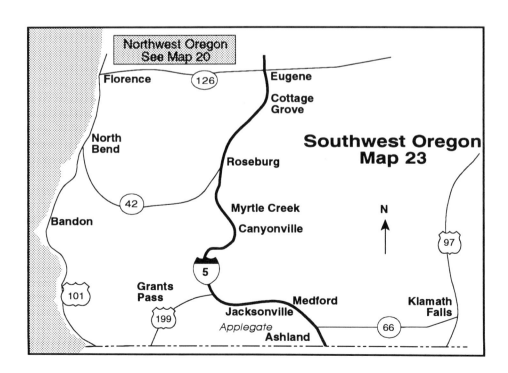

Eugene
(Map 23, page 333)

Black Sun Books
2455 Hilyard Street 97405

Open Shop
(541) 484-3777

Collection:	General stock of used and new hardcover and paperback.
# of Vols:	7,000-10,000
Hours:	Tue-Sat 10-6:30. Sun 12-6. Extended hours in Dec.
Services:	Appraisals, accepts want lists.
Travel:	30th Ave exit off I-5. West on 30th Ave. Right on Hilyard.
Credit Cards:	Yes
Owner:	Peter J. Ogura
Year Estab:	1992
Comments:	Stock is approximately 60% used and 60% hardcover.

The Book Fair
1409 Oak Street 97401

Open Shop
(541) 343-3033

Collection:	General stock of paperback and hardcover.
Specialties:	Auto repair; Christian books; language dictionaries; needlecrafts.
# of Vols:	15,000-20,000
Hours:	Mon-Thu 10-5:30. Fri 10-7. Sat 10-5.
Services:	Appraisals, search service, accepts want lists, mail order, book repair.
Travel:	From I-5 northbound: 30th Ave exit. Cross over Fwy to Amazon Pky. Left at 19th, right at Oak to 14th.
Credit Cards:	Yes
Owner:	Jerry D. Leedy
Year Estab:	1966
Comments:	Try visiting this shop on a cool day. When we arrived during a mid July hot spell, the absence of any cooling system or apparent ventilation only served to exacerbate the difficulty of maneuvering through a cluttered shop with narrow aisles and piles of boxes. What we did manage to see was an eclectic collection that included serious books for serious readers as well as a sampling of CDs and yes, even comic books.

The Book Station
606 Blair Boulevard 97402

Open Shop
(541) 345-6211

Collection:	General stock of paperback and hardcover.
# of Vols:	2,000-3,000
Hours:	Mon-Sat 10-6.
Travel:	On southwest corner of 6th and Blair between 6th & 7th.
Year Estab:	1980
Comments:	Stock is approximately 60% paperback.

Buck's Book Store
769 Highway 99 N 97402

Open Shop
(541) 689-6976

Collection:	General stock of mostly paperback.
Hours:	Mon & Sat 12-5. Tue-Fri 12-7.

Daniel Conner
4820 Garnet Street 97405

By Appointment
(541) 334-6891

Collection:	General stock.
Specialties:	Art; music; Orientalia; Western Americana.
# of Vols:	5,000
Services:	Appraisals, search service, accepts want lists, mail order.
Credit Cards:	No
Year Estab:	1992

Hungry Head Books
1212 Willamette Street 97401

Open Shop
(541) 485-0888

Collection:	Specialty. Mostly new and some used.
Specialties:	Counter culture.
# of Vols:	8,000
Hours:	Mon-Sat 10:30-6. Sun 12-5.
Services:	Search service.
Travel:	Between 11th & 13th Streets.
Credit Cards:	Yes
Owner:	Brian Wilga
Year Estab:	1988

J. Michaels Books
160 East Broadway 97405

Open Shop
Fax: (503) 342-2002   (541) 342-2002

Collection:	General stock of mostly used.
Specialties:	Art; architecture; photography.
# of Vols:	10,000
Hours:	Mon-Thu 10-5:30. Fri & Sat 10-9. Sun 11-5.
Services:	Appraisals, search service.
Travel:	From I-5 southbound: City Center Mall exit. Right on 8th, left on Pearl, right on Broadway. From I-5 northbound: Eugene exit feeds into Franklin Blvd which becomes Broadway.
Credit Cards:	Yes
Owner:	Jeremy Nissel
Year Estab:	1975
Comments:	Most used book stores carry some showcase books. This shop seems to thrive on them. In addition to its showcase stock, it's sometimes difficult to distinguish between the new and used books as the latter are in such good condition. In addition to the specialties noted above, the collection has a heavy emphasis on literature and non fiction. We agree with the lettering on the awning outside the front door that says there are "fine books" inside.

T.W. Palmer Books
259 West 23rd Avenue 97405

By Appointment
(541) 343-6536

Collection:	Specialty
Specialties:	Western Americana; voyages; exploration; surveys; natural history; railroads; (all related to the west); cartography; maps; atlases; facsimiles.

(Eugene)

# of Vols:	4,000
Services:	Accepts want lists, mail order.
Owner:	Theodore W. Palmer
Year Estab:	1985

Smith Family Bookstore   **Open Shop**
768 East 13th 97401   (541) 345-1651

Collection:	General stock of hardcover and paperback.
# of Vols:	243,000
Hours:	Mon-Sat 9-5:30.
Services:	Appraisals, search service, mail order.
Travel:	University of Oregon exit off I-5. Follow Univ. of Oregon signs to East 13th. Left on East 13th. Shop is between Alder and Hilyard Streets on second floor. (Elevator is available.)
Credit Cards:	Yes
Owner:	Delbert & Misao Smith
Year Estab:	1974
Comments:	Similar to the Willamette Street shop (see below) with perhaps a greater emphasis on scholarly titles. The books in this bi-level shop are meticulously sorted for easy locating. One can easily spend a great deal of time browsing shelves displaying both academic and non academic titles.

Smith Family Bookstore II   **Open Shop**
525 Willamette 97401   (541) 343-4717

Collection:	General stock of hardcover and paperback.
# of Vols:	140,000
Hours:	Mon-Sat 9:5:30, except Fri till 9.
Services:	Appraisals, search service, mail order.
Travel:	I-105 exit off I-5, then downtown exit. Bear right onto 6th Ave, then right on Willamette. Shop is across from post office on second floor. (Elevator is available.)
Credit Cards:	Yes
Owner:	Delbert & Misao Smith
Year Estab:	1974
Comments:	This large shop is divided into three rooms, each brimming over with books in almost every field one can imagine. Lots of old magazines and a reasonable number of paperbacks. While most of the stock could be considered relatively recent, the shop did have its share of older items and collectibles. Visiting dealers will be disappointed to discover that discounts are not available.

Windows Booksellers   **Open Shop**
790 East 11th Avenue 97401   Fax: (541) 465-9694   (541) 485-0014

Collection:	Specialty hardcover and paperback.

Specialties: Theology; church history; biblical studies; philosophy.
# of Vols: 9,000-10,000
Hours: Mon-Fri 10-5. Sat 12-4.
Services: Catalog, accepts want lists.
Travel: I-5 to I-105. 7th Ave exit off I-105. Left on 7th, right on Patterson, left on East 12th, left on Hilyard, right on East 11th.
Credit Cards: Yes
Owner: Church of the Servant King
Year Estab: 1988

Florence
(Map 23, page 333)

The Bay Window
1308 Bay Street
Mailing Address: PO Box 5 Florence 97439

Open Shop
(541) 997-2002

Collection: General stock and ephemera.
Specialties: Art; illustrated.
# of Vols: 200+
Hours: Mon-Sat 10-5. Sun 12-5. Other times by appointment.
Services: Appraisals
Travel: From Hwy 101 in Florence, follow "Old Town" signs to Bay St at the river.
Credit Cards: Yes
Owner: John & D'Ann Stone
Year Estab: 1975
Comments: Primarily a print and painting shop with a small, select stock of used books.

Books 'N Bears
1255 Bay Street
Mailing Address: PO Box 2326 Florence 97439

Open Shop
(541) 997-5979

Collection: General stock of mostly used paperback.
Hours: Mon-Sat 10-5. Sun 11-5.

Forest Grove
(Map 20, page 345)

Chapter II Bookstore
2038 Main Street 97116

Open Shop
(503) 359-5673

Collection: General stock of used and new paperback and hardcover.
Hours: Mon-Sat 10-5:30.
Services: Appraisals, search service, catalog, accepts want lists.
Travel: Hwy 47 into town. Shop is one block north of Pacific Ave at 21st and Main.
Credit Cards: Yes
Year Estab: 1989
Comments: Stock is approximately 75% used and 70% paperback.

Garibaldi

Country Store
406 Garibaldi Avenue 97118

Open Shop
(503) 322-3225

Collection: General stock.
# of Vols: 500
Hours: Mon-Sat 10-5. Sun 11-5.

Gaston

Western Book Company
PO Box 271 97119

By Appointment
(503) 662-3618

Collection: Specialty
Specialties: Railroads
Services: Appraisals, catalog, accepts want lists.
Owner: Pam Konschu

Grand Ronde
(Map 20, page 345)

Jim's Trading Post
29335 Salmon River Highway 97347

Open Shop
(503) 879-5411

Collection: General stock of new, remainders and used paperback and hardcover.
# of Vols: 100,000
Hours: Daily 9-6.
Travel: On Hwy 18, one mile west of Grand Rondoe. Look for a one story stand alone building.
Credit Cards: Yes
Owner: Jim E. Hosley
Year Estab: 1958
Comments: A wide variety of popular titles (new and used) that would appeal to buyers looking for both serious and light reading matter. Most of the used hardcover volumes we saw were of recent vintage and in fairly good condition. If the shop has any rare or collectible items, we missed them.

Grants Pass
(Map 23, page 333)

Golden Gull Bookstore
1889 NE 7th Street 97526

Open Shop
(541) 476-7323

Collection: General stock of new and mostly used paperbacks.
Hours: Mon-Fri 9-9. Sat 9-6. Sun 11:30-5.

Yellow Pages Used Books
111 SE G Street 97526

Open Shop
(541) 474-5514
E-mail: wdoody@magick.net

Collection: General stock of paperback and hardcover.

Specialties:	Science fiction; fantasy; military.
# of Vols:	45,000
Hours:	Mon-Sat 10-5:30. Sun and evenings by appointment.
Services:	Appraisals, search service, mail order.
Travel:	Southbound on I-5: Grants Pass exit. Proceed on 6th St to G St (the exit becomes 6th St after the first light). Left on G. Shop is on the right. Northbound on I-5: Grants Pass Pky exit. Right on E St, left on 6th, left on G.
Credit Cards:	No
Owner:	William G. Doody, Jr.
Year Estab:	1981
Comments:	At least 75% (perhaps more) of the stock in this shop consists of paperbacks and there is not much depth in the hardcover sections, with the exception of the military and science fiction sections. A nice touch was an attractive round green doorway leading to a rear room that emulated the gateway to the City of Oz. And, there were even some older Oz books under glass in that section of the shop.

Gresham
(Map 22, page 366)

Coffee House Books
901P SW Highland Drive 97080

Open Shop
(503) 661-6250

Collection:	General stock of used paperback and hardcover.
Specialties:	Regional and local authors.
# of Vols:	26,000
Hours:	Mon-Fri 9-7. Sat 9-5. Sun 11-5.
Services:	Search service, catalog in planning stage, accepts want lists.
Travel:	SE Powell Blvd to SE 181st St. Shop is in Highland Falls Shopping Center.
Credit Cards:	Yes
Owner:	Richard & Betty Morris
Year Estab:	1993
Comments:	Stock is approximately 70% paperback.

Interzone Comics
403 East Powell 97080

Open Shop
(503) 661-1815

Collection:	Specialty paperbacks.
Specialties:	Science fiction; fantasy.
Hours:	Daily 1-6.

Lang Syne Books
43 NW Third Street 97030

Open Shop
(503) 665-7472

Collection:	General stock of mostly hardcover.
Specialties:	Scotland; books by Scottish authors; Celtic history.
# of Vols:	15,000
Hours:	Mon-Thu 9-5:30. Fri & Sat 10:30-5:30. Sun by appointment.
Services:	Search service, accepts want lists.

Travel:	From Portland, proceed east on Hwy 26 (Powell Blvd) to Main St in Gresham. Left on Main, then left on 3rd St.
Credit Cards:	Yes
Owner:	George Taylor
Year Estab:	1992
Comments:	Some nice quality titles in good condition. While most of the hardcover items were of fairly recent vintage, we spotted some older items and some collectibles. A constructive criticism might be to leave a bit more space between some of the shelves for more comfortable browsing. The shop offers some paperbacks but they don't overwhelm the visitor.

Hillsboro
(Map 22, page 366)

K & D Main Street Books **Open Shop**
211 East Main Street 97123 (503) 648-9216

Collection:	General stock of paperback and hardcover.
Hours:	Mon-Fri 10-6. Sat 10-5.
Travel:	Cornelius Pass exit off Hwy 26. Follow signs to Hillsboro. Once in town, turn right on Main.
Comments:	Stock is approximately 70% paperback.

Hood River
(Map 20, page 345)

Artifacts **Open Shop**
209 Oak Street 97031 (541) 387-2482

Collection:	General stock of paperback and hardcover and some political ephemera.
# of Vols:	20,000
Hours:	Daily 10-6.
Travel:	Exit 63 (City Center) off I-84. Proceed on 2nd for two blocks, then right on Oak St. Shop is upstairs.
Credit Cards:	Yes
Owner:	Tom Murray
Year Estab:	1992
Comments:	A small shop offering a selection of mostly recent paperbacks (but NO romances) and a modest selection of hardcover volumes, also mostly recent titles. Reading copies to meet the community's needs. The shop also features a collection of "bad art."

The Old Trunk **Open Shop**
2958 Dee Highway 97031 (541) 354-1911

Collection:	General stock of hardcover and paperback, ephemera, sheet music and magazines.
# of Vols:	250,000
Hours:	Daily 9-6.

Services:	Appraisals, accepts want lists, mail order.
Travel:	City Center exit off I-84. Proceed on 2nd to Oak. Right on Oak and left on 13th St which becomes Tucker Rd. After crossing bridge, bear right on Dee Hwy.
Credit Cards:	No
Owner:	Evahn Paetehr
Year Estab:	1980
Comments:	A collection of mostly older, mostly worn (with exceptions) hardcover volumes and a similar selection of paperbacks. We saw most subjects on display in the two buildings that house this "out-of-the-way" collection and even spotted some titles that could be considered both interesting and desirable; we only wish they had been in better condition. Considering the above observation, we also believe that some prices were unrealistic. (If you want to mix book hunting with a scenic drive along the Columbia River and a view of Mt. Hood, this shop fits both categories.)

Jacksonville
(Map 23, page 333)

Christian Discount Books
225 West California
Mailing Address: PO Box 1241 Jacksonville 97530

Open Shop
(541) 899-8044
(800) 380-8044

Collection:	Specialty new and used.
Specialties:	Religion.
# of Vols:	10,000 (used)
Hours:	Mon-Fri 10-6. Sat 12-5.

Jacksonville Books
120 East California Street
Mailing Address: PO Box 716 Jacksonville 97530

Open Shop
(541) 899-8520

Collection:	General stock of used and new hardcover and paperback and ephemera.
Specialties:	Civil War; children's.
# of Vols:	5,000
Hours:	Jan-May: Wed-Sun 10:30-4:30. Jun-Dec: Tue-Sun 10-5 and open some Mondays.
Services:	Accepts want lists.
Travel:	Medford (Barnett Rd) exit off I-5. West on Barnett, right on Riverside (Hwy 99) and left on Main which turns into Hwy 238. Continue on Hwy 238 to Jacksonville.
Credit Cards:	Yes
Owner:	Gene & Jean Chase
Year Estab:	1994
Comments:	Located in an old fashioned general store setting in an historic town, the number of new books and memorabilia in this shop far outnumber the used volumes (and are also more interesting).

The Three Gables Antiques   **Open Shop**
305 South Oregon   (541) 899-1891
Mailing Address: PO Box 577 Jacksonville 97530

Collection:	General stock, ephemera and magazines
# of Vols:	1,000+
Hours:	Summer: Daily 10-4. Winter: Daily 10-4.
Credit Cards:	No
Owner:	Emilie Oliver
Comments:	This primarily antique/collectibles shop also stocks a small number of older volumes in mixed condition with an emphasis on Americana. If you're passing through Jacksonville and are looking for older titles, you might want to stop here for a brief visit.

Turner House Antiques   **Open Shop**
120 North Fifth Street   (541) 899-1936
Mailing Address: PO Box 1113 Jacksonville 97530

Collection:	General stock and ephemera.
Specialties:	Children's; Western Americana.
# of Vols:	4,000-5,000
Hours:	Summer: Mon-Sat 10:30-5:30. Winter: By appointment.
Credit Cards:	No
Owner:	David Ralston
Year Estab:	1983
Comments:	At the time of our visit, there were several boxes of weather damaged books for sale on the front lawn, plus additional books (mostly older and in mixed condition), ephemera and some interesting collectibles available on the first floor of this private residence.

Keizer

Booksmart   **Open Shop**
4908 River Road North 97303   (503) 393-2899

Collection:	General stock of mostly used paperback.
Hours:	Mon-Sat 10-6.

Klamath Falls
(Map 23, page 333)

Ashurst Books   **Open Shop**
1006 Main Street 97601   (541) 883-1442

Collection:	General stock of hardcover and paperback.
Specialties:	Western Americana.
# of Vols:	10,000
Hours:	Tue-Sat 10-5:30.
Services:	Search service, accepts want lists, mail order.
Travel:	Downtown exit off Hwy 97. Proceed east on Klamath Ave, then left on 11th St and right on Main.

Credit Cards: No
Owner: Aaron Ashurst
Year Estab: 1991
Comments: The stock is approximately 60% hardcover.

Basin Book Trader   **Open Shop**
4846 South 6th Street 97603   (541) 884-0197

Collection: General stock of paperback and hardcover.
# of Vols: 40,000
Hours: Mon-Sat 10-5.
Travel: South 6th St is the main highway between Bend and Reno.
Credit Cards: No
Owner: Sheryl Van Fleet
Year Estab: 1991
Comments: Stock is approximately 60% paperback.

La Pine

La Pine Book Exchange Plus   **Open Shop**
16388 Third Street   (541) 536-5580
Mailing Address: PO Box 1623 La Pine 97739   Fax: (541) 536-5673

Collection: General stock of mostly paperback.
Hours: Mon-Fri 10-5. Sat 10-3.

Lake Oswego
(Map 22, page 366)

Booktique   **Open Shop**
3975 Mercantile Drive 97035   (503) 699-9109

Collection: General stock of hardcover and paperback.
# of Vols: 30,000
Hours: Tue-Sat 11-3.
Travel: Exit 292 off I-5. Proceed east on Hwy 217 (Kruse Way) to Lake Oswego. At end of Kruse Way, turn right, then immediate right again on Mercantile.
Comments: Operated by the Friends of the Lake Oswego Public Library.

Lincoln City
(Map 20, page 345)

Brady Books   **Open Shop**
1530 SE Highway 101   (541) 994-4599
Mailing Address: PO Box 959 Lincoln City 97367

Collection: General stock of hardcover and paperback.
# of Vols: 10,000
Hours: Mon-Fri 10-6, except sometimes closed Wed. Sat 10-6. Sun 10-5.
Owner: Glenn Cobb
Year Estab: 1995

Comments: Most of the hardcover volumes we saw were of recent vintage and in fairly good condition. Little in the way of depth (except for a nice mystery section) and less still in terms of rare or collectible items. An adequate neighborhood shop providing reading copies.

L & M Treasures **Open Shop**
2065 NW 34th Street 97367 (541) 994-5428

Collection: General stock.
Specialties: Children's
# of Vols: 8,000
Hours: Daily 10-5.
Services: Accepts want lists.
Travel: Located on corner of Hwy 101 and 34th Ave in the north end of town.
Credit Cards: No
Owner: Lyle Guthrie
Year Estab: 1986
Comments: Despite the above hours, given to us by the owner, the shop was closed on the day we were in town.

Robert's Book Shop **Open Shop**
3412 SE Highway 101 97367 (541) 994-4453

Collection: General stock of hardcover and paperback and ephemera.
Specialties: Americana; guns; hunting; technical; cookbooks; mystery; detective; art.
# of Vols: 100,000
Hours: Daily 10:30-5:30.
Services: Mail order.
Travel: At South 35th Street.
Credit Cards: Yes
Owner: Bob Portwood
Year Estab: 1988
Comments: A Class A shop with a generous collection in almost every genre of both vintage and newer items and at reasonable prices. Absolutely worth visiting. We spent considerable time here and would have spent even more time had we not been forced to stick to a rigid schedule. A visit here is an absolute must if you're anywhere near the Oregon coast.

McMinnville

Philip J. Pirages Rare Books **By Appointment**
2205 Nut Tree Lane (503) 472-0476
Mailing Address: PO Box 504 McMinnville 97128 Fax: (503) 472-5029

Collection: Specialty
Specialties: Early printed books; British and American literature; fine bindings; illustrated; private press (modern); illuminated manuscript leaves.
# of Vols: 1,000
Services: Appraisals, catalog, accepts want lists.
Credit Cards: Yes

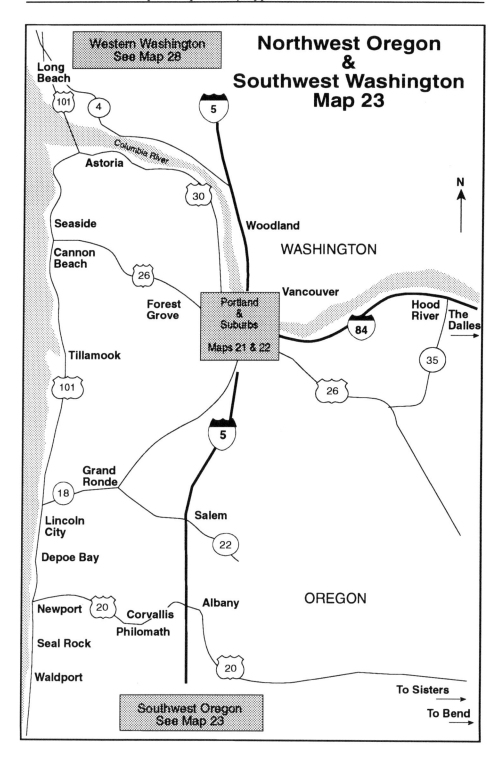

Medford
(Map 23, page 333)

Bartlett Street Book Store   **Open Shop**
16 South Bartlett Street 97501   Fax: (541) 772-8049   (541) 772-8049

Collection: General stock of mostly hardcover.
Specialties: Children's; illustrated.
# of Vols: 18,000
Hours: Mon-Sat 10:30-5:30.
Services: Appraisals, search service, book repair and binding.
Travel: Medford exit off I-5. Proceed on Barnett. Left on Riverside, left on Main and left on Bartlett. Shop is 1/2 block ahead on right.
Credit Cards: No
Owner: Kenneth Corliss
Year Estab: 1974
Comments: A tightly packed shop with a strong stock: a small representation of paperbacks and an overwhelmingly good representation of hardcover books of mixed vintage and in generally good condition. We saw several volumes that could certainly be viewed as collectibles. This is a shop we believe experienced book people will appreciate.

Village Books   **Open Shop**
1310 B Center Drive 97501   (541) 779-7576

Collection: General stock of paperback and hardcover.
# of Vols: 60,000
Hours: Mon-Sat 10-6. Sun 12-5.
Travel: Exit 27 off I-5. Follow signs to Visitor's Center. Shop is located in Harry & David's Country Village shopping center.
Credit Cards: Yes
Owner: Loren & Jeanne Otto
Year Estab: 1994
Comments: A standard shopping center format with paperbacks along the center aisles and hardcover volumes along the side and rear walls. The shop has a better balance between older and newer hardcover items than we have seen in similar shops. Several sets and other attractive items on hand.

Monmouth

Dog Eared Editions   **Open Shop**
183 Main Street West 97361   (503) 838-0269

Collection: General stock of mostly paperback.
Hours: Mon-Fri 9-6. Sat 9-5.

Second Chance Books   **Open Shop**
309 North Pacific Avenue 97361   (503) 838-5279

Collection: General stock of mostly paperback.

# of Vols:	20,000
Hours:	Mon-Sat 10-6. Sun 11-5.
Services:	Accepts want lists, mail order.
Travel:	On Hwy 99W (Pacific Ave) at corner of Powell.
Credit Cards:	Yes
Owner:	Steve & Dina Carter
Year Estab:	1994
Comments:	An overwhelmingly paperback shop with perhaps 500 or so hardcover books, most of which were of recent vintage and would fall into the "reading copy" classification.

Myrtle Creek
(Map 23, page 333)

Mike's Books & Espresso **Open Shop**
217 NW 2nd Avenue (541) 863-3545
Mailing Address: PO Box 928 Myrtle Creek 97457

Collection:	General stock of hardcover and paperback.
Specialties:	Western Americana; American and English history; psychology; sciences.
# of Vols:	20,000
Hours:	Mon-Fri 8:30-6. Sat 10-5.
Services:	Search service, catalog, accepts want lists.
Travel:	Exit 108 off I-5. Just off Main St.
Credit Cards:	No
Owner:	Mike & Kathi Justman
Year Estab:	1995
Comments:	One of the few combination book store/cafes that we actually had lunch at. (The food was good.) We suspect that the books, some paperbacks, lots of hardcover fiction and an interesting mystery section, are designed to appeal primarily to local interests. We also spotted some classics and a few items that looked as though the owner would have to wait for an out-of-the-area buyer. While the number of books on hand was relatively small, they did reflect the taste of a veteran book person enjoying a new phase in his life. If you happen to be on I-5, you may well enjoy a visit here.

Nehalem

Mystery Treasure House **Open Shop**
35870 Highway 101 97131 (503) 368-6219

Collection:	Specialty new and used, paperback and hardcover.
Specialties:	Mystery
Hours:	Daily 10-5.
Credit Cards:	Yes
Owner:	June Geislinger
Year Estab:	1977
Comments:	Stock is approximately 25% used, 60% of which is paperback.

Newport
(Map 20, page 345)

Newport Book Center   **Open Shop**
823 SW Hurbert Street 97365   (541) 265-8971

Collection: General stock of paperback and hardcover.
Specialties: Western Americana; children's.
Hours: Mon-Fri 10-5:30. Sat 10:30-5. Sun (summer and special weekends only) 1-4.
Travel: Just off Hwy 101.
Credit Cards: Yes
Owner: Patrick & Martha Hannan
Year Estab: 1985
Comments: Nice reading copies of mostly more recent titles. Don't expect rare items here, although, one never knows what a dealer may acquire and make available to his customers after one's visit.

Nye Book House   **Open Shop**
727 NW 3rd Street 97365   (541) 265-6840

Collection: General stock of mostly paperback.
Hours: Sun-Wed 11-5. Thu-Sat 10-6.

North Bend
(Map 23, page 333)

Pirate Cove   **Open Shop**
1987 Sherman Avenue 97459   (541) 756-6163

Collection: General stock of mostly used paperback and hardcover.
Hours: Mon-Sat 10-5. Sun 12-4.
Services: Accepts want lists, mail order.
Travel: On Hwy 101.
Credit Cards: Yes
Owner: Gary & Janice Jadin
Year Estab: 1981
Comments: Stock is approximately 60% paperback.

Yesterday's Books   **Open Shop**
1988 Sherman Avenue 97459   (541) 756-7214

Collection: General stock of paperback and hardcover.
# of Vols: 40,000
Hours: Mon-Sat 11-5:30. Sun 1-5.
Travel: At corner of Virginia and southbound side of Hwy 101.
Comments: Stock is approximately 60% paperback.

Ontario

Per USED Books
2022 SW 4th Avenue 97914

Open Shop
(541) -88-1-1221

Collection: General stock of mostly paperback.
Hours: Mon-Fri 10-6.

Philomath
(Map 20, page 345)

Beehive Books and Arts
1233 Main Street
Mailing Address: PO Box 1636 Philomath 97370

Open Shop
(541) 929-5027

Collection: General stock of mostly hardcover.
Specialties: Travel; languages; gardening.
# of Vols: 6,000
Hours: Mostly daily 12-6, or ring the doorbell.
Services: Book binding and repair.
Travel: Hwy 34 exit off I-5. Proceed thru Corvallis to Philomath. Shop is on right after the 13th St traffic light.
Credit Cards: No
Owner: Marion McKinsey
Year Estab: 1993
Comments: The books we saw in this shop were, for the most part, rather ordinary, but the shop itself was by no means ordinary. In addition to a modest collection of hardcover books (some older and very possibly collectible), at least half the shop is devoted to a beautiful display of quilts (the shop offers quilting classes) and a fascinating collection of old sewing machines. Whether or not you purchase a book, regardless of your gender, you should enjoy a visit here.

In Between Times
1144 Main 97370

Open Shop
(541) 929-3394

Collection: General stock of mostly paperback.
# of Vols: 20,000
Hours: Mon-Sat 12-6.
Travel: See Beehive above.
Credit Cards: No
Owner: James & Sherrill Kvidt
Year Estab: 1992
Comments: A small shop dominated by paperbacks with 100 or so hardcover books, some very old (primarily fiction) and some newer. Basically reading copies.

Portland
(Map 21, page 352 and Map 22, page 366)

Armchair Family Bookstore   **Open Shop**
3205 SE Milwaukie Avenue 97202   (503) 238-6680

Collection: General stock of mostly paperback.
Specialties: Vintage paperbacks.
Hours: Mon-Fri 10-9. Sat 10-6. Sun 12-6.

Author's Ink   **Open Shop**
13611 NW Cornell Road 97229   Fax: (503) 626-4743   (503) 626-4743

Collection: General stock of paperback and hardcover.
Specialties: Pacific northwest; cookbooks; classics.
# of Vols: 25,000-30,000
Hours: Mon-Thu 10-6. Fri 10-7. Sat 10-5.
Services: Appraisals, search service, accepts want lists, mail order.
Travel: Hwy 26 west from Portland. Murray Blvd exit. North on Murray, left on Cornell then right into shopping center.
Map Ref: Map 22, page 366, #2.
Credit Cards: Yes
Owner: Harold Walkup
Year Estab: 1982
Comments: An overwhelmingly paperback shop. The hardcover titles, with the exception of some best sellers, seemed to fall into the category of "practicality," e.g., real estate, crafts, how-to, etc. If you live locally and your free public library doesn't have what you're looking for, you could possibly find it here.

The Author's Bookstore   **Open Shop**
4625 SE Woodstock Boulevard 97206   (503) 777-4644

Collection: General stock of mostly paperback.
Hours: Mon-Sat 10-7.

Autumn Leaves Bookstore   **Open Shop**
2512 SE 122nd Street   (503) 760-5607
Mailing Address: 1951 SE 135th Portland 97233

Collection: General stock of paperback and hardcover.
# of Vols: 120,000
Hours: Mon-Sat 10-7. Sun 12-5.
Travel: Division St exit off I-205. Proceed east on Division. Shop is at Division and 122nd. Turn right into shopping center.
Map Ref: Map 21, page 352, #4.
Credit Cards: No
Owner: Sharon L. Garner
Year Estab: 1985
Comments: If you're home is within a mile or two or three of this shop and you like to read, you can find paperbacks galore here, plus some hardcover mysteries, older books in mixed condition and a variety of more recent titles. If you're

traveling from a longer distance and decide to stop by, it's certainly possible that a title of interest to you may be on hand - but don't get your hopes up too high.

Blumenkron & Ramirez Books
PO Box 10163   97210

By Appointment
(503) 291-7112

Collection:	Specialty
Specialties:	Modern first editions; rare books in a variety of subject areas.
# of Vols:	2,000
Services:	Occasional catalog, accepts want lists.
Credit Cards:	No
Owner:	Art Blumenkron & George Ramirez
Year Estab:	1985

Book City Paradise
3315 SE Hawthorne Boulevard
Mailing Address: 606 SE Madison Street Portland 97214

Open Shop
(800) 356-5202   (503) 234-6003
Fax: (503) 235-1979

Collection:	General stock of hardcover and paperback.
# of Vols:	100,000+
Hours:	Mon-Fri 9:30-9. Sat 10-8. Sun 11-7.
Services:	Accepts want lists, mail order.
Travel:	"Omsi" exit off I-5. Proceed straight on Belmont to 20th St. Right on Belmont then left on Hawthorne. Shop is at 33rd St.
Map Ref:	Map 21, page 352, #5.
Credit Cards:	Yes
Owner:	N.W. Raintree, Inc.
Year Estab:	1988
Comments:	If you're looking for volume, this shop has it. Lots of paperbacks, but certainly a fair collection of hardcover books (mostly reading copies) in mixed condition and of mixed vintage. We did spot a few titles that looked interesting enough to catch the attention of a scout but these could be long gone by the time you visit.

Books/Art
6802 SE Milwaukie Avenue   97202

Open Shop
(503) 236-8345

Collection:	General stock of new and used paperback and hardcover.
# of Vols:	3,000 (used)
Hours:	Mon-Sat 10-6.
Travel:	Milwaukie/McLaughlin exit off I-5. Proceed south on McLaughlin, then south on Milwaukie.
Map Ref:	Map 22, page 366, #7.
Comments:	Stock is approximately 50% used, 65% of which is paperback.

Cal's Books and Wares
732 SW 1st Avenue   97204

Open Shop
(503) 222-5454

Collection:	General stock.
Specialties:	Vintage magazines.

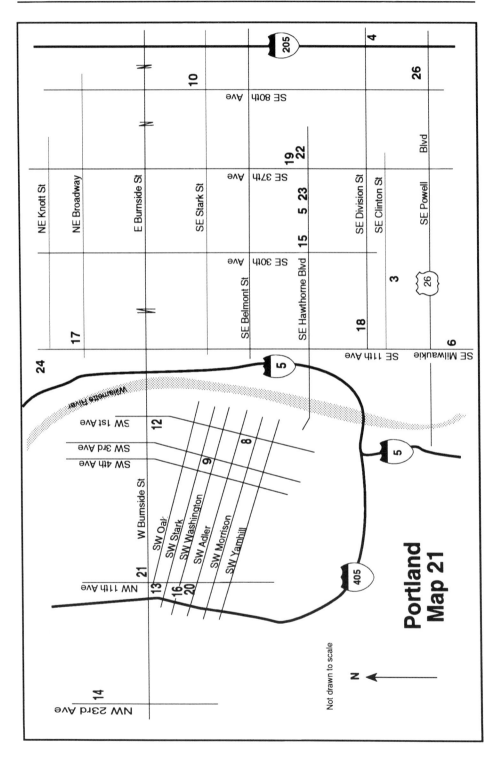

# of Vols: 1,000+
Hours: Mon-Fri 10:30-5:30. Sat 11-4.
Travel: Downtown, between Yamhill and Morrison.
Map Ref: Map 21, page 352, #8.
Credit Cards: Yes
Owner: Dana Hancock
Year Estab: 1963
Comments: The shop also sells antiques.

Cameron's Books   Open Shop
336 SW 3rd Avenue 97204   (503) 228-2391

Collection: General stock of hardcover and paperback.
Specialties: Magazines; vintage paperbacks.
# of Vols: 50,000 (books only)
Hours: Mon-Sat 10-6. Sun 12:30-4:30.
Services: Search service, mail order.
Travel: Downtown, between Washington and Burnside.
Map Ref: Map 21, page 352, #9.
Credit Cards: Yes
Owner: Jeff Frase
Year Estab: 1938
Comments: A crowded shop with lots of paperbacks and a smaller number of hardcover books (mostly reading copies) in mixed condition. Little to excite the eye. While back issues of popular magazines are on display, most of the magazines, vintage paperbacks and pulps are not available for causal browsing.

Collectors Antique Marketplace   Antique Mall
338 NW Fifth Avenue   (503) 227-7789

Collection: General stock.
Hours: Mon-Sat 10-6. Sun 12-5.

Barbara Cutts-UK/USA Bookdealer   By Appointment
2206 NE 40th Avenue 97212   (503) 288-9301

Collection: Specialty new and used.
Specialties: Celebrity signed books; arts and crafts; literature; performing arts; United Kingdom imports.
# of Vols: 5,000
Services: Appraisals, search service, catalog, accepts want lists.
Credit Cards: No
Year Estab: 1985

Dee's Books & More   Open Shop
8021 SE Stark 97215   (503) 255-4547

Collection: General stock of hardcover and paperback.
# of Vols: 8,000-10,000
Hours: Mon-Sat 9-6.
Travel: Stark St exit off I-205. Proceed west on Stark to 80th St.

(Portland)

Map Ref: Map 21, page 352, #10.
Year Estab: 1994
Comments: Stock is approximately 60% hardcover.

Excalibur Books & Comics   Open Shop
2444 SE Hawthorne Boulevard 97214   (503) 231-7351

Collection: Specialty
Specialties: Horror; science fiction; fantasy.
Hours: Mon-Wed 11-7. Thu 11-8. Fri & Sat 10-8. Sun 11-6.

Fritzler's Books   Open Shop
3286 NE Killingsworth Street 97211   (503) 287-3736

Collection: General stock of paperback and hardcover.
# of Vols: 30,000
Hours: Tue-Sat 10-5.
Travel: Killingsworth exit off I-5. Proceed east on Killingsworth to 33rd St.
Map Ref: Map 22, page 366, #11.
Owner: Ken Fritzler
Comments: Predominately paperback, with perhaps several hundred hardcover books of little or no distinction.

Future Dreams/Gateway   Open Shop
10508 NE Halsey 97220   (503) 255-5245

Collection: Specialty new and used.
Specialties: Science fiction; fantasy; horror and related art work.
Hours: Thu-Mon 12-7.
Travel: In northeast Portland, at 102nd St and Halsey.

Future Dreams/Burnside   Open Shop
1800 East Burnside 97214   (503) 231-8311

Collection: Specialty used and new. Mostly paperback.
Specialties: Science fiction; fantasy; horror; comics.
Hours: Mon-Fri 10-7. Sat & Sun 10-6.

Charles Garvin, Books   Open Shop
104 SW 2nd Avenue 97204

Collection: ??
Travel: Downtown, between Burnside and Ankney.
Map Ref: Map 21, page 352, #12.
Comments: Another dealer without a phone. We were advised, however, by area dealers that the shop is open for business, although with irregular hours. If you have some extra time while in downtown Portland, you may want to stop by. If you do, let us know what you find.

Robert Gavora, Bookseller   Open Shop
4514 East Burnside Street 97215   Fax: (503) 231-7338 (503) 231-7338

Collection:	Specialty
Specialties:	Science fiction; mystery; railroads; western fiction; Western Americana.
# of Vols:	3,000
Hours:	Wed-Sat 11-5. A call ahead is advised.
Services:	Catalog
Travel:	Downtown, at 45th Street.
Credit Cards:	Yes
Year Estab:	1984

The Great Northwest Bookstore   Open Shop
1234 SW Stark 97205   (503) 223-9474
                                              E-mail: gnwdt@teleport.com

Collection:	General stock of hardcover and paperback.
Specialties:	Western Americana.
# of Vols:	150,000
Hours:	Mon-Fri 9-7. Sat 11-7. Sun 12-5.
Services:	Appraisals, catalog (Americana and Western Americana), on line search service, accepts want lists.
Travel:	Downtown, just off intersection of Burnside and 13th St.
Map Ref:	Map 21, page 352, #13.
Credit Cards:	Yes
Owner:	Phil Wikelund
Year Estab:	1977
Comments:	In addition to a strong collection in the specialty noted above, the shop displays a very fine general collection. We were impressed by the balance between vintage titles and more recent items. If you can demonstrate that you're a "serious buyer," you should be able to visit the rare book room located on the shop's second floor. We think you'll be impressed.

Hanson's Books   Open Shop
814 NW 23rd 97210   (503) 223-7610

Collection:	General stock of hardcover and paperback.
Specialties:	Art; literature; history; science; philosophy.
# of Vols:	7,500
Hours:	Sun-Thu 11-8. Fri & Sat 11-10.
Services:	Appraisals, accepts want lists, mail order.
Travel:	From I-405 northbound: Everett St exit. Go past Everett and turn left on Glisan and proceed to 23rd. Right on 23rd. Shop is 3½ blocks ahead.
Map Ref:	Map 21, page 352, #14.
Credit Cards:	Yes
Owner:	Steve Hanson
Year Estab:	1992
Comments:	A small collection of quality books, most of which looked well cared for. While most subjects were covered, the only ones that appeared to be covered in any depth were the specialties listed above.

(Portland)

Hawthorne Boulevard Books
3129 SE Hawthorne Boulevard 97214

Open Shop
(503) 236-3211

Collection:	General stock of mostly used.
Specialties:	Western Americana; illustrated; limited editions.
# of Vols:	25,000
Hours:	Tue-Sun 11-6.
Services:	Appraisals, search service, accepts want lists, mail order.
Travel:	See Book City Paradise Avenue. Shop is between 31st St & 32nd St.
Map Ref:	Map 21, page 352, #15.
Credit Cards:	Yes
Owner:	Roger & Isle Roberts
Year Estab:	1984
Comments:	Our kind of bookstore. Not huge but crammed full of quality titles in almost every field. Particularly strong in scholarly and vintage items. Don't miss it.

Hey Joe Used Books & Records
4019 SE Hawthorne Boulevard 97214

Open Shop
(503) 234-8843

Collection:	Specialty paperback and hardcover and magazines.
Specialties:	Mari Suona; rock n roll; counter culture.
Hours:	Daily 11-6.
Services:	Accepts want lists, mail order.
Travel:	See Book City Paradise above.
Credit Cards:	Yes
Owner:	Joseph Lipkind
Year Estab:	1989

Holland's Books
527 SW 12th 97205

Open Shop
(503) 224-4242

Collection:	General stock of hardcover and paperback.
Specialties:	History; social theory; literature; philosophy.
# of Vols:	15,000
Hours:	Mon-Sat 11-6.
Services:	Appraisals, accepts want lists.
Travel:	Downtown, between Washington and Alder.
Map Ref:	Map 21, page 352, #16.
Credit Cards:	No
Owner:	Stephen Holland
Year Estab:	1980
Comments:	An overwhelmingly scholarly stock, with quite interesting titles, most of which were in quite good condition. Even the more general collection consisted of interesting titles. Worth a visit, particularly as it's close to several other quality dealers.

Irvington Booknook
1115 NE Broadway 97232

Open Shop
(503) 284-6457

Collection:	General stock of mostly hardcover.
Specialties:	Aviation; maritime; railroads; automotive.
# of Vols:	25,000
Hours:	Daily 11-6.
Services:	Appraisals, accepts want lists.
Travel:	Between 11th & 12th Avenues.
Map Ref:	Map 21, page 352, #17.
Credit Cards:	No
Owner:	Talbot V. Ridgway
Year Estab:	1994
Comments:	Stock is approximately 80% hardcover.

JP Books
1601 SW Pendleton Court
Mailing Address: PO Box 10884 Portland 97210

By Appointment
(503) 227-3308

Collection:	Specialty
Specialties:	Mountaineering; Central Asia; exploration; polar; skiing.
# of Vols:	3,500
Hours:	Available Sep-Jun only.
Services:	Appraisals, search service, accepts want lists.
Credit Cards:	No
Owner:	Jim Petroske
Year Estab:	1989

Raymond Kimeldorf
1925 SE 59th Avenue 97215

By Appointment
(503) 236-1848

Collection:	General stock.
Specialties:	Judaica; business; college and university histories.
# of Vols:	3,000
Hours:	Mon-Thu 7pm-10pm. Sun 9-9.
Services:	Appraisals, search service, accepts want lists, mail order.
Credit Cards:	No

Longfellow's Books
1401 SE Division Street 97202

Open Shop
Fax: (503) 239-5222 (503) 239-5222

Collection:	General stock and ephemera.
Specialties:	Children's series; *National Geographic*; modern first editions; *Oregon* magazine; sheet music.
# of Vols:	20,000
Hours:	Mon-Sat 12-5:30. Sun by appointment.
Services:	Appraisals, search service, accepts want lists, mail order.
Travel:	See Book City Paradise above. Continue on 20th to Division. Right on Division.
Map Ref:	Map 21, page 352, #18.
Credit Cards:	Yes

(Portland)

Owner:	Jon Hagen
Year Estab:	1981
Comments:	We arrived at this shop at 2:45pm on a Thursday in July only to find a sign on the front door reading: "Closed. Too Hot." Apparently the owner of this establishment believes book hunters are as intimidated by the weather as he is. If you're planning to visit here, our advice is to first check with the weatherman. Then call the shop.

David Morrison Books   **Open Shop**
1420 SE 37th Avenue 97214   Fax: (503) 233-5868   (503) 233-5868
E-mail: morrison@teleport.com

Collection:	General stock.
Specialties:	Photography; architecture; decorative arts; art.
# of Vols:	40,000
Hours:	Daily 10-7.
Services:	Appraisals, search service, subject catalogs, accepts want lists.
Travel:	See Book City Paradise above. Shop is just north of Hawthorne Blvd SE.
Map Ref:	Map 21, page 352, #19.
Credit Cards:	Yes
Owner:	David Morrison
Year Estab:	1991
Comments:	When we visited this shop, the number of books on hand was substantial and yet we had the impression that changes had either just occurred or were about to occur. The books (all hardcover) were in good to very good condition and represented both vintage and more recent titles. Most subject areas were well represented and there was certainly a good supply of collectibles and desirable items. We even made a modest purchase. With changes in the book world as frequent as they are, you may want to call ahead to be certain that the shop you visit is the same one we saw.

Murder By The Book   **Open Shop**
7828 SW Capitol Highway 97219   (503) 293-6507

Collection:	Specialty new and used and related items.
Specialties:	Mystery; detective; crime; spy.
Hours:	Mon-Sat 10:30-6. Sun 12-5.
Services:	Appraisals, search service, catalog, accepts want lists, newsletter.
Travel:	Southbound on I-5: Multnomah exit. Right on 36th, right on Capitol Hwy.
Credit Cards:	No
Owner:	Carolyn Lane & Jill Hinckley
Year Estab:	1983

Murder By The Book   **Open Shop**
3210 SE Hawthorne Boulevard 97214   (503) 232-9995

Collection:	Specialty new and used and related items.
Specialties:	Mystery; detective; spy; crime.

Hours: Mon-Sat 10:30-6:30. Sun 12-5.
Services: Appraisals, search service, catalog, accepts want lists, newsletter.
Travel: See Book City Paradise above.
Credit Cards: No
Owner: Carolyn Lane & Jill Hinckley
Year Estab: 1983
Comments: An overwhelmingly paperback shop with the hardcover titles taking up a limited space against the back wall. We saw three times as many hardcover mysteries in a general shop almost directly across the street as we saw here. So much for "specialty" shops.

Nineteenth Century Prints **By Appointment**
2732 SE Woodward Street 97202 Fax: (503) 234-3538 (503) 234-3538

Collection: Specialty
Specialties: Limited stock of illustrated; children's; natural history books. Larger stock of maps and prints.
Services: Accepts want lists, mail order.
Credit Cards: Yes
Owner: Elisabeth Burdon
Year Estab: 1981

Old Friends Library **Open Shop**
3370 SE Milwaukie 97202 (503) 231-9992

Collection: General stock.
# of Vols: 5,000
Hours: Daily 7am-6pm.
Travel: Four blocks south of Powell. See Book City Paradise above.
Map Ref: Map 21, page 352, #6.
Owner: John Asparro
Year Estab: 1995

Old Oregon Book Store **Open Shop**
1128 SW Alder 97205 (503) 227-2742

Collection: General stock.
Specialties: Pacific Northwest; Western Americana; Russia.
# of Vols: 60,000
Hours: Mon-Sat 11-5. (See Comments)
Services: Appraisals, accepts want lists, mail order.
Travel: Downtown, between 11th & 12 Sts.
Map Ref: Map 21, page 352, #20.
Credit Cards: No
Owner: Preston & Phyllis McMann
Year Estab: 1949
Comments: The shop (actually two adjacent storefronts that are not connected to each other) is heavily into the specialties listed above, plus strong sections in American history and biography and a smaller sampling of more popular subjects. The quality of the collection, in terms of both condition and

(Portland)

uniqueness of title, should tempt many a university library. Note: A call ahead is advised as the owner, a veteran book dealer, may be retiring in the near future.

Panurge Emporium Books   **Open Shop**
1005 NW 16th 97209   (503) 248-6905

Collection: Specialty new and some used.
Specialties: Occult
Hours: Tue-Thu 11-7. Fri & Sat 11-8. Sun 12-6.
Travel: At corner of Lovejoy.

The Paper Moon Bookstore   **Open Shop**
2504 SE Clinton Street 97202   Fax: (503) 236-3444   (503) 239-1984
E-mail: paprmoon@teleport.com

Collection: General stock of hardcover and paperback.
Specialties: Children's; illustrated.
# of Vols: 25,000
Hours: Mon-Sat 10-6. Sun 12-5. Best to call ahead.
Services: Appraisals, catalog, accepts want lists, search service.
Travel: From I-5, see Book City Paradise above. Shop is two blocks south of Division between 25th & 26th Streets.
Map Ref: Map 21, page 352, #3.
Credit Cards: Yes
Owner: Andrea Drinard
Year Estab: 1983

Periodicals Paradise   **Open Shop**
3366 SE Powell 97214   (800) 356-5202   (503) 236-8370
Fax: (503) 235-1979

Collection: Specialty
Specialties: Magazines.
# of Vols: 1 million+
Hours: Daily 9-9.
Travel: See Book City Paradise above. At 33rd St.
Credit Cards: Yes
Owner: N.W. Raintree, Inc.
Year Estab: 1988

Pilgrim Discount Book & Bible Supply   **Open Shop**
9003 SE Stark 97216   (503) 255-7620

Collection: Specialty new and used.
Specialties: Religion (Christian evangelical).
# of Vols: 16,000 (used)
Hours: Mon-Thu 10-6. Fri 10-8. Sat 10-5.
Travel: Downtown
Year Estab: 1988

Powell's City of Books
Open Shop
1005 West Burnside Street 97209
Fax: (503) 228-4631 (503) 228-4651
E-mail: ping@powells.portland.or.us

Collection:	General stock of new and used, hardcover and paperback.
# of Vols:	1 million+
Hours:	Mon-Sat 9am-11pm. Sun 9am-9pm.
Services:	Appraisals, search service, mail order.
Travel:	Southbound on I-5: St. Helens (I-405) exit. Cross Fremont Bridge, then Burnside exit off I-405. Left on Burnside. Shop is four blocks ahead. Northbound on I-5: City Center (I-405) exit, then Everett exit off I-405. Right on Everett, right on 11th. Shop is three blocks ahead. Free parking is available on 11th St between Couch and Burnside.
Map Ref:	Map 21, page 352, #21.
Credit Cards:	Yes
Owner:	Michael Powell
Year Estab:	1975
Comments:	The vastness of this shop's collection (the three story building takes up an entire city block) perhaps explains the popularly and aura surrounding this shop that we sensed in our travels long before we arrived in Portland. Dealers all along the Pacific Coast asked if we had visited Powell's yet and told us that we would certainly be impressed. They were right. You will certainly not find every title you're looking for here. We didn't. But, what you will find is perhaps one of the most extensive collections of used books found anywhere in the country. In addition to its very strong collection of post World War II titles (and an even stronger collection of publications from the 1970's-1990's), you'll also find interesting selections of older volumes, albeit not in large numbers. Even if you don't find the title you've been searching for for years, if printer's ink runs through your veins, you should very much enjoy your visit here. We stayed 1½ hours and obviously wish we could have stayed much much longer. The collection is meticulously organized in a series of color coded rooms and numbered aisles and specific subjects are easy to find with the aid of a handy map (copies supplied) listing in excess of 100 different subject categories. The shop's rare book room displaying older volumes of interest to more serious collectors is open Thu-Sun from 10-7 and other times if staff is available.

If you don't see the book you're looking for here (or at any of the other Powell's stores you visit) ask one of the employees to check if the book is available at one of the other locations. If the book is available, it will be delivered to the Powell's store of your choice within 24 hours. Now that's service.

Powell's Books for Cooks
Open Shop
3747 SW Hawthorne Boulevard 97214
Fax: (503) 238-4427 (503) 235-3802

Collection:	Specialty new and used, hardcover and paperback and ephemera.
Specialties:	Cookbooks; gardening.
# of Vols:	20,000

(Portland)

Services:	Appraisals, search service, catalog, accepts want lists.
Travel:	See Book City Paradise above. At 37th St.
Credit Cards:	Yes
Year Estab:	1988
Comments:	Stock is approximately 25% used, 80% of which is hardcover. The shop also sells an array of attractive non book items related to its specialties.

Powell's on Hawthorne   **Open Shop**
3723 SE Hawthorne Boulevard 97214   (503) 235-3802   (503) 238-1668

Collection:	General stock of mostly used hardcover and paperback.
# of Vols:	60,000
Hours:	Mon-Thu 9am-10pm. Fri & Sat 9am-11pm. Sun 9am-8pm.
Services:	Appraisals, search service, accepts want lists.
Travel:	See Book City Paradise above. At 37th St.
Map Ref:	Map 21, page 352, #22.
Credit Cards:	Yes
Year Estab:	1988
Comments:	A particularly nice shop that combines some new books with a good selection of used hardcover volumes and paperbacks in mostly very nice condition. A most helpful and friendly staff. New and used books are shelved separately and the sections are well labeled for easy browsing. While the selection may not be as overwhelming as the Burnside Avenue location downtown, the collection is certainly large and varied enough to make a visit here most worthwhile.

Powell's Technical Books   **Open Shop**
33 NW Park Avenue 97029   (503) 228-3906   (800) 225-6911
Fax: (503) 228-0505
E-mail: ping@technicall.powells.Or.us

Collection:	Specialty new and used hardcover and paperback.
Specialties:	Technology; computers; electronics; physical science; engineering; math; metallurgy; construction; radio.
# of Vols:	100,000
Hours:	Mon-Sat 9-9. Sun 12-7.
Services:	Accepts want lists, mail order.
Travel:	Downtown
Credit Cards:	Yes
Year Estab:	1986
Comments:	Stock of about evenly divided between new and used. Used stock is approximately 60% hardcover.

Powell's Travel Store   **Open Shop**
701 SW 6th Avenue 97204   Fax: (503) 228-7062   (503) 228-1108

Collection:	Specialty paperback and hardcover. Mostly new.
Specialties:	Travel

Hours:	Mon-Fri 9-7. Sat 10-7. Sun 10-5.
Services:	Mail order.
Travel:	City Center exit off I-5. Shop is at corner of 6th & Yamhill in Pioneer Courthouse Square.
Credit Cards:	Yes
Year Estab:	1985

Second Story Booksellers   Open Shop
3325 SE Hawthorne 97214   (503) 234-0343

Collection:	General stock of hardcover and paperback.
Specialties:	Beat generation; expatriates.
# of Vols:	10,000
Hours:	Mon-Thu 11-5. Fri & Sat 11-7. Sun 12-6.
Services:	Accepts want lists.
Travel:	See Book City Paradise above.
Map Ref:	Map 21, page 352, #23.
Credit Cards:	No
Owner:	Barbara Wahr
Year Estab:	1988
Comments:	A relatively small shop, and except for the owner's specialties, a fairly limited stock of mostly common titles. However, since the shop is just steps away from a larger book dealer, you can't go wrong stopping by once you've visited the neighboring shop.

Charles Seluzicki Fine and Rare Books   By Appointment
3733 NE 24th Avenue 97212   (503) 284-4749

Collection:	Specialty
Specialties:	19th and 20th century first edition literature; author archives; fine press; history of ideas.
# of Vols:	4,000-5,000
Services:	Appraisals, occasional catalog, search service (better books only), accepts want lists.
Credit Cards:	No
Year Estab:	1975

Bill Swing Rare & Fine Books   By Appointment
917 SW Oak Street, Ste. 213 97205   (503) 228-5520

Collection:	Specialty
Specialties:	19th & 20th century literature.
# of Vols:	5,000
Services:	Appraisals, catalog, search service, accepts want lists.
Year Estab:	1990

Title Wave Bookstore   Open Shop
216 NE Knott Street 97212   (503) 248-5021

Collection:	General stock of library discards.
Hours:	Mon-Sat 10-4.

(Portland)

Travel:	One block west of Martin Luther King, Jr. Blvd between Fremont and Broadway. Located in an old library building.
Map Ref:	Map 21, page 352, #24.
Comments:	Operated by volunteers for the benefit of the Multnomah County Library.

Waking Dream Books　　　　　　　　　　　　　　　　　　　　**Open Shop**
927 SW Oak Street 97205　　　　　　　　　　　　　　　　　(503) 223-2784

Collection:	Specialty
Specialties:	Art; design.
# of Vols:	500
Hours:	Mon-Sat 12-6.
Services:	Appraisals, catalog, search service in special areas only, accepts want lists.
Travel:	Downtown, between 9th & 10th Sts.
Credit Cards:	Yes
Owner:	Mary Mason Carr
Year Estab:	1985

Webfoot Bookman　　　　　　　　　　　　　　　　　　　　　**Open Shop**
8235 SE 13th Avenue 97202　　　　　　　　　　　　　　　　(503) 239-5233

Collection:	General stock and ephemera.
Specialties:	Oregon; Western Americana; hunting; fishing; first editions; performing arts.
# of Vols:	15,000
Hours:	Wed-Sun 10-5.
Services:	Appraisals, search service.
Travel:	Shop is located on Sellwood's Antique Row. From Hwy 43, cross Sellwood Bridge and proceed to first light. Turn right and proceed two blocks.
Map Ref:	Map 22 page 366, #25.
Credit Cards:	No
Owner:	Charles Gould
Year Estab:	1979
Comments:	A relatively small shop (with fewer volumes on display than indicated above) with a good collection of older collectible books, several sets and several rare titles. Lots of vintage items in addition to some newer volumes.

Wrigley-Cross Books　　　　　　　　　　　　　　　　　　　**Open Shop**
8001A SE Powell Boulevard 97206   (See Comments)　　　(503) 775-4943

Collection:	General stock of new and used hardcover and paperback.
Specialties:	Science fiction; fantasy; mystery; horror; cookbooks. Stock includes small press and British imports in all above fields except cookbooks.
# of Vols:	40,000
Hours:	Mon-Thu 10-7. Fri 10-9. Sat 10-7. Sun 12-5. Longer hours in summer and Dec.
Services:	Search service, catalog, accepts want list.

Travel:	Powell Blvd exit off I-205. Proceed west on Powell. After crossing 82nd Ave, turn right into shopping center.
Map Ref:	Map 21, page 352, #26.
Credit Cards:	Yes
Owner:	Debbie Cross & Paul M. Wrigley
Year Estab:	1987
Comments:	With the exception of the new and used books in the specialty areas listed above, the remainder of the shop's used stock was overwhelmingly paperback with the hardcover books falling mainly into the practical, e.g., how-to category plus some fiction (including science fiction and mystery). An interesting shop to visit if you're into the shop's specialty areas. Note: At the time of our visit, the owners were considering relocating in Portland. You may wish to call ahead to confirm the shop's location and hours.

Prineville

Wayne Kee Books **By Appointment**
618608 O'Neil Highway 97754 (541) 447-7403

Collection:	Specialty
Specialties:	Western Americana; Pacific Northwest.
# of Vols:	3,000
Services:	Mail order, search service, accepts want lists.
Credit Cards:	No
Year Estab:	1992

Reedsport

Reedsport Books & Tapes **Open Shop**
439 Fir Avenue 97467 (541) 271-2555

Collection:	General stock of mostly paperback.
Hours:	Mon-Fri 9:30-5:30. Sat 10-4.

Roseburg
(Map 23, page 333)

While Away Books **Open Shop**
932 West Harvard Boulevard 97470 (541) 957-1751

Collection:	General stock of paperback and hardcover.
# of Vols:	35,000
Hours:	Mon-Fri 6:30am-7pm. Sat 10-6. Sun 12-4.
Services:	Accepts want lists.
Travel:	Exit 124 off I-5. West on Harvard. Shop is on right in a shopping center.
Credit Cards:	Yes
Owner:	Karen Tolley
Year Estab:	1994
Comments:	Stock is approximately 65% paperback. The shop also has an espresso bar.

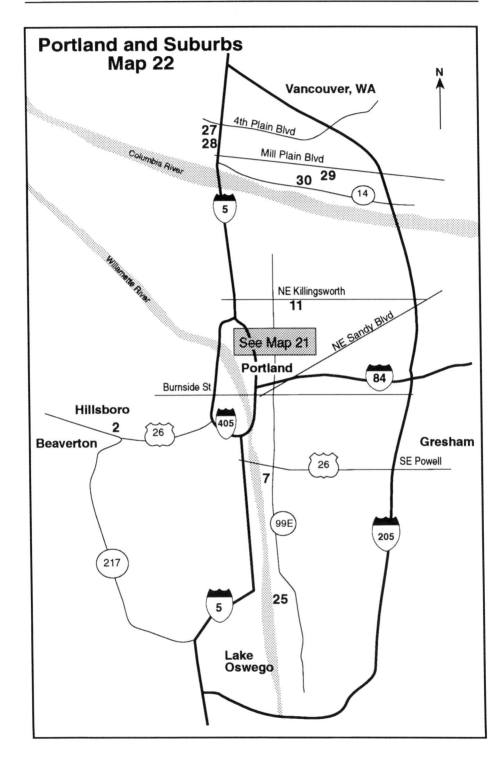

Salem
(Map 20, page 345)

The Book Bin
450 Court Street, SE 97301

Open Shop
(503) 361-1235

Collection:	General stock of hardcover and paperback.
# of Vols:	100,000
Hours:	Daily 9:30-6.
Travel:	Hwy 22/99E exit off I-5. Proceed west on Hwy 22 toward city center. Right on Liberty and proceed to Court. Shop is 1/2 block east of Liberty.
Credit Cards:	Yes
Owner:	Robert Baird
Year Estab:	1995
Comments:	The newest of the three Oregon Book Bins with a similar ambience and mix of books. (See Albany and Corvallis.) A mezzanine level was devoted to bargain books with some excellent titles being offered for $1.95 each. We would definitely recommend a visit.

The Book Habit
390 Liberty Street SE 97301

Open Shop
(503) 581-3637

Collection:	General stock of hardcover and paperback.
# of Vols:	15,000
Hours:	Mon-Sat 10:15-5:30. Sun 12-5.
Travel:	See Book Bin above. Shop is located on lower level of Pringle Park Plaza.
Credit Cards:	Yes
Owner:	Bess Reynolds
Year Estab:	1985
Comments:	The majority of the books were in good condition and of fairly recent vintage although we did see some older and more interesting items, some fine bindings and even some collectibles. The shop uses just about every square inch of space, including a loft area reached via a winding staircase.

Books Welred
3070 River Road North 97303

Open Shop
(503) 371-6525

Collection:	General stock of paperback and hardcover.
Hours:	Mon-Sat 11-5.

Budget Books
3934 Commercial Street, SE 97302

Open Shop
(503) 585-1178

Collection:	General stock of used and new, mostly paperback.
Hours:	Tue-Sat 10-6. Sun 11-5.

Jewell Collector Reference Books
265 Court Street NE
Mailing Address: PO Box 4514 Salem 97302

Open Shop
(503) 362-9903

Collection:	Specialty new and used.
# of Vols:	2,000

(Salem)

Hours:	Mon-Sat 10-5.
Services:	Subject lists, search service, accepts want lists.
Travel:	See Book Bin above. Shop is between Commercial and Front.
Owner:	Jewell Gowan
Year Estab:	1980
Comments:	If you're a collector, regardless of the nature of what you collect, chances are there are publications, perhaps price guides, that provide information regarding your interest. This shop specializes in such publications, both new and used. While the shop is interesting to visit because it will give you a chance to view the wide array of publications covering many fields of interest, you might save yourself time and energy by phoning ahead to determine whether the shop stocks an item related to your particular interest.

Magic Door Books **By Appointment**
PO Box 4422 97302 (800) 261-7508   (503) 362-7508

Collection:	Specialty
Specialties:	American and English 20th century literature; philosophy; Hemingway; baseball fiction; French Foreign Legion; lost world fiction; H. Rider Haggard; Talbot Mundy; P.C. Wren; George MacDonald Fraser; A. Conan Doyle. All first editions.
# of Vols:	2,000
Services:	Appraisals, catalog, accepts want lists.
Owner:	Walt Barrie
Year Estab:	1994

Michael's Book Shop **Open Shop**
115 Liberty Street NE 97301 (503) 585-8239

Collection:	General stock of hardcover and paperback and records.
Specialties:	Literature; history; music; scholarly; 1960's politics and culture.
# of Vols:	10,000
Hours:	Mon-Sat 11-5. Sun by chance or appointment.
Services:	Appraisals, search service, accepts want lists, catalog (1960's only), mail order.
Travel:	See Book Bin above.
Credit Cards:	Yes
Owner:	Michael Karn
Year Estab:	1992
Comments:	A compact bi-level shop with a strong emphasis on the specialties listed above. The books were mostly of mixed vintage and in mixed condition. The shop is just around the corner from another book shop so you can't go wrong combining visits.

Readers Guide to Recycled Literature **Open Shop**
1105 Edgewater NW 97304 (503) 588-3166

Collection:	General stock of hardcover and paperback.

Specialties:	Mystery; children's; fiction.
# of Vols:	70,000
Hours:	Mon-Sat 10-6. Sun 12-5.
Travel:	Southbound on I-5: Salem Pky/Ocean Beaches. Proceed on Salem Pky to Marion St bridge. Cross bridge and follow signs to West Salem, then Edgewater. Northbound: See Book Bin, then proceed to Marion St bridge.
Credit Cards:	Yes
Owner:	Jo & Tim Hannan
Year Estab:	1983
Comments:	A quite nice, quite good sized shop with lots of little alcoves and small rooms to get lost in. The hardcover books represent most subject areas and are, for the most part, in good condition. While there are plenty of paperbacks on hand, they do not necessarily overwhelm the visitor. We saw lots of interesting titles and believe this is a place that a true book lover would enjoy browsing. The shop has more than its share of collectibles along with a healthy number of reading copies.

Dale C. Schmidt-Books   **By Appointment**
610 Howell Prairie Road SE 97301   Fax: (503) 585-3071 (503) 364-0499

Collection:	Specialty
Specialties:	Americana; Pacific Northwest Americana; Alaska; sausage making; aviation; genealogy; wooden runabout inboard boats.
Services:	Appraisals, accepts want lists, mail order.
Credit Cards:	No
Year Estab:	1980

Seal Rock
(Map 20, page 345)

Antiques, Etc.   **Open Shop**
Highway 101   (541) 563-2242
Mailing Address: 587 North Beaver Valley Drive Seal Rock 97376

Collection:	General stock of mostly hardcover and some vintage paperback.
# of Vols:	3,000
Hours:	Summer: Daily 11-4. Winter: Fri-Mon 11-4.
Credit Cards:	No
Owner:	Martina Hauser
Year Estab:	1975

Seaside
(Map 20, page 345)

Buck's Book Barn   **Open Shop**
1023 Broadway 97138   (503) 738-4246

Collection:	General stock of hardcover and paperback.
# of Vols:	15,000
Hours:	Daily 9-4.
Travel:	One half block from Hwy 101.

Credit Cards: No
Year Estab: 1993
Comments: Stock is evenly divided between hardcover and paperback.

U Shop   **Open Shop**
2281 Beach Drive 97138   (503) 738-8224

Collection: General stock of hardcover and paperback.
# of Vols: 2,000
Hours: Thu-Mon 10-6.
Travel: Hwy 101 to U Avenue. Proceed west on U. Shop is at Beach and U.
Credit Cards: No
Owner: Jim Licht
Year Estab: 1994
Comments: Stock is evenly divided between hardcover and paperback.

Sheridan

Main Street Books   **Open Shop**
142 East Main Street 97378   (503) 843-4510

Collection: General stock of mostly paperback.
Hours: Wed-Sat 12-6.

Sherwood

Second Time Around Books   **Open Shop**
16400 SW Langer Drive 97140   (503) 625-2112

Collection: General stock of mostly paperback.

Sisters
(Map 20, page 345)

Lonesome Water Books   **Open Shop**
255 West Cascade   (541) 549-2203
Mailing Address: PO Box 1268 Sisters 97759

Collection: General stock of mostly hardcover.
# of Vols: 3,000-5,000
Hours: Best to call for current hours.
Travel: On main street in town.
Owner: Tom Hughes
Year Estab: 1988

Stayton

Gerry Aboud-Back Issue Magazines   **By Appointment**
836 East Kathy 97383   (503) 769-7505

Collection: Specialty
Specialties: Magazines (general interest, pre-1955).
Year Estab: 1975

Oregon Territorial Books **By Appointment**
265 East Ida (503) 769-7356
Mailing Address: PO Box 22 Sublimity 97385

Collection:	Specialty
Specialties:	Western Americana; fur trade; exploration; private press (western).
# of Vols:	5,000
Services:	Appraisals, search service, catalog, accepts want lists.
Credit Cards:	Yes
Owner:	Dennis Stadler
Year Estab:	1978

Stayton Books **Open Shop**
281 North 3rd Avenue 97383 (503) 769-2327

Collection:	General stock of mostly paperback.
Hours:	Mon-Sat 10-5.

The Dalles
(Map 20, page 345)

Bargain Barn Books **Open Shop**
1431 West 2nd Street 97058 (541) 298-5782

Collection:	General stock of mostly paperback.
Hours:	Mon-Fri 10-5. Sat 10-1.

Klindts, Booksellers **Open Shop**
319 East 2nd Street 97058 (541) 296-4342

Collection:	General stock.
# of Vols:	5,000
Hours:	Mon-Sat 10-5:30.
Services:	Search service, accepts want lists, mail order.
Travel:	Eastbound on I-84: City Center exit. Proceed east on 2nd St which becomes 3rd St. Left on Federal and left on 2nd.
Credit Cards:	Yes
Owner:	Linda Klindt
Year Estab:	1993
Comments:	Not a single paperback in the shop! The collection is modest in size and divided between recent titles in generally quite good condition and some older items, more than a few of which have collectible interest. Reasonably priced. If you're out this way, we think you should stop by for a visit. The shop also sells antiques and collectibles.

Tigard

... and Books, too! **Open Shop**
12260 SW Scholls Ferry Road 97223 (503) 590-7120

Collection:	General stock of mostly paperback.
Hours:	Mon-Fri 10-6. Sat 10-5.

Tillamook
(Map 20, page 345)

An-Tiki Books and Collectables   **Open Shop**
4720 Highway 101 North 97141   (503) 842-4772

Collection: General stock of hardcover and paperback.
Hours: Hours vary. Call ahead.
Comments: We're sorry we can't provide a bit more information about this shop which we were unable to visit. In addition to being vague about hours, the owner did not provide us with more details about the stock. So if you have the time and/or the inclination for a visit here, let us know what we missed.

Rainy Day Books   **Open Shop**
2015 Second Street 97141   (503) 842-7766

Collection: General stock of mostly used paperback and hardcover.
Hours: Mon-Fri 10-5:30. Sat 10-5.

Waldport
(Map 20, page 345)

Nautical Wheelers Books & Gifts   **Open Shop**
440 Commercial Street   (541) 563-3310
Mailing Address: PO Box 184 Waldport 97394

Collection: General stock of mostly used paperback and hardcover.
# of Vols: 3,000 (used)
Hours: Mon-Sat 10-5. Sun by chance (Memorial Day-Labor Day).
Services: Accepts want lists, mail order.
Travel: At corner of Hwy 34 and Commercial St, 1/2 mile east of Hwy 101.
Credit Cards: No
Owner: Richard D. & Blanche E. Mevis
Year Estab: 1989
Comments: We would be quite surprised if the number of used hardcover books (mostly fiction, old, in only fair condition and undistinguished) on display in this shop amounted to more than 500. There were at least three to four times the number of used paperbacks. Need we say more.

Winston

Sandy's Corner Book Nook   **Open Shop**
131 NE Main   (541) 679-0121
Mailing Address: PO Box 1306 Winston 97496

Collection: General stock of mostly paperback.
Hours: Mon-Sat 9:30-5:30, except Fri till 6. Sun 12-4.

Antiques & Artifacts (541) 935-1619
20457 Highway 126 Noti 97461

Collection: Specialty
Specialties: Railroads and related subjects (e.g., telegraphy); some transportation.
Services: Catalog
Credit Cards: Yes
Owner: Scott Arden & Barrie Arden-Gendel
Year Estab: 1971

Joe Armstrong
PO Box 10641 Eugene 97440

Collection: Specialty new and used.
Specialties: Morals and dogma; science fiction.
# of Vols: 5,000
Services: Search service, accepts want lists.
Credit Cards: No
Year Estab: 1967

Backstage Books
PO Box 3676 Eugene 97403

Collection: Specialty
Specialties: Performing arts; theater; opera; concerts; dance; circus; music hall; music in performance; plays.
# of Vols: 16,000
Services: Catalog
Credit Cards: No
Owner: Howard L. Ramey
Year Estab: 1977

Carol Barnett, Books (503) 282-7036
3562 NE Liberty Street Portland 97211

Collection: Specialty
Specialties: Gardening; botany.
Services: Catalog
Credit Cards: No
Year Estab: 1985

Beth L. Bibby-Books (541) 855-1621
1225 Sardine Creek Road Gold Hill 97525

Collection: Specialty new and used.
Specialties: Gardening; horticulture; natural history.
# of Vols: 2,500
Services: Catalog, accepts want lists.
Credit Cards: No
Owner: George A. Bibby
Year Estab: 1965

Cellar of Books (541) 343-0262
PO Box 10863 Eugene 97440

Collection:	Specialty
Specialties:	Children's; Northwest Americana; cookbooks.
# of Vols:	20,000
Services:	Appraisals, catalog, accepts want lists.
Credit Cards:	No
Owner:	C.J. Houser
Year Estab:	1979

Columbia Books (503) 638-2926
PO Box 1686 Lake Grove 97035

Collection:	Specialty
Specialties:	Journalism; advertising; public relations; communications; broadcasting.
# of Vols:	5,000
Services:	Appraisals, search service, catalog, accepts want lists.
Credit Cards:	No
Owner:	Leonard W. Lanfranco
Year Estab:	1989

Corls Books (541) 753-7277
PO Box 2298 Corvallis 97339

Collection:	Specialty
Specialties:	First editions; limited editions; art; Oregon; Western Americana.
# of Vols:	1,000
Services:	Accepts want lists.
Credit Cards:	No
Owner:	Robert & Maud Corl
Year Estab:	1950's
Comments:	Collection may be viewed by appointment.

Eldora's Books (503) 538-1279
311 South Edwards Newberg 97132

Collection:	General stock of hardcover and paperback.
Specialties:	Children's
# of Vols:	4,000+
Services:	Search service.
Credit Cards:	No
Owner:	Eldora Acott
Year Estab:	1978

Great Outdoors Book Exchange (503) 245-1315
PO Box 223 Lake Oswego 97034

Collection:	Specialty
Specialties:	Fly fishing.
# of Vols:	1,000

Services: Appraisals, search service, catalog, accepts want lists.
Credit Cards: No
Owner: William S. Hotine
Year Estab: 1989

Lawrence Hamman Fine Books (503) 646-1530
2335 SW Briggs Rd, #33 Beaverton 97005

Collection: General stock.
Specialties: Americana; illustrated; private press; literature.
# of Vols: 5,000
Year Estab: 1974

Main Street Books (541) 336-2977
1252 SE 18th Toledo 97391

Collection: General stock.
# of Vols: 2,000-3,000
Services: Subject, fiction or non fiction lists; occasional catalog, accepts want lists.
Credit Cards: No
Owner: Pat Kaiser
Year Estab: 1990

Marc Paulsen Bookseller (503) 292-2266
10220 SW Melnore Street Portland 97225

Collection: General stock.
# of Vols: 5,000

Larry W. Price Books (503) 221-1410
353 NW Maywood Drive Portland 97210

Collection: Specialty
Specialties: Natural history; travel; Americana; mountaineering; polar regions.
# of Vols: 10,000
Services: Catalog
Credit Cards: No

Truman Price (503) 838-5452
7210 Helmick Road Monmouth 97361

Collection: General stock.
Specialties: Children's (literature and picture books); Western Americana.
# of Vols: 8,000
Services: Search service, catalog, accepts want lists.
Credit Cards: No
Year Estab: 1993

Washington
Map 24

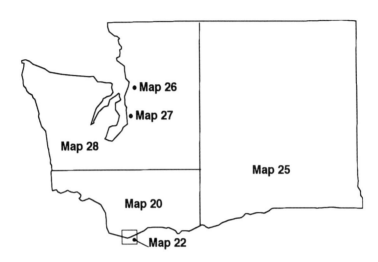

Map 20
Long Beach
Vancouver
Woodland

Map 22
Vancouver

Map 25
Cheney
Clarkston
Ellensburg
Pasco
Prosser
Richland
Selah
Spokane
Sunnyside
Yakima

Map 26
Seattle

Map 27
Tacoma

Map 28
Anacortes
Auburn
Bainbridge Island
Bellevue
Bellingham
Bremerton
Burlington
Centralia
Duvall
Edmonds
Enumclaw
Everett
Federal Way

Gig Harbor
Kent
Kirkland
Lynnwood
Mercer Island
Milton
Mount Vernon
Olympia
Port Angeles
Port Orchard
Port Townsend
Poulsbo
Puyallup
Seattle
Silverdale
Snohomish
Tacoma
Tukwila
Woodinville

Washington

Alphabetical Listing By Dealer

Aero Book Club	384	Book World	400
Agathon Books	435	Book World II	400
AJ's Cookbooks	436	The Book Worm	440
Alcove Books	396	The Bookcyclers	409
Alfi News & Books	411	Bookmark	408
American Booksellers	383	Books For Change	389
An Odd Volume	411	Books Northwest	389
Anchor In Time	395	Books, Etc.	391
Arlington Book Store	384	The Bookshop	402
The Arthur H. Clark Company	435	Booktique	443
Arundel Books	411	The Bookworm	396
Auntie's Bookstore	435	Bookworm	409
Automotive Bookstore	412	Bookworm	400
B & M Book Store	392	Bowie & Company Booksellers	415
Gene W. Badde, Books on the West	445	Bristol Antiques and Books	389
Ballard Books	412	Broad Horizons	409
Bauhaus Books & Coffee	412	Browsers' Book Shop	404
Beatty Book Store	413	Buffalo Gals' Trading Co.	398
Beauty and the Books	413	Colin Bull, Polar Books	445
Bellingham Bay Collectibles	388	The Business	383
Benicia Books	406	Buy The Book	388
Best Read Books	433	Calendula Horticultural Books	393
Between the Covers	443	Cardinal Books	441
Bev's Book Shoppe	400	Chameleon	415
Beyond the Closet Bookstore	414	Chapter Two	443
Bibelots & Books	414	Cheshire Books	444
Blackberry Books	389	Cinema Books	416
Book & Bean Espresso Co.	414	Clark's Book Store	435
Book Affair	414	Louis Collins Books	416
Book Discoveries	415	The Comic Character Shop	416
Book Exchange of Lynnwood	402	Comstock's Bindery & Bookshop	384
Book Feire	437	Corner Books	417
Book Nook	409	Costless Books	403
Book Quest	392	Couth Buzzard Used Books	417
Book Recylcer Bookstore & Cafe	393	Cal's Books	435
Book Stop	398	C. Dave's Books	441
Book Stop	408	Don Johnson's Ambience	417

Don Quixote Bookstore	396	The Jabberwocky	399
Duvall Books	394	Jan's Book Rack	397
Earth Bound Used Books	383	JNJ Books	401
Earth Light Books	443	Jomar	407
Easton's Books	404	King Tree Book Company	446
Edmonds Olde Bookstore	394	Know Thy Self Afrikan Book Center	437
Gary L. Estabrook-Books	445	Lady Jayne's Comics and Books	438
Fairlook Antiques	417	Ladybug Books	422
Fantasy Illustrated	417	Lake City Books	423
Fillipi Book & Record Shop	418	Larson Books	397
First Edition Books	436	Left Bank Books	423
Fleetstreet	385	Leisure Books	423
Flora & Fauna Books	418	Michele Leroux Fine Old Books	399
Folio Books	418	Lost and Found Books	400
Fortner Books	386	Magus, Inc.	423
Four Winds Bookstore and Cafe	395	P.T. Mallahan, Bookseller	446
Fox Book Co.	437	Michael Maslan Historic Photographs,	
Gary's Books & Collectibles	397	Postcards & Ephemera	424
Gemini Book Exchange and		MasterPieces Unlimited	446
Comic Center	418	Robert W. Mattila, Bookseller	424
Globe Bookstore & Bindery	419	Carol D. McKinley, Bookseller	446
Golden Age Collectables	419	Melville & Co Books	407
Goodwill Store	397	Michael's Books	390
Goodwill Store	440	Miner's Quest	446
Goodwill Store	419	MisterE Books	424
Goodwill Store	403	Mostly Books	398
Great Epic Books	403	Mountainbooks	425
Anthony Greene	445	Multi Books	425
Greenwood Books	420	Mysteries Unlimited	425
Gregor Books	420	O'Leary's Books	438
Half Price Books	440	The Old Fool's Bookstore	395
Half Price Books	395	The Old London Bookshop	390
Half Price Books	388	Olympic Supply - Used Book Store	433
Half Price Books	437	Open Books: A Poem Emporium	426
Half Price Books	420	Orca Books	405
Helen Harte, Bookseller	420	Orpheus Books	395
Henderson Books	390	Orpheus Books	447
Hidden Treasures	440	Simon Ottenberg, Bookseller	447
High Latitude	386	Page One Book Exchange	388
J.D. Holmes	445	Page 2 Book Exchange	426
Horizon Books	421	Page Two Bookstore & Craft Shop	386
Horizon Books/Greenwood	421	Pages Books	434
Horizon Books/Roosevelt	421	Paper Horn	434
Huckleberry Books	392	Pegasus Book Exchange	426
Iconoclast Books	421	Peggatty Books	393
Inland Bookstore	436	Pelican Bay Used Books	384
Inlet Books	405	The Penny Box Used Books	401
Inquisitive Sportsman Books	399	Dick Perier Books	441
Interim Books	391	Pilchuck Books	397
David Ishii, Bookseller	422	Pioneer Square Books	426
Island Books	403	Pistil Books & News	427

The Play's The Thing	427	Swans's Comic & Magazine Mart	439
Puyallup Book Mark	409	Shop & Save Thift Store	391
Puzzle Book Store	407	Tacoma Book Center	439
Quiet Companion Books	438	Tales of Kirkland	401
Railroad Street Books	396	Tennant's Aviation Books	385
Raindance Books	404	Third Street Book Exchange	403
Rainy Day Books	427	Tilikum Books	406
Ravenna Rare Books	427	Titlewave Books	430
The Reading Lamp	447	George H. Tweney, Antiquarian Bookseller	431
Recollection Fine Used Books	428	Twice Sold Tales/Capitol	431
Red & Black Book Collective	428	Twice Sold Tales/Downtown	431
Renaissance Books	447	Twice Sold Tales/Wallingford	431
Mike Robertson Books	447	Upper Case Books	434
Sandpiper Books	401	Upper Room Christian Bookstore	385
Allen Sarno Books About Latin America	428	Uptown Bookshelf	442
Seattle Book Center	428	Used Book Store	388
Seattle Mystery Bookshop	429	Vandewater Books	432
The 2nd Generation	441	Village Books	391
Second Hand Prose	442	Vintage Books	442
2nd Look Books	436	Violet Books	448
Sherburne Antiques & Fine Art	405	Way's Magazines Unlimited	448
Shop & Save Thift Store	385	Well Read Books	404
Shop & Save Thrift Store	401	Wessel & Lieberman Booksellers	432
Shorey's Book Store	429	West Coast Books	403
Signature Bound Bookseller	430	Westside Stories	432
Sirius Books	398	The Whale's Tale	402
Spectrum of Rainbows	447	William James Bookseller	407
Spencers Bookstore	442	Ye Olde Book Peddler	439
Kirk Stines Collectible Books & Toys	430	Zephyr Used & Rare Books	444
Storment Library	406		

Alphabetical Listing By Location

Aberdeen
American Booksellers   383
Anacortes
The Business   383
Earth Bound Used Books   383
Pelican Bay Used Books   384
Arlington
Aero Book Club   384
Arlington Book Store   384
Auburn
Comstock's Bindery & Bookshop   384
Shop & Save Thift Store   385
Tennant's Aviation Books   385
Upper Room Christian Bookstore   385
Bainbridge Island
Fleetstreet   385
Fortner Books   386
High Latitude   386
Battle Ground
Page Two Bookstore & Craft Shop   386
Bellevue
Buy The Book   388
Half Price Books   388
P.T. Mallahan, Bookseller   446
Orpheus Books   447
Page One Book Exchange   388
Used Book Store   388
Bellingham
Bellingham Bay Collectibles   388
Blackberry Books   389
Books For Change   389
Books Northwest   389
Bristol Antiques and Books   389
Henderson Books   390
Michael's Books   390
The Old London Bookshop   390
Village Books   391
Bremerton
Books, Etc.   391
Interim Books   391
Burien
Shop & Save Thift Store   391
Burlington
B & M Book Store   392
Centralia
Book Quest   392
Huckleberry Books   392
Chehalis
Calendula Horticultural Books   393

Cheney
Book Recylcer Bookstore & Cafe   393
Clarkston
Peggatty Books   393
Deer Park
King Tree Book Company   446
Duvall
Duvall Books   394
Edmonds
Edmonds Olde Bookstore   394
Half Price Books   395
J.D. Holmes   445
Orpheus Books   395
The Reading Lamp   447
Ellensburg
Anchor In Time   395
Four Winds Bookstore and Cafe   395
The Old Fool's Bookstore   395
Enumclaw
Railroad Street Books   396
Everett
Alcove Books   396
The Bookworm   396
Don Quixote Bookstore   396
Gary's Books & Collectibles   397
Goodwill Store   397
Jan's Book Rack   397
Larson Books   397
Pilchuck Books   397
Sirius Books   398
Federal Way
Book Stop   398
Gig Harbor
Buffalo Gals' Trading Co.   398
Mostly Books   398
Granite Falls
Inquisitive Sportsman Books   399
Issaquah
The Jabberwocky   399
Michele Leroux Fine Old Books   399
Lost and Found Books   400
Kelso
Bev's Book Shoppe   400
Kennewick
Bookworm   400
Kent
Book World   400
Book World II   400
JNJ Books   401

Kirkland
The Penny Box Used Books	401
Shop & Save Thrift Store	401
Tales of Kirkland	401

Long Beach
Sandpiper Books	401
The Whale's Tale	402

Longview
The Bookshop	402

Lynnwood
Book Exchange of Lynnwood	402
Goodwill Store	403
Great Epic Books	403

Maple Valley
Mike Robertson Books	447

Marysville
Third Street Book Exchange	403
West Coast Books	403

Mercer Island
Island Books	403

Milton
Costless Books	403

Moses Lake
Well Read Books	404

Mount Vernon
Easton's Books	404

Mountlake Terrace
Raindance Books	404

Olympia
Browsers' Book Shop	404
Inlet Books	405
Carol D. McKinley, Bookseller	446
Orca Books	405
Sherburne Antiques & Fine Art	405
Tilikum Books	406

Pasco
Storment Library	406

Port Angeles
Benicia Books	406
Puzzle Book Store	407

Port Orchard
Jomar	407

Port Townsend
Melville & Co Books	407
William James Bookseller	407

Poulsbo
Book Stop	408

Prosser
Bookmark	408

Puyallup
Broad Horizons	409
Puyallup Book Mark	409

Renton
Gene W. Badde, Books on the West	445
The Bookcyclers	409

Richland
Book Nook	409
Bookworm	409

Rolling Bay
Colin Bull, Polar Books	445

Seattle
Alfi News & Books	411
An Odd Volume	411
Arundel Books	411
Automotive Bookstore	412
Ballard Books	412
Bauhaus Books & Coffee	412
Beatty Book Store	413
Beauty and the Books	413
Beyond the Closet Bookstore	414
Bibelots & Books	414
Book & Bean Espresso Co.	414
Book Affair	414
Book Discoveries	415
Bowie & Company Booksellers	415
Chameleon	415
Cinema Books	416
Louis Collins Books	416
The Comic Character Shop	416
Corner Books	417
Couth Buzzard Used Books	417
Don Johnson's Ambience	417
Fairlook Antiques	417
Fantasy Illustrated	417
Fillipi Book & Record Shop	418
Flora & Fauna Books	418
Folio Books	418
Gemini Book Exchange & Comic Ctr	418
Globe Bookstore & Bindery	419
Golden Age Collectables	419
Goodwill Store	419
Anthony Greene	445
Greenwood Books	420
Gregor Books	420
Half Price Books	420
Helen Harte, Bookseller	420
Horizon Books	421
Horizon Books/Greenwood	421
Horizon Books/Roosevelt	421
Iconoclast Books	421

David Ishii, Bookseller	422
Ladybug Books	422
Lake City Books	423
Left Bank Books	423
Leisure Books	423
Magus, Inc.	423
Michael Maslan Histor Ephemera	424
MasterPieces Unlimited	446
Robert W. Mattila, Bookseller	424
MisterE Books	424
Mountainbooks	425
Multi Books	425
Mysteries Unlimited	425
Open Books: A Poem Emporium	426
Simon Ottenberg, Bookseller	447
Page 2 Book Exchange	426
Pegasus Book Exchange	426
Pioneer Square Books	426
Pistil Books & News	427
The Play's The Thing	427
Rainy Day Books	427
Ravenna Rare Books	427
Recollection Fine Used Books	428
Red & Black Book Collective	428
Renaissance Books	447
Allen Sarno Books About Lat Amer	428
Seattle Book Center	428
Seattle Mystery Bookshop	429
Shorey's Book Store	429
Signature Bound Bookseller	430
Kirk Stines Collectible Books & Toys	430
Titlewave Books	430
George H. Tweney, Bookseller	431
Twice Sold Tales/Capitol	431
Twice Sold Tales/Downtown	431
Twice Sold Tales/Wallingford	431
Vandewater Books	432
Violet Books	448
Way's Magazines Unlimited	448
Wessel & Lieberman Booksellers	432
Westside Stories	432
Sedro Woolley	
Best Read Books	433
Selah	
Olympic Supply - Used Book Store	433
Sequim	
Spectrum of Rainbows	447
Silverdale	
Pages Books	434
Snohomish	
Paper Horn	434
Upper Case Books	434
Spokane	
Agathon Books	435
The Arthur H. Clark Company	435
Auntie's Bookstore	435
Clark's Book Store	435
Cal's Books	435
Inland Bookstore	436
Miner's Quest	446
2nd Look Books	436
Sunnyside	
First Edition Books	436
Tacoma	
AJ's Cookbooks	436
Book Feire	437
Fox Book Co.	437
Half Price Books	437
Know Thy Self Afrikan Book Center	437
Lady Jayne's Comics and Books	438
O'Leary's Books	438
Quiet Companion Books	438
Swans's Comic & Magazine Mart	439
Tacoma Book Center	439
Ye Olde Book Peddler	439
Tonasket	
Hidden Treasures	440
Tukwila	
Goodwill Store	440
Half Price Books	440
Vancouver	
The Book Worm	440
Cardinal Books	441
C. Dave's Books	441
Gary L. Estabrook-Books	445
Dick Perier Books	441
The 2nd Generation	441
Second Hand Prose	442
Spencers Bookstore	442
Uptown Bookshelf	442
Vintage Books	442
Walla Walla	
Booktique	443
Earth Light Books	443
Wenatchee	
Chapter Two	443
Woodinville	
Between the Covers	443
Woodland	
Zephyr Used & Rare Books	444
Yakima	
Cheshire Books	444

Aberdeen

American Booksellers **By Appointment**
102 West 11th (360) 532-2099
Mailing Address: PO Box 1497 Aberdeen 98520

Collection: Specialty books and ephemera.
Specialties: Maritime; exploration; pirates; South Pacific; boat building; yachting; World War I & II; Civil War; Americana; children's; illustrated.
# of Vols: 30,000
Services: Search service, catalog, accepts want lists.
Credit Cards: Yes
Owner: Kaye & Carl Weber
Year Estab: 1989
Comments: Owners also operate a Bed & Breakfast. For travelers who buy $350 or more worth of books, the night's stay is free.

Anacortes
(Map 28, page 387)

The Business **Open Shop**
1717 Commercial Avenue 98221 (800) 901-9788 (360) 293-9788

Collection: General stock of hardcover and paperback, records and ephemera.
# of Vols: 10,000-15,000
Hours: Mon-Sat 8-8. Sun 10-6.
Services: Appraisals, search service, accepts want lists.
Travel: Burlington exit off I-5. Proceed west on Hwy 20 to Anacortes.
Credit Cards: Yes
Owner: Glen Des Jardins, Bret Lunsford, & Kecia Fox
Year Estab: 1978
Comments: A rather eclectic shop that sells photographic equipment, CDs and records, has an espresso bar and cafe, and, also sells used books. The hardcover collection (probably closer to 5,000-10,000 volumes) consisted of older items in mixed condition at quite reasonable prices. If one searches, one might even find a collectible or two.

Earth Bound Used Books **Open Shop**
619 Commercial Avenue 98221 (360) 293-5908

Collection: General stock of paperback and hardcover.
Specialties: Art; sailing and boating; classic literature; metaphysics.
# of Vols: 5,000
Hours: Mon-Sat 10:30-5. Also, Sun (Jul & Aug) 12-4, but best to call ahead.
Services: Accepts want lists, mail order.
Travel: See The Business above.
Credit Cards: Yes
Owner: Maria & Jack Papritz
Year Estab: 1991

Comments: If we were inventing a new metaphor for shops, we might refer to this one as a potpourri with few sections containing enough volumes to represent any significant number. The collection was a mix of newer and vintage items in varying condition. One section displayed some older literary sets.

Pelican Bay Used Books   **Open Shop**
410 Commercial Avenue 98221   (360) 293-1852

Collection:	General stock of paperbacks and hardcover.
# of Vols:	3,000
Hours:	Mon-Sat 9:30-5:30. Sun (summer only) 12-5.
Travel:	See The Business above. Between 4th & 5th Streets.
Credit Cards:	No
Owner:	Kevin Green
Year Estab:	1994
Comments:	A small collection with hardcover books of mixed vintage and in mixed condition, plus some Franklin Mint and Easton leather bindings. While we didn't see much to excite us, book people never know when the next surprise may be purchased by such a store and placed in the "new arrivals" bin.

Arlington

Aero Book Club   **Open Shop**
At Arlington Airport   (360) 435-5290
Mailing Address: PO Box 146 Lynnwood 98036   Warehouse: (360) 368-0198

Collection:	Specialty new and used.
Specialties:	Aviation
# of Vols:	4,000
Hours:	Thu-Sun.
Services:	Mail order, accepts want lists.
Credit Cards:	Yes
Owner:	"Red" MacLane
Year Estab:	1990

Arlington Book Store   **Open Shop**
427 North Olympic 98223   (206) 435-2742

Collection:	General stock of mostly used paperback.
Hours:	Tue-Sat 10-5.

Auburn
(Map 28, page 387)

Comstock's Bindery & Bookshop   **Open Shop**
257 East Main 98002   (206) 939-8770

Collection:	General stock of hardcover and paperback.
Specialties:	Aviation; military; maritime; American history; railroads; magazines (primarily aviation and railroad).
# of Vols:	100,000

Hours:	Mon-Sat 10-6.
Services:	Appraisals, search service, accepts want lists, mail order.
Travel:	Hwy 18 exit off I-5. Proceed east on Hwy 18, then Auburn Way exit off Hwy 18. North on Auburn Way, then left on Main.
Credit Cards:	Yes
Owner:	David & Anita Comstock
Year Estab:	1973
Comments:	A very attractive shop that should be a pleasure to visit whether or not you make a purchase. The books were well organized, in generally good condition and we saw quite a few unusual titles. While there were plenty of paperbacks on hand and not all of the subject categories falling outside of the shop's specialties were covered in great depth, what was available, does make a visit well worth while.

Shop & Save Thrift Store
102 Cross Avenue Southeast 98002

Open Shop
(206) 939-4245

Collection:	General stock of hardcover and paperback.
Hours:	Mon-Sat 9-9. Sun 10-6.

Tennant's Aviation Books
PO Box 1695
Mailing Address: 2867 Forest Ridge Drive, SE Auburn 98092

By Appointment
(206) 833-7506

Collection:	Specialty used and new.
Specialties:	Aviation
# of Vols:	3,000
Services:	Appraisals, search service, catalog, accepts want lists.
Credit Cards:	No
Owner:	George B. Tennant
Year Estab:	1965

Upper Room Christian Bookstore
707 Auburn Way North, Ste. B 98002

Open Shop
(206) 838-8797

Collection:	Specialty used and new.
Specialties:	Religion.
# of Vols:	12,000 (used)
Hours:	Mon-Sat 10-6. Other times by appointment.
Travel:	15th St NW exit off Hwy 167. Proceed east on 15th St, then right on Auburn Way north. Shop is on second floor.
Credit Cards:	No
Owner:	Karen & Ernest McIntyre
Year Estab:	1982

Bainbridge Island
(Map 28, page 387)

Fleetstreet
100 North Madison Avenue 98110

Open Shop
(206) 842-7488

Collection:	General stock and prints.

Specialties:	Travel; voyages.
# of Vols:	3,000
Hours:	Mon-Sat 10-5.
Services:	Appraisals, accepts want lists, catalog.
Travel:	In downtown. See Fortner Books below.
Credit Cards:	Yes
Owner:	Christopher Charles
Year Estab:	1977

Fortner Books   **Open Shop**
220 Winslow Way 98110   Fax: (206) 780-5872   (206) 780-2030

Collection:	General stock of hardcover and paperback and remainders.
Specialties:	Gardening; Pacific Northwest; maritime; literature; cookbooks.
# of Vols:	25,000
Hours:	Mon-Fri 10-6. Sat 9:30-6. Sun 10-5.
Services:	Appraisals, search service, mail order.
Travel:	A short walk from the Seattle ferry or by car from Hwy 305 on the Kitsap Peninsula.
Credit Cards:	Yes
Owner:	Robert & Nancy Fortner
Year Estab:	1992
Comments:	Finding a shop with so many nice titles (the vast majority of which were of more recent vintage) that were also in such good condition in an island setting was a pleasure as well as a pleasant surprise. Many subject areas were represented but few in great number. One could easily walk out of this shop with a dozen or more books that would make nice additions to one's library, whether or not they fell into the rare or collectible categories.

High Latitude   **By Appointment**
PO Box 11254 98110   Fax: (206) 842-6101   (206) 842-0202

Collection:	Specialty
Specialties:	Polar regions; Alaska; Eskimos; whaling.
# of Vols:	2,000
Services:	Appraisals, catalog.
Credit Cards:	Yes
Owner:	Bob Finch
Year Estab:	1978

Battle Ground

Page Two Bookstore & Craft Shop   **Open Shop**
121 North Parkway Drive 98604   (360) 687-6088

Collection:	General stock of mostly paperback.
Hours:	May-Oct: Daily 10-6. Nov-Apr: Daily 10-5.

Open Shops and By Appointment Dealers

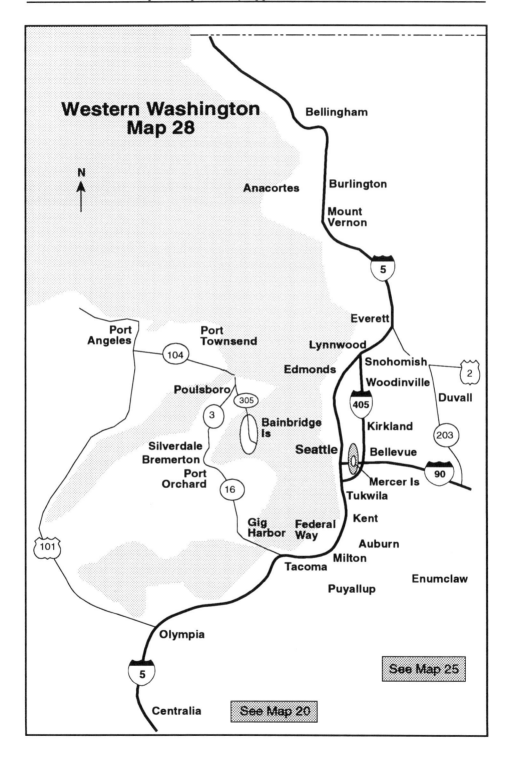

Bellevue
(Map 28, page 387)

Buy The Book **Open Shop**
820 102nd Avenue NE 98004 (206) 451-7793

Collection: General stock of paperback and hardcover.
# of Vols: 20,000
Hours: Tue-Fri 10-5:30. Sat 11-5.
Travel: NE 8th St exit off I-405. Proceed west on 8th, then right on 102nd.
Comments: Stock is about 60% paperback.

Half Price Books, Records, Magazines **Open Shop**
15600 NE 8th Street, Ste F2 98008 (206) 747-6616

Collection: General stock of new, used and remainders.
Hours: Sun-Thu 9-9. Fri & Sat 9-10:30.
Travel: In Crossroads Shopping Center at corner of NE 8th St.

Page One Book Exchange **Open Shop**
14220 NE 20th Street 98007 (206) 747-6165

Collection: General stock of mostly paperback.
Hours: Mon-Fri 10:30-5. Sat 10-5.

Used Book Store **Open Shop**
10133½ Main Street 98004   Voice Mail: (206) 450-9936   (206) 453-8297

Collection: General stock of paperback and hardcover.
# of Vols: 5,000
Hours: Mon-Sat 10-6.
Travel: Bellevue Way exit off I-90 or Hwy 520. Proceed on Bellevue Way to Main St, then west on Main.
Credit Cards: No
Owner: Anita U. Emel
Year Estab: 1990
Comments: What we would call a "quaint" little shop. One hundred or so paperbacks and the rest mostly older hardcover volumes, some of which might fall into the collectible category and some just falling into the "old and mostly forgotten" classification.

Bellingham
(Map 28, page 387)

Bellingham Bay Collectibles **Open Shop**
314 West Holly Street (360) 676-9201

Collection: General stock of hardcover and collectibles.
# of Vols: 1,000
Hours: Mon-Sat 10:30-6.
Travel: See Bristol Antiques and Books below.

Comments: We're not experts on the non book collectibles which made up the majority of this shop's stock (furniture, clothing, glassware, trinkets, etc.). With regard to the books we saw, however, we can say that they were few (perhaps 1,000 or so) and consisted of paperbacks and older hardcover items with very little "collectible" interest.

Blackberry Books
1323 Cornwall Avenue 98225

Open Shop
(360) 671-8940

Collection:	General stock of paperback and hardcover and ephemera.
Specialties:	Political science; suspense; military; literary criticism; literature.
# of Vols:	9,000+
Hours:	Mon-Sat 10-6. Sun 12-5.
Services:	Accepts want lists.
Travel:	Lakeway Dr exit off I-5. Proceed west on Lakeway which becomes Holly, then right on Cornwall.
Credit Cards:	No
Year Estab:	1992
Comments:	A relatively small shop with limited stock and a higher proportion of paperbacks to hardcover items. Both older titles and newer items (in about equal numbers), some older sets and some books that had seen better days.

Books For Change
1 Bellis Fair Parkway, Ste. 436 98226

Open Shop
(360) 734-8661

Collection:	General stock of new and mostly paperback used.
Hours:	Mon-Sat 9:30-9. Sun 11-6.

Books Northwest
2500 Cedarwood 98225

Open Shop
(206) 647-1747

Collection:	General stock of mostly used paperback.
Hours:	Mon-Fri 7am-9pm. Sat & Sun 8am-9pm.

Bristol Antiques and Books
310 West Holly Street 98225

Open Shop
(360) 733-7809

Collection:	General stock of used and some new, hardcover and paperback.
Hours:	Mon-Sat 11-5.
Services:	Accepts want lists, mail order.
Travel:	Lakeway exit off I-5. Left on Lakeway which becomes Holly St.
Credit Cards:	No
Owner:	Estella G. Gelder
Year Estab:	1972
Comments:	Passing by this shop prior to its scheduled opening time and glancing through the windows, we were able to see lots of antiques and collectibles and three bookcases with what appeared to be older books. Clearly, we can make no assessment with regard to the books and can only generalize that our experience when visiting this type of shop has rarely been positive.

(Bellingham)

Henderson Books
112 Grand Avenue 98225

Open Shop
(360) 734-6855

Collection:	General stock of hardcover and paperback.
Specialties:	Art; literature; history; cookbooks; gardening.
# of Vols:	175,000
Hours:	Mon, Thu-Sat 9-6. Sun 11-6. Tue & Wed by chance.
Travel:	Lakeway Dr exit off I-5. Proceed on Lakeway which becomes Holly. Right on Bay St, right on Champion and left on Grand. Shop is on right.
Credit Cards:	Yes
Owner:	Robert R. Henderson & Barbara Meyers
Year Estab:	1986
Comments:	When we visited this shop, it was just getting ready to open an annex next door and things were spic and span. The books at both sites were meticulously shelved, well labeled, generally in good condition and represented both newer items and vintage titles. We were impressed with the depth of the collection. While there were probably as many paperbacks on hand as hardcover volumes, the more traditional buyer would have no trouble finding desirable items here. We certainly didn't. The owners smile when they tell visiting dealers that they do not offer dealer discounts.

Michael's Books
109 Grand Avenue 98225

Open Shop
(360) 733-6272

Collection:	General stock of hardcover and paperback.
# of Vols:	200,000
Hours:	Mon-Sat 9-7. Sun 12-7.
Travel:	See Henderson Books above.
Credit Cards:	Yes
Owner:	Michael Elmer
Year Estab:	1983
Comments:	Directly across the street from another used book dealer, this shop has volume in terms of the number of books on display and also depth of subject matter. The books are probably a bit less expensive than at its "across the street competitor" but then again the books are less meticulously displayed. (Every once in a while someone should come in and straighten out the shelves.) When visiting Bellingham, neither of these two shops should be missed.

The Old London Bookshop
111 Central Avenue
Mailing Address: PO Box 922 Bellingham 98227

By Appointment
(360) 733-7273
Fax: (360) 647-8946

Collection:	Specialty
Specialties:	Scholarly; modern first editions; signed.
# of Vols:	30,000
Services:	Appraisals, catalog, accepts want lists.
Credit Cards:	No

Owner: Michael & Marlys Schon
Year Estab: 1988

Village Books   **Open Shop**
1210 11th Street 98225   (360) 671-2626

Collection:	General stock of mostly new and some used paperback and hardcover.
# of Vols:	5,000 (used)
Hours:	Mon-Sat 9am-10pm. Sun 10am-8pm, except till 10 during summer.
Services:	Search service, accepts want lists, mail order.
Travel:	Exit 250 off I-5. Proceed south on Old Fairhaven Pky then right on 12th and left on Harris. Shop is at corner of Harris and 11th.
Credit Cards:	Yes
Owner:	Chuck & Dee Robinson
Year Estab:	1980

Bremerton
(Map 28, page 387)

Books, Etc.   **Antique Mall**
At Perry Mall Antiques, 2901 Perry Avenue 98310   (360) 377-0162

Collection:	General stock.
Hours:	Mon-Sat 10-6. Sun 12-6.

Interim Books   **Open Shop**
322 Pacific Avenue   (360) 377-4343
    E-mail: elde@aol.com

Collection:	General stock of hardcover and paperback.
Specialties:	Naval; military.
# of Vols:	12,000
Hours:	Mon-Sat 11-5.
Services:	Accepts want lists, mail order.
Travel:	From Hwy 3, Kitsap Way exit. Follow Kitsap to downtown. Right on Pacific. Shop is between Burwell and 4th.
Credit Cards:	Yes
Owner:	Nancy Filler
Year Estab:	1981
Comments:	We visited this shop shortly before its move to a larger bi-level location. The hardcover books we saw were in generally good condition and several of the titles were of note in terms of collectibility. Although the collection is modest in size, a visit here could prove fruitful.

Burien

Shop & Save Thrift Store   **Open Shop**
16033 1st Avenue South 98148   (206) 246-6608

Collection:	General stock of hardcover and paperback.
Hours:	Mon-Sat 9-9. Sun 10-6.

Burlington
(Map 28, page 387)

B & M Book Store   **Open Shop**
686 McCorquedale Road 98233   (360) 757-7800

Collection: General stock of paperback and hardcover.
# of Vols: 300,000
Hours: Mon-Fri 10-5.
Comments: Approximately 70% of stock is paperback. All books are from trades.

Centralia
(Map 28, page 387)

Book Quest   **Open Shop**
105 West Main Street 98531   Fax: (360) 736-9773   (360) 736-823

Collection: General stock of hardcover and paperback.
Specialties: Modern first editions.
# of Vols: 30,000-40,000
Hours: Mon-Sat 9-5.
Services: Search service, mail order.
Travel: Harrison St exit off I-5. Proceed east on Harrison for about one mile. Harrison becomes Main.
Credit Cards: No
Owner: William E. Foster & Roger J. Stewart
Comments: At the time of our visit, the shop was in transition. We saw a nice selection of older hardcover books, quite reasonably priced, along with a good sized collection of more recent titles (many in dust jackets). We found interesting titles here, made at least one purchase, and feel this shop has promise for the traveling book buyer. Reorganization plans include displaying the shop's better books one flight up, setting up a paperback display in the front of the shop and moving hardcover books to an expanded area in the rear. The owners also display at a nearby antique mall.

Huckleberry Books   **Open Shop**
505 North Tower Avenue 98531   (360) 736-8796

Collection: General stock of paperback, hardcover, sheet music and CDs.
# of Vols: 5,000
Hours: Mon-Fri 10:30-5:30. Sat 10:30-4:30.
Services: Search service, accepts want lists.
Travel: See Book Quest above. From Main, make left on Tower Ave.
Credit Cards: Yes
Owner: Bill Moeller
Year Estab: 1994
Comments: Having previously visited the other used book dealer in town, we were anxious not to miss this one and indeed were pleased to find the shop open 15 minutes before its stated opening time. In the words of those who

describe the Mary Robert Rhinehart mysteries as "Had I but known...," had we known about the content of this shop, we might not have stopped here. While the shop does offer some hardcover books in generally good condition (and a much larger selection of paperbacks), the titles were not of sufficient interest to justify a visit if you're on a tight schedule.

Chehalis

Calendula Horticultural Books **By Appointment**
160 SW Alfred Street 98532 (360) 740-0903

Collection:	Specialty
Specialties:	Gardening; horticulture; flower arrangements; landscape architecture; North American wildflowers; birds.
# of Vols:	3,000
Services:	Catalog, accepts want lists.
Credit Cards:	No
Year Estab:	1987

Cheney
(Map 25, page 433)

Book Recylcer Bookstore & Cafe **Open Shop**
1953 1st Street 99004 (509) 235-8295

Collection:	General stock of mostly used paperback and hardcover.
# of Vols:	9,000 (used)
Hours:	Mon-Fri 9-7. Sat 10-6.
Travel:	Hwy 904 into Cheney.
Credit Cards:	No
Owner:	Robert Bobincheck
Year Estab:	1991
Comments:	Used stock is approximately 65% paperback.

Clarkston
(Map 25, page 433)

Peggatty Books **Open Shop**
609 Maple Street 99403 (509) 758-9517

Collection:	General stock of mostly used hardcover and paperback.
Specialties:	Pacific Northwest, military.
# of Vols:	22,000 (used)
Hours:	Summer: Mon-Sat 12-6. Winter: by chance or appointment. (Seasons coincide with change to daylight savings time.)
Services:	Appraisals, search service; accepts want lists, mail order.
Credit Cards:	Yes
Owner:	Peggy Behrens
Year Estab:	1975

Duvall
(Map 28, page 387)

Duvall Books   **Open Shop**
Main Street
Mailing Address: PO Box 307 Duvall 98019

Collection: General stock of hardcover and paperback, sheet music and ephemera.
# of Vols: 15,000
Hours: Daily 10-5:30, except Sat till 9.
Travel: Hwy 520 to end. At light at end of highway, continue straight on Avondale to first "T" intersection. Right on Woodinville-Duvall Road and continue to Duvall. Right on Main.
Credit Cards: No
Owner: Mike & Vickie Elledge
Year Estab: 1977
Comments: A sleeper? Several area dealers mentioned this shop to us as one that was "out of the way" and also one that "offered great buys." We couldn't resist the temptation so we made the trip. The shop is indeed out of the way and the prices are indeed inexpensive. Based on what we saw during our visit, though, our guess is that the secret of the shop's existence has long since been uncovered. The hardcover volumes we saw were mostly, but not exclusively older and we didn't really see anything here that might not have been found elsewhere, albeit at a higher price. But there is a certain charm in traveling to an out of the way village to a shop without a phone (or cash register) to make one's discovery.

Edmonds
(Map 28, page 387)

Edmonds Olde Bookstore   **Open Shop**
9679 Firdale Avenue 98020   (206) 542-8636

Collection: General stock.
Specialties: Children's; cookbooks; Pacific Northwest.
# of Vols: 20,000
Hours: Wed-Sun 11-7. Mon & Tue by appointment.
Services: Search service, catalog, accepts want lists.
Travel: North 205th St exit off I-5. Proceed west on 205th St. Stay in left lane at "Y" intersection. Bear left, continuing on 205th St which becomes Firdale. Shop is in rear of a shopping center.
Credit Cards: No
Owner: Janice & Wayne Williams
Year Estab: 1981
Comments: An interesting collection of mostly hardcover books with a clear emphasis on the specialties listed above but with other titles, both common and unusual. If your eye is quick and you're a patient browser you should be able to find some worthwhile items here.

Half Price Books, Records, Magazines   Open Shop
23632 Highway 99, Ste M 98026   (206) 670-6199

Collection: General stock of new, used and remainders.
Hours: Mon-Sat 9 am-10pm. Sun 9-8.
Travel: Located in Aurora Market Place, between 236th St & 238th St.

Orpheus Books   By Appointment
23907 80th Place W 98026   (206) 776-4912

Collection: Specialty
Specialties: Classical music, including opera, history, theory, biography.
# of Vols: 3,500
Services: Catalog, search service.
Owner: Irving & Rita Goldstein
Year Estab: 1986

Ellensburg
(Map 25, page 433)

Anchor In Time   Open Shop
310 North Main 98926   (509) 925-7067

Collection: General stock.
Specialties: Natural history; travel; fine bindings; poetry.
# of Vols: 2,000
Hours: Daily 9-6.
Services: Appraisals, accepts want lists.
Travel: Either Ellensburg exit off I-90. Follow signs for downtown.
Credit Cards: Yes
Owner: Bruce Magnotti
Year Estab: 1988

Four Winds Bookstore and Cafe   Open Shop
200 East Fourth 98926   (509) 962-2375

Collection: General stock of mostly used paperback.
Hours: Mon-Fri 9-5:30. Sat 10-5. Sun 12-4.

The Old Fool's Bookstore   Open Shop
112 East 3rd 98926   (509) 925-4480

Collection: General stock of mostly hardcover.
Specialties: Philosophy; literature; classics; Shakespeare; ecology.
# of Vols: 25,000
Hours: Mon-Sat 10-5. Sometimes on Sun, or by appointment.
Services: Appraisals, search service, accepts want lists.
Travel: Either Ellensburg exit off I-90. Proceed to downtown. Shop is next to post office.
Credit Cards: Yes
Owner: Tom Dell
Year Estab: 1990

Enumclaw
(Map 28, page 387)

Railroad Street Books
1634 Railroad Street 98022

Open Shop
(360) 825-6724

Collection: General stock of hardcover and paperback.
# of Vols: 10,000
Hours: Mon-Sat 10-6.
Travel: Hwy 410 into town. Left on Roosevelt, right on Griffin, left on Railroad.

Everett
(Map 28, page 387)

Alcove Books
1001 North Broadway 98201

Open Shop
(206) 258-9390

Collection: General stock of hardcover and paperback.
# of Vols: 25,000
Hours: Mon-Sat 10:30-6. Sun 1-5.
Travel: See Don Quixote Bookstore below. At 10th & Broadway.
Year Estab: 1994
Comments: Stock is evenly divided between hardcover and paperback.

The Bookworm
2829 Wetmore Avenue 98201

Open Shop
(206) 252-8593

Collection: General stock of paperback, hardcover and comics.
# of Vols: 6,000
Travel: See Pilchuck Books below.
Hours: Mon-Fri 10-6. Sat 10-5.
Owner: Dave Halvorsen
Comments: Far more paperbacks than hardcover books, with the latter consisting of mostly newer items. Not much here for the seasoned book person.

Don Quixote Bookstore
2709 Wetmore 98201

Open Shop
(206) 259-5432

Collection: General stock of hardcover and paperback.
# of Vols: 130,000
Hours: Mon-Sat 11-6.
Services: Appraisals, search service, accepts want lists.
Travel: From I-5 northbound: Broadway exit. Continue on Broadway for about 14 blocks, then left on Everett and left on Wetmore. From I-5 southbound: Exit 198. Continue on Broadway. Right on Everett, left on Wetmore.
Credit Cards: Yes
Owner: Neal & Kimberly Cox
Year Estab: 1979
Comments: A bi-level shop with a good sized collection. The stock is about 50% paperback but there are certainly enough hardcover volumes that standing by

themselves would make a respectable shop. While most of the books were in quite good condition and of recent vintage, the shop does have enough older volumes to make browsing a challenge. Most subjects are covered.

Gary's Books & Collectibles   **Open Shop**
1904 Hewitt Avenue 98201   (206) 258-4233

Collection: General stock of mostly paperback.
# of Vols: 5,000
Hours: Mon-Sat 11-6.
Comments: If your field is science fiction, you may be willing to work your way through some of the crowded aisles to view four or five dozen used hardcover books. Or, if you're into children's literature and you don't mind getting copies not in the best condition, you might also decide that a visit here might be worth the effort. Unless paperback science fiction and/or comics are your thing, we would suggest you move on.

Goodwill Store   **Open Shop**
3002 Hoyt Avenue 98201   (206) 743-647

Collection: General stock of hardcover and paperback.
Hours: Mon-Sat 9-6.

Jan's Book Rack   **Open Shop**
2531 Broadway Avenue 98201   (206) 339-1197

Collection: General stock of paperback and hardcover.
Hours: Mon-Sat 10-5:30.
Travel: See Don Quixote Bookstore above. Shop is at 26th St in Broadway Mall.
Credit Cards: No
Owner: Jan Haney
Year Estab: 1992
Comments: If you live in town, or in one of the surrounding towns, and are looking for some light reading, Jan's has a nice supply of paperbacks and a few hardcover volumes (reading copies) that she can offer. If your wants are more special, we doubt if you will find them here.

Larson Books   **Open Shop**
1513 23rd Street 98201   (206) 252-6866

Collection: General stock of hardcover and paperback.
# of Vols: 7,000
Hours: Daily 10-10:30.
Comments: Stock is approximately 50% paperback.

Pilchuck Books   **Open Shop**
2821 Wetmore Avenue 98201   (206) 303-0345

Collection: General stock of used and new hardcover and paperback.
# of Vols: 5,000-7,000
Hours: Mon-Sat 11-6.
Services: Search service, accepts want lists.

Travel: See Don Quixote Bookstore above. Shop is between Hewitt and California.
Credit Cards: Yes
Owner: Ken Bosman
Year Estab: 1995
Comments: An exception to the general rule (prejudice?) that we sometimes apply to bookstore/cafe combos. We didn't taste the food, but we did look at the books. While the collection is modest in size, the quality of many of the titles we saw was such as to suggest that book people would not regret a visit here. The hardcover titles ran the gamut from vintage to newer titles.

Sirius Books **Open Shop**
9109 Evergreen Way 98204 (206) 355-9756

Collection: General stock of mostly paperback.
Hours: Mon-Fri 11-7. Sat 10-6. Sun 12-5.

Federal Way
(Map 28, page 387)

Book Stop **Open Shop**
29007 Military Road South 98003 (206) 941-2960

Collection: General stock of paperback and hardcover.
# of Vols: 46,000+
Hours: Mon-Sat 10-7. Sun 12-6.
Travel: 272nd St exit off I-5. Proceed east to Military Rd. Right on Military, then right into Lakecrest Shopping Center.
Credit Cards: Yes
Year Estab: 1993
Comments: Stock is approximately 75% paperback.

Gig Harbor
(Map 28, page 387)

Buffalo Gals' Trading Co. **Open Shop**
Harborview Drive (203) 858-2994
Mailing Address: PO Box 52 Gig Harbor 98335

Collection: General stock of hardcover and paperback.
# of Vols: 2,000
Hours: Wed-Sun 10-5.
Travel: Located a few doors from Mostly Books (see below).
Comments: One sign on the door read: "Wed-Sun 10-5 while a second read: "We'll be closing for a show on July 22 & 23rd." One more reason to call ahead before making a trip, unless that is, you're planning a vacation nearby.

Mostly Books **Open Shop**
3126 Harborview Drive (206) 851-3219
Mailing Address: PO Box 428 Gig Harbor 98335

Collection: General stock of new and used hardcover and paperback.

Specialties:	Pacific Northwest.
# of Vols:	7,000
Hours:	Mon-Fri 9:30-5:30. Sat 9:30-5.
Services:	Informal search service.
Travel:	Hwy 16 exit off I-5. Proceed on Hwy 16 to City Center exit. At waterfront, left on Harborview.
Credit Cards:	Yes
Owner:	Harry Dearth
Year Estab:	1969
Comments:	This mostly new book shop had about four bookcases of used hardcover titles on display at the time of our visit (although we were advised that there were more used books in storage). The titles ranged from the serious to the lighter but all appeared to be reading copies.

Granite Falls

Inquisitive Sportsman Books   **By Appointment**
PO Box 1811 98252   Fax: (360) 691-7540   (360) 691-7540

Collection:	Specialty. Mostly used and ephemera.
Specialties:	Fishing; hunting; signed.
# of Vols:	3,000-10,000
Hours:	Mon-Fri 4pm-6pm & 6pm-8:30pm. Sat 1pm-8pm. Sun 9am-11.
Services:	Appraisals, search service, catalog, accepts want lists, collection building
Credit Cards:	No
Owner:	Stephen P. Gill
Year Estab:	1983

Issaquah

The Jabberwocky   **Open Shop**
99 Front Street North 98027   (206) 557-0230

Collection:	General stock of mostly used paperback.
Hours:	Daily, except closed Tue, 11-8.

Michele Leroux Fine Old Books   **By Appointment**
710 Fifth Avenue, NW 98027   (206) 392-9536

Collection:	Specialty and limited general stock.
Specialties:	Children's; illustrated; fine bindings; books about books; books by and about women..
# of Vols:	4,000
Services:	Accepts want lists, mail order.
Credit Cards:	No
Year Estab:	1985

Lost and Found Books
485 Front Street North 98027

Open Shop
(206) 391-7151

Collection: General stock of mostly paperback.
Hours: Mon-Thu 10-7. Fri & Sat 10-6.

Kelso

Bev's Book Shoppe
410 South Pacific Avenue 98626

Open Shop
(360) 577-8620

Collection: General stock of mostly paperback.
Hours: Mon-Sat 10-5.

Kennewick

Bookworm
101 North Union, # 209 99336

Open Shop
(509) 735-9016

Collection: General stock of new and primarily paperback used.
Hours: Mon-Fri 10-6. Sat 12-6.

Kent
(Map 28, page 387)

Book World
23406 Pacific Highway South 98032

Open Shop
Fax: (206) 824-9422   (206) 824-9422

Collection: General stock of used, new and remainders hardcover and paperback.
Specialties: Children's; science fiction.
# of Vols: 100,000+
Hours: Mon-Sat 10-9. Sun 10-7.
Services: Accepts want lists, mail order.
Travel: Des Moines exit off I-5. Proceed west one block to Pacific Hwy, then left on Pacific. Shop is immediately ahead, on left, in shopping center.
Credit Cards: Yes
Owner: Rick & Leatha Traphagan
Year Estab: 1973
Comments: First impressions can be deceiving. When approaching this shop, one can easily believe that its concentration will be new books and other related items. However, at least one third of the shop is devoted to a substantial collection of used paperbacks and hardcover volumes in most categories. The hardcover items, in generally good condition, are of mixed vintage, with the majority of them being of more recent vintage. The shelves were well labeled and the shop was easy to browse.

Book World II
23824 104th SE 98031

Open Shop
(206) 859-5826

Collection: General stock of hardcover and paperback.
# of Vols: 150,000 (used)
Hours: Mon-Sat 10-9. Sun 12-6.

Services: Accepts want lists, mail order.
Travel: Kent exit off I-5. Proceed east on Kent/Des Moines Rd. Left on Washington. Right on James. Shop is at corner of 104th and James in Benson Shopping Center.
Owner: Rick & Leatha Traphagen

JNJ Books   **Open Shop**
302 West Harrison 98032   (206) 854-5405

Collection: General stock of paperback and hardcover.
# of Vols: 40,000
Hours: Mon-Sat 10-6, except Thu till 9.
Travel: Kent exit off Hwy 167. Proceed toward town. Shop is at corner of West Harrison and 2nd North.
Comments: Stock if approximately 70% paperback.

Kirkland
(Map 28, page 387)

The Penny Box Used Books   **Open Shop**
10052 NE 137th Street 98034   (206) 820-0226

Collection: General stock of paperback and hardcover.
Specialties: Science fiction; local interest.
# of Vols: 25,000
Hours: Sun & Mon 11-6. Tue-Thu 10-8. Fri & Sat 10-9.
Services: Accepts want lists.
Travel: Exit 22 off I-405. Proceed west two miles. Shop is on right in shopping center.
Owner: Robin, Russ & Heather Van Steenburgh
Year Estab: 1994
Comments: Stock is approximately 70% paperback.

Shop & Save Thrift Store   **Open Shop**
6613 132nd Avenue NE   (206) 881-0803

Collection: General stock of hardcover and paperback.
Hours: Mon-Sat 9-9. Sun 10-6.

Tales of Kirkland   **Open Shop**
12100 NE 85th Street 98033   (206) 822-7333

Collection: General stock of mostly paperback.
Hours: Mon-Sat 10-6. Sun 11-5.

Long Beach
(Map 20, page 345)

Sandpiper Books   **Open Shop**
114 South Pacific Highway   (360) 642-4969
Mailing Address: PO Box 1439 Long Beach 98631   Fax: (360) 642-4451

Collection: General stock of mostly used hardcover.

Specialties:	Pacific Northwest; fantasy; mystery; modern first editions; mythology; Sherlock Holmes; children's; illustrated.
# of Vols:	15,000
Hours:	Jun-Aug: Daily 10-6. Remainder of year: Thu-Tue 10-6.
Services:	Appraisals, search service, catalog, accepts want lists.
Travel:	Hwy 103 exit off Hwy 101. Proceed into town.
Credit Cards:	Yes
Owner:	Paul & Ginny Merz
Year Estab:	1991
Comments:	The good news is that this shop, located in a tourist community, has a nice collection of hardcover volumes, most of which were in good to better condition. (A small room in the back offers a limited number of paperbacks.) If you're in town, you may just find the book you've been looking for. The less positive news is that several of the volumes we saw were priced higher than we've seen in less "touristy" locations.

The Whale's Tale   **Open Shop**
620 South Pacific Highway   (360) 642-3455
Mailing Address: PO Box 1520A Long Beach 98631   Fax: (360) 642-2626

Collection:	General stock of hardcover and paperback.
Specialties:	Cookbooks; mystery.
# of Vols:	5,000-8,000
Hours:	Mon-Sat 10-6. Sun 10-5.
Services:	Service, accepts want lists, mail order.
Travel:	See Sandpiper Books above.
Credit Cards:	Yes
Owner:	Norma Wadler
Year Estab:	1991
Comments:	About an equal mix of hardcover and paperback. Most of the hardcover volumes we saw were of recent vintage and in good condition. Most were reading copies although there were a few collectibles under glass. While the number of volumes was not large, the books were reasonably priced. If you're in the neighborhood, stop by.

Longview

The Bookshop   **Open Shop**
1203 14th Avenue 98632   (360) 636-3820

Collection:	General stock of mostly paperback.
Hours:	Mon-Fri 10-5:30. Sat 10-5.

Lynnwood
(Map 28, page 387)

Book Exchange of Lynnwood   **Open Shop**
6725-B 196th Street, SW 98036   (206) 775-2377

Collection:	General stock of paperback and hardcover.
Hours:	Mon-Sat 10-6.

Goodwill Store **Open Shop**
19505 52nd West 98036 (206) 774-6157

Collection: General stock of hardcover and paperback.
Hours: Mon-Sat 9-6.

Great Epic Books **By Appointment**
15918 20th Place, West 98037 Fax: (206) 745-9520 (206) 745-3113

Collection: Specialty and limited general stock.
Specialties: Africa; T.E. Lawrence; Ireland.
# of Vols: 20,000
Services: Appraisals, catalog, accepts want lists.
Credit Cards: Yes
Owner: Dr. Donal A. Brody
Year Estab: 1984

Marysville

Third Street Book Exchange **Open Shop**
1615 Third Street 98270 (360) 659-8734

Collection: General stock of mostly paperback.
Hours: Mon-Fri 10-6:30. Sat 10-5:30. Sun 10-5.

West Coast Books **Open Shop**
1206-H State Avenue 98270 (360) 659-5626

Collection: General stock of mostly paperback.
Hours: Mon-Sat 10-5, except Tue till 5:30.

Mercer Island
(Map 28, page 387)

Island Books **Open Shop**
3014 78th SE 98040 (206) 232-6920

Collection: General stock of new and some used.
# of Vols: 1,500 (used)
Hours: Mon-Fri 9:30-6, except Thu till 8. Sat 9:30-5:30. Sun 12-5.
Travel: Island Crest Way exit off I-90.
Comments: Used stock is all hardcover.

Milton
(Map 28, page 387)

Costless Books **Open Shop**
2800 Milton Way 98354 (206) 952-6858

Collection: General stock of hardcover and paperback.
# of Vols: 15,000-20,000
Hours: Mon-Sat 11-9. Sun 11-6.

Travel: Milton exit off I-5. Proceed uphill toward town. Left on Meridan. Shop is in Milton Plaza.
Year Estab: 1995
Comments: Stock is approximately 65% hardcover.

Moses Lake

Well Read Books   **Open Shop**
222 West 3rd Avenue 98837   (509) 766-1950

Collection: General stock of mostly paperback.
Hours: Winter: Mon-Sat 10-5. Summer: Mon-Fri 10-6. Sat 10-5.

Mount Vernon
(Map 28, page 387)

Easton's Books   **Open Shop**
223 South First Street 98273   (360) 336-2066

Collection: General stock of hardcover and paperback.
# of Vols: 35,000
Hours: Mon-Sat 10:30-5.
Services: Appraisals, search service, accepts want lists.
Travel: Kincaid exit off I-5. West on Kincaid, then right on 1st.
Credit Cards: No
Owner: David & Dianna Cornelius
Year Estab: 1976
Comments: A very neat shop in terms of appearance and the quality of most of its hardcover books. While there were subject category signs on the walls above the bookcases, unfortunately, these signs did not necessarily indicate where in the shop those categories were on display. An astute browser taking his time or inquiring of the owner could, of course, locate the sections he was interested in but we believe it would have been nicer (and made browsing easier) for the actual sections to have been labeled. There were plenty of paperbacks on hand for those interested in lighter reading.

Mountlake Terrace

Raindance Books   **Open Shop**
22803 44th Avenue West 98043   (206) 775-1819

Collection: General stock of mostly used paperback and some new.
Hours: Mon-Fri 7am-9pm. Sat 11am-9pm.

Olympia
(Map 28, page 387)

Browsers' Book Shop   **Open Shop**
107 North Capitol Way 98501   (360) 357-7462

Collection: General stock of paperback and hardcover.
# of Vols: 10,000

Hours:	Mon-Sat 10-6, except Fri till 8. Sun 12-4.
Services:	Appraisals, search service, accepts want lists.
Travel:	Port of Olympia exit off I-5. Proceed on Plum St, then left on Legion Way to Capitol Way.
Credit Cards:	No
Owner:	Jenifer Stewart
Comments:	A pleasant, mostly paperback shop with a relatively small selection of hardcover books, few of which could be considered rare or collectible. This is the kind of shop that offers reading copies for the local community.

Inlet Books

210½ West 4th Street 98501

Open Shop
(360) 357-6608

Collection:	General stock of hardcover and paperback.
# of Vols:	5,000
Hours:	Mon-Sat 10-5:30.
Travel:	Port of Olympia exit off I-5. Proceed on Plum St. Left on State, left on Water and left on 4th. Shop is between Columbia and Water.
Credit Cards:	Yes
Owner:	Frank Dodson
Year Estab:	1993
Comments:	A relatively small shop with a relatively small collection. Most of the stock appeared to be of recent vintage and not particularly distinguished. A few older items were on hand.

Orca Books

509 East 4th Avenue East 98502

Open Shop
(360) 352-0123

Collection:	General stock of paperback and hardcover.
# of Vols:	60,000
Hours:	Mon-Thu 10-8. Fri & Sat 10-9. Sun 12-6.
Services:	Search service.
Travel:	Port of Olympia exit off I-5. Proceed on Plum St, then left on Legion Way, right on Jefferson and right on 4th.
Credit Cards:	Yes
Owner:	Linda Berentsen & Cori Christiansen
Year Estab:	1992
Comments:	In terms of size, the largest shop in Olympia. Paperbacks and hardcover volumes were intershelved, and except for fiction, the books in most other categories were represented in less volume and clearly less depth. Most of the books we saw were reading copies although there were some older volumes and collectibles on hand. Reasonably priced.

Sherburne Antiques & Fine Art

100 East 4th Avenue 98501

Open Shop
(360) 357-9177

Collection:	Specialty
Specialties:	Government reports, surveys and explorations, primarily pre-20th century western United States.
Hours:	Mon-Sat 10-4.

Travel:	Port of Olympia exit off I-5. Proceed on Plum St, then left on Legion Way, right on 4th.
Owner:	S.F. Cook
Year Estab:	1980

Tilikum Books   **Open Shop**
115 Legion Way SW 98501   (360) 956-0432

Collection:	General stock of hardcover and paperback.
Specialties:	Nautical; natural history; science; cookbooks.
# of Vols:	20,000
Hours:	Mon-Sat 10:30-5:30.
Services:	Accepts want lists.
Travel:	Port of Olympia exit off I-5. Proceed on Plum then left on Legion Way. Shop is between Columbia and Capitol Way.
Credit Cards:	Yes
Owner:	Larry Martin
Year Estab:	1990
Comments:	The hardcover books were in generally good condition and reasonably priced. Most subjects were covered but few in depth.

Pasco
(Map 25, page 433)

Storment Library   **Open Shop**
7617 West Court 99301   (509) 547-5375

Collection:	General stock.
Specialties:	Northwest Americana.
# of Vols:	34,000
Hours:	Call for hours.
Credit Cards:	No
Owner:	Eugene & Edith Storment
Year Estab:	1983

Port Angeles
(Map 28, page 387)

Benicia Books   **Open Shop**
222 North Lincoln 98362   Fax: (360) 417-0421   (360) 452-8302

Collection:	General stock and ephemera.
Specialties:	Aviation; military; guns; hunting.
# of Vols:	1,000
Hours:	Summer: Tue, Wed, Sat, Sun 10-5. Thu & Fri 11-7. Win: Wed-Sun 10-5.
Services:	Appraisals, search service, catalog, accepts want lists.
Travel:	Located in Harbortowne Mall, across from ferry terminal.
Credit Cards:	Yes
Owner:	Richard M. Merrill
Year Estab:	1987

Puzzle Book Store   **Open Shop**
117½ West 1st Street 98362   (360) 457-7071

Collection:	General stock of mostly paperback.
Hours:	Mon-Sat 9-4. Sun 10-4.

Port Orchard
(Map 28, page 387)

Jomar   **Open Shop**
713 Bay Street 98366   (360) 895-8462

Collection:	General stock of hardcover and paperback.
# of Vols:	50,000
Hours:	Mon-Sat 10-6.
Travel:	Off Hwy 16, in center of town.
Year Estab:	1993
Comments:	Stock is approximately 75% hardcover.

Port Townsend
(Map 28, page 387)

Melville & Co Books   **Open Shop**
914 Water Street 98368   (360) 385-7127

Collection:	General stock of hardcover and paperback.
Specialties:	Fiction; literature.
# of Vols:	10,000+
Hours:	Daily 11-5.
Services:	Appraisals, occasional catalog, mail order.
Travel:	See William James Bookseller below.
Credit Cards:	No
Owner:	Bob Deweese
Year Estab:	1975
Comments:	If you visit this shop at the height of the summer season, and in the middle of the day when it's likely to be crowded with visitors, you no doubt will find it difficult, as we did, to maneuver the narrow aisles and/or find the subject categories you're looking for on shelves that were not always well labeled or organized. While there certainly may have been some titles worth examining or purchasing here, browsing for them under the above conditions was not a pleasant chore and we did not stay long. Perhaps a true book person would see more and appreciate more during a less busy time of the day or during the off season.

William James Bookseller   **Open Shop**
829 Water Street 98368   Fax: (360) 379-8946   (360) 385-7313

Collection:	General stock of hardcover and paperback.
# of Vols:	30,000
Hours:	Daily 11-5.

Services:	Accepts want lists, mail order.
Travel:	Hwy 104 to Hwy 19. North on Hwy 19 which merges with Hwy 20 which becomes Water St in downtown.
Credit Cards:	Yes
Owner:	Jim Catley
Year Estab:	1987
Comments:	Shortly after visiting the shop listed above we visited this establishment. Our impressions were completely different. This shop was larger (but hardly enormous), the books were meticulously shelved and for the most part were in good condition and chairs were available for the browser's comfort. We saw some older volumes, some collectibles and some remainders. Even in the height of the summer season, this shop was far easier and more pleasurable to browse than its neighbor.

Poulsbo
(Map 28, page 387)

Book Stop **Open Shop**
18954-A Front Street NE (360) 779-9773
Mailing Address: PO Box 1823 Poulsbo 98370

Collection:	General stock of paperback and hardcover.
Specialties:	Cookbooks; nautical; children's.
# of Vols:	13,000
Hours:	Mon-Sat 10-5:30. Sun 12:30-5. Longer hours in summer.
Travel:	Take ferry from Seattle to Bainbridge Island, then proceed north on Hwy 305. In Poulsbo, proceed west on Hostmark St to downtown. From Kitsap peninsula: Finn Hill exit off Hwy 3. Follow signs to city center.
Credit Cards:	Yes
Owner:	Megan Holmberg
Year Estab:	1983
Comments:	The sign in the front window read: "Used Books" and that's exactly what the store sells. There were lots of used paperbacks (far more than hardcover volumes), plus book club editions, a goodly share of Stephen King and other recent best sellers, and even a few Franklin Mint and Readers Digest leather bindings. We did see some older books but these had little to distinguish them. If you're in town on vacation and have forgotten to bring some reading matter along, you might want to stop by here and purchase a book you could read during your leisure hours.

Prosser
(Map 25, page 433)

Bookmark **Open Shop**
611 6th Street 99350 (509) 786-2626

Collection:	General stock of new and hardcover used.
# of Vols:	1,500 (used)

Hours: Mon-Sat. Hours vary so best to call ahead.
Travel: Prosser exit off I-82. Proceed on 6th St into town.
Credit Cards: Yes
Owner: Mary DaCorsi & John Koenig
Year Estab: 1959

Puyallup
(Map 28, page 387)

Broad Horizons   Open Shop
1823 East Main Avenue 98372   (206) 845-1565

Collection: General stock of mostly paperback.
Hours: Mon-Sat 9-6.

Puyallup Book Mark   Open Shop
715 39th Avenue SW 98373   (206) 840-0209

Collection: General stock of paperback and hardcover.
# of Vols: 20,000+
Hours: Tue-Sat 9:30-5:30.
Comments: Stock is approximately 75% paperback.

Renton

The Bookcyclers   Open Shop
327 Williams Avenue South 98055   (206) 226-2711

Collection: General stock of mostly paperback.
Hours: Mon-Fri 10-5:30. Sat 10-3.

Richland
(Map 25, page 433)

Bookworm   Open Shop
1908-D George Washington Way 99352   (509) 946-0898

Collection: General stock of new and primarily paperback used.
Hours: Mon-Fri 10-6. Sat 12-6.

Book Nook   Open Shop
2143 Van Glesen 99352   (509) 946-2477

Collection: General stock of paperback and hardcover.
# of Vols: 20,000
Hours: Mon-Sat 10-6.
Credit Cards: Yes
Owner: Ann Evans
Year Estab: 1984
Comments: Stock is approximately 65% paperback.

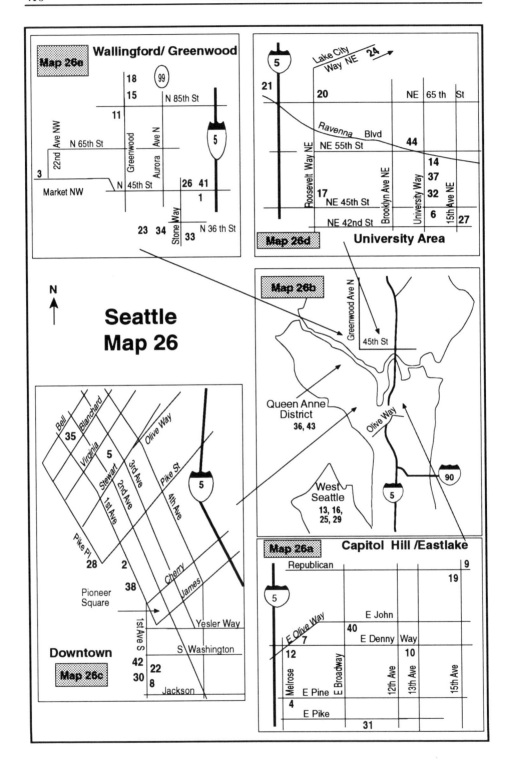

Seattle
(Map 26, page 410 & Map 28, page 387)

Alfi News & Books
1717 North 45th Street 98103

Open Shop
(206) 632-9390

Collection:	General stock.
Specialties:	Sets
# of Vols:	2,000
Hours:	Mon-Fri 9am-10pm, except Fri till 11pm. Sat 8:30am-11pm. Sun 8-8.
Services:	Appraisals, accepts want lists.
Travel:	45th St exit off I-5. Proceed west on 45th St.
Map Ref:	Map 26e, page 410, #1.
Credit Cards:	Yes
Year Estab:	1990
Comments:	We were most pleasantly surprised to find that this shop, which sells newspapers, magazines (new) and greeting cards also had quite a collection (several dozen) of literary sets with fine bindings, as well as other older volumes, some more modern leather bound books and a modest sized general stock collection. Perhaps it was the non traditional book store-like setting that made the literary sets stand out so and made us wonder how many folks purchase these sets for reading as opposed to decorative purposes. Regardless of one's motives, they were extremely attractive.

An Odd Volume
1309 NE Ravenna Boulevard 98105

Open Shop
(206) 522-2137

Collection:	General stock.
# of Vols:	25,000
Hours:	Tue-Sun 11-7.
Travel:	In University District. In an alley between University Way and Brooklyn.
Map Ref:	Map 26d, page 410, #44.
Credit Cards:	Yes
Owner:	Thomas Schellhase & Christine Notske
Year Estab:	1995

Arundel Books
1309 First Avenue 98101

Open Shop
(206) 624-4442

Collection:	General stock of hardcover and paperback.
# of Vols:	25,000+
Hours:	Mon-Sat 10-9, except Thu till 10. Sun 10-6:30.
Travel:	Downtown, across from the Seattle Art Museum.
Map Ref:	Map 26c, page 410, #2.
Credit Cards:	Yes
Owner:	Phillip Bevis
Year Estab:	1995
Comments:	At the time of our visit, the shop had been in operation for only two months and only a portion of its collection was on display. The hardcover books we did get to see were mostly in good to excellent condition, most subject

(Seattle)

areas were represented, the shelves were well labeled and the books moderately priced. Although the shelves are high, rolling ladders are available. Based on our discussion with the owner and our earlier visit to his shop (with the same name) in Los Angeles, we firmly believe that the growth and development of this establishment will be such as to merit a visit by the discriminating book person.

Automotive Bookstore **Open Shop**
1830 12th Avenue 98122 (206) 323-6719

Collection:	Specialty books (mostly paperback) and magazines.
Specialties:	Automobiles, trucks and motorcycles. Factory and aftermarket repair manuals.
# of Vols:	20,000
Hours:	Mon-Fri 10-4. Weekends by appointment.
Travel:	Denny Way exit off I-5. Proceed east on Denny to 12th Ave.
Credit Cards:	Yes
Owner:	William Morris
Year Estab:	1984

Ballard Books **Open Shop**
2232 NW Market Street 98107 (206) 782-0820

Collection:	General stock of hardcover and paperback.
# of Vols:	20,000
Hours:	Mon-Sat 10-8. Sun 12-6.
Services:	Accepts want lists.
Travel:	45th St exit off I-5. Proceed west on 45th St until it becomes Market St (cross under Hwy 99, staying in right lane.) Shop is between 22nd NW and 24th NW.
Map Ref:	Map 26e, page 410, #3.
Credit Cards:	Yes
Owner:	Jaclyn Brandt
Year Estab:	1993
Comments:	A neighborhood shop with a mixed collection of hardcover volumes, most reading copies of recent vintage, paperbacks in good condition and some signed first editions behind glass. The store is easy to browse, and with perhaps a few exceptions, we saw little here that should cause one to travel out of one's way to visit.

Bauhaus Books & Coffee **Open Shop**
301 East Pine 98122 (206) 625-1600

Collection:	General stock of hardcover and paperback.
Specialties:	Art; architecture; counter culture; design.
# of Vols:	2,000-3,000
Hours:	Mon-Fri 6am-1am. Sat & Sun 8am-1am.
Travel:	Olive Way exit off I-5. Proceed east on Olive then south on Melrose.

Map Ref: Map 26a, page 410, #4.
Credit Cards: No
Owner: Joel Radin, Mike Klebeck, Chris Vonoy
Year Estab: 1994
Comments: We visited this shop on a rather hot day and found several customers taking advantage of the refreshments sold here rather than perusing the books on the 10 foot high bookcases. Foregoing a climb up the library style rolling ladder to examine the titles more carefully, we were satisfied, after a quick glance at the volumes on the lower shelves, that the hardcover books were in good condition and represented the specialties listed above, but clearly not in significant numbers.

Beatty Book Store **Open Shop**
1925 Third Avenue 98101 (206) 728-2665

Collection: General stock.
# of Vols: 100,000
Hours: Mon-Sat 11-6.
Services: Accepts want lists, mail order.
Travel: Downtown, between Virginia and Stewart.
Map Ref: Map 26c, page 410, #5.
Credit Cards: No
Year Estab: 1968
Comments: We hope the owner does not take offense at our viewing this shop as a classic "old fashioned" book shop; it holds so many volumes that would truly touch the soul, as well as the palette, of veteran book lovers. While the shop has its share of more recent items, its real treasures are its older volumes, generally in good condition, and in almost every field. Lots of literary sets, antiquarian items and collectibles. If you enjoy books that have been around for a while but that are still well cared for, you'll have fun here. We wish we could have stayed longer.

Beauty and the Books **Open Shop**
4213 University Way NE 98105 (206) 632-8510

Collection: General stock of hardcover and paperback, ephemera and records.
Specialties: Western Americana; literature; science fiction; autographs.
# of Vols: 150,000
Hours: Daily 10-10.
Services: Appraisals
Travel: 45th St exit off I-5. Proceed east on 45th St, then right on University. Shop is 1½ blocks ahead on right.
Map Ref: Map 26d, page 410, #6.
Credit Cards: No
Owner: Richard Leffel
Year Estab: 1979
Comments: This shop offers a substantial collection of mixed vintage hardcover volumes in mixed condition in most subject categories. While the books were

(Seattle)

organized by subject and were reasonably easy to locate, the condition of the shelves reflected either lack of care or too much customer handling without appropriate tidying up afterwards.

Beyond the Closet Bookstore **Open Shop**
1501 Belmont Avenue 98122 (206) 322-4609

Collection: Specialty. Primarily new with some used.
Specialties: Homosexuality
# of Vols: 500 (used)
Year Estab: 1987

Bibelots & Books **Open Shop**
1530 Eastlake East, #207 98102 (206) 329-6676

Collection: Specialty
Specialties: Children's; children's series; illustrated.
# of Vols: 10,000
Hours: Thu-Sat 12-5.
Services: Search service, accepts want lists, mail order.
Travel: Roanoke exit off I-5. Proceed south for 1/2 mile.
Credit Cards: Yes
Owner: Shirley Schneider
Year Estab: 1977

Book & Bean Espresso Co. **Open Shop**
1635½ East Olive Way 98102 (206) 325-1139

Collection: General stock of paperback and hardcover.
# of Vols: 2,000-3,000
Hours: Daily 7am-midnight, except Fri & Sat till 1am.
Travel: From I-5 northbound: Stewart/Denny St exit. Proceed two blocks then left on Denny. Continue over freeway, then left on East Olive. Southbound on I-5: Exit 166 (Olive St). At second light, continue up hill which is East Olive. Shop is between Belmont and Summit.
Map Ref: Map 26a, page 410, #7.
Credit Cards: Yes
Owner: Dan Johnson
Year Estab: 1994
Comments: We did not count the number of books in this shop but we would estimate there were 1,500 or so, with fewer than 200 hardcover volumes. Quite possibly, in the future, that number may grow. Our advice is that unless you're anxious for a cup of espresso, you'd be better off investing your browsing time in some of Seattle's other, more established book shops.

Book Affair **Open Shop**
15203 Military Road South 98188 (206) 241-0629

Collection: General stock of mostly paperback.

# of Vols:	10,000
Hours:	Mon-Sat 10-6.
Travel:	Hwy 518 exit off I-5. Proceed west on Hwy 518 to Hwy 99. North on Hwy 99 to 152nd St. Left on 152nd. Left on Military Rd.
Credit Cards:	Yes
Owner:	Vickie Brock
Year Estab:	1984
Comments:	Close to 90% paperback with the few hardcover volumes on display consisting of some older (but undistinguished) titles and recent fiction. Also back issues of girlie magazines. Not a shop we would urge you to get off the highway to visit.

Book Discoveries   **By Appointment**
7730 36th Avenue NE 98115   (206) 522-2640

Collection:	General stock.
Specialties:	Biography; travel; science; cookbooks; mystery; science fiction. Most first editions and fine bindings.
# of Vols:	6,000
Services:	Search service, catalog, accepts want lists.
Credit Cards:	No
Owner:	Allan & Phyllis Michaels
Year Estab:	1989

Bowie & Company Booksellers   **Open Shop**
314 First Avenue South 98104   Fax: (206) 223-0966   (206) 624-4100

Collection:	General stock.
# of Vols:	25,000
Hours:	Mon-Sat 10-6. Sun 12-6.
Services:	Appraisals, catalog, search service, accepts want lists.
Travel:	In Pioneer Square area. See Wessel & Lieberman below.
Map Ref:	Map 26c, page 410, #8.
Credit Cards:	Yes
Owner:	M. Taylor Bowie
Year Estab:	1976
Comments:	An immaculate shop where the books are extremely well organized and the shelves well labeled. Regardless of the age of the books, we saw very few that were not in excellent condition. Almost every subject was covered. We saw many collectibles and certainly items that might be considered rare and desirable. A stop here should not disappoint you.

Chameleon   **Open Shop**
514 15th Avenue East 98112   (206) 323-0154

Collection:	General stock of hardcover and paperback.
Specialties:	Art; medicine; Africa.
# of Vols:	10,000-15,000
Hours:	Mon-Fri 11-9. Sat & Sun 11-6.
Services:	Accepts want lists.

(Seattle)

Travel:	Denny St exit off I-5. East on Denny then left on 15th Ave East.
Map Ref:	Map 26a, page 410, #9.
Credit Cards:	Yes
Owner:	Alan D. Frank
Year Estab:	1989
Comments:	A modest sized shop with a neat collection of attractively displayed books. Most of the books we saw were in good to excellent condition and were reasonably priced. Some collectibles on hand as well as an interesting selection (for sale) of African art.

Cinema Books   **Open Shop**
4753 Roosevelt Way NE 98105   (206) 547-7667

Collection:	Specialty books and magazines. Mostly new and some used.
Specialties:	Film; television; theater.
Hours:	Mon-Sat 10-7.
Services:	Catalog, accepts want lists.
Travel:	50th St exit off I-5. Proceed east for three blocks.
Credit Cards:	Yes
Owner:	Stephanie F. Ogle
Year Estab:	1977

Louis Collins Books   **Open Shop**
1211 East Denny Way 98122   Fax: (206) 323-8233   (206) 323-3999

Collection:	General stock.
Specialties:	Anthropology
# of Vols:	10,000
Hours:	Mon-Fri 12-5. Sat by chance or appointment.
Services:	Appraisals, search service, catalog, accepts want lists.
Travel:	Denny exit off I-5. East on Denny. Shop is between 12th & 13th Avenues.
Map Ref:	Map 26a, page 410, #10.
Credit Cards:	Yes
Year Estab:	1969
Comments:	Away from the bustle of downtown Seattle traffic, this is a relatively modest shop with quality titles in quality condition in many areas but particularly strong in its specialty area. Devotees of anthropology should enjoy the pleasure of visiting the two rooms that are devoted exclusively to this subject; they are universal in terms of coverage.

The Comic Character Shop   **By Appointment**
110 Alaskan Way South   (206) 283-0532
Mailing Address: PO Box 99142 Seattle 98199

Collection:	Specialty
Specialties:	Cartoons; animation; children's; illustrated.
Owner:	Dennis Books
Year Estab:	1980

Corner Books
6521 NE 181st Street
Mailing Address: PO Box 82676 Kenmore 98028

Open Shop
(206) 486-6485

Collection: General stock of mostly paperback.
Hours: Mon-Fri 10:30-6. Sat 10:30-5:30. Sun 12-5.

Couth Buzzard Used Books
7221 Greenwood Avenue North 98103

Open Shop
(206) 789-8965

Collection: General stock of paperback and hardcover.
# of Vols: 125,000
Hours: Mon-Thu 12-8. Fri-Sun 10-6.
Travel: 80th St exit off I-5. Proceed west on 80th St, then south on Greenwood to 73rd St.
Map Ref: Map 26e, page 410, #11.
Credit Cards: Yes
Owner: Gerald Lovchik & Marilyn Stauter
Year Estab: 1988
Comments: This shop certainly has volume, including a huge amount of paperbacks. The hardcover books were in mixed condition and represented mixed vintages. Prices were reasonable and the shelves were well labeled. Most of the books were reading copies although we did spot a few scarce and collectible items in our journey down the various aisles.

Don Johnson's Ambience
7700 Greenwood Avenue North 98103

By Appointment
(206) 784-0712

Collection: Specialty books and prints
Specialties: Illustrated; signed.
# of Vols: 2,000+

Fairlook Antiques
81½ South Washington Street 98104

Open Shop
(206) 622-5130

Collection: General stock and ephemera.
# of Vols: 300
Hours: Wed-Sat 10:30-5. Sun 11-4
Travel: In Pioneer Square area between First Ave and Alaskan Way. See Wessel & Lieberman below.
Credit Cards: Yes
Year Estab: 1970

Fantasy Illustrated
8408 Greenwood Avenue North
Mailing address: PO Box 30183 Seattle 98103

Open Shop
(206) 784-7300
Fax: (206) 782-2844

Collection: Specialty
Specialties: Vintage paperbacks; pulps; comics.
Hours: Mon-Fri 11-7. Sat 11-5.
Services: Appraisals, catalog, accepts want lists.
Credit Cards: Yes

(Seattle)

Owner: David Smith
Year Estab: 1979

Fillipi Book & Record Shop
1351 East Olive Way 98122

Open Shop
(206) 682-4266

Collection:	General stock, magazines and records.
# of Vols:	100,000
Hours:	Tue-Sat 10-5.
Travel:	Just off Olive Way exit off I-5.
Map Ref:	Map 26a, page 410, #12.
Credit Cards:	No
Owner:	Brenda & Nikki Fillipi
Year Estab:	1935
Comments:	A hidden jewel with a collection that makes a visit here well worthwhile. One is initially impressed by the number of records on display. However, as you walk around the first floor and then climb to the second floor, you begin to realize that the collection of hardcover books is equally substantial and that every important category is represented in depth by a combination of older and more recent titles. The books are well organized and most reasonably priced. The shop also sells old piano rolls and magazines.

Flora & Fauna Books
121 First Avenue South 98104

Open Shop
(206) 623-4727

Collection:	Specialty. Mostly new and some used.
Specialties:	Horticulture; ornithology; mammalogy; botany; ecology; marine sciences; geology; entomology; nature; art; literature.
Hours:	Mon-Sat 10-6.
Services:	Appraisals, search service, catalog, accepts want lists.
Travel:	In Pioneer Square area. See Wessel & Lieberman below.
Credit Cards:	Yes
Owner:	David Hutchinson
Year Estab:	1983

Folio Books
527 1st Avenue N, #101 98109

By Appointment
(206) 283-9332

Collection:	Specialty
Specialties:	Western Americana; Pacific exploration.
Services:	Catalog
Credit Cards:	No
Owner:	Rip Kirby
Year Estab:	1968

Gemini Book Exchange and Comic Center
9614 16th Avenue SW 98106

Open Shop
(206) 762-5543

Collection:	General stock of paperback, hardcover and comics.

Specialties:	Science fiction; westerns; mystery; adventure.
# of Vols:	50,000+
Hours:	Mon-Sat 10:30-6. Sun 11-3.
Map Ref:	Map 26b, page 410, #13.
Credit Cards:	No
Year Estab:	1972

Globe Bookstore & Bindery

Open Shop

5220B University Way NE 98105

(206) 527-2480

Collection:	General stock of hardcover and paperback.
Specialties:	Eastern philosophy, religion and languages; western philosophy; native Americans; history; literature; travel; exploration; children's; cookbooks; mystery; classics.
# of Vols:	40,000
Hours:	Mon-Sat 11-6. Sun 1-6.
Services:	Appraisals, search service, catalog, accepts want lists, book binding.
Travel:	45th St exit off I-5. Proceed east on 45th St then left on University Way.
Map Ref:	Map 26d, page 410, #14.
Credit Cards:	Yes
Owner:	John & Carolyn Siscoe
Year Estab:	1980
Comments:	A relatively small shop packed full of what we would call "serious" literature and difficult to browse in parts because of the way the books are displayed. A sampling in more subject areas was available but little in the way of volume. Most of the books were of mixed vintage and in good condition. We would estimate the shop as having not more than 15,000-20,000 volumes. If more books were available, they were out of sight.

Golden Age Collectables

Open Shop

1501 Pike Place Market, #401 98101   Fax: (206) 622-2749   (206) 622-9799

Collection:	Specialty
Specialties:	Science fiction; fantasy; horror; pulps; autographs.
Hours:	Mon-Sat 10-5:30. Sun 11-5.
Services:	Appraisals, mail order.
Travel:	Located in Pike Place Market. From I-5 southbound: Stewart St exit. Proceed on Stewart St to Market. From I-5 northbound: Seneca St exit. Follow signs to Market.
Credit Cards:	Yes
Owner:	Roderick Dyke
Year Estab:	1971

Goodwill Store

Open Shop

1400 South Lane Street 98144

(206) 329-1000

Collection:	General stock of hardcover and paperback.
Hours:	Mon-Fri 10-8. Sat 9-5. Sun 10-5.

(Seattle)

Greenwood Books
8536 Greenwood Avenue North 98103

Open Shop
(206) 784-4660

Collection:	General stock of paperback and hardcover.
# of Vols:	25,000
Hours:	Mon-Thu 11-7. Fri & Sat 11-9. Sun 12-6.
Travel:	85th St exit off I-5. Proceed west on 85th St. Right on Greenwood.
Map Ref:	Map 26e, page 410, #15.
Credit Cards:	No
Owner:	Bruce McKinney
Year Estab:	1987
Comments:	Stock is approximately 75% paperback.

Gregor Books
3407 California Avenue SW 98116

Open Shop
Fax: (206) 932-1077   (206) 937-6223

Collection:	General stock of hardcover and some paperback.
Specialties:	Literary first editions; Vietnam War; signed books, literature in translation; authors' first books.
# of Vols:	20,000
Hours:	Mon-Sat 11-7. Sun 12-5.
Services:	Catalog, accepts want lists.
Travel:	Exit 163A off I-5. Proceed west across west Seattle Fwy. Take Admiral Way exit. At intersection of Admiral Way and California Ave turn south on California Ave. Shop is four blocks ahead.
Map Ref:	Map 26b, page 410, #16.
Credit Cards:	Yes
Owner:	David Gregor
Year Estab:	1987
Comments:	A quality shop with an excellent selection of books in the specialties listed above. There are lots of scarce and collectible items here "for the right price."

Half Price Books
4709 Roosevelt Way NE 98105

Open Shop
Fax: (206) 547-1611   (206) 547-7859

Collection:	General stock of used, new and remainders, hardcover and paperback.
# of Vols:	100,000+
Hours:	Daily 10-10.
Travel:	50th St exit off I-5. Proceed east on 50th then south on Roosevelt.
Map Ref:	Map 26d, page 410, #17.
Credit Cards:	Yes
Year Estab:	1972

Helen Harte, Bookseller
6525 51st Avenue NE 98115

By Appointment
(206) 526-5284

Collection:	Specialty
Specialties:	Irish books.
# of Vols:	1,500

Services: Catalog, accepts want lists.
Year Estab: 1981

Horizon Books **Open Shop**
425 15th Avenue East 98112 (206) 329-3586

Collection: General stock of hardcover and paperback.
Specialties: Literature; literary criticism; humanities; philosophy.
# of Vols: 40,000
Hours: Mon-Fri 10-10. Sat & Sun 10-9.
Services: Mail order.
Travel: Denny St exit off I-5. East on Denny. Left on 15th East. Shop is between Harrison and Republican.
Map Ref: Map 26a, page 410, #19.
Credit Cards: Yes
Owner: Donald Glover
Year Estab: 1971
Comments: A store that we enjoyed visiting and, in our judgment, is well worth a stop. The shop is far deeper, both in size and the quality and texture of its books than is initially apparent upon entering. The sections are well organized and labeled (although perhaps a bit too compactly shelved). Most of the books we saw were in quite good condition. We purchased books from the owner by mail many years ago when the shop specialized in science fiction and fantasy and it is clear that over the years the owner has expanded his stock to include strong sections in more scholarly areas. The owner has two other shops by the same name elsewhere in Seattle. (See below)

Horizon Books/Greenwood **Open Shop**
8570 Greenwood Avenue North (206) 781-4680

Collection: General stock of hardcover and paperback.
# of Vols: 25,000+
Hours: Mon-Sat 11-5:30
Travel: Between 85th & 87th Streets.
Map Ref: Map 26e, page 410, #18.
Credit Cards: Yes
Year Estab: 1995

Horizon Books/Roosevelt **Open Shop**
6512 Roosevelt Way NE 98115 (206) 523-4217

Collection: General stock of hardcover and paperback.
# of Vols: 30,000
Hours: Mon-Fri 10-10. Sat & Sun 10-9.
Travel: Between 65th & 67th Streets.
Map Ref: Map 26d, page 410, #20.

Iconoclast Books **Open Shop**
7209 Woodlawn Avenue NE 98115 (206) 525-1619

Collection: General stock of hardcover and paperback.

(Seattle)

Specialties:	Emphasis on literature; poetry; philosophy; cookbooks; travel; eastern religions.
# of Vols:	6,000-7,000
Hours:	Mon-Sat 11-8. Sun 11-3.
Travel:	Northbound on I-5: Ravenna Blvd/65th St exit. Proceed north on Ravenna, then right on Woodlawn. Southbound on I-5: 70th St exit. Proceed right on 70th St, then right on Woodlawn.
Map Ref:	Map 26d, page 410, #21.
Credit Cards:	Yes
Owner:	Henry W. Taylor, III
Year Estab:	1993
Comments:	A small two room shop with the first room devoted to serious literature and scholarly titles and the rear room displaying less serious subjects. The stock was about evenly divided between hardcover volumes (reading copies), paperbacks and trade paperbacks.

David Ishii, Bookseller **Open Shop**
212 First Avenue South 98104 (206) 622-4719

Collection:	General stock.
Specialties:	Western Americana; northwest Americana; Asian Americana; fly fishing; baseball; Japan; China.
# of Vols:	15,000-20,000
Hours:	Mon-Sat 10-6. Sun 10-5.
Services:	Appraisals, search service, mail order.
Travel:	Pioneer Square area. See Wessel & Lieberman below.
Map Ref:	Map 26c, page 410, #22.
Credit Cards:	No
Year Estab:	1972
Comments:	A tightly packed bi-level shop with mostly older volumes representing many subject areas, although not many in great depth. The titles were interesting, the books in mixed condition, and if you don't mind the shop's cluttered appearance, you might well find an item or two worth taking home.

Ladybug Books **Open Shop**
465 North 36th Street 98103 (206) 632-3170

Collection:	General stock of paperback and hardcover.
Hours:	Wed-Sun 12-6. Other times by appointment. Closed in Jan.
Services:	Accepts want lists, mail order.
Travel:	45th St exit off I-5. West on 45th St, left on Fremont, right on 36th St.
Map Ref:	Map 26e, page 410, #23.
Credit Cards:	No
Owner:	Kirby Lindsay
Year Estab:	1992
Comments:	Stock is approximately 55% paperback.

Lake City Books **Open Shop**
11032 Lake City Way NE 98125 (206) 363-3232

Collection:	General stock.
Specialties:	History; military; travel.
# of Vols:	1,000+
Hours:	Mon-Fri 11-5. Sat 12-4.
Services:	Accepts want lists.
Travel:	From I-5 northbound: Lake City Way NE exit. Proceed north on Lake City Way. Shop is set back from road.
Map Ref:	Map 26d, page 410, #24.
Credit Cards:	No
Owner:	F. Ghoddousi, owner. David Ghoddousi, manager
Year Estab:	1992
Comments:	When we visit book dealers who display in antique malls, we frequently find that the books are older, sometimes (but not too often) unusual, often not in the best condition and generally not in very significant numbers. (Of course, there are always exceptions.) At least on such trips we know what to expect and we often get to see some interesting collectibles at the other booths. If you decide to visit here, you'll probably see as many non book collectibles as books and the few books you will see will make you almost wish you were at an antique mall.

Left Bank Books **Open Shop**
92 Pike Street 98101 (206) 622-0195

Collection:	General stock of new and primarily paperback used.
Hours:	Mon-Sat 10-9. Sun 12-6. Hours vary slightly depending on season. Best to call ahead.

Leisure Books **Open Shop**
4461 California Avenue SW 98116 (206) 935-7325

Collection:	General stock of paperback and hardcover.
# of Vols:	10,000
Hours:	Mon-Sat 10-6, except Fri till 7. Sun 10-6.
Services:	Accepts want lists, mail order.
Travel:	West Seattle Fwy to end, then right on Oregon. Shop is at corner of Oregon and California.
Map Ref:	Map 26b, page 410, #25.
Credit Cards:	Yes
Owner:	Margarita & Curtis Clement
Year Estab:	1989
Comments:	A community bookshop with hardcover volumes of mostly recent vintage (many representing best selling authors) and in very good condition. Some collectibles but most items were basically reading copies.

Magus, Inc. **Open Shop**
1408 NE 42nd Street 98105 (206) 633-1800

Collection:	General stock of paperback and hardcover.

(Seattle)

# of Vols:	65,000
Hours:	Mon-Wed 10-8. Thu & Fri 10-10. Sat 11-6. Sun 12-8.
Travel:	45th St exit off I-5. East on 45th, right on University Way and left on 42nd.
Map Ref:	Map 26d, page 410, #27.
Credit Cards:	Yes
Owner:	David L. Bell
Year Estab:	1978
Comments:	This shop offers a large number of books, both paperbacks and hardcover (mostly reading copies). The shelves are well labeled and easy to browse. Most subjects are covered. While most of the books we saw were in reasonably good condition, the manner in which they were displayed gave us the impression that some of them had seen better days. Some worthwhile items if you know your field.

Michael Maslan Historic Photographs, Postcards & Ephemera   Open Shop
1216 Third Avenue   (206) 587-0187
Mailing Address: PO Box 20639 Seattle 989102

Collection:	General stock of ephemera.
Specialties:	Western Americana.
Hours:	Mon-Wed 11:30-5. Thu, Fri and weekends by chance or appointment.
Services:	Accepts want lists.
Travel:	Downtown Seattle.
Credit Cards:	Yes
Year Estab:	1980's

Robert W. Mattila, Bookseller   Open Shop
121 First Avenue South   (206) 622-9455
Mailing Address: PO Box 4038 Seattle 98104

Collection:	Specialty
Specialties:	Alaska; Arctic; Antarctic; Washington; WPA.
# of Vols:	2,000
Hours:	Mon-Sat 10-6.
Services:	Appraisals, catalog, accepts want lists.
Travel:	In Pioneer Square area. See Wessel & Lieberman below.
Credit Cards:	Yes
Year Estab:	1976

MisterE Books   Open Shop
1501 Pike Place Market, #432 98101   (206) 622-5182

Collection:	General stock of new and used paperback and hardcover and records.
Specialties:	Mystery; some modern first editions.
# of Vols:	10,000
Hours:	Daily 9:30-5:30.
Services:	Appraisals, search service, accepts want lists, catalog.
Travel:	First floor "down under" in Pike Place Market.

Map Ref: Map 26c, page 410, #28.
Credit Cards: Yes
Owner: Ed Leimbacher & Sandra Wilcox
Year Estab: 1992
Comments: The shop is actually more of a general new book store that also carries some older used items, including some vintage mysteries and related items behind glass. Whether or not your visit to this shop proves fruitful, if you have any sense of fun, adventure or curiosity, you should plan to spend an hour or two wandering through the many levels of the market. You'll find the experience unique indeed.

Mountainbooks **By Appointment**
PO Box 27734 98125 Fax: (206) 365-9106   (206) 365-9192

Collection: Specialty
Specialties: Mountaineering
# of Vols: 8,000-9,000
Services: Search service, appraisals, accepts want lists.
Credit Cards: No
Owner: John Pollock
Year Estab: 1979

Multi Books **Open Shop**
4748-A University Way NE 98105 (206) 522-2488

Collection: General stock of hardcover and paperback.
Specialties: Vintage paperbacks; multilingual books and tapes (new and used).
# of Vols: 10,000
Hours: Mon-Fri 10-8. Sat 10-6. Sun 12-6.
Services: Search service, accepts want lists, mail order.
Travel: Exit 169 (50th St west) off I-5. Proceed east on 50th. Shop is on south corner of University Way and 50th NE.
Map Ref: Map 26d, page 410, #37.
Credit Cards: Yes
Owner: Tom Tomkins
Year Estab: 1992
Comments: We visited this shop just prior to the owner's reorganization. The hardcover books we saw were of mixed vintage and in mixed condition. We noted several items that fell into the collectible category and believe that while the number of volumes on display is limited, there are certainly titles here that a discriminating book person might want to walk away with.

Mysteries Unlimited **Open Shop**
18820 Aurora Avenue North 98133 (206) 546-8853

Collection: Specialty. Mostly paperback.
Specialties: Mystery; science fiction.
Hours: Tue-Fri 12-7. Sat & Sun 11-5.

(Seattle)

Open Books: A Poem Emporium
2414 North 45th Street

Open Shop
(206) 633-0811

Collection:	Specialty new and used.
Specialties:	Poetry and poetry related subjects, e.g., biographies of poets.
# of Vols:	3,500
Hours:	Mon-Sat 11-6, except Fri till 8.
Travel:	In Wallingford district between Sunnyside and Eastern.
Credit Cards:	Yes
Owner:	John Marshall
Year Estab:	1988
Comments:	Stock is approximately 30% used.

Page 2 Book Exchange
15706 First Avenue South 98148

Open Shop
(206) 248-7248

Collection:	General stock of mostly paperback.
Hours:	Mon-Sat 9:30-6. Sun 12-5.

Pegasus Book Exchange
4553 California Avenue SW 98116

Open Shop
(206) 937-5410

Collection:	General stock of paperback and hardcover.
Hours:	Mon-Sat 10-6. Sun 12-5.
Travel:	West Seattle Fwy exit off I-5. Continue on freeway (which becomes Alaska) to California. Right on California.
Map Ref:	Map 26b, page 410, #29.
Credit Cards:	Yes
Owner:	Fred Epps
Year Estab:	1980
Comments:	Stock is approximately 75% paperback.

Pioneer Square Books
213 First Avenue South 98117

Open Shop
(206) 343-2665

Collection:	General stock of hardcover and paperback.
Specialties:	Science fiction; mystery; art; nature; cookbooks; general fiction.
# of Vols:	40,000
Hours:	Mon-Sat 10-6. Sun 12-6.
Services:	Accepts want lists, mail order.
Travel:	In Pioneer Square area. See Wessel & Lieberman below.
Map Ref:	Map 26c, page 410, #30.
Credit Cards:	Yes
Owner:	Steve Zemke
Year Estab:	1992
Comments:	A moderate sized "general shop," quite heavy in paperbacks, with reading copies of mostly recent hardcover items. The shelves are well labeled and hold a limited number of selections in many different categories. Fine for the average reader looking for something that is not very scarce.

Pistil Books & News
1013 East Pike 98122

Open Shop
(206) 325-5401

Collection:	General stock of paperback and hardcover.
Specialties:	Literature; poetry; erotica; gay and lesbian; art.
# of Vols:	20,000
Hours:	Daily 10-10, except till midnight on Fri & Sat.
Services:	Accepts want lists.
Travel:	James St/Cherry St exit off I-5. Proceed east to 12th Ave, left on 12th to East Pike. Shop is between 10th & 11th.
Map Ref:	Map 26a, page 410, #31.
Credit Cards:	Yes
Owner:	Amy Candiotti & Sean Carlson
Year Estab:	1993
Comments:	A small shop located in Seattle's "alternative lifestyles" neighborhood with a mixed collection of paperbacks and hardcover volumes, as well as magazines (new) and newspapers. The number of hardcover books on hand does not allow for depth in many subjects except the shop's specialties. If these are of interest to you, this is your shop.

The Play's The Thing
514 East Pike 98122

Open Shop
(206) 322-7529

Collection:	Specialty new and used hardcover and paperback.
Specialties:	Theater
# of Vols:	Limited (used)
Hours:	Mon & Tue 10-10. Wed-Sun 12-5.
Travel:	Madison St exit off I-5. Proceed east on Madison than north on Summit.
Credit Cards:	Yes
Owner:	Robin Kilrain
Year Estab:	1990
Comments:	Used stock is approximately 50% paperback.

Rainy Day Books
8329 15th Avenue NW 98117

Open Shop
(206) 783-3383

Collection:	General stock of primarily paperback.
Hours:	Tue-Sat 11-4.

Ravenna Rare Books
5639 University Way NE 98105

By Appointment
Fax: (206) 525-3777   (206) 525-3737

Collection:	General stock and ephemera.
Specialties:	History of law and crime; autobiography; food history; oddities and eccentricities of human behavior.
# of Vols:	15,000
Services:	Appraisals, search service, accepts want lists.
Credit Cards:	No
Owner:	Russell Johanson
Year Estab:	1971

(Seattle)

Recollection Fine Used Books
4519 University Way NE 98105

Open Shop
(206) 548-1346

Collection:	General stock of hardcover and paperback.
# of Vols:	25,000
Hours:	Mon-Sat 11-9. Sun 12-6.
Services:	Search service, accepts want lists, catalog.
Travel:	45th St exit off I-5. East on 45th, then left on University Way.
Map Ref:	Map 26d, page 410, #32.
Credit Cards:	No
Owner:	David Brown
Year Estab:	1995 (See Comments)
Comments:	A recently established quality shop owned by an experienced book person (formerly the owner of a.k.a. Books). The bi-level shop offers good copies of books in almost every category ranging from scholarly items to more popular titles. Most of the books we saw were in quite good condition, nicely displayed and reasonably priced. Some collectibles.

Red & Black Book Collective
432 15th Avenue, East 98112

Open Shop
(206) 322-7323

Collection:	Specialty. Primarily new.
Specialties:	Homosexuality.
# of Vols:	Limited used stock
Hours:	Mon-Thu 10-8. Fri & Sat 10-9. Sun 11-7.

Allen Sarno Books About Latin America
5510 37th Avenue NE
Mailing Address: PO Box 45154 Seattle 98105

By Appointment
(206) 527-6319
Fax: (206) 524-3430

Collection:	Specialty
Specialties:	Latin America: All areas of interest. Popular and scholarly works.
# of Vols:	2,000+
Services:	Appraisals, search service, catalog, accepts want lists.
Credit Cards:	No
Year Estab:	1991

Seattle Book Center
3530 Stone Way North 98103

Open Shop
(206) 547-7870

Collection:	General stock.
Specialties:	History; science fiction; philately.
# of Vols:	15,000
Hours:	Mon-Sat 10-6. Sun 11-4.
Services:	Catalog, accepts want lists.
Travel:	45th St NE exit off I-5. Proceed west on 45th St to Stone Way. Left at light and proceed nine blocks to 36th and Stone Way.
Map Ref:	Map 26e, page 410, #33.
Credit Cards:	Yes

Owner: John Polley & Al Worden
Year Estab: 1980
Comments: Susan had to drag me kicking and screaming from this store after spending considerable time here buying fewer books that I would have liked to and still not being satisfied that I had seen all of the titles of the books that were of interest to me. It was just time to move on. The shop is not enormous; only four or five small rooms. However, the quality of the stock in the specialties listed above, as well as the general stock, was such that true book aficionados will want to visit here. You will not be disappointed. Prices reflect the difficulty of finding some of the titles.

Seattle Mystery Bookshop **Open Shop**
117 Cherry Street 98104 (206) 587-5737

Collection:	Specialty new and used, paperback and hardcover.
Specialties:	Mystery; detective.
# of Vols:	10,000
Hours:	Mon-Sat 11-6, Sun 12-5.
Services:	Search service, accepts want lists, mail order, newsletter.
Travel:	James St exit off I-5. West on James to end. Right on First. Right on Cherry.
Credit Cards:	Yes
Owner:	Bill Farley
Year Estab:	1990
Comments:	Stock is approximately 70% new and 60% paperback. The used stock includes both collectibles and reading copies.

Shorey's Book Store **Open Shop**
1109 North 36th Street 98103 * * (206) 624-0221

Collection:	General stock, ephemera and magazines.
# of Vols:	750,000
Hours:	Mon-Sat 10-6. Sun 12-6.
Services:	Appraisals, search service, catalog, accepts want lists.
Travel:	45th St exit off I-5. West on 45th, left on Stone Way and right on 36th.
Map Ref:	Map 26e, page 410, #34.
Owner:	John W. Todd
Year Estab:	1890
Comments:	When we had the good fortune of visiting this shop, viewing its collection and chatting briefly with its owner, we learned that the shop would be moving to a new location (the above address). While we can't comment on the new site, we're told that it will be a larger stand alone building with its own parking. We can only believe that a visit to this new site will be even more pleasant for the dedicated bookaholic than our visit to its former location where we enjoyed browsing a huge collection of well organized, mixed vintage, reasonably priced hardcover books.

* The new location will be operational on or about December 1, 1995. The phone number may change.

(Seattle)

Signature Bound Bookseller
2222 Second Avenue 98121

Open Shop
(206) 441-3306

Collection:	General stock of paperback and hardcover.
Specialties:	20th century fiction; beat generation; poetry; art; drama; French language.
# of Vols:	40,000
Hours:	Mon-Fri 10-6. Sat 12-6. Sun 12-5:30.
Services:	Appraisals, catalog, accepts want lists.
Travel:	Downtown, between Blanchard and Bell Streets.
Map Ref:	Map 26c, page 410, #35.
Credit Cards:	No
Owner:	Dean Wynveen & Gregor Jamroski
Year Estab:	1992
Comments:	On the morning we attempted to visit this shop, Second Avenue was undergoing some construction work and although most of the shops on the street were open, a sign on the door of this shop advised its customers that during construction the shop's regular hours would be changed to 2-8pm. Looking through the front window there was no way we could comment on the quality of the books inside, except to say that they appeared to be neatly shelved and that the store appeared to be "well cared for."

Kirk Stines Collectible Books & Toys
5119½ 27th NE 98105

By Appointment
(206) 524-5355

Collection:	Specialty
Specialties:	Children's
# of Vols:	300
Services:	Appraisals, search service, accepts want lists, mail order.
Year Estab:	1985

Titlewave Books
7 Mercer Street 98109

Open Shop
(206) 282-7687

Collection:	General stock of hardcover and paperback.
Specialties:	Arts; literature; cooking; children's.
# of Vols:	30,000+
Hours:	Tue-Sat 10:30-7, except Fri till 10. Sun 12-6. Memorial Day-Christmas: Also open Mon 12-6.
Services:	Search service, accepts want lists, mail order.
Travel:	Queen Anne district, between First Ave North and Queen Anne Ave North.
Map Ref:	Map 26b, page 410, #36.
Credit Cards:	Yes
Owner:	Nickie Jostol
Year Estab:	1985
Comments:	A moderate sized shop that looks like it sells new books because its books, most of which were of recent vintage, were in such nice condition. At least one third of the stock was paperback. While many subjects were covered, few were covered in great depth.

George H. Tweney, Antiquarian Bookseller   By Appointment
16660 Marine View Drive SW 98166   (206) 243-8243

Collection:	Specialty books and ephemera.
Specialties:	Western Americana; voyages; exploration; Lewis & Clark; bibliography; books about books.
# of Vols:	3,000
Services:	Mail order.
Credit Cards:	No
Owner:	George H. & Maxine R. Tweney
Year Estab:	1959

Twice Sold Tales/Capitol   Open Shop
905 East John Street 98102   (206) 324-2421

Collection:	General stock of hardcover and paperback and some new.
Specialties:	Literature; new age; philosophy; esoterica, "general weird stuff."
# of Vols:	60,000
Hours:	Mon-Thu & Sat 10-2 am. Fri - 24 hours. Sun 10am-midnight.
Travel:	Olive Way exit off I-5. Proceed east on Olive to Broadway. Shop is first shop on right after Broadway. (Note: Olive becomes John after crossing Broadway.)
Map Ref:	Map 26a, page 410, #40.
Credit Cards:	Yes
Owner:	Jamie Lutton
Year Estab:	1990
Comments:	Most of the hardcover volumes we saw were in good to better condition, of more recent vintage and reasonably priced. The owner, who has two other similar shops with the same name elsewhere in Seattle (see below), has a most vivacious personality and if you're fortunate enough to meet her, you should enjoy hearing some of her "biblio-war" stories.

Twice Sold Tales/Downtown   Open Shop
815 First Avenue   (206) 625-1611

Collection:	General stock of hardcover and paperback.
# of Vols:	50,000
Hours:	Mon-Fri 8-8. Sat & Sun 12-6.
Travel:	Near Marion.
Map Ref:	Map 26c, page 410, #38.
Credit Cards:	Yes
Year Estab:	1994

Twice Sold Tales/Wallingford   Open Shop
2210 North 45th Street 98103   (206) 545-4226

Collection:	General stock of hardcover, paperback and some new.
# of Vols:	25,000
Hours:	Sun-Thu 12-8. Fri 12-10. Sat 10-10.
Travel:	Near Bagley.
Map Ref:	Map 26e, page 410, #26.

(Seattle)

Credit Cards: Yes
Year Estab: 1992

Vandewater Books
1716 North 45th 98103

Open Shop
(206) 633-3040

Collection:	General stock of paperback and hardcover.
# of Vols:	5,000-6,000
Hours:	Sun & Mon 10-6. Tue-Sat 10-8.
Services:	Accepts want lists.
Travel:	45th St exit off I-5. Proceed west on 45th.
Map Ref:	Map 26e, page 410, #41.
Credit Cards:	No
Owner:	Marla Vandewater
Year Estab:	1994
Comments:	A nice bi-level shop with a good, although limited, collection about equally divided between hardcover books in good condition and of good quality and paperbacks. Prices are most reasonable.

Wessel & Lieberman Booksellers
121 First Avenue South 98104

Open Shop
(206) 682-3545

Collection:	General stock.
Specialties:	Pacific Northwest; Western Americana; native Americana; books about books; book arts; literary first editions; poetry.
# of Vols:	10,000
Hours:	Mon-Sat 10-6. Other times by appointment.
Services:	Appraisals search service, catalog, accepts want lists.
Travel:	In Pioneer Square area. From I-5 southbound: James St exit. Proceed west on James to First Ave. From I-5 northbound: Fourth Ave south exit. Left at bottom of ramp onto Jackson, then left on Jackson and right on First.
Map Ref:	Map 26c, page 410, #42.
Credit Cards:	Yes
Owner:	Michael Lieberman & Mark Wessel
Year Estab:	1993
Comments:	A shop that looks very much like a specialized library/art gallery with quality titles and a heavy emphasis in the shop's specialties. Almost without exception the volumes were in pristine condition. What adds most positively to a visit here are the many attractive exhibits of book art.

Westside Stories
12 Boston Street 98109

Open Shop
(206) 285-2665

Collection:	General stock of mostly used hardcover and paperback.
Specialties:	Emphasis is on the arts.
# of Vols:	10,000
Hours:	Tue, Wed, Fri, Sat 10-6. Thu & Sun 12-5.
Services:	Search service, accepts want lists.

Travel: At northeast corner of Boston and Queen Anne Ave.
Map Ref: Map 26, page 410, #43.
Credit Cards: Yes
Owner: Beth Dunn
Year Estab: 1992
Comments: Stock is approximately 50% hardcover.

Sedro Woolley

Best Read Books **Open Shop**
122 State Street 98284 (360) 855-2179

Collection: General stock of mostly used paperback.
Hours: Mon-Fri 10-5. Sat 10-2.

Selah
(Map 25, page 433)

Olympic Supply - Used Book Store **Open Shop**
414 South 1st Street 98942 (509) 697-8239

Collection: General stock of paperback and hardcover.
# of Vols: 30,000+
Hours: Mon-Sat, except closed Thu, 10-6.
Travel: Selah exit off I-82. Proceed east to Harrison Rd, then east on Harrison, south on Wenas Rd, and east on Waches and south on First.
Owner: Kay Shemanski
Year Estab: 1991
Comments: Stock is approximately 70% paperback.

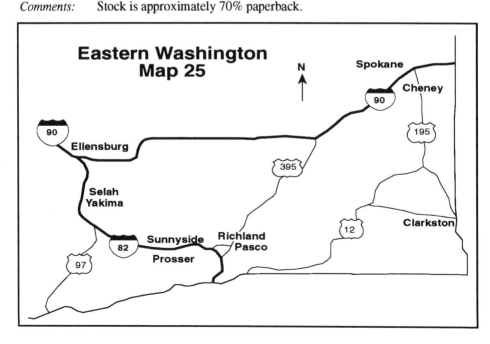

Silverdale
(Map 28, page 387)

Pages Books — **Open Shop**
10406 Silverdale Way NW 98366 — (360) 692-3352

Collection:	General stock of used and new.
# of Vols:	25,000 (used)
Hours:	Mon-Sat 10-6. Sun 12-4.
Travel:	Newberry Hill Rd off Hwy 3. North on Newberry which becomes Silverdale Way.
Credit Cards:	Yes
Owner:	Denise Myers
Year Estab:	1987
Comments:	Stock is approximately 70% paperback.

Snohomish
(Map 28, page 387)

Paper Horn — **Antique Mall**
At Star Center Antique Mall, 829 2nd Street — Mall: (206) 402-1870
Mailing Address: 8235 Interlake North Seattle 98103 — Home: (206) 527-1123

Collection:	Specialty books and ephemera.
Specialties:	Children's series.
# of Vols:	300+
Hours:	Sun-Fri 10-5. Sat 10-8.
Services:	Accepts want lists, mail order.
Travel:	See Upper Case Books below.
Credit Cards:	Yes
Owner:	Darrell Lehman
Year Estab:	1983
Comments:	Collection can also be viewed by appointment.

Upper Case Books — **Open Shop**
121 Glen Avenue, #3 98290 — (360) 568-5987

Collection:	General stock of hardcover and paperback.
# of Vols:	50,000
Hours:	Daily 11-6.
Services:	Search service, accepts want lists, mail order.
Travel:	From Everett, Snohomish exit off Hwy 2. Proceed on Avenue D to 2nd St. Left on 2nd, right on Union, left on Glen.
Credit Cards:	Yes
Owner:	Dee Halley
Year Estab:	1989
Comments:	A crowded shop with a reasonable supply of vintage hardcover books, including some good titles that could be considered collectible. The collection did not appear, to us at least, to be strong in any one area. No distinction was made between various forms of fiction e.g., literature and mystery were shelved together.

Spokane
(Map 25, page 433)

Agathon Books
PO Box 8645 99203

By Appointment
(509) 624-5624

Collection:	Specialty
Specialties:	Modern first editions; signed; 19th & 20th century literature; philosophy.
# of Vols:	3,000
Services:	Appraisals, catalog, accepts want lists.
Owner:	Scott Kramer & Deborah Kyle
Year Estab:	1989

The Arthur H. Clark Company
9017 East Euclid
Mailing Address: PO Box 14707 Spokane 99214

Open Shop
(509) 928-9540
Fax: (509) 928-4364

Collection:	Specialty books and some ephemera.
Specialties:	Western Americana.
# of Vols:	15,000
Hours:	Mon-Fri 8:30-4:30. Sat by appointment.
Services:	Appraisals, search service, catalog, accepts want lists.
Travel:	Argonne exit off I-90. Proceed north on Argonne, then left at Euclid.
Credit Cards:	Yes
Owner:	Robert A. Clark
Year Estab:	1902

Auntie's Bookstore
402 West Main 99201

Open Shop
(509) 838-0206

Collection:	General stock of new and mostly used paperback.
Hours:	Mon-Sat 9-9. Sun 11-5.

Clark's Book Store
12724 East Sprague Avenue 99216

Open Shop
(509) 924-0737

Collection:	General stock of hardcover and paperback.
Specialties:	Western Americana; military.
# of Vols:	16,000+
Hours:	Call for hours.
Services:	Accepts want lists, search service.
Travel:	Pines exit off I-90. Proceed south on Pines, then left on Sprague.
Credit Cards:	No
Owner:	Robert Hammer
Year Estab:	1910
Comments:	Stock is approximately 60% hardcover.

Cal's Books
N 2174 Hamilton 99207

Open Shop
(509) 487-1206

Collection:	General stock of primarily paperback.
Hours:	Mon-Fri 9-6. Sat 9-5.

Inland Bookstore   **Open Shop**
123 South Wall Street 99204   (509) 624-9064

Collection: General stock of hardcover and paperback.
# of Vols: 25,000-30,000
Hours: Mon-Sat 12-6 and some evenings.
Travel: Division St exit off I-90. Proceed north on Division, left on 2nd St and right on Wall. Shop is between 1st & 2nd St.
Credit Cards: No
Owner: Jerome Carlson
Year Estab: 1955
Comments: Stock is evenly divided between paperback and hardcover.

2nd Look Books   **Open Shop**
2829 East 29th Avenue 99223   Fax: (509) 448-1491 (509) 535-6316

Collection: General stock of paperback and hardcover.
# of Vols: 88,000
Hours: Mon-Fri 9-9. Sat 9-8. Sun 11-6.
Services: Search service, accepts want lists (but please call first), mail order.
Travel: Exit 283B (Freya St/Thor St) off I-90. Proceed south on Thor up hill to light at 29th St. Right on 29th for three blocks to Regal, then turn into shopping center.
Credit Cards: Yes
Owner: Ann Simpson & Terry Gregory
Year Estab: 1982
Comments: Stock is approximately 75% paperback.

Sunnyside
(Map 25, page 433)

First Edition Books   **Open Shop**
2010 Yakima Valley Highway 98944   (509) 839-2665

Collection: General stock of hardcover and paperback.
# of Vols: 10,000
Hours: Mon-Fri 10-8. Sat 10-6. Sun 12-5.
Travel: Exit 69 off I-82. Proceed north on Yakima Valley Hwy for about two miles. Shop is on right in Mid Valley Mall.
Credit Cards: Yes
Owner: Donna VanRuiten
Year Estab: 1993
Comments: Stock is approximately 60% hardcover.

Tacoma
(Map 27, page 438 & Map 28, page 387)

AJ's Cookbooks   **By Appointment**
PO Box 45375 98444   Fax: (206) 537-4899 (206) 537-4899

Collection: Specialty

Specialties: Cookbooks.
Services: Appraisals, search service, catalog, accepts want lists.
Credit Cards: Yes
Owner: Anna Davis
Year Estab: 1990

Book Feire
3818 North 26th Street 98407

Open Shop
(206) 759-4680

Collection: General stock of new and used hardcover and paperback.
Hours: 10-6 Mon-Fri. Call for weekend hours.
Travel: At Proctor.
Comments: A store in transition in terms of the types of books and other products it will be selling. Even the name may change. We suggest you call ahead to verify the hours as well as the current mix of books.

Fox Book Co.
737 St. Helens Avenue 98402

Open Shop
(206) 627-2223

Collection: General stock.
Specialties: Northwest Americana; sets; first editions.
# of Vols: 100,000
Hours: Mon-Sat 10-6.
Services: Catalog
Travel: City Center exit off I-5, then A St exit. Left on 9th, right on St. Helens.
Map Ref: Map 27, page 438, #1.
Credit Cards: Yes
Owner: Barbara Fox
Year Estab: 1939
Comments: A nice solid used book shop with a quality stock. Well organized and more than a few truly rare and collectible items. In our view well worth a visit. (At the time of our visit, the number of books on display was less than the number noted above.)

Half Price Books, Records, Magazines
6409 Sixth Avenue, Ste M 98406

Open Shop
(206) 566-1238

Collection: General stock of new, used and remainders.
Hours: Mon-Sat 10-10. Sun 12-8.
Travel: See Ye Olde Book Peddler below. Shop is in Discovery Place Shopping Center between Mildred & Pearl.
Map Ref: Map 27, page 438, #2

Know Thy Self Afrikan Book Center
317 South 11th Street 98405

Open Shop
(206) 572-8186

Collection: Specialty
Specialties: Black studies.
Hours: Tue-Sat 10-7.

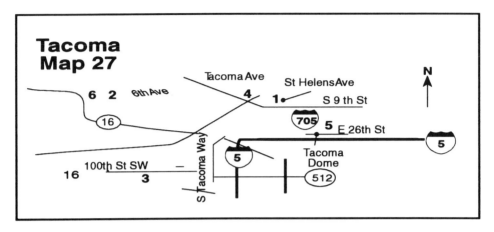

Lady Jayne's Comics and Books
5969 Sixth Avenue 98406

Open Shop
(206) 564-6168

Collection: Specialty new and used. Primarily paperback.
Specialties: Science fiction; fantasy.
Hours: Mon-Fri 10-8. Sat 10-6. Sun 12-5.

O'Leary's Books
3828 100th Street SW 98499

Open Shop
Fax: (206) 589-9115   (206) 588-2503

Collection: General stock of paperback, hardcover, comics, collectibles, magazines and records.
# of Vols: 20,000 (hardcover)
Hours: Mon-Fri 9-9. Sat 10-9. Sun 10-6. Closed only Christmas, July 4th, Thanksgiving and Easter.
Services: Mail order.
Travel: Exit 127 (South Tacoma Way) off I-5. Right on South Tacoma Way, then left at first light (100th St). Shop is 1/2 block ahead on left.
Map Ref: Map 27, page 438, #3.
Credit Cards: Yes
Owner: Ron & Barbara Trimble
Year Estab: 1977
Comments: About 40% of the stock in this shop consists of used paperbacks and comics with an additional 20% devoted to new paperbacks, magazines and other new items. The remaining 40% consists of used hardcover books, most in good condition, and including some vintage items. On balance, the hardcover selection is large enough to satisfy most tastes and is definitely worth browsing if you're in Tacoma.

Quiet Companion Books
21 Tacoma Avenue North 98403

Open Shop
(206) 272-2929

Collection: General stock of hardcover and paperback.
Specialties: Economics; Pacific northwest.
# of Vols: 45,000

Hours: Mon-Sat 10:30-6:30.
Services: Appraisals, accepts want lists.
Travel: City Center exit off I-5 to Stadium Way exit. Right on Stadium and proceed four blocks. Left on Tacoma Ave.
Map Ref: Map 27, page 438, #4.
Credit Cards: No
Owner: Jesse B. Jolibois
Year Estab: 1975
Comments: On the day we visited Tacoma, we found the shop closed and a sign on the window announcing that the owner was having a moving sale. We hope that if you visit the shop at its new location (listed above), you'll find it open.

Swans's Comic & Magazine Mart
2608 6th Avenue 98406

Open Shop
(206) 627-3028

Collection: Specialty
Specialties: Magazines dating back to pre-1900; vintage paperbacks; pulps; private press; H. Werner Mun.
Hours: Sat 10-5. Weekdays by appointment or chance.
Owner: Charles Burris
Year Estab: 1930

Tacoma Book Center
324 East 26th Street 98421

Open Shop
(206) 572-8248

Collection: General stock of hardcover and paperback and remainders.
Specialties: Children's; military; literature; mystery.
# of Vols: 200,000
Hours: Mon-Sat 10-6. Sun 12-5.
Travel: Tacoma Dome exit off I-5. Right at end of exit ramp onto 26th St. Shop is 1½ blocks ahead. Parking is available on side of building.
Map Ref: Map 27, page 438, #5.
Credit Cards: No
Owner: Larry Jezek & David Killian
Year Estab: 1983
Comments: The largest used book dealer in Tacoma. Plan to come early and spend a good deal of time. The shelves are well labeled, not only by subject but frequently also by author or sub category. The books are in generally very good condition and are moderately priced. The majority of the books are of recent vintage but there were some oldies. The one constructive criticism we could make is that there could have been more ladders as many of the bookcases are very high and sighting titles on the upper shelves can be a problem. (There were lots of stools but alas, unless you're very tall, these didn't provide enough extra height to reach the upper most shelves.)

Ye Olde Book Peddler
6603 6th Avenue 98406

Open Shop
(206) 564-3932

Collection: General stock of hardcover and paperback.

# of Vols:	15,000
Hours:	Mon-Fri 11-6. Sat 11-5.
Services:	Search service, mail order.
Travel:	6th Ave exit off Hwy 16. Shop is on right at corner of Mildred St.
Map Ref:	Map 27, page 438, #6.
Credit Cards:	Yes
Owner:	Becky Koertge
Year Estab:	1994
Comments:	The hardcover books were not shelved in any discernibly rational manner (e.g., biography, humor and fiction were all mixed together) and several were priced higher than we have seen in many other shops in the same or better condition. The shop does offer some collectibles. If you live in the area or are traveling through, stop by. If you're thinking of making a special trip, think twice.

Tonasket

Hidden Treasures Open Shop
31580 Highway 97 North (509) 486-4496
Mailing Address: PO Box 424 Tonasket 98855

Collection:	General stock of mostly new and some used.
# of Vols:	100 (used)
Hours:	Mon-Sat 9:30-5:30.

Tukwila
(Map 28, page 387)

Goodwill Store Open Shop
1174 Andover Park 98188 (206) 575-4944

Collection:	General stock of hardcover and paperback.
Hours:	Mon-Sat 10-8. Sun 11-6.

Half Price Books, Records, Magazines Open Shop
16828 Southcenter Parkway 98188 (206) 575-3173

Collection:	General stock of new, used and remainders.
Hours:	Daily 9am-10pm.
Travel:	Located in a strip mall near Strander.

Vancouver
(Map 22, page 366 & Map 20, page 345)

The Book Worm Open Shop
13023 NE Highway 99 98686 (360) 573-0426

Collection:	General stock of mostly used paperback and hardcover.
# of Vols:	30,000

Hours: Mon-Fri 11-7. Sat 10-5. Sun 1-4.
Travel: 134th St exit off I-5. Shop is located in Salmon Creek Plaza.
Credit Cards: No
Owner: Mary Santa
Year Estab: 1983
Comments: Stock is approximately 75% used, 65% of which is paperback.

Cardinal Books **By Appointment**
4010 NE 136th Street 98686   Fax: (360) 576-0475   (360) 576-9070

Collection: Specialty
Specialties: Mystery; detective.
# of Vols: 8,000
Services: Catalog, accepts want lists.
Credit Cards: No
Owner: Larry & Linda Johnson
Year Estab: 1986
Comments: Stock is primarily used hardcover titles.

C. Dave's Books **Open Shop**
109 West 7th St 98660   (360) 699-6239

Collection: General stock of new and used paperback and hardcover.
Hours: Mon-Fri 10-5:30. Sat 10-4.
Comments: Stock is about 50% used, 75% of which is paperback.

Dick Perier Books **By Appointment**
PO Box 1 98666   (360) 696-2033

Collection: Specialty
Specialties: Alaska; Pacific Northwest; Western Americana; cookbooks.
# of Vols: 5,000
Services: Catalog, accepts want lists.
Credit Cards: No
Year Estab: 1971

The 2nd Generation **Open Shop**
1911 Main Street 98660   (206) 695-5291

Collection: General stock of hardcover and paperback.
# of Vols: 5,000-7,000
Hours: Tue-Sat 11-5:30.
Services: Search service, accepts want lists.
Map Ref: Map 22, page 366, #28.
Credit Cards: No
Owner: Carol Tappe
Year Estab: 1994
Comments: A nice little shop with a small but healthy collection of hardcover titles, including some vintage items. Most of the books were in reasonably good condition. The haystack here was small enough for us to have been able to find one worthwhile needle. We wish you equal or better luck.

(Vancouver)

Second Hand Prose
713 Grand Boulevard 98661

Open Shop
(360) 693-9344

Collection:	General stock of paperback and hardcover.
# of Vols:	60,000+
Hours:	Mon-Sat 10:15-5.
Travel:	From Hwy 14, at light turn north on Grand Blvd. Shop is at intersection of Grand and Evergreen.
Map Ref:	Map 22, page 366, #30.
Credit Cards:	No
Owner:	Sally Jewett
Year Estab:	1986
Comments:	Stock is approximately 70% paperback.

Spencers Bookstore
10411 NE 4th Plain, Ste. 126 98662

Open Shop
(360) 892-9862

Collection:	General stock of mostly paperback.
Hours:	Mon 10-5. Tue-Fri 10-8. Sat 10-4.

Uptown Bookshelf
2312 Main Street   Fax: (360) 254-7245

Open Shop
(360) 699-1636

Mailing Address: 7807 NE Loowit Loop, #106 Vancouver 98662

Collection:	General stock of hardcover and paperback.
Specialties:	Children's; political science; mystery.
# of Vols:	10,000
Hours:	Mon-Fri 10:30-6>30. Sat 10:30-5.
Services:	Accepts want lists.
Travel:	4th Plain exit off I-5. Proceed west on 4th Plain to Main St, then south on Main for one block. Shop is located on corner of Main and 24th St.
Map Ref:	Map 22, page 366, #27.
Credit Cards:	No
Owner:	Lew & Ann Patry
Year Estab:	1994
Comments:	Although the collection is not large enough to offer much depth, we did see an interesting selection of titles in most fields that could well be of interest to collectors suggesting that a brief stop here would not be out of order.

Vintage Books
6613 East Mill Plain Boulevard 98661   Fax: (360) 694-7644

Open Shop
(360) 694-9519

Collection:	General stock of mostly used paperback and hardcover.
Specialties:	Automobiles
# of Vols:	200,000
Hours:	Mon-Fri 10-8. Sat 10-6. Sun 12-5.
Services:	Accepts want lists.

Travel:	From I-5: Proceed east on Mill Plain for 2½ miles. From I-205: Mill Plain west exit. Proceed west on Mill Plain 2¼ miles. Shop is in Heights Shopping Center.
Map Ref:	Map 22, page 366, #29.
Credit Cards:	Yes
Owner:	Becky & Alec Milner
Year Estab:	1974
Comments:	A large shop with much to see. Paperbacks and hardcover books (mostly reading copies) are well organized and intershelved. The majority of the hardcover volumes we saw were newer items (to some extent contradicting the name of the shop.) There were, of course, some vintage items and special displays of more collectible items but these represented only a small portion of the stock. The shop also sells used magazines. All in all, because of the number of books on hand (usually a factor that should increase the likelihood of your finding a book of interest to you) we think a stop here would be appropriate.

Walla Walla

Booktique — Open Shop
214 East Main Street 99362 — (509) 525-2421

Collection: General stock of primarily paperback.
Hours: Mon-Thu 10:30-5. Fri & Sat 10-5:30.

Earth Light Books — Open Shop
321 East Main Street 99362 — (509) 525-4983

Collection: General stock of mostly used paperback and some new.
Hours: Mon-Fri 10-6. Sat 10-4.

Wenatchee

Chapter Two — Open Shop
109 Yakima Street 98801 — (509) 662-2093

Collection: General stock of primarily paperback.
# of Vols: 35,000
Hours: Tue-Fri 9:30-5:30. Sat 9:30-4.

Woodinville

(Map 28, page 387)

Between the Covers — Open Shop
14450 Woodinville-Redmond Rd, Ste 200 98008 — (206) 481-9117

Collection: General stock of paperback and hardcover.
Specialties: Children's; non fiction.
Hours: Tue, Wed, Sat 10:30-5:30. Thu & Fri 12-8. Sun 11-4.

Services:	Accepts want lists; monthly newsletter lists wants.
Travel:	Bothell-Woodinville exit (Hwy 522) off I-405. Proceed on Hwy 522 to Woodinville. Right on Hwy 202 (Woodinville-Redmond Rd). Shop is in Redwood Shopping Center.
Credit Cards:	Yes
Owner:	Barbara & Ronald Hammond
Year Estab:	1989
Comments:	Stock is approximately 75% paperback.

Woodland
(Map 20, page 345)

Zephyr Used & Rare Books   **Open Shop**
607 Goerig Street 98674   (360) 225-7444

Collection:	General stock of hardcover and paperback.
Specialties:	Children's; illustrated; history; biography; fine printing.
# of Vols:	25,000
Hours:	Mon-Sat 10-7.
Services:	Appraisals, search service, accepts want lists; mail order.
Travel:	Exit 21 off I-5. West on Goerig. Shop is about 1/2 mile from freeway, in a shopping center on the right.
Credit Cards:	No
Owner:	Kol Shaver
Year Estab:	1994
Comments:	A nice shop with somewhat fewer books on display for browsing than the number indicated above. The books were in generally good condition, represented several eras and included a number of items that one would certainly consider collectible. We made a satisfactory purchase here and wish you the same good fortune. Very reasonably priced.

Yakima
(Map 25, page 433)

Cheshire Books   **Open Shop**
310 East Yakima Avenue 98901   (509) 457-0930

Collection:	General stock of mostly used hardcover and paperback.
Specialties:	Children's; Pacific Northwest.
# of Vols:	30,000 (used)
Hours:	Mon-Sat 9-5.
Services:	Search service, accepts want lists, mail order.
Travel:	City Center exit off Hwy 97. Proceed west on Yakima Ave.
Credit Cards:	No
Owner:	Walter Toop
Year Estab:	1983
Comments:	Stock is approximately 60% hardcover.

Gene W. Badde, Books on the West (206) 271-6481
824 Lynnwood Avenue, NE Renton 98056

Collection: Specialty
Specialties: Western Americana. Primarily non fiction.
# of Vols: 3,000
Services: Catalog, accepts want lists.
Credit Cards: No
Year Estab: 1988

Colin Bull, Polar Books (206) 842-9660
PO Box 4675 Rolling Bay 98061

Collection: Specialty
Specialties: Arctic; Antarctic.
# of Vols: 6,000
Services: Appraisals, accepts want lists.
Credit Cards: No
Owner: Colin Bull
Year Estab: 1986

Gary L. Estabrook-Books (360) 699-5454
PO Box 61453 Vancouver 98666

Collection: Specialty books and collectibles
Specialties: Sports; fishing; hunting.
# of Vols: 35,000
Services: Search service, catalog, accepts want lists.
Credit Cards: No
Year Estab: 1973
Comments: Collection can also be viewed by appointment.

Anthony Greene (206) 324-9351
PO Box 4551 Seattle 98104

Collection: General stock.
Specialties: Modern first editions.
# of Vols: 10,000
Services: Occasional catalog, accepts want lists.
Credit Cards: No
Year Estab: 1990

J.D. Holmes (206) 771-2701
PO Box 623 Edmonds 98020   Fax: (206) 771-2701

Collection: Specialty
Specialties: Metaphysics; occult; religion; Orientalia; alchemy; hermetica.
# of Vols: 5,000
Services: Catalog, accepts want lists.
Credit Cards: Yes
Year Estab: 1971

King Tree Book Company (509) 276-7182
West 217 6th Street, Box 580 Deer Park 9900

Collection:	Specialty. Mostly new and some used.
Specialties:	Natural history; country living; educational resources in science and nature.
Services:	Search service, catalog, accepts want lists.
Credit Cards:	Yes
Owner:	Craig Palmer
Year Estab:	1993

P.T. Mallahan, Bookseller (206) 454-1663
307 130th Avenue SE Bellevue 98005

Collection:	Specialty
Specialties:	World War I (military, social and political history).
# of Vols:	5,000
Services:	Appraisals, catalog.
Credit Cards:	No
Owner:	Patrick Mallahan
Year Estab:	1975

MasterPieces Unlimited (206) 932-4927
5945 47th SW Seattle 98136

Collection:	General stock.
# of Vols:	2,000
Services:	Search service, accepts want lists.
Credit Cards:	No
Owner:	Guy L. Peck & Delores Peck-Johnson
Year Estab:	1992

Carol D. McKinley, Bookseller (360) 786-8074
2908 Sherwood Drive Olympia 98501

Collection:	Specialty
Specialties:	Women's studies; Pacific Northwest.
# of Vols:	5,000
Services:	Appraisals, search service, catalog, accepts want lists.
Credit Cards:	No
Year Estab:	1976

Miner's Quest (509) 327-2897
3015 West Weile Spokane 99208

Collection:	General stock and ephemera.
Specialties:	Mining (history and technical).
# of Vols:	1,000+
Services:	Appraisals, search service, catalog, accepts want lists, reference library.
Credit Cards:	No
Owner:	Robert D. Weldin
Year Estab:	1993

Orpheus Books (206) 451-8343
11522 NE 20th Street Bellevue 98004

Collection: Specialty new and used.
Specialties: Signed first editions; modern literature.
Services: Catalog, accepts want lists.
Credit Cards: No
Owner: Don Stutheit & Barbara Wight
Year Estab: 1992

Simon Ottenberg, Bookseller (206) 720-7150
PO Box 15509 Seattle 98115

Collection: Specialty
Specialties: African art, music, dance, archaeology, folklore, literature and cookbooks.
Services: Catalog, appraisals.
Year Estab: 1969
Comments: Collection can be viewed by appointment.

The Reading Lamp (206) 776-1902
24032 79th Place West Edmonds 98026

Collection: Specialty
Specialties: Modern writers; first editions; signed; mystery; nature; fiction.
Credit Cards: No
Owner: Joe Spitz
Year Estab: 1991

Renaissance Books (206) 523-1712
5554 27th NE Seattle 98105

Collection: Specialty
Specialties: History of ideas, including philosophy; theology; social theory.
Services: Catalog, accepts want lists.
Credit Cards: Yes
Owner: David Anthony
Year Estab: 1991

Mike Robertson Books
PO Box 372 Maple Valley 98038

Collection: Specialty books and ephemera.
Specialties: Pulps; comic books and related original art; science fiction; mystery; movie and television ephemera.
Services: Catalog, accepts want lists.
Credit Cards: No
Year Estab: 1972

Spectrum of Rainbows (360) 683-2559
PO Box 1958 Sequim 98382   Fax: (360) 683-2559

Collection: Specialty
Specialties: American illustrators (1890's-1980's).

# of Vols: 7,000
Services: Catalog
Owner: Denis Jackson
Year Estab: 1983

Violet Books (206) 726-5924
PO Box 20610 Seattle 98102 Fax: (206) 324-3420

Collection: Specialty
Specialties: Supernatural literature, especially the short story.
# of Vols: 2,000
Services: Appraisals, catalog, accepts want lists.
Owner: Jessica Salmonson
Year Estab: 1986

Way's Magazines Unlimited (206) 633-2262
PO Box BHP-193 Seattle 98111

Collection: Specialty
Specialties: Magazines
Owner: Jack E. Way, Jr.
Year Estab: 1947

A book lover's paradise

Specialty Index

Adventure
Fantasy Etc.   222
Gemini Book Exchange & Comic Ctr   418
Africa
Chameleon   415
Ethnographic Arts Publications   136
Peter R. Feltus   53
Great Epic Books   403
Simon Ottenberg, Bookseller   447
Schoyer's Books   307
Agriculture and water issues
AG Access   79
R.G.I. Book Co.   137
Alaska
Alaska Book Store   14
Alaskan Heritage Bookshop   13
Alaskan Renaissance Books   11
Alaskana Bookshop   11
Apollo Book Shop   74
High Latitude   386
Lost Horizon Books   14
Martin's Books   13
Robert W. Mattila, Bookselle   424
The Observatory   14
Parmer Books   208
Dick Perier Books   441
Dale C. Schmidt-Books   369
Title Wave Used Books   12
Alcoholics Anonymous
Sol J. Grossman, Bookseller   275
La Mesa Used Books   109
Safari Out of Print Bookstore   209
American history
American-European Books   120
Comstock's Bindery & Bookshop   384
Mike's Books & Espresso   347
American literature
Authors Of The West   333
The Brick Row Book Shop   219
Dirk Cable, Bookseller   170
Harold B. Diamond, Bookseller   61
Thomas A. Goldwasser Rare Books   224
Magic Door Books   368
Philip J. Pirages Rare Books   344
Americana
Albany Book Company   325
American Booksellers   383
Avocet Used Books   331
Roy Bleiweiss-Fine Books   292
Bolerium Books   216
The Book Broker   202
Book Depot   51
The Book Nook   158
Virginia Burgman Rare Books   293
Dirk Cable, Bookseller   170
Encore Books   182
Grapevine Books   237
Green Ginger Bookshop   66
Lawrence Hamman Fine Books   375
Emmett Harrington Rare Books   299
David Hecht Antiquarian Books   225
Historicana   63
Houle Rare Books & Autographs   126
Kauai Fine Arts   317
Parmer Books   208
Past Times Bookshop   65
Larry W. Price Books   375
Robert's Book Shop   344
Dale C. Schmidt-Books   369
Schoyer's Books   307
Nancy Stewart-Books   329
Jeffrey Thomas   230
Ancient civilizations
Archaeologia   155
Eric Chaim Kline Bookseller   251
Papyrus Books   304
Animation
The Comic Character Shop   416
Anthropology
Louis Collins Books   416
Ethnographic Arts Publications   136
Antiques
A Time For Books   198
Alan S. Bamberger Books   216
Greyhavens Books   183
San Fernando Book Co.   211
Applied arts
Art Books Only   243
L. Clarice Davis   296
Weinstein & Ruhl Fine Books   65
Aquariums
The Aquatic Book Shop   291
Archaeology
Archaeologia   155
Charles Lewis Best   201
Bluff Park Rare Books   117
Ethnographic Arts Publications   136
Eric Chaim Kline Bookseller   251

Libros Latinos	181	Adobe Bookshop	213
Malter Galleries	84	Aftermore Books	117
Papyrus Books	304	Afterwords	238
Archaic skills		Aladdin Books	94
Argus Books & Graphics	188	Aldine Books	120
Architecture		Allred Books	278
Arcana: Books on the Arts	249	Anchor Book Shop	91
Arundel Books	120	Arcana: Books on the Arts	249
Alan S. Bamberger Books	216	Art Books Only	243
Bauhaus Books & Coffee	412	Arundel Books	120
Roy Bleiweiss-Fine Books	292	Avocet Used Books	331
Carl Blomgren-Fine Books	239	Ronald J. Ballou, Bookman	187
The Book Broker	202	Alan S. Bamberger Books	216
The Book Den	243	Bargain Books	273
L. Clarice Davis	296	Bauhaus Books & Coffee	412
Hennessey & Ingalls	250	The Bay Window	337
Richard Hilkert, Bookseller	225	Roy Bleiweiss-Fine Books	292
J. Michaels Books	335	Carl Blomgren-Fine Books	239
Kenneth Karmiole, Bookseller	250	Book Alley of Old Pasadena	169
Eric Chaim Kline Bookseller	251	The Book Broker	202
Lost Horizon Bookstore	244	Book City Of Burbank	60
Moe's Books	54	The Book End	140
David Morrison Books	358	The Book Gallery	196
J. B. Muns Fine Arts Books	54	Book Mall of Ventura	274
Murphy's Books	145	Book Time	159
Phoenix Bookstore	236	Booklegger	86
Richard L. Press, FineBooks	193	Books & Company	217
Prufrock Books and Etc.	172	Books On The Boulevard	259
Kenneth Starosciak	229	Books Past & Present	83
William Stout, Books	229	Brannan Books	96
Joseph Tabler Books	210	Broadway Booksellers	204
Turtle Island Booksellers	57	Chameleon	415
Van Norman-Booksellers	311	Chanticleer Books	261
Alan Wofsy Fine Arts	231	Chelsea Books	220
Arctic		Chimaera Books & Music	166
Alaska Book Store	14	Daniel Conner	335
Alaskan Renaissance Books	11	Corls Books	374
Blue Dragon Bookshop	326	W & V Dailey	124
Colin Bull, Polar Books	445	L. Clarice Davis	296
Ethnographic Arts Publications	136	Harold B. Diamond, Bookseller	61
High Latitude	386	Richard Dix, Illustrated Books	329
JP Books	357	Earth Bound Used Books	383
Martin's Books	13	The Eclectic Collector	104
Robert W. Mattila, Bookseller	424	871 Fine Arts Gallery and Bookstore	222
The Observatory	14	Encore Books	182
Parmer Books	208	Essence Gallery	297
Larry W. Price Books	375	Ethnographic Arts Publications	136
Area studies		Flora & Fauna Books	418
D.A. Sachs - Books	157	Godfather's Books & Espresso Bar	328
Armed services editions		Goldwasser & Wilkinson Books	224
James M. Dourgarian, Bookman	280	Green Ginger Bookshop	66
Armenia		Greyhavens Books	183
Armenian Coins & Books	174	Hanson's Books	355
Arms and armor		Henderson Books	390
El Dorado Books	125	Hennessey & Ingalls	250
Art		Heritage Books	85
Acorn Books	213	Michael S. Hollander Rare Books	240
Acquitania Gallery	213	Iliad Bookshop	150
		J. Michaels Books	335
		Kenneth Karmiole, Bookseller	250

Samuel W. Katz	127	Ethnographic Arts Publications	136
Eric Chaim Kline Bookseller	251	Forest Books	223
Valerie Kraft, Fine Books	164	Hammons Archives	193
Lemon Grove Bookstore	114	Michael S. Hollander Rare Books	240
Libros Latinos	181	J.D. Holmes	445
Lost Horizon Bookstore	244	David Ishii, Bookseller	422
Laurence McGilvery	108	JP Books	357
Frank Mikesh	281	Netkin Fine Arts	303
Moe's Books	54	Oriental Book Store	172
David Morrison Books	358	Rare Oriental Book Co.	45
Mountain Light Books	153	Renaissance Bookshop	186
J. B. Muns Fine Arts Books	54	Schoyer's Books	307
Murphy's Books	145	Tusitala Bookshop	316
Netkin Fine Arts	303	Graeme Vanderstoel	312
The Odyssey Bookshop	240	**Asians in America**	
Old Master Gallery	113	Steven G. Doi-Books	296
Otento Books	207	David Ishii, Bookseller	422
Papyrus Books	304	Oriental Book Store	172
Phoenix Bookstore	236	Sun Dance Books	309
Pictus Orbis Collectors Books	267	**Assassination**	
Pioneer Square Books	426	Atlantis Book Shop	59
Pistil Books & News	427	**Astronomy**	
Richard L. Press, Fine Books	193	B & L Rootenberg Rare Books	259
Prufrock Books and Etc.	172	E. Louis Hinrichs	116
R. Franklin Pyke, Bookseller	48	**Atlases (See Maps)**	
Robert's Book Shop	344	**Austin, Mary**	
Russian Hill Bookstore	228	Pacific Rim Galleries	68
Sam's Book City	151	**Authors' first books**	
Sam's Book Company	286	Gregor Books	420
Signature Bound Bookseller	430	The Invisible Bookman	301
Kenneth Starosciak	229	**Autographs**	
Sullivan Goss Books & Prints	245	A Time For Books	198
Sunset Bookstore	229	Beauty and the Books	413
Michael R. Thompson, Bookseller	129	Stan Beecher	292
Titlewave Books	430	Benedikt & Salmon	201
Torrance Book Buddy	269	Roy Bleiweiss-Fine Books	292
Turtle Island Booksellers	57	Richard Callaway, Rare Books	294
Vagabond Books	59	Channel Island Books	294
Van Norman-Booksellers	311	Golden Age Collectables	419
Graeme Vanderstoel	312	Heros & Legends	41
Vigne Co.	68	Houle Rare Books & Autographs	126
Walden Pond Books	157	Larry's Books & Autographs	301
Waking Dream Books	364	J. B. Muns Fine Arts Books	54
Weinstein & Ruhl Fine Books	65	Pepper & Stern Rare Books	305
West L.A. Book Center	283	Randall House	245
West Portal Books	230	Kenneth W. Rendell Gallery	58
Westside Stories	432	Christophe Stickel Autographs	308
Alan Wofsy Fine Arts	231	**Automotive**	
Artist's books		Auto-Bound Inc.	41
Art Books Only	243	Automotive Bookstore	412
Califia Books	219	Automotive Book Stop	60
871Fine Arts Gallery & Bookstore	222	Automotive Information	291
Arts and crafts		The Book Fair	334
American Bookstore	92	Day's Past	179
Books In Transit	269	Green Ginger Bookshop	66
Barbara Cutts-UK/USA Bookdealer	353	Irvington Booknook	357
Asia		Vintage Books	442
Book Depot	51	Yesterday's Books	138
Daniel Conner	335		

Aviation

Aero Book Club	384
Automotive Book Stop	60
Aviation Bookmobile/H.Miller	152
Books Bargain Books	273
Barnstormer Books	87
Benicia Books	406
Comstock's Bindery & Bookshop	384
Crawford-Peters Aeronautica	295
Irvington Booknook	357
John Roby	306
Dale C. Schmidt-Books	369
Tall Stories	230
Tennant's Aviation Books	385
William Byrd Aviation Books	115

Baja California

Books By Mail	204
John Cole's Book Shop	107
Jim Hansen Books	67
Old California Store	276

Balkan

Schoyer's Books	307

Beat generation

Black Ace Books	121
Broadway Booksellers	204
Exploded Views Books	150
The Fool's Progress	298
Mike's Memories	303
Red House Books	227
Saint Adrian Company	228
Second Story Booksellers	363
Signature Bound Bookseller	430
Skyline Books	89
Sun Moon Bear Rare Books	309

Biblical studies

The Archives Bookshop	169
Cornerstone Books	242
Windows Booksellers	336
Yesterday's Books	138

Bibliography

The Brick Row Book Shop	219
Serendipity Books	56
George H. Tweney	431
Jeff Weber Rare Books	99

Biography

Alouette Antiques	200
Aracia Avenue Books	260
Ronald J. Ballou, Bookman	187
Book Discoveries	415
The Book Shop	280
Book Stop	112
Celebrity Bookstore	164
Drama Books	221
The Eclectic Collector	104
Richard Glassman Books	73
Movie World	62
Mystery & Imagination Bookshop	99
Open Books: A Poem Emporium	426
Orpheus Books	395
Ravenna Rare Books	427
Ed Smith Books	152
Theater Book Shop	310
Valdez Books & Bindery	285
Van Norman-Booksellers	311
West Portal Books	230
Zephyr Used & Rare Books	444

Black studies

Bibliomania	155
Barbara Bilson-Books	250
Bolerium Books	216
The Book Shelf	293
Richard Gilbo-Bookseller	69
The Invisible Bookman	301
It Is Written Bookstore	113
Key Bookshop	156
Know Thy Self Afrikan Book Center	437
Kongo Square Gallery	128
Lee-Gannon Booksellers	142
Moondance Bookshop	252
P.F. Mullins Books	108
Prufrock Books and Etc.	172
Rykken And Scull	102
Marvin Stanley, Bookseller	153
Sylvester & Orphanos Booksellers	309
Taugher Books	50
Third World Ethnic Books	129
Waverley Books	252
Weinstein & Ruhl Fine Books	65

Books about books

Bolerium Books	216
Dirk Cable, Bookseller	170
Barry Cassidy Rare Books	191
Harold B. Diamond, Bookseller	61
Heron House	300
Michele Leroux Fine Old Books	399
Robert Perata	305
Richard L. Press, Fine Books	193
The Printers' Shop	306
Safari Out of Print Bookstore	209
Serendipity Books	56
Sleepy Hollow Books	308
Taugher Books	50
George H. Tweney, Bookseller	431
Valdez Books & Bindery	285
Van Norman-Booksellers	311
Wessel & Lieberman Booksellers	432

Botany

Carol Barnett, Books	373
Brooks Books	72
Flora & Fauna Books	418

Braille/large print

Sacramento Surplus Book Room	194

Brautigan, Richard

James M. Dourgarian, Bookman	280

British history

Mike's Books & Espresso	347

Thorn Books	143	Monroe Books	93
Broadsides		Mountain House Books	147
Caravan Book Store	123	P.F. Mullins Books	108
Bull fighting		Murphy's Books	145
Fat City Books	264	Murphy's Stage Stop	145
Maurice F. Neville Rare Books	245	Old California Store	276
Burroughs, William S.		Past Times Bookshop	65
Exploded Views Books	150	R. Franklin Pyke, Bookseller	48
Burton, Sir Richard		Schoyer's Books	307
Trophy Room Books	41	Sleepy Hollow Books	308
Business		Jack L. Stone, Bookseller	262
Columbia Books	374	Sullivan Goss Books & Prints	245
John T. Hamilton III	108	Thorn Books	143
Raymond Kimeldorf	357	Time Tested Books	194
Wall Street Books	313	Tin Can Mailman	46
California		Paul von Ahnen Books	312
Again Books	242	Wahrenbrock's Book House	210
Robert Allen/Books	168	**Camping and hiking guides**	
Anderson Valley Books	58	Uptown Books	262
Apollo Book Shop	74	**Caribbean**	
Argonaut Book Shop	214	Kauai Fine Arts	317
Argus Books & Graphics	188	Kongo Square Gallery & Gift Shop	128
Ronald J. Ballou, Bookman	187	**Cartoons**	
Charles Lewis Best	201	The Comic Character Shop	416
Bonanza St. Books	280	**Cats**	
Book Alley of Old Pasadena	169	Bibliomania	155
The Book Den	243	**Celtic history**	
Book Depot	51	Lang Syne Books	339
The Book End	140	**Central Intelligence Agency**	
The Book Shop	76	Atlantis Book Shop	59
Books By Mail	204	Tom Davis Books	44
The Bookstall	218	David Park Books	305
Dirk Cable, Bookseller	170	**Chess**	
Cahill's Book Store	91	Bolerium Books	216
Calico Cat Bookshop	275	**Chicano studies**	
California Collectible Books	133	Sun Dance Books	309
Caravan Book Store	123	Waverley Books	252
Derail Books	254	**Children's**	
El Dorado Books	125	Noreen Abbot Books	290
Eureka Books	86	Affordable Books & Collectibles	136
Ferndale Books	88	Again Books	242
Garcia-Garst, Booksellers	271	Robert Allen/Books	168
Geiger's Books	298	Alouette Antiques	200
Goldwasser & Wilkinson Books	224	Alta's	290
Great Overland Book Co.	257	American Booksellers	383
Jim Hansen Books	67	American Bookstore	92
Emmett Harrington Rare Books	299	Ames Bookstore	101
Hein & Co.	177	An Oasis Bookstore	200
Dave Henson-Books	299	Ander's Attic	185
Jack London Bookstore	98	Apex Books	290
George Robert Kane, Fine Books	247	Arkadyan Books & Prints	215
Lincoln Avenue Books	232	Avocet Used Books	331
Live Oak Booksellers	99	Balbontin Books	172
Lorson's Books & Prints	96	Ronald J. Ballou, Bookman	187
Lost Horizon Bookstore	244	Bargain Books	277
E. Lubbe Books	302	Bargain Books	273
Maxwell's Bookmark	265	Barnstormer Books	87
Memorabilia of San Jose	233	Bartlett Street Book Store	346

Bell's Book Store	165	Readers Guide to Recycled Literature	368
Between the Covers	443	Rocky's Antiques & Books	208
Bibelots & Books	414	Rykken And Scull	102
Bibliomania	155	Salty's Record Attic	138
Black Swan	155	Sam's Book City	151
Bluff Park Rare Books	117	Sandpiper Books	401
The Book Collector	190	Sleepy Hollow Books	308
The Book End	140	Smith & Co. Booksellers	266
The Book Review	190	Solvang Book Company	260
Book Stop	408	Nancy Stewart-Books	329
The Book Tree	72	Kirk Stines Collectible Books	430
Book World	400	Tacoma Book Center	439
Booklegger	86	Tall Stories	230
The Bookstall	218	Titlewave Books	430
Virginia Burgman Rare Books	293	To & Again Books	311
Cellar of Books	374	Toad Hall	311
Cheshire Books	444	Turner House Antiques	342
Cliff's Books/Records/Comics	170	Uptown Bookshelf	442
The Comic Character Shop	416	Volume One Used Books	146
Dorothy G. Cook-Rare Children's Books	247	Joy A. Wheeler-Books	333
Ursula C. Davidson Books	239	Wonderland Books	83
Diesel, A Bookstore	155	Woodie's Collectibles	313
Discoveries Music & Books	173	Zephyr Used & Rare Books	444
Richard Dix, Illustrated Books	329	**Children's illustrated**	
Carol Docheff-Bookseller	110	Acquitania Gallery	213
Edmonds Olde Bookstore	394	Blue Goose Books	326
El Dorado Books	125	Book Treasury	118
Elaine's Books	187	Sol J. Grossman, Bookseller	275
Eldora's Books	374	Heritage Books	85
Encore Books	182	My Book Heaven	41
Fifty Thousand Books	82	Van Norman-Booksellers	311
First Street Books & Antiques	297	**Children's series**	
Garcia-Garst, Booksellers	271	Anmar' Children's Series Books	184
Richard Glassman Books	73	Bibelots & Books	414
Globe Bookstore & Bindery	419	Garcia-Garst, Booksellers	271
Grapevine Books	237	Longfellow's Books	357
Jacksonville Books	341	Paper Horn	434
Josef's Books	185	The Prince and the Pauper	208
George Robert Kane, Fine Books	247	Select Press	74
Eric Chaim Kline Bookseller	251	**Churchill, Winston**	
Valerie Kraft, Fine Books	164	Blenheim Books	257
Gen Krueger Books	301	Churchilliana Co.	192
L & M Treasures	344	**Circus**	
Last Seen Reading	302	Aladdin Books	94
Michele Leroux Fine Old Books	399	Backstage Books	373
Lincoln Avenue Books	232	Elliot Katt, Bookseller	127
Magnolia Park Book Shop	62	**Civil War**	
Margaret Mannatt Fine Books	207	American Booksellers	383
Monroe Books	93	American-European Books	120
Mystery & Imagination Bookshop	99	Ronald J. Ballou, Bookman	187
Newport Book Center	348	Barnaby Rudge Bookseller	111
Nineteenth Century Prints	359	Book Depot	51
Otento Books	207	Barry Cassidy Rare Books	191
Pages of Time	137	The Eclectic Collector	104
The Paper Moon Bookstore	360	Encore Books	182
Joan Perkal-Books	305	History Focused	300
Phantom Bookshop	276	Jacksonville Books	341
Pictus Orbis Collectors Books	267	Monroe Books	93
Truman Price	375		
Prince and the Pauper Children's Books	208		

Specialty Index

Wallace D. Pratt, Bookseller	305
2nd Edition Books	69

Classical studies

Turtle Island Booksellers	57

College and university histories

Raymond Kimeldorf	357

Comics

FootNote Books	206
Mike Robertson Books	447
West Portal Books	230
Woodie's Collectibles	313

Communications

Columbia Books	374
Powell's Technical Books	362

Computers

E. Louis Hinrichs	116
Powell's Technical Books	362

Conspiracy

Aftermore Books	117
Atlantis Book Shop	59
E. Louis Hinrichs	116
David Park Books	305

Cookbooks

AJ's Cookbooks	436
Albatross Book Co.	214
Author's Ink	350
Avocet Used Books	331
Bargain Books	273
Best Books	113
Book Box	189
Book Discoveries	415
Book Mall of Ventura	274
The Book Nook	84
Book Stop	408
Books & Company	217
Calico Cat Bookshop	275
Caravan Book Store	123
Cellar of Books	374
Chanticleer Books	261
Cliff's Books/Records/Comics	170
Cook Books - By Janet Jarvits	61
The Cook Book Lady	295
Craig Books	295
Curran & Hermes Books	295
Edmonds Olde Bookstore	394
Elaine's Books	187
Encore Books	182
Fortner Books	386
Richard Gilbo-Bookseller	69
Peter Glaser Bookseller	257
Richard Glassman Books	73
Globe Bookstore & Bindery	419
Goldwasser & Wilkinson Books	224
Grapevine Books	237
Green Ginger Bookshop	66
Henderson Books	390
Household Words	300
Iconoclast Books	421
Jane's Books	329
Valerie Kraft, Fine Books	164
Mary Mason Bookseller	303
Otento Books	207
Pages of Time	137
Dick Perier Books	441
Pioneer Square Books	426
Powell's Books for Cooks	361
Prufrock Books and Etc.	172
Ravenna Rare Books	427
Robert's Book Shop	344
Rocky's Antiques & Books	208
Second Time 'Round Quality Used Books	308
Marvin Stanley, Bookseller	153
Tilikum Books	406
Titlewave Books	430
Treehorn Books	255
Volume One Used Books	146
Western Sport Shop	241
The Whale's Tale	402
Joy A. Wheeler-Books	333
Wrigley-Cross Books	364

Costume design

Dorothy G. Cook-Rare Children's Books	247
Drama Books	221
Golden Legend	126
Elliot Katt, Bookseller	127
Lincoln Avenue Books	232
Margaret Mannatt Fine Books	207
B. Vasin Bookseller	312

Counter culture

Bauhaus Books & Coffee	412
Black Ace Books	121
Exploded Views Books	150
Flashback Books	297
The Fool's Progress	298
Hey Joe Used Books & Records	356
Hungry Head Books	335
Iliad Bookshop	150
Michael's Book Shop	368
Red House Books	227
Saint Adrian Company	228
Skyline Books	89

Cowboys

Bookends	255
El Dorado Books	125
Old California Store	276

Dance

Backstage Books	373
Barbara Cook Modern 1st Editions	295
Drama Books	221
Golden Legend	126
Elliot Katt, Bookseller	127
Movie World	62
J. B. Muns Fine Arts Books	54
Netkin Fine Arts	303
Opera Shop of Los Angeles	128

Martin A. Silver, Musical Literature	100
Van Norman-Booksellers	311
Darwin, Charles	
Don Conner Fine Books	192
Harold B. Diamond, Bookseller	61
Decorative arts	
Art Books Only	243
Avons Research Publications	291
Alan S. Bamberger Books	216
L. Clarice Davis	296
Eric Chaim Kline Bookseller	251
Lost Horizon Bookstore	244
David Morrison Books	358
Richard L. Press, Fine Books	193
Kenneth Starosciak	229
Deserts	
Ravens Bookshop	272
J. Arthur Robinson, Bookseller	287
Sagebrush Press Bookstore	288
Design	
Arcana: Books on the Arts	249
Alan S. Bamberger Books	216
Bauhaus Books & Coffee	412
Drama Books	221
William Stout, Books	229
Waking Dream Books	364
Disney	
Stan Beecher	292
Woodie's Collectibles	313
Dogs	
Bookends	255
Doyle, Arthur Conan	
Phillip Gold-221 Books	299
Magic Door Books	368
Dreams	
Regent Press	157
Drug literature	
Flashback Books	297
Early printed books	
Barnaby Rudge Bookseller	111
The Brick Row Book Shop	219
W & V Dailey	124
David Hecht Antiquarian Books	225
George Robert Kane, Fine Books	247
Kenneth Karmiole, Bookseller	250
Samuel W. Katz	127
Krown & Spellamn	58
Philip J. Pirages Rare Books	344
Bernard M. Rosenthal	55
John Windle, Bookseller	231
Ecology	
Flora & Fauna Books	418
The Old Fool's Bookstore	395
Economics	
Harold B. Diamond, Bookseller	61
Quiet Companion Books	438
Renaissance Bookshop	186

English literature	
Stuart Bennett Rare Books	135
Brigadoon Books	147
The Brick Row Book Shop	219
Brigadoon Books	147
Dirk Cable, Bookseller	170
Harold B. Diamond, Bookseller	61
Thomas A. Goldwasser Rare Books	224
Magic Door Books	368
Philip J. Pirages Rare Books	344
Tavistock Books	309
Valdez Books & Bindery	285
Erotica	
Harold B. Diamond, Bookseller	61
Exploded Views Books	150
The Fool's Progress	298
Pistil Books & News	427
Ivan Stormgart-Books	309
Europe	
American-European Books	120
Book Depot	51
Volkoff & von Hohenlohe	312
Exhibition catalogs	
L. Clarice Davis	296
871 Fine Arts Gallery and Bookstore	222
Laurence McGilvery	108
Expatriates	
Charmed Circle Books	191
Second Story Booksellers	363
Exploration	
American Booksellers	383
Berkelouw Books	121
The Bookstall	218
El Dorado Books	125
Folio Books	418
Globe Bookstore & Bindery	419
JP Books	357
Oregon Tertitorial Books	371
T.W. Palmer Books	335
Trophy Room Books	41
George H. Tweney, Bookseller	431
Facsimiles	
T.W. Palmer Books	335
William Thomas	310
Fairy tales	
Smith & Co. Booksellers	266
Fantasy	
A Wrinkle In Time	78
Aladdin Books	94
Altair-4 (Knights Cross Books)	159
Anderson's Bookshop/BooksFantastique	284
Apex Books	290
Basement Books	291
Book Carnival	159
Book Oasis	114
The Book Symposium	293
Donald W. Cannon Bookseller	96
Cobblestone Books	192

Specialty Index

Copper Dragon Books	265	Sam's Book City	151
Harold B. Diamond, Bookselle	61	Starworld	106
Richard Dix, Illustrated Books	329	Super Collector	91
Elsewhere Books	222	Torrance Book Buddy	269
Excalibur Books & Comics	354	Donald J. Weinstock Books	313
Fantasy Etc.	222	**Fine bindings**	
Far Mountain Books	197	Anchor In Time	395
Flights of Fantasy Books	250	Arkadyan Books & Prints	215
Flip Side	266	Ronald J. Ballou, Bookman	187
J. Joseph Flynn Rare Books	297	Barnaby Rudge Bookseller	111
FootNote Books	206	Book Discoveries	415
Future Dreams/Burnside	354	Richard Callaway, Rare Books	294
Future Dreams/Gateway	354	Caravan Book Store	123
Galactic Archives	43	Thomas A. Goldwasser Rare Books	224
Golden Age Collectables	419	Houle Rare Books & Autographs	126
Heros & Legends	41	Michele Leroux Fine Old Books	399
Inkworks Rare & Collectible	300	Philip J. Pirages Rare Books	344
Books Interzone Comics	339	Toad Hall	311
Lady Jayne's Comics and Books	438	**Fine printing**	
Barry R. Levin Science Fiction Books	251	Roy Bleiweiss-Fine Books	292
Magic Door Books	368	Dawson's Book Shop	125
Merlin's Bookshop	116	Richard Glassman Books	73
Kai Nygaard, Bookseller	303	Heron House	300
The Other Change of Hobbit	55	Kenneth Karmiole, Bookseller	250
Diane Peterson - Booklady	134	The Printers' Shop	306
Sam: Johnson's Bookshop	129	John Scopazzi Gallery	229
Sandpiper Books	401	John Windle, Bookseller	231
Swans's Comic & Magazine Mart	439	Zephyr Used & Rare Books	444
Torrance Book Buddy	269	*(See also Private Press)*	
Violet Books	448	**First editions**	
Waverley Books	252	Acorn Books	213
Wrigley-Cross Books	364	Agathon Books	435
Yellow Pages Used Books	338	Alaskan Renaissance Books	11
Federal Writer's Project		Anacapa Books	51
Bolerium Books	216	Anacapa House	242
Schoyer's Books	307	Andy's Books	290
Fiction (older)		Apex Books	290
James M. Dourgarian, Bookman	280	Aracia Avenue Books	260
Live Oak Booksellers	99	Authors Of The West	333
Sleepy Hollow Books	308	Avocet Used Books	331
Film		Bad Moon Books	291
Aladdin Books	94	Ronald J. Ballou, Bookman	187
Barbara Bilson-Books	250	Bargain Books	277
Book Alley of Old Pasadena	169	Stan Beecher	292
Books On The Boulevard	259	Black Oak Books	51
Donald W. Cannon Bookseller	96	Black Swan	155
Cinema Books	416	Roy Bleiweiss-Fine Books	292
Collectors Book Store	105	Blue Goose Books	326
Grayson D. Cook, Bookseller	124	Blumenkron & Ramirez Books	351
Drama Books	221	Book Baron	43
Iliad Bookshop	150	The Book Collector	190
Elliot Katt, Bookseller	127	Book Discoveries	415
Larry Edmunds Cinema & TheatreBooks	106	Book King	74
Limelight Bookstore	225	Book Mall of Ventura	274
Movie World	62	The Book Merchant	146
Nothing's New	198	Book Quest	392
Other Times Books	282	The Book Shelf	293
Pepper & Stern Rare Books	305	The Book Shop	76
Mike Robertson Books	447	The Book Store	75

Book Time	159	Nix Books	161
Book Treasury	118	The Old London Bookshop	390
Book'Em	52	Orpheus Books	447
Booklegger	86	Past Times Bookshop	65
Books Revisited	239	Pepper & Stern Rare Books	305
Books, Etc.	218	Diane Peterson - Booklady	134
The Brick Row Book Shop	219	Pettler & Lieberman Booksellers	128
Virginia Burgman Rare Books	293	The Reading Lamp	447
John R. Butterworth	294	Sam's Book City	151
Buy The Book	294	Sam's Book Company	286
Cahill's Book Store	91	Sandpiper Books	401
California Collectible Books	133	Charles Seluzicki Fine and Rare Books	363
Richard Callaway, Rare Books	294	Serendipity Books	56
Channel Island Books	294	Nancy Stewart-Books	329
Channel Isles Books	177	Sun Moon Bear Rare Books	309
Chanticleer Books	261	Sylvester & Orphanos Booksellers	309
Charmed Circle Books	191	Tall Stories	230
Collectors' Library	148	Taugher Books	50
Grayson D. Cook, Bookseller	124	Jeffrey Thomas, Fine & Rare Books	230
Barbara Cook Modern 1st Editions	295	Title Wave Used Books	12
Copperfield's Annex	254	Turtle Island Booksellers	57
Corls Books	374	Len Unger-Rare Books	130
Craig & Craig Booksellers	165	Vagabond Books	59
Robert Dagg Rare Books	296	Wahrenbrock's Book House	210
W & V Dailey	124	Waverley Books	252
James M. Dourgarian, Bookman	280	Webfoot Bookman	364
Dutton's Books/North Hollywood	149	Wessel & Lieberman Booksellers	432
Encore Books	182	West Portal Books	230
Estates Gallery	90	Wonderland Books	83
First Street Books & Antiques	297	**Fishing**	
Fox Book Co.	437	Adams Angling and Hunting Books	50
Fuhrman & Fuhrman	298	Alaskana Bookshop	11
Geiger's Books	298	Don Conner Fine Books	192
Richard Gilbo-Bookseller	69	Day's Past	179
Thomas A. Goldwasser Rare Books	224	El Dorado Books	125
Goldwasser & Wilkinson Books	224	Gary L. Estabrook-Books	445
Great Overland Book Co.	257	Richard Gilbo-Bookseller	69
Anthony Greene	445	Great Outdoors Book Exchange	374
Gregor Books	420	Inquisitive Sportsman Books	399
Heritage Books	85	David Ishii, Bookseller	422
House Of Books	275	Frank Mikesh	281
The Invisible Bookman	301	Murphy's Books	145
Joseph the Provider/Books	244	Webfoot Bookman	364
Gerry Kleier	301	Western Sport Shop	241
Susan J. Klein, Bookseller	232	**Folk arts**	
Larry's Books & Autographs	301	Folk Motif	298
Lawrence's Books	302	**Fore-edge paintings**	
Lee-Gannon Booksellers	142	George Robert Kane, Fine Books	247
Barry R. Levin Science Fiction Books	251	Jeff Weber Rare Books	99
Longfellow's Books	357	**Foreign language books**	
Margaret Mannatt Fine Books	207	Beehive Books and Arts	349
Merlin's Bookshop	116	The Book End	140
Monroe Stahr Books	259	The Book Review	190
Moondance Bookshop	252	Columbus Books	220
P.F. Mullins Books	108	Harold B. Diamond, Bookseller	61
Murphy's Books	145	Globus Slavic Bookstore	223
Mystery & Imagination Bookshop	99	E. Louis Hinrichs	116
Maurice F. Neville Rare Books	245	Eric Chaim Kline Bookseller	251
Nick Adams & Co Rare Books	187	Multi Books	425

Diane Pyke-Books	306	**Government publications**	
Renaissance Bookshop	186	Alaskana Bookshop	11
D.A. Sachs - Books	157	Rock of Ages	306
Signature Bound Bookseller	430	Sherburne Antiques & Fine Art	405
Szwede Slavic Books	167	**Graphics**	
Ten O'CLock Books	310	Book City Of Burbank	60
Forestry		**Greek and Latin**	
AG Access	79	Black Oak Books	51
Brooks Books	72	**Guns**	
French ForeignLegion		Benicia Books	406
Magic Door Books	368	Day's Past	179
Fur trade		Robert's Book Shop	344
Beaver Books	292	Western Sport Shop	241
Oregon Tertitorial Books	371	World Wide Hunting Books	313
Gambling		**Haggard, H. Rider**	
Byron's Magic Books	234	Phillip Gold-221 Books	299
Gardening and horticulture		Magic Door Books	368
AG Access	79	Phantom Bookshop	276
Carol Barnett, Books	373	**Hawaii (See South Pacific)**	
Beehive Books and Arts	349	**Health**	
Bell's Book Store	165	E. Louis Hinrichs	116
Beth L. Bibby-Books	373	Shambhala Booksellers	57
Books By Mail	204	**Hemingway, Ernest**	
Brooks Books	72	Magic Door Books	368
Calendula Horticultural Books	393	Nick Adams & Co Rare Books	187
Chimney Sweep Books	246	**History**	
Flora & Fauna Books	418	Aftermore Books	117
Fortner Books	386	Allred Books	278
V.L.T. Gardner	244	American Bookstore	92
Richard Glassman Books	73	Atlantis Book Shop	59
Henderson Books	390	Avon Book Shop	60
Powell's Books for Cooks	361	Bart's Books	158
Quest Rare Books	263	The Book Gallery	196
R.G.I. Book Co.	137	Dirk Cable, Bookseller	170
Rocky's Antiques & Books	208	Calico Cat Bookshop	275
William Stout, Books	229	Channel Isles Books	177
Toad Hall	311	Chanticleer Books	261
Gemology		Chimaera Books & Music	166
The Gemmary Inc.	182	Coffee & Classics	79
Geoscience Books & Print	298	Collected Thoughts Bookshop	53
Peri Lithon Books	305	Harold B. Diamond, Bookseller	61
Pleiadian Dreams	45	Richard Glassman Books	73
Rock of Ages	306	Globe Bookstore & Bindery	419
Twelfth Street Booksellers	132	Greyhavens Books	183
Genealogy		Hanson's Books	355
Canyonville Books & Videos	330	Henderson Books	390
Dale C. Schmidt-Books	369	Heritage Books	85
Geology		Holland's Books	356
Flora & Fauna Books	418	Julia Houdek Books & Search Service	80
Hammons Archives	193	House of Fiction	171
Peri Lithon Books	305	Lake City Books	423
Rock of Ages	306	Lemon Grove Bookstore	114
Gold rush		Michael's Book Shop	368
Hein & Co.	177	Mountain Light Books	153
Mountain House Books	147	Nix Books	161
Murphy's Stage Stop	145	The Odyssey Bookshop	240
Uptown Books	262	Phoenix Bookstore	236
		Renaissance Bookshop	186

Russian Hill Bookstore	228	**Horses**	
Sam's Book Company	286	Bookends	255
Seattle Book Center	428	Phoenix Books/Mind & Body	130
Marvin Stanley, Bookseller	153	R.G.I. Book Co.	137
Joseph Tabler Books	210	**Humanities**	
Michael R. Thompson, Bookseller	129	Chimaera Books & Music	166
Time Tested Books	194	Horizon Books	421
Torrance Book Buddy	269	**Hunting**	
Volkoff & von Hohenlohe	312	Adams Angling and Hunting Books	50
Donald J. Weinstock Books	313	Alaskana Bookshop	11
Wessex Books & Records	134	Benicia Books	406
Zephyr Used & Rare Book	444	Don Conner Fine Books	192
Hollywood		Day's Past	179
Aftermore Books	117	El Dorado Books	125
Apex Books	290	Gary L. Estabrook-Books	445
Bluff Park Rare Books	117	Richard Gilbo-Bookseller	69
Heros & Legends	41	Inquisitive Sportsman Books	399
Monroe Stahr Books	259	Frank Mikesh	281
Waverley Books	252	Murphy's Books	145
Homosexuality		Robert's Book Shop	344
Beyond the Closet Bookstore	414	Safari Press	307
Bolerium Books	216	Trophy Room Books	41
Books & Company	217	Webfoot Bookman	364
Books Bohemian	123	Western Sport Shop	241
Books, Etc.	218	World Wide Hunting Books	313
Phoenix Bookstore	236	**Illustrated**	
Pistil Books & News	427	Noreen Abbot Books	290
Red & Black Book Collective	428	Affordable Books & Collectibles	136
Horror		American Booksellers	383
A Wrinkle In Time	78	Arkadyan Books & Prints	215
Anderson's Bookshop/Books Fantastique	284	Ronald J. Ballou, Bookman	187
Andy's Books	290	Bartlett Street Book Store	346
Apex Books	290	The Bay Window	337
Bad Moon Books	291	Bibelots & Books	414
Basement Books	291	Book City Of Burbank	60
Black Moon Books	202	The Bookstall	218
The Book Symposium	293	Richard Callaway, Rare Books	294
Books, Etc.	218	The Comic Character Shop	416
Donald W. Cannon Bookseller	96	Grayson D. Cook, Bookseller	124
Cobblestone Books	192	W & V Dailey	124
Copper Dragon Books	265	Ursula C. Davidson Books	239
Elsewhere Books	222	Richard Dix, Illustrated Books	329
Excalibur Books & Comics	354	Don Johnson's Ambience	417
Fantasy Etc.	222	El Dorado Books	125
Flights of Fantasy Books	250	First Street Books & Antiques	297
Future Dreams/Burnside	354	Garcia-Garst, Booksellers	271
Future Dreams/Gateway	354	Thomas A. Goldwasser Rare Books	224
Golden Age Collectables	419	Greyhavens Books	183
Inkworks Rare & Collectible	300	Lawrence Hamman Fine Books	375
Books Know Knew Books	166	Hawthorne Boulevard Books	356
Barry R. Levin Science Fiction Books	251	Heldfond Book Gallery	196
Merlin's Bookshop	116	George Robert Kane, Fine Books	247
Mystery & Imagination Bookshop	99	Samuel W. Katz	127
Kai Nygaard, Bookseller	303	Eric Chaim Kline Bookseller	251
Jim Orbaugh, Bookseller	304	Valerie Kraft, Fine Books	164
Sam: Johnson's Bookshop	129	Michele Leroux Fine Old Books	399
Smith & Co. Booksellers	266	Margaret Mannatt Fine Books	207
Violet Books	448	Mystery & Imagination Bookshop	99
Wrigley-Cross Books	364	Nineteenth Century Prints	359

The Paper Moon Bookstore	360	**Labor history**	
Joan Perkal-Books	305	Anderson Valley Books	58
Pictus Orbis Collectors Books	267	Bolerium Books	216
Philip J. Pirages Rare Books	344	**Latin America**	
Prufrock Books and Etc.	172	Ethnographic Arts Publications	136
Rykken And Scull	102	Ferndale Books	88
Sandpiper Books	401	Howard Karno Books	273
John Scopazzi Gallery	229	Libros Latinos	181
Spectrum of Rainbows	447	Allen Sarno Books About Latin America	428
Nancy Stewart-Books	329	Sun Dance Books	309
Tall Stories	230	**Latin American literature**	
Jeffrey Thomas, Fine & Rare Books	230	Latin Blood Books	302
West Portal Books	230	Valdez Books & Bindery	285
John Windle, Bookseller	231	Waverley Books	252
Wonderland Books	83	**Law**	
Zephyr Used & Rare Books	444	Harold B. Diamond, Bookseller	61
Indian Wars		Meyer Boswell Books	227
Wallace D. Pratt, Bookseller	305	Ravenna Rare Books	427
Intellectual History		**Lawrence, D.H.**	
Renaissance Books	447	The Book Shop	280
Charles Seluzicki Fine and Rare Books	363	**Lawrence, T.E.**	
Interior design		Great Epic Books	403
Richard Hilkert, Bookseller	225	**Lewis & Clark**	
Ireland		George H. Tweney, Bookseller	431
Brigadoon Books	147	**Lewis, C.S.**	
Carroll's Books	220	Authors Of The West	333
Channel Isles Books	177	J. Joseph Flynn Rare Books	297
Great Epic Books	403	**Limited editions**	
Helen Harte, Bookseller	420	Book'Em	52
Jewelry		Caravan Book Store	123
The Gemmary Inc.	182	Corls Books	374
Peri Lithon Books	305	Sol J. Grossman, Bookseller	275
Rock of Ages	306	Hawthorne Boulevard Books	356
Twelfth Street Booksellers	132	Jim Orbaugh, Bookseller	304
Journalism		**Linguistics**	
Columbia Books	374	Multi Books	425
Joyce, James		Turtle Island Booksellers	57
Shakespeare & Co - A Bookstore	327	**Literary criticism**	
Judaica		Blackberry Books	389
American-European Books	120	Horizon Books	421
Harold B. Diamond, Bookseller	61	The Invisible Bookman	301
Historicana	63	The Literary Guillotine	248
Raymond Kimeldorf	357	Charles Seluzicki Fine and Rare Books	363
Eric Chaim Kline Bookseller	251	Paul von Ahnen Books	312
Richard L. Press, Fine Books	193	Wessex Books & Records	134
Volkoff & von Hohenlohe	312	**Literature**	
Juggling		Abandoned Planet Bookstore	213
Byron's Magic Books	234	Adams Avenue Bookstore	199
Kennedy, John F.		Affordable Books & Collectibles	136
Tom Davis Books	44	Agathon Books	435
David Park Books	305	Aladdin Books	94
King Arthur		Robert Allen/Books	168
Camelot Books	279	Allred Books	278
Thorn Books	143	American Bookstore	92
Klondike		Anacapa Books	51
Alaskan Heritage Bookshop	13	Arundel Books	120
Jack London Bookstore	98	Author's Ink	350

Avocet Used Books	331	Mountain Light Books	153
Bart's Books	158	P.F. Mullins Books	108
Beauty and the Books	413	Mystery & Imagination Bookshop	99
Bibliomania	155	Nix Books	161
Blackberry Books	389	Ocean Beach Books	207
Bleak House Books	267	The Odyssey Bookshop	240
Bluff Park Rare Books	117	The Old Fool's Bookstore	395
The Book Broker	202	Oliver's Books	196
The Book End	140	Orpheus Books	447
Book Harbor	95	Other Times Books	282
The Book Nook	84	Phoenix Bookstore	236
Book Re-View	112	Pistil Books & News	427
The Book Shelf	293	Prufrock Books and Etc.	172
Book Time	159	The Reading Lamp	447
Book Worm	195	Red House Books	227
Books On The Boulevard	259	Renaissance Bookshop	186
The Bookstall	218	Sam's Book City	151
By The Way Books	172	Sam's Book Company	286
Calico Cat Bookshop	275	Sam: Johnson's Bookshop	129
California Collectible Books	133	John Scopazzi Gallery	229
Cape Cod Clutter	205	Serendipity Books	56
Barry Cassidy Rare Books	191	Skyline Books	89
Chanticleer Books	261	Ed Smith Books	152
Chelsea Books	220	Sun Moon Bear Rare Books	309
Chimaera Books & Music	166	Bill Swing Rare & Fine Books	363
Claremont Books & Prints	71	Tacoma Book Center	439
Coffee & Classics	79	Michael R. Thompson, Bookseller	129
Collected Thoughts Bookshop	53	Title Wave Used Books	12
Columbus Books	220	Titlewave Books	430
Counterpoint Records & Books	105	Toad Hall	311
Barbara Cutts-UK/USA Bookdealer	353	Turtle Island Booksellers	57
Gene de Chene, Bookseller	282	Twice Sold Tales/Capitol	431
Earth Bound Used Books	383	Len Unger-Rare Books	130
Encore Books	182	Vigne Co.	68
Encyclopedias Bought & Sold	242	Paul von Ahnen Books	312
Exploded Views Books	150	Wahrenbrock's Book House	210
Flora & Fauna Books	418	Donald J. Weinstock Books	313
Fortner Books	386	Weinstein & Ruhl Fine Books	65
Globe Bookstore & Bindery	419	Wessex Books & Records	134
Godfather's Books & Espresso Bar	328	West L.A. Book Center	283
Phillip Gold-221 Books	299	D.G. Wills Books	109
Gregor Books	420	Ye Bookstore	278
Lawrence Hamman Fine Books	375	Yesterday's Books	138
Hanson's Books	355	Zeno's	232
Henderson Books	390	**London, Jack**	
Heritage Book Shop	126	James M. Dourgarian, Bookman	280
Heritage Books	85	Jack London Bookstore	98
Historicana	63	Phantom Bookshop	276
Holland's Books	356	Plaza Books	262
Horizon Books	421	Treehorn Books	255
Julia Houdek Books & Search	80	**Magazines**	
Houle Rare Books & Autographs	126	Gerry Aboud-Back Issue Magazines	370
House of Fiction	171	Ander's Attic	185
Iconoclast Books	421	Benedikt & Salmon	201
Iliad Bookshop	150	Book Baron	43
Susan J. Klein, Bookseller	232	The Bookie Joint	184
Lemon Grove Bookstore	114	Virginia Burgman Rare Books	293
Melville & Co Books	407	Cal's Books and Wares	351
Michael's Book Shop	368	Cameron's Books	353
Mike's Memories	303		

Specialty Index

Comstock's Bindery & Bookshop	384
Exploded Views Books	150
Hans Kuperus-Periodicals	163
La Mesa Used Books	109
The Magazine	225
Magazine Baron	43
McDonald's Bookshop	226
Periodicals Paradise	360
Saint Adrian Company	228
The Second Time Around Bookshop	276
Marvin Stanley, Bookseller	153
Swans's Comic & Magazine Mart	439
Way's Magazines Unlimited	448
Zeitlin Periodicals Co.	130

Magic

Aladdin Books	94
Byron's Magic Books	234

Manuscript leaves

Krown & Spellman, Booksellers	58
Philip J. Pirages Rare Books	344

Manuscripts

Roy Bleiweiss-Fine Books	292
David Hecht Antiquarian Books	225
Barry R. Levin Science Fiction Books	251
Nick Adams & Co Rare Books	187

Maps and atlases

Acquitania Gallery	213
Arkadyan Books & Prints	215
Barnaby Rudge Bookseller	111
Basically Books/Book Finders of Hawaii	316
Calico Cat Bookshop	275
Kauai Fine Arts	317
Manning's Books	163
Nineteenth Century Prints	359
The Observatory	14
Pacific Shore Maps	208
T.W. Palmer Books	335
R. Franklin Pyke, Bookseller	48
Robert Ross & Co.	63
Barry Lawrence Ruderman Old Maps	108
Sacramento Surplus Book Room	194
John Scopazzi Gallery	229

Maritime

American Booksellers	383
Apollo Book Shop	74
Armchair Sailor Bookstore	256
Charles Lewis Best	201
Book Stop	408
Cape Cod Clutter	205
Caravan Book Store	123
Chamasha Books	294
Channel Isles Books	177
Comstock's Bindery & Bookshop	384
Earth Bound Used Books	383
El Dorado Books	125
Fortner Books	386
Green Ginger Bookshop	66
Harvard Used Book Store	264
Irvington Booknook	357

Pacific Shore Maps	208
Dale C. Schmidt-Books	369
Seabreeze Limited	209
Southwest Instrument Co.	238
Tilikum Books	406
Van Norman-Booksellers	311
Whaling Research	313

Mathematics

B & L Rootenberg Rare Books	259
Black Oak Books	51
E. Louis Hinrichs	116
Merlin's Bookshop	116
Powell's Technical Books	362

Medicine

Alouette Antiques	200
B & L Rootenberg Rare Books	259
The Bookstall	218
John Caius-Books	219
Chameleon	415
Harold B. Diamond, Bookseller	61
Edwin V. Glaser Rare Books	256
Peter Glaser Bookseller	257
Jeremy Norman & Co.	227
Jeff Weber Rare Books	99

Medieval history

Black Oak Books	51
Serendipity Books	56
Turtle Island Booksellers	57

Metallurgy

Powell's Technical Books	362
Rock of Ages	306

Metaphysics

Allred Books	278
An Oasis Bookstore	200
Apex Books	290
Bearded Giraffe	256
Being Books Inc.	151
Blue Dragon Bookshop	326
Bodhi Tree Bookstore	123
The Book Nook	84
Books Past & Present	83
Cal's Books	180
Channel Book Shop	332
Cliff's Books/Records/Comics	170
Controversial Bookstore	205
Earth Bound Used Books	383
East West Bookshop	134
Estates Gallery	90
Fields Book Store	223
Fifty Thousand Books	82
Gateways Book & Gift	247
Golden Bough Bookstore	144
J.D. Holmes	445
La Mesa Used Books	109
Lodestar Books	225
Minerva Books	167
New Age World Services & Books	107
Open Secret Bookstore	241

The Phoenix Bookstore	252	Once Read Books	112
Pleiadian Dreams	45	Peggatty Books	393
Ravens Bookshop	272	Wallace D. Pratt, Bookseller	305
The Second Time Around Bookshop	276	Red Star Military Museum & Sales	77
Shambhala Booksellers	57	Tacoma Book Center	439
Vicarious Experience Books	76	Tall Stories	230
Visions & Dreams	75	Tusitala Bookshop	316
Mexico		Yellow Pages Used Books	338
Libros Latinos	181	**Miller, Henry**	
Sun Dance Books	309	Lighthouse Books	141
Wahrenbrock's Book House	210	Pacific Rim Galleries	68
Microscopy		**Miniature books**	
The Gemmary Inc.	182	Dawson's Book Shop	125
Peri Lithon Books	305	Lorson's Books & Prints	96
Middle East		Diane Peterson - Booklady	134
Oriental Book Store	172	The Printers' Shop	306
Margaret Mannatt Fine Books	207	**Mining**	
Scattergood Research	307	Argus Books & Graphics	188
Schoyer's Books	307	Day's Past	179
Military		The Gemmary Inc.	182
Acorn Books	213	Geoscience Books & Prints	298
Again Books	242	Hammons Archives	193
Albany Book Company	325	Miner's Quest	446
Altair-4 (Knights Cross Books)	159	Peri Lithon Books	305
Amadeus Books	110	Rock of Ages	306
American Bookstore	92	**Modern Library**	
American-European Books	120	Books, Etc.	218
Ander's Attic	185	Richard Glassman Books	73
The Antiquarian Archive	119	**Mountaineering**	
Atlantis Book Shop	59	Blue Dragon Bookshop	326
Aviation Bookmobile/H. Miller Books	152	Richard Gilbo-Bookseller	69
Ronald J. Ballou, Bookman	187	JP Books	357
Benicia Books	406	Mountainbooks	425
Bibliomania	155	Larry W. Price Books	375
Blackberry Books	389	Toad Hall	311
Black Swan	155	Van Norman-Booksellers	311
Blenheim Books	257	**Muir, John**	
The Book Broker	202	Diane Peterson - Booklady	134
Book Depot	51	**Music**	
Book Stop	112	Ronald J. Ballou, Bookman	187
Broadway Booksellers	204	Backstage Books	373
Channel Isles Books	177	Bell's Book Store	165
Clark's Book Store	435	Benedikt & Salmon	201
Comstock's Bindery & Bookshop	384	The Book Shop	76
El Dorado Books	125	Daniel Conner	335
Estates Gallery	90	Drama Books	221
Fifty Thousand Books	82	Eureka Books	86
Gaslamp Books, Prints & Antiques	206	Theodore Front MusicalLiterature	274
Greyhavens Books	183	Hey Joe Used Books & Records	356
Interim Books	391	Iliad Bookshop	150
Kaiser Bill's Military Emporium	178	Elliot Katt, Bookseller	127
Lake City Books	423	Michael's Book Shop	368
Last Grenadier	61	J. B. Muns Fine Arts Books	54
The Last Post Military Antiques	173	Opera Shop of Los Angeles	128
Lawrence's Books	302	Orpheus Books	395
Los Osos Book Exchange	131	Pages of Time	137
E. Lubbe Books	302	Salty's Record Attic	138
Magnolia Park Book Shop	62	Sam: Johnson's Bookshop	129
P.F. Mullins Books	108		

Martin A. Silver, Musical Literature	100	Mystery & Imagination Bookshop	99
Michael R. Thompson, Bookseller	129	Maurice F. Neville Rare Books	245
Donald J. Weinstock Books	313	New Albion Bookshop	88
Yesterday's Books	138	M.C. Newburn Books	42
(See also Performing arts)		Nick Adams & Co Rare Books	187
		Pepper & Stern Rare Books	305
Mystery and detective		Phantom Bookshop	276
Aardvark Books	199	Pioneer Square Books	426
Aladdin Books	94	Ravens Bookshop	272
Alibi Mystery	258	Ravenscar Books	306
Allred Books	278	The Reading Lamp	447
An Oasis Bookstore	200	Readers Guide to Recycled Literature	368
Anderson's Bookshop/Books Fantastique	284	Robert's Book Shop	344
Andy's Books	290	Mike Robertson Books	447
Apex Books	290	Sam's Book Company	286
Bad Moon Books	291	Sam: Johnson's Bookshop	129
Stan Beecher	292	San Francisco Mystery Bookstore	228
Betty's Bookstore	202	Sandpiper Books	401
Barbara Bilson-Books	250	Seattle Mystery Bookshop	429
Blackberry Books	389	Secondhand Prose	46
Bloody Dagger Books	202	2nd Edition Books	69
Blue Sky Books	216	Second Time 'Round Quality Used Books	308
Bluff Park Rare Books	117	Serendipity Books	56
Book Carnival	159	Sleepy Hollow Books	308
Book Discoveries	415	Tacoma Book Center	439
Book King	74	Tall Stories	230
Book Passage Used & Rare Books	73	Taugher Books	50
The Book Shelf	293	Rik Thompson Books	311
Book Time	159	Len Unger-Rare Books	130
Book'Em	52	Uptown Bookshelf	442
Boulevard Books	293	Vagabond Books	59
Caernarvon Press	294	Waverley Books	252
Camelot Books	279	Donald J. Weinstock Books	313
Donald W. Cannon Bookseller	96	The Whale's Tale	402
Cardinal Books	441	Wrigley-Cross Books	364
Cobblestone Books	192	Donald Yates	314
Grayson D. Cook, Bookseller	124	Yesterdays Used Books & Coffee House	183
Elsewhere Books	222	*(See also Sherlock Holmes)*	
Fantasy Etc.	222	**Mysticism**	
Fuhrman & Fuhrman	298	By The Way Books	172
Robert Gavora, Bookseller	355	Calico Cat Bookshop	275
Geiger's Books	298	**Mythology**	
Gemini Book Exchange & Comic Ctr	418	Sandpiper Books	401
Globe Bookstore & Bindery	419	**Napoleon**	
Phillip Gold-221 Books	299	Volkoff & von Hohenlohe	312
Grounds for Murder Mystery Book Store Willis E. Herr, Bookseller	207 300	**National Geographic**	
House Of Books	275	Longfellow's Books	357
I Love A Mystery	300	Village Books	94
Gerry Kleier	301	**Native Americans**	
Last Seen Reading	302	Allred Books	278
Latin Blood Books	302	Ronald J. Ballou, Bookman	187
Mary Mason Bookseller	303	The Book Collector	190
MisterE Books	424	Channel Book Shop	332
Mitchell Books	171	F. Wayne Edmunds - Bookseller	47
Murder By The Book	358	El Dorado Books	125
Murder By The Book	358	Ethnographic Arts Publications	136
Mystery Treasure House	347	Globe Bookstore & Bindery	419
Mysteries Unlimited	425	Great Overland Book Co.	257
Mysterious Bookshop West	281	Murphy's Stage Stop	145

R. Franklin Pyke, Bookseller	48	El Dorado Books	125
Sun Dance Books	309	Exotica Fine Books	297
Paul von Ahnen Books	312	Eye of the Cat	118
Waverley Books	252	Fields Book Store	223
Wessel & Lieberman Booksellers	432	Heros & Legends	41
		J.D. Holmes	445
Natural history		New Age World Services & Books	107
Adams Angling and Hunting Books	50	Panurge Emporium Books	360
Aldine Books	120	The Phoenix Bookstore	252
Anchor In Time	395	Pleiadian Dreams	45
Anderson Valley Books	58	**Oregon**	
Avocet Used Books	331	Albany Book Company	325
B & L Rootenberg Rare Books	259	Canyonville Books & Videos	330
Beth L. Bibby-Books	373	Corls Books	374
Don Conner Fine Books	192	Webfoot Bookman	364
Curran & Hermes Books	295	Joy A. Wheeler-Books	333
Harold B. Diamond, Bookseller	61	**Ornithology**	
Flora & Fauna Books	418	Books By Mail	204
King Tree Book Company	446	Calendula Horticultural Books	393
Lee-Gannon Booksellers	142	Curran & Hermes Books	295
Frank Mikesh	281	Flora & Fauna Books	418
Natural History Books	150	Richard Glassman Books	73
Nineteenth Century Prints	359	**Outlaws and lawmen**	
Jeremy Norman & Co.	227	Monroe Books	93
The Odyssey Bookshop	240	**Oz**	
T.W. Palmer Books	335	Book Treasury	118
Larry W. Price Books	375	Phantom Bookshop	276
Tilikum Books	406	Prince and the Pauper Children's Books	208
Van Norman-Booksellers	311	Woodie's Collectibles	313
Nature		**Pacific Northwest**	
Crabtree's Collection	89	Author's Ink	350
Flora & Fauna Books	418	Cellar of Books	374
Richard Glassman Books	73	Cheshire Books	444
King Tree Book Company	446	Edmonds Olde Bookstore	394
Murphy's Stage Stop	145	Fortner Books	386
Once Read Books	112	Fox Book Co.	437
Pioneer Square Books	426	David Ishii, Bookseller	422
The Reading Lamp	447	Wayne Kee Books	365
Secondhand Prose	46	Robert W. Mattila, Bookseller	424
Western Sport Shop	241	Carol D. McKinley, Bookseller	446
Needlecrafts		Mostly Books	398
The Book Fair	334	Old Oregon Book Store	359
Richard Glassman Books	73	Peggatty Books	393
New England		Dick Perier Books	441
Cape Cod Clutter	205	Quiet Companion Books	438
Newspapers		Sandpiper Books	401
Jim Lyons Historical Newspapers	302	Dale C. Schmidt-Books	369
Nostalgia		Storment Library	406
Nothing's New	198	Wessel & Lieberman Booksellers	432
Numismatics		**Paleantology**	
John T. Hamilton III	108	Peri Lithon Books	305
George Frederick Kolbe	77	**Performing arts**	
Malter Galleries	84	Abandoned Planet Bookstore	213
Papyrus Books	304	Aladdin Books	94
Occult		Backstage Books	373
Bart's Books	158	Benedikt & Salmon	201
Bodhi Tree Bookstore	123	Book City Of Burbank	60
John Caius-Books	219	Book City Of Hollywood	105
Cliff's Books/Records/Comics	170		

Books On The Boulevard	259	Book Alley of Old Pasadena	169
Chimaera Books & Music	166	Book City Of Burbank	60
Collected Thoughts Bookshop	53	L. Clarice Davis	296
Collectors Book Store	105	Dawson's Book Shop	125
Columbia Books	374	871 Fine Arts Gallery and Bookstore	222
Counterpoint Records & Books	105	El Dorado Books	125
Barbara Cutts-UK/USA Bookdealer	353	Goldwasser & Wilkinson Books	224
Houle Rare Books & Autographs	126	Iliad Bookshop	150
Elliot Katt, Bookseller	127	J. Michaels Books	335
Mountain Light Books	153	Eric Chaim Kline Bookseller	251
The Odyssey Bookshop	240	Lighthouse Books	141
Salty's Record Attic	138	Carl Mautz, Vintage Photographs	147
Sam's Book City	151	Moe's Books	54
Titlewave Books	430	David Morrison Books	358
Graeme Vanderstoel	312	Mr. Nichols	254
Webfoot Bookman	364	J. B. Muns Fine Arts Books	54
Westside Stories	432	Netkin Fine Arts	303

(See also Dance, Music, Theater)

		Pacific Rim Galleries	68
Pets		Phoenix Bookstore	236
R.G.I. Book Co.	137	Richard L. Press, Fine Books	193

(See also Aquariums, Dogs, Cats)

		Rykken And Scull	102
Philately		Ed Smith Books	152
Peter R. Feltus	53	Turtle Island Booksellers	57
Seattle Book Center	428	Van Norman-Booksellers	311
		Walden Pond Books	157
Philosophy		**Pirates**	
Adams Avenue Bookstore	199	American Booksellers	383
Adobe Bookshop	213	El Dorado Books	125
Agathon Books	435	**Poetry**	
The Archives Bookshop	169	Alaskan Renaissance Books	11
Being Books Inc.	151	Allred Books	278
Stuart Bennett Rare Books	135	Am Here Books	174
Book Worm	195	American Bookstore	92
By The Way Books	172	Anacapa Books	51
Fields Book Store	223	Anchor In Time	395
Globe Bookstore & Bindery	419	Stuart Bennett Rare Books	135
Hanson's Books	355	Bleak House Books	267
Holland's Books	356	Bluff Park Rare Books	117
Horizon Books	421	Book Worm	195
Iconoclast Books	421	By The Way Books	172
The Literary Guillotine	248	Collected Thoughts Bookshop	53
Magic Door Books	368	Counterpoint Records & Books	105
The Odyssey Bookshop	240	Diesel, A Bookstore	155
The Old Fool's Bookstore	395	Richard Glassman Books	73
The Phoenix Bookstore	252	Iconoclast Books	421
Renaissance Books	447	The Invisible Bookman	301
Renaissance Bookshop	186	Larry's Books & Autographs	301
Sam's Book Company	286	Mystery & Imagination Bookshop	99
Sunrise Bookshop	57	Open Books: A Poem Emporium	426
Michael R. Thompson, Bookseller	129	Pages of Time	137
Twice Sold Tales/Capitol	431	Pacific Rim Galleries	68
Donald J. Weinstock Books	313	Pistil Books & News	427
D.G. Wills Books	109	Saint Adrian Company	228
Windows Booksellers	336	Sam's Book Company	286
		Serendipity Books	56
Photography		Signature Bound Bookseller	430
Aladdin Books	94	Sun Moon Bear Rare Books	309
Arcana: Books on the Arts	249	Wessel & Lieberman Booksellers	432
Alan S. Bamberger Books	216	D.G. Wills Books	109
Black Swan	155		
Carl Blomgren-Fine Books	239		

Politi, Leo
Sol J. Grossman, Bookseller 275
Political science
Atlantis Book Shop 59
Blackberry Books 389
The Book Nook 158
Collected Thoughts Bookshop 53
Harold B. Diamond, Bookseller 61
Phoenix Bookstore 236
Time Tested Books 194
Uptown Bookshelf 442
Popular culture
Aladdin Books 94
The Bookie Joint 184
Other Times Books 282
Presentation copies
Robert Dagg Rare Books 296
Harold B. Diamond, Bookseller 61
Latin Blood Books 302
Press books
Claremont Books & Prints 71
Robert Perata 305
Private press
The Antiquarian Archive 119
Arundel Books 120
Roy Bleiweiss-Fine Books 292
Califia Books 219
Goldwasser & Wilkinson Books 224
Sol J. Grossman, Bookseller 275
Lawrence Hamman Fine Books 375
Michael S. Hollander Rare Books 240
George Robert Kane, Fine Books 247
Lorson's Books & Prints 96
Jim Orbaugh, Bookseller 304
Oregon Tertitorial Books 371
Philip J. Pirages Rare Books 344
Charles Seluzicki Fine and Rare Books 363
Sleepy Hollow Books 308
Sun Moon Bear Rare Books 309
Swans's Comic & Magazine Mart 439
Jeffrey Thomas, Fine & Rare Books 230
(See also Fine printing)
Proofs
Books Revisited 239
Monroe Stahr Books 259
Ed Smith Books 152
Propaganda
Tom Davis Books 44
Scattergood Research 307
Psychology
Being Books Inc. 151
By The Way Books 172
La Mesa Used Books 109
Mike's Books & Espresso 347
The Phoenix Bookstore 252
Sam's Book Company 286
Shambhala Booksellers 57

Pulps
Altair-4 (Knights Cross Books) 159
Fantasy Illustrated 417
Golden Age Collectables 419
Mike Robertson Books 447
Swans's Comic & Magazine Mart 439
Radical studies
Anderson Valley Books 58
Bolerium Books 216
Exotica Fine Books 297
Red House Books 227
Renaissance Bookshop 186
Treehorn Books 255
Walden Pond Books 157
Railroads
Acorn Books 213
Alta's 290
Antiques & Artifacts 373
Ronald J. Ballou, Bookman 187
Bookmine 190
Caravan Book Store 123
Comstock's Bindery & Bookshop 384
Derail Books 254
Robert Gavora, Bookseller 355
Hammons Archives 193
Irvington Booknook 357
T.W. Palmer Books 335
San Diego Model Railroad Museum 307
Turn Table Books 81
Walden Pond Books 157
Western Book Company 338
Reference books
The Book Fair 334
Encyclopedias Bought & Sold 242
Magnolia Park Book Shop 62
Sacramento Surplus Book Room 194
Uptown Books 262
Religion
Adams Avenue Bookstore 199
Aftermore Books 117
Again Books 242
American Bookstore 92
The Archives Bookshop 169
Joe Armstrong 373
Bart's Books 158
Being Books Inc. 151
Best Books 113
Bethel Antiquarian Books 292
Bodhi Tree Bookstore 123
The Book Fair 334
The Book Gallery 196
The Book Review 190
Book Worm 195
Broadway Booksellers 204
By The Way Books 172
Canyonville Books & Videos 330
Chimney Sweep Books 246
Christian Discount Books 341
Christian Discount Book Center 77, 283, 284

Specialty Index

Collected Thoughts Bookshop	53
Cornerstone Books	242
Globe Bookstore & Bindery	419
Hessel and Taylor Books	180
J.D. Holmes	445
Iconoclast Books	421
Josef's Books	185
La Mesa Used Books	109
One Way Book Shop	87
Pages of Time	137
Pilgrim Discount Book & Bible Supply	360
Renaissance Books	447
St. Francis Book Store	198
Shambhala Booksellers	57
Marvin Stanley, Bookseller	153
Sunrise Bookshop	57
Upper Room Christian Bookstore	385
Volkoff & von Hohenlohe	312
Donald J. Weinstock Books	313
Windows Booksellers	336

Roosevelt, Theodore

Don Conner Fine Books	192

Royalty

Aftermore Books	117

Russia

Globus Slavic Bookstore	223
Old Oregon Book Store	359
Scattergood Research	307

San Francisco

Acquitania Gallery	213
Book Depot	51
Sun Moon Bear Rare Books	309
West Portal Books	230

Saroyan, William

Monroe Books	93

Satire

Stuart Bennett Rare Books	135

Sausage making

Dale C. Schmidt-Books	369

Scandinavia

Solvang Book Company	260

Science

Allred Books	278
American Bookstore	92
Avocet Used Books	331
B & L Rootenberg Rare Books	259
Black Oak Books	51
Book Discoveries	415
The Book Gallery	196
Books From Bree	149
The Bookstall	218
John Caius-Books	219
Cliff's Books/Records/Comics	170
Coffee & Classics	79
The Gemmary Inc.	182
Edwin V. Glaser Rare Books	256
Peter Glaser Bookseller	257
Hanson's Books	355
E. Louis Hinrichs	116
King Tree Book Company	446
Merlin's Bookshop	116
Mike's Books & Espresso	347
Jeremy Norman & Co.	227
Phoenix Bookstore	236
Powell's Technical Books	362
Tilikum Books	406
Volkoff & von Hohenlohe	312
Jeff Weber Rare Books	99
D.G. Wills Books	109

Science fiction

A Wrinkle In Time	78
Aardvark Books	199
Aladdin Books	94
Altair-4 (Knights Cross Books)	159
An Oasis Bookstore	200
Anderson's Bookshop/Books Fantastique	284
Another World Comics & Books	120
Apex Books	290
The Armchair Adventurer	43
Bookstore Joe Armstrong	373
Bad Moon Books	291
Basement Books	291
Beauty and the Books	413
Stan Beecher	292
Betty's Bookstore	202
Book Carnival	159
Book Discoveries	415
Book King	74
Book Oasis	114
The Book Shop	76
The Book Symposium	293
Book World	400
Caernarvon Press	294
Donald W. Cannon Bookseller	96
Cobblestone Books	192
Copper Dragon Books	265
Harold B. Diamond, Bookseller	61
Elsewhere Books	222
Excalibur Books & Comics	354
Fantasy Etc.	222
Far Mountain Books	197
Fifty Thousand Books	82
Flights of Fantasy Books	250
Flip Side	266
FootNote Books	206
Future Dreams/Burnside	354
Future Dreams/Gateway	354
Galactic Archives	43
Robert Gavora, Bookseller	355
Gemini Book Exchange & Comic Ctr	418
Phillip Gold-221 Books	299
Golden Age Collectables	419
Heros & Legends	41
Inkworks Rare & Collectible	300
Books Interzone Comics	339
Gerry Kleier	301
Know Knew Books	166

Lady Jayne's Comics and Books	438	Collectors' Library	148
Barry R. Levin Science Fiction Books	251	Barbara Cutts-UK/USA Bookdealer	353
Merlin's Bookshop	116	Robert Dagg Rare Books	296
Mysteries Unlimited	425	Harold B. Diamond, Bookseller	61
Mystery & Imagination Bookshop	99	Don Johnson's Ambience	417
New Albion Bookshop	88	Gregor Books	420
Kai Nygaard, Bookseller	303	Sol J. Grossman, Bookseller	275
The Other Change of Hobbit	55	Inquisitive Sportsman Books	399
The Penny Box Used Books	401	Latin Blood Books	302
Diane Peterson - Booklady	134	Mary Mason Bookseller	303
Pioneer Square Books	426	Moondance Bookshop	252
Ravens Bookshop	272	The Old London Bookshop	390
Renaissance Bookshop	186	Jim Orbaugh, Bookseller	304
Mike Robertson Books	447	Orpheus Books	447
Sam's Book Company	286	Pepper & Stern Rare Books	305
Seattle Book Center	428	The Reading Lamp	447
2nd Edition Books	69	Kenneth W. Rendell Gallery	58
Second Time 'Round Quality Used Books	308	Rykken And Scull	102
Serendipity Books	56	Ed Smith Books	152
Sleepy Hollow Books	308	Christophe Stickel Autographs	308
Super Collector	91	Len Unger-Rare Books	130
Tall Stories	230	Vagabond Books	59
Rik Thompson Books	311	Westside Books	130
Vagabond Books	59	**Slavic countries**	
Donald J. Weinstock Books	313	Szwede Slavic Books	167
Wrigley-Cross Books	364	**Social movements**	
Yellow Pages Used Books	338	Stuart Bennett Rare Books	135
Yesterdays Used Books & Coffee House	183	Bibliomania	155
Yesterday's Books	138	D.A. Sachs - Books	157
Scotland		**Social sciences**	
Lang Syne Books	339	Claremont Books & Prints	71
Brigadoon Books	147	Harold B. Diamond, Bookseller	61
Service, Robert W.		Holland's Books	356
Alaskan Heritage Bookshop	13	Renaissance Books	447
Sets		Donald J. Weinstock Books	313
Alfi News & Books	411	**South Pacific**	
Fox Book Co.	437	American Booksellers	383
Houle Rare Books & Autographs	126	Apollo Book Shop	74
Shakespeare		Basically Books/Book Finders of Hawaii	316
Blue Dragon Bookshop	326	Berkelouw Books	121
Harold B. Diamond, Bookseller	61	The Book Bin	331
The Old Fool's Bookstore	395	Ethnographic Arts Publications	136
Shakespeare & Co - A Bookstore	327	Island Books	317
Sherlock Holmes		Jack London Bookstore	98
Phillip Gold-221 Books	299	Kauai Fine Arts	317
Pepper & Stern Rare Books	305	Susan Mast Enterprises	303
Sandpiper Books	401	Parmer Books	208
Sleepy Hollow Books	308	Tusitala Bookshop	316
Smith & Co. Booksellers	266	**Southern Americana**	
Signed		American-European Books	120
Agathon Books	435	**Southwest Americana**	
Book Mall of Ventura	274	Books By Mail	204
The Book Shelf	293	Gaslamp Books, Prints & Antiques	206
Book Time	159	Jim Hansen Books	67
Book'Em	52	Sun Dance Books	309
Books Revisited	239	**Space**	
Virginia Burgman Rare Books	293	Aviation Bookmobile/H.Miller Books	152
Channel Island Books	294	Crawford-Peters Aeronautica	295
Charmed Circle Books	191		

Spanish Civil War
Bibliomania	155
Bolerium Books	216
Scattergood Research	307

Sports
Bibliomania	155
Books on Sports	123
El Dorado Books	125
Gary L. Estabrook-Books	445
Godfather's Books & Espresso Bar	328
Goodwin Goldfaden	259
Grand Slam Sports Books	299
House of Fiction	171
David Ishii, Bookseller	422
JP Books	357
Valerie Kraft, Fine Books	164
Magic Door Books	368
Martin's Books	13
Maxwell's Bookmark	265
Frank Mikesh	281
On The Cover	132
R. Plapinger Baseball Books	327
Sam's Book City	151
Monroe Stahr Books	259
Joseph Tabler Books	210
Waverley Books	252

Stegner, Wallace
James M. Dourgarian, Bookman	280
First Street Books & Antiques	297
Diane Peterson - Booklady	134

Steinbeck, John
The Book Nest	119
James M. Dourgarian, Bookman	280
Lighthouse Books	141
P.F. Mullins Books	108
Nick Adams & Co Rare Books	187
Pacific Rim Galleries	68
Diane Peterson - Booklady	134

Technology
Avocet Used Books	331
B & L Rootenberg Rare Books	259
Bargain Books	273
Books From Bree	149
Cliff's Books/Records/Comics	170
Encore Books	182
Green Ginger Bookshop	66
E. Louis Hinrichs	116
Johnson Books & Collectibles	244
Lawrence's Books	302
Live Oak Booksellers	99
Jeremy Norman & Co.	227
Powell's Technical Books	362
Reade Moore Books	173
Robert's Book Shop	344

Television
Donald W. Cannon Bookseller	96
Cinema Books	416
Collectors Book Store	105
Limelight Bookstore	225
Mike Robertson Books	447

Textiles
Lincoln Avenue Books	232
Dennis B. Marquand	128
Kenneth Starosciak	229
B. Vasin Bookseller	312

Theater
Backstage Books	373
Book Alley of Old Pasadena	169
Boulevard Books	293
Cinema Books	416
Drama Books	221
Golden Legend	126
The Invisible Bookman	301
Elliot Katt, Bookseller	127
Larry Edmunds Cinema & Theatre Books	106
Limelight Bookstore	225
Margaret Mannatt Fine Books	207
Movie World	62
The Play's The Thing	427
Shakespeare & Co - A Bookstore	327
Signature Bound Bookseller	430
Tall Stories	230
Theater Book Shop	310
Donald J. Weinstock Books	313

(See also Performing Arts)

Tobacco
Roy Bleiweiss-Fine Books	292

Tolkien, J.R.R.
J. Joseph Flynn Rare Books	297

Trade catalogs
Argus Books & Graphics	188

Transportation
The Antiquarian Archive	119
Antiques & Artifacts	373
Aviation Bookmobile/H. Miller Books	152

Travel
Acquitania Gallery	213
Anchor In Time	395
Basically Books/Book Finders of Hawaii	316
Beehive Books and Arts	349
Book Discoveries	415
Dirk Cable, Bookseller	170
Cape Cod Clutter	205
Barry Cassidy Rare Books	191
Collected Thoughts Bookshop	53
El Dorado Books	125
Peter R. Feltus	53
Fleetstreet	385
Richard Gilbo-Bookseller	69
Richard Glassman Books	73
Globe Bookstore & Bindery	419
Goldwasser & Wilkinson Books	224
Greyhavens Books	183
David Hecht Antiquarian Books	225
Michael S. Hollander Rare Books	240
Iconoclast Books	421

Kauai Fine Arts	317	George H. Tweney, Bookseller	431
Kenneth Karmiole, Bookseller	250	Wahrenbrock's Book House	210
Lake City Books	423	**Wells, H.G.**	
The Odyssey Bookshop	240	Phillip Gold-221 Books	299
Powell's Travel Store	362	**Western Americana**	
Larry W. Price Books	375	Acorn Books	213
Schoyer's Books	307	Adams Avenue Bookstore	199
Jeffrey Thomas, Fine & Rare Books	230	Albatross Book Co.	214
Trophy Room Books	41	Amadeus Books	110
Wahrenbrock's Book House	210	American Bookstore	92
True crime		Ames Bookstore	101
Atlantis Book Shop	59	Anderson Valley Books	58
Bloody Dagger Books	202	Anderson's Bookshop/Books Fantastique	284
Exotica Fine Books	297	The Antiquarian Archive	119
Latin Blood Books	302	Argonaut Book Shop	214
Mitchell Books	171	Argus Books & Graphics	188
Murder By The Book	358, 358	The Arthur H. Clark Company	435
Ravenna Rare Books	427	Ashurst Books	342
Smith & Co. Booksellers	266	Authors Of The West	333
West Portal Books	230	Gene W. Badde, Books on the West	445
Twain, Mark		Ronald J. Ballou, Bookman	187
Bleak House Books	267	Beauty and the Books	413
UFOs		Book Alley of Old Pasadena	169
Apex Books	290	The Book Collector	190
Atlantis Book Shop	59	Book Depot	51
Tom Davis Books	44	Book Mall of Ventura	274
New Age World Services & Books	107	The Book Merchant	146
The Second Time Around Bookshop	276	The Book Shop	76
University press		Book Time	159
Coffee & Classics	79	Bookmine	190
University Press Books	58	Dirk Cable, Bookseller	170
Wessex Books & Records	134	Cahill's Book Store	91
Ventriloquism		Caravan Book Store	123
Byron's Magic Books	234	Barry Cassidy Rare Books	191
Vietnam War		Claremont Books & Prints	71
Bibliomania	155	Clark's Book Store	435
Gregor Books	420	Daniel Conner	335
Tavistock Books	309	Copperfield's Annex	254
Waverley Books	252	Corls Books	374
Vintage paperbacks		Dawson's Book Shop	125
Apex Books	290	Day's Past	179
Armchair Family Bookstore	350	Derail Books	254
Black Ace Books	121	Harold B. Diamond, Bookseller	61
Book'Em	52	F. Wayne Edmunds - Bookseller	47
Cameron's Books	353	El Dorado Books	125
Cliff's Books/Records/Comics	170	Elaine's Books	187
Fantasy Illustrated	417	Eureka Books	86
Multi Books	425	Ferndale Books	88
My Book Heaven	41	Folio Books	418
Recyclepedia Bookstore	252	Garcia-Garst, Booksellers	271
Marvin Stanley, Bookseller	153	Robert Gavora, Bookseller	355
Swans's Comic & Magazine Mart	439	Geiger's Books	298
Voyages		Michael Gibbs, Books	298
Barry Cassidy Rare Books	191	Goldwasser & Wilkinson Books	224
Fleetstreet	385	The Great Northwest Bookstore	355
David Hecht Antiquarian Books	225	Green Ginger Bookshop	66
T.W. Palmer Books	335	Hammons Archives	193
Parmer Books	208	Emmett Harrington Rare Books	299
		Hawthorne Boulevard Books	356

Dave Henson-Books	299	**Westerns**	
David Ishii, Bookseller	422	Apex Books	290
Jan's Book Nook	81	The Armchair Adventurer	43
Josef's Books	185	Bookstore Bookends	255
Wayne Kee Books	365	Robert Gavora, Bookseller	355
Live Oak Booksellers	99	Gemini Book Exchange & Comic Ctr	418
Lorson's Books & Prints	96	Houle Rare Books & Autographs	126
Lost Horizon Bookstore	244	Waverley Books	252
E. Lubbe Books	302	**Weston, Edward**	
Michael Maslan Historic Ephemera	424	Pacific Rim Galleries	68
Maxwell's Bookmark	265	**Whaling**	
Memorabilia of San Jose	233	High Latitude	386
Mike's Books & Espresso	347	Whaling Research	313
Monroe Books	93	**Whitman, Walt**	
Mountain House Books	147	By The Way Books	172
Murphy's Books	145	**Wine**	
Newport Book Center	348	Albatross Book Co.	214
Northwest Books	156	Caravan Book Store	123
Old Oregon Book Store	359	Cook Books - By Janet Jarvits	61
Once Read Books	112	Curran & Hermes Books	295
Oregon Tertitorial Books	371	Fat City Books	264
Pa-Has-Ka Books	304	Peter Glaser Bookseller	257
T.W. Palmer Books	335	Goldwasser & Wilkinson Books	224
Robert Perata	305	Household Words	300
Dick Perier Books	441	Plaza Books	262
Diane Peterson - Booklady	134	Second Harvest Books	308
Plaza Books	262	Treehorn Books	255
Truman Price	375	**Women's studies**	
R.G.I. Book Co.	137	Anacapa House	242
Ross Valley Book Co.	56	Betty's Bookstore	202
Sagebrush Press Bookstore	288	Barbara Bilson-Books	250
Schoyer's Books	307	The Book Shelf	293
Secondhand Prose	46	Booklegger	86
2nd Edition Books	69	Chimney Sweep Books	246
Serendipity Books	56	Gene de Chene, Bookseller	282
Sherburne Antiques & Fine Art	405	Herland Book-Cafe	247
Sleepy Hollow Books	308	Michele Leroux Fine Old Books	399
Solvang Book Company	260	Carol D. McKinley, Bookseller	446
Jack L. Stone, Bookseller	262	Schoyer's Books	307
Sullivan Goss Books & Prints	245	Volkoff & von Hohenlohe	312
Thorn Books	143	**World War I & II**	
Time Tested Books	194	Albany Book Company	325
Treehorn Books	255	American Booksellers	383
Turner House Antiques	342	Book Depot	51
George H. Tweney, Bookseller	431	Harold B. Diamond, Bookseller	61
Valdez Books & Bindery	285	The Eclectic Collector	104
Van Norman-Booksellers	311	Encore Books	182
Vigne Co.	68	P.T. Mallahan, Bookseller	446
Paul von Ahnen Books	312	**WPA**	
Wahrenbrock's Book House	210	Robert W. Mattila, Bookseller	424
Webfoot Bookman	364	**Yosemite**	
Wessel & Lieberman Booksellers	432	Argus Books & Graphics	188
Wonderland Books	83		

Keeping Current

As a service to our readers, we're happy to make available, at cost, Supplements for each of our guides.

The Supplements, published annually, provide our readers with additional listings as well as information concerning dealers who have either moved or gone out of business.

Much of the information in the Supplements comes to us from loyal readers who, in using our guides, have been kind enough to provide us with this valuable data based on their own book hunting experiences.

Should you wish to receive the next Supplement for the book(s) you currently own, complete the Order Form below and enclose $1.00 for each Supplement, plus postage. The Supplements will be mailed as they become available.

ORDER FORM

Book Hunter Press
PO Box 193 • Yorktown Heights, NY 10598
(914) 245-6608

Supplement	Price	Please Send	Cost
Pacific Coast	1.00		
New England	1.00		
Mid-Atlantic	1.00		
South Atlantic	1.00		
Midwest	1.00		
		Subtotal	
Postage: 50¢ per Supplement		Postage	
		TOTAL	

Name_____

Company_____

Address_____

City_____ State_____ Zip_____

Phone_____